# FEMININE
# INGENUITY

# FEMININE INGENUITY

## WOMEN AND INVENTION IN AMERICA

*Anne L. Macdonald*

BALLANTINE BOOKS
NEW YORK

All rights reserved under International and Pan-American Copyright Conventions.
Published in the United States by Ballantine Books, a division of Random House, Inc.,
New York, and simultaneously in Canada by Random House of Canada Limited, Toronto.

Library of Congress Cataloging-in-Publication Data
MacDonald, Anne L., 1920–
    Feminine ingenuity : women and invention in America / Anne
MacDonald. — 1st ed.
        p.   cm.
    Includes bibliographical references and index.
    ISBN: 0-345-35811-2
    1. Women inventors—United States.   2. Inventions—United States.
I. Title.
T36.M33   1992
609.2′273—dc20
    [B]                                                        91-55502
                                                                    CIP

Text design by Beth Tondreau Design / Mary A. Wirth

Manufactured in the United States of America
First Edition: May 1992
10 9 8 7 6 5 4 3 2 1

*Once again, for Peter*

WE HOLD THESE TRUTHS
TO BE SELF-EVIDENT THAT
ALL MEN AND WOMEN
ARE CREATED EQUAL

Declaration of Rights and Sentiments
First Women's Rights Convention
Seneca Falls, New York, July 19–20, 1848

# CONTENTS

# ACKNOWLEDGMENTS

$\mathcal{S}$o many have helped me in the writing of this book that I hesitate to cite any lest I omit others. I wrote letters, placed calls, traveled miles, haunted reading rooms, explored library stacks, opened dusty boxes, and tracked leads and no one ever turned me down. Even stamped self-addressed envelopes I enclosed with written queries came back stuffed with reams of material or "Sorry, I don't know, but have you tried . . . ?" Writers appended, "Let me know what you find out!" I hope that *Feminine Ingenuity* will accomplish just that.

At the National Archives, I am especially grateful for the help of Marjorie Ciarlante, Claudia Nicholson, and John Butler.

At the Smithsonian Institution, I relied upon Deborah Warner and Barbara Jansen at the National Museum of American History; at the Air and Space Museum's library, on Brian Nichols and Chris King; at the Anacostia Museum, on Portia James for information on black women inventors.

At the Library of Congress, I am not only grateful for the shelf and desk space that Bruce Martin of Reader Services has made available to me but for his never-failing interest in the subject I have been pursuing. I can't say enough for the incredible research librarians, who combine their awesome knowledge of materials in the collections with a joyous determination to see that nothing comes between me and my quarry.

At the United States Patent and Trademark Office, Anne Kelly, Donald Kelly, Marion Canedo, Ruth Nyblood, Jane Myers, Commissioner Donald Quigg, Janice Pickering, Martha Crockett, Bernard Thomas, and James Davie have seen to it that I had whatever materials I needed.

Beyond Washington, many other institutions arranged for me to study there or sent me material: the Huntington Library in San Marino, California; the Schlesinger Library at Radcliffe College; the Baker Library at Harvard University Graduate School of Business Administration; the Atlanta Historical Society; the Cincinnati Historical Society; the Catholic University of Washington, D.C.; the New Jersey Historical Society; the Missouri Historical Society; the Georgia Department of Archives and History; the New York Historical Society; the Maine Historical Society, Portland; the Rennselaer County Historical Society and Lansingburgh Historical Society, Troy, New York; the Louisiana Historical Society in New Orleans; the Tennessee Historical Society, Nashville; Kimball House Historical Society of Battle Creek, Michigan; the Colorado Historical Society; the Ohio Historical Society, Columbus; the Hagley Museum and Library, Wilmington, Delaware; the General Electric Hall of History, Schenectady, New York; the Whittier Historical Society, California; the Searls Historical Library, Nevada City, California; the B & O Historical Society; the B & O Museum; the Wethersfield Historical Society; the Connecticut Historical Society; the Cincinnati Art Museum; and the Mannequin Museum.

These public and private libraries have been of inestimable assistance: Maud Preston Palenske Memorial Library in Saint Joseph, Michigan; Pennsylvania Historical Society Library; Mount Holyoke College Library/Archives; Goucher College Library; Chalmers Memorial Library, Kenyon College; San Jose Public Library; Brooklyn Public Library; Phillips County Historical Society, Helena, Arkansas; Nashville Public Library; Willard Library, Battle Creek, Michigan; Denver Public Library; Framingham Public Library, Massachusetts; Public Library of Charlotte and Mecklenburg Counties, Charlotte, North Carolina; Davidson College Library; Whittier Public Library, California; Carnegie Free Library of McKeesport, Pennsylvania; Moline Public Library, Illinois; Yuba County Library, Marysville, California; Public Library of Oakland, California; Kalamazoo Public Library; Three Rivers Public Library, Michigan; Davenport Public Library, Iowa; Library of the Association of American Railroads; Public Library of Springfield, Massachusetts; Monteagle Public Library, Tennessee; Birmingham Public Library and Jefferson Country Free Library, Alabama; Niles Community Library, Michigan; Ottumwa Public Library; Chicopee Public Library, Massachusetts; Pollard Memorial Library, Lowell, Massachusetts.

Individuals who have been especially helpful are Cliff Peterson, who owns the largest private collection of patent models; Fred Amram, who has been studying this subject for over a decade and is incredibly generous with his materials; Anne Whitehead, United States Department of Agriculture, Agricultural Research Service; and James W. Gandy, Oberlin Smith Society.

My literary agent, Leona Schechter, is always helpful—from concept to negotiation to creation.

I want to thank Michelle Russell, whose early enthusiasm for this book helped me begin it, and Ballantine's editor-in-chief, Joelle Delbourgo, whose steadfast belief that I could pull it all together—even after a violent storm wiped out half our house while I was at my computer—sustained me. For helping me so improve its final form, I am deeply grateful for the graceful touch and positive suggestions of my editor, Beth Rashbaum.

Other than Beth Rashbaum, Joelle Delbourgo, Ravin Korothy (my eagle-eyed copy-editor), and myself, only one other person already knows everything in this book. My husband has heard me describe each day's finds as he met me at library steps, planes, buses, and subways; he's listened to endless tales of "my" inventors; he's heard the computer go beep in the night. My heart goes out to him—also my thanks!

Anne L. Macdonald
Bethesda, Maryland

The author and her patented knitting device.

# INTRODUCTION

$\mathcal{W}$henever I talk about having written a book on American women inventors, someone always pipes up, "Well, what *did* women invent? Anything really important?" Though I console myself that no one seriously questions women's ability to invent, I can count on one hand those who know the name of even one American woman who actually did. When I explain that I have narrowed my subject to women who actually received patents for their inventions, my audience is further nonplussed. "Is this a very recent development, women getting patents?" asked one. A friend who has practiced patent law for four decades said he has never represented a female inventor. Others ask me to name a few patentees, and I am tempted to roll out the big names, whether their inventions broke important ground or not. A trio of actresses might do: Take Hedy Lamar, whose patent was for a secret wartime communications system; or May Robson, who invented a false leg for stage use; or Lillian Russell, who received a patent for a clever wardrobe trunk that could double as a bureau when she was on tour. Even one of Rudolph Valentino's wives, Winifred Hudnut Gugliemi—professionally known as Natacha Rambova—had a patent (for a coverlet and doll).

I must admit that before I undertook this project I, too, knew the names of only a few women patent holders, and one of those names was mine. When I extol my invention's virtues (it enables hand knitters to avoid tangling the colored yarns they use to knit geometric patterns), the eyes of nonknitters glaze over, their eyebrows lift, they sigh—"Oh, well, is *that* all?"—as if to say "Oh, a *woman's* thing!" and I grow defensive. Never mind that knitting is done by men as well as women; what's wrong with inventing a woman's thing? Why should it be more significant to invent something less "domestic," perhaps more "industrial," perhaps more "masculine"? Inventing is inventing. Put an ingenious person in intimate contact with a problem and he or she will invent a solution—for everything from corralling the baby to damming a river to extracting gold from ore (all women's inventions).

Without getting into the *value* of women's inventions—I leave that to others in my book—there is a common bond among all of us patenting inventors, whether of dams or of knitting devices. We know from personal experience that having a great idea (the "Eureka!" or light-bulb moment) is only the first step in a process that requires considerable hard work, staying power, and determined hanging-on, plus hard cash to invest in patenting costs and—if we get the patent—in manufacturing and marketing. We have suffered through the anxieties of hoping that no one else has already patented the idea we were fully convinced was ours alone. We have had to explain our idea clearly enough so that patent examiners familiar with the state of the art could determine whether our idea really is "new and useful"; we've learned to work with the draftsman who illustrates the workings of the device in action. And many of us, myself included, have gone through the experience of working with a patent attorney as well. Like others in the same situation, once I realized that my application would have to conform to Patent Office rules about everything from the phrasing of the description to the weight and color of the paper on which it was submitted, I decided a patent attorney would speed things along.

I eventually got the patent, and I love having my name attached to number 4,548,055. It was, however, no snap getting it there. After being turned down twice, I dispensed with the attorney's further services, boned up on how to restate my claims, honed my arguments, practiced my presentation, and personally appeared before the examiners to demonstrate and defend my invention. Greatly encouraged by their reception, I asked another attorney to restate my claims. I got the patent that time around, and in return for divulging how my invention works for the information of anyone who cares to look at the particulars, I can sit tight and know that until the year 2002 I alone can sell the device, which has become the core of a modest mail-order business. It's no wonder that when I read another inventor's application file, I can read between the lines the anxiety and agony that has prompted her correspondence with Washington.

In this book I write about women patentees rather than women inventors in general, not just because of my personal empathy with patentees but for the practical reason that I can be sure that the woman patentee actually is the inventor. In patenting, she has taken an oath that she alone (or, in cases of co-patenting, in combination with a partner) is responsible for having reduced inspiration to practice, as we say in the trade. By putting her own name on her patent (some even edited patent application forms to read "inventress" rather than "inventor" and substituted "her" and "she" for masculine pronouns), she has enshrined that name on an official United States government list. Even if future historians find no other information on her, having an assigned patent number means that the particulars of her invention can be traced. That number is the key that will unlock her patent case file, complete with descriptions and illustrations of her invention, and often rife with succulent tidbits of correspondence between her and the examiners (for applications before 1918, the only ones so far accessioned by National Archives). Also in the National Archives can be found the records of any negotiations she conducted regarding the transfer or sale of her patent rights, and any statements she or any other party made if she was involved in a patent interference suit.

It was such a patent interference suit, for example, that led me to pursue the events leading to Susan Hibbard's 1876 patent. Susan's husband, George, felt no compunction about attesting to "his" new method for processing formerly discarded turkey wing and tail feathers into usable feather dusters, though Susan had actually figured out the process. But when a competitor alleged that he had the idea first and hauled Hibbard before the patent examiners, George confessed that the idea *was* Susan's: "My wife suggested the idea. If the one who suggested the splitting of the feathers is the inventor, then I am not the one." Susan revealed why she let George do it: "I didn't understand the patent laws—[knew] nothing about them" but volunteered, "I have no particular occupation but I know a lot about feathers; I did the experiments myself. I said take a knife and try to split them." Susan's meticulous records of her invention's trial-and-error phase effectively documented the priority of the Hibbard invention, and Susan won number 177,939 in her own name, leaving the stranded counsel for the plaintiff to snivel, "Mrs. Hibbard's claim is simply a put-up affair . . . conceived in dishonesty and fraud." To no avail; Susan had made her case.

Of course, thousands of women inventors undoubtedly made critical suggestions to relatives and employers—or even employees—that resulted in patents for others, but it is difficult to assign credit without indisputable evidence of their role. Take Eva Landman's case. The name of Max Landman, her husband, appears on the 1935 patent for what was at the time quite an innovation—an umbrella with a built-in transparent "windshield" to deflect rain and wind while still providing the carrier with a clear view of potential hazards. The idea was definitely Eva's, but her ingenuity would have gone unrecorded (except, perhaps, in family lore) were it not for a story in a popular magazine of the time, *Invention and Finance.* It related how Eva darted across the street in a rainstorm, collided with a truck, and spent three months recovering in the hospital. There she incubated her concept of a windowed umbrella and told her husband about it. He took it from there, and the patent is in his name. Mr. Landman was no miscreant bent on robbing his wife of credit; he simply brought her idea to its patentable stage. Still, many partners and spouses would have listed the idea's originator as co-patentee. He didn't. So, the woman behind the man got what? Well, Eva got in this book, if that's any consolation.

Women's names may not have made it to the patent list for another reason. Many undoubtedly concurred with the opinion of a nineteenth-century patent commissioner that a woman's name might jeopardize an application's success. Quoth the commissioner: "If it had been known [that it was] the invention of a woman, it would have been regarded as a failure." But if a woman shielded the fact of her ingenuity by not demanding official recognition at the time of patenting, she paid the consequence of leaving it to posterity to debate what role she played.

Take Katherine Greene and the cotton gin, for example. Everyone agrees that Greene (widow of one of General Washington's high-ranking military adjutants) and her manager (and later, husband), Phineas Miller, urged Eli Whitney, the newly hired, Yale-educated, skilled mechanic at her Mulberry Grove plantation, to try to perfect what all planters wanted, a machine to separate seed from cotton. Whitney built a model, but progress ground to a halt when the cotton clogged the wooden teeth instead of slipping between them and passing through the slate of the rollers. There is disagreement about events that followed. Some say that Kitty Greene surveyed the problem and asked, "Why don't you use wire instead of wooden teeth?" He did. It worked. Others contend that even if Greene *did* suggest wire (and few concede that much), her suggestion was not really "inventing" and no claim should be made that it was.

Still, stories of Greene's ingenuity persisted, the first written mention that I have located being almost four decades after the Whitney patent: an 1832 letter from George Scarborough of Georgia to the magazine *Southern Agriculturalist.* Scarborough claimed that he had it on good authority ("derived from a much esteemed and lamented friend, who was the family physician and intimate friend of Mr. Phineas Miller") that when the cotton clogged the wooden teeth of Whitney's model, Greene remarked laughingly, "What! Allow such a trifle as that worry you? Trust to a woman's wit to find the cure," seized the wire hearth-brush, and suggested to Whitney that he use it to comb through the cotton. Whitney gallantly replied, "Thank you for the hint. I think I have it now," and repaired to his workshop where he eventually developed the machine he patented—the one with wire teeth. According to Scarborough's source, no one could have been more surprised at this achievement than Greene herself, for she had been "perfectly unconscious" that her advice to use the broom could possibly inspire a breakthrough when she meant it only as a playful comment to relieve Whitney's chagrin over his inventive stalemate. All this, of course, was the opinion of the "intimate" source, and the rest is history. Eli Whitney's history.

A month after Scarborough's story appeared, however, an anonymous "subscriber" wrote *Southern Agriculturalist* to pass on what *he* had heard, though admittedly from sources he couldn't vouch for: When Phineas Miller handed Whitney the pod of green seed cotton and asked him, in Mrs. Greene's presence, whether he could invent a

machine to separate the cotton from the seed, Whitney examined it
carefully and then asked Mrs. Greene for a *pin*—which he used to pick
off the cotton. Then, related the subscriber:

> At this moment [with pin in hand], the idea flashed across his mind,
> that a machine composed of instruments with sharp points, which in
> the course of rapid revolutions, should tear off the cotton from the
> seed, would accomplish the object in view. He retired to his room
> with the idea in his mind, and never abandoned it until, by successive
> improvements, he brought the cotton gin to . . . perfection.

"Subscriber" felt the incident proved that even a small hint can
stimulate the mind of a genius to produce the "most magnificent
results" and waxed eloquent over how "the widow's mite of experience" offered by the humblest individual might lay the foundation of
"great and lasting benefits to mankind." So there was one early
"maybe" vote for Greene.

Although no one claimed that Greene did more than offer a suggestion, the story (with variations) has been repeated so often that it's
obvious that, at the very least, it has been irresistible to those who have
wished to stress the necessity for women's social, political, and economic assertiveness. The story was a natural for a feminist with the
sentiments of Matilda Joslyn Gage, once a happy housewife until her
consciousness was raised at an Akron, Ohio, women's rights convention
where she noted in her maiden address that there were "mountains of
established laws and custom to overcome; a wilderness of prejudice to
be subdued . . ." Her conscience stayed raised for the remainder of the
century, and her tombstone inscription reflected her emancipation:
"There is a word sweeter than Mother, Home, or Heaven; that word
is Liberty." Shortly after the Civil War, Gage, by then active in the
newly formed National Woman Suffrage Association, entertained no
doubts that Greene was an INVENTOR in the full sense of the word and
championed her in an article decisively headlined "The Cotton Gin
Invented by a Woman" in *The Revolution,* the Association's newspaper.
She pressed the issue again two years later by featuring Greene in the
star-studded roster of innovators that appeared in her widely-read
suffrage tract, *Woman as Inventor.* One should not be deterred by
Whitney's name on the patent, advised Gage, for "[W]omen's inven-

tive ideas are sometimes allowed to take form in the hands of a practical mechanic," fair warning to inventive women to assert themselves and protect their interests.

Jumping on the Greene bandwagon was Charlotte Smith, whose efforts on behalf of industrial women will be described often in this book. Smith said that Greene allowed Whitney to patent what was really her idea because of her "fear of ridicule because of her social position." Also in Greene's corner was Frances Willard, well-known nineteenth-century educator and speaker, social reformer, temperance leader, woman's suffrage protagonist, chronicler of women, and the first woman honored with a statue in the United States Capitol—just the kind of woman to take up the cause. Willard declared unequivocally that "[c]otton became king because of woman's thought" but, like Smith, excused Greene for not publicly proclaiming her inventiveness because of the climate of the time: "Had she done so, the ridicule and scorn of every man and woman who knew her name would have been heaped upon her. She would have been looked upon as a monstrosity of unwomanliness and presumption."

It's important to note that the flurry over Greene's contribution to the invention of the cotton gin occurred *decades* after Whitney's patent, but since the canon that mechanics was "unwomanly" *still* prevailed, feminists liked to point out that womanliness never won any prizes in the business world. Others raised the issue for their own reasons. One such person was Russell Conwell, a Baptist clergyman and famed public lecturer of the Chautauqua movement, who included Greene in his most popular lecture, "Acres of Diamonds" (a metaphor for the opportunity for riches in everybody's backyard). Conwell filled the halls with his soul-stirring talks about American get-up-and-go. By giving full credit to "Mrs. General Greene" for the idea and castigating Whitney, who, "like a man, seized it," Conwell, who is said to have delivered the "Acres of Diamonds" talk over six thousand times to packed halls, perpetuated the story and stirred the ambitions of many a female listener. As an extra bonus, Conwell needled Elias Howe, his Civil War tentmate and "recognized" inventor of the sewing machine. As Conwell told it, Howe described his fourteen unsuccessful years of trying to develop a sewing machine until "his wife made up her mind one day that they would starve to death if there wasn't something or other invented pretty soon, and so in two hours she invented the sewing-machine. Of course he took out the patent in his name. Men always do that."

There are probably hundreds more stories like Greene's and, perhaps, Howe's, but latter-day compensatory recognition is tricky business. Absent the official acknowledgment that names on patents afford, it is almost impossible to corroborate that behind a patent bearing a man's name was the hand or mind of a woman. How can one, for example, give proper credit to unidentified female factory workers who made suggestions, and in some cases even constructed models, for time-saving and labor-saving devices? If they were lucky, the employers who took out the patents paid them a fee for the exclusive use of their ingenious ideas. If they weren't, factory managers simply appropriated without compensation.

Despite such obstacles, thousands of women nonetheless had the drive not only to invent but to patent their own ideas in areas from which women were traditionally excluded. And in doing so, they left an incontrovertible and enviable record of ingenuity and ambition.

# FEMININE
# INGENUITY

# 1

# FOREMOTHERS OF
# AMERICAN INVENTION

$\mathcal{A}$lthough women have invented since the beginning of time, it seems as if full recognition of their role has been painfully slow. Even after English King George I acknowledged the critical role that colonist Sybilla Masters played in the development of Pennsylvania's economy by citing her as the inventor of the new way "for cleaning and curing the Indian corn growing in several colonies in America," he nonetheless issued the patent itself to her husband, Thomas Masters. One should not be surprised. That was business as usual—certainly for 1715—and it would be almost a century before an American woman would succeed in gaining a patent in her own name. Then it would be 1809, and it would not be a king but the United States government which would grant one to Mary Kies for a straw-weaving process she had invented.

There was nothing in the law that precluded women from benefitting from the Founding Fathers' concern for property rights—rights that, owing largely to the urging of the Constitutional Convention's senior delegate, Benjamin Franklin, the noted inventor of devices as varied as bifocal glasses and a rocking chair, were to include protection for one's inventions, what became known as "intellectual property." Determined to free inventors from dependency

upon political favor by opening a patent system to all on equal footing, the newly independent states delegated the authority to "promote the progress of science and useful arts" to a *national* Congress
rather than continuing to allow each state legislature to award patents valid only within its boundaries. By remaining silent on gender,
the Patent Act of 1790, one of the first pieces of legislation of the
newly constituted Congress, therefore offered women the same patenting privileges as men, though the serious social, psychological,
and economic obstacles that stood in women's paths prevented them
from availing themselves of those privileges for some years—until
Mary Kies took the initiative. There was no specific lobbying to ex-
tend these patent rights for women, but certainly early legislators
were mindful that female descendants of the Revolution's plucky
Daughters of Liberty should, as Abigail Adams coached her husband,
be "remembered." Therefore, all individuals, women included, would
obtain exclusive rights to their respective writings and discoveries for
a stipulated number of years, even though state laws severely limited
married women's rights to own property.

The Patent Office offered a good bargain: In return for disclosing
full particulars on the invention, for defining how it worked, and for
supplying specifications and drawings and (usually) a model so that
anyone skilled in that particular art could understand it, an inventor
gained a protected interval in which to develop the product for commercial use free of competition. Prospective patentees (all male)
rushed to submit their applications the moment President Washington
signed the Patent Act on April 10, 1790.

Since the secretary of state doubled as administrator of the patent
system in its first years, it fell to the prolifically inventive Thomas
Jefferson to examine those first applications. The Patent Board, made
up of Jefferson, Secretary of War Henry Knox, and Attorney General
Edmund Randolph, examined each model and written description to
ascertain whether an invention was both novel and useful enough to
receive a patent. The task swamped leaders already burdened with
other rigorous duties, and within three years the process was so simplified that an inventor needed pay only a thirty-dollar registration fee
to secure a patent from a State Department clerk. By 1802, the number
of applications so deluged the State Department that Secretary of State
James Madison decided to create a separate Patent Office within the

department and appointed his Georgetown neighbor, Dr. William Thornton, the original designer of the United States Capitol, to head it as Superintendent of Patents.

Mary Kies might not hold the record as the first woman to gain a United States patent from the new Patent Office had inventor Betsey Metcalf of Providence followed up on the new method of braiding straw she first discovered in 1798. Though she didn't even apply for a patent, I exempt Metcalf from my rule about limiting my scope to patenting women because her invention of a new way to make the popular Italian "leghorn" hats (large circles of straw brimming a central skullcap)—which American women adapted to local taste by attaching ribbons to the sides and pulling them into "gipsy hats" or whacking off the back section to form bonnets—was to have far-reaching consequences for the local economy—and beyond. Metcalf taught her method to everyone, and the fad was on: Children straw-plaited at school, sewing circles converted to braiding bees, and braiding almost edged out knitting and crocheting as women toted bonnets along with butter and eggs to exchange for other articles at

Bonnet-making fostered some of the earliest inventions by women.

village markets. So many women were engaged in the business of cutting, boiling, dyeing, flattening, splitting, braiding, and bleaching that many New England towns were known as "straw towns."

The flourishing bonnet industry provided employment to thousands of women and filled state treasuries; it is no wonder that Rhode Island's Society for the Encouragement of Domestic Industry not only preserved a replica of Betsey Metcalf's first bonnet (now enshrined at the John Brown House, Rhode Island Historical Society, Providence), but also commissioned a portrait of her in 1858 that was donated by the governor. Since Metcalf was satisfied with her earnings ("I could easily earn one dollar per day, and sometimes one dollar and fifty cents, for several weeks at a time"), she never applied for a patent for the method that pumped such life into the local industry. Furthermore, she hated the idea of the public role into which she feared patenting would cast her. When she explained some years later, "Many said I ought to get a patent; but I told them I did not wish to have my name sent to Congress," she epitomized the dread of the public eye that checked the ambition of many inventive women.

Betsey may have inveighed against having her name before Congress, but Mary Dixon Kies, of Killingly, Connecticut, showed no such reluctance about her own work in straw. When Kies patented her process of weaving straw with silk or thread in 1809, she was fortunate in her timing. The federal government had just embargoed importation of European goods in an attempt to isolate this nation's affairs from the Napoleonic wars, and, to compensate, newly elected President Madison's worried administration was eager to stimulate native industry. Hearing of the straw-weaving invention, President Madison's wife, Dolley, who might have been aware that Kies was the first woman to receive a patent, commended her genius in discovering a process to boost New England's hat industry. During the War of 1812, the hat industry would be one of the few that continued to prosper, while other industries foundered so badly that most of the New England states were on the brink of secession when the war ended. The Patent Office itself was at risk, for British troops occupying Washington were poised to torch it and were dissuaded only by Patent Commissioner Thornton's desperate plea that they should spare the nation's treasures.

Within a few years another woman inventor from Connecticut who

Sophia Woodhouse's "Wethersfield Bonnet."

worked in straw would also receive notice from Washington. After Sophia Woodhouse of Wethersfield substituted a native grass for straw and won a premium for the "Best Grass Bonnet" at Hartford County's Society for Promoting Agriculture and Domestic Manufactures, she dispatched a sample to the British Society of Arts, which found it so "superior in color and fineness to the best Leghorn Straw" that it awarded her a silver medal and twenty guineas (enclosed in a splendid morocco case) in return for the seed and a description of her process so that British merchants could import and cultivate the grass. By that time, she had to tell them that she had patented it. End of negotiations.

But it was not the end of fame. A New York businessman who learned of her process of boiling and drying the grass, treating it with a solution of pearl ash, fumigating it with brimstone, braiding, sewing, shaping, and then refumigating it before ironing it into final shape, thought that if he could attract attention, he could promote the product to advantage. His solution was to send a "Wethersfield" bonnet to Louisa Adams, wife of Secretary of State John Quincy Adams, probably with the hope that she would wear it. I don't know whether she actually wore it, but contrary to his customary practice of returning all gifts, Madison allowed his wife to keep the bonnet because, as he explained in his diary, it was such "an extraordinary specimen of American manufacture . . . [and] ingenuity of our country." Adams made no mention of its being invented by a woman, but, interestingly, since he was secretary of state, his signature is on the patent along with that of President James Monroe.

In the thirty-two years following Kies's patent in 1809, twenty-one other women received patents, four of which dealt with the hat industry. The others, such as that for Elizabeth Adams's 1841 pregnancy corset, were also mainly clothing related. The wording of one of Adams's claims for her garment hints that she recognized from personal experience the need for "looseness above the abdomen [to allow] the parts to rise upward, in case the patient is in a sitting or stooping posture."

In the following decade, fourteen more women gained patents for devices ranging from Mary Ann Woodward's motion-activated fan attached to a rocking chair to a truly remarkable submarine lamp and telescope used to illuminate the ocean depths. This latter was developed by Sarah Mather and celebrated by Matilda Gage in her *Woman as Inventor*, the previously mentioned suffrage tract which was published in 1870: "We deem the telescope which examines the heavens a wonderful invention . . . but how much greater the scientific genius must these women possess who have invented an instrument for bringing to view the depths of the ocean, and making its wonders as familiar to us as those of dry land." There was also a device for freezing ice cream, celebrated even 145 years later, in an article on homemade ice cream, as the creation of Nancy Johnson, who "invented the hand-crank ice cream maker as we know it. The

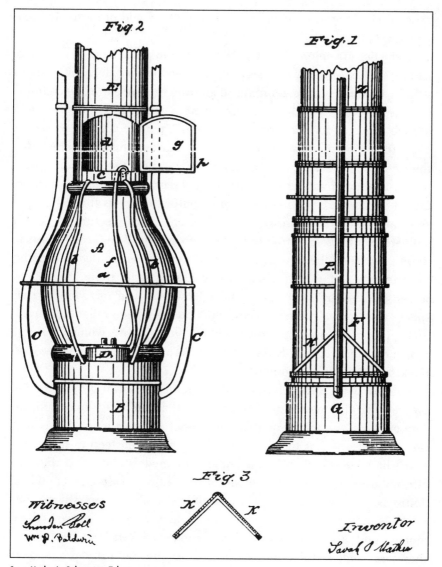

Sara Mather's Submarine Telescope.

machine, with a crank and dasher, made ice cream easier to produce at home while opening a wealth of commercial possibilities." Johnson reputedly sold her patent rights for fifteen hundred dollars, a goodly sum for mid-century, although a *Harper's Bazaar* journalist, writing some years afterward and with the benefit of hindsight, deemed her "not so wise as her sisters," who would presumably have struck a better deal.

In the decade before the Civil War began in 1861, women inventors patented twice as many devices as in the previous decade, most of them still for feminine apparel but also including such practical mechanical devices as a reaping and mowing machine. Though patenting had been a male preserve for the first two decades after the act was passed in 1790, more and more women discovered that only tradition precluded their entering the field. But the tradition that held that woman's place was in the home was firmly entrenched. George Washington Burnap, famed Unitarian clergyman and contributor to various literary magazines and journals, expressed it well in one of the lectures he often delivered on his tours through the eastern states: "The God who made them knew the sphere in which each of them was designed to act, and he fitted them for it by their physical frames, by their intellectual susceptibilities, by their tastes and affections." And for women, that sphere was home! Those who clung to that conviction relied so heavily upon quotations from Scripture that a good many women's rights proponents, particularly Elizabeth Cady Stanton, blasphemed the Good Book for denigrating women.

The few who were willing to defy tradition had also to overcome the considerable obstacles presented by the patenting process itself. One of those obstacles was that the Patent Office, though increasing the value of a patent by upping the grant from fourteen to seventeen years, had reinstated the requirement for models and ruled that applicants must furnish an extra set of drawings in case one should be destroyed by fire. Since my study of women's patents shows that most women relied upon professional assistance to prepare these models and drawings, fees for the model makers and draftsmen, therefore, added still another expense to the daunting problem of raising investment capital.

Still, one can understand the new regulation, since fire was more than a vague threat. In 1836, just as ground was being broken for a completely new Patent Office building a block away, fire swept through Blodgett's Hotel (actually a theater at the northeast corner of Washington's E and Eighth streets Northwest), to which the Patent Office had moved after the aisles of its previous building became jammed with boxloads of models, even though models were no longer required. The Blodgett's fire destroyed all the Patent Office's records and seven thousand pieces of its priceless model collection (records that have, over the years, been partially restored through the donation and restoration of patentees' original drawings, specifications, and models).

In addition to model makers and draftsmen, women had to depend upon other expert help. It was widely available—at a price, of course. Most commonly, they relied upon agents to act as go-betweens in their dealings with the Patent Office. They could easily locate such agents through city directories or through advertisements in magazines targeted toward inventors. Some agents boldly offered "no patent, no pay" deals, but these were risky since the claims in such patents were often so limited in outlining the scope of the device's potential use that they offered scant protection to the inventor. Sometimes the magazines themselves ran patent agencies on the side. The *Inventor,* one of the early technical magazines catering to prospective clients, for instance, assured inventors in an 1857 issue that it could handle the entire business by mail.

If a woman could afford a patent attorney, she engaged one, since an attorney could handle her case in court if need be, while an agent could represent her only with the Patent Office. It is interesting to note that although earlier in this century bar associations reprimanded or disbarred members who advertised their services, it was such a common nineteenth-century practice that attorneys' cards flutter out like moths from the "Inventor" file of the Smithsonian's Warshaw Collection of business ephemera. The largest firms, both agents and attorneys, maintained branch offices handy to the Patent Office.

One of these was Munn & Company, an outgrowth of the magazine *Scientific American,* which had been founded in 1845 by a not very successful but nonetheless prolific inventor who subtitled his publication "The Advocate of Industry and Journal of Mechanical and Other Improvements." In addition to providing news about developments in industry, it condensed general news of passing events and appealed to the whole family by including material deemed "suitable for Sunday reading" since it avoided "the disgusting and pernicious details of crime." *Scientific American* gained a double stake in invention in 1846 when its owners found themselves so besieged by inventors clamoring to learn how to patent that, organizing as Munn & Company, they established their own patenting agency, eventually the largest in the world.

Part of the agency's eminence may have stemmed from the fact that Munn, in a kind of mutual assistance pact, offered its patrons at least a line or so, or, if the invention warranted it, a complete article in *Scientific American*, its house organ. Among its clients over the years were thousands of obscure and unsuccessful inventors, but it also snagged stars such as Edison, whose "talking machine" earned full coverage in 1877. Boasting that its branch office's choice location "directly opposite the Patent Office in Washington" allowed it to furnish the inventor the most reliable advice if the inventor submitted a drawing, a description or a model, and five dollars, Munn also wooed women clients by highlighting their achievements in issues of *Scientific American*. The number of women's patents bearing the familiar "Munn & Co." endorsement indicates that Munn's service paid handsome dividends. A good example of the agency's appeal to women is this front-page article headlined WOMEN'S RIGHTS in *Scientific American* in 1861:

> Women can also apply for and obtain patents upon the same terms as the sterner sex. We frequently take out patents for ladies; but they do not exercise their ingenuity as much as they ought. If the woman-patentee is of age she can transfer a patent legally, and enjoy all the rights and privileges of any one.

What Munn failed to mention was that in many states it was marital status rather than age that determined the "rights and privileges" a woman could enjoy. In all states, a single woman patentee could do as she saw fit with her patent rights—manufacture and sell her device herself or contract with another party to do so in exchange for a set fee, a percentage of profits, or stock in the company. The situation for married women, however, was quite different. Most states had laws that either transferred ownership of a married woman's property to her husband outright or empowered him to make decisions about its disposition. It wasn't until around mid-century that states began to repeal property laws that discriminated against married women, a process that took about fifty years before universal acceptance. At the time of the advertisement, there were still a good many states to go. The

Men's absence during the Civil War required women to understand mechanical devices.

advertisement was otherwise well timed, for it appeared at the beginning of the Civil War, and Munn thought, quite rightly, that women, now faced with mechanical work their husbands had previously performed, might have good ideas for improvement; in filing, they could take up the wartime slack.

They were certainly taking up the slack elsewhere. The prewar cult of "true womanhood," which extolled the womanly virtues of piety, purity, submissiveness, and domesticity, found its most fertile ground in rural America, where the good old American traits of endurance, independence, hard work, and thrift underlay the agrarian image. But the war forced even those "true" women to master enough basic mechanics to operate and repair plows, harvesters, and reapers in addition to their household chores. One company capitalized on the metamorphosis by depicting a woman driving her horse with its attached "patented spring steel tooth sulky rake" in its advertisement. In an accompanying "balloon," the woman driver explained: "My brother has gone to the war." It was a scene played out throughout the country.

Husbands such as Union Corporal George B. Phifer might have tried to tell their harried wives to limit themselves to the basics ("I don't expect you to do the same amount of work we have all done when I was at home"), but most wives, like his wife, Louisa, knew that keeping the farm together was their best investment for the future:

> We intend to take as good care of things as is possible till you get back. George if there is anything you want done that We have not done Write and let us know what it is for We want to do the things as you want them done.... It is too wet to plow next Tuesday. When spring Work does commence it will make a very hurrying time for I think from the looks of the Wheat that it will be an early harvest. But I think if we keep at the work Steady we will do a great deal in the course of the Summer.

Farm wives were not the only ones working hard. All women assumed extra burdens at home, provided emergency clothing and rations to the men at the front, and faithfully attended local aid society meetings, burdens that were both exhausting and empowering. For four terrible years, they maintained meticulous records, not only of donors and donations but also of collaboration for the common cause, of shared grief, of the newly forged bonds of sisterhood. In the South, women worked primarily in their local groups, but in the North they augmented their local work with a series of "Sanitary Fairs" in the large cities, to raise funds for the government-sponsored United States Sanitary Commission, which was charged with coordinating and monitoring donations and providing hospital care for the troops. Though the prevailing myth until that time had been that women's sphere was rightly the home, given their capacities and predelictions, times—and tunes—had changed now that women were needed in the public sphere. As the Reverend Byron Sunderland said in his opening remarks at one such fair held in the Patent Office in Washington and attended by President and Mrs. Lincoln and their elder son, Robert: "It would be strange, indeed, if woman should not have found her mission in times like this."

That mission involved traveling to local aid societies to collect whatever bounty the local groups had assembled to be sold to aid their soldier boys. From the ranks of these organizers rose a cadre of talented speakers and writers, women, such as Mary Livermore, who in coming decades would turn their talents to a series of social and political reforms, and to the improvement of their own status. They had a new authority born of their wartime work. They had wheedled store owners into providing free supplies and pastors into rigging church sanctuaries with tables for cutting, sewing, knitting, boxing, and shipping; they had commandeered town halls from aldermen; they had sweet-talked railroad men into free transportation for Aid Society boxes bound for the front and for themselves when bound for regional meetings; they had cajoled into acquiescence those husbands who thought it unseemly for their wives to be saleswomen.

Among the women partially liberated from domestic circles were the relatively few inventors who had tackled specific wartime problems. Overall, the number of patenting women increased sharply during the war, and the fact that the rate continued to rise in the years immediately following verifies that the flurry of patenting activity reflected the elevation of women's position in society. There was still a sharp gap, however, between the number of women who invented "domestic improvements" and the much smaller number who addressed war-related problems.

But women were still responsible for a range of inventions related directly to the fighting of the war. New Yorker Mary Jane Montgomery, for example, patented improved planking of iron- or steel-armored war vessels to discourage barnacles, oysters, and other sea animals from attaching themselves to the hull and hindering the sailing capacity of a ship. Sarah Mather improved upon her own 1845 invention of a submarine telescope for locating and studying underwater objects. Temperance P. Edson invented a "Self-inflator" for raising sunken vessels. Sarah Hussey, noting from her experience as an army hospital nurse that "sick soldiers suffer unnecessary bodily pain from the want of a suitable head and foot rest, and are subjected to many inconveniences from the want of a table directly over the bed," combined those requirements into a hospital table that served in all capacities: head and foot rest, drawer space for personal articles, book rest with pivots to hold the book open, even as a sling to elevate or lower injured limbs. Though Clevelander Sarah Mossman's contribution was nothing mechanical, it was a welcome addition to a soldier's gear—a folding waterproof cover and neckpiece that could be attached to a military cap and, when unfurled, converted it from dress cap to foul-weather gear.

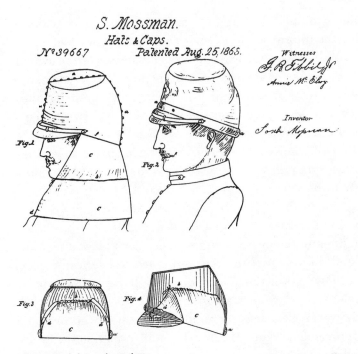

A hat invented during the Civil War.

Also directly related to the war were the famous Coston pyrotechnic night signals, a system employing different-colored pyrotechnical fires, coded so that senders and receivers could communicate between distant points. The patent was issued to Martha Coston, whose husband had first tested the signals under navy auspices at Hampton Roads, Virginia, two decades before the Civil War. When he died before perfecting or patenting the system, he left his young widow only a rough chart of the idea, but it was she who worked out a way to put his concept into practice. Since the inventor is whoever "reduces to practice" the idea, a process that can range all the way from working out the details that make the invention actually *work* to simply applying for the patent, Martha Coston more than qualified to have obtained the patent in her own name. But she deferred to her deceased husband in the patent (she received it as the "administrix" of his estate) because he had a well-established reputation that gave her special credibility—and respectability. The socially and politically well-connected widow even had John Quincy Adams witness her patent application.

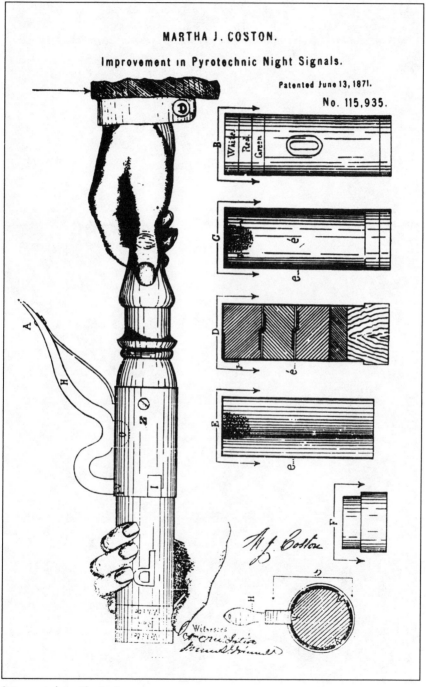

Coston pyrotechnic night signals.

Martha Coston, inventor of pyrotechnic night signals.

Coston had never been a shrinking violet. Having fallen in love with the dashing young inventor at sixteen, she eloped with him only a few years later in defiance of parental wishes. The secret out, the couple moved to Washington, where he worked for the navy and she cut such a social swath that her husband, she wrote in her autobiography, considered her "the very queen of women." The social and political connections she formed in the nation's capital (Henry Clay was only one of the many names she dropped) provided much-needed assistance to the social monarch when less than five years after their wedding her husband's sudden death left her with four small children and without "good recipes for the perfect combination of chemicals" for the signals.

The bereft widow spent many discouraging years hiring chemists and conducting tests. Then a massive fireworks display in honor of Cyrus Field, who had successfully conveyed a message to Queen Victoria on his Atlantic cable, convened the nation's greatest pyrotechnists in New York. Among them, she discovered men skillful enough to help solve the enigma of her husband's invention. The problems settled, she concluded a sale of three hundred sets of signals to the navy for about five thousand dollars and took out patents in the United States and most other maritime nations. At the onset of the Civil War, the government bought the American rights for twenty thousand dollars and contracted with her to build the flares. Her reputation and fortune were made, and she became an enduring symbol for those working to belie continuing claims that women never invented anything.

No such success awaited Clarissa Britain, who began her professional life as a Yankee schoolmistress but later, due to the exigencies of wartime, turned to invention. Britain, whose brother had laid out the streets of the original village of Saint Joseph, Michigan, was so proud of the work she had done as principal of the Niles Female Seminary in Niles, Michigan, that she was not embarrassed to advertise in the *Niles Republican* in 1843 that she had, "by her kindness, industry and perseverance as an instructress," created such a splendid school that "parents wishing to give their daughters an education, can find no institution more desirable, or place them under a person better qualified for the duty."

After moving to South Carolina to continue her teaching, Britain found herself in alien territory when the Civil War broke out, and returned north to Saint Joseph. Being jobless and dependent upon family members at forty-nine must have wounded her pride, for it was at that time that she began her patenting efforts in an apparent attempt to become self-supporting again. She first patented a floor warmer, but when she received the papers, she "found to my great chagrin that the figures were bottom-upward," making the warmer "utterly worthless." She begged the commissioner of patents to let her redraft the drawings. The harried commissioner responded that he could not change a patent once granted but would recommend she reapply. He enclosed "rules and directions for your perusal." She never responded, either for lack of time or funds.

Instead, she turned her attention to an ambulance. She was obviously aware of the difficulty of maneuvering ambulances onto the battlefield and thus designed what she described in her patent as a "safe, cheap, and comfortable" ambulance whose framework, compactly collapsed, could be hauled to the site and re-erected on top of wagon bodies the army used to transport the sick and wounded. Bearers could remove the stretchers from the racks, load the wounded onto them on the battlefield, and, without transferring the injured, return the stretchers to their slots in the ambulance framework and thus avoid unnecessary jostling.

Moving from battlefield to kitchen, Britain concentrated on a "New and Improved Potato Boiler" that vented steam out of the room and whose inner kettle the cook could easily raise from the boiling pot to prevent scalding her hands. The schoolteacher, accustomed to having her instructions heeded and positive that "the female half of the population [would] welcome" her boiler, twitted her Munn & Company attorney to pester the patent examiners to proceed on her patent application. Accordingly, the attorney apprised the commissioner: "She has apprehensions that her invention will not be fully appreciated by the male portion of society because they are freed from the steaming and scorching effects of the kitchen." She received the patent forthwith.

Britain subsequently patented two improvements to the boiler, a dinner pail with a lantern (recommended for miners), and a combination lamp-burner. Since assignment files at the National Archives yield no evidence of transactions for the sale of rights to any of her seven patents, one can assume that Britain never benefitted financially from her ingenuity. Nor did she become known for her work, even locally. At her death near the close of the century, at the age of seventy-nine, the local Saint Joseph paper summarized only: "She was a fine lady and esteemed by all who knew her."

Rebecca Sherwood had better luck—but she had to work for it. With wartime shortages of materials, Sherwood's invention for reducing straw to pulp and then substituting it for wood pulp might well have been applauded, but when she asked her husband to run tests of it at the local mill where he worked, his fellow workers gathered around to guffaw and jeer that no *woman* could improve upon their methods. The Sherwoods accepted the ribbing; but when the mill owner himself tried to patent a suspiciously similar process, the combative Rebecca Sherwood slapped him with an "interference" suit and, in the testimony assembled for the case, thus preserved for posterity the steps in her invention's incubation.

After the mill owner's attorney repeatedly referred to the patent application for her "so-called" invention as being so "exceedingly vague that [it] baffles all ingenuity," he called for some show of "reliable evidence." Sherwood produced it. She told how she, the inventive housewife, converted her clothes boiler to hold a steaming cauldron of "a pretty strong soapy solution" in which she boiled straw until it was pulpy enough to substitute for wood pulp. *And* she had witnesses! A gaggle of neighbors backed her up, supplying specific dates and descriptions of unusual kitchen commotion. Recalled one:

> [S]he was attending to her household duties, but she apologized for her dirty stove and said she had been boiling her straw on it and it had boiled over. . . . Some of the preparations were in teacups and bowls scattered around on the window sills and tables and on the mantel piece. . . . She told me she knew how to make paper pulp. She was very positive of getting a patent and said she should have one.

Another witness told how Sherwood had inadvertently dropped a piece of straw into her wash and found that it turned white and pulpy. All she had to do was try to duplicate the process:

> She [Sherwood] said she was trying to produce a pulp for making paper. She also showed me some of the straw that she had boiled the

> color from and the water that she boiled it in, but she would not tell me what was in it [because] she was afraid that I would be trying to get out a patent, so I received no information. . . . We hardly ever met but that she had something to say about getting out a patent right for that paper pulp.

Providentially, Sherwood had preserved those pulp samples she showed disbelieving friends ("some in small sheets and pieces—balls like—and some in boxes with other specimens") and produced them as prima facie exhibits for the patent examiners. She won her case, and her straw pulp samples still remain in a National Archives file, though there are no records of her having sold the rights to the process.

Though there were important exceptions, many women, who during the Civil War developed technical know-how from running, repairing, or replacing mechanical implements their absent husbands and sons formerly manipulated, regressed to more dependent roles in the peace that followed. This withdrawal of women from fields in which they had finally validated their skills alarmed feminists, who campaigned for educational reforms in the future. Matilda Gage, who had entered the suffrage movement at the National Woman's Rights Convention at Syracuse in 1852 and had since been one of its most ardent advocates, wrote that women's lack of scientific and mechanical training reminded her of the friend whose "perfect passion for engineering" would have led her into engineering had "she" been a "he":

> But she was a woman. She had been taught from her earliest childhood that to make use of this talent which God had endowed her, would be an outrage against society; so she lived for a few years, going through the routine of breakfasts and dinners, journeys and parties, that society demanded of her, and at last sank into her grave, after having been of little use to the world or herself.

Gage's story appeared in one of the first issues of the new weekly journal *The Revolution*, founded in 1868 with a circulation of around two thousand and edited by Elizabeth Cady Stanton and Parker Pillsbury, a Massachusetts reformer who had been active in the anti-slavery crusade. Susan B. Anthony, its manager and financial strategist, was listed on the masthead as "Proprietor." The paper, whose motto was "Men, their rights and nothing more; women, their rights and nothing less," included news of anything related to the women's rights cause.

It was, therefore, the ideal medium in which to paint the grim picture of the predicament of bright girls with mechanical skills. With none of the educational advantages of their brothers or the encouragement of society, they proceeded to a bleak adulthood that stifled their once-promising ingenuity, mired them in the torpor of conventional activities, and left their ambitions unrealized. They succumbed at last to depression—and death. The utter waste was too much for Gage, who wrote of her friend: "What a benefit she might have been to her sex had she dared to exercise her powers. Her example would have opened the way for hundreds more to find health and wages and freedom, in some congenial occupation outside of the prescribed limits."

Outside those "prescribed limits," however, women's experiences were woefully inadequate to deal with business matters, and *The Revolution*'s editors, always concerned about the vulnerability of un-suspecting women, had advice for them. In "Let Every Woman Be Her Own Adviser," women were told to purchase a copy of *Every Man His Own Lawyer* so that they could protect their own property, rights, and privileges. Inventive women, newly embarked in the business world, would need just such grounding in the law.

# AFTER THE WAR: INVENTING WITHIN WOMAN'S SPHERE

*I*n the political and social ferment of the post–Civil War years, women's rights leaders, most of whom were deeply committed to the Abolitionist cause, were incensed when the Reconstruction era's Fifteenth Amendment enfranchised black men but left women—black and white—without the vote. So outraged were Elizabeth Cady Stanton and Susan B. Anthony that they demanded a separate amendment that would simultaneously enfranchise women in all states. Without such an amendment, getting the vote for women would have to proceed by the slower route of gradually amending state constitutions, as they were already trying to do to achieve property and divorce law reform. Support for the woman suffrage amendment was scattered, however, and a discouraged Stanton warned that it would probably be a century before women could vote. She was almost right. The schism that developed within the suffrage movement over both means and methods deeply grieved the politically inclined—since it was already hard to convince women to change the status quo at a time when their immediate goal was to return to their prewar domestic scene. With most women willingly exchanging soldiers' aid society meetings for home-centered activities, those who might have been inventing important machines were instead devising better feather dusters.

Even farm women, whose wartime independence had been especially pronounced, chose to peruse columns such as "Aunt Hattie's Household Talks" in *American Agriculturalist* rather than suffrage tracts. While their husbands pored over articles and ads for the latest equipment in their farm magazines (there were three or four in every leading farm state), they devoured articles on a broad range of domestic topics, from food preparation to medicine, from fiction to gardening, from etiquette to sewing and cleaning. Farm magazines obviously knew their quarry, for their woman readers may have aspired to the "new order" about which the suffragists preached, but, freighted with a sentimentalized tradition that viewed them as provincial angels warming hearths, baking bread in scoured kitchens, solacing the discouraged, ministering to the sick, and sacrificing for everyone, they demanded few changes in the "woman's place is in the home" canon by which they had been raised. They seldom dreamed of political equality, for rural America was essentially traditional, conservative. Stanton's own father, Judge Cady, unable to tolerate her radicalism, once barred her from visiting (and presumably embarrassing) him at their home in "sleepy old Johnstown."

Rural women would probably have traded the long-range benefits of suffrage for the immediate ones of technology—had anybody offered them the choice. Men and women alike had only the most rudimentary tools to aid them in their work. In the post–Civil War era, running water was primarily an urban luxury; only a few farmhouses boasted so much as an inside pump. If husbands wanted hay balers, wives wanted indoor plumbing. If husbands wanted log-cutters, wives wanted cooking ranges. Women demanded and got a good many pieces of labor-saving "domestic machinery," from apple peelers to sewing machines, but, as Norton Juster pointed out in his study of farm women, they used the time saved to take on new tasks for which they previously had been too busy.

Still, Juster points out, these new devices improved their outlook on life, and that was not all bad, for farm women's work was ceaseless drudgery, menial labor so backbreaking that it drove thousands of younger rural women to seek urban factory jobs. Those who remained

A farm woman's work is never done.

tried to convince themselves they were in a far better place than those who had left only to find that they had exchanged one form of enslavement for another, but the flip side of dreams of healthful recreation and happy evenings beside cozy firesides was long, dreary, exhausting hours.

The following complaints voiced in farm journals cover only a range of several years, but they aptly describe a generations-old condition. Wrote one correspondent: "My weary limbs are scarcely stretched for repose, before red dawn peeps into my chamber window, and the birds, in the whispering leaves over the roof, apprise me by their sweetest notes that another day of toil awaits me. I arise, the harness is hastily adjusted and once more I step upon the tread-mill." Another agreed: "I am fifty years of age and a farmer's wife. I have never known anything but hard work." When *Cosmopolitan* magazine sponsored a contest for the best essay depicting the life of a farm woman, it awarded the prize to the contestant who limned a similarly bleak outlook: "There are times when heart and hands are filled with cares so heavy that she doubts her ability to lift the burdens, much less carry them safely to a hopeful ending of all trouble."

It was natural that farm women, being intimately acquainted with farm work, addressed its problems creatively and patented their solutions. Anna Corey Baldwin of Newark, New Jersey, is a good example of a woman determined to maximize the profits of a family business via her own creativity. Between 1869 and 1879 she received four patents, all based upon her knowledge of her husband's dairy. In one process, she boiled milk with water, cooled it to recover the floating bone marrow, boiled the marrow to drive off further moisture, and used the end product for ointments or pomatum, a key ingredient for pommades widely used to set or "slick" coiffures. Practicing the old maxim "Waste not, want not," she churned the remaining mixture into butter.

In another process, the inventive Baldwin allowed raw milk to stand for two or three days, retrieved whey from the curds, dripped it through a series of perforated shelves, and further drained off the precipitate through gauze-covered faucets. Whatever curd remained she turned into cheese or fed to the chickens. By fermenting the precious whey with brown sugar, she produced "an excellent cordial, or at the pleasure of the operator, a good strong vinegar." Her patent even supplied the recipe: for cordial, one pound of sugar to six quarts of whey; for vinegar, one pound of sugar to sixteen quarts of whey, though she added firmly, "I desire it to be distinctly understood that I do not confine myself to any given quantities, as climate temperature, &c. may necessitate different proportions."

She also had an idea for cooling milk quickly. She introduced a tube filled with cold water or ice into the cooling vessel and added a lid with paddles attached to agitate the milk and force more of its particles against the cold surface. The device was very similar to the hand-cranked ice cream freezer, except that in the latter the ice is on the outside and the cream in the inner tube.

Within a few years, though she had not sold rights to any previous patents, Baldwin patented again, this time her "Hygienic Glove-Milker," guaranteed to "do the work many times faster than the old hand process, and at a great saving of tax on the hands of the milker." It was simple but effective: an elastic rubber sack was secured against the udder with a constricting band that terminated in four tubes for teats; each tube discharged into a larger tube, which connected to an adjacent suction pump—all, explained Baldwin, like an inverted glove—the upper part the hand on the udder, the tubes and bands, the thumb and fingers on the teats. Phyllis Schlafly, a twentieth-century writer and political activist, saluted Anna Baldwin over a century later as the inventor of the first suction milking machine, perhaps a bit of an overstatement, since several men also patented similar devices before her 1879 "cow-milker." There is no record that Baldwin sold her milker.

Baldwin was undoubtedly typical of the many farm wives who rose shortly after four each morning, built the fires, and milked from four to eight cows before preparing breakfast at six—after which she churned, and churned and churned. One exhausted churner once reported, "[M]any are the books of poems, histories, stories and newspapers I have read through while churning!" Then as now there was no lack of pressure on the weary domestic worker to keep up her personal appearance in the midst of chores. A "Mrs. H. M. R." (wisely anony-

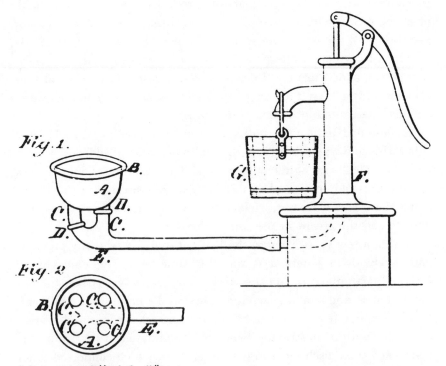

Dairywoman Anna Baldwin's Cow-Milker.

Churning butter: a steady job for mother.

mous) wrote in *American Agriculturalist:* "The first thing in the morning, *see that your hair is neatly combed and put up,* and your toilet made in such a way that you would not be ashamed to see anyone. Of course, you will dress according to your business, but always clean, whole and tidy." The author's tirade against personal sloth ("There is no excuse for going with the hair looking like a fright") was too much for one woman, "An Overworked Farmer's Wife," who demanded that Mrs. H. M. R. explain to her how she could get everything done *and* look great without mechanical help with her churning!

Her outrage smacked of the same bitterness Iowan Emily Hawley Gillespie felt upon hearing that a neighbor woman had been committed to an asylum. Gillespie, who skimmed and washed twenty-four milk pans every day and churned several times a week in addition to all her other farm chores, groaned in her diary: "I only wonder that more women do not have to be taken to that asylum, especially farm wives. No society except hired men to eat their meals. Hard work from the beginning to the end of the year. Their only happiness lies in their children with fond hopes that *they* may rise higher." The desolation was palpable.

A few women tried to develop farm projects into paying businesses, hence the spate of patents for chicken coops, egg crates, and apiaries. As early as the Civil War, Thiphena Hornbrook, who knew her bees, patented a ventilated case that looked like a shed to enclose one or two hives. From outside, the beekeeper could not only reach through a slot to remove the dirt tray from the bottom of the hive without touching the hive itself but also could place food for the bees in a feeding trough attached to the door of the shed. Many other women followed her patenting trail, for society considered beekeeping an essentially "feminine" occupation; the constant care involved in maintaining colonies of bees was perceived to be more in line with a woman's nurturing side. Moreover, beekeeping was said to be therapeutic as well: Attending to the needs and harvesting the honey of the busy little workers put roses in the cheeks by keeping the tenders in the fresh air. And selling honey was thoroughly genteel.

The surest source of pride and outside income for the farm woman was from the sale of butter. As early as mid-century, *People's Journal* reported that 350 million pounds of butter were made annually, requiring an "expenditure of considerable physical force," and another writer called the American appetite for butter one of the wonders of the modern world. Competition for prizes at agricultural fairs was keen because, as one farm magazine pointed out, "the finest butter neatly stamped in golden balls is certain to be looked at, and the maker to be inquired for."

Well she might be inquired for, but, asked "H. M. Robinson" in "A Word to the 'Men Folks' " in *American Agriculturalist,* would she get paid for it? How many men, she asked, took into account the strenuous work that went into churning the special "rosy" butter that commanded at least five or ten cents more per pound at market? Did a farmer simply pocket the profit or did he allow his wife to "spend it as she thinks best?" It was a question many churners must have asked. Opportunities abounded for inventors to improve churns, and during the next few decades there were nearly twenty-five hundred churn patents, many by women such as Brooklynite Sarah Saul, who had obviously spent too many hours over a churn. Saul attached a handle to her churn, she explained in her patent claims, to allow the operator to work "while in the act of sitting, thereby rendering the work far less laborious than usual." She added a hand rest to ease discomfort.

As for urban women, though their wartime activities had equipped them for assuming leadership roles, they had scant time or energy to devote to their own causes when there was so much to be done just to ensure survival in the difficult years following. Virginia Penny, who during that period scouted prospects for jobs for hard-pressed women, particularly bereft widows, noted how many women, consumed by the subject of domestic contrivances, pinned their hopes on inventing a simple, cheap, easily manufactured device that would simplify the domestic grind and then on finding someone to manufacture it for them.

In her book *Think and Act*, in which she condensed material gleaned from interviews with hundreds of manufacturers, Penny learned that such opportunities were rare and urged those women with mechanical aptitude to produce and sell their own inventions rather than wait for a manufacturer to take over the project. Even then, she was not optimistic that invention was the route to economic security and speculated that while those with mechanical genius could accomplish wonders, it would be another generation before they did. Her acknowledgment that it would take another generation was born of many other observations that women were so bogged down with household responsibilities that they had scant time to devote to such projects. Though household inventions appeared to make life easier for her, they ironically resulted in more work. If a new stove facilitated baking bread, the housewife did not divert the time gained to pursue other avenues. She simply baked more bread or baked more often.

This fetish for increased production made overwrought housewives increasingly dependent upon outside help, a paradox journalist Jane Croly noted when she estimated that it took "at least two domestics to accomplish the work formerly done by the mistress of the household." Croly, née Jane Cunningham, was once a harried housewife herself until she started a newspaper career by selling articles first to the *New York Tribune* and then to other leading newspapers. Eventually she had her own column directed specifically to women under the pseudonym "Jennie June," which, in true "ladylike" fashion, preserved her anonymity.

Croly struggled to combine marriage and motherhood with a busy journalistic career, and in doing so became an important voice for ambitious women, particularly in the women's club movement. In 1868, the New York Press Club sponsored a reception and banquet for

Charles Dickens at Delmonico's but failed to include women journalists until they were shamed into it by the refusal of Horace Greeley,
then editor of the *Tribune* and the banquet chairman, to attend otherwise. Three days before the affair, the capitulating committee sent
Croly a note saying, "If a sufficient number of ladies can be found, to
prevent each other from feeling lonesome, who are willing to pay
fifteen dollars each for their tickets, they will be allowed to purchase
them." Her anger unassuaged, Croly declined the ungracious invitation: "The ladies feel that they have not been treated like gentlemen
and refuse to avail themselves of a possible opportunity so reluctantly
given."

After that experience, Croly, along with other ostracized female
journalists and leaders in all aspects of New York's social and business
life (including Ellen Demorest, with whom Croly was closely associated in business), met to lay the groundwork of their own woman's
club. They gave it the name Sorosis, which Croly fancied "for its full,
appropriate signification, its unhackneyed character and sweet sound
. . . full of all gracious meaning." A few members thought the name
sounded like a skin disease, and the viciously witty magazine *Pun-
chinello* nicknamed the group "Sore-eye Sissies," but Sorosis it remained, and the group pointedly held its first official meeting at
Delmonico's.

It was not long before men applied for membership, and Croly
composed a standard rejection that stated that the club respected the
applicant's stellar qualities, but for "the unfortunate fact of your being
a man," and continued:

> We willingly admit, of course, that the accident of your sex is on your
> part a misfortune and not a fault; nor do we wish to arrogate any-
> thing to ourselves, because we had the good fortune to be born
> women. . . . Sorosis is too young for the society of gentlemen and
> must be allowed time to grow. By and by, when it has reached a
> proper age, say twenty-one, it may ally itself with the Press Club or
> some other male organization of good character and standing. But for
> years to come its reply to all male suitors must be, "Principles, not
> men."

By the time Croly assumed the editorship of *Demorest's Illustrated
Monthly Magazine,* published by William Jennings Demorest and his

wife, Ellen, she had become a feminist stalwart whose pronouncements on everything from women's clothes to women's work found a wide audience through the pages of *Demorest's* and her own books.

Ellen Demorest, Croly's employer and fellow founder of Sorosis, was the daughter of a well-to-do Saratoga, New York, hat manufacturer. She began her business life as the leading milliner for wealthy summer visitors, and moved her business to New York, where she met and married William Jennings Demorest, a dry goods merchant with a penchant for promoting new ideas, one of which was to upgrade plain Mrs. Demorest to "Mme. Demorest" to connote Parisian chic for her Emporium of Fashions. A friend thought the name especially fitting: "Personally, she is the French style of beauty. Full erect and graceful, with sparkling blue eyes, rather prominent nose, smiling expression and a profusion of flossy black hair, with very easy conversational powers, she is a most charming and agreeable woman beloved by all who know her."

When Demorest observed a maid cutting a dress from a crude pattern, she enlisted her sister's help in adapting foreign styles to suit American taste, and thrifty sewers were soon using the Demorests' familiar tinted tissue paper dress patterns to copy high-styled couture dresses, which they then ran up on their home sewing machines. Patterns became the most lucrative part of the Demorest business, but they were unable to patent their invention because New England tailor Ebenezer Butterick, who had begun by selling men's clothes patterns during the Civil War and then edited the rival *Delineator* magazine, had already received a patent. It was not, however, the end of Ellen Demorest's inventive career.

She invented, but did not patent, an inexpensive hoop skirt, which won prizes at many fairs, and an "Imperial Dress Elevator," a device to hoist long skirts. The dress elevator was so popular that "Imperial" became the code name for any device that raised a skirt. When women asked each other, "Are you wearing your Imperial today?" they knew what they meant. Demorest did patent two items—a floor for an elevator shaft and a "puff" for arranging hair—but neither enjoyed the commercial success of the other, heavily advertised but unpatented, devices.

Inventor Demorest, entrenched though she was in the world of fashion, was a socially conscious woman eager to provide work for other women, and with the aid of wealthy feminist Susan King, she established the Woman's Tea Company to import tea for impoverished gentlewomen to sell on commission. In 1872, they fitted out and renamed an old Spanish bark the *Madame Demorest* and hired a crew of women. When the ship was ready to leave, even jaded New Yorkers who had called the venture "a mere school girl's romance" and "a funny joke" jostled the press, bankers, and merchants to board launches for the send-off party. A minister blessed the ship as an "evangel to preach a new gospel, not the gospel of women's rights but of women's acts"; a newspaper writer lauded women's achievements in the "great business world, where thought, energy, judgment, industry, management, discretion and physical endurance are indispensible to the gaining of a fortune, representation and power." As the ship sailed off, Demorest delivered a commendable credo:

> I do not claim that all women, or a large portion of them, should enter into independent business relations with the world, but I do claim that all women should cultivate and respect in themselves an ability to make money.

Demorest and "Jennie June" Croly might appear to today's feminists to be fence-straddlers in their attitude toward what constituted woman's natural sphere, but they were both unequivocal in their support of a woman's right to choose her sphere, even if they themselves tended toward conventional views. Though Croly's feminist principles might have made her an enemy of housewifery, for example, she hoped that if her publications could elevate housework to a field in which women aspired to become specialists, their attention would return to the home.

Ennobling the performance of household tasks was not a new idea. George Washington Burnap, who laid the groundwork in his lectures on the perimeters of woman's special sphere, intoned: "It is no degradation to the finest lady to know all the details of domestic affairs. . . . A woman, though she may be as wise as Minerva, and as accomplished as the Graces, ought to know all the details of house affairs." Mrs. Cornelius's still-popular *Young Housekeeper's Friend* had assured its readers that God smiled upon those who faithfully and cheerfully discharged their duties, "however lowly." And Croly at this stage of her life was inclined to agree. Though Stanton had argued that the only reason women performed household tasks was because men wouldn't,

The famous corner: Washington Office of Munn & Co.

or at least didn't, Croly claimed that Providence endowed women with "a natural instinct of cleanliness" that made them willing disciples of housekeeping. Inborn proclivity or not, however, she worried that some women carried their devotion too far. Being too ardent a votary of housekeeping, she warned, might actually drive prospective husbands away. While swains might respect them as "good girls," they invited their "pretty, stylish, useless sisters" to the ball, for, said Croley, "Men generally fall in love as stupidly as possible, and marry the objects of their affection—if they can. In almost every instance where a man marries a sensible woman, it is after he has met with a severe disappointment in not marrying a fool."

Her own predelictions aside, Croly was well aware of the chorus of other voices saying that not every woman was cut out for the task, and a few years later, in her book *For Better or Worse*, artfully subtitled *A Book for Some Men and All Women*, she allowed this "natural vagabond" her say: "I hate living in a house to which one is tied by the necessity of keeping it and taking care of it. . . . I never was so happy as when I was first married, and we lived, Bohemian fashion, in two rooms, and took our dinners at a restaurant." Croly began more and more to sympathize with "good women, faithful wives and conscientious mothers, who, at times, are wrought up to a pitch almost of insanity by the wearing and eternal recurrence of petty cares and duties."

As others, such as Transcendentalist Abby Morton Diaz, reported that overworked and compulsive housekeepers filled the women's wards in New England insane asylums, Croly took heart from the prospect that labor-saving devices would soon free women to perform more important service, especially improving their minds and overseeing their children's education. In a few years, her optimism waned as she observed that middle-class women made a pitiable swap by trading emancipation from housework for servitude to fashion and endless hours of work for unproductive leisure. With an enlightened Ellen Demorest giving her wide latitude as social critic, Croly moved from discussions of housekeeping to use *Demorest's* to espouse higher education for women, equality in marriage, career training for all young women, improved working conditions, and entrance into the professions.

Though Croly moved on to discussing other roles for women, there is no question that society as a whole continued to consider housekeeping woman's primary obligation. After the four long years of Civil War conflict, postwar women gave first priority to reestablishing their sway over the domestic realm, and the vast number of women's inventions dealing with the house reflect that commitment. There were, nevertheless, sea changes in the way women perceived themselves, for the Civil War had catapulted them into serious activities beyond their domestic life, and inventive women in particular prospected for wider opportunities in the peacetime economy. Seeking their patronage, Munn & Company, in a booklet of patent information for inventors, made sure such women understood that patent law made no distinction based on age or gender. Munn assured them in its monthly, *Scientific American*, that its experience with women clients contradicted the common bias against their inventive talents:

> In our practice as patent solicitors we have frequently been called upon to prepare applications for female inventors . . . and we can say to those who are unbelievers in regard to the power of women to achieve . . . anything higher than a pound-cake or a piece of embroidery, that the inventions made by women, and for which they solicit patents through our agency, are generally found to be in their practical character . . . fully equal to the same number of inventions selected at random from among those made by men.

Munn & Company accounted for a fourth of all patents ever issued up to that time. Women trusted mighty Munn, and rightly so, but they needed more than Munn. Other books and pamphlets also solicited women inventors' attention: *Snook's Inventors' Helper*, in supplying lists of "needed" inventions, prompted, "Inventors, as you read and re-read the following list, your pulse will quicken more than once as an idea of 'how it can be done' flashes with lightning vividness across your mind." Interestingly, among the ideas for invention were several for which women actually *did* acquire patents: "a non-counterfeiting paper for National and bank-bills," "a better method of fastening down carpets than with tacks," and "a successful plan for the controlling of smoke and cinders so annoying to railroad and steamboat travelers."

Women, like men, invented in whatever field they had the greatest experience. With nursing one of women's primary responsibilities, they quite naturally invented slings and pulleys to tilt, turn, or lift patients; ingenious bedside writing tables with drawers and slots for writing equipment; book racks; eating trays; stools; overhead exercise bars; room ventilators; even trapdoors under the patient for disposing of human waste.

Since women inventors naturally looked for solutions to problems indigenous to their gender, they considered "managing their monthlies" a field particularly suited to their genius. Though few women were doctors, they understood their own physical hygiene enough to envision that by relieving their sisters of discomfort with improved "Monthly Protectors," "Catamenial Sacks," "Bags," "Napkin Belts," "Safety Skirts," and "Safety Belts," they would find a ready commercial market for their inventions. Sanitary napkins were simply cloth bandages suspended from a waistband and drawn between the legs, but the manner in which inventors described the central features of their improvements reveal their concerns: "eases the wearer's discomfort, particularly in the act of sitting down"; a shape "to conform more closely to the body"; "fine, flexible, pure, odorless, and durable"; "a sack conveniently carried between the legs of the user"; "prevents the pin and its frame from abrading the body"; "a ready supply of diaper cloths when traveling or absent from their homes"; "relieving her of much anxiety as to accidents and of much trouble and embarrassment."

In addition, there were accouchement beds and a variety of gyneco-

logical devices, with an emphasis upon douche pans and vaginal irriga-
tors but extending to pessaries as well. Dr. Edward B. Foote's widely
read *Medical Common Sense*, published in 1864, recommended a pessary as a "womb veil" to prevent conception, and as the crusade for
limiting family size ("Voluntary Motherhood") gradually drew more
supporters, middle-class and upper-class women undoubtedly used pessaries for this purpose regardless of how they were described in their
patent claims.

Emeline Brigham was, for example, undoubtedly aware of the contraceptive possibilities of her "Improved Pessary," but described it
simply as "a support and covering to the mouth and neck of the uterus
in cases of female weakness, falling of the womb, and other affections
of the same." For good reason. In 1868, New York State banned
contraceptive devices, and other states soon followed. After a wave of
moral indignation against contraception, the federal government
branded birth control devices "articles for immoral use" and banned
advertisements or even information on them in the U.S. mails. With
moral reformers like Anthony Comstock ever alert to such transgres-
sions, inventors, knowing that their dual-purpose devices could be used
perfectly legally for treating "women's complaints," disavowed any
possible contraceptive intent by describing them simply as "Vaginal
Irrigator and Urinal"; "Combined Aspirator and Concealed Uterine
Cauterizer"; "Vaginal Syringe" ("to cure affectations of the uterus)";
and, simply, douche pans.

As is to be expected, the greatest number of women inventors made
articles for the home. Mary Evard, a milliner by trade, for example,
had a jeweler (probably her husband, since that was his trade) construct a tiny eighteen-by-eighteen-inch model oven and demonstrated
it to judges at a Saint Louis fair. They were incredulous at the model's
delicacy and the ingenious way she had divided the stove with movable
partitions so that wood burned in one side while coal glowed in the
other. By adding front-to-back partitions, Evard made one half suitable
for dry baking and the other for moist. Flushed with pride over its
reception at the fair and its subsequent patent, she and her husband
manufactured and sold the "Reliance Cook Stove" and demonstrated
to customers that it could simultaneously cook three pounds of lamb,
a spring chicken, soup, coffee, several varieties of vegetables, and a
small pound cake. They could hardly keep apace of the avalanche of

initial orders, but business fell off as competition heightened. Before long, the credit rater for R. G. Dun & Co., the nationwide firm whose agents regularly evaluated the stability of commercial enterprises (and the progenitor of the current Dun and Bradstreet ratings), wrote in his notebook: "Does very small business, advise care in crediting." Soon they were out of business entirely—the usual saga of good product, inadequate capitalization.

Stoves also inspired Elizabeth Hawks of Troy, New York. With heating stoves having by that time replaced the open hearth in most homes, Hawks, then fifty-seven and of "no particular occupation except as housekeeper to my family," had a "vision" of a baking attachment to her heating stove ("it was clear in my mind. . . . I had no thought of what its use was for"). Since Ann Braude, in her recent study of spiritualism, indicates that in that period, and particularly in that section of New York State, belief in such spiritual counsel was widespread, one can assume that Hawks's claim to a divine origin for her idea was sincere.

In the course of obtaining her patent and then defending it, Hawks left a trail through Patent Office files that not only limns the background of her invention but illustrates the often adversarial relationship between female applicants and male examiners. As Clarissa Britain had been sure no male could appreciate her potato boiler, Hawks was convinced that the delay in receiving her patent stemmed from men's lack of experience with household stoves. Surely, if women were patent examiners, she reasoned, they would not only recognize the merits of her invention but would not view it with a jaundiced eye because it came from a woman. It is interesting to note that all patent examiners *were* male until the appointment of Anna Nichols of Melrose, Massachusetts, in 1873.

Hoping to appeal to the examiners' sympathies, Hawks wrote them of her "debilitated state of health," her poverty, and her invention's "divine" genesis: "I called on God for help for some way to be opened for me for means desperately [needed] as we have been very unfortunate since the beginning of the war. . . . Therefore I consider it a gift from Heaven." Fortunately, her vision delineated the stove's dimensions so precisely that Hawks was able to translate those celestial instructions to a local tinsmith, who made a model for her stove with its special air chamber. She observed with delight that it "baked

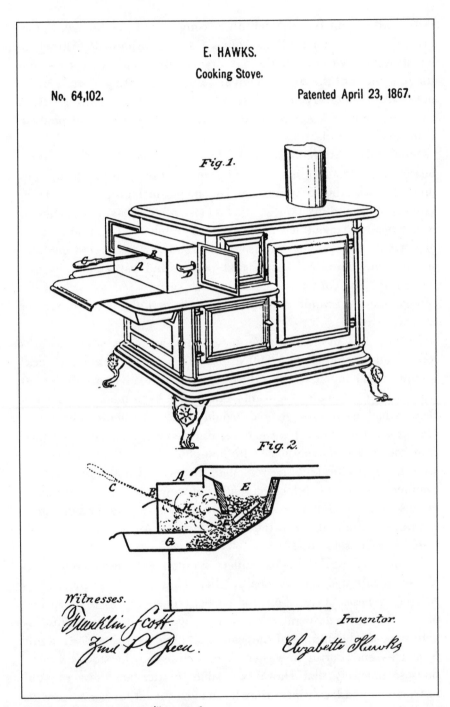

**E. HAWKS.**

Cooking Stove.

No. 64,102.

Patented April 23, 1867.

*Fig. 1.*

*Fig. 2.*

Elizabeth Hawks's stove: a "spirited" invention?

differently from what it did without it . . . baked the bread all the way through, leaving a tender crust on top." Fortified by further successful experiments, she engaged a local attorney to draw up the patent application for a stove that would, she asserted, prove a boon to "every housekeeper in the country" since dust and ashes would not scatter about the room when the baker raked or dumped the coal grate. Like many patentees, she dismissed her lawyer in favor of representing herself and proceeded to send reworded parts of her application to the commissioner of patents (who routinely turned her letters over to the examiner who handled the case). Undaunted by his refusal to add the new sections on the grounds that it was not the Patent Office's respon-sibility, she continued to add modifications, reminded him that she was in very poor health and needed the money the invention would bring, and implored him to issue the patent "at the earliest possible moment."

That moment was not yet to be. Rejected once again, the ailing inventor fired another salvo at the commissioner and accused the examiner of thickheadedness in failing to see the difference between her *heating* stove (no mention now of the crusty bread) and the *cooking* stove to which he compared it. "It has," she argued, "been approved by all that has seen and used them. It has been said by many that the invention is the greatest blessing to a sick room that was ever known for it equalizes the heat through the room."

Perhaps her husband presumed that masculine endorsement would speed the granting, for Mr. Hawks appended this on the reverse side of her letter:

> As this matter is closely connected with myself (the inventor being my wife) I take the liberty to say a few words in regard to it. . . . However simple the [illegible: method?] may appear to you it has astonished many men that has been in the stove business for many years. Many stove men has been to my place to see it say that it is the latest improvement and a good one, and parties stand ready here also in Chicago & Erie Penn to adopt and cast it with the stove.

The inventor's tale of ill health and the Lord's will, climaxed by her husband's sales pitch about eager buyers, so offended the examiner that he chastised Elizabeth Hawks, writing that his office could judge an invention only by the strictest rules as to novelty and utility and could not allow "the personal matters of which you speak to have any weight in influencing its discussions." Three months later, however, the patent was finally allowed, and she jauntily dispatched her twenty-dollar fee with instructions to "[p]lease forward as soon as possible as there are parties wishing to see the specification." Shortly thereafter, Matilda Gage, writing in *Woman as Inventor,* said that she had read in a Troy newspaper that the Empire Foundry that manufactured Hawks's auxiliary stove chamber had sold two thousand within months of its introduction and, when the model was updated, had sold two thousand more, bringing Hawks hefty royalties. Observing that the "genius of women applied to a small article" accounted for the foundry's success, Gage asked rhetorically, "Who says women cannot invent?"

And Elizabeth Hawks kept right at it, or claimed she did, because a few years later she importuned the Patent Office to add even more specifications to her original patent. An inventor who was a neighbor of Hawks in Troy, however, claimed the changes were inspired not by another visitation from the Lord but by her visit to his house where she studied his model. It appears that the patent commissioner believed him, for, in denying her additional patent coverage, he scoffed at her claim to divine inspiration: "It requires no deep research into the 'laws of psychology' to come to a pretty correct conclusion as to the cause and source of her 'vision' or impression." He was not alone in believing that spiritualism was "hokum," but from reading the Hawks files, one cannot question the sincerity of her gratitude for "divine inspiration." It is a phrase many inventors use when trying to explain where they get their problem-solving insight. In a period when thousands were drawn to the spiritualist movement, it is not surprising that Hawks would rely upon such an "unscientific" explanation.

Within the domestic realm, a good many women confined there by societal norms, choice, or circumstance must have wondered why, if they were in charge of the house, they should not design it themselves. Although not the first woman to design a house, Harriet Irwin was the first one to patent her design. Irwin was the frail third child in the family of Robert Hall Morrison, a highly respected minister and founder and first president of Davidson College in North Carolina. But even after she obtained a patent on a house and actually had it constructed, most men still thought the field should be reserved to the male of the species—for women, they asserted, could neither understand the mathematics of stress nor tramp around to supervise the job of construction.

The battle lines were, not surprisingly, drawn by gender. Noted architect Calvert Vaux pointed out in his mid-century publication *Villas and Cottages* that women would be inappropriate in a profession that called for "climbing ladders [and] mingling with the mechanics and laborers during the progress of the works." Women, however, were likely to feel that no one had a clearer idea of what should go into the design of a home than a woman. In 1848, Louisa Tuthill dedicated her tome on the history of architecture: "To the Ladies of the United States of America, the Acknowledged Arbiters of Taste." And during the Civil War years Harriet Beecher Stowe, who with her sister Catherine Beecher authored many articles and books about houses and house-keeping, longed for the day when women could put their practical wisdom into action: "One of the greatest reforms that could be, in these reforming days . . . would be to have women architects. The mischief with the houses built to rent is that they are all male contrivances."

With all modesty, however, Harriet Irwin never laid claim to being an architect or even to being "first" in design. As indicated by her patent's title, *"Improvement* in the Construction of Houses" (italics added), she was aware that the house was not entirely original but was an improvement upon previously constructed octagonal and hexagonal houses. However, it seems remarkable that in a period when men spoke snidely of women's "little house plans," Irwin, without benefit of formal training, not only planned and patented her house, she *built* it, at 912 West Fifth Street in Charlotte. Though not corresponding exactly to her patent drawings' compact design, its lozenge shape was achieved by avoiding a central hall, and it saved space, materials, and heat while affording superior ventilation and lighting. It also avoided corners, for Irwin, a scrupulous housekeeper, wanted none "for the dirt to get in."

The following year her husband and his brother-in-law formed the General Land Company and, as Hill & Irwin, advertised their hexagonal houses in the Charlotte *Southern Home* as "the most economical, most durable, and most elegant mode of building yet practiced." In an article that *Southern Home* reprinted from the Huntsville, Missouri, *Herald,* a reporter proclaimed that Irwin's designs (news of which had

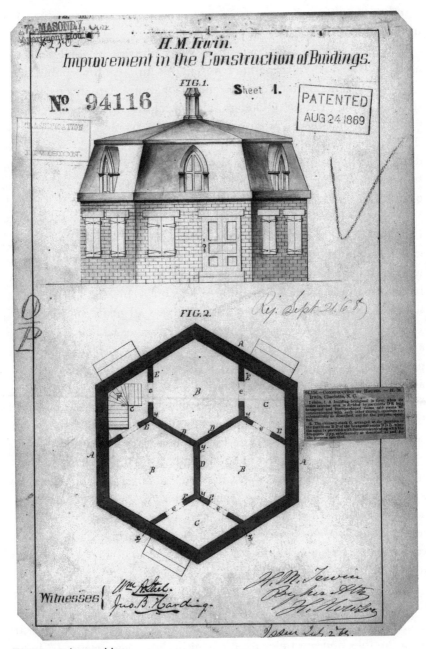

Harriet Irwin's hexagonal house.

The Irwin house in Charlotte, N.C.

obviously spread) opened "a new era in architecture" because of their highly economical use of space: the rooms fit together so neatly that an eighty-foot exterior hexagonal wall enclosed a third more space than a wall of equal length in a square configuration. According to the *Herald*, Mrs. Irwin guaranteed her buildings would also be far handsomer than quadrangular ones if the plans were "in the hands of a good architect."

A century later, many Charlotte residents were still fond of the two-story, mansard-roofed house topped with a central tower. Irwin's name, too, survived, for in 1962, when the *Charlotte News*'s "Chatter Box" columnist asked her readers, "Who is Harriet Irwin?" telephone calls and letters swamped the switchboard. Harriet Morrison Irwin, bearing the names of two prominent North Carolina families, the

Morrisons and the Irwins, left descendants who knew her story well, particularly her proud grandson, who supplied many details of her life. Though other Irwin houses had already fallen to the wrecking ball by 1962, the *Charlotte News* announced HARRIET MORRISON IRWIN'S HOUSE STILL STANDS, a testament to her inventive genius. Only one major change was visible: The front yard and original porch steps had been sacrificed to municipal improvements. As the population of the small town of less than four thousand burgeoned over the years, the once narrow lane the house faced had given way to a four-lane highway that necessitated relocating the entrance to the side. Since then, the whole house, Harriet Irwin's "first," has been razed in the name of progress.

The woman behind this patented house was a genteel Southerner whose father was committed to the education of women. "Educate the women," he often expounded, "and you elevate the whole race of mankind." After home instruction, his daughter progressed with her sisters to the Moravian church's Institution for Female Education at Salem, North Carolina (later Salem College). There, the "Morrison girls" expanded the limited curriculum centered on "woman's sphere" with their own voracious reading. Blessed with intellectual vigor, Harriet was an eminently successful student whose early passion for reading compensated for the lifelong frail health that limited her physical activities. That yen for knowledge and her authorship of articles for magazines and newspapers on colonial and revolutionary America and Charlotte's early history brought her a well-earned reputation as a scholar and historian.

At twenty she married a well-to-do Mobile cotton manufacturer and moved to Alabama for a short time until her delicate health prompted their return to North Carolina, where she lived a conventional Southern girl's life as wife, mother, and housekeeper for two decades, decades that brought death in infancy to four of her nine babies and deprivation and family losses during the Civil War, including the battlefield demise of her brother-in-law, General Stonewall Jackson, whose daughter was born in Irwin's house during the conflict.

After the war, discouraged farmers who abandoned their wasted acreage and flocked to the city of Charlotte fostered an industrial boom there. Seeing the new market for housing, Harriet Irwin, at forty still the consummate Southern gentlewoman and listing herself in census records as "keeping house," signed "H. M. Irwin" to a patent application proposing "an entire revolution in the method of building houses" and became the first woman to patent architectural drawings. The Society of Architectural Historians, concurring with a much earlier writer's summation that: "The planning of houses . . . is not architecture at all; and the ability to arrange a house conveniently does not in the least make an architect," rightfully points out that Irwin should not be labeled the first woman architect: "[O]ne invention does not make a professional architect." Irwin's 1869 patent is still remarkable, however, in light of women's all but total exclusion from the field of architecture until then. Though women knew firsthand what they needed in domestic architecture and they scribbled, sketched, calculated, provided drawings, and even built houses, Irwin was the first to claim the credit a patent could bestow.

By the close of the 1860s, the number of patents issued to women had increased sharply to 441 from the previous decade's total of 28. Among the patentees were women who explored fields of invention far removed from their domestic confines. They were still, however, distinctly in the minority.

# 3

# NEW FIELDS
# OF INVENTION

*A*ny post–Civil War woman who dared to adapt for industrial use the devices she regularly used at home, such as sewing machines and fruit canners, faced tough competition, not to mention ridicule, from male counterparts who considered it unseemly of her to transcend the bonds of her sex to invent in areas considered far beyond what they considered her sphere—and her capabilities. In other words, she had threatened *their* sphere. Such resistance didn't daunt the brave, but it did plunge them into the middle of the highly charged "woman question." Magazine articles and stump orators demanded to know what would happen if women became inventors. What *else* would they dare? Where would it all end?

The anonymous *Scientific American* author who addressed such questions, in an article titled "Female Inventive Talent," was not encouraging about the prospect of women entering occupations calling for courage, daring, and combativeness. These were qualities, he opined, that were guaranteed to "engrave lines of character in the faces of women, and develop peculiarities and manner, which are little admired by men." In deference to the fact that women were important and lucrative clients of Munn & Company, however, he saw no threat to their entering those "creative or imitative arts which . . . give scope to the imagination" but do not unduly challenge the body or the spirit. As for his article's title, "Female Inventive Talent," he magnanimously concluded that *Scientific American*'s experience had long ago established that "women have as much inventive talent as men" but that "the circumstances under which most of them pass their lives prevent an equal manifestation on their part."

That was just it—the circumstances under which most women passed their lives. Matilda Gage, in her suffrage tract on women inventors published that same year—1870—wondered why the ancient Greeks idolized Minerva for embodying women's power and intuition while Americans looked askance at inventive women and suppressed them as inappropriate to their sex. Genius, said Gage, was an honor to their sex and should not be hidden from the light. Tracing women's inventions from ancient to contemporary times, Gage lauded women's accomplishments and countered men's sneers that women had no mechanical genius with the "Katherine Green Story" about the genesis of the cotton gin.

Given the uncertainties of Kitty Green's claim on the cotton gin, Gage might better have focused on Martha Coston, who had taken out the original patent on her maritime signals in the name of her deceased husband but then struck out on her own. After moving with her children to Europe, where she sold the signals, she hobnobbed with European royalty and glitterati and accumulated a good-sized fortune before returning to the Washington residence she christened the Villa Coston. In 1871, she patented, in her own name, a holder for pyrotechnic material, which, when twisted, caused the signal to ignite. Proud of her improvement, she compiled and distributed enthusiastic testimonials from newspapers, people who had used the signals to locate people lost at sea, marine insurers, the New York Chamber of Commerce, shipping masters and crewmen, members of Congress, yacht clubs, and the United States Navy. Hers is a success story, but in her autobiography, *Signal Success: The Work and Travels of Mrs. Martha J. Coston,* she minced no words about the tough climb to the top:

> We hear much of chivalry of men towards women; but let me tell you, gentle reader, it vanishes like dew before the summer sun when one of us comes into competition with the manly sex. Let a woman sit, weep, wring her hands, and exult in her own helplessness, and the

modern knight buckles on his imaginary breastplate and draws his
sword in her behalf; but when the woman girds up her loins for the
battle of life, ready to fight like a lioness, if need be, to put food in
the mouths of her children, let her select for her field the living-room
or the cooking range.

Still, Coston hoped her struggle might serve as encouragement to her
sisters who, "stranded upon the world with little ones looking to them
for bread may feel, not despair but courage rise in their hearts; confident that with integrity, energy, and perseverance they need no extraordinary talents to gain success and place among the world's
breadwinners."

While Coston might have believed that integrity, energy, and perseverance could compensate for extraordinary talents, this was not borne
out by the experiences of other women who invented in unusual areas.
They needed every ounce of technological expertise they could muster,
not to mention enough courage and determination to fight off would-
be male claimants to their inventions who knew they could count on
a modicum of skepticism about women's innate abilities to give cre-
dence to their claims, no matter how unfounded. Undoubtedly the best
known of those inventors, then and now, was Margaret Knight. She
was and is so well known that over a century after she patented the
process she sold (for figures variously reported at anywhere from
twenty to fifty thousand dollars), Ernest Heyn, the author of *Fire of
Genius,* was still commending her achievement: "Every shopper who
loads up at the supermarket," he wrote, "is indebted to her" because
it was she who invented the machine that folded and glued paper to
form the "satchel-bottomed" brown paper grocery bags so ubiquitous
today. Knight was able to enjoy her success during her lifetime, for her
machine attracted extraordinary attention when it first appeared, both
in Europe and America, and even the news that the machine could do
the work of thirty persons alarmed no one. Such progress, after all, was
in the "spirit of America."

Knight became the role model for other women inventors, and she
remained a popular subject among writers for decades. In 1912, two
years before her death, her "persistency and remarkable competency"
and her ability to convert disbelievers into disciples drew kudos from
Notre Dame theologian John Augustine Zahm, who wrote *Women in
Science* under the pseudonym H. J. Mozans. The 1967 *American*

*Woman's Gazetteer* even went so far as to apprise feminist pilgrims of the street address of the house in Framingham, Massachusetts, where Knight spent her last twenty-five years—southwest corner of Hollis and Charles. At her death, the newspaper in Framingham dubbed her a "woman Edison" and expansively, though erroneously, attributed to her eighty-seven patents (a much inflated figure) and the distinction of being the first woman to receive an American patent (also clearly incorrect). Still, there was a solid foundation to the stories of her inventive prowess, and celebrants of women's achievements feature her for good reason.

Her rags-to-riches story was fodder for feminists who recognized in the child mill-worker transformed into woman inventor a rousing good saga, one that Knight herself loved to tell. The basic account appears in many publications, but the original source for it appears to have been an interview Knight gave to the feminist publication *Woman's Journal* in which she was asked how an uneducated woman with no training in mechanics could develop such a machine. She replied:

> It is only following out nature. As a child, I never cared for things that girls usually do; dolls never possessed any charms for me. I couldn't see the sense of coddling bits of porcelain with senseless faces: the only things I wanted were a jack-knife, a gimlet, and pieces of wood. My friends were horrified. I was called a tomboy; but that made little impression on me. I sighed sometimes, because I was not like other girls; but wisely concluded that I couldn't help it, and sought further consolation from my tools. I was always making things for my brothers: did they want any thing in the line of playthings, they always said, "Mattie will make them for us." I was famous for my kites; and my sleds were the envy and admiration of all the boys in town. I'm not surprised at what I've done. I'm only sorry I couldn't have had as good a chance as a boy, and have been put to my trade regularly.

This inventive youngster with a knack for tools entered Manchester, New Hampshire's, cotton mills at nine or ten, saw a steel-tipped shuttle topple out of its loom and injure a worker whom it penetrated with its steel tip, and shortly thereafter devised her first invention—a shuttle-restraining device. After working in the mills until her late teens, she took on various short-term jobs and duties, which included learning the upholstery trade; doing light work at her brothers' homes ("my health being rather poor at that time"); repairing a house in Holyoke; learning daguerreotype, ambrotype, and photography; engraving letters on silver; and "trying to negotiate for a thread and trimming store." About two years after the Civil War, with ten years of such piecemeal jobs under her belt, she went to work for the Columbia Paper Bag Company in Springfield, Massachusetts, though she was still in frail health. There she joined a largely female labor force that was paid a third less than men who did the same job because managers at such manufacturing companies considered women inept at keeping machines in order. One superintendent interviewed by writer Virginia Penny gave an additional reason for penalizing women: "Their dress is objectionable, particularly their hoops, which take up much room, and are in danger of getting in the machinery."

If Knight wore a hoop—there is no record one way or another—it was no deterrent to her operating or trying to improve upon the machines. After initially skeptical fellow workers saw her experimenting with a machine that could cut, fold, and paste bag bottoms itself, thus bypassing time-consuming hand work, they gave her what they must have believed to be the ultimate compliment—they said that she had "a keener eye than any man in the world." When her employer complained about company time spent on her experiments, she intimated she might sell him the rights if her ideas proved feasible. He was interested. After making thousands of trial bags on a wooden model, she commissioned a Boston machinist to produce an iron model for patenting purposes. But before she could apply for the patent, she learned that a man who had studied her model of the machine while at the machinist's on other pretexts had subsequently patented a machine suspiciously like hers. The feisty Knight, just turned thirty-three and struggling to raise funds by working as a broker in commercial real estate, sought legal remedy through a patent interference suit against the interloper, Charles F. Annan.

Bluntly accusing him of copying her model and uncowed by his claim to priority of invention, she pitted her Washington patent attorney against Annan's legal eagle from Boston and spent one hundred dollars a day, plus expenses, for sixteen days of depositions from herself, Annan, and key Boston witnesses. Knight played to win and amply demonstrated that despite meager schooling she knew her machines. When Annan insinuated that Knight could not possibly have

Model for Margaret Knight's paper-bag machine.

designed the machine herself and attributed it to the model maker, her Washington attorney, a Mr. Stanbury, rolled out Knight's former employer, who scotched the accusation: "The idea of a machine for the manufacture of square-bottomed bags originated in conversation between Miss Knight and myself. . . . I saw them folded myself and most certainly there is no doubt that it was her idea." Moreover, her Boston mechanic testified that since the wooden model was already making bags when she brought it to him and the no-nonsense Knight had ordered him to comply with her instructions "absolutely—whether right or wrong," the minor changes he suggested never altered the fundamental principle. While he had tried to shroud the model from public view, he said, his was still an "open shop" where Annan, representing that he had no personal interest in such a machine, had had ample opportunity to inspect it on his frequent visits there.

When the defense continued to assault her grasp of mechanical principles, the indignant inventor countered: "I have from my earliest recollection been connected in some way with machinery. I have worked in manufacturing departments where both wood and iron machinery was used for the purpose of manufacturing different kinds of articles and goods, in Manchester, New Hampshire. . . . I have worked at almost everything where machinery is employed." Machinery, in other words, was her business, and to authenticate the priority of her invention she produced her exhibits: 1867 drawings, paper patterns ("I made a great many drawings and illustrations about that time, but have preserved only a few which I cut out in paper"), sketches of experiments, parts of her first wooden model, paper bags made both the old way and her "new" way, wooden cog wheels, sketches of the cog's teeth, four photographs of the original iron machine, original patent drawings and paper bags made from the machine, and lastly, 1867 entries from her personal diary, so intimate, she demurred, that she permitted only the magistrate to read them in private.

A number of the diary's carefully dated notations not only corroborate priority of invention but exemplify Knight's diligence and optimism: "Heigh ho, can't see how to turn that fold back—unless . . ."; "I am told that there is no such machine known as a square-bottomed machine. I mean to [try?] away at it until I get my ideas worked out"; "I've been to work all this evening trying the clock work arrangement for making the square bottoms. It works well so far, so good. Have done enough for one day"; "Have got now 12 made. Shall have to make more I suppose—just like these. Heigh ho, if I could only draught, it would save labor." It was an impressive array of proof, from genesis to manufacture.

In the course of the hearings, Knight described not only every step of the process that led to the invention but the kind of total absorption in the details of production that eventually made her own innovations possible: "I had plenty of leisure time for making observations, and such time was employed in watching the movement of the machines, and the manufacture of the square bottom bags by hand." When one of Annan's witnesses characterized her wooden model as a "rickety wooden thing, all shaky," she snapped that, after all, her assistant had used it to make "thousands of bags—not perfect bags, since they lacked the paste [but] good, handsome bags."

Corroborating Knight's claim that she been working on the process long before Annan viewed her iron model, Eliza McFarland of Springfield, with whom Knight boarded in 1867, testified that she had known of the invention from the beginning: "She told me she had a plan for making square bottom bags, like those she pointed out here [the bags in the exhibits], by machinery. Afterwards she explained her ideas with paper and with a paper tube. She folded up a newspaper in the form of a tube to convey the idea. . . . I saw her wooden model." McFarland also backed Knight's contention that the original machine was complete with "guide fingers," a pasting apparatus, and a "plate-knife folder," additions Annan claimed he had made himself. Despite a grilling cross-examination, McFarland remained unshakable: "I know what I saw. . . . I saw her making drawings continually . . . always of the machine. She has known nothing else, I think."

The issue turned on whether the interim between conceiving the invention and applying for the patent was too long. The Patent Office examiners sided with Knight, reasoning that she had exerted enough "proper diligence" to protect her invention: conducting sufficient experiments with the wooden model to prove its feasibility; placing it in the hands of a skilled machinist; firing him for working only "whenever it suited him best"; engaging a more efficient worker. Still, the examiners concluded that they would not have allowed the time span between the completion of the model and patent filing "were the inventor a man of business." Since *this* inventor was not a "man of business," the examiners relied upon other factors: her "inexperience in business, as well as the embarrassments to which her sex subjected Miss Knight" and the difficulties she faced in enforcing her claims "with the persistence that one of the other sex might use." Rather than charging Knight with laxity in pressing her interests, they gave her the benefit of the doubt and awarded her the patent, a decision the commissioner of patents sustained, adding that under the circumstances she had exercised diligence of "most notable character." Then, in an obiter dictum that must have outraged Knight, he added: "Considering her little practical acquaintance with machinery, her success in overcoming the many difficulties encountered is a matter of great surprise." Her victory was otherwise sweet.

Her patent and its improvements protected, she went into partnership with a Newton businessman who provided the financial assistance to have her first machines manufactured at Ames Manufacturing in Chicopee, Massachusetts. They then established the Eastern Paper Bag Company of Hartford, Connecticut, and hammered out agreements for the patent rights: Eastern paid Knight $2,500 outright, agreed to a royalty of twenty-five cents for every thousand flour sacks (made with satchel bottoms) and five cents for every thousand smaller bags made by the machine until the accumulated royalties reached $25,000. Knight also received 214 shares of the company's capital stock, on which she would receive quarterly dividends. It is no wonder that Knight acknowledged "satisfaction of the covenants and agreements." In the coming decades, she moved into other fields of invention.

While certainly not as famous or as successful as Knight, several other women in this period invaded male-dominated fields, including mining. With one prerequisite for invention being an opportunity to study the need, women who accompanied their husbands to mining outposts had ringside seats from which to observe the difficult work of separating valuable ore from its matrix, so it makes sense that several of them obtained patents for metallurgical processes. One of these, Elizabeth Burns, was the wife of a California gold prospector.

She and her husband were part of the gold rush that occurred when newly discovered western ore deposits beckoned adventurers and investors with the lure of great wealth. Whole families moved to isolated mining camps in the Sierras, where on-site separators were built to extract the precious metal from the ore's worthless constituents. Sometimes this was accomplished manually in a slow and costly process by which workers picked out the gold and discarded the refuse. Sometimes the ore was smelted to isolate the metal. The preferred method was the one in which ore was ground into lumps that were then immersed and stirred in a chemically suitable "broth." Agitating the lumps in the broth floated the gold to the top and deposited the gangue, or residue, at the bottom, where workers drew it off. Finding the magic combination of the right chemical broth and the most efficient method of agitation was the prospectors' Holy Grail.

Elizabeth Burns thought for a while that she had found it. She had accompanied her husband, Robert, to the mountainous Meadow Lake gold country of California, potentially the state's richest mining district, where miners struggled to extract gold from rich, auriferous quartz veins. Investment companies built mills to reduce the ores, and families poured in, keeping in touch with the outside world through the Central Pacific Railroad, which was operated except in the most severe winter storms. The optimistic Burns family moved there shortly after the Civil War and barely survived the next year's disastrous winter when twenty-five-foot snows remained frozen until July. As one survivor remarked, "A Winter on the summit of the Sierras is by no means a desirable thing, and every one who could afford to leave the business of mines, to spend the winter months in a more genial clime, departed."

Unfortunately, the hard-pressed Burns family could not afford a more "genial clime." Everyone waited eagerly for the thaw because the previous season's take from the mines indicated the rich ore's potential. The quartz matrix was obdurate, however, and sulfur fleurets dissolved in the chemical broth to loosen the gold washed too high a percentage of it down the drain. Another terrible winter, followed by a catastrophic summer fire, left the town with "two restaurants, four stores, six saloons, a post office, two breweries and a milkman . . . [with a population of] about one hundred and fifty men, women and children, three horses, four cows, four dozen chickens, forty dogs, one pig and a Chinaman." Still, in that lot were Elizabeth and Robert Burns and their children, who once again braved the brutal winter in the hope that some new process could be discovered for "bringing out" the precious gold from Meadow Lake's veins.

It was at this juncture, when the town was, according to a correspondent from the nearby *Grass Valley Union,* about "ready to shuffle off its immortal coil . . . never again, we fear, to return," that Elizabeth Burns, who supported her husband and several children by taking in laundry, announced some electrifying news. Out of the blue, she proclaimed that she had discovered a new process for taming the "rebellious ore." The process involved the use of a mixture of sulfur, arsenic, antimony, and other minerals. Everyone was dying to know how she had thought of it, but Burns gave a far from satisfactory answer. The idea, she claimed, came to her by way of a voice from the great beyond—that of her dead brother! To a newspaper correspondent who had rushed to Meadow Lake to interview the unlikely inventor, she recounted her equally unlikely story. It was while brooding about her brother's recent death and despairing over the dwindling mining fortunes of her husband, she explained, that her mind suddenly "became absorbed in other matters besides her regular duties" and she learned the secret of the new process as a revelation—every single detail of which was crystal clear—from her brother. One wonders whether the "revelation" was her way of explaining to the world an invention that she knew would otherwise be denounced as the product of a mere woman's brain or whether it was how she explained to herself one of those mysterious flashes of insight that come to inventors who have long grappled with a problem. At any rate, as she described it to the reporter, something in her mind had urged her to get some rock to try the process. When she found that it destroyed the sulfur and left the rock in a condition to be worked by an ordinary mill process, she deemed the chemical solution a discovery of major import.

Many locals, suspicious of her version of the discovery, and keeping in mind that she took in laundry, guessed that it had come about as she made soap and watched what happened when heated quartz crystals came in contact with concentrated lye. Whatever the source of her inspiration, husband Robert grasped its significance and had it patented in San Francisco—in her name. As news of her secret chemical solution spread, capital flooded into the almost moribund town, causing the *Nevada City Transcript* to rejoice that "Meadow Lake will soon be a prosperous place, and the fact that [the process] was dreamed out and invented by a woman will be no detriment if only it saves gold."

With optimistic assay reports, samples of Burns's desulfurized ores on display at Collins's hat store, and a "company of influential and moneyed gentlemen . . . making full preparations for desulphurizing ore by the new process on a large scale," the expectant town almost doubled in size as backers built new roasting furnaces. The outlook for Meadow Lake denizens seemed rosy—but not for long, for, despite successful tests on small amounts of ore, the Burns process proved too expensive for large quantities. It was a short-term victory for Elizabeth and Robert Burns, who left the area soon thereafter. They weren't alone in their exodus. Within three years, the city looked as if it had been evacuated at a moment's notice, its residents leaving behind freshly made beds, larders still full, and crockery pots and pans laid out in preparation for meals. The Burns process died with the town.

The needle trades, which employed thousands, mainly women, provided a far more receptive field for mechanically gifted women. Sewing, after all, was considered woman's work (even if it was done in a factory), and sewing proficiency was an important feminine attribute. But there were many women who objected to having it assigned to their domestic realm. One young woman from South Carolina, where a young lady's accomplishments always included being able to sew a fine seam, complained in her diary (the only place she dared complain?) that she feared her genius would be "stitched entirely away." She was not alone in her dissatisfaction. To those who argued that a woman could always make a little money by sewing should hard times hit, Sarah Hamer, who in *What Girls Can Do: A Book for Mothers and Daughters* advised young women to prepare to be self-supporting should necessity strike, cautioned, "[T]he needle has proved a very poor weapon of defense for her. . . . More than that, it makes no call on the powers of a woman's mind."

But the invention of the sewing machine, largely credited to Elias Howe's patent of 1846, Singer's of 1852, and Wilson's of 1852, drastically revised women's daily sewing boredom and drudgery. By midcentury, when New York City had about two hundred sewing machines, *Scientific American* prophesied that the invention would "create a social revolution, for a good housewife will sew a fine shirt, doing all the seams in fine stitching . . . in a single hour. The time thus saved to wives, tailors, and seamstresses of every description is of incalculable importance, for it will allow them to devote their attention to other things, during the time which used to be taken up with dull seaming." *Godey's* magazine optimistically forecast that the sewing machine, "the Queen of Inventions," would, at the very least, provide women enough leisure to indulge in outdoor exercise.

A decade after Singer's and Wilson's patents, sewing machines were the leading attraction for women visitors at London's International Exhibition in 1862. The exhibition catalog noted that sewers, no longer content with simple stitching, now demanded that machines be adapted to "do all that human fingers can accomplish with a common needle and thread. They intend that the machine should embroider, work plain stitches, hem a handkerchief, do the gathering of a skirt, ornament the uppers of my ladies' slippers, or do the sterner duty of securing the soles and other parts of my lord's boots and shoes." A twentieth-century male historian, looking back over those expectations, anointed the sewing machine the "Servant in the House"—but it was a servant that, rather than saving time, often cost time in that it created higher expectations for the quality of workmanship.

Whatever the dividend in increased leisure may have been for the woman sewing at home, there certainly was no such leisure for the thousands of sewers who bent over machines and pedaled the treadle in factories. A member of the Massachusetts Board of Health, viewing their contorted positions and their "sickly worn-out aspect," listed the following roster of complaints as indicative of "sewing machine diseases": "indigestion due to the constrained posture, close confinement and defective hygienic arrangements; muscular pains of the legs and trunk, caused by over exertion of the treadle; uterine and ovarian disorders, aggravated though not originated through this occupation, and alleviated by its discontinuance; general debility, the result of over-work and confinement."

Regardless of their effect on workers, sewing machines could have such dramatic effects on production, hence profits, that both men and women alike were drawn to inventing improvements on the machines themselves and a variety of attachments for specialized jobs. The treadle-activated wheel of the sewing machine was also adapted by some of the more imaginative inventors to run everything from winding Granny's yarn to whipping Cook's eggs—and even honing knives via an attached emery-edged wheel. While housewives enjoyed their home machines and clever attachments, factories were the most promising customers for enterprising inventors since one factory alone might purchase hundreds of machines.

Into that commercial sewing machine field came Helen Augusta Blanchard, no child of the factory like Knight but the daughter of Nathaniel Blanchard, of Portland, Maine. Blanchard was Portland's best known shipbuilder and owner of packet steamers, a prominent and much honored businessman until his business collapsed during the financial panic of 1866. After his death, his mechanically oriented daughter, destitute and with only her inventive genius to support herself, invented the precursor of the modern zigzag machine, an overseaming machine that simultaneously sewed and trimmed knitted fabrics. She was later to invent at least twenty-six other mechanical sewing contrivances that performed such functions as crocheting edges and making buttonholes.

Profits from her privately held Blanchard Over-Seam Company of Philadelphia (from which other industries sprang), along with fat royalties from the many patent rights she sold, provided her with such a healthy income that she was able to retrieve the family homestead her father had sold at the nadir of his fortunes—a remarkable recovery for the woman who had been forced to borrow money for her first

Helen Augusta Blanchard.

Patent Office fee. Secure in the social position her background and prosperity warranted, she did not forget those less fortunate than herself but generously supported other struggling women. According to Frances Willard, who lauded her as "a benefactor of her sex" in her biographies of important nineteenth-century women, Blanchard, even in affluence, never lost her qualities of "gentleness, dignity and modesty."

Harriet Tracy of New York made her mark in the sewing machine field with her popular Tracy "Lock and Chain Stitch Machine," but not

Helen Blanchard's sewing machine model.

before she learned the patenting ropes through an earlier misadventure. As Tracy recounted that experience, she had invented a combination bureau and trunk but knew nothing about patenting and therefore allowed an impoverished young pedagogue who taught mathematics and military tactics at a nearby military academy to take the invention through the patenting process in exchange for a fifty-fifty share of the profits. Having no special interest in having her own name on the patent ("It was a matter of indifference"), Tracy allowed him to take her model to Munn & Company to apply for the patent in his own name. When she learned that the law required patent applicants to swear that they were the true inventors, Tracy brought suit to have the patent reissued in her name but explained that she could not argue the case in person because of personal problems ("I have been in feeble health much of the time since the model was finished [and] in very limited pecuniary circumstances"). Fearing that her absence would prejudice the case, she wrote the patent examiner: "Women cannot always do just as they would—they are sometimes incapacitated for all work physical and mental."

The schoolmaster's attorney countered that Tracy was nothing more than a "confidence woman" who appropriated the entire idea from the poor scholar who had originated the concept, and Tracy could offer no real evidence of experimentation to support her claim, saying only that the idea appeared in a "nighttime moment of flash of thought." Though Tracy remained resolute and blamed her illness for her inability to quash the defendant's arguments ("My case is so plain that I am sorry to lose it from circumstances over which I have no control"), her case was *not* plain to the examiners, for she provided no proof beyond claiming the flash of insight. The patent remained in the agent's name, and Harriet Tracy never forgot that lesson. In coming years, when she became a major inventor and manufacturer of sewing machines and attachments, she not only saw that she alone held the patents but that each machine prominently displayed the name Tracy.

Although Blanchard and Tracy invented machines for both domestic and industrial use, prolific inventor Mary Carpenter (later, Hooper) made her mark primarily in industrial machinery. *Scientific American* assigned prime position and illustration space to news of her self-threading and self-setting sewing machine needles, which displayed "a

Mary Carpenter's model for braid-sewing machine.

great deal of ingenuity and inventive capacity" since the operator could thread them easily and their increased elasticity made constant readjustment unnecessary. The magazine reported that in an experiment on the heaviest kind of shoes, a Hooper needle stitched sixty pairs in a single day without breakage or inconvenience. The final accolade was a sure boost to sales: "By its use, neither the eyes nor the patience of the operator is tried in threading, or setting the needle, each of which manipulations may be performed in a perfect manner in a moment of time, by the most inexperienced person." A week later, in an article on women inventors, the lofty periodical bestowed what it must have considered ultimate kudos on her invention: "[It] would not do discredit to the most experienced and ingenious male inventor."

Carpenter also patented such diverse devices as an ironing and fluting machine, an improved mop wringer, a sewing machine needle and arm, an improvement in sewing machine feeding mechanisms, a button, a grated shovel, a "device for numbering houses," and a "netting canopy for bedsteads." Another Carpenter machine, smaller than a typewriter, braided and then sewed straw, making it possible to convert expensive and intricate hatmaking into a smooth process of sewing the hat from crown tip to outer edge in one continuous motion without removing it from the machine. According to *Inventive Age*, an important late-nineteenth-century "invention magazine" edited by Robert DuBois, a champion of women inventors, it so revolutionized the industry within two decades of its patenting that "not an inch of straw braid sewn into hats by machine anywhere in the world does not employ a part of Mrs. Hooper's invention to accomplish the work." The fact that her invention was in a field "into which women always venture at a risk of being suspected of scant knowledge and less experience—mechanics" impressed the editors even more.

The straw-braiding invention spawned an elaborate and lengthy patent interference suit when Carpenter took legal action against a former employee ("this vile perjurer") for stealing her ideas. Prosperous enough from sales of her previous patents to be able to afford squads of attestants to her mechanical skills, she must have gloried in their accounts. Henry McCabe told the examiners: "That was Mrs. Carpenter's machine, all right; we often talked that it was wonderful that a woman could produce such a machine. . . . She was always managing and directing . . . the head and front of everything, directing the construction of this machine . . . and working the machine to show me what it could do."

Bristling at the defendant's claim that she didn't understand her own invention, Carpenter retorted,

> I took that machine to England and sold the English Patent . . . for $10,000, and I went alone, unaided, and returned within 30 days after leaving New York. . . . [T]hey bought the machine provided I would go back to England at their expense, paying all my expenses at the hotel while there, that I could teach the men to build it and operators to use it; I remained five months in the factories in Oldham, in Manchester, and the machine proved a success.

Answers to other questions evoked the information that all her previous machines had been sold under the name of "the Carpenter Straw Sewing Machine" ("after me, the patentee") and that she couldn't remember just how many other patents she had been granted previously—"eight or nine, I think about nine." The examiners, convinced that she was no neophyte inventor, voted in her favor.

Of all those unusual women inventors who moved beyond the traditional domestic perimeters, undoubtedly the quirkiest of the lot was Amanda Theodosia Jones, who, like a number of her contemporaries, ascribed her inventing spark to a message from another realm. Though she exhibited no signs of mechanical proclivities in youth and was embarked upon a literary life when she received her first "message," Jones was to become a leader in the burgeoning canning industry. Reared in a small town in New York State, she and her brother attended school together until the day when he suddenly died at school and a terrified teacher left her to cope with making all the notifications and arrangements. This experience was so traumatic that it might have prompted the physical breakdown she suffered at age seventeen and from which she never entirely recovered. It surely contributed to her interest in spiritualism, for she would later attend séances to try to communicate with her brother. She eventually became so convinced of her special sensitivity to knockings and voices that she became a medium herself.

Despite her frailties, Jones graduated from a state normal school and became a teacher, the most common form of employment for intellectual young women, and wrote poetry on the side. Shortly after her first poem appeared in the *Methodist Ladies' Respository,* she abandoned teaching in favor of writing, and *Frank Leslie's Weekly* published her series of "war songs" during the Civil War. Afterward, she divided her time between editorial positions at *Western Rural* and *Bright Side,* a magazine for children. Her developing interest in spiritualism, however, gave her life a new energizing force, and she soon tired of her work at *Western Rural.* Urged by her *Bright Side* publisher to follow up on that interest, she immersed herself completely and was astonished when her new spiritual mentor, the unseen "Dr. Andrews," whose "trenchant words" came to her out of the blue, urged her to invent and patent. Jones recounted the experience in her autobiography:

> Now, I confess this seemed so far from what I most desired, I never dreamt [the message] was for me. Since I, in very truth, was no inventor. No flounce of mine had ever brushed a Patent Office door-jamb, or caught in court-house palings. Then one night, the voice spoke again: "Friends, do you know there is a way of canning fruit without cooking it?"

Though she had never canned so much as a jar of fruit, she made up for lost time in her experiments. The art of canning was called "Appertizing" after Frenchman Nicolas Appert, who wrote in his 1810 book, *The Art of Preserving All Kinds of Animal and Vegetable Substances,* that food placed in hermetically sealed containers and heated high enough and long enough would keep indefinitely. William Underwood further developed the principle in his famous Boston canning business a decade later, and Underwood's Deviled Ham is still a market staple. Most foods were placed in metal containers or tins, but glass was also used for "putting up," and it was for glass canning that Jones hit upon a kind of vacuum pack. While she credited the spirit with telling her to invent, she was adamant that he hadn't been in cahoots with her over *how* to do it: "*No spirit told me this.* . . . To every patent application I have taken the oath, unperjured: 'This is my invention. This I claim.' "

Her cousin Leroy C. Cooley, from Albany, New York, gave her valuable practical assistance, and as a result the two divided their

Amanda Theodosia Jones.

patenting rights on terms that appear to have been mutually agreeable: He assigned rights to one of his patents to Jones, co-patented another, and listed only himself on one for exhausting air from fruit cans. Between them, they received seven patents in the field in 1873 alone, and with patent control over the "Jones Process" of exhausting air by raising the temperature of the vessel containing food and its juices from 100 degrees to 120 degrees Fahrenheit, she was primed to storm the canning industry and lay the foundation of her enormous pure-food industry—what she called "a traffic in the very means of life."

Jones launched the newly incorporated Woman's Canning and Preserving Company, whose charter stated that its purpose was "to manufacture, sell and deal in canned, bottled or otherwise preserved foods

A product of Amanda T. Jones's Woman's Canning and Preserving Company.

of all kinds; to acquire, purchase or control letters-patents . . . relating to methods, processes, machinery, apparatus and devices for preserving foods of all kinds; to establish and operate branch factories for canning, boiling or otherwise preserving foods, under protection of letters-patents." Wanting to capitalize the company at one million dollars, she sold forty thousand shares at twenty-five dollars a share to thirty-seven women, but most of them purchased only one or two shares. Her cousin's wife, Rossa M. Flack Cooley, purchased four; two women whose names were followed by the medical suffix "M.D." each took two. Jones herself subscribed to the remaining shares to reach the necessary million-dollar goal.

All officers and employees of the new company were women except for "Mike," who fired the boiler, and cousin Cooley, the only one trusted to operate the precious preserving mechanism. Ann Braude's book on spiritualism provides a valuable clue to what motivated Jones to take the strong feminist stand of establishing a *woman's* company. Women mediums like Jones were committed to the right of a woman to control her own body, to wear garments of an unconstricting nature, to gain custody of her children, and, most important in the material realm, to own property. Defying society's strictures against women in business out of a conviction that it was her spiritual mentors who had urged her into her profitable pursuit, Jones therefore addressed her employees: "This is a woman's industry. No man will vote our stock, transact our business, pronounce on women's wages, supervise our factories. Give men whatever work is suitable, but keep the governing power. This is a business training school for working women. . . . Here is a mission; let it be fulfilled."

Her woman's company prospered enough to advertise in national magazines; to expand operations to plants in Aurora, Illinois, and Montello, Wisconsin; and to hire a professional processor from the Union Stock Yards to help with what became her palatable, popular, and profitable "lunch tongues," a noticeable improvement over the unappealing rice and tapioca puddings with which she had started. *New Ideas* magazine later called the company women "Real Women" and reported that they hoped to double their 1895 output of 200,000 cans in the next year. It hadn't always been easy, the magazine reported: "At the start each woman had a different way for preparing the fruits and vegetables and 'fastening up' the cans, but a uniform plan was finally agreed upon, and then everything went along smoothly and without trouble."

Not completely without trouble, however. As business grew, a rival carped that the process was unduly complex, that operating the "Jones Exhauster" required no more than four of its thirty valves, the surplus serving only to camouflage the mechanism and deter copiers. He scoffed, "Of course, all this exhausting could have been done in a fraction of the time given it, and at much less expense with a simple air pump. But it would not have been 'scientific.' "

Although Hawks, Burns, Tracy, and Jones attributed their sparks of inspiration to otherwordly sources, they still had to do the rest of the work themselves, and Jones maintained in her autobiography that her inventions were "as much my own as are my many poems—mostly studied out by slow and painful process, often at bitter cost." Despite her inventive feats and patronage of women in business, however, Jones never took part in suffrage activities, and that, in addition to a probable reluctance to have their movement identified with spiritualism, may account for the fact that feminist publications never cited her among the women inventors they featured.

By the time of the nation's centennial, they had found more suitable candidates for stardom and decided to provide them with a showcase for their inventive talents.

*4*

# CENTENNIAL
# SISTERHOOD

*T*hough women inventors them-
selves were, of course, in favor of women's rights, they never organized
themselves, either professionally or politically, into any kind of special-
interest group. Feminists, however, once they were ready to take up the
banner again for issues they had shelved temporarily during the Civil
War, viewed the inventors' virtuoso assemblage of talent as prime
evidence that women were equal to men. By portraying them as
paradigms of the useful talents necessary to an industrializing nation,
suffragists nourished the inventors with publicity and acclaim and
made them both a cause and a symbol of the women's movement. The
inventors, in turn, were grateful for the support and basked in the
sisterhood's blessing. They were ready for the spotlight, for in the ten
years since the close of the war, the number of patents issued to them
had increased by 566 percent, a figure more than double the rate of
increase for those issued to men during the same period.

In the mid-1870s, the leaders of the resurgent suffrage movement
still sprang from the ranks of women who had honed their organiza-
tional skills during the war, and there can be no better illustration of
the benefits of wartime seasoning for postwar authority than Mary
Livermore. The wife of an Illinois clergyman, during the war she had

organized soldiers' aid societies, visited soldiers and nurses, distributed supplies at the front, and, through hundreds of lectures, quickened interest and enthusiasm for the Sanitary Commission's work by relating her own experiences and observations. Despite early prejudice against women speakers, thousands flocked to hear her tell stories in the public lecture series then taking the country by storm, after which they donated their admission fees to the commission.

Although few women were involved in such a broad range of wartime activities as Livermore, for all women the war was a transformative experience, altering their roles in such a way that each woman developed, in the words of Livermore, "potencies and possibilities of whose existence she had not been aware." For Livermore herself, the war had provided what feminist Julia Ward Howe described as a "new sense of the moral power of her sex," a conviction that she should maximize women's new promise into a movement that would make equality with men its first priority.

During the suffrage movement's earlier incarnation, Livermore had thought Lucretia Mott and Elizabeth Cady Stanton were far too radical in their demands at the 1848 Seneca Falls Convention. If women simply *explained* their need for enfranchisement, she blithely assumed, during what she later came to regard as those naive and "verdant" prewar days, men would promptly confer it. Her conversion she attributed in large part to her wartime discovery that without a male guarantor, even she, acting in her capacity as chairman of the Great Western Sanitary Fair in Chicago, was nonetheless enjoined by the laws of Illinois from signing a contract to authorize a builder to erect exhibition space:

> Here was a revelation. We two women were able to enlist the whole Northwest in a great philanthropic, money-making enterprise . . . and had the executive ability to carry it forward to a successful termination. We had money of our own in a bank, twice as much as was necessary to pay the builder. . . . Later in the conversation, we learned that we had no legal ownership in our minor children. . . . They too were the property of our husbands.

Describing that central moment in her political development, she wrote: "I registered a vow that when the war was over I would take up a new work—the work of making law and justice synonymous for women. I have kept my vow religiously."

And indeed she had. Larding her writing and lectures with such charged metaphors for women's political enslavement as "manacles" and "yokes," the suffrage convert promulgated her views in the Chicago press and her husband's church organ, *New Covenant*; arranged a suffrage convention in Chicago that attracted like-minded women (notably Stanton and Susan B. Anthony) from other parts of the country; and, at her own cost and considerable risk, established her own newspaper, the *Agitator*, which espoused temperance along with suffrage.

Other suffrage leaders also had their own newspapers. The sixteen-page weekly *Revolution*, Stanton's and Anthony's joint venture, was interested in far more than suffrage. In addition to news of working women's organizations, women pioneers in new fields, and the first women's clubs, it dealt vehemently with such issues as sex discrimination in the workplace, partiality given to men in divorce proceedings, biblical injunctions on women's inferior position, and the evils of prostitution. These issues, in addition to disagreement over the quickest way for women to get the vote, caused the major breach in the women's movement, the split that put Livermore in the opposite camp from Anthony and Stanton.

Noting the preponderance of men in the Equal Rights Association (which had been formed at the close of the Civil War to further the rights of both women and Negroes), Anthony and Stanton suspected that Lucy Stone and Julia Ward Howe had been hoodwinked by their male mentors into toning down their demands and accepting a slower route to woman suffrage. Still, the break that came in 1869 might not have occurred had Anthony's and Stanton's demand for immediate suffrage by national amendment been the only issue. Rejection by the Stone and Howe Boston contingent of their aggressive campaign for social reforms for women—be they "fallen," divorced, underpaid, non-unionized, or unemployed—brought it to a head.

In May 1869, Stanton and Anthony quit the ranks of the Equal Rights Association and formed the National Woman Suffrage Association, which excluded men from its membership—not surprising since Stanton so often called them "tyrants." Woman suffrage was one objective of the new organization, said Stanton, but not the only one: "[It] is a question covering a whole range of woman's needs and demands . . . including her work, her wages, her property, her education, her physical training, her social status, her political equalization, her marriage and her divorce." Thus, by championing economically and socially exploited women as well as demanding an immediate suffrage amendment to the Constitution rather than slower state-by-state enfranchisement, the "National" was deemed radical.

The final break between the two groups—what Stanton described as "a division in the ranks of the strongminded"—took place six months later. At the November 1869 convention in Cleveland (held there to garner Midwestern support), the group led by Stone and Howe, fearing that sponsoring broad social change would drive away men and women who would otherwise support the single issue of woman suffrage, established the rival American Woman Suffrage Association and placed a man, the famous minister Henry Ward Beecher, at its head. The split would rend the women's movement for the next twenty years. Membership in the "American"—conservative about everything except its commitment to woman suffrage—became attractive to more traditional women, who, though emerging into greater economic and political freedom, were still hesitant to demand immediate political and economic equality.

When the suffrage movement fractured, Livermore, who had represented her home state of Illinois at the Cleveland meeting, threw in her lot with the conservatives. That support made her an attractive candidate for the job of editor of a new feminist weekly periodical, which was not to be an arm of the American but would be closely identified with its principles. Its backers, members of a newly founded joint-stock company in Boston, who included Julia Ward Howe, Thomas Higginson, and William Lloyd Garrison, approached Livermore with an offer to purchase the *Agitator*. Their offer was conditional upon her agreement to move to Boston for a year and, at a reasonable compensation, assist their proposed publication by serving as editor-in-chief and speaking in behalf of woman suffrage at conventions. Chief among the backers of the new periodical was Lucy Stone. Stone was the first woman to earn a college degree in Massachusetts and the first married woman to keep her own name. The "morning star of the woman's rights movement," the movement for which she had lectured to enormous audiences throughout the country, she was a gifted fund-raiser who, after an initial gift of one thousand dollars from her husband, Henry Browne Blackwell (whom she had met when she was an Oberlin student and he a young Cincinnati abolitionist), had raised most of the remaining money for the new paper herself. Somewhat overwhelmed at joining so "brilliant a coterie of men and women" as that comprised by Stone, Howe (whom Stone had converted to the cause), Higginson, and Garrison, yet secure that her experience and stature supported the decision, Livermore accepted, and moved with her husband to Melrose, Massachusetts. Julia Ward Howe's "Salutatory" in the first issue, January 8, 1870, of the new publication, *Woman's Journal,* appealed to "our sisters, of whatever kind or degree, to make common cause with us." That cause was woman suffrage.

The paper, ensconced in what Howe described as a "pleasant, prettily fitted up, lower front room," was a joint tenant of 3 Tremont Place along with the New England Women's Club and the American Woman Suffrage Association, a place where visitors could pick up the latest tracts, papers, and petitions. Howe envisioned the paper as a "sort of social centre for women" and assured its readers, "You will be sure to like us." Just as the *Journal* debuted, *Revolution,* saddled with debt, acquired a new editor whose charter was to emphasize not only women's rights but also women's *duties,* such a change in complexion that by 1872 it merged with *Liberal Christian,* a periodical with a decidedly Unitarian slant. That left the field open to *Woman's Journal,* which, by appealing to women who coveted the vote but shunned affiliation with the more radical wing, became the principal suffrage periodical for half a century, with a commitment not just to suffrage but to temperance, dress reform, improvement in women's health, and better business, technical, and higher education for women. Though Livermore's editorship lasted only two years, because the paper's finances became so strained that it could not afford to pay her, the *Journal* would serve as a voice for women for many decades to come. In 1917, on the forty-seventh anniversary of its founding, the founder's daughter, Alice Stone Blackwell, eulogized the "noble band of pioneers" whose names "have been written into history and are now written into the book of light."

*Woman's Journal* is of particular interest in the study of women inventors because it was the perfect vehicle for vaunting their accomplishments. Correspondents sent in local news items about inventors; Washington women scanned the patent lists for names to dispatch to 3 Tremont Street; editors and contributors extolled inventors' achievements and recommended their products to readers. To the great profit of the inventors, the paper offered testimony to their intelligence, ingenuity, and business acumen; to the benefit of equal rights proponents, their inventions were tangible confirmation of women's creative ability beyond the womb, which until then was the only creative zone in which legislative solons granted them ascendancy.

It was in this setting of burgeoning interest in their position and rights that women were emboldened to demand that the forthcoming 1876 celebration of independence, planned as a mammoth trade fair, should take suitable notice of their gender's contribution to the nation's progress. The break in the women's movement, however, worked against a unified approach. Feminists were of two minds about the celebration. The radicals argued that there was little to celebrate when women were still disenfranchised and that the trade fair format presented little opportunity to display the prodigious output of unrecognized industrial women. On the other hand, not participating would rob them of a chance to proselytize the throngs who would attend. The more conservative admitted that factory women's work was difficult to isolate (since the products of factories owned by men would be viewed as men's accomplishment), and thought that this was indeed a shame, but they still did not see this as any reason not to highlight the contributions of women inventors, who might be considered industrial women themselves—too mired in making a living to be in the forefront of the suffrage movement. Featuring inventors would, in the long run, reflect well on women as a whole. Other complaints came from a few financially strapped Southern women who were reluctant to participate with "those Yankee women" because, as one woman from Florida explained, they had become accustomed to being "ostracized from our country's bosom" and therefore needed persuading to "gather once more with our sisters of the North, East and West."

In the end, enough women lobbied so strongly for participation in the Centennial exposition that a women's committee was set up under Benjamin Franklin's granddaughter, Elizabeth Duane Gillespie, the organizer of Philadelphia's 1864 Sanitary Fair. They finally decided to ask for a separate building to exhibit women's unique contributions even though they might appear picayune compared to men's work. Poor women who earned only a scanty subsistence (usually by sewing), Gillespie argued, would be inspired by seeing what women were capable of attaining in other and higher branches of industry and thus the "more timid sisters" would be spurred to greater achievement.

Gillespie soon earned her sobriquet, "Imperial Wizard of the Centennial," when, after space allotted to women was first too small and then eliminated entirely as too costly, she urged the rejected women to build a Woman's Pavilion devoted exclusively to the results of women's labor. Told they could have it if they paid for it, she organized committees in each state to raise over one hundred thousand dollars, a princely sum in an economy still reeling from the panic of 1873. They sponsored concerts and art shows, nationwide benefits, bazaars, and patriotic "Martha Washington tea parties" at which ladies in colonial dress sold twenty-five-cent teacups commemorating the centennial of the Boston Tea Party. The radicals, who had initially opposed the idea of a women's building but loyally subscribed to large blocks of centennial stock nonetheless, almost boycotted the pavilion itself as a protest against the male planners who had included women in Centennial plans only as an afterthought. It was, cracked Elizabeth Cady Stanton, too much like the afterthought that "theologians claim woman herself to have been."

Building a woman's building was one thing; filling it with "suitable" exhibits was another. Antoinette Brown Blackwell, minister, author, lecturer, sister-in-law of Lucy Stone, and regular contributor to *Woman's Journal*, issued this call at a planning session: "Let every woman in the country who has made anything, or who can make anything worth exhibiting as a credit to womanhood, send it forward in demonstration of womanly capacity as applied outside the nursery. . . . [I]t will be a practical assertion that a woman, matron or spinster, is no longer a nonentity outside the household." Blackwell's call for proof of capacities outside the nursery and the household added to organizers' qualms that a flood of atrocious knickknacks would swamp the pavilion. That a good many did is attested to by the fact that William Dean Howells (expressing a tacit belief in the notion that men did not belong in woman's sphere) commented that some of the women's needlework products were so bad that they were "no better than if men had made them."

Hoping that serious works would compensate for the trivial, Gillespie dispatched a flurry of letters to prospective contributors, among them the expatriate neoclassical sculptor Harriet Hosmer, then studying in Rome, who wrote back enthusiastically: "We had a fright here that there was not to be a Woman's Department, which disappointed us all, me in particular, because I don't think I shall trouble myself to send anything to a *General* Exhibition, whereas for the women I shall send every thing I can make and scrape together. I have a truly American subject in hand now, and I shall certainly send that; I must try and find a good woman-subject."

Matilda Gage, partially reconciled to the Woman's Building concept, proposed adopting Abigail Adams's feisty words for their Centennial credo: "We are determined to foment a rebellion, and will not hold ourselves bound by laws in which we have no voice or representation." Others chose not to use the Centennial as a platform for the suffrage

The Women's Centennial Executive Committee.

Woman's Pavilion.

agenda and selected instead a theme taken from the Thirty-first Proverb: "Give her of the work of her hands, and let her own works praise her in the gates." Accordingly, "Her Works Do Praise Her in the Gates," was inscribed on panels on each side of the doors in English, French, German, Italian, Spanish, and Swedish. Hosmer, hearing of the theme, subsequently promised her sculpture *Gates* to the Centennial. When the voyage proved too risky for that piece, she substituted *The Triton.*

The committee was delighted to have the work of Hosmer, undoubtedly the best known woman artist of the period and an anomaly in a field dominated by men. Indeed, she was such a rarity that a decade before, when she was selected to sculpt a figure of Missouri's late Senator Benton, she had thanked the judges for their lack of prejudice not only against her youth but against her gender: "[K]nowing what barriers must in the outset oppose all womanly efforts, I am indebted to the chivalry of the West, which has first overleaped them." At the opening ceremonies for the Benton statue in Saint Louis's Lafayette Park in 1868, her mentor, famous sculptor John Gibson, remarked, "Americans may now boast of possessing what no nation in Europe possesses—a public statue by a woman—a little woman—young, with great talent and love of her art." Hosmer, who from childhood liked to work with her hands, was not only an artist but a "fixer" who contrived ingenious household devices and machines and conducted mechanical experiments, and interestingly, in the context of the subject of this book, patented a method of making artificial marble three years after the Centennial.

Hosmer's road had not been smooth, but she was fortunate in having the support and encouragement of an adoring father, ever bent upon providing her with rich educational experiences, who once helped her to enroll in an anatomy course at Saint Louis Medical School since young women could not receive such instruction elsewhere. As *Success* magazine pointed out half a century later, "Every medical college closed its doors against her, in horror at one 'so out of her sphere.' What right had a woman to know anything about the construction of the human body, or to be a sculptor?" By 1852, she had embarked for Rome to study under Gibson. She stayed there thirty years, building a solid reputation, which brought her a number of important commissions and enabled her to entertain at her studio such political and literary figures as British prime minister Gladstone, Robert and Elizabeth Browning (the cast of whose clasped hands she presented to the Chicago Art Museum in 1894), the Longfellows, the Bryants, and the Trollopes.

Though she was very successful in her lifetime, she was not without detractors. When a rival sculptor charged that Hosmer attracted attention more for the uniqueness of her career than for her talent, Lydia Maria Child (the famous abolitionist and author who once lived next door to the coltish young Hosmer) rebuked the slur: "I observed a degree of pique in his tone, which mediocrity is not apt to excite." Agreeing, the Reverend R. B. Thurston, writing on Hosmer in *Eminent Women of the Age*, pointed out that because she was "positive, piquant, and unique," because some called her "masculine and strong minded," because she defied convention and was "self-sustained, bold, and dashing," those who feared her poaching upon their preserve were bound to carp at her success.

Hosmer was a great catch for the committee—a success story of a woman who had triumphed over sexism, hence a living symbol of hope. Eager to speak out about the injustice done to Hosmer, Phebe Coffin Hanaford, the noted lecturer and Universalist preacher who once removed her church's services to the town's public hall when her congregation split over the women's rights issue, interviewed her for the book she was then compiling on prominent American women. In it, Hosmer recounted that she learned the painful lesson of what happened to a woman who stepped out of her sphere when "brother artists" accused her of not doing her own work: "I felt that I must have made some progress in my art; otherwise they would not have been so ready to attribute that work to one of their own sex." To Jane DeForest, a well-known suffrage advocate whose lectures were, according to an Ohio newspaper, "spiced with a vein of sarcasm," Hosmer explained that any woman artist who received frequent commissions was "an object of peculiar odium." In Philadelphia, however, Hosmer found only honor.

Searching for other women of accomplishment to participate in the Centennial Exposition, Gillespie wrote to a list of women patentees supplied her by the Patent Office. Of the many enthusiastic respondents, eighty-five exhibited, but there are no figures on which ones personally accompanied their inventions, though some who did are mentioned in local periodicals. Most came from Pennsylvania (twenty-five), New York (twenty-one), the Middle West (thirteen), and Massachusetts (nine). The majority of their inventions dealt with domestic affairs: six with laundry; eight with sewing; seven with garment cutting; thirteen with kitchen devices (including three stoves and two dishwashers); six with corsets; eighteen with furniture or building materials; five with hair or flower decoration; two with medicine. Fifteen won special Centennial awards.

Fifty-nine woman exhibitors of inventions held patents or soon would (of that number, twenty-five held more than one patent); two later received patents (though not for the work they showed at Philadelphia); two were sisters who patented jointly; two were friends who co-patented; approximately one fourth were widows or spinsters. One was a French citizen living in New York, Celine Laumonier, whose folding combination travel bag and chair must have been a boon since fair-going was exhausting business despite the three-mile-long narrow-gauge, double-track steam railroad that ferried riders about the sprawling grounds of Fairmount Park for five cents. Laumonier's bag, when opened, was a seat "with a certain amount of rigidity"; closed, it was a satchel with attached bags for stowing books, papers, and whatnots collected at the exposition.

Another of the inventions that was put to use in the course of the exposition was Hannah Suplee's "Suplee Patent Open-Eye Easy-Threading Needle," which was used to sew the exposition's captive hot-air balloons. These balloons could carry eight or ten intrepid fairgoers at a time in a basket tethered with a strong rope to a steam windlass, and it was of course crucial that the balloons be well constructed so that no disasters befell the passengers on their twenty-minute flight. Professor John Wise, who supervised the manufacture of the three balloons used, had them sewn on machines fitted with Hannah Suplee's award-winning needle without a single needle breaking, a remarkable feat, since the professor's niece had never completed even one of her uncle's balloons without breaking several. Suplee, who had patented her needle seven years before, bragged in an advertisement in *Sewing Machine Journal* that one needle had taken "two million nine hundred and fourteen thousand and four hundred stitches" through sixteen hundred yards of stout balloon cloth without bending, and the magazine elsewhere reported that the Centennial proved a "big success" for "Madame Suplee," who did a "nice trade" with the largest notion houses. A customer who tried one of her needles complimented, "[N]o one who can feel the needle can fail to thread it." Suplee had, it was reported, gone to San Francisco to locate a clever Chinese draftsman to follow her drawings explicitly, with the felicitous result that her needles merged "Yankee training and Chinese skill."

Though the radical suffragists still complained that Centennial fever would make women overlook "the manacles which are goading many a mother and sister into despair of their country," they realized what a golden opportunity it was to gather the faithful in Philadelphia and to recite their Declaration of Independence for Women at dinners and picnics in the city's town halls and nearby groves. On the Glorious Fourth itself, they planned to follow the reading of the original Declaration with a woman's version that impeached the Fathers and their male descendants for "injustice and oppression." Applying to the Centennial Commission for an opportunity to participate in the official ceremonies, they defended their right to equal time as representatives of half the nation; the commission rebuffed them firmly but politely.

Not to be denied, when the day came a resolute delegation of five headed by Susan B. Anthony and Matilda Gage broke into the official ceremonies and made their way down the aisle to the platform just as Richard Henry Lee closed his reading of the Declaration of 1776 with "our lives, our trust, and our sacred honor." As Anthony thrust a copy of the Woman's Declaration into the hands of the startled presiding officer, the women turned on their heels, retraced their steps down the aisle, and scattered printed copies to outstretched hands while the chairman shouted, "Order, order!" Once outside, they mounted the band platform erected on the square in front of Independence Hall, and Anthony (whom *Scientific American* had proposed as commissioner of patents only three years before), shielded by Gage's umbrella from the blazing sun, read their declaration to an applauding audience while other sweltering fair visitors revived themselves (perhaps with Mary Foster's and Anna Thomas's patented hatchet-shaped fans with Mount Vernon on one side and Martha and George Washington on the other).

Both Anthony and Stanton were disappointed in the overall caliber of women's work shown, the only bright spot for Stanton being one of the exposition's most popular attractions: Emma Allison of Grimsby, Iowa, an engineer who operated the Baxter portable engine supplying power to the Woman's Pavilion machinery. Clad in a dainty, light brown, neatly trimmed dress, described by one enraptured spectator as being "as smooth and clean as though the wearer were a flower-girl instead of an engineer," she was as competent as she was attractive, dispelling the fears of those who had protested that she might blow the building to smithereens by reading novels instead of monitoring the steam gauge. Allison enjoyed all aspects of her work, from starting the fire in the morning to blowing off the steam at night, and did not find it wearing. It was, she said, far easier than nursemaiding and less fatiguing than bending over a kitchen stove. According to one male chronicler, "[I]f she does nothing else, she offers an example worth following to the engineers in the neatness of her dress and the perfection of cleanliness exhibited in both engine and engine-room." Another fan allowed, "She is no low, vulgar woman, but an educated and accomplished lady." She was that, but her higher education was of a kind available to few other young women of the period—for she had been given the same engineering course that her brother had taken. Though she saw no reason why women should not enter the profession and even operate engines on ocean liners, she herself left the business after the exposition and started a literary magazine in San Francisco.

As for the inventions in the Woman's Pavilion, the general press provided a few interesting tidbits on clever inventions but assigned

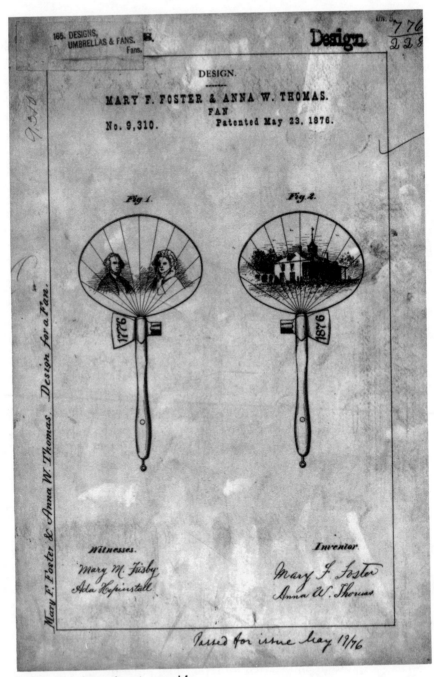

Mary Foster's and Anna Thomas's patented fan.

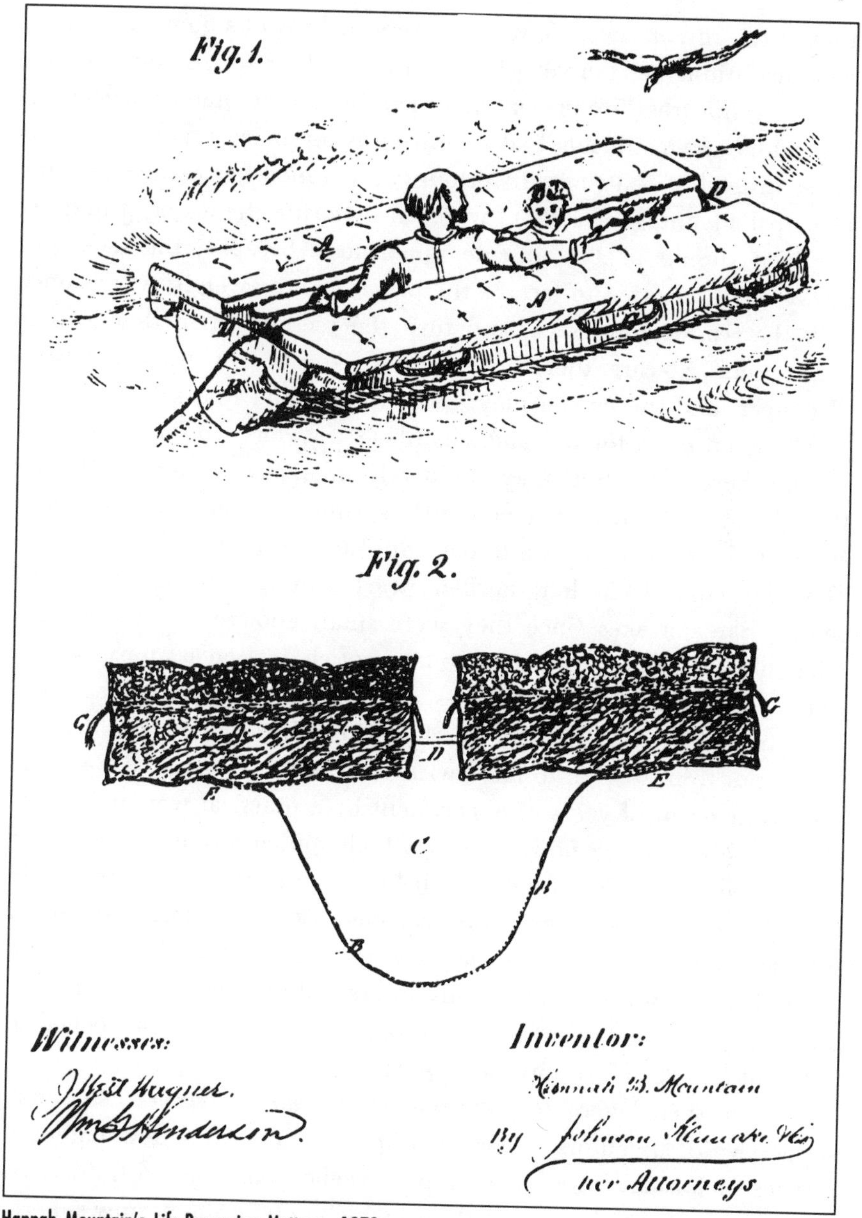

Fig. 1.

Fig. 2.

Witnesses:

Inventor:

Hannah Mountain's Life-Preserving Mattress, 1873.

them little importance. Newspapers reported visitors queueing up for demonstrations of Hannah Mountain's deer hair (or sometimes cork shavings) mattress/life preserver, which the United States Supervising Inspectors of Steamboats had approved as auxiliary lifesaving appliances instead of boats or rafts. Mountain claimed her reversible raft's principal advantage was that "when thrown into the water, it matters not if it should be bottom-side uppermost [because] the sack will always be in position to receive the person, whose weight will at once sink the [connecting] sack, and turn the sections upon their center connections. No care, therefore, need be taken in launching it in time of danger, and the person may jump upon it and find safety. . . ."

The good news for rail and steamboat travelers who drew duty in the top berth, was that they could rely upon Sarah Siegel's "happy thought . . . a neat and handy little spring step" attached to upper berths to help them vault into position. Elizabeth Harley's "Complete Darners," shaped like long-necked dwarf gourds, were reported to be selling like hotcakes since they were small enough and priced low enough for a sightseer to tuck one into her chatelaine as an exposition souvenir. Various other novelties received some attention as well. Margaret Colvin's "Triumph Washing Machine," which could clean all fabrics from carpets to laces without rubbing, was praised as "the successful result of years of experiment by a practical woman." Mary Pierce's self-draining flower stand, which spilled any overflow water into its own catch basin without dribbling onto the carpet, was duly noted. The versatile Pierce also displayed a cleverly designed thread and needle bank, with places for sewing accessories, and then, to the astonishment of a reporter already impressed with her "rather inventive turn of mind," calmly set up a parlor handsaw and proceeded to turn out "work of extraordinary delicacy."

Despite such favorable press notices, *Woman's Journal*, usually so supportive of inventors, reported limply, "There are a few patented articles such as a dish-washer, carpet-sweeper, bedstead with drawers, a new model to cut dresses by, things which help in the narrow sphere, which has been called woman's—that of housekeeping" and pointed out that such "pots and pans" exhibits simply reinforced men's conviction that women should stay within their sphere no matter "how insipid the lives of many of them are." *Centennial Eagle* bluntly charged that pitifully few of the women's inventions could withstand being "gauged by higher standards than the frying pan and the cradle." The Quaker periodical *Friends' Intelligencer,* already showing its feminist colors by rapping the needlework display for demonstrating how "the industry and nerve force of women has been so misdirected," rated the women's inventions on display a painful disappointment, unlikely to spark much interest in women's advancement. *Arthur's Illustrated Home Magazine* surmised that the "strong" women of the country must have decided not to exhibit in the pavilion since what was displayed was "only the inferior and most useless labors of her sex." Frank Leslie, publisher of *Leslie's Historical Register of the Centennial Exhibition* and a regular weekly, might have agreed but backpedaled because his wife, Miriam, was a strong feminist. He gallantly attributed the preponderance of domestic inventions to the fact that the exhibit plan had "commenced at a very late period, and it was prosecuted by the women under a good many disadvantages without outside assistance."

The women in charge, however, had their own press to rebut the snipes from some of the male press ("those pests of journalism"). *New Century for Women,* a daily that was printed on presses operated within the pavilion, carried articles on equal pay for equal work, lauded woman's "new" role without quite explaining what it was, and urged businesswomen to drop off advertisements and "cards" for inclusion in the paper. A good many patentees obliged: Mrs. C. L. Slade advertised her child's "Combination Desk & Slate," sold by the Instructive Toy Company in New York, as the "[b]est article of its kind ever invented. Everybody likes it"; Mary A. E. Whitner promoted her "Multiscope," "the cheapest arrangement for viewing packs of pictures without disturbing their order in the packs."

Visitors were interested enough in viewing many of these inventions to thread their way through acres of such needlework treasures as tatted antimacassars, knitted bootees and crocheted "bosom friends," and dolls, paintings, sculpture, and pictures worked in human hair, not to mention a chair upholstered in black satin decorated with oil paintings, bouquets of waxed flowers, toilet articles fashioned entirely of fish scales, and a whistle made of a pig's tail. When they finally located the inventions, they found, quite literally, devices that pertained to everything from the cradle to the grave. At one end of life's spectrum, for enclosing a cemetery plot, florist Mary Stigale displayed an ornamental rail perforated to hold vases of memorial flowers; at the other, Jane Wells showed her portable baby holder-jumper, which she claimed an infant could operate "from the time it can sit erect until it walks" since the child's toes could reach the floor and swing it around in any direction, thus providing, she said, a "healthy and safe amusement, and relieving parents and nurses from much care and labor." Though a card accompanying it emphasized that the chair was wholly the invention of one woman and that nearly all the work of producing it was done in a factory employing only women, Wells chose anonymity and tagged her jumper the invention of a "Chicago mother," an abnegation of identity that peeved the reporter for *New Century for Women*, who demanded, "Why does she not give her name?" She may not have given it, but history preserved it. A century later, columnist Erma Bombeck, who rated women's inventions more practical than men's, wrote of Wells: "Jane Wells was the first to acknowledge that children did not sit in seats, they jumped in them and bounced off the ceiling; so she invented the jumper seat."

Unlike Wells, other inventor/entrepreneurs incorporated their names into trade names to lend authority or perhaps a touch of hominess, to wares identified with women's work. By attaching her name to her flat ("sad") iron, Mary Potts implied she was a veteran ironer with a trustworthy product—which must have seemed like a good idea in trying to sell a new iron at a time when women had irons for every purpose. There were crimpers for pushing into ruffles or frills, fluting irons for wider parallel grooves (Henrietta Cole's fluting iron was commended for its "originality in construction in the lever pressure, so that the lightest texture of fabric can be fluted without injury"), "goffering" tongs to set smaller frills in curtains and neckpieces, mangles for smoothing flat work such as sheets and table linen by running them through rotating rollers of polished wood, and flat irons for general use.

Ironers kept several sad irons in service, one in active use and two heating on the stove in preparation. It took an experienced practitioner to get the plate hot enough to remove wrinkles while keeping the handle cool enough to hold. Potts (née Webber) patented her first iron at nineteen in Ottumwa, Iowa. To keep it from scorching clothes and to buffer the hand from its heat, she built a pasteboard rim around the iron and filled it with plaster of paris, with which she had gained some

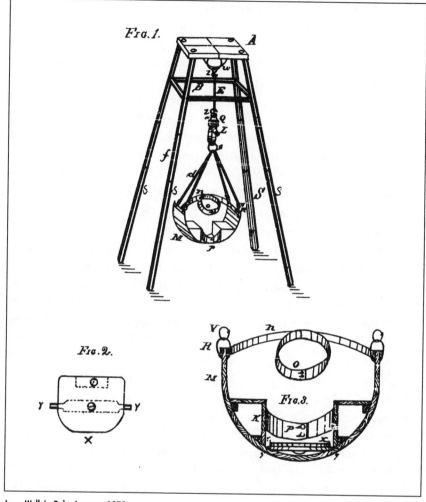

Jane Wells's Baby-Jumper, 1872.

familiarity from her father, who was a plasterer. She later redesigned the shape of the body and replaced the heat-retaining iron handle with a detachable wooden one. First marketing "Mrs. Potts' Sad Iron" in Ottumwa, she faced a credit crunch and imminent foreclosure but must have spun a sad but optimistic tale to R. G. Dun & Company's credit rater, who concluded: "[W]e thk [think] if they have time they may get through." He was wrong. Potts and her husband, a dry goods clerk, went bankrupt and tried to cover liabilities at fifty cents on the dollar. They were still upbeat enough that on his next call the rater postulated: "[They] will probably go into bus again after bankruptcy." It was not long before they did, but only after moving to her husband's native Philadelphia, where the American Enterprise Manufacturing Company, which sold many other household aids, took over sales.

A fanfare of advertising made Mrs. Potts' Sad Iron not only an exposition best-seller but a household word. American Enterprise leafleted exposition visitors with so many varieties of Mrs. Potts's trade cards that fairgoers could collect them like modern baseball cards. Some bore her portrait; most were gimmicky cartoons such as Jolly Old Santa with his reindeer trooping across while Saint Nick shouted, "Hi-Ho. Hurry up my hearties. The demand for the Mrs. Potts's Irons is so great we'll have to make two trips this year, one with them along and another with the toys." Another showed Mrs. Potts' Sad Iron on the bowsprit of a ship bound for the North Pole: "The problem solved. Uncle Sam has caught the idea. The Mrs. Potts' Irons retain the heat and melt icebergs." Marking the visit of the President to the Centennial, a card, labeled "President and Mrs. Hayes' Visit to Philadelphia," shows the First Lady (holding a Sad Iron) saying to her bearded spouse, "We cannot leave until we visit Enterprise Manufacturing Company and order some of Mrs. Potts' Cold Handle Irons like this." The President informs his wife, "But my dear, they are for sale by all Hardware Stores in this country." While that may have been an exaggeration in 1876, it was certainly not by the end of the century.

The true showstopper of the Woman's Pavilion, however, was Caroline Brooks's bust of *Dreaming Iolanthe,* made entirely of butter by a method for which she was just then applying for a patent. Despite the Arkansas artist's painstaking packaging of *Iolanthe* for her two-thousand-mile train trip to the exposition, a brawny baggage handler mistook the tin box for a seat, plumped his massive two-hundred-pound frame onto it, and crashed through to the dreamer's face. After speedy restoration, Brooks pronounced *Iolanthe* perfect again. When word spread that the Woman's Pavilion sported a *butter* sculpture, crowds collected, finally becoming so unwieldy that anxious officials relocated the figure to the top floor of the larger Memorial Hall, where Centennial guards regulated the jostling pack impatient to see "the Butter Lady" ("undoubtedly the cream of both buildings," as one wag quipped) and perhaps hoping to catch a glimpse of the much-acclaimed twenty-six-year-old sculptor. To everyone's surprise, and despite soar-

The Butter Lady herself:
"Iolanthe Dreaming."

ing temperatures, the liberal and regularly replenished supply of ice packed in the tin frame beneath *Iolanthe* kept her frozen for the entire six months of the display.

Although it was the butter sculpture itself that drew the crowds, Brooks intended it to be only the first stage in a process for creating plaster casts. The butter sculpture was the model over which she pressed plaster until it hardened, after which she melted the butter, drained it away through a hole, filled the now-empty cast with plaster, removed the hardened plaster shell, and achieved a plaster cast that she could copy in marble. It was an ingenious method of using what she, as a farmer's wife, had at hand—butter! Wrote the inventor in her patent:

> I have found, after repeated practical tests, that butter possesses properties which render it particularly available as material for the formation of delicate and perfect designs. . . . The best butter should be selected for the purpose, and it should be as free as possible from foreign matter and impurities. . . . The butter may be combined with lard, or lard alone, or other fatty substances which will melt when subjected to heat, may be used; but after many experiments I have found that pure butter is the best substance wherewith to carry my invention into effect.

The ingenuity of the technique was forgotten, however, in the midst of the excitement generated by the artist's creation. One beholder related the sculpture's attraction to fairgoers: "Thousands wondered 'how she did it.' The 'lovelies' and 'oh mys' were scattered promiscuously around the building. 'Did she churn it?' 'Was it Butter?' " In fact, Brooks had to field so many questions that she finally distributed a small explanatory booklet, in addition to doing a step-by-step enactment of her working method. With broom straws and a butter paddle as instruments, she demonstrated to several enthralled commissioners, Women's Centennial committees, and the press how she first packed small bits of butter into a granite basin until she had about a dozen pounds. After refrigerating it, she worked with the cooled "shapeless golden mass" with her tools and transformed it into the sleeping beauty in about an hour and a half. One witness exclaimed that from "a goodly supply of Bethlehem butter, a sweet angelic face popped out, complete in all its details." A Philadelphia writer hailed Brooks as an "unconscious artist of the West . . . with that plastic skill which has been the guiding star to fame of many sculptors." The critic for *Leslie's Historical Register of the Centennial Exhibition* urged that though one had to take into account the difficulties encountered in such a medium, still "the work itself is one exhibiting the highest degree of talent, a fine ideal feeling, as well as exceeding delicacy and brilliancy of manipulation." Another viewer deemed Brooks's "exquisite head carved in butter . . . an exhibition of native talent, as the lady had no regular instruction in her art."

Instruction she lacked, but she came by her inventive faculties quite naturally, for her father, Abel Shawk, invented the first successful steam fire engine in the United States and discovered copper fields in the Lake Superior region. Her raw materials were from the farm she lived on with her husband, Samuel Brooks, a former railroad man turned "substantial and progressive farmer . . . thoroughly posted in all public affairs as well," who owned his own large farm and managed additional acreage belonging to a local doctor. From those farms, his wife had built up a nice butter business, and when she carved the face of the invalid wife of a well-known judge in a large pat of butter, the grateful spouse urged her to send it to the Centennial.

Caroline Brooks, Sculptor of the "Butter Lady."

In exhibits representing fields in which women were rare participants, Martha Coston's improved Coston Signals won an award and
elicited praise from *Demorest's Monthly:* "[S]he stands today the most
remarkable instance of woman's capacity for inventing and producing,
and successful achievement, through ability, great intelligence, perseverance, and extraordinary diplomacy. She should be as bright as one
of her own signals, to guide and encourage other women in business."

Also outside the household realm was Elizabeth Stiles. A business-woman originally from Vermont, Stiles established and supplied furniture to library reading rooms as far away as the territories of Minnesota and Dakota, and shortly before the exposition had furnished one in Philadelphia for the Ladies' Christian Association. Since the Philadelphia room was overcrowded, she talked a carpenter into combining several separate pieces of furniture into a single one that could be approached from all four sides. Folded, it was only eighteen inches deep, six feet wide, and seven feet high. When it was unfolded its depth was extended to seven feet and it was seen to consist of adjustable, tiltable tables (complete with inkstands on pivots to keep them right side up); small closets; slots; shelves; drawers; racks; twenty-six pigeonholes; a wastebasket; and space on top to display busts, bronzes,

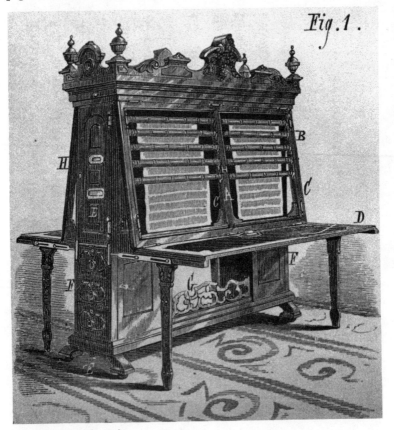

The prize-winning Stiles Desk.

Elizabeth Stiles, inventor of the Stiles desk.

or other ornamental library furnishings behind the carved molding. Families in urban areas who required such multifunction, space-saving furniture for their homes could order it in smaller sizes. "[S]hould a lady wish one in her apartment," said Stiles in her patent, she could add mirrors and other conveniences. Delighted association members pressed her to patent her multifunctional desk, and one semiofficial observer of the Centennial rated it "probably the most successful invention, in every point of view, in the Woman's Building." Judges accorded it the overall highest award in the invention category.

Moving on from exhibits of items for the home, thirty-year-old Mary Nolan, a member of the Saint Louis Board of Lady Commissioners for the Centennial Exposition, sent a model that depicted materials of which the home itself could be constructed. The model brick structure she sent to the exposition carried with it her highest hopes. The daughter of two Irish immigrants, her father a contractor, Nolan had spent years experimenting with interlocking hollow blocks of various substances until she hit upon a compound of native Missouri materials that she named "Nolanum" for herself. She constructed her model exclusively of Nolanum and proudly arranged for a public display in advance of its trip to Philadelphia. After the viewing, a reporter for the *Missouri Republican* expansively predicted that Nolanum's interlocking bricks would halve building expenses and revolutionize building. The hollow, fireproof walls could cool a house in summer and warm it in winter, and, because Nolanum was nonabsorbent and "vermin free," it could replace hospitals' papered walls, thought to spread communicable diseases. Nolan explained to viewers that Nolanum, formed into hollow walls of a uniform surface and finished appearance, required neither paint, plaster, nor wallpaper and could thus be easily washed down in sickrooms.

The distinctively configured and prominently labeled Nolanum house model sent to Philadelphia was eighteen inches long, nine inches wide, thirteen inches deep, and constructed of tiny interlocking blocks that Nolan claimed were harder than marble, nonabsorbent, and noncombustible. Although Nolan made much of the composition of the bricks, her patent was actually on the size and shape that made interlocking possible. The model, which can be identified in the accompanying photograph at left center, drew a good deal of attention, particularly from members of the awards committee, who singled it out from the more traditionally "feminine" inventions:

> Nolanum is a novel method of obtaining with great simplicity and economy a very thorough ventilation within the walls of houses from foundation to roof, thus promoting health and comfort, as such walls, being filled with air, would necessarily be better non-conductors of heat. One important novelty claimed for Nolanum is that the blocks

Inside the Woman's Pavilion. Mary Nolan's "Nolanum" and Elizabeth Stiles's desks are in foreground.

constitute the entire thickness of the wall, and form, as soon as laid in position, finished surfaces inside and out, thus needing no plastering, mastic, paper hanging, or other covering. Its fire-proof qualities and great strength of material, when burnt, constitute in it an additional recommendation. The application of kaolin clays in the construction of dwellings is novel, and may lead to important results.

Exuberant at news of her award and dreaming of "important results," Nolan wrote the exposition's director general: "Your favor giving text of award for Nolanum is received. Will you have the kindness to send the diploma and medal. I desire to place them on exhibition as soon as possible." She presumably displayed them to further sales of the material; unfortunately, her patent was not granted until two weeks *after* she signed the receipt for delivery of the medal. Meanwhile, according to William C. Breckenridge, one of her contemporaries, others saw her expensive model, "recognized its possibilities," and stole the idea behind her not-yet-patented invention. Breckenridge later recounted: "Her lack of business acumen and her big heart brought her to poverty in her old age."

It was a sad end for the inventor whom Breckenridge remembered as a "little lame Irish woman, highly educated and a genius," whose bookstore near Saint Louis University cornered sales to undergraduates and enabled her to carry on her many other activities. Before she burst on the scene as an inventor, Nolan had formed an ill-starred partnership to publish *Inland* magazine, the nation's first magazine produced *completely* by women, from typesetter to editor and publisher. Nolan was the editor; the publisher was Charlotte Smith, a New Orleans widow who had moved to Chicago to open a bookstore, lost it in the Chicago fire, and moved to Saint Louis for a fresh start. As coincidence would have it, this same Charlotte Smith later did more than almost any other woman to promote the interests of women inventors by focusing national attention on them and prodding the inventors themselves to demand equality with men. She will receive further attention in later chapters.

In 1872, however, both women had focused their interest on *Inland,* and its inaugural editorial introduced the new magazine as an important literary monthly that, its founders forthrightly hoped, would improve their own financial condition. They were, they reported, delighted that instead of receiving brickbats from "gentlemen members of the press . . . ungallant enough to throw obstacles in the way of woman's success," their magazine was receiving a cordial welcome "for what it is rather than who is its Editor, publisher or proprietor." The brickbats, however, were soon to come—not from outside but from Nolan herself, who dissolved the partnership (avowedly "by mutual consent") after only a few months.

A staunch Catholic, Nolan saw no humor in an "amusing piece" called "My Idees [*sic*] About Free Love" signed by the anonymous "Josiah Allen's Wife," the pen name of humorist Marietta Holley. Angry with Smith for including the Holley piece and pained by various other disagreements, Nolan left the magazine she had founded but eschewed a fight for the *Inland* name, to which she held copyright. Explaining that she was "constitutionally opposed to disputes," she instead soloed with her own *Central* Magazine, dedicated to upholding "strictly Christian morality" and "all the old-fashioned virtues, which gave to woman the halo of her highest glory." She added, pointedly, "We wish it distinctly understood that articles tinctured with free-love doctrine, blasphemy, or infidelity, will not be accepted from any contributor to this magazine." The indignant Smith rejoined that "a lady . . . should have known better" than to circulate such reports. Unchastised, Nolan pledged her new *Central* would give no space to "unripe essays on crude subjects [which] would give our readers the colic" and launched her monthly with a cover that boasted a physical map of North America in which all roads, railroads, and the great Father of the Waters converged upon . . . Saint Louis. It was "central" indeed.

*Central*, like *Inland*, was written, typeset, printed, and mailed entirely by women, and Nolan demonstrated her complete allegiance to feminism by printing pictures showing the all-female work force in the magazine's composing rooms. It was in *Central* that Nolan publicized her first invention. Prompted by news stories of heavy losses sustained by city hotels when steam fire engines couldn't direct water to the tops of buildings, she devised and applied for a patent for "portable reservoirs" to carry additional water to the site of fires. As papers across the country reprinted articles on the reservoirs from the Saint Louis *Republican* and *Times*, Editor Nolan promised an illustration in *Central* "when we have perfected it." Unfortunately for Nolan, the patent never came through and no illustration was forthcoming. That interest in fighting fires, however, must have generated her later invention of fireproof building blocks.

Nolan continued to publish *Central*, at least until December 1875, when the representative of the national credit-rating firm R. G. Dun & Company completed his call on the Catholic Book Store and penned in his notebook: "Miss Mary Nolan who is the Editor Publisher of the Central Magazine . . . has a small place . . . [small capital invested] which is the extent of her resources . . . is a woman of good character and very industrious . . . is sometimes a little slow to pay."

That snaillike pace changed little, but nine months later the creditrater saw a ray of hope: "Miss Mary . . . has invented a new building material which she called 'Nolanum.' The whole family has great expectations therein." The expectations, however, never materialized. Though Nolan had received favorable publicity and won an award, she had not yet been issued a patent when she showed in Philadelphia. With no protection from the predatory competition and with meager sources for raising the capital to advance Nolanum, she suffered such financial losses that in the next few years Dun's representative successively predicted: "too weak to advise credit"; "not responsible. no credit"; "no improvement"; "poor but honest"; and "cr[edit] weak."

By 1880 the business had expanded to "Books and Millinery" after a friend retired from millinery and left his business to Mary's sister, Teresa Nolan—who paid all bills promptly. When the Dun agent returned the next year, he recorded: "Miss Mary Nolan is not in business; has been an invalid for past two years and is supported by her sister Teresa." There is only one more public mention of inventor Mary Nolan; her name appears among the subscribers to the 1904 Louisiana Purchase Exposition—a fitting position for an inventor whose model attracted such attention at the Exposition of '76.

It is impossible to omit from Centennial mention Elizabeth French, even though she didn't "show" her patented invention in the Woman's Building. Rather, she advertised it in *New Century for Women* and treated fair visitors with it at her "electrical clinic" at 1609 Summer Street. French was one of the many American apostles of Friedrich Mesmer, whose doctrine of universal magnetic force attracted thousands of believers. French advocated hygiene and physical culture in addition to electrotherapy, and when she embarked on her numerous lecture tours, armies of "witnesses" besieged her with offers to testify to their recovery through her treatments.

She trained a corps of practitioners (charging female students five hundred dollars, males, a thousand) to follow her methods, self-published *A New Path in Electrical Therapeutics* in 1873, and two years later patented her "Improvement in Electro-Therapeutic Appliances" in which she proposed three metals or alloys rather than the usual two to "convey currents from a separate source of electricity to any desired part of the body." Specializing in cranial diagnosis, French charged patients with "nervous headache" five dollars for an examination, five dollars for treatment, five dollars for written diagnosis, and ten dollars for house calls. Standard treatment was to administer a three-to-five-minute electrical current "as strong as it can be borne without pain" between a sponge cup at the base of the brain and an electrode held between the palms of the hands. She also dispensed, for a sum, "Dr. Elizabeth J. French's Anti-Dyspeptic Electric Baking Powder" to make "palatable, nutritious, and anti-dyspeptic" bread.

Although cranial distress was French's specialty, she echoed the concerns of her temperance movement sisters about inebriation and used the same galvanic energy to treat overimbibers. If overconsumption of alcohol was chronic rather than periodic, she simply extended her "infallible" treatment over a longer period of time:

> Set up a current from the plate on the stomach to the base of the brain as strong as can be borne. Change from base of brain to palms of hands—five minutes. Let the patient eat a dry cracker during the treatment. At meals, drink little or no water, but take a cup of strong coffee, sweetened to the taste, but without milk. Eat also slices of bread toasted very brown. Carefully abstain from any drink except this coffee and a little water. Keep dry crackers about the person, to eat whenever a sense of thirst arises. Continue this treatment with electricity and diet for from three to seven days, and the cure is effected.

Proponents of the Woman's Pavilion were disappointed that so many fairgoers would go home with memories of "mottoes worked in worsted on card-board" and "useless objects which have not even the merit of artistic beauty to recommend them," rather than of displays that enhanced women's position both politically and industrially. Though most called the inventions exhibit mediocre, Reverend Phebe Hanaford, perhaps because of her ministry more charitable than others, commented in her book: "The question is sneeringly asked sometimes, Can a woman invent? The Great Centennial Exposition answered the question satisfactorily to the believer in women's capabilities; and those who saw and heard the dish-washer and other women who were displaying their own inventions there will not soon forget them." Hanaford argued that genius inhabited both sexes equally but that women diverted their initiative and genius into particular channels, notably the home. Angry that they received scant recognition for their ingenious contributions in that realm, she threw down the gauntlet to future historians: "Some woman with sufficient leisure would do royal service to her sex and the cause of woman, if she would prepare a volume in which, with all detail, it might be shown the help of women in the onward progress of society in regard to household and other conveniences."

Hanaford's invitation to historians rankled the radical feminists, who hoped that no one *ever* had sufficient leisure to report on women's inventions of "household and other conveniences," since they considered domestic work a badge of slavery and thus the ultimate inhibitor of woman's creativity. To glorify those inventions would drive one more nail into the coffin of the women's rights cause.

While opinions diverged about the value of individual exhibits and the unfortunate predominance of "minor" domestic contrivances among the inventions, science historian Deborah Jean Warner, writing with the benefit of one hundred years of hindsight, stresses the Woman's Pavilion's "synergistic effect" in assembling inventors, writers, suffragists, reformers, artists, businesswomen, and professionals. By bringing such a remarkable group of women together for the first time, the pavilion forged friendships and cemented participants' commitment to active work on behalf of women's future political and economic progress. This politicization had a much more direct effect on those who were already active in women's rights issues than on women inventors, however. Though some of the inventors already knew each other from years of exhibiting in regional fairs, and the exposition furthered their sense of fellowship and sisterhood by helping them to establish additional contacts with whom they could discuss their mutual problems, most viewed themselves not as feminists committed to a cause but as businesswomen trying to capitalize on their inventions. As such, they regarded the Centennial as an opportunity to generate publicity for their devices and garner public attention for themselves as well as their products. If a powerful sisterhood was something they could profit from, then it must be a good thing.

In short, while happy to be beneficiaries of the women's movement, most women inventors showed little interest in it. They might have been simply too preoccupied with their businesses to devote time to a wider cause, or leery of group action since the nature of the invention process itself is solitary—and often secret. In the meantime, however, if feminists wished to celebrate them as examples of women's brain power, industry, and ingenuity, so be it.

# 5

# PATENTING
# DRESS REFORM

*A*t the same time that women were organizing to display proofs of their achievements in the Woman's Pavilion, they and legions of their strong-minded sisters were also bent upon liberating themselves from the bondage of constricting clothing. Convinced that they would ultimately have to address the issue of the long skirts that hampered their movement but chastened by the experiences of women who had tried unsuccessfully to popularize bloomers two decades before, they chose instead to begin on the inside—with "reform" undergarments. Intending to free their bodies from the harnessing effects of conventional foundation wear, reformers had two powerful arguments for adopting the new garments: improved health and the mobility that was necessary to participate in the formerly precluded activities that many of them were eager to embrace. When it came to new garments, the inventors were there with ready solutions.

The health issue was a timely one. Gymnastics had already attracted many devotees, and magazines such as *Godey's* had for years published illustrated instructions to show readers how to perform calisthenics in home gymnasia. There was an increasing number of health evangelists gaining prominence as well, among them Dio (for Dioclesian) Lewis, one of the pioneers of the physical culture movement. Lewis organized gymnasium classes in Boston shortly before the Civil War, enrolled hundreds of men and women in his Boston Normal Institute for Physical Education, published *New Gymnastics* to spread the gospel of fitness, and conducted a health retreat in Lexington, Massachusetts, the same city in which he ran a girls' school. Based on his experience and observations, Lewis blamed most of women's weaknesses on their poor physical conditioning and the impediments of their conventional dress.

Other groups, even if they were sympathetic to the need for greater physical freedom, used the health issue as a weapon against those who argued for intellectual freedom for women. Such renowned doctors as Harvard Medical School physician Edward Hammond Clarke submitted that women had a different "organization" (a code word for women's reproductive system) from men, so different that they (and their menfolk as well) should take on only those jobs suitable to their gender. Clarke wrote in his *Sex in Education: Or, a Fair Chance for the Girls*, "[I]f, on the whole, her husband can hold best the plough, and she ply best the needle, they should divide the labor. He should be master of the plough, and she mistress of the loom." Claiming that advanced education made physical and emotional wrecks of women and endangered their later fecundity, Clarke laced his book with shocking case studies providing medical "proof" that the pressures of academic life made too great a demand on women during their menstrual periods. "The brain is dependent upon blood—but if blood supply is low as in the menstrual period, the brain suffers, and mental power is lost. . . . As the blood, so the brain; as the brain, so the mind."

As was expected, Clarke's efforts to oppose higher education for women on the grounds of health did not go unopposed. Elizabeth Stuart Phelps (christened Mary Gray Phelps but, after the death of her mother, a popular fiction writer, choosing to use her mother's name instead of her own) regularly wrote a column on women for *The Independent* and took the first page of its January 1, 1874, issue to speak up for what she termed the "silent majority." In "A Word for the Silent," Phelps retorted that women wouldn't believe Clarke ("simply because they know better. . . . Their unlearned experience stands to them in refutation of his learned statements") and disputed his contention that women who had completed rigorous studies later became ill because their mental efforts had devastated their bodies. Quite the reverse, she believed: "Does it not look as if women were sick because they *stopped* studying?" With few options available to these educated women, they were sick, she said, not from study, as Clarke would have it, but from "perplexed disappointments, baffled intelligence, unoccupied powers and blunted aspirations." Similarly, an anonymous contributor to *Woman's Journal* wrote: "Looking over families and schools that I have known, I certainly cannot say that the young girls who have become invalids were the most studious—quite as often the contrary!"

Whatever the medical men may have believed, the dress reformers unequivocally rejected advanced education as the cause of invalidism and other female ills, instead laying the blame on unsuitable clothing. But it took a while for the movement to spread. In the 1850s the only women strong-minded enough to disregard the dictates of fashion tended to be suffragists—Lucy Stone, for example, who wrote to Susan B. Anthony: "Women are in bondage. Their clothes are a great hindrance to their engaging in any business which will make them pecuniarily independent." Feminist leaders daringly promoted "Turkish" trousers tied at the ankle, a style eminently suitable to and attractive on the trim reformer Amelia Bloomer, who wore one version, but not on the corpulent Elizabeth Cady Stanton, who wore them nonetheless. Bloomer had not herself designed the more comfortable costume that came to be identified with her name, but since she had spoken out in its behalf in her magazine, *The Lily* (whose masthead read "Devoted to the Interests of Women" and which published Stanton's directions on how to make the new garment) reporters christened it with Bloomer's catchy name and incorporated it into such doggerel as

Heigh ho
Through sleet and snow
Mrs. Bloomer's all the go.
Twenty tailors take the stitches
Plenty of women wear the britches
Heigh ho, Carrion crow!

Though many wore the new garb because it was comfortable, the nervier adopted it as a symbol of revolt against all restrictions against women in general, a stance that caused the public to equate "bloomerism" with the fight for equal rights. Although men might have accepted shorter, less voluminous skirts, they wouldn't countenance

modified trousers even for comfort's sake. Those initial efforts to reform women's dress therefore boomeranged as bystanders and press
hooted at women in liberated garb. A New York State legislator was
so offended by men who allowed their wives to wear the newfangled
outfit that he recommended that such men switch to petticoats while
their wives wore pants to "indicate to their neighbors and the public
the true relation in which they stand to each other." The *New York
Herald* viewed women "vagabondizing over the country . . . in eccentric habiliments" with "aversion and disgust." Nevertheless, "rational
dress" had its proponents. When organizers of an antislavery convention questioned whether Lucy Stone should speak because she was
wearing bloomers, famed abolitionist Wendell Phillips rejoined,
"Well, if Lucy Stone cannot speak at that meeting, in any decent dress
that she chooses, I will not speak either." They needed him; they took
Stone, bloomers and all.

Eventually, however, after what Stone described as "three years of
petty derision," even the most dedicated disciples capitulated and
renounced the "freedom dress" in favor of long skirts. Though the
movement foundered after the 1850s, Stanton, in her old age, still
recalled those halcyon bloomered days: "What incredible freedom I
enjoyed for two years! Like a captive set free from his ball and chain,
I was always ready for a brisk walk through sleet and snow and rain,
to climb a mountain, jump over a fence, work in the garden, and, in
fact, for any necessary locomotion." Lucy Stone, her compatriot in
creating "that wholesome discontent which would compel [women] to
reach out after better things," recalled her own exhilaration: "We
could go upstairs without stepping on ourselves, and go downstairs
without being stepped on. But useful as the bloomer was, the ridicule
of the world killed it. It suffered the usual fate of anything that is forty
years ahead of its time."

With skirt length and shape appearing to be nonnegotiable and the
movement temporarily sidetracked for another two decades, women
inventors followed the fashions and stuck with patenting minor variations on the same old nursing dresses, corsets, petticoats, patterns for
laying out and cutting garments, and such body and garment aids as
bosom pads, corset stays, hip padding, dress elevators, and bustles.
Though one would think that the new roles played by women during
the Civil War might have provoked a revival of the dress reform

movement, women shuttled between home and Soldiers Aid Society meetings, packed and shipped huge boxes to the front, visited camps and hospitals, and assembled and sold vast quantities of goods at local and regional fairs—all the while clad like "ladies" in trailing or hooped skirts. There were very few exceptions. Some tried "bifurcated skirts" or even outright trousers—surgeon Mary Walker, who would win the Congressional Medal of Honor (the first of her sex to do so), eventually wore full male attire on the battlefield, saying that she was, after all, engaged in a man's service. Most women, however, continued to burnish the "girl he left behind him" image even when warned that their shackling garments would "trip them into eternity when stepping into a car."

When reformers decided that women were too spineless to shorten trailing skirts, they switched their focus to the abominations beneath and found their most powerful weapon in the battle was the charge of unhealthfulness. One even equated corsets with liquor and opium as "injurious to society." Mary Livermore, in her lecture "What Shall We Do with Our Girls," which she delivered over eight hundred times from Maine to California, blamed tight garments for limiting a girl's freedom of movement, contributing to her "feebleness" and "ship-wreck[ing] our young daughter before she gets out of port." There was also concern about the moral effects of such trussing: Popular phrenologist Orson S. Fowler charged corsets and tight lacing with exciting "impure desires" and begged: "Unloose your corset strings. Forsake corset stores . . . remember that you are born, not to be courted and pleased by fashionable rowdies, but to become *wives* and *mothers*." To matrimonially inclined men, he warned: "See to it that you shun tight-lacers, and get 'NATURAL WAISTS or *no wives.*'"

Reformers found plenty of support within the medical profession. Dr. Clarke, the same doctor who harbored misgivings about the effects of women's advanced education, was also concerned on their behalf about invalidism caused by "[c]orsets that embrace the waist with a tighter and steadier grip than any lover's arm"; Dr. John Harvey Kellogg, founder of the famous Battle Creek health center, scolded that heavy skirts were "enough to drag the life out of a Hercules" and recommended suspending them from the shoulders rather than the waist. With the medical profession's backing, therefore, the dress reform movement not only revived but flourished. Its leadership came

# FRANK LESLIE'S
# ILLUSTRATED
# NEWSPAPER

Entered according to the Act of Congress, in the year 1874, by FRANK LESLIE, in the office of the Librarian of Congress, at Washington.

No. 977—Vol. XXXVIII.]     NEW YORK, JUNE 20, 1874.     [PRICE, 10 CENTS.

Ladies' Dress Reform Meeting at Freeman Place Chapel, Boston.

from the New England Women's Club's Dress Reform Committee, which functioned as a bureau of correspondence with other like-minded women. Founded by Julia Ward Howe in 1867, the New England Women's Club on Park Street in Boston worked in tandem with Sorosis (which Jane Croly launched a month later in New York), the flagship of the network of women's clubs that in the postwar period penetrated every section of the country. Describing the movement their mother inaugurated, two of Julia Howe's daughters later described the club movement:

> To thousands of elder women in the late sixties and early seventies it came like a new gospel of activity and service. They had reared their children and seen them take flight; moreover, they had fought through the war, their hearts in the field, their fingers plying needle and thread. They had been active in committees and commissions, the country over; had learned to work with and beside men, finding joy and companionship and inspiration in such work. How could they go back to the chimney-corner of life of the fifties? In answer to their question—an answer from Heaven, it seemed—came the women's clubs, with their opportunities for self-culture and for public service.

Dress reformers would have agreed with Edward Everett Hale, Unitarian clergyman and writer, who remarked, "When I want anything in Boston remedied, I go down to the New England Woman's Club!" The club's Dress Reform Committee spun into action under the chairmanship of Elizabeth Stuart Phelps, whose 1873 address to the club on "Dress as It Affects the Health of Women" was published in four parts in *The Independent* magazine and reprinted in book form as *What to Wear*. Phelps complained that when women hiked up their skirts to climb into horse-, street-, and railroad cars, male bystanders gleefully gathered below to eyeball off-limits expanses. "It is not," she tartly opined, "in our drawing-rooms that we should look to judge of the intrinsic worth of any style of dress. The street-car is a truer crucible of its inherent values." In her own dress she practiced what she preached, and once wrote a friend from her seaside retreat in Gloucester: "You should see us down here in our beach dresses—short, loose and not uncomely to my fancy."

The committee, however, concentrated on undergarments rather than outer garments and approved patterns, bought fabrics, negotiated for patent rights to designs, opened a store on Winter Street to sell endorsed garments, and held a mass meeting for women to demonstrate the approved undergarments (on large dolls, since it was unseemly to display them on even a life-size replica of the human form). The stamp "Approved," chairman Phelps explained, meant "suspend[ing] every single article of clothing you wear, even to your flannels, from the shoulder, by some device or other, if you would attain any approach to comfort."

At the behest of the dress reformers, a number of inventor/corsetieres focused their ingenuity on the design of nonconstricting, "healthful" foundation wear that they could license to the committee in exchange for what they assumed would be fair remuneration for use of their ideas. When the committee rejoined with a "we are all sisters on a joint crusade" appeal to have them *donate* their patterns, or at least take lesser compensation for something that was beneficial to all womankind, the inventors indignantly accused the reformers of greed. This was not one of the happier moments in the relations between women inventors and women reformers.

A prime example of a woman who came to feel exploited by the reformers was inventor Olivia Flynt, a Boston dressmaker of twenty-five years' pre-reform experience in compressing waists into eighteen-inch girths. By 1876 she had patented her "Flynt Waist" or "True Corset," which allowed the waist "natural circulation, perfect respiration, and freedom for every muscle" while at the same time imparting "an artistic contour and elegance of motion, that all corsets utterly destroy." Not unmindful of the less endowed, she saw to it that her waist had a "very nice provision . . . [for] extra fullness where sufficient development is lacking." The "Flynt Waist" became so popular that even two decades later an observer noted that "girls go to college and train for a year or two, and don Flynt waists."

Flynt's *Manual of Hygienic Modes of Under-Dressing for Women and Children* ("mailed free to any physician or lady" and therefore not available to the prurient) abounded with vivid accounts of women ruined by their corsets: a musician forced to relinquish the piano for life, French-corseted maidens too weary to frolic, a mother's thickened

Olivia Flynt's dictum on hygienic clothing, opposite.

# MANUAL

OF

# Hygienic Modes of Under-Dressing

FOR

## WOMEN AND CHILDREN.

Pat. Jan. 6, 1874.

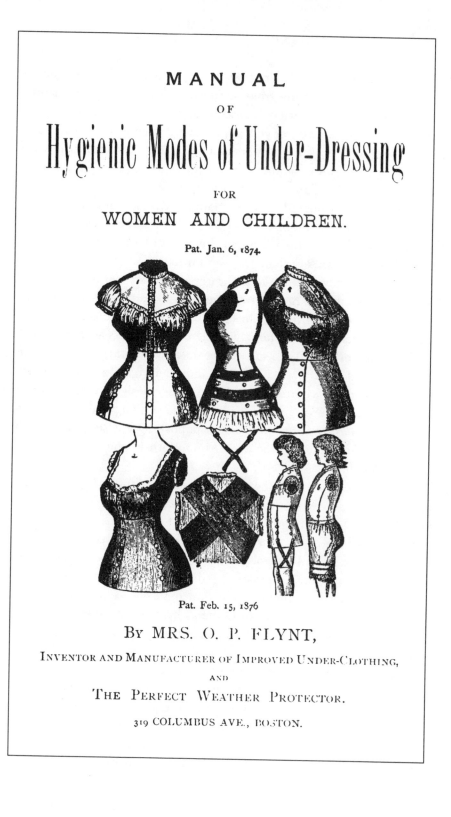

Pat. Feb. 15, 1876

## BY MRS. O. P. FLYNT,

INVENTOR AND MANUFACTURER OF IMPROVED UNDER-CLOTHING,

AND

THE PERFECT WEATHER PROTECTOR.

319 COLUMBUS AVE., BOSTON.

heart valves attributed to her "compressing machine." The decision to invent, wrote Flynt, came from a customer invalided by the painful weight of her unsupported breasts, and she promised the stricken woman: "I will [invent], for you and for every other woman who wants it. . . . [W]hen I took my scissors to fashion the garment, in just ten minutes I had it, although in a crude state, but the principle the same as it is today." She patented that principle.

Flynt further patented a "Hose Supporter," the garment that became a bone of contention between her and the committee. With her garments already patented prior to the committee's formation, Flynt advertised them widely, lent the committee a pattern/diagram, and hoped their store would make and carry it and pay her a commission on each garment. The members, however, viewing themselves as missionaries to women in need, objected to the patent protection, which made her patterns as "unattainable to Dress Reformers as if they were made on the moon." Flynt, suspecting that the stocking supporter the committee did finally sell infringed upon her rights as an inventor, baldly accused the committee of copying her designs, asked for the return of her pattern, and warned: "The laws that regulate Patents compel me to ask you to refrain from publishing a description of my invention in any manner whatever. Also to forbear your copying them in whole or in part."

Abba Woolson, a well-known New England journalist and the committee member to whom the complaint was addressed, shot back, "I am sure that you will agree with me that I have not infringed upon your patents." Her own stocking supporter, she maintained, was "entirely different." While Woolson handled Flynt with kid gloves and praised her "unrivalled originality, skills and taste as an inventor and maker of women's garments," she fumed to one committee friend, "Mrs. Flynt's thunderings seem to me as harmless as they are ridiculous. If we infringe her patents . . . then she has power to stop every workshop in the world." To another, Woolson reported that she had fended off the insults and falsehoods "with more forbearance and kindly feeling than, perhaps, I ought to have shown" and hoped that "the cause" would not be harmed by "the wrath of such ignorant pretenders as Mrs. F. and other selfish speculators on our ideas."

Woolson was equally harsh with those who hoped to capitalize on the practice of stamping garments "Dress Reform Committee." But, without having registered the label as a trademark, she was outmaneuvered. A case in point was Mrs. H. S. Hutchinson, who copyrighted the phrase herself when the committee dallied too long in registering it. Owning the trademark, she could exact a fee from any who used it, including the committee that had initiated it. Members howled that by trying to line her own pockets Mrs. Hutchinson was endangering the whole reform movement. Hutchinson, however, remained resolute: She had paid her own thirty-five dollars for protection and planned to look out for herself.

Susan Taylor Converse of nearby Woburn became even more of a problem to the committee. Converse held three patents: a body-covering combination union suit, skirt-supporting corset, and corset cover; a later improvement in cotton or linen; and a top ("Emancipation Waist") whose bodice protected the breasts from "compression and irritation." According to Converse, the committee asked her to display this last garment ("the results of years of practical study in a school of heavy affliction"), and she carefully spelled out her terms beforehand: She would show it *only* if doing so did not endanger her rights and if she received twenty-five cents for each one sold. That said, and secure in the knowledge that each committee member was a "lady of culture and honor who with sincerity equal to my own was laboring to bring the emancipation of woman—beginning with the body," she exhibited her garment. To her horror, even before she left the room, she noted others studying how to copy it and knew that the promise of protection was "as forcible as a rope of sand." Desperately needing the income, however, she accepted their proposal, and the shop was soon selling "Emancipation Waists" along with "Union Under-Flannels, Emancipation Suits, Dress Drawers, Chemiloons, &c., Made to Order on Short Notice, on Hygienic principles, as recommended by the Committee."

Suspecting the store was selling garments made according to her patterns without paying her royalty and hearing that committee members had accused her of being greedy and overcharging for her patterns, she angrily withdrew the "Emancipation Suit" from further sale and submitted a bill for those the shop had sold. How could the committee, she asked, expect her to *donate* her patterns after she had spent so much to protect herself by patent? "Did they," she steamed, "with any kindness of heart look the pattern over and see the amount of work there is in preparing it—carefully, for *perfect fitness,* that it might

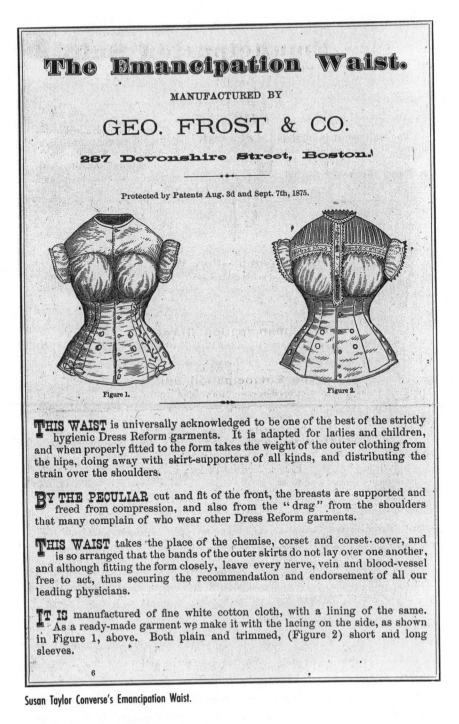

# The Emancipation Waist.

MANUFACTURED BY

## GEO. FROST & CO.

### 287 Devonshire Street, Boston.

Protected by Patents Aug. 3d and Sept. 7th, 1875.

Figure 1.          Figure 2.

**THIS WAIST** is universally acknowledged to be one of the best of the strictly hygienic Dress Reform garments. It is adapted for ladies and children, and when properly fitted to the form takes the weight of the outer clothing from the hips, doing away with skirt-supporters of all kinds, and distributing the strain over the shoulders.

**BY THE PECULIAR** cut and fit of the front, the breasts are supported and freed from compression, and also from the "drag" from the shoulders that many complain of who wear other Dress Reform garments.

**THIS WAIST** takes the place of the chemise, corset and corset. cover, and is so arranged that the bands of the outer skirts do not lay over one another, and although fitting the form closely, leave every nerve, vein and blood-vessel free to act, thus securing the recommendation and endorsement of all our leading physicians.

**IT IS** manufactured of fine white cotton cloth, with a lining of the same. As a ready-made garment we make it with the lacing on the side, as shown in Figure 1, above. Both plain and trimmed, (Figure 2) short and long sleeves.

6

Susan Taylor Converse's Emancipation Waist.

appear before an awakening public, to approach, as near as possible, to the highest standard of hygienic excellence?" She turned the sword in the breast of committee members: "With all their zeal for woman, did they ever ask why one woman like myself should give of her head and hand labor, without fair compensation?"

To this letter, along with other Dress Reform material now in committee archives at the Schlesinger Library, is appended a member's comment whose signature is illegible but whose sentiments are clear: "In our zeal for woman we did *not* ask 'why one woman should give head and hand and heart,' for we were all giving it and expected others to do so. There was *no* intimation . . . that the thing was patented." Eventually the committee paid up—but not without grousing from the treasurer: "I think the sooner we get her off our hands the better."

Though unappreciated by the committee, Converse must have relished the accolade of a correspondent to *Woman's Journal:* "I have worn the 'Emancipation Suit' for over three years, and I daily bless the woman who invented it. . . . We must do real missionary work, and make it a matter of conscience not to sin against our own physical well-being, even at the risk of being called 'odd.' "

Clara Clark's path with the committee was smoother. Her patented boneless and wireless "Combination Shoulder Brace Corset" and a variety of other braces and stocking and skirt supporters sold both in the committee rooms and at Boston's well-known George Frost and Company and New Haven's Foy, Harmon and Chadwick. Emmaline Philbrook's inventions were also carried by Frost and Company and other companies, and testimonials abounded for her popular "Equipoise Waist" with attached stocking supporters: "They are highly recommended by physicians of this city in whose practice they are used"; "They have satisfied all our customers who have tried them; and we think they will soon come into favor with ladies and misses who cannot wear corsets." One Frost and Company advertisement depicted two women, one pertly cheerful, the other bedraggled after an exhausting shopping trip. Bedraggled wore only a regular corset for support while Light and Lively wore the "fashionable corset substitute [the Equipoise] . . . as comfortable to the tired as to the rested."

In New York, patentee Catherine ("Madame") Griswold rode the wave of dress reform's popularity and designed corsets to "keep the chest erect and effectively prevent stooping . . . [especially] students, sewing women, or any whose occupation obliges them to sit or stoop." She had the Worcester Corset Company manufacture them and stimulated nationwide sales by employing "Lady Agents" to call on customers. Such work, said Griswold, was "a very appropriate and congenial occupation for women," each of whom she required to order a corset in her own size so that she could "fully test its merits, and be better prepared to recommend and fit it to others." Her physician-endorsed "Abdominal Corset," with "all weight suspended from the Shoulders, preventing any pressure on the Spine or Kidneys," promised "relief and cure of the many forms of female weakness" and sold well.

Despite having enlisted many women in their movement and making some modest improvements in foundation construction, dress reformers concluded that as long as more conventional women continued to shroud their legs with "ladylike" long skirts, they would never become emancipated. A woman doctor who ran the New England Hygienic Home in Concord, Vermont, saw women's clothing as undermining more than health and expounded to *Woman's Journal*: "Society is accustomed to keep woman in her place by the rules of propriety." Reformers had made a stab at change, but if street filth still clung to their hems, if they tripped over curbs and doorsills, if they sweltered in summer under layers of petticoats and skirts, if, because of their clothes, they could be only spectators of active sports rather than participants, if the only advancement in their dress had to occur where it wouldn't show, then there was still a fight to be waged. It would take a while to regroup, but in a few years the reformers would return to the battlefield.

# 6

## PUBLICIZING, PROSELYTIZING, AND EDUCATING: UPLIFTING THE POSITION OF WOMEN BEGINS

*T*he mutual support that women gained from working together in the reform movement—whether for suffrage, better working conditions, more liberal divorce laws, legalization of contraception, attention to physical fitness, equalization of property laws, or changing clothing styles they felt were designed to keep them in their place—gave them the courage to speak up forcefully against the way society disparaged women's achievements. Women inventors were certainly women of achievement, but since they seldom crusaded for women's causes, it fell to the movement's activists to argue that regardless of the negligible number of patents issued to women compared to those issued to men, and despite the fact that the majority of their patents dealt with women's conventional realm, women's creativity was still no less than men's. Though all feminists confronted the issue of society's belittlement of women's inventive skills, they seldom agreed on the best way to counteract it.

The more conservative feminists, who still subscribed to the conventional "woman's place is in the home" doctrine, found no cause for embarrassment either in the lesser number of women's patents or in the plethora of their household inventions. They celebrated women's ingenuity wherever it was displayed. The more radical feminists rationalized the discrepancy in numbers and concentration in household devices by charging that being mired in domestic detail stifled women's creativity, and they demanded equality of opportunity, which would, they asserted, enable women to invent in *any* field. They pointed out that society, which lionized the male inventor, notwithstanding the fact that his single-minded pursuit of his invention might force his family to the brink of destitution, would denounce a similarly driven woman inventor for callous abdication of familial obligations. As one woman wrote to *Woman's Journal,* "If a woman was spending her fortune, and wearing out her life, in unraveling some mechanical prize . . . the doors of the insane asylum would shut her off from indulging in such vagaries." In the next few decades, the two groups argued. One, tired of being constantly reminded of the numerical chasm separating men's and women's inventions and of the profusion of household devices, preferred to focus on the positive, on triumphs achieved in the face of obstacles regardless of whether their inventions had to do with the traditionally female concerns or not. The other, demanding major societal changes to allow women to move beyond domestic perimeters, minimized inventions of "women's things," focused on those with no connotation of gender, and singled out the few women who invented in fields normally reserved for men as proof that widening women's horizons would allow them to reach their creative potential.

In 1877, Ida Tarbell, a young writer who believed that the home was, and should be, woman's primary sphere, tried to counter the radicals' arguments in her article "Women as Inventors." She chose her venue wisely by giving these relatively conservative views in *Chautauquan* magazine, the monthly supplement for subscribers to the popular four-year adult education plan begun in 1874 in Chautauqua Lake, New York. Though affiliated with the Methodist Episcopal church, the nondenominational Chautauqua movement initially offered formal classes, conferences, lectures, and recreation at its lakeside retreat. By 1880, the Chautauqua Literary and Scientific Circle had enrolled thousands of ambitious students in its home reading course, which covered a few contemporary topics but concentrated on English, American, European, and classical history and literature. Tarbell's article, therefore, had a relatively cultivated audience of around a hundred thousand readers who devoured the magazine as homework for the Chautauqua diplomas they would earn at the end of four years of required study. By her calculation, 95 percent of the circle's members were women. There was a good deal of Methodism in *Chautauquan*, especially the selected Sunday readings, so that there is no doubt that its women readers, though eager to improve themselves through study, were traditional women whose primary interest was the home.

Tarbell must therefore have had a receptive audience to her argument that housework offered women considerable scope for their inventiveness, as their many patents on household devices indicated. As to whether these inventions were worthy of women's talents, she declared: "Invention is an invention whether it be for housework or mill-work, and the mental quality it requires is the same." She announced that any woman who could transform a dress she and her daughters had worn into a quilt lining or could festoon an old dry goods box with cretonne for "an enviable result" was a bona fide inventor. She nonetheless did allow that women's circumscribed lives blinded them to the possibilities of increasing the family fortune by patenting a clever device, that their fear of ridicule for presuming to engage in the business arena cut deep, that their ignorance about how to secure patents was abysmal, and that their skepticism about being able to raise money for a model and legal fees was well founded, given the prejudice that existed against women.

Still, on the basis of her own observations, she did not agree with the bleak picture presented by the militant suffragists. Not only did she resist their carping disparagement of women's household inventions, she doubted the accuracy of the statistics they quoted: only around three hundred patents granted to women since passage of the Patent Act in 1790. Even the nonmilitant feminist Mary Lowe Dickinson, writing in an 1886 issue of *Chautauquan*, the very magazine for which Tarbell wrote, classified the majority of women's inventions (except the dishwasher—which she allowed was a boon to women whose thrice daily confrontations with dishes made anyone wish that "dishes grew on trees") as "trifles," and declared that only 334 patents, most of them for household articles, had "as yet" been issued to women. This led Dickinson to conclude: "Evidently the field of invention is one to which the feminine mind has not yet largely turned." Tarbell magnanimously called Dickinson "one of our noblest and best informed advocates for more work and better wages for women," but disputed the accuracy of her figures, suspecting them of having been supplied by radicals who were shrewdly undercalculating the number of women patentees to clinch their arguments that men deliberately and jealously excluded women from their patent duchy. Tarbell felt that what had been intended to stir women to action had backfired instead, for it discredited women's creativity, a creativity she felt was properly centered in "the most delicate, complex, and essential of all creative tasks—the making of a home."

Recognizing that she needed figures and facts to refute the radicals' allegations, Tarbell headed straight for the Patent Office in Washington to conduct her own research. It is well to note that some years later, this same kind of dedication to the facts characterized Tarbell's research on the Standard Oil Company's practices and made her a standard-bearer among the twentieth-century "muckrakers." So what would have been a tremendously audacious act for most women at that time was, to Tarbell, simply the act of a professional reporter digging for facts. As she later related in her autobiography, she got them: "I was able to put my finger at once on over two thousand patents, enough to convince me that, man-made world or not, if a woman had a good idea and the gumption to seek a patent, she had the same chance as a man to get one."

Since in 1875 Elizabeth Duane Gillespie had received from the Patent Office a list of women patentees whom she could solicit for Centennial Exposition exhibits, and a couple of years later Tarbell went to Washington and put her finger on over two thousand patentees "at once," it is obvious that even though there was still no *official* Patent Office list by gender, there *was* some kind of list. In her 1877 "Women as Inventors" article, Tarbell gave the credit to R. H. Gill, longtime head of the Patent Office's Model Hall, for toiling three years to compile "the *first* and *only*" such list. Perhaps Gill had also helped Gillespie. He certainly seems to have had the interests of women at heart, telling Tarbell that he hoped his list of women patentees would inspire other women to use their ingenuity to raise themselves from "overwork and poverty."

Armed with the statistics she had gathered, Tarbell established that far more women invented than was popularly believed (six times more than the figure cited by Dickinson and others), made a case for the value of those household inventions the feminists so regularly deplored ("An article that will lighten and brighten the housewife's grind is a national blessing"), and inspired women to ignore all obstacles:

> The world sensibly says, Do whatever you can do well. How, not what, shall decide your fitness. A woman who has inventive skill may easily find a place in which to exercise it. . . . No improvement which a woman can originate will be slighted because it comes from the hand of a woman. It only remains for her to take full possession of a field in which there is abundant opportunity for her to win great successes and do great good.

In addition, Tarbell argued that the relatively few who actually patented were only a drop in the bucket compared to the hundreds of thousands of their fellow women who approached their quotidian tasks with the same "flash of genius" that characterized patenting women. To Tarbell, creativity itself was central, its application peripheral. It mattered little whether the flash was beamed toward a better feather duster or a telescope. Still, Tarbell agreed with the radicals that one major spur to ingenuity was lacking—technical education for girls. One of Tarbell's friends, a woman who was partner and joint manager of a large paper mill, wrote her: "Girls are so entirely and totally ignorant of practical mechanics that it is about as astonishing a feat for them to originate any invention as it would have been for Noah to have invented a steam-engine for his ark." Though Tarbell admitted and deplored society's failure to train women in mechanics, she felt that they nonetheless gained remarkable dexterity in handling tools in the course of their housewifely pursuits by doubling regularly as carpenters, locksmiths, and tinners. "If she can learn to split her own kindling wood," maintained Tarbell, "she can learn to handle a saw and hammer."

Most women inventors would have felt that this was not enough, for those with no training in mechanics were at an obvious disadvantage not just in their ability to invent in the first place but in the extra expenses they had to bear in hiring a local handyman/carpenter or a professional model maker to translate their concepts into working prototypes. A petition by a group of inventors asking Congress to rescind requirements for models because they imposed "a serious tax on inventors" drew the fervent support of women inventors. They might better have focused on education, however, as many feminists did. Since schools taught girls to bake and sew rather than work with tools, mechanically inclined girls, without the kind of manual training in wood or metal that the feminists were advocating, had little hope of becoming inventive women unless they had parents who encouraged them. Otherwise, they had to learn on the job as factory workers (like Margaret Knight) or be trained in a family business that depended upon such skills.

Though they were rare, there were a few parents who nurtured their daughters' native mechanical talents. In the case of Harriet Hosmer, it was her father who, having observed his child's surprising affinity for mechanics, whetted her appetite for tinkering. Many years later, as an expatriate sculptor living in Rome, Hosmer devised a way to make artificial limestone. Being no stranger to the world of business, unlike some of her inventing sisters, she apprised her American attorney of the "purely private and confidential matter" and engaged him to proceed immediately to protect her invention. Hosmer kept the draft letter for her own file, marking the outside with underlined and bolded instructions: "PETRIFIED MARBLE PATENT IMPORTANT KEEP." Ordering him not to "reveal the secret of the invention to *anyone*" and relying implicitly upon his "discretion and faithfulness," she divulged the secret of making "petrified marbles," not as others had done by coating cement or plaster with enamel to simulate natural marble, but by converting limestone to marble through a "petrifying" process. Her experiments indicated that if she heated limestone in hot water under high atmospheric pressure for twelve to eighteen hours, then colored it with dyes specifically formulated for each desired shade, the product would bear a close resemblance to real marble.

Hosmer was already popular with feminists for sculpting a special piece for the Woman's Building at the Centennial, and even though she never turned her invention into a commercial success (concentrating instead on modeling in plaster of paris), feminist lecturers starred

Harriet Hosmer.

her in their roster of famous women patentees. One of them bragged, "When Harriet Hosmer took her Yankee brains to Rome, she found out the way to make marble from limestone, which the Italian government had long been seeking." In her later years, Hosmer was absorbed in trying to construct a perpetual motion machine with magnets, and told a magazine writer, "Anyone can do sculpture; what I shall try for now is original work."

Unwilling to rely on such rare anomalies of fortune and fathering as Hosmer enjoyed, feminist leaders urged reforms in the education system so that women, whose training generally ended after secondary school and did not include any of the traditionally male skills, could both enroll in mechanical training classes *and* matriculate in college. An editorial in the 1870 inaugural issue of *Woman's Journal* lamented that "existing customs and methods of education stunt [a woman's] soul. . . . Her sphere is prescribed to her, and she is fitted to the procrustean bed, be it too long or too short for her natural proportions." But even among women themselves changes were slow to take root, in part because of events like the Boston symposium the Woman's Education Association sponsored two years later, at which the roster of speakers was exclusively male. If college campuses were to be potential training grounds for the leaders of social and political reform, said the editor of *Woman's Journal* in a spirited attack on that gathering, then women should consult educators of their own sex: "If Harvard College can do nothing more for women, let it at least serve them as an awful warning against caste, exclusion, and the unsympathetic dictation of a fancied superiority to the world that has outgrown its acknowledgement."

Unwilling to wait for the gates of men's institutions to open, by the mid-1870s women had established several major institutions devoted *solely* to woman's higher education: Mount Holyoke, Vassar, Wellesley, and Smith. Such women's colleges, however, clung to liberal arts rather than offering any vocational training for technical or professional careers. Most of them patterned their entrance requirements after those of the most selective men's colleges, but since girls rarely received a sufficiently thorough grounding in their secondary schools, most (at least in their first few years) had to maintain "preparatory departments" to help students meet standards for college work. They provided a rich intellectual atmosphere for those lucky enough to enroll—so rich that some of the parents feared that their daughters would be enticed down paths leading far away from the domestic circle where tatting, embroidery, and the stitching of crazy quilts kept most young women safely occupied.

Sophia Smith, founder of Smith, attempted to assuage such fears: "It is not my design to render my sex any less Feminine, but to develop as fully as may be the powers of womanhood, and furnish women with the means of usefulness, happiness and honor, now withheld from them." Wellesley College, founded to educate young women to lead "lives of noblest usefulness," required that students learn domestic work by serving meals and doing light housework on campus. When the college entered its exhibit at the Centennial, the judges soberly agreed with Wellesley's housekeeping requirements, "established for the beneficial influence of the discipline of domestic work upon the moral nature, while conducing to a better preparation for domestic and social life," and bestowed a high award. Actually, Wellesley's founders had their own reasons for the housekeeping requirement: The money saved by the use of student labor allowed them to reduce fees and thus attract poor but able girls. There was another dimension to the house- work requirement: Wellesley's founders believed it fostered a sense of community interdependence among students and minimized financial differences in their backgrounds. To ensure that this was so, the admin- istration staunchly refused bribes from wealthy parents to free their daughters from such domestic chores by paying a higher fee.

With or without a housekeeping requirement, higher education and the professional opportunities it offered remained beyond the reach of all but a few women. The welcome mat was out, however, for women who wanted to teach in the lower schools—for women have always had opportunities in fields that pay little. Teaching was also an accept- able extension of woman's work in rearing children and a training ground for what Catherine Beecher (herself a teacher) called "life's great purpose . . . the 'happy superintendence of a family.' " Young middle-class women with modest education found their most likely employment in teaching, where women had gradually replaced school- masters since about 1830 and would outnumber them, two to one, by 1890. With not even a high school diploma required until 1907, when Indiana became the first state to require one, teaching was more "calling" than profession, and despite wages a third to half of what men commanded, women flocked to teaching because it was usually the only profession open to them. Society appeared to justify its low pay to teachers, a profession it purportedly ranked high, even noble, by intimating that teachers were rewarded by the "psychic benefits" they got from watching their little charges flourish (another characteristic of fields open to women).

The psychic benefits may have indeed been considerable, but so was the wear and tear. With little academic training, these women needed every ounce of ingenuity they possessed to instruct, if not to foil their willful little scholars. Virginia Penny, that gold mine of information on nineteenth-century job opportunities for women, ruled out as candidates for the teaching profession those lacking patience and tenderness, and anyone "whose feelings can in an hour change from the boiling to the freezing point." But many of the school-related inventions designed by women seemed tacitly to acknowledge the inevitability of such lapses, while attempting to remedy the circumstances that gave rise to them. Patents taken out by those grappling with the challenges of the classroom make savory reading for anyone who has ever taught the young.

Philadelphian Anna M. Breadin, for instance, had no doubt gone from freeze to boil after hearing a desk top slam once too often, and therefore invented a "noiseless desk" about which she wrote in her patent: "One object of my invention is to so construct a school-desk as to prevent or lessen to a great extent the noise caused by the slamming of slates or books upon the desks, or the dropping of the slates into the slate-wells." To muffle the noises of the "restless or nervous scholar," she covered the desk top and lined the bottom of the well into which the slates fit with an easily washed rubber sheet, and, for good measure, tacked it down tightly enough to deter even the most "mischievous scholars" from destroying it. Breadin's design also made it easy for the teacher passing along the aisle between rows to open and inspect the inner portion of the slate well. Breadin's intimate acquaintance with rambunctious students resonates throughout her patent, and when one learns that her first job upon completing school was teaching boys in a "House of Refuge"—probably an orphanage or a home for delinquent minors—one fathoms the desperation that must have inspired her inventing.

Teachers also patented items such as the "Scholar's Companion," which held such paraphernalia as pencils, pens, erasers, sponges, and lunch bags. But it was in the field of actual instruction in the basics of reading, writing, arithmetic, and geography that their genius flowered, resulting in new copybooks, slates, pencil holders, alphabet and number devices, blackboards, and globes. To describe but a few: teachers rotated a ratchet wheel to lower a ruler from a case mounted above the

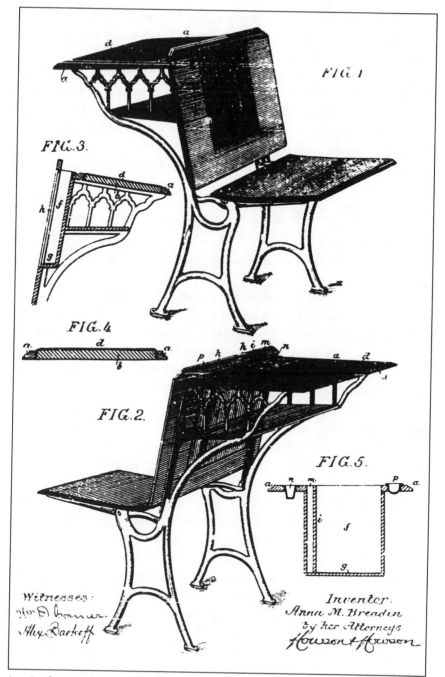

Anna Breadin's "noiseless" school desk.

blackboard so that they could draw parallel lines at any desired distance from each other; copybooks with detachable trial pages enabled students to tear out messy trial sheets and hand in a vastly tidier book; letters permanently "sand-blasted" into the students' slates could be filled in with a pencil as a guide to those still unable to shape them correctly; letters suspended on a wire, abacus-style, could be arranged into several different words. Teachers used a variety of games ("educational appliances") to make it easier to learn letter combinations, grammar, and arithmetic ("With a device of this character a child will become interested, and the learning will be found a pleasure rather than a drudgery as practiced by the common method of teaching arithmetic to primary scholars"); students learned the difference between rotation and revolution of the earth and the consequent day and night and progression of seasons through ingenious attachments to globes.

Ellen E. Fitz showed one of the best mounted globes at the Centennial, one that demonstrated both the 23 ½-degree inclination of the earth's axis and, through various markings, its rotation around that axis and its revolution about the sun. Though her patent claims comprised a good beginner's course in geography (replete with "tracing the sun's diurnal course," the "twilight circle," and "terrestrial positions"), Fitz called it only a skeletal adjunct to her accompanying manual—*Handbook of the Terrestrial Globe, or Guide to Fitz's New Method of Mounting and Operating Globes,* later published in Boston during the 1880s—which, she demurred, was "manifestly too prolix" to put into her patent specification.

China painting, like teaching, was another field that offered impecunious men and women the opportunity of earning a modest living and inventing women a rich vein to mine. Though inventing in this field required knowledge of chemistry and, in the case of firing kilns, of mechanics, a number of women, including Susan Stuart Frackelton, Laura Fry, and Mary Louise McLaughlin, excelled at it. Frackelton, who was conceded to be the first major woman potter of the period, was born in Milwaukee and attended art school in New York, but was largely self-taught. At the beginning of her work as a china painter, she ground her own clay in a coffee mill and rolled it out with a pastry roller; when she saw the need for a portable gas kiln to fire her work, she promptly invented one and sold it in this country and abroad.

China decorator and inventor, Susan Stuart Frackelton.

Frackelton's work was exhibited in all the major expositions and fairs, and at the Centennial was the only china painted by a woman to be exhibited alongside men's work. Primarily a teacher, she taught classes to women who wanted to support themselves by selling their products, and she reached thousands more through her widely used book on the craft, aptly titled *Tried by Fire*. In it, she even included such practical advice as what to wear when potting: "The first thing to be provided with is a calico gown . . . in 'Mother Hubbard' design . . . a yoke with a long ample skirt open down the front, so that it may be donned and doffed readily, a sleeve buttoned at the wrist."

Having begun her career as a china painter in 1874, Frackelton continued to exhibit for the remainder of the century, garnering cita-

Mary Louise McLaughlin, potter and inventor.

tions throughout the world and serving as the first president of the
National League of Mineral Painters. By the time she became head of
a successful china coloring and decorating business, a writer for *Success*
magazine called her "a notable example of feminine genius"; Frances
Willard credited Frackelton's success "to her own temperament and
the full use of all the opportunities for developing her own genius."

The other two major figures in the field, Laura Fry and Mary Louise
McLaughlin, were Cincinnati friends of long standing, initially
brought together through their early interest in wood carving at which

Fry's father, William Fry, who taught at Cincinnati's Art Academy until he was ninety-six, was an expert. In fact, at the Centennial Exposition, McLaughlin showed a carved cabinet she credited to his direction, but it was her painted china that attracted the attention of visitors. Fairgoers in Philadelphia who viewed this American ceramic work for the first time compared it favorably to Limoges and Haviland faience exhibits and snatched up every available piece. McLaughlin's twelve decorated egg cups, according to Laura Fry, commanded a "fabulous price." Although her display never matched the popularity of the Butter Lady's, McLaughlin's delicately painted panels, plates, cups, teapots, stands, and decorated egg cups won enough prizes to establish her firmly as a specialist in a field that, within another two decades, would attract over twenty-five thousand Victorian women who gloried in embellishing everything in sight. Two years after the Centennial, the *Cincinnati Enquirer* still gushed that McLaughlin's Centennial vases were the "sensation of the hour" and that everybody kept asking: "Who is Miss McLaughlin, of Cincinnati? Is she poor? Is she rich? Does she want to come to New York and teach a class? Does she want to start a pottery manufactory?"

This last question was not too far off the mark, for when McLaughlin saw the Haviland exhibit of Limoges porcelain (painted in ceramic colors on white and later covered with glaze) at the Centennial, she decided to duplicate it in America and began her experiments. Shortly thereafter, in the frontispiece to her 1877 book, *China Painting: A Practical Manual for the use of Amateurs in the Decoration of Hard Porcelain*, she quoted the words of H. Taine (whom she did not identify) to describe her own experience: "Success depends on knowing how to be patient, how to endure drudgery, how to unmake and remake, how to recommence and continue without allowing the tide of anger or the flight of the imagination to arrest or divert the daily effort."

McLaughlin's satisfaction in duplicating Limoges ware in America turned into a nightmare ("something I would like to forget") when she discovered that a newcomer to Cincinnati, Thomas Wheatley, had placed pottery suspiciously like hers in a local store window. The enraged McLaughlin and her coterie of faithful supporters charged Wheatley with copying her color formulas. Wheatley, maintaining that he had discovered how to make the china three years before while living in New York, had already applied for a patent, secured financial backing from a Cincinnati capitalist to enlarge his pottery, engaged artists to make it, and threatened to sue those who were using "his" invention. The issue, of course, hinged on priority of invention, and McLaughlin's loyalists rallied to her defense, one claiming, "I even knew the secrets before he did. I don't see how he could get out a patent. . . . I don't care [if he sues]. I shall go on building my pottery and I hope to have the first fire in the kiln in a month's time."

When a Cincinnati paper headlined a story about the fracas WAR AMONG THE POTTERS, McLaughlin's brother, who had carefully recorded his sister's step-by-step experiments and could therefore document the time (and priority) of invention, had to explain to the press that the reason his sister had not applied for a patent was that he had advised her that he didn't think the mixture itself was patentable. He called Wheatley's patent "not worth the paper it is written on" and his chances for making money from the patent "about equal to that of being struck by lightning." To Wheatley he fumed, "It is very easy to get a patent, but it is hard to sustain one." Though confident of the priority of her invention, McLaughlin had neither the commercial ambition nor the financial urgency to press her suit and turned instead to porcelain artware, in which medium she did receive a patent.

McLaughlin's lifelong friend and fellow inventor, Laura Fry, began her artistic career not only in her father's footsteps but also in those of her paternal grandfather, Henry L. Fry, who carved much of the wood in the British Parliament (including the throne chair used by Queen Victoria and her father). She branched out from wood carving to pottery through courses at New York's Art Students League and practical experience in pottery making in New Jersey before returning to Cincinnati to set up her studio and to work with McLaughlin. Over the years, she conducted the question-and-answer "China Painter's Column" in *The Young Ladies Magazine,* for which she supplied the questions as well as the answers until she developed a steady readership.

Fry's and McLaughlin's ability to achieve novel effects with their glazes won them great renown. By 1879, Fry, along with McLaughlin, who was president, and ten others became charter members of the Cincinnati Pottery Club, the first such club in the country, and she later widened her reputation by winning a silver medal for a "most meritorious piece of sculpture" from the University of Cincinnati School of Design. Working for the newly established Rookwood Pottery, Fry proposed applying background color to soft clay by blowing it or spraying it onto the surface, a suggestion the company president scoffed at and then tried to patent herself despite Fry's counterclaim. Said Fry, "Since I used my own tool, an atomizer to spray charcoal drawings, I could claim the legal right of invention." The controversy lasted ten years, with Rookwood Pottery retaining the legal services of the prominent William Howard Taft (later President of the United States). The Patent Office, having the last word, finally ruled that spraying the color on was simply a new use for an old tool, the atomizer, and granted no patent.

Both McLaughlin and Fry hoped to improve not just the method but the aesthetics of pottery painting, for the decorating craze resulted in so many tasteless bibelots that McLaughlin moaned, "Women are inclined sometime so to decorate these articles that the original is lost sight of. In this, to our shame, let it be said we fall behind our aboriginal models, who in their simplicity never lost sight of the fitness of things." Fry, pointing out the difference between *painting* and *decorating*, pleaded for restraint: "I take this opportunity to protest against flowers on a flower pot and portraits in the middle of dinner plates. Think of eating off the portrait of a king!"

As for china-decorating inventions, however laudable and lucrative, however indicative of women's mastery of chemistry and mechanics, militant feminists still viewed them as minor accomplishments compared to a breakthrough such as Mary Walton's method for deflecting smokestack emissions from industrial buildings into water tanks and flushing them into city sewers. Now, this was evidence of woman's creative genius at work in a "man's world"! Feminists rushed to embrace the ingenious Walton, whose work reinforced their claims that mechanical education would not be wasted on women and that women were fully the equals of men in their inventive capabilities.

In 1883, Matilda Gage, the suffragist colleague of Susan B. Anthony and Elizabeth Cady Stanton who had already written a suffrage tract on women inventors in 1870, recycled much of that material for an article on women and invention for *North American Review*, an avowedly unbiased magazine that tried to promote free discussion by presenting both sides of arguments, among them women's rights. This time, Gage added several sources whose flattering evaluations of women's inventive capacity spoke directly to her purpose. *Scientific American* was quoted to the effect that "in their personal character and in their adaptation of means to effect a definite purpose, they [women] fully equal the same number of inventions made by men." The former commissioner of patents, the Honorable Samuel Fisher, weighed in with: "Any sketch of American inventions would be imperfect which failed to do justice to the part taken by woman." And a *New York Times* editorial was put to good use too:

> The feminine mind is, as a rule, quicker than the masculine mind; takes hints and sees defects which would escape the average man's attention. Women frequently carry the germs of patents in their head, and cause some rude machine to be constructed which serves their purpose. If women would fix their minds on inventions, it is entirely probable that they would distinguish themselves in this line far more than they have done hitherto.

In addition to the testimony of contemporaries, Gage relied upon the ancients, as she had in her suffrage tract, to provide such examples of inventive and creative women as Isis in Egypt, Minerva and Ceres in Greece, the mother of the Incas in Peru, and several empresses of China. She also expanded her earlier listing of examples to include more unusual devices, and cited machinists' appraisals of Harriet Hosmer's work with magnets as "one of the most important inventions of the century [whose] influence upon the world is likely to be far reaching and extraordinary." Gage renewed her earlier charge that many women's ideas were appropriated by men ("A very slight investigation proves that patents taken out in some man's name are, in many instances, due to women") and laid special emphasis on patenting as an indicator of a nation's superiority—a superiority that could be achieved, she vowed, only when inventors of both sexes had full freedom to exercise their powers and to enjoy a warm welcome for their ideas. Since inventions were, according to Gage, a measure of the freedoms enjoyed by a people, the statistical gap between the number of men and women who had been granted patents in the United States illuminated not the differences in their respective abilities but the disparity in the educational, industrial, and political opportunities available to them. It had been only thirty years since the first state protected a married woman's right to her brain's product, and more than half the states still withheld that right. What incentive did wives in those states have to patent, she asked.

While celebrating the inventive achievements of the few, Gage made the political emancipation of the many her main goal. Without it, a woman, "trained to seclusion, dependence, and abeyance of thought," had to endure "contempt of her sex, open and covert scorn of womanhood, depreciatory allusions to her intellectual powers—all tending to hamper the expression of her inventive genius," and thus hampering "the growth of the nation as well." To Gage, the solution was political: enfranchised, women would parallel men's patenting record, not only in number but in *significance*. Although she didn't spell it out in so many words, Gage aspired to see women enter the *same* fields as men, not fritter their inventive talents on a mélange of housekeeping devices.

Though Gage and like-minded feminists flailed at the inconsequence of such inventions, they still accounted for the majority of women's patents, and many of them were obviously valuable both in and of themselves and as outlets for women's stifled ingenuity. This, after all, was a time when men like Dr. William Alexander Hammond, noted neurologist and professor at New York City University, argued that the household was where women belonged and the only healthful place for them. Warning that "[A] peculiar neurotic condition called the hysterical is grafted on the organ of woman," Hammond limned a debilitating prospect for those who dared to thwart "nature." That so many women inventors continued to thwart it and to go outside their sphere, if only by taking to the road to exhibit their generally household-oriented inventions at the various industrial expositions that proliferated after the Centennial, is a tribute to their persistence in the face of such prejudice.

The expositions were a major opportunity for women to make their inventive talents more widely known. Many were old hands on the exposition trail, exhibiting at such well-known venues as New York's American Institute and Cincinnati's industrial fair. The latter city, aptly calling itself "The Gateway to the South" since railroad and steamship lines passed through on their way to southern markets, flexed its industrial muscle in annual expositions. Although *most* women made contributions that landed in the Ladies' Articles department and consisted of waxwork, tatting, "hair work," knitting, crocheting, quilting, embroidery, and the like, others showed their inventions alongside men's and formed a nucleus around whom other women gathered for advice and encouragement.

By the middle of the 1880s, New Orleans, eager to show off her post–Civil War economic resurgence, proposed an exposition of her own and successfully lured as chairman of its Women's Department Julia Ward Howe, who had recently presided over the science fair in Boston that had successfully deployed a number of exhibits ("of an industrial nature . . . requiring brain effort") to demonstrate that women had an excellent grasp of the mysteries of science. For New Orleans, Howe lobbied Congress for fifteen thousand dollars, arranged a series of entertainments (including one of her own lectures, "Is Polite Society Polite?") to raise money for the cause, and sallied forth to meetings in the major cities of the East to solicit interest among women's groups. She discovered, as the Centennial organizers had, that in choosing what to exhibit it was difficult to unravel the thread of women's work from men's, but decided that a segregated showing would make a more distinct impression upon viewers.

Each state's Lady Manager (as they were so quaintly called) urged her constituents to send pieces of their work, but shortness of time and the difficulty of actually locating women inventors proved daunting. Indiana women, who had no trouble finding needlework to display ("Because," one of them said, "apparently, the needle is the heritage of women"), complained that they were stumped tracking down their state's women inventors without laboriously searching Patent Office records and noting female names—"a task about equivalent to reading a dozen large dictionaries in succession." They still managed to send more inventions than most states and prayed they would correct "the common impression that women have no inventive faculty." One of those inventions, Mrs. Marion I. Remy's "Columbia Ironer," so impressed a writer for *Industrial America* that he pronounced it "one of the most useful and excellent articles of house furnishings invented by woman."

New Jersey's chairman sent circulars to five thousand New Jersey women for anything "that shall do credit to our industry . . . [to] prove our women honorable alike to our State and our sex," and specifically asked for "any useful inventions of labor-saving contrivance for the home." She received only one. A calamitous wreck of the train bearing Iowa's inventions left many articles damaged, destroyed, or utterly lost. Nebraska women, hoping to counter the perception of Easterners who considered "Western" a synonym for "a crude, uncultivated civilization," proudly explained that Nebraska girls enjoyed educational advantages equal to those of boys and that independent Nebraska women could earn their own support without injuring their social standing, but then pleaded they had not had time to send any inventions. New Hampshireites had time to collect only four inventions, two of which were patented: Charlotte Stewart's "Dust Repeller" and Adelaide Palmer's decorator's easel for painting china. Virginia's only patentee was Mrs. Henrietta A. Dangerfield, who showed a car seat. Massachusetts listed twenty-two inventors, including Olivia P. Flynt of Flynt Waist fame and the inventors of a smattering of household devices, including two broom holders. Rhode Island bragged of Marin L. Ghirardini's "Improved Ventilating-Chimney." Illinois's chairman complained that lack of time combined with lack of money for manufacturing suitable models deprived the Women's Department of valuable and remarkable inventions. The few sent, she hoped, would "result in substantial benefit to [the] inventors." Among them was Mrs. Nettie Rood's "Portable Wire-Screen, Insect-Proof Summer-House," noted to be "a cottage made by a woman of Illinois, furnished with furniture made by her—with even a patent washing machine in its kitchen, made by her; and the cottage is a patent, and can be packed up, carted off, and set down in the prairies."

The California women's committee sent several inventions, all useful but hardly breaking new ground for women. Harriet Strong, whose unusual inventing career will be discussed in a later chapter, sent her "Bedford Window Attachment" for raising and lowering fine plate-glass windows such as those in church or school windows or transoms, as well as a "Hook and Eye" that worked as readily on the trappings one might wish to affix to a harness as it did on the dainty doilies frequently attached to chair arms.

Of all the patented inventions shown, only a few already enjoyed commercial success. Pennsylvania's chairman rightly boasted of the practicality and success of Maria Beasley's barrel-hooping machine,

Helen Blanchard's crochet and braiding machine, and Josephine Davis's hot-air vapor bath apparatus, but since no models were available, they were shown only in photographs. From New York, Mary Carpenter exhibited her machine for sewing straw braid and Nancy M. Fitch, her "Parlor-Kiln" for firing china (praised by no less an authority than Mary Louise McLaughlin).

Looking at the inventions, which seemed to have been chosen because they could be shipped easily or would appeal (and thus sell) to the mostly female visitors to the Women's Building, Howe said they represented an "interesting range" of patents but then seemed unable to find any better example of women's ingenuity than a set of drawers designed to hold voluminous ball dresses! True, the exposition's commissioner-general, after viewing the same exhibits, announced gallantly that he was proud to declare himself a women's rights man, but ardent feminists felt the exhibits failed to demonstrate the true range of women's innate talents and creativity.

Given the apparent lack of progress in women's inventing achievements, feminists would have to take heart from other developments that might bode well for the future, such as a new and relatively nonsexist children's magazine, *Saint Nicholas*, first published in 1873 in the midst of one of the nation's most severe financial panics. This publication was a daring move by Scribners to break the tradition of morally uplifting but hardly electrifying fare for young readers. While still extolling the good old American virtues of country, flag, family, moral rectitude, and hard work, the founders wanted to supplant anesthetizing pontification with imaginatively illustrated stories and articles written by noted authors, and the whole publication was designed to appeal to and inspire both boys and girls. The years of *Saint Nicholas* became, according to Henry Steele Commager, historian and editor of an anthology of the best of the magazines, a time "when majors wrote for minors."

As editor, Scribners chose Mary Elizabeth ("Lizzie") Mapes Dodge, who gained her first editorial experience on her father's and brother's magazine, *Working Farmer.* Widowed early, she wrote and sold stories she had first tried out on her young sons, then branched out to write books for children, the most enduring of which was *Hans Brinker; or the Silver Skates,* which came out in 1865 and went into over a hundred editions during her lifetime. Before taking the *Saint Nicholas* job she joined the editorial staff of the magazine *House and Home*, co-edited by Harriet Beecher Stowe.

Despite the hard times during which it was founded, *Saint Nicholas* was eminently successful. Dodge saw to it that children dined on victuals served by distinguished literary figures, such as Mark Twain, Rudyard Kipling, and Louisa May Alcott, and on visual delights provided by America's best known illustrators. Her own children must have thrived in such company, for years later Mark Twain called her son James "the greatest story teller in America." James must also have tweaked his mother's interest in invention—or vice versa—for the mechanically ingenious youth went on to become a famous inventor himself. He patented not only several kinds of links and sprocket wheels for belt chains used to convey anthracite coal but also the folding theater seat whose back became vertical when the seat was depressed. A wire hat rack fit under the seat.

Dodge's magazine affirmed the interests and talents of both its boy and its girl readers. In her "Jack-in-the-Pulpit" editor's column Dodge discussed everything from cooking to making everyday articles such as buttons. Children interested in botany and geology could join the magazine's Agassiz Society, named for the famous Swiss-American naturalist (and founder of the Museum of Comparative Zoology at Harvard), whose lectures and essays in magazines brought science to the attention of the American public. The Historical Girls series provided girls with important role models. A national writing contest inspired boys and girls between thirteen and seventeen. The "How to Do and Make It" column appealed to both genders. So did some of the advertisements. American Writing Machines, for example, addressed both "Boys and Girls of St. Nicholas" in pushing a writing aid that would help them "to stand at the head of the next generation of business men and women!"

Since patenting was an equal opportunity activity, Dodge saw to it that her writers appealed to inventive girls and boys alike. In the fictional "Elsie's Invention" (1888), a young girl invented a special hammock chair to make her crippled brother more comfortable. To inspire budding inventors, the story provided illustrations of the chair's construction, along with a note at the end explaining just how a child could make one at home. Its rendering of the moment of inspiration, as Elsie spontaneously describes the proposed chair to her brother, followed by the working out of the details for putting the idea into practice, is an excellent introduction to the mental processes involved in inventing:

> "[M]elt the rocking chair and the hammock into one. Yes, and the easy-chair and the bed too!" And she gave a little skip as her idea took definite shape. "It won't take long to do it, and you can help. You know how we netted the hammock. Well, our new contrivance can be made in the same way. There is some twine left. I'll get the needles and mesh-sticks, and we will go right at it."

The invalid's increased comfort was so marked that Elsie and her brothers rigged similar hammock backs for other camp stools so that their brother could rest comfortably in any part of the house or yard. The story continued: "It is very singular, but he [the invalid] began to gain from that very day, and even the doctor says the improvement is due largely to Elsie's invention." Nor was that the end of Elsie's invention: Elsie's brother's doctor introduced such devices at the local hospital; the state medical inspector mentioned them in his official report; and Elsie's father offered her the sort of advice that *Saint Nicholas*'s inventive young readers would do well to follow: "Elsie has made an invention," the story related, "and her papa, who is a lawyer, declares that she must have it patented, because if *she* does not, somebody else will, as soon as it is seen in public."

Elsie's father never mentioned that Elsie, in inventing, might be out of her sphere; instead, he thought so well of his daughter's ingenuity "in the matter of girlish devices" that he even hoped she might expand her interests and become a doctor.

Elsie's story was quintessential *Saint Nicholas* material: realistic, inspiring, sympathetic, and affirming. But despite its endorsement of a variety of options for girls, the magazine also published a series of "Little Housekeeping" songs that appear in hindsight to have been aimed at impounding young girls within domestic perimeters. One must remember, however, that this was the nineteenth century, that Dodge had apprenticed under the aegis of one of the famous Beecher sisters (whose reverence for competent housewifery was a given), and that she therefore saw no harm in happifying such domestic functions for little girls who loved to play grownup. Thus, while Elsie was inventing, little housekeepers within the magazine's pages were trilling ("animato") Mary Jacques's "Washing Dishes" verses, which began: "With a skip and a hop, And a jolly dish mop, And a pan of bubbling water." Or they were play-ironing dollies' clothes (perhaps with the toy "Mrs. Potts' Sad Iron" Mother ordered from Montgomery Ward), all the while chirping: "First your iron smooth must be . . . Rub away! Rub away! Rust and irons disagree . . . Rub away! Rub away!"

Such sing-alongs for children might have satisfied tradition-minded women, but they were red flags to those who clamored for mechanical education for their daughters, among them Mary Livermore (who was still asking, "How far may girls and young women be included in this preparation for modern industrial pursuits?"), to those who thirsted for examples of atypical rather than conventional roles, to those who winced at the number of inventions for household use, and to those who scoured the patent list for names of women inventors engaged in fields far removed from the domestic scene to which these little girls seemed to aspire.

In July 1888, the Patent Office made it easier to locate such names by publishing an official chronological compilation of all women granted patents since the office's establishment in 1790. Since unofficial lists had been available for some time (Gillespie and Tarbell had both used them), the task of compilation was not as monumental as it would otherwise have been. Nor was it as rigorous as it might have been. Four clerks, who spent ten days and were paid about three hundred dollars to cull women's names from the almost half a million patentees, relied on their sense of what *sounded* like women's names. By comparing the official, cumulative 1888 list to annual lists, one can find a good many omissions, even when the inventors bore such obvious first names as Mary and Sarah. But one can only be grateful that this record, flawed though it is, exists. Besides this list, and its updated appendices in 1892 and 1895, the Patent Office published no comparable study until its bicentennial in 1990, when it published "From Buttons to Biotech," which provides important statistics but does not list inventors by name.

The genesis of that 1888 list is a story in itself, since it was almost single-handedly forced upon the office by the determined Charlotte Smith, erstwhile co-founder (with Mary Nolan) of the ill-fated *Inland*

# WOMEN INVENTORS

396

TO WHOM

# PATENTS

HAVE BEEN GRANTED BY THE UNITED STATES GOVERNMENT.

## 1790 TO JULY 1, 1888.

COMPILED UNDER THE DIRECTION OF THE COMMISSIONER OF PATENTS.

WASHINGTON:
GOVERNMENT PRINTING OFFICE.
1888.

The famous list.

Visiting the Patent Model Hall.

magazine. By 1888, Smith was forty-seven years old, a veteran of numerous other battles to champion the rights of working women, and eager to advance the cause of women inventors. Her own experiences had taught her the art (and difficulties) of survival: early widowhood with two young sons to support and no marketable skills; a bookstore leveled in the Chicago fire; and the ultimate demise of the all-woman *Inland* after its move from Saint Louis to Chicago. When *Inland* failed, she moved to Washington and tried to force the newly organized national unions to accept working women into their ranks. The unions were resistant, and young women (especially those in typical women's positions such as office work) were apathetic about long-range goals since industry-labor was viewed as only temporary. Frances Willard later described a woman as thinking of work as "something which must be done to bridge over a certain time of waiting . . . until such time as the coveted position of wife is open to her."

With the 1880 census reports showing that, such views notwithstanding, some two and a half million women were employed in "gainful occupations," Smith founded the Women's National Industrial League, an alternative for women excluded by the unions. It was an ambitious organization that never achieved national significance, probably because Smith's political alliances with leaders of the Populist movement—vilified as "hayseed Socialists" by Democratic party regulars who feared the third party would cause a split that would deny them victory at the polls—eventually weakened its support. In her 1915 study of women in trade unions, Alice Henry (an Australian who came to America to work in the suffrage movement, joined the Women's Trade Union League in 1907, and edited its newspaper, *Life and Labor*) referred to the league as merely "one of those hopeful undertakings." Still, it was taken more seriously in its time, if only as fuel for the ambitions of others. Terence V. Powderly, Knights of Labor leader, saw inclusion of its members as a way to widen his own organization's base and affirmed to them that they would find him committed to their cause: "There was a time when I was laughed at, and by some of your own sex as a 'woman's rights' man, but that day has gone by. . . . I am not a woman's right's man but *an equal rights* man, and equal rights cannot be obtained while woman is oppressed."

In her capacity as league president, and with the support of Powderly's wing of the labor movement, Smith badgered the other union leaders and regularly attended congressional hearings on behalf of working women. Buttonholing legislators to pass laws to improve wages, she warned that without such help those poorly paid wretches had no other recourse than to descend into a life of sin. She also lobbied the American Federation of Labor for the right of women to participate in such exclusively male trades as mining, building, ironworking, and bricklaying, and when she wasn't busy with all these other activities, she tried to bring women inventors into the Industrial League, where they could better promote their special interests. To help them do so, she targeted the commissioner of patents to publish a list of women's inventions, and she put the squeeze on various Capitol Hill supporters, especially the Populist Party senator from Kansas, "Sockless Jerry Simpson," to appropriate money to authorize the study.

Though I have been unsuccessful in discovering evidence of how the Patent Office decided to compile the list or anything about the manner in which Smith might have pressed her case, I *have* found other material in the papers of several patent commissioners that suggests that the list of women inventors was only one item on her agenda. Among the many pamphlets and copies of speeches she dropped off or mailed, there is one letter tartly recommending that the commissioner hire ten charwomen and one woman superintendent, each with thirty days' annual leave. The only evidence of her activity on behalf of the list is a brief letter the commissioner of patents later wrote (and Smith later published) in which he acknowledged that he remembered her visits well and "how earnest and persistent you were in urging the compilation."

That persistence paid off. By forcing the government to publish the cumulative list of women inventors to 1888, Smith not only gained official, and now public, acknowledgment of women's inventive activity, but also names she could tap for membership in her Women's National Industrial League. She spent the next few years corresponding with many of the more recent inventors—whose names, patent numbers, and hometowns she got from the list—and featured their most poignant and dramatic responses in the first major tribute to them, the periodical she herself would publish in 1891—*Woman Inventor.*

# INVENTING
# OUTSIDE AND BEYOND
# WOMAN'S SPHERE

*W*ith the published lists of women inventors in hand, feminists (and anyone else who wished to know) could now locate the names of women who had invented an impressive array of devices transcending their gender's domestic perimeters. Though in absolute numbers the inventors, and their devices, were few, the variety of fields they had entered was broad enough to gratify the fondest hopes of the most enthusiastic women's rights advocates.

By the 1880s, Amanda Jones (of canning and preserving fame) had branched into another unusual field. Still immersed in spiritualism, she heeded her guru's instructions to go to Pennsylvania's new oil fields and invent a way that drillers could safely burn the crude oil they were extracting without risking hideous accidents. If she could, oil would become a reliable fuel for industry. Her "Automatic Safety Burner," a kind of safety valve to control the amount of oil released from the pipe (or other container), was Jones's answer, one quite obvious to her but so ingenious to the five hundred men who watched her demonstration that, she reported, they "stood around agape." The United States Navy, then hoping to use oil to replace coal in powering its ships but reluctant to do so because of the danger, grasped the potential of the safety burner and bestowed official praise upon it.

Such acclaim helped Jones to win a fat contract with an "invisible [albeit corporeal] partner," one she expected to be so remunerative that she would be able to underwrite her favorite charity—homes for needy city girls. The bubble burst, however, when the Stock Exchange wiped out her partner, and she had to go forward without his support. Alone, and conceding that her views might "invite the ridicule of men," she argued that "each inventor is entitled to his own ideal, though it may seem to all others a mere will o'the wisp" and continued to extol the superiority of liquid fuel. Not one to give up on something, even though it had failed commercially, decades later she was still stoutly proclaiming her belief in her burner when she wrote her *Psychic Autobiography*. Published in 1905, when its author was seventy-five, it contained a vivid chronicle of a life filled with uncanny experiences, premonitions, previsions, "astral excursions," precognitions, and extraordinary beyond-the-grave conversations with such departed souls as President John Adams, as well as her defense of the safety burner, which, she claimed, could run not only mills but battleships.

So long as other women had intimate contact with the problems that needed solution, flashes of inspiration—though not usually astral ones—helped them to invent in nontraditional areas. When horse-drawn carts were the norm, women patented nets and shades to protect their horses from the elements, flying vermin, and street muck. Sarah Ruth had her "Sun-Shade for Horses," with a "bonnet" in front and a scalloped canopy elevated above the girth. Elizabeth Stryker had her "Fly-Net for Horses," a dangling cover of flexible straps that undulated with shifting breezes or equine movement and whisked away flies and insects while allowing the circulating air to cool the horse's body. To deal with the problems caused when a horse-drawn railway car "jumped track," Maria Ghirardini recommended setting grooved rails almost flush with each other so that if a car did jump, it would simply fall into the next. By inserting into a railroad car wheel a small ball of lead that would rotate over rather than scrape against rail surfaces, Evelyn and Milton Clifford French created a "Sound-Deadening Attachment for Railway Cars," which they patented in 1880.

The introduction of electric railways in 1886, however, caused trans-

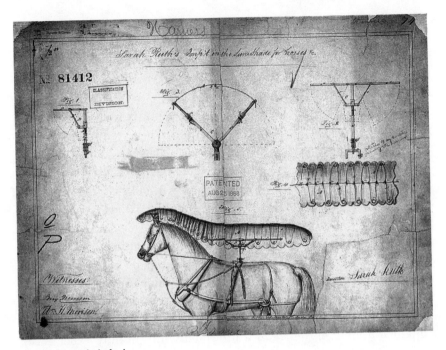

Sarah Ruth's sunshade for horses.

portation problems those earlier inventors could never have foreseen. When congestion, noise, and dirt from the speedier electrified railways became unbearable, engineers in the larger cities simply raised the roadbeds and supported railways on iron posts. As trains roared over elevated tracks laid across wooden cross-ties, however, the rattle and vibrations apparently drove some residents to bizarre behavior. George M. Beard, in his *American Nervousness: Its Causes and Consequences,* attributed many neuroses to the cacophony of the "els" and told of a patient who was normally "tough and wiry" but became so unnerved by the noise that he refused to approach the street where the trains ran. As one physician observed, there was little chance of a gentle decline into old age in New York City, where "the constant din of travel and traffic, borne for a time without evidence of injury, suddenly shows itself in a shattered nervous system and imminence of dissolution."

It was just this din which drove Manhattan resident Mary Walton, who had previously invented the antipollution device for smokestacks, to invent what had so far eluded Edison and other important inventors—a method for muffling the sound of the "els" rattling by at window level. Experimenting in her basement, she set up two barrels, stretched a piece of planking across them, used side edges as "stringers"

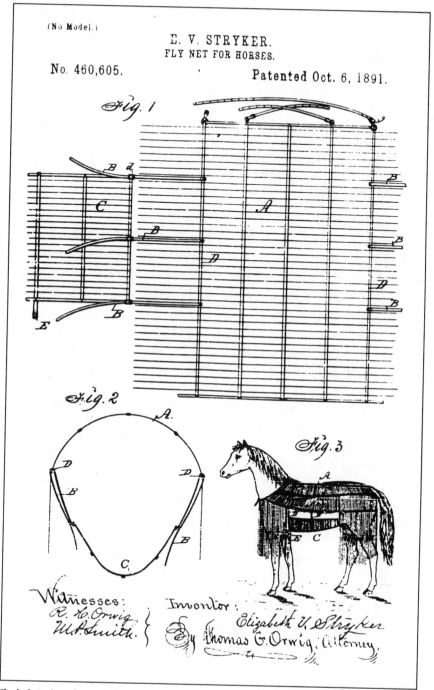

Elizabeth Stryker's fly net for horses.

(boards that ran parallel to the track), overlaid short pieces of wood across the planking to act as ties, and then nailed two pieces of railroad iron to the ties. Having simulated a "railroad track," she faced the crux of the problem, how to absorb sound as the wheels passed over the rails at high speed. She described her next steps:

> I sawed pieces of board and nailed them in between the ties and underneath the stringers; I then bought at a drug store a bottle of tar, and painted the inside of the box with the tar; then I took a roll of cotton and lined the inside of the box with a thin lining of cotton, and tightly packed it with sand, covering the top with cotton and tar [to keep the sand from flying].

Importuning a workman who was cleaning her cellar to strike the iron rails with as much force as he could wield while she sped upstairs to her kitchen to audit the noise, she found she could scarcely hear it. She told the manager of the Metropolitan Railroad what she had discovered by comparing her method to a violin: "When you stopped your air passages, you stopped your music, and the stringers acted as sounding boards." Impressed, he agreed to let her test her experiment on his rails, with the proviso that she first obtain a patent and promise to sell him the rights if the test was successful.

When tests proved her right, she received a patent for her method—arranging ties and longitudinal guards to enclose sand or sandlike materials—and sold the rights to the Metropolitan Railroad, leaving her competitors to complain that the company had afforded her a testing opportunity it denied them. Walton smugly told them she did what any persevering inventor/entrepreneur would have done under the circumstances—trounced her rivals! Almost two decades later, *Woman's Journal* was still bragging about that accomplishment: "The most noted machinists and inventors of the century had given their attention to the subject without being able to furnish a solution, when, lo, a woman's brain did the work, and her appliance proving perfectly successful, was adopted by the elevated roads, and she is now reaping the rewards of a happy thought."

One woman who, alas, did not reap any such rewards was Chicagoan Carrie Everson, though her invention in the field of metallurgy helped certify that mining was not an exclusively male fraternity. Everson knew mining only through her husband's investments but had learned

Elevated Railroad, New York City.

a good deal about chemistry, and by 1886 she knew enough to be able
to improve upon previous processes of recovering ore from its matrix—a process in which the raw material was plunged into an oil
mixture, then agitated until the oil attracted the sulfides and floated
them to the top, leaving the heavier metal (either gold or silver) to sink
to the bottom, where it could be recovered. Everson discovered that by
altering the bath's chemical formula (primarily by adding acid), the
flotation process became far more effective. At the time she received
the patent for this new formula, her innovation, though startling, made

no waves in an industry where ore was so plentiful that no one worried about extracting every ounce. Perhaps even if ore had been scarce, the fact that there was then no technology for mechanical devices to deliver the proper mix of solids, liquids, and gases would still have postponed its use.

Decades later, when ore was no longer plentiful enough to allow waste, mining men decided to use the Everson method (although it pained them to admit that a woman had done something so useful as to invent the process) and were immensely relieved to learn that her patent had expired and no royalties would have to be paid. Theodore Hoover, the seminal writer on the flotation process, did allow that she had patented the process, but found a way of explaining her genius away that assuaged any possible wounds to the male ego: He chose to believe the story circulating in mining circles that she had inadvertently discovered the flotation process by laundering ore concentrate sacks in the office of her brother, a local assayer. A man, so the rationalization ran, would simply shake out the ore bags before reusing them; a *woman* would *launder* them. As she immersed the greasy ores into her washtub and agitated them sufficiently, Hoover opined several decades after the supposed event, "it only required the customary acuteness of observation of the Western lady-schoolteacher to grasp the essential facts of sulphide flotation." A very neat explanation, but for the facts that Everson was not a schoolteacher and did not have an assayer brother.

It was not until a few years later, after much of her real history had been revealed, that another mining historian could report, "There is probably no figure in metallurgical history about whom there has been so much belated interest as Mrs. Everson, nor is there any one, probably, about whom so many erratic statements have been made." Those "erratic statements" simply grew from the general conviction that a woman could not have invented the process. Still, her name *was* on the patent lists for it, and in 1915 Colorado metallurgy leaders decided to honor the inventor of the revolutionary process, one that had not only brought enormous profits to miners but had also fostered an economic revival in states that produced the wood oils, wood creosote, turpentine, and other oil products used in the oil baths. Belatedly they wanted to ensure that she, who had never profited financially from her invention,

"Mystery Woman" Carrie Everson.

was not in any economic distress. If she was alive, they would bestow a sizable fortune on her; if she was dead, they would build a memorial to her ingenuity.

*Engineering and Mining Journal* searched relentlessly for Everson, hoping to "pierce the veil of mystery surrounding the patentee of this far-reaching metallurgical discovery" but found no trace of the "little woman . . . very modest and retiring of disposition . . . a most lovable character," a sterling character, a "quiet, self-sacrificing woman who devoted her life to those less favored than the majority." Denver newspapers leaped into the fray. Recognizing a good story, they dubbed Mystery Woman Everson the "Madame Curie of Colorado" and ran headlines announcing MOTHER OF NEW GOLD TREATING PROCESS LOST: RICHES AWAIT CARRIE EVERSON, INVENTOR OF FLOTATION PROCESS OF EXTRACTIONS. They interviewed everyone who might have known the "Denver nurse who, while washing greasy ore sacks in her brother's assay office, discovered the affinity of oil for gold and was clever enough to get out patents on her discovery." Actually, Everson's patent was based on the addition of specified chemicals to the oil bath, not on oil's affinity for gold, but the press didn't want to quibble with details of a long-ago patent. The "schoolteacher" had by this time become "Denver nurse" because the

Visiting Nurse Association had identified her name on its rolls; but "brother" continued on as an "assayer."

Denver bank bookkeeper Everett Fay, at whose home Everson once lived, surfaced to supply the detail that the Eversons had moved to Denver because of her doctor husband's poor health, and to deny that the invention was solely Carrie's, telling the press that Everson herself had always given her husband credit for the germ of the idea. The *Denver Times* snatched that tidbit and rushed into print—DR. EVERSON AND NOT HIS WIFE FOUND ORE METHOD—and featured a photograph of Carrie Everson, supplied by Fay, on the front page. When Fay was confronted with the fact that Carrie's name alone appeared on the patent and that moreover she was a co-patentee of a later patent that did not involve her husband, he backtracked and conceded: "She was a woman of high education, entirely capable of having thought out the whole thing, herself." With such conflicting testimony, the Colorado Scientific Society dug in its heels: If honor was due to her husband, it would bestow a joint award. As Western newspapers picked up the Denver story, several readers supplied the *Engineering and Mining Journal* with the name and address of the son with whom Everson lived in San Anselmo, California.

When contacted, John Everson, the only survivor of Carrie Everson's five children, revealed that his mother had died two years before the search began. He also filled in many of the other details of her life, and scotched the rumor of his father's participation in the invention by recounting how his mother ground ore with mortar and pestle and then examined it with his father's microscope. His mother, born in Sharon, Massachusetts, attended high and normal school there and, instead of becoming a teacher (as was later conjectured because of that normal school education), married Dr. W. K. Everson in Chicago in 1864. Her husband, a general physician, druggist, and chemist, tutored his wife first in medicine and then in chemistry, a science in which she soon surpassed her teacher. When her husband invested in Colorado and Mexico mining ventures, she turned to mineralogy as a practical means of bolstering his work. When she began her experiments of adding chemicals to the oil baths used in flotation and agitation, she decided to test her method only on ore samples bearing gold, silver, and copper, since no other metallic yields were valuable enough to justify the expense of the special equipment needed to implement her process.

Before Everson could perfect her discovery, her husband invested and lost their entire fortune of about forty thousand dollars in the Golden Age Mining Company, one of famed Denver promoter "Brick" Pomeroy's disastrous business ventures. Dr. Everson then went to Mexico, presumably for his health, and his wife, who stayed behind, redoubled her research in the hope that her metallurgical process could recoup their lost funds. She hired Chicago lawyer M. E. Dayton to represent her in her patent application, and Dayton earned every dollar. After rewriting section after section to satisfy the patent examiner, whose five separate letters complained about the application's "lack of specificity," the attorney reasonably concluded that he had dispelled every possible objection. Then came the examiner's clincher: He had run tests according to her descriptions; all had failed. Dayton defended his client: "[I]t appears possible that the manipulation of the Examiner may have been faulty at some point. . . . It is quite reasonable that a failure should result the first time of trial by the Examiner as would happen to a housewife in making her first batch of bread, though further trials would be successful." This attribution of blame could not endear him to the examiner, who, after all, held the patent's future in his hands, so Dayton hedged that perhaps the trial had not worked because the concentrating compound had deteriorated "as occasionally, though rarely, a batch will do." He further declared that he and Everson would amend if need be, because a delay in getting the patent was "greatly to be deprecated . . . for several very important personal reasons."

Need for money in the wake of the Eversons' financial reverses was, of course, the paramount "personal reason." After a few t's were crossed and i's dotted, the patent was duly granted, about a year and a half after the application was first filed; but Dr. Everson died a couple of years later, and his widow, by then forty-six and with little hope of receiving anything from their soured investments, was forced to become an obstetrical nurse to support herself and her young son.

The years passed and Everson continued to believe in her process. She searched for a backer and found one in Denver capitalist Thomas Criley. With her seventeen-year-old son assisting her, she conducted further experiments in Silver Cliff, Colorado, which were impressive enough to draw press attention. After seeing the Eversons' eight-hundred-gallon tank with revolving paddles and an adjustable horizontal partition, the Denver *Daily News* apprised its readers: "So far, the experiments have proved a perfect success." When tested again in Baker City, Oregon, the "Criley and Everson Oil Process" drew attention from potential investors in Portland and Walla Walla, inflating the hopes of Baker citizens looking for jobs in the demonstration plant. But Criley soon died, leaving Everson to untangle the mess of their joint affairs. After making one last stab at interesting other mining companies in her oil froth method, she finally turned her attention to another method, a dry process of flotation that she co-patented in 1892 with Charles B. Hebron of Denver.

The much-needed financial backing of another investor fizzled when she and Hebron quarreled over division of the still-to-be-earned riches from the process, and the discouraged Everson abandoned further hope of financial benefit from her patents. For three years she worked as a visiting nurse for the Denver Flower Mission and for two years as a teacher of physiology and hygiene in the State Reformatory for Girls at Morrison, Colorado, her only teaching experience. The next year she moved to San Anselmo, California, to live with her son. According to her son, his mother was aware in her later years that others were earning millions by using her process to recover ore from once-worthless "tailings" and was proud that her belief in her invention had been vindicated, even though the patent had expired.

With the discovery of Everson's son, the search for the mystery-shrouded inventor was over. The metallurgical profession cited Carrie Everson for standing "in the position of an originator of the process of concentrating mineral by oil flotation" and added that she was "generally credited with having disclosed in 1886 all the essential elements of the process as practised to-day." As the phrase "generally credited" implies, not all metallurgists agreed. One flotation process expert argued that she never really quite knew what she had invented. He was soon joined by the editors of the respected *Mining and Scientific Press,* who, in an article titled "The Everson Myth," denigrated her work as the "amateur experiments . . . [of an] intelligent earnest woman," and permitted themselves to "laugh at those who have exaggerated her ineffective attempt into a great invention." Mindful of the public clamor to recognize Everson's contribution, the magazine backtracked to this extent: "Meanwhile we congratulate the Colorado Scientific Society on its course of action and hope that it will not abate in its intention to do honor to a woman who was an investigator, a nurse, a teacher, a good wife, and a devoted mother. That is more than being a bubble in the froth of litigation."

Old legends never die, however. Two decades later, in 1933, a *Rocky Mountain News* writer, trying to recapitulate Everson's work for another generation, still characterized her as the "young Colorado school teacher" who washed her assayer brother's ore sacks and whose system was "a complete failure" even though she had the "basic idea." By 1952, when a reader wrote in to ask about the woman inventor to whom a tour conductor at Kennecott Copper's Bingham, Utah, mine credited the flotation process, the *News* replied that Mrs. Everson had no formal education but learned chemistry "because it was an allied subject of her husband's medical knowledge" and that since she was interested in his investments in mining processes, she took a keen interest and also worked in his laboratory. *Full* credit seems always to elude Carrie Everson! Her achievement just doesn't seem credible to those convinced that only a man could be its author.

Of all the women who patented inventions "out of their sphere" during the 1880s, none was further "out" than Mary ("Carlotta") Myers. When the Massachusetts *Berkshire Courier* reported the ascent of "Madame Carlotta," the best known "lady balloonist" of her day, it noted that she was co-patentee of a "Guiding Apparatus for Balloons." Myers claimed her apparatus allowed her to guide her hydrogen-filled balloon at will; the *Courier* said she understood the balloon "as if it were part of herself"; a bystander marveled that she stepped into her basket "with no more concern than most ladies would exhibit on entering a carriage for a drive"; the *Daily Saratogan* reported: "Mlle. Carlotta may be said to be a veritable high flyer."

High flyer "Madame" or "Mademoiselle" Carlotta was no European miss or missus—or even "Carlotta," for that matter—but, according to a local historian, the "handsome and highly intellectual" Mary Breed Hawley Myers, a descendant of the Bostonian Breeds of Breeds' Hill fame now married to and full partner of her husband, Carl Myers, the mechanically gifted aeronautics pioneer who owned and operated Balloon Farm in New York's Mohawk Valley. There he conducted experiments, manufactured various forms of lighter-than-air craft, and, to underwrite those ventures, offered at open-air events such attractions as parachute drops, captive balloon rides, aerial weddings, and the

"Balloon Farm."

spectacle of his attractive wife's daring unmoored ascents. Mary *be-came* Carlotta the Aeronaut, even to the point of signing her patent "Carlotta" rather than "Mary." At the farm where the professor and his wife took in paying guests ("No more cheering place for a country residence or summer sojourn can be found . . . the scenery in all directions from the elevation of the housetop is only exceeded by the balloon views from above it"), hundreds of spectators gaped as she rose from the farm's "Balloon Lawn Parties." Tens of thousands watched at local fairgrounds; all were dumbfounded at her aptitude for landing at predetermined sites with the precision, said one observer, "of a foot-passenger selecting his particular street-car."

Carlotta saw nothing to it, modestly disclaiming, "The small, light balloon responds like an intelligent horse to the slightest suggestions." But, of course, she relied upon her thorough grounding in aeronautical theory, her intimate experience in constructing balloons, the steering device she and her husband co-patented in 1885, and—a particularly handy attribute for a skyward traveler—"an abundance of health such as comparatively few women are blessed with."

In *Aerial Adventures of Carlotta or Sky-Larking in Cloudland, Being Hap-Hazard Accounts of the Perils and Pleasures of Aerial Navigation,* the book she wrote about the adventures leading up to their invention, she explained how she tested one steering apparatus after another during her flights, hoping to find a simple, lightweight appliance that would allow her to use the erratic winds that bore her aloft. It was not enough to experience "rapturous sensations of floating freely in space"; she wanted to control her course. After many tries, she thought she had the answer, what she first called "Sky-Lark" and, later, "Flying Dutchman." With it, she and her husband claimed that a pilot standing on a tiltable half-inch board bottom supported by a twine hammock rather than the usual wicker basket could navigate by manipulating the "screw-sail and rudder-kite" until it caught the breezes and controlled direction. Since no one understood enough about aeronautical principles in 1885 to question their assertion that this external "appliance" could indeed enable a pilot to direct the flight of a hydrogen-filled balloon, the patent examiners must have scratched their heads over the claims, muttered "Why not?" and granted the patent. Later experiments with internally powered dirigibles made it clear that the Myerses' appliance was unworkable, and today Claudia Oaks, curator of the Aeronatics National Department at the National Aviation and Space Museum of the Smithsonian Institution, says that while further experimentation invalidated their invention, they carried out their "Dutchman" trials in good faith.

In the 1880s, however, their stock was high. On her first ascent at a Fourth of July spectacular in Little Falls, New York, in 1880, "Queen of the Air" Carlotta released a covey of homing pigeons to report her flight progress back to anxious fans whose "prayers ascended with the bold lady who made this her first venture in the clouds, and who did it so beautifully and so successfully."

In the next decade she completed more hydrogen balloon ascents (typically lasting several hours) than any other living person and more than all the other women in the world combined. At one such event, fifteen thousand persons crowded the pavilion, two bandstands, and chairs and settees scattered on the fairground and took to the surrounding hillsides to watch the woman one reporter declared "pretty as a picture . . . a strong, healthy lady, though not at all masculine, with features betokening great courage and decision of character, and, in the opinion of several marshals and officers, expressing considerable attractiveness." To each reporter, however, his own taste. An *Albany Argus* reporter who detailed her "simple flannel dress of blue, with plain

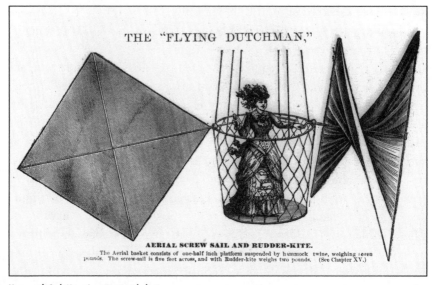

Mary and Carl Myers' navigational device.

waist, and no wrap . . . her hair neatly arranged in the double knot now so much affected, encircled by a blue ribbon" saw the thirty-three-year-old aeronaut as "plain in appearance." The stung high flyer groaned, "Ah me! How aeronautical experience does wreck one's charms, to be sure!" But another reporter noted that her short-skirted and braid-trimmed blue suit revealed "neat-fitting gaiters" and admired her "nobby sailor's hat of plaited straw [that] crowned the whole and gave her face a boyish piquancy." Carlotta explained of that ever-present hat, "Even my nobby sailor hat is a little paddle."

After a decade of virtually accident-free "skylarking"—once with her three-year-old daughter (appropriately middle-named Aeriel), Carlotta retired from performances. She continued testing new devices, however, taking in-flight measurements and helping her husband (by then deeply interested in using balloons for rainmaking experiments) for two more decades.

Though never borne aloft like Myers, Harriet Strong was equally remarkable in her own way. An inventor of water-conservation techniques, she was also a businesswoman of considerable talent. In the early days of her inventing career, she sent to the New Orleans Fair housekeeping items that were but faint precursors of her later patents.

Mary ("Carlotta") Myers (her husband is in right foreground).

Those early patents, however, marked her determination to rescue herself and her four young daughters from the financial morass into which her husband's suicide had plunged her. Her patents were not the ultimate source of her financial salvation, but they did reveal one of the many talents of this remarkably independent, resourceful woman, who once advised those who might someday face a situation like her own:

Harriet Strong and her daughters.

> The pink and white, helpless prettiness, the delicate, fainting, cling-
> ing doll is fast becoming a thing of the past. . . . It is quite possible
> for every gentlewoman to make herself familiar with business meth-
> ods, papers etc.; to prepare herself for any and all emergencies, so that
> if the head of the house be removed, the home that he established
> may be kept intact, may be preserved on its financial basis.

Born in Buffalo, the future wealthy and influential southern California
businesswoman and her family went west in 1844 in what she described as the "plushiest wagon ever to cross the plains," and moved
from the San Francisco Bay area to Carson City, Nevada, where her

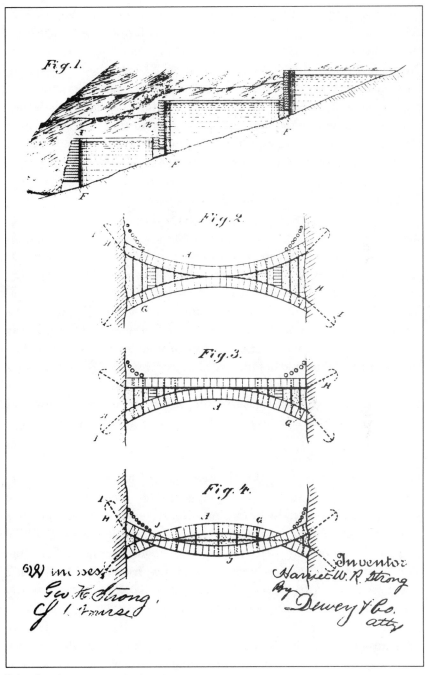

Harriet Strong's water conservation invention.

father was engaged in silver mining. Sent to board at Miss Atkin's Seminary for Young Ladies in Bernicia, California, she earned high marks in academic subjects and in Faithfulness, Politeness, Stillness, Neatness, Punctuality, and Deportment. In Nevada, she met and married wealthy Charles Lyman Strong, eighteen years her senior and superintendent of a large Nevada City mining company. His health, both physical and emotional, was so debilitated that within a year of their marriage they moved from Nevada to Oakland and then to southern California, where, through personal friendship with Governor Don Pio Pico, they bought acreage from his San Gabriel Valley "Ranchito" and named it "Rancho del Fuerte."

His health somewhat restored, Charles Strong joined the Nevada and California mining rushes, leaving a lonely Harriet to manage the ranch, tend their babies, and pen almost daily letters complaining: "My husband is far away . . . and we—his babies—are lonely and feel almost sometimes forsaken with no one to love us or care for us"; "Must I say good-bye for this whole long Summer—I cannot"; "You say not one word about coming home—This *cannot, must not be!!!!*" But it was. Though the couple had four daughters in their short period together, the marriage foundered, a fact that Harriet acknowledged sorrowfully: "You have told me too many times you have no love to give me—I am but half a being without the sustaining satisfying love of my husband. . . . To think I who have been loved always should live [as] an unloved wife."

As their romance deteriorated, so too their fortunes, and the despondent husband wrote his wife, "I hope you will hang on to every cent you possibly can as there's no knowing when or where another dollar will come." Despite tight funds, his wife, suffering from excruciating headaches, chronic back pain, and nervous exhaustion, went to Philadelphia for protracted treatment by the famous neurologist Dr. Silas Weir Mitchell. It was to him that a family friend sent this fateful telegram: PLEASE INFORM MRS. C. L. STRONG OF HER HUSBAND'S SUDDEN DEATH THIS MORNING. REMAINS WILL BE DEPOSITED IN TOMB AT OAKLAND.

What the telegram didn't say was that he had shot himself. Daughter Hattie tried to console her mother: "Everyone thinks Papa's brain gave way under the pressure of care and over work, and because he thought things were all wrong. . . . You remember how anxious we were about him last March. . . . Don't worry—we have many good gentlemen friends to stand up for our rights and lots of ladies for sympathy." Gentlemen friends and ladies' sympathy, however, were not what Harriet Strong needed. Though Charles had left paid-up life insurance, his debts were so large that the ranch was in danger of foreclosure.

With her husband's mines and land in litigation, and four children to support, the once semiinvalided widow summoned the energy to return to California, where she set vigorously to work on the inventions that she hoped would redeem their fortunes. Applying from Oakland, she received three patents. She might have planned to sell the one for hooks and eyes herself, since Sargent & Company of New Haven and New York wrote her: "We send you by to-days mail a sample of hook as we propose to make them if you like the designs. . . . We will fill your order as agreed if new design suits. We await your reply." There is, however, no evidence that any of her three early inventions were profitable.

She did have one tangible asset—the ranch. As a friend remembered, "She did not turn to relatives for aid. She did not go out to do plain sewing. She did not take in boarders. To one of these three things most women turn in an hour of need. She determined to cultivate her land." On her acreage, she planted a few orange trees but filled the remainder with walnut trees, fifty half-mile-long rows of irrigated trees, which made it the largest single walnut orchard in the world. Utilizing the spaces between, she bordered the avenues of walnuts with crops eminently suitable to the arid climate: fast-growing pomegranates and pampas, the latter a plume to provide a cash crop (four thousand dollars the second year) until the walnuts bore. The plumes were an enormous hit; when customers wanted them colored and with a silky finish, she developed a new curing and dyeing process. Her white pampas plumes, incidentally, figured prominently in the 1884 presidential campaign of "Plumed Knight" James G. Blaine and decorated her friend Theodore Roosevelt's Bull Moose insignia in 1912.

Strong visited northern and eastern markets to learn the trade and successfully employed agents to sell her crops, plowing her profits into the purchase of additional acres to lease for truck farming, forming the Paso de Bartolo Water Company, and creating an oil company that drilled three successful wells. Living as she did in the semiarid San Gabriel Valley and witnessing the damage done by torrential spring rains and the devastation of the dessicating summer heat, she had firsthand understanding of her crops' dependence upon consistently delivered and flood-protected water, and she went to work on the two inventions that led to her most famous patents. The first was a series of dams, one above the other in a canyon or water-course so that the water filling the lower dam extended up the face of the next higher dam and thus braced and supported it; the other was a water-storage system to be used in conjunction with the dam. Though she experimented in a small canyon near the ranch, she could not convince local politicians to implement the plans in the foothill area.

She nonetheless clung resolutely to the principles behind her inventions and fought to reactivate them in the next century, a topic to be discussed later in this book. Strong epitomized the transformation of a once typically vulnerable, dependent, aching "neurasthenic" into an optimistic, self-reliant, resourceful trailblazer, the most prominent woman civic leader in southern California, and an extremely successful businesswoman whose fortune was due entirely to the efforts of her own superior brain. She became an exemplary feminist heroine.

# 8

## CELEBRATING WOMEN'S INGENUITY: EXPOSITIONS, FAIRS, AND PATENT OFFICE LISTS

*E*ven the unusual inventions of such protagonists as Walton, Everson, Myers, and Strong did little to stanch the flow of snide remarks about women's inventive faculty. It was business as usual in 1890 when a Providence newspaper editor declared that women's faculties were inferior, but at least an irate reader was there to snap back that no one should dare to compare woman's work to man's until woman had been given equality—at which time she could develop her latent powers "not as [man's] rival, but as the complement of his real being." She spoke to the same point feminists had long made: that until women enjoyed social, political, and economic equality, they could not demonstrate their talents—in inventing or any other field. That millennium still seemed eons away.

What was not eons away, however, was the Patent Office's imminent celebration of the beginning of its second century, an occasion made to order for Charlotte Smith, founder of the National Woman's

Industrial League and the driving force behind the 1888 official compilation of the list of women patentees. To Smith, needy industrial women were always the primary concern, and among those needy she counted the over five thousand women patentees whose contributions society had been negligent in recognizing. Though the Patent-Office's Centennial celebration would provide an ideal forum for bringing that lapse to the attention of the hundreds of delegates converging on Washington, the circumstances were not auspicious for Smith's purpose—invitations for the gala reception read: "Dear Sir . . . . The Executive Committee requests the presence of yourself and ladies at a reception." The *Washington Star* welcomed "The Patent Men" to Washington, ran biographies of prominent male inventors, described the reception for "inventors and manufacturers and the ladies who accompany them," and provided fashion commentary on the gowns of the wives of important officials. The *Washington Post* headlined its coverage: MANY MEN WITH BRAINS: INVENTORS GATHER TO CELEBRATE THE PATENT CENTENNIAL. Notable among the brainy, albeit of the opposite sex, was the well-connected Martha Coston, but she was described as "the widow with four children [who] singlehanded and alone, visited all the European courts and secured by personal solicitation the adoption of her husband's invention by all the maritime countries"—as though her only contribution to the process was her vigorous championship of her husband's work. With the invitations directed only to men, one must assume that Coston came as the guest of an invitee.

Perhaps it was just as well that women inventors were not present to hear Professor Otis T. Mason, curator of the United States National Museum, address one august gathering and deliver this morsel about woman's *real* patent:

> The man who made the best weapons killed the most game, from that game he got better food, that food made him stronger, that strength made him chief, that chieftancy gave him more wives, more children, more cohorts to support his throne. The best woman to cook or sew or carry loads got the best husband. That was her patent.

It was certainly not the patent Charlotte Smith had in mind; nor had she been napping during preparations for the gala event. Drawing upon her previous experience in publishing the all-woman *Inland* in

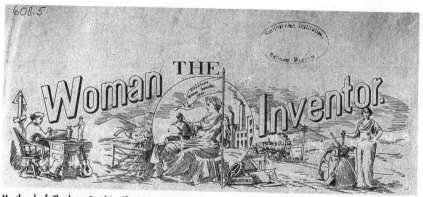

Masthead of Charlotte Smith's *The Woman Inventor.*

Saint Louis, she produced two issues of a four-page newssheet titled *Woman Inventor,* whose columns listed many of the most notable inventions of women inventors, broadcast women's complaints about their unequal position, and enabled its subscribers to exchange information on invention. Its publication reflected months of corresponding with inventors, lobbying legislators, importuning Patent Office officials to update the 1888 list of women inventors, and soliciting newspapers and magazines to publish material from its pages. Many did so, and the archivist quickly recognizes not only Smith's rhetoric and style but also her lists of specific inventors in articles such as the *Washington Post*'s "Women as Inventors: They Have Turned Their Bright Ideas into Actual Results."

Smith leafleted centennial attendees with copies of her newsletter, and she and her supporters tried to talk to as many delegates as possible. Explaining that women had much catching up to do since it had been only a little over a quarter of a century since the first state in the Union protected a married woman's property, *Woman Inventor* also carried Smith's "Memorial and Petition to the Members of the Centennial Celebration." The term "memorial," used to denote a statement of facts, was, in Smith's case, a women's rights polemic describing the plight of women inventors constantly beleaguered by financial woes. The petition asked the Patent Office not only to reduce women's application fees but also to allocate its million-dollar surplus to provide women money to protect their inventions. It also charged that unscrupulous attorneys collected their fees but failed to steer women's applications through the Patent Office, and pleaded that the Patent Office assign a special official exclusively for women's affairs, devote a

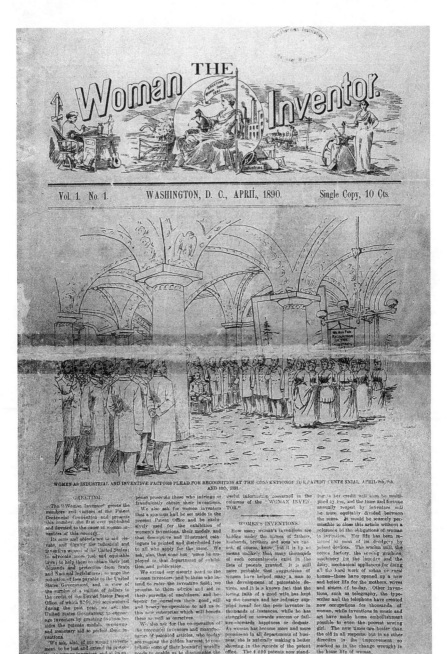

Full page of Charlotte Smith's *The Woman Inventor*.

"spacious hall" (staffed only by women) to display their inventions, and establish a cut-rate "Woman's National Patent Agency"—all this as a means of encouraging them to invent.

Smith wanted her publication to speak not just to the powerful about the need for reform but to the nascent inventor about the need for hope: "Let us cheer on the heavily laden heart of the embryo inventor, let us all aid her by word and deed, and although her ambition will stumble over some disappointment, she will ten to one reach that so much coveted success." At the centennial's final session, when about a hundred inventors met to organize an association of inventors and manufacturers, Smith (who had wangled an appearance if not an invitation to the reception that preceded it) won passage of a resolution inviting women inventors to join the association. That achievement speaks volumes for Smith's political skills, for unless women reformers conducted themselves in the most refined, re- strained, and "ladylike" manner (even when protesting egregious sex discrimination), they made little headway. An engraving depicting the subsequent "cordial reception" of women inventors into the formerly all-male sanctuary graced the front page of the second issue of *Woman Inventor*, published in June, two months after the centennial, and Smith's text paid lavish praise ("staunch defender of woman," "earnest and sincere advocate of woman's industrial advancement," and so forth) to the men who had supported her in her efforts to include women in the association.

She saved most of her praise for Virginia's Senator John W. Daniel, thanking him for the tribute he paid in his speech to industrial women in general, and to one Southern woman—whom he called the first native-born woman patentee—in particular. The woman to whom he referred was Agdalena Goodman of Duval County, Florida, who pat- ented a broom-duster in 1849, but she was by no means the first native-born patentee, even if Mary Kies (of straw-weaving fame) were discounted. Smith did not, however, quibble. She was grateful for Daniels's support—after all, he had also told the delegates that when women turned to mechanical invention, their achievements would "surpass the scope of prophecy"—and chose to capitalize on his tribute to Southern women. "[T]o-day the women of the South," said Smith in *Woman Inventor*, "are hand in hand with their sisters of the North in the advancement of industrial education and are now awakening to the requirements of the age . . . to accomplish practical education for women in the colleges of the New South." In case any Southern women missed the first page, Smith (originally from New Orleans) wrote on the second: "The editor of *Woman Inventor* is also a Southern woman and the *Woman Inventor* is the first paper of the kind ever published in the United States or Europe. So let it be recorded in history that Southern women are ahead as pioneer inventors."

Both issues of the paper provided names and anecdotes about inventors and inventions and reviewed common inventors' complaints, particularly that men often had robbed them of the fruits of their own minds. "How many women's inventions are hidden under the name of fathers, husbands, brothers and sons we cannot, of course, know," Smith lamented. Stories of financial despair buttressed her pleas for monetary help to struggling inventors, one of the most wrenching of these being the sad plight of Ellen F. Eglin, a black woman who had sold her clothes wringer invention to an agent for eighteen dollars. It made money—but not for her. Eglin told *Woman Inventor:*

> You know I am black and if it was known that a Negro woman patented the invention, white ladies would not buy the wringer. I was afraid to be known because of my color in having it introduced into the market, that is the only reason. I am working on another invention and have money to push it after the patent is issued to me, and the invention will be known as a black woman's[.] I am looking forward to exhibiting the model at the Woman's International Industrial Inventors Congress to which women are invited to participate regardless of color lines.

Smith took Eglin under her wing and told a *Washington Post* reporter that Eglin was having a special dress made for President Harrison's reception for the inventors and planned to accompany Smith to that event. Eglin, listed at that time in the Washington, D.C., directory as either "charwoman" or "domestic," within three years rose to clerk in the census office, probably as a result of her association with Smith. But there is no record of a patent ever being issued to her.

The second issue of *Woman Inventor* reprinted editorial comments from other papers regarding the Patent Office centennial and Smith's efforts to include women in its celebration. The suffragist paper *Woman's Tribune* found it ironic that the celebrants, who had not invited women inventors to their banquet, nonetheless depicted the "Genius of Invention" as a woman on the menu card; it was further outraged that in all the centennial speeches the only *mention* of a woman's invention was Senator Daniels's reference to the broom as "one of the brightest laurels in the crown of woman's inventive genius" (this in a speech in which he extolled Eli Whitney's invention of the cotton gin). As far as *Woman's Tribune* could see, the only bright spot was that by gaining admission to the Association of Inventors, women had gained their "just desserts."

Other publications, although less fervent, commended Smith's work and the talents of the women she championed. The *Marshall County News* in Iowa commented, "Charlotte has a good field"; the *Washington Post* said, "The workingwomen of the United States have no truer, braver, more helpful, and practical friend than Charlotte Smith, and their help and good wishes should be with her in her new enterprise." It is no wonder that Smith spoke highly of that paper's "genial" editor as a "friend and well-wisher." The *Omaha World Herald* credited her with gaining a congressional appropriation for the 1888 compilation of women inventors, a list that would be "astonishing to those who imagine that it is only men who understand the wider utilitarian concerns of life" and noted her continuing efforts to have that list updated from 1888. The *Herald* picked up on that portion of the "Memorial and Petition" that asked for more equitable laws for women since too many states still allowed husbands to control their wives' property. A number of other papers also joined in with support and praise from which she quoted lavishly.

Since Smith solicited correspondence, and there were many eager to recount their own experiences in print, *Woman Inventor*'s two issues provide a rich cache of first-person narratives about invention. Harriet Brown wrote in to protest her exclusion from mention in Smith's earlier issue. She wanted it known that numerous diplomas and awards had singled out her successful Boston Dress-Cutting College as superior to others in its methods. Justifiably proud of her work ("My patents were said to be superior to any thing ever granted to a woman . . . [and I] stand at the head of the only dresscutting and making college in the United States"), Brown apprised Smith that her preeminence had come about only because of her incredible persistence and her ability to pay large sums to her attorney to remain in Washington to defend her

Harriet A. Brown.

ideas. She blamed what she considered the unconscionable delay in obtaining her patent on her gender ("If I had been a man, there would have been no problem"), but her patent case file indicates that her patent examiner originally denied her patent for "lack of inventiveness" until convinced that her process was new. By 1891, Brown had won several other patents in the field and, at forty-three, wrote Smith, "I have defeated them all. . . . I was left with some money to battle with the world when quite young, and at the present time have much to feel proud of. . . . The Lord gave me talent, and I know I have done good with it. . . . For my brains have made me quite independent and without the help of any man."

While Brown chafed at her exclusion from Smith's publication, Anna Connelly gloried in "the nice notice you gave my invention the fire escape," sought to distribute extra copies of *Woman Inventor* (available for ten dollars per hundred), promised Smith a circular with further details of her invention, and praised her for "calling the attention of the most distinguished minds of Europe and America to women's inventive genius." Connelly was one of many women (nine in the ten years between 1878 and 1888 alone) who invented bridges, chutes, ladders, cages, and alarms in response to the widespread concern about fires in urban areas. The press had given wide coverage to major fires such as Chicago's, where flames tore through the city with death-dealing ferocity; Jacob Riis's photographs and accompanying text had further alarmed people by depicting the tinderbox conditions prevailing in tenement buildings where children were left in makeshift playpens on fire escape landings. Connelly's "bridge" (equipped with guard rails) rested upon the roof of an adjacent building, allowing occupants of the burning building to head across the bridge to safety on the other side, where they rang a bell to alert someone to let them in. Never missing a chance to promote its editor, *Woman Inventor* announced that Smith herself had pressed for enactment of a District of Columbia fire escape law.

A letter from Mary E. Thomas, the thirty-two-year-old widow of a doctor/inventor, related how, within a year of her husband's death, she "picked up the tangled threads" of his work in electrotherapy, patented a battery to treat kidney disorders (which won a gold medal and diploma from the Paris Academy of Inventors, of which she was subsequently made a life member), and went on to patent such a successful foot-warming "galvanic insole" that she raised funds to build a factory to produce both inventions by selling half interest in the business. Citing her own experience, Thomas tried to encourage others of her sex: "I know that women little know of the ability of their powers until tried and tested."

Eliza Wood, describing herself as a fifty-year-old farmer's wife who knew nothing but hard work, explained that she was unable to raise the money necessary to improve her already patented mop pail and that although her patent attorney found "no competition in the Patent Office" for two other "equally as good" ideas, she had lost her faith in attorneys: "I receive so many letters and also warnings to let them alone that one is afraid. . . . [C]ertainly there must be someone who can be trusted to do this work. . . . I have gone without the comforts of life to get my patents, and is it any wonder that they bring heart-aches. This letter is not dictated, but from the brain and pen of your humble correspondent." Following the letter she published from Wood, Smith made this optimistic reply: "Mrs. Eliza Wood: We shall in the near future establish an agency which will help you materially, we are now perfecting all the necessary preliminaries and shall then aid you in obtaining the just rewards for your toils and struggles." Such an agency was one of the items in her petition, though it was never to be.

Emma Watrous of Homer, New York, wrote the most appealing letter of all, touching upon every significant aspect of the struggle for patenting equality. Speaking of the general needs of women inventors, she asked that the Patent Office set up a special department run by and for women to which women could send their inventions for evaluation and direction, not only in raising capital for the patent procedure but in manufacturing and distributing their inventions as well. Speaking of her personal needs, Watrous was looking for a "partner who has money and push" to help her exploit the commercial potential of her two existing patents. She was turning to *Woman Inventor* for help, she explained, because "I have no one in the world to tell it too [*sic*] . . . in this country town where no one is posted on these things" and her friends laughed at any mention of patent rights. Then came the words that seemed to spring from Everywoman:

> I do not want to be covetous, but I think I speak the minds of many a wife and mother when I say I would willingly work hard as possible all day and all night, if I might be sure of a small profit, but have worked hard for twenty-five years and have never known what it was to receive a financial compensation and to have what was really my own. Should I ever succeed, the interest of women shall share my success, and whenever I read the sympathetic words which your paper contains my heart always goes out to the women, and I feel like putting my hands in my pocket and helping them.

Maria Littleton wrote that despite her discouragement over a competitor's infringement upon her patent, "since reading your paper think I will battle on." This was exactly the reinforcement Smith needed to keep her at her task, to "battle on" herself.

The Patent Centennial behind her, Smith urged her congressional contacts to have the Patent Office update its original list of women inventors, which they did in 1892. As her obituary recalled many years later, she knew how to get things done: "Mrs. Smith personally knew every national leader of Congress during that remarkable period in the country's history . . . [and] wielded a big influence in the legislative lobby and with committeemen." Indeed she did. But the next big fair at which women inventors played a role was one she would be forced to sit out.

By this time, Chicago had won official endorsement as the city to sponsor a fair to mark the four-hundredth anniversary of Columbus's trip to the New World—a voyage about which a wry woman's rightist carped, "In 1492 a woman sent Columbus to discover a continent wherein, four hundred years later, woman should discover herself." There seemed no better opportunity for celebration of women's ingenuity, and the issue of which of the rival suffrage groups would sponsor such displays was now moot, for the two groups had recently united into an organization with a decidedly more conservative—or conventional—posture.

Several factors had combined to effect the change. One was that the number of Socialists involved in the wave of railroad strikes in the 1870s and 1880s and the Haymarket Riots in Chicago in 1886 had made the public panic that labor unions and anarchism went hand in hand. When the National Woman's Suffrage Association favored unionizing low-paid women workers, therefore, it had raised fears that it endorsed militant socialism. It now recognized the need to lessen those fears by adopting a more conservative stance. Another factor was the change in leadership of the women's movement from its more radical pioneers, who espoused the causes of women of meager means and limited education who could not speak for themselves, to women of more substantial incomes (much of it earned through their own professional work), who tended to gravitate to causes common to women of their own class. Too, the proposition that women should vote had gained enough respectability—if not yet adoptability—that younger leaders felt they could tone down their demands for broad social reform and thus avoid antagonizing the male legislators whose actions could bestow or withhold the vote.

With social reform less an issue between the two rival suffrage organizations because of all these changes, Alice Stone Blackwell, Lucy Stone's daughter, editor of *Woman's Journal,* and secretary of the American, broached the subject of rapprochement to the larger National in 1887. Three years later, after going back and forth about leadership, the two groups united under the banner of the National American Woman Suffrage Association (NAWSA) with Elizabeth Cady Stanton as president. But Stanton harbored misgivings about the alliance: too many timid conservatives, too many temperance advocates, too much psalm-singing and praying at meetings. Three years before her eightieth birthday, she decided not to run for reelection and delivered her stirring "The Solitude of Self" address to NAWSA delegates at the 1892 convention. With what her biographer, Elisabeth Griffith, calls "feminine ferocity," Stanton declared that the patriarchal society had so isolated and subordinated women that they must learn to depend only upon themselves. She bowed out of NAWSA, leaving Susan B. Anthony to lead an organization with a much narrower base than the one she and Stanton had so optimistically started over two decades before.

When word reached Anthony that the federal government might fund the quadricentennial of Columbus's discovery of America at Chicago, she, who had delivered the women's manifesto on the occasion of the national centennial over two decades before, decided to tap Congress to support women's affairs at the fair. To aid her cause, she discreetly courted wives and daughters of senators, congressmen, Supreme Court justices, cabinet officers, and military leaders, asking them to petition their relatives to place women on the fair's governing commission. Congress duly authorized the newly established all-male National Commission to appoint a "Board of Lady Managers," a title that seemed so demeaning to one feminist that she could only say: "I am truly grateful to know that the women are not accountable for that title 'Board of Lady Managers' and that it was the men which put that word lady in place of the word woman."

The 115 women representing the states and territories conferred with influential women's organizations both in the United States and abroad (this was, after all, a *world's* fair) and were soon debating the same issue that had beset women in 1876—whether to show women's work along with men's or separately. Women's work fell into two categories: the scientific and artistic work of skillful—and independent—women, and the work of unskilled factory women that would otherwise be credited to manufacturers—who were almost always men. Showing the works of the skilled would remove the impression that women were capable of only menial work, but showing products of the unskilled would be a sign of support for those less fortunate sisters who had to work for measly pay because they were poor and unorganized—and lacked other alternatives to starvation. Some continued to argue that featuring woman's work separately implied that the public should give women preferential rather than *equal* treatment, a bias they feared might hurt them politically, but the Lady Managers, as they had done at Philadelphia and New Orleans, finally decided to exhibit women's work separately to make it more obvious that ability did not depend upon gender.

They convinced the fair's directors to sponsor a women-only architectural competition for the design of their building. The contest was won by recent MIT graduate Sophia Hayden of Boston, though she might have had mixed feelings about her triumph because the one-thousand-dollar prize money the committee offered her was trifling compared to the flat ten thousand dollars it paid each male architect for his "personal artistic service" in designing the fair's ten other large buildings. Harriet Irwin, the first woman to patent an architectural drawing but too ill to attend the fair, was not represented by her work in architecture but did dispatch to the Woman's Building library a copy of her fictional *The Hermit of Petraea*, poignantly subtitled *A Tale Written with the Hope of Throwing a Charm Around the Out-door Life So Necessary to Invalids*, which she completed two years after obtaining her patent.

As plans crystallized for exhibiting women's work at the Chicago World's Fair, Charlotte Smith hoped to find her niche in the inner circle headed by Bertha (Mrs. Potter) Palmer, but circle members mistrusted her for her close friendship with Phoebe Couzins (her former attorney and current secretary of the Lady Managers), whose rivalry with Palmer provided grist for the gossip mills of Chicago salons and newspaper columns. Smith also inadvertently got drawn into a dispute between Palmer and cosmetologist/inventor "Madame Yale."

In the course of demonstrating her "sweating machine" (guaranteed to remove wrinkles and other impediments to beauty) to a group in Pittsburgh one night, Yale spotted Smith in the audience and called upon her to explain why she hadn't forced the Board of Lady Managers to rescind Palmer's barring of cosmetic wares in the Woman's Building. The face-off between the dowdily dressed reformer, described by a fascinated *Pittsburgh Union Leader* reporter as "[l]arge and rather stout [in] a black wool gown, her plain black bonnet pulled slightly awry" and with no sign of "all the merely pretty feminine ways and graces, with which most of her sister women occupy themselves," and Yale, "young, pink, and white, with masses of soft blond hair, a black velvet gown with an Elizabethan collar of ostrich tips," culminated in Smith's capitulating and carrying the banner for Yale. She protested the unfairness of Palmer's allowing a French firm to exhibit while denying space to the American Yale. Palmer countered that *no* cosmetic woman, American or French, would show, since the board did not feel that displays of cosmetics would enhance woman's position. The unmollified Yale dispatched samples to Palmer and argued that anything that helped women "make the most of their appearance and retain their youth" indeed contributed to women's elevation, a stand corroborated by a *Chicago Times* correspondent who wrote, "Men are fickle and children are selfish, and the woman who wants to keep her hold on them must make up—and make up well and make up all the time." But the exclusion stood.

Despite such pre-exhibition altercations, all agreed that women's inventions (other than cosmetics) should play an important part in the Woman's Building, and, two years before the exposition opened, Mary Lockwood, the District of Columbia's member of the Board of Lady Managers, began preparing a lecture on women as inventors from the time of the Garden of Eden to the Columbian Exposition, complete with pictures projected on a screen by a stereopticon (or "magic lantern") to illustrate "the thorny path [woman] has travelled while filling the place God assigned to her in the world's progress." Lockwood, a Washington writer revered as the beloved "Little Mother" of the National Society of the Daughters of the American Revolution (she had published in the *Washington Post* a call to descendants of patriots to hold their first meeting in her home), had hoped to have the Smithsonian include examples of women's work as part of its government exhibit, but an official of that institution informed her that he had no time to conduct a search and advised that if the women themselves could not find "something superior," they should just stick to "bonnets, trimmings, dresses and wearing apparel."

Scouting for a more agreeable agency, the offended Lockwood asked the commissioner of patents (a new appointee since the lists had been published) to suggest which women's inventions they should feature, and when he replied that he too lacked the time and the money to help, she felt sure that *Inventive Age*, already supportive of women, would print her complaints. Its editor, James DuBois, who had earlier editorialized that women should be allowed to work "on equal terms with their brothers"—in other words, with equal pay—and, at the time of the Patent Centennial, proposed that fame and fortune resulting from inventions should be "more equitably divided between the sexes," accepted the article and headlined it WOMAN AS AN INVENTOR: SHALL SHE BE GIVEN A REPRESENTATION AT THE COLUMBIAN EXPOSITION? Lockwood recited a litany of wrongs by charging the Patent Office with making no "visible sign of diligent or casual research . . . in woman's domain" and concluded: "With due respect to the gentleman in charge and his protest, we expect to go right on showing what the Patent Office will lose, what the Government will lose if this historic lesson is not translated to show . . . woman's share in the world's progress." With no help from Washington, Lockwood, acting for the board, made her own decisions and drew up an invitation list.

Enough inventors accepted to warrant a special "Inventions Room" on the second floor, where one viewer reported seeing 335 inventions, though the official catalog lists many less. Not all were noteworthy. Ellen Henrotin, prominent Chicago clubwoman and one of the Lady Managers, wrote for *Cosmopolitan* that the inventions shown in the room were scant acknowledgment of women's accomplishments since none had any scientific value. Press and public reaction was generally more favorable. Lydia Hoyt Farmer, a contributor to newspapers and popular magazines who compiled *What America Owes to Women* as an exposition souvenir, described the women inventors as engaged in "unusual and interesting lines of work" and credited them with dispelling "existing misconceptions as to the originality and inventiveness of women."

Most reporters who investigated the inventions area enthusiastically

The Invention Room at the Chicago World's Fair, 1893.

cited Olivia Flynt's Flynt Waist and Martha Coston's Night Signals, as well as a variety of baking, sewing, and laundry aids and china decorated according to the newly patented process of Mary Louise McLaughlin, "that gifted Cincinnati girl," who had studied the Limoges pottery exhibited at the Centennial and then reproduced it. A *Woman's Journal* reporter gave top marks to Josephine Cochran's dishwashing machine, which resembled a large glass box with inside racks for cups, saucers, plates, and glasses. Cochran's Crescent Washing Machine Company manufactured her dishwasher and sold many large-size models to Chicago hotels and restaurants, but it found few customers willing to pay the steep price ($250) for a smaller size suitable for home use. The reporter, however, felt that the problem might have more to do with management than pricing: "I wish that women alone might form the stockholders. There is money in it if it is properly managed." The reporter who examined Margaret Wilcox's combination stove and house heater pronounced it "so perfect in its arrangement that a house of 10 rooms can be heated by it and in 24 hours the cooking of the family done besides, with only 4 scuttlefuls of coal."

When inventor Harriet Tracy heard of plans for the Woman's Building, she foresaw an ideal showcase for her recently patented "Tracy Gravity Safety Elevator," whose special safety mechanism retarded the descent of the cage in case of power failure, and speedily bid for the contract. Reminding the board of recent elevator disasters ("A car falling through a lofty shaft has sent one or more persons into eternity or crippled them for life; or a man has fallen down an unguarded shaft; or a small fire in a basement mounts by an elevator shaft and spread through the whole building") and guaranteeing that her company alone could guarantee passenger safety, she won the right to install it. It must have seemed a foregone conclusion to the discouraged but still gallant male inventor who bid against her: "It seems presumptuous for a humble man like myself to attempt the elevation of woman."

While her elevator safely whisked visitors to the roof-top restaurant of the Woman's Building, Tracy chose to exhibit her other inventions alongside men's, and her trade cards urged visitors to go to the "Northeast corner of the Liberal Arts Building" to see them. The most prominent was the "Tracy Lock-Stitch and Chain-Stitch Sewing Machine" whose rotary shuttle mechanism accommodated the new bobbin she had invented, one that held one thousand yards of thread. Since a bobbin with that capacity could significantly reduce the time and inconvenience of replacing bobbins, Tracy's brochure, not immodestly, waxed eloquent over her ability to solve the long-baffling problem: "But wonders have not yet ceased upon the earth, and the alleged impossibility has been actually accomplished." Chicago newspaper correspondents also reported so generously on her inventive exploits that she duly reprinted their most eloquent passages and distributed them to potential customers. Chicago's *Mail* hailed her rotating shuttle and bobbin as the solution to problems vainly addressed by the most skilled mechanics: "It is one of the most novel, simple, efficient and ingenious devices in the World's Fair. . . . All ladies who see the machine are delighted with it and her other meritorious inventions, and proud that a woman has accomplished what man failed to do. . . ." *Inter Ocean* recorded that the Fair's Association of American exhibitors had elected the "born genius" and "Queen of Inventors" to honorary membership. The *Herald* not only praised the bobbin ("She has triumphed in what a generation of skilled inventors have failed") but went so far as to say that "None can truly say that woman has never invented anything valuable after seeing Mrs. Tracy's inventions," all of which were marked with "great originality, ingenuity and utility." When the *Herald* further reported that Tracy, who had been gently reared in antebellum Charleston with aristocratic "ancestors who lived at ease regardless of practical effort" and therefore never studied mechanics, was nonetheless known from childhood as a "born genius," I perked up. By adding that to *Inter Ocean*'s mention that among Tracy's childhood inventions was one for a "gimlet-eyed screw," I became convinced that it was the young Harriet Tracy to whom several nineteenth-century writers on invention had namelessly referred when they wrote of a girl inventor of just such an object.

Also showing outside the Woman's Building was Annie H. Chilton, who exhibited her model of "Horse-Detacher and Brake" (a device for unfastening a carriage from a runaway horse to avoid "the danger of vehicles turning over or of shafts being broken after the animal has been released") in the Invention Room, and demonstrated it in the Transportation Building, where a rider showed how to uncouple a real cart from a model horse should a horse bolt. Caroline Westcott Romney, editor of a journal for the porous earthenware industry, showed her foot-warming stone for use in frigid railway cars in the Transportation Building and her milk cooler/refrigerator in the dairy and dairy products section of the Agriculture Building. In the Machinery Building, Harriet Strong won medals for her models of water storage and dam construction. An engineer charged with preparing a report to the Nicaraguan government on the feasibility of a canal took the water-storage model with him for further study and concluded that her system would make such a route possible. Her pampas grass (hardly an

Annie Chilton's Horse Detacher and Brake shown in Chicago.

invention but cured in an innovative way) was so popular that daughter Hattie, who accompanied her mother to Chicago, was able to give a very favorable report to her younger sister back home about the value of sales taking place in the Horticultural Hall, the Public Comfort Hall, the Woman's Building, and the California Building (where an entire "pampas palace" had been created). Her mother, ever the supporter of working women, assigned all profits from exposition sales to establish Queen Isabella colleges, where the Ladies' Business League would teach classes in business methods.

Overall, feminists considered that the Columbian Exposition showed inventive women in a good light. Even humorist Marietta Holley, still writing under the pseudonym "Josiah Allen's wife" (as she had two decades before when she published her notorious free love satire in *Inland Magazine* and thereby precipitated the estrangement of Mary Nolan and Charlotte Smith), seems to have been impressed, judging from the words she put in Josiah Allen's mouth:

> By crackey! not a bit of lace or tattin,' not a streamer of ribbon; [women] have riz up for once above gauzes, and flummerie, and ornaments. . . . By Jocks! I hadn't no idea that wimmen had ever done so much work that is usefull as well as ornamental. . . . I hadn't no idee that they wuz a'goin' to swing out and make such a successful show as this. . . . why, the very elevator you rode up to the ruff garden on wuz made by a woman.

When the Woman's Building opened, one woman was so exuberant over women's new opportunities that she predicted that in the next century women would occupy every field then monopolized or at least dominated by men, even to serving in "the senate and house; probably the Supreme bench, possibly in the cabinet, and perhaps in the president's chair." As of 1991, her prediction was off by only one office.

The high-water mark of the fair was the World Congress of Women, a week-long symposium at which delegates from 126 organizations, fifty-six of them from the United States, gathered to discuss issues common to women all over the world. A remarkable roster of 331 women presented papers on topics that ranged from "The Glory of Womanhood" to "The Financial Independence of Woman," helping their listeners to assess how far women had come and how much farther they needed to go. For the inventors in the audience, a speaker on "Woman's Sphere from a Woman's Standpoint" put her finger on their most common predicament—the obstacles put in their path by society's attitude toward creative women: "[I]f one possessed of inventive genius fashioned a new and useful device, even her nearest male relatives and friends advised her to patent it in the name of some man, as it would not be compatible with womanly modesty to attain such notoriety as a patent to herself would bring." But most talks carried an onward and upward theme, and the more conservative women's rights leaders were in a euphoric mood because—with Stanton not even in attendance—leadership of the suffrage movement had quietly passed from the proponents of radical change to the more conservative, wealthy, and socially prominent middle-class and upper-class women epitomized by Lady Managers chairman Bertha Palmer, who had somehow managed to hold the coalition together.

The year of the fair was also the year Mary Livermore and Frances Willard, in a further display of optimism, published *A Woman of the Century*, a compendium of 1,470 alphabetically arranged biographical sketches, almost all accompanied by portraits. It was needed, they said, to fill a "vacant niche in the reference library," to record not only what women had accomplished after four centuries of life in the New World but to peer into the "marvelous promise" of the next century. Livermore and Willard revised the book in subsequent editions to include an appendix of categories in which women were prominent, a broad spectrum that ranged from "Invention" to "Bee-keeper" (which listed only one woman, prominent apiarist and publisher of *Beekeepers' Journal* Ellen Smith Tupper, who was known as "Queen Bee"). *A Woman of the Century* found eight women inventors to commend as leaders in their field, and its editors deemed the nineteenth century "woman's century."

There was indeed much for inventing women to celebrate: The *New York Tribune* specifically lauded such "unusual" women's inventions as agricultural implements, mining machinery, electrical contrivances, and railroad and mill machinery; *Success* magazine, devoted to "Education, Enterprise, Enthusiasm, Energy, Economy and Self-respect, Self-reliance, Self-help, Self-culture and Self-containment," discussed women's patenting accomplishments in a column titled "Woman's Widening Field"; and many other publications applauded women's contributions as well.

But, on the down side, the field of invention for women, while enlarging, was still narrow. When the *Chautauquan* commissioned writer Leon Mead to write on woman inventors the year after the fair, he sulked over his assignment and importuned the newly appointed commissioner of patents to send him *any* information on the subject, grousing that it was "a sorry task at best" to cover a topic of such "limited scope." If the commissioner sent the 1892 figures, figures that amply corroborated the sheer quantity of devices women had invented, Mead was not impressed: "Generally speaking, there is not a wide range covered by these creations of the daughters of Eve." To realize their "bright and glorious" future, he said, they would have to familiarize themselves with the country's commercial and industrial needs and "cope with mechanical complexities." Eve's inventive daughters had coped as best they could in an educational system that excluded them from the very courses they needed to develop their talents. Until such time as a proper education was available to them, their attempts to shift for themselves in the business world would be badly undermined.

Hope sprang eternal, however. In 1895 women inventors had another chance to promote their interests when Atlanta hosted the Cotton States and International Exposition—"international" because of the desire of the sponsors to tap Central, Southern, and Latin American markets as well as domestic ones. Like their Northern sisters, Southern women opted for a separate Woman's Building "filled with the wonders of woman's work, with gems of her brain and her hand," to display women's role in the regeneration of the South after the Civil War. The very existence of such a building was a sign of changing times in the South, since it had required considerable effort on the part of women heretofore confined to their homes. As one weary husband said at the building's dedication: "I have no doubt that a great many of the gentlemen here have had to stay at home nights to take care of the babies [laughter] and attend to other domestic duties." Though the exposition program described members of the Board of Women Managers in such distinctly unmanagerial-sounding phrases as "singularly blessed with beauty, intellect, wealth and social position," "The Star of the South," and "a brilliant woman who was a noted belle and beauty. . . . [P]ractical matters had never entered into the unruffled currents of her life," the women themselves did not necessarily view these words as complimentary. She whose "unruffled currents" had never been marred by practical affairs, for example, saw herself in quite different terms: "I'm tired of being told how people think I've developed and broadened through this work. . . . I had it all to start with, but this is the first thing that called forth that side of my nature."

In charge of inventions, now a routine feature of expositions, were Mrs. William Grant and her co-chairman, from Washington, D.C., Mary Lockwood, the same Mary Lockwood who earlier created the lecture and accompanying stereopticon display that had informed Chicago audiences of women's progress. Grant went to Washington in person to deal with the powers that be, and her pass to the gallery of the United States Senate Chambers for July 2, 1895, is still among her papers in the archives of the State of Georgia. In Washington, Lockwood, described once as "a charming picture with her white hair and sweet face," obviously focused her charms upon "Mr. Seymour" of the Patent Office, for he promised forthwith to send the Woman's Building 125 models of women's inventions, nine of them by women who had exhibited at the Centennial almost two decades before.

Most of Seymour's choices were models of inventions that eased domestic tasks, but among them were five safety devices and five dealing with railroads (including Louisa Simpson's apparatus for destroying vegetation on railroads, Augusta Rodgers's for conveying smoke and cinders from locomotives to the roadbed below, and Eleanor McMann's guard for sleeping-car berths). Others in unusual fields were Mary Jane Montgomery's war vessel patented during the Civil War,

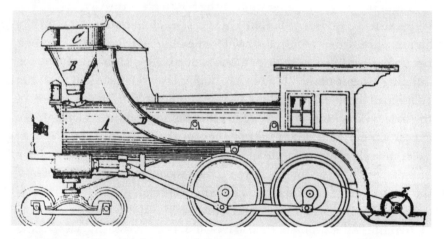

Augusta Rodgers's Smoke and Cinder Conveyer shown in Atlanta.

Bill of lading for a model bound for the Atlanta Fair, 1895.

Emily Tassey's method of propelling ships, Sarah Mather's submarine telescope and lamp, Mary Walton's sound-deadening construction of rails for an elevated railway, and Margaret Knight's three models for paper bag machines.

To supplement the government exhibit, Co-chairman Grant energetically corresponded with inventors to announce that she would "gladly and proudly welcome . . . all patents by women; for this department of scientific invention represents the highest order of woman's work" and reminded them that the Southern Railway & Steamship Association would provide free transportation for patents bound for the Woman's Department. Most of what inventors sent in appeared in "theme settings" such as the one in which a wax-figured grandmother sat at her patented folding worktable that could convert to a trunk, her finger sporting a patented thread cutter, a patented receptacle for waste needles and pins nearby, along with (in the words of the *Atlanta Constitution*) a "chatelaine with all kinds of sewing implements, held in the mouths of little dogs and piglings."

When the Cotton States Exposition closed, the magazine *New Ideas* stated that women should no longer serve as the butt of their masculine competitors' "semi-contemptuous references," for the displays of women's patents had done "much to dissipate the popular misconception of feminine talent." A more far-reaching, heavily documented means of dissipating that misconception was the recently published second appendix to the list of women inventors, updated to March 1, 1895. Probably still under pressure from Charlotte Smith, the Patent Office this time classified patents not only by name of inventor but also by field of invention. That was a mixed blessing to feminists. It was easier to locate women's inventions in atypical fields, but the fact that there *were* no close seconds to the number of entries in the "Wearing Apparel and Culinary Utensils" field was also made obvious. This didn't surprise the *Portland Oregonian*, which stated that "woman's attention is devoted chiefly to things in these lines, and very little to large machinery, to extended mechanical appliances or to experiments in dynamics."

That conclusion was corroborated by the subsequent exhibit of women's inventions at the Tennessee Centennial Exposition two years later. Though Nashville women expected the displays to prove that their gender had "invaded and mastered this field of human action" and the local newspaper loyally pronounced that invention was "an integral part of the life of a modern woman," that "field of action" and that "integral part of life" were, to judge from the number of household inventions shown in the Woman's Building, notably limited to the domestic arena. It was undoubtedly this fact that led women organizers of future expositions to re-study the advisability of displaying examples of women's industry in their own space, apart from men's.

Still, the separate women's buildings at Philadelphia, New Orleans, Chicago, Atlanta, and Nashville had served as much more than just exhibits of woman's work. By providing space for women's club members, educators, artists, missionaries, suffragists, philanthropists, physical culture proponents, journalists, scientists, temperance advocates, and divorce and dress reformers to meet and exchange ideas, they had empowered what Bertha Palmer called "the freemasonry among women."

# 9

# STILL A LONG
# WAY TO GO

$\mathcal{B}$y the end of the century, feminists could congratulate themselves all they liked on the giant strides their sex had taken, could point with pride to their increased educational opportunities and the larger numbers of women in the professions of medicine or law, but society as a whole had changed little in its perspective on women's proper role. As for women inventors, their number was greater, the fields in which they invented broader, the utility of the devices designed (even if most of them were still for women's exclusive use) undeniable—for why knock anything that liberated women from cumbersome clothing or alleviated the grind of housekeeping? But while feminists loyally disseminated information on various newly patented devices as examples of women's creative genius, trying as hard as they could to focus on the occasional nondomestic inventions, the accomplishments of these women were not enough to shake society's conviction that the hub of women's universe was naturally, and properly, their homes, rather than the business world, which was the domain of men.

So, while an optimistic speaker at the Congress of Women in Chicago might pronounce that the "domestic shrine" was past history, in actuality women were still expected to worship there. Social Darwinism exponent Lester Ward could rail all he liked that if "this vicious dogma that woman's place is in the house is persisted in for a few more centuries, there can be no escape from a general physical and intellectual degeneracy of the whole human race," but the dogma continued to thrive. If a woman wanted to invent, so opinion went, she could invent in her home—and for her home. "A woman knows intuitively what is needed in a house," said the *New York Tribune. Patent Record* queried, "[W]ho knows better than a woman what will lighten the burdens of the housewife in the kitchen and dining room?" A Michigan woman's suggestion to put glass doors on ovens was a typical woman's invention, said *New Ideas*, for "[f]rom [a woman's] practical knowledge of the work, she is better qualified than her brother of the sterner sex." Even the few women who defied the domestic stereotype to invent such urban necessities as street cleaners were pictured at the time as simply broom-wielding housekeepers on a larger than usual scale, rather than pioneers in a new field. For example, *Success* magazine, though usually a proponent of progress, scored a point for traditional roles for women by wondering why anyone should be surprised that a woman headed Chicago's street cleaning department: "Why should [women] not vent a little of their enthusiasm for scrubbing upon the places where it is most needed?"

This is not to deny that progress had been made. On the positive side, there were notable changes in women's position. Three decades had passed since Vassar's first graduates were regarded, recalled one of them, "as something in the nature of freaks." Three decades had also elapsed since Virginia Penny, an otherwise forward-thinking writer who urged women to enter new fields, had opined that for a woman to become an attorney and argue in a courtroom was "scarcely compatible with the reserve, quietude, and gentleness that characterize a woman of refinement." By 1895, only about half a dozen colleges or universities still closed their doors to women, and, noted *Success*, even the venerable Harvard could hear "the tramp of progress through the halls of Radcliffe." Despite such headway, a mistrustful public, fearing that to develop women's intellectual capabilities would be to defeminize them, continued to ridicule the few who hoped to escape their stereotyped role as keepers of the hearth and home.

With many parents prizing domestic skills above scholarly achievement for their daughters, a good many schools of otherwise high academic standards hedged their bets by having seasoned teachers conduct supplementary classes in housewifery as diligently as they taught geography and arithmetic. When Dwight Moody's Northfield, Massachusetts, seminary added classes in washing, ironing, sewing, and setting a fine table to its curriculum, a shocked woman writer for *Harper's Bazaar* wondered why girls were shunted into housekeeping while boys were given manual training: "But what of women? . . . Have they a like opportunity to learn their part in life? Our daughters and sisters are not less dear to us." *Success* raised the same issue, going so far as to endorse a Virginia educator's proposal for "Schools of Invention" for both sexes. But the time was not yet ripe, and few parents defied the conventional wisdom that daughters would profit from courses in the domestic realm. They dutifully enrolled them in schools founded on the Moody model—thereby raising yet another generation of young women who were denied the mechanical and manual training lavished upon their brothers.

Housewifery was so in the ascendancy that even Mount Holyoke continued to maintain its Domestic Department "for its advantageous influence upon the lives and characters of its students," and students at most of the other women's colleges still had to serve meals and do light housework in order to learn something of domestic work. Wellesley finally broke the pattern by hiring servants to relieve students "from the thraldom of housework" and enable them to devote more time to their rigorous academic studies. Hedging, however, the college established a course in domestic science, a field being pioneered by MIT chemist Ellen Richards, who in time extended the turf to include public health. Domestic science seemed safe since it strengthened girls' knowledge of the "feminine" roles their gender destined them to fill at that time: wives, mothers, teachers.

In the face of such compromise, and even capitulation, it is not surprising that most nineteenth-century women regarded their education as an embellishment of their traditional role in the domestic sphere rather than a means of emancipating themselves from it. It was far easier to progress to marriage and motherhood than to risk the loss of their femininity by teetering on the brink of intellectualism. All this was enough to make educator and women's rights leader Emma Willard (no relation to Frances Willard), speaking before the New York legislature, explode: "The education of females has been exclusively

**Blue Monday.**

directed to fit them for displaying to advantage the charms of youth
and beauty. . . . Though well to decorate the blossom, it is far better
to prepare for the harvest." Willard never backed off from her commitment to women's education, but she did not yet speak for society as a
whole.

Thus, although it was perfectly acceptable for women to invent
domestic "novelties" (as magazines often called them), when one of
them turned out to be a masterpiece of mechanical complexity that
enjoyed great commercial success, few but dedicated feminists acknowledged the fact. Margaret Colvin created such a marvel to contend

# The Enterprise
# Family Outfit of

# Sad Irons

## A Handsome Wedding
## or Christmas Present

No. 330 – Nickel-Plated, $3.75
No. 335 — Polished,    3.50

Mrs. Potts's Irons.

with one of the most abominable jobs assigned to woman's sphere—laundry. Victorian women were steeped in such maxims as "Dirt wouldn't stick to her" and "Cleanliness is Godliness," or at least next to it. And, since birth control was still largely confined to the upper classes, the average woman had to do laundry for six or more children, as well as for grandparents or other relatives who lived with the family, and the servants who were hired to lessen housework's load but nonetheless contributed to the laundry basket. Moreover, skirts were long and wide, multiple petticoats were commonplace, and starched bosoms (shirt fronts) and cuffs were de rigueur for businessmen.

Home magazines, etiquette books, and laundry manuals dispatched hints to the housewives to stock veritable pharmacopoeia of such cleansing agents as salt, vinegar, borax, naptha, hydrochloric acid, alum, wax, blueing, starch, ammonia, oxalic acid, French Javelle water (a form of bleach), and bran in cheesecloth bags for light starching. One would think that anyone who could invent a washing machine to lighten this burden would be a local heroine, but, for all the sophisticated mechanical knowledge Margaret Colvin displayed in inventing the washing machine that won plaudits at both the Centennial and the Chicago fair and was successfully marketed by the Triumph Washing Machine Company, her own hometown newspaper had little to say about any of this in her obituary. Only a passing reference to being "clear headed and sensible" in business marked her inventive career; to the home folks she was just "one of the old fashioned women, whose influence is pure and sweet and good."

Things went better for Mary Potts, whose sad iron had been the toast of the Centennial when Enterprise Manufacturing Company made her product a household word to the collectors of trade cards that touted the product's effectiveness through catchy cartoons and jingles. Enterprise continued to advertise the Potts product skillfully for the remainder of the century. By dubbing the iron a "labor-saving machine," the company lured customers into buying more than one size by creatively packaging several different sizes in an elegantly fitted case called a "Family Outfit"—an ideal wedding or Christmas gift or simply "a convenient article for the tidy housekeeper." With such promotion, Potts's invention could not help being, according to one of her proud townsmen, "the most popular and the most widely used of all the articles in that line."

The field of needle arts was also considered an ideal field for women, and professionals, whose special stitches, patterns, and techniques constituted the heart of their businesses, relied upon patenting to protect the expertise on which their reputations rested. Candace Wheeler and her former employee, Mary Tillinghast, two such professional needlewomen, provided original, custom-made needlework pieces for the elegant homes of wealthy customers, and they soon faced off in a suit over priority of invention.

Fifty-five-year-old Wheeler, the doyenne of "artistic embroideries" and a partner with painter and glassmaker Louis J. Tiffany and painters Samuel Colman and Lockwood deForest (the latter specializing in carved and ornamental woodwork) in a prominent New York interior decorating firm known as Associated Artists, was a formidable plaintiff. She was known for her good works. Having seen how London's newly founded Kensington School of Art Needlework provided work for needy ladies (designated "decayed gentlewomen" by the British), Wheeler established the New York Women's Exchange, where refined women "cramped by untoward circumstances" could sell their painted pictures, china, or needlework. Since the needle-woven method of ornamenting fabrics that she had invented attracted lucrative orders for Associated Artists, Wheeler was also able to provide financial help to such women by hiring expert stitchers to make products under her direction.

Mary Tillinghast was exactly the kind of young woman Wheeler wanted to help: no ordinary shop girl but an ambitious, cultured, once-monied, well-traveled young woman who could deal with Tiffany's elite clientele. Unknown to Wheeler, the future employee had taken a Grand Tour of Europe in 1872, where she had studied the Gobelin tapestries with the idea of duplicating the work in America, until the foundering of the family fortune shattered that dream. Instead of having the necessary leisure to develop her method, Tillinghast was then forced to become the principal support of her parents and six siblings. Working as a teacher-companion to a New York family whose young children she tended from early morning until almost midnight, she nonetheless worked steadily to perfect her Gobelin-inspired method but was unable to find the funds to finance a patent application for the new method of stitchery she was confident she had invented.

Candace Wheeler offered her a job that enabled her to pad out a basic nine-dollar-a-week salary with sales commissions and profits from the sale of her own designs, until she eventually netted enough to apply for a patent. When Wheeler got wind of Tillinghast's sideline business and her patent application for a method Wheeler was sure duplicated the one she herself had already patented in England and had applied for in America, she sued to quash Tillinghast's application and charged that Tillinghast "acquired her special knowledge of this invention whilst in my employ and has surreptitiously and fraudulently attempted to produce for herself letters patent therefor."

Both women swamped the patent examiners with samples of their separate work (which remain in the National Archives file today), Wheeler trying to convince the examiners of the similarity of their work, Tillinghast, the difference. Finally, fearful that Tillinghast's arguments and woeful tales of financial plight were tilting the examiners to decide in her behalf, Wheeler agreed to a joint stipulation that dissolved the suit: "The inventions sought to be patented and claimed are not the same but distinct and dissimilar." The patent suit might have been only a flyspeck in Wheeler's career, but with her reputation at stake, she could ill afford a loss. Six months later, each needlewoman, on the same day, received a patent for "her" method. To the uninitiated, the two methods seem to bear a marked resemblance to each other. Within two weeks, a patent that had pended for a different type of embroidery was granted to Wheeler.

Later separating amicably from her partners and taking the Associated Artists name with her to a four-story brownstone on New York's East-Twenty-third Street, Wheeler founded an all-female business to supply textiles, carpets, artwork (including embroideries), and wallpaper, all in original American designs. Of these efforts to wed art and industry in a business she considered a "natural field" for women of cultivation and taste, she boasted, "We added interior decoration to our list of accomplishments, and had much to do with making that form of art a profession for women."

Wheeler, who lived almost a full century and doted upon her grandchildren (one of whom, Henry L. Stimson, became President Hoover's secretary of state and President Franklin Roosevelt's secretary of war), was tireless in pursuit of her professional goals. She advised home and needlework magazines, wrote *The Development of Embroidery in America*, and crystallized the essence of her career in *Principles of Home Decoration*. Today, textile collectors still cherish the method of embroidery she patented, which is known as "Wheeler Work." Tillinghast's name also survived the patent tiff without tarnishing, and a few years later she turned her artistic talents to designing stained-glass windows. Her window *Jacob's Dream*, in Grace Church, New York City, was the first one to have been set by a woman, and she was also well known for her design and supervision of the complete interior of Saint Stephen's Church in Pittsfield, Massachusetts, including the altar, pulpit, and five stained-glass window panels.

Doyenne of Needle Arts, Candace Wheeler.

If needlework was woman's business, certainly women's clothing fell into the same category—one in which women inventors could make a strong statement in behalf of reform. Yet it seems as if women wore the impractical clothes they did because men liked to see them that way! Although some women had in earlier years converted to healthful underclothes such as Converse's "Hygienic Waist," their outer clothes had changed so little by 1890 that seasoned critic Elizabeth Stuart Phelps, once the chair of Boston's Dress Reform Committee, wrote in *Forum*, a magazine devoted to contemporary issues, that women were wearing even more impractical and outrageous clothes than ever. To counter this tendency, Annie Jenness Miller of the Jenness-Miller School of Physical Culture lectured in all the major cities on "Artistic and Healthful Dress." Her packed audiences sometimes contained men, in which case she asked them to leave when it was time for her to model intimate garments, such as Emmaline Philbrook's vaunted "Equipoise Waist" (which Frost & Company advertised frequently in *Jenness-Miller Magazine*). Modeling undergarments "live" was in itself a radical departure from the 1870s, when Boston dress reformers dared to show them only on dolls. Miller drew large audiences and was by no means sympathetic to those who considered her hundred-dollar lecture fee excessive "for a woman," since, she maintained, "[n]o man of equal reputation as a speaker accepts less."

Dressmakers with originality, instinct, and artistic ability were eager to design the kind of healthful and practical clothes Miller advocated, but, as Annie Meyers, doyenne of dressmaking and author of several books on the subject, predicted, a woman would undoubtedly achieve the "right to the ballot-box before she is given the right to appear in them." The Congress of Women's Dress Reform Committee at the Chicago fair in 1893 tried to drive home to audiences that if progress were to be made, "womanly modesty"—and reluctance to brave ridicule—were no longer acceptable. Frances Russell, the committee chairman whose "Syrian costume" harem pants were gathered at the ankle, full above, dejectedly counted the few with courage to change from the voluminous skirts worn by the many and pleaded: "No one is asked to make a martyr of herself. . . . What we seek especially is a wide awakening and the impetus of numbers, so that those who want freedom of their limbs may find liberty and not ostracism." A trousered librarian from Wichita defended dress reformers (" 'cranks' as some people call those of us who take an advanced view of things in this world") for giving her the courage to wear her ensemble to work.

Some speakers inveighed against corsets and bragged they wore none. Ellen Hayes, a professor of mathematics and astronomy at Wellesley College, predicting that women would never wield power

Pneumatic Dress Form.

until they added pockets to their clothes, appeared in a blue serge suit conspicuously adorned with ten. When models in Dress Reform Committee–approved gear mounted chairs and tables at one session to show the audience how cleverly their full-cut outfits defied detection as trousers, one viewer marveled that the models looked "just like people who are not reformers"—the ultimate accolade from one still apprehensive about flouting convention. Timidity reigned: For each woman who begged the models for patterns to copy, another hesitated. Celia Whitehead, who described her own "Eight Months of Experiences in the Syrian Costume" in a dress reform symposium sponsored by *Arena* magazine, expected more of women. Their excess modesty, she said, put her in mind of the story of the stocking manufacturer who sent the Queen of Spain a few examples of his company's wares as a gift. The queen's minister returned them with this curt message: "The Queen of Spain *has* no legs." To Whitehead, it was obvious that "[u]ntil woman is allowed to have ankles, there is no hope for her brain."

The "hygienic" dress movement might have succumbed had it not been for the bicycling craze that captured the nation in the 1890s. The bicycle industry, too insignificant to tally in the census of 1880, by 1897 included not only ten thousand businesses that carried bicycles as part of their stock in trade but also peripheral industries that had sprung up to manufacture steel tubing for the frame, chains for the driving gear, wood rims for the wheels, steel balls for the bearings, pneumatic tires, bicycle saddles, and such necessaries as cyclometers, tool kits, lamps, locks, baskets, racks, and even sunshades. All this, said the commissioner of patents in his annual report for that year, had caused the number of patents for bicycles and their equipment to skyrocket "due to the enormous accession of thinkers to the ranks of those who use them."

Among those thinkers were a good many women. During the craze, which lasted only about five years, hordes of shop girls, clerks, typists, and housewives took a new lease on life from cycling, which, summarized one health culture devotee, "gives them a kind of 'paddle your own canoe' feeling which makes them less like clinging vines." The only problem for the feminine contingent was the lack of suitable outdoor gear for the new sport. The *New York Herald* quickened interest in developing an appropriate outfit by conducting a design contest and awarded a fifty-dollar prize to Mrs. Marie Reideselle for the best cycling costume, even though the designer felt compelled to cover the trousers with a long skirt when she was off the wheel. Fearful of censure if they chose garb that might appear too masculine, women cyclists compromised: a divided skirt or trousers for straddling the saddle and pedaling the wheel but a camouflage to disguise the division when they dismounted. Most patented bicycle suits of the period, therefore, had some kind of overlay that, when released on cue, descended over the offending pants.

The most prolific patentee of such clothing was Brooklynite Lena Sittig, who developed a rainy-day combination trouser and skirt overdress. The skirt folded into a pocket when not in use. Though she originally designed it as simply a waterproof outfit whose trousers were made of what she called "duck's back" waterproof cloth, she quickly recognized that the outfit could double as a rain garment for the obsessed "women of the wheel" who wanted to face downpours with as much impunity as their pedestrian sisters. Her attorney duly explained such possibilities to the patent examiner and explained that the suit was so in demand that it was important for the Patent Office to act with speed: "She cannot get them manufactured fast enough to supply the demand." The patent issued, Sittig sold the rights for the design and the special fabric to Best and Company, which coined the word "cravenetted" to describe the fabric's imperviousness to water.

Impressed by Sittig's invention, the exclusive Cycle Club of Brooklyn, which met at the local skating rink so that members could master bicycle-riding before venturing out onto busy roads, invited her as their weekly Saturday night attraction. There Sittig exhibited her "Duplex Bicycle Skirt," a genteel but sporting outfit she had designed with the knowledge that most women shrank from donning trousers of any kind. A mannequin draped in one of the outfits enabled members to conduct a close-up inspection of the garment, while two similarly clad young friends of the inventor pedaled about the rink to allow each guest to see for herself that a cyclist in action could be "as gracefully and modestly dressed as though in [her] own parlor." The fact that Sittig was prominent in Brooklyn civic affairs undoubtedly helped her to attract press attention, including that of editor and author "Jennie June" Croly, who had already endorsed the garment, which, in turn, made it easier for Sittig to approach such companies as Best and Company.

Though others lacked Sittig's entrée to the business world, about thirty women inventors received patents for similarly ingenious solutions to the skirt/trouser question, and the explanations in their patents reflect the concerns of their prospective clients. Alice Nash knew that

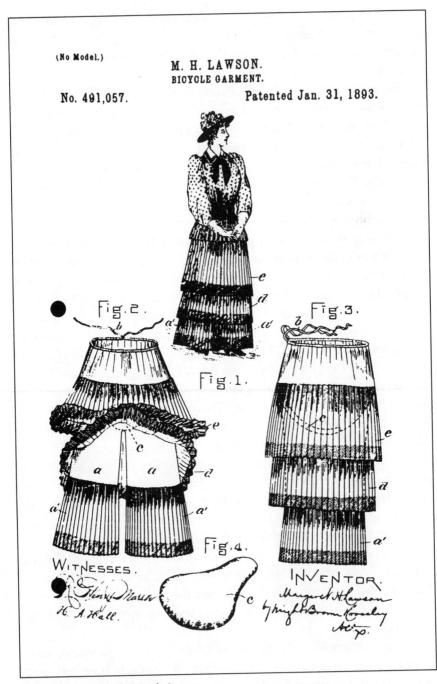

(No Model.)

M. H. LAWSON.
BICYCLE GARMENT.

No. 491,057.

Patented Jan. 31, 1893.

Fig. 2.

Fig. 3.

Fig. 1.

Fig. 4.

WITNESSES.

INVENTOR.

Margaret Lawson's "lady-like" Bicycle Garment.

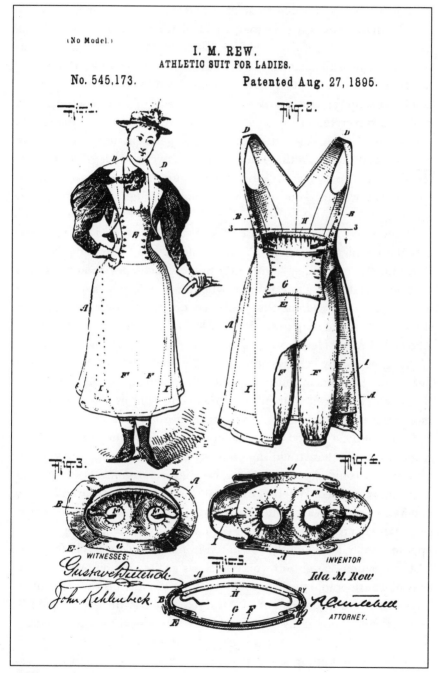

**Another version from Ida Rew.**

bloomers were preferable to skirts, which became entangled in the bicycle chain, but, since women disliked their "mannish look," she disguised them carefully. Clarissa Ellen Dockham recognized that some women so disliked the idea of pulling on trousers like a man that her trousers opened flat so that the cyclist could slip them on over her head and snap the crotch afterward. Margaret Hobbs Lawson placed a pillow in the crotch of the trouser to ease the discomfort of the saddle and so neatly concealed the "bifurcated" garment under decorative pleating and flouncing that the "division between the legs" was undetectable. Pauline B. Hercht's ingenious manipulation of drawstrings to transform a walking suit into a cycling habit brought kudos from *New Ideas.*

While few women invented cycles, *New Ideas* singled out for mention those who turned their inventive talents to accessorizing them. It was, said the magazine, "eminently proper" that they should do so, a comment that makes one wonder whether it was proper only as long as they invented gadgets that appealed mainly to their own gender, since the ones the magazine cited all fell in this category. The magazine called Mary Henderson's tricycle with armrests "A woman's Tricycle," presumably because only a woman would need such support for her limbs. Henderson's other invention, a form-fitting attachment to the saddle, answered women's common complaint of "local pains of a more or less passing nature" from uncomfortable seats.

Incidentally, a few edgy gynecologists, eyeing women's surge to the wheels, warned that straddling pommels led to involuntary masturbation, which could greatly compromise their later delicate adjustment to the marriage bed. Whether aware of this aspect or not, Sarah L. Naly and Mary Scott Jones widened the front end of the seat, explaining that seats which projected forward to a narrow point were fine for the opposite sex but "obviously not suited to female riders." What's more, such projections caught on women's skirts as they got on or off, "often causing considerable mishap, to say nothing of mortification." Sarah S. Howarth wrote in her patent of "[b]icycle riders [who] are frequently attacked and injured by vicious dogs while traveling over country roads." To repel "dogs of this class," she attached to the handlebar a set of boxes containing snuff or pepper. A squeeze of a bulb released the pepper and "immediately cause[d] a dog to desist from further attack." As *New Ideas* put it, "The curs require one dose, and this can be administered without looking back."

While dress reform and cycling captured the interest of a good many women inventors in the century's last decade, Cynthia Westover was on another track. When she patented a street-cleaning apparatus in 1892—what the *New York Times* later credited as being the "first wheelbarrow to collect dirt from streets"—not only did she gain national respect for suggesting a solution to a major urban problem, but she became to feminists a symbol of emancipated womanhood. As a motherless child, she was often the only female in the vicinity as she and her father, a noted geologist, prospected in the American and Mexican West before they finally settled in Colorado. She rode, fished, swam, and became such a crack shot that the buffalo she had felled at the age of twelve was made part of Colorado's exhibit at the Centennial. With solid credentials from a commercial college—where she was considered a skilled mathematician—and a diploma from Colorado State University in Boulder's first class, she headed for New York, where she studied music, sang in church choirs, and acquired a Bachelor of Arts degree in literature from Alfred University. To support herself, she worked as a customshouse inspector and quickly learned French, German, and Italian and perfected her Spanish. Long impressed with Westover's skills, the surveyor of the port of New York appointed her his private secretary when he became New York's commissioner of street cleaning, making her the first woman appointee in any city department. Her linguistic ability (Frances Willard wrote that the young woman was "on speaking terms with most of the nationalities coming to our shore") helped her to quell a threatened strike of sanitation workers when she addressed the grievances of the primarily Italian force in their native tongue.

Despite the fact that by this time electricity was beginning to supplant horsepower in drawing New York's street railways, a large number of the horse-drawn railways, not to mention horse-drawn carts and carriages, still remained, making filth-clogged streets a threat to health as well as to sensibilities. Standing on the City Hall steps one windy day, Westover observed a worker sweeping up the same pile of dirt five times and resolved to invent an efficient, labor-saving device that would not only speed the process but make it possible for horses to make the haul up the steep inclines to department dumps without rupturing from the strain of pulling heavy loads. Her patented derrick-operated swinging cart (or "dingey"), which dumped loads into a scow, was soon a fixture on city streets in all the major cities of the world, and though as a city employee she could claim no monetary reward for her ingenuity, she did receive honorable membership and a gold medal from the French Academy of Inventors. Her invention's reputation lives on. As recently as 1981, Westover's "cart to dump as well as carry dirt" made it into the brief list of inventions in the "Mothers of Invention" section of *Womanlist*, an annual compendium of accomplishments by women.

Although her inventing career ended with the swinging cart, Westover never retreated to anonymity. As a journalist and photographer, she assembled material on public questions for the editor of *Harper's Weekly*, wrote short autobiographical stories for the *New York Recorder*, and published several tales about a charming young woman nicknamed "Bushy," the same name her father had conferred on her when an Indian tribal chieftain told him that with her marksmanship and fluency they would adopt her into their tribe were it not for her bushy blond hair. In *Bushy: A Romance Founded on Fact*, published in 1896, Westover recalled her own Rocky Mountain adventures and cloaked her heroine with the "habit of self-dependence, the perpetual exaltation of the practical." The *Detroit Free Press* thought: "The story is told with a rush and whirl that takes the reader off his feet. Bushy is a fine character." The *Boston Herald* applauded Bushy as "the sturdiest little woman who ever brought sunshine to a miners camp." The *Saint Louis Globe Democrat* annointed her the "prodigy of Feminine Courage," all characteristics of the plucky inventor herself.

By 1895, Westover was editing the woman's page at the *Recorder*, the first full page to be devoted exclusively to women's affairs. The next year, this "essentially womanly . . . very handsome, magnetic woman, who wins all with whom she comes in contact" married one of those she had beguiled—John Alden, an editorial writer for the *Recorder* and descendant of colonist John Alden. The newspaper's staff gave them a handsome silver service; Morse and Company, her "Bushy" publishers, gave a set of French china, something they could well afford, since her "Bushy" books and "Bushy" posters were extraordinarily popular. My mother, an independent-minded young woman

Cynthia Westover (Alden).

who would one day become an engineer and architect, remembered the inspiration she gained from Bushy's spirit of buoyant optimism and perseverance.

Westover also wrote a history of New York that grew from lectures she delivered to the weekly meetings of the Professional Woman's League and, upon the demise of the *Recorder*, edited the woman's page of the *New York Tribune* and later the *Ladies' Home Journal.* In her

*Women's Ways of Earning Money,* she rallied "progressive womanhood" to enter new fields of endeavor, as she herself had done throughout her life ("It is my firm belief that every woman not an invalid can
earn her own living if she really wants to do so"), and praised wage-
earning women for their intelligence as well as their womanly virtues.
"Though I often had to prove by my work what would have been taken
for granted in a man," wrote Westover, "my sober judgment is that
they [wage-earning women] are rather above the average of their sex,
not merely in mental keenness but in gentleness, dignity and strength.
They are not injured by business contact with men." In the preface to
the book, her editor described her as a "breezy, confident, and reassuring" woman who could show other women that if they wanted to
achieve distinction and receive salaries, they must not be afraid to work
hard, "in the open, as men do."

Certainly Westover had earned money in more varied occupations
than almost any other woman in America. Her editor listed them in
the introduction to Westover's *Women's Ways of Earning Money:*
"cooking for sixteen farm hands on a Western ranch, teaching a
borderland school, singing in church and concert, 'matron' in a great
tent factory, superintendent in a metropolitan candy factory, inspec-
tress in the New York Customs House, Secretary in the Street Cleaning
Department, a busy reporter with note-book and camera, as editor on
a daily newspaper." She omitted mention of the street-cleaning invention, perhaps because Westover had earned no money from it.

In her later years, after Westover and her husband moved to Brooklyn (where he worked on the *Brooklyn Eagle*), she devoted most of her
time to the Sunshine Society, a charitable group active on behalf of
blind babies. Unfortunately, the Sunshine Society was more ardent in
its sympathies than it was punctilious in its accounts, which was to
cause Westover considerable trouble, though even a man with the soul
of an accountant should have known better than to call her integrity
into question. When a member of a public accounting firm not only
testified to the society's sloppy bookkeeping practices but implied that
the books had been "willfully altered" for Mrs. Alden's personal benefit, a claque of outraged Sunshiners rose as one and shouted, "Shame!
Shame!" at the traitor. When he attempted to apologize to Westover,
she gave him no quarter: "I do not care to have an apology. God in His
time will attend to Mr. Suffern." Poor bookkeeping, however, was

intolerable, and Westover agreed, through her lawyer, to "rearrange the bookkeeping system in any manner satisfactory to state authorities." She emerged unscathed, and years later, at her death in 1931, her hometown newspaper hailed her numerous careers—naturalist, musician, linguist, city employee, inventor, journalist, and philanthropist— and called them a remarkable achievement for a time "when careers for women were extremely rare."

They would not have been rare if that other remarkable career woman, Charlotte Smith, had had her way. Unfortunately, however, by the turn of the century Smith was losing the shaky hold she had on some of her constituency. Even some of her most ardent supporters must have flinched at one of her proposed solutions for redressing society's wrong's—a law to compel men to marry so that women who could not support themselves alone could avail themselves of their husband's income. The *New York Times* blasted her plan as "extravagantly grotesque," branded her loyal followers "shrieking sisters," and put Smith down as a "flamboyant reformer . . . whose theories and whims have made a lot of 'good stuff' for the sensational press." Undaunted, the next year Smith attacked the government for erecting statues and buildings to commemorate men's achievements while ignoring women's, and she proposed and was granted a meeting to map out plans for a permanent Washington exhibit "to show the world that woman possesses Industry, Inventive genius [and] is skilled in the Arts, versed in Science, and proficient in Manufacture." The session was presumably one of the many activities cancelled when a snowstorm paralyzed Washington for several days—"presumably" because the local press made no mention of it. Smith faded from the press but apparently not from the Patent Office, for files of the commissioner of patents in the last decade of the century yield several memoranda that she either brought or sent to keep the commissioner abreast of her activities on behalf of needy women. With her credibility diminished by the negative reaction to her more eccentric proposals, however, Smith had lost her effectiveness as a spokeswoman for women inventors.

Luckily, someone else moved into the breach—a woman of the cloth. In 1899 Mary Livermore introduced the Reverend Ada C. Bowles to speak to the members of the Fortnightly of the Massachusetts Woman Suffrage Association, not on spiritual matters but on the topic she had researched for twelve years—"Women as Inventors." Bowles, a schoolteacher at fifteen and a newspaper writer until her marriage to a minister at twenty-two, had herself begun to fill vacant pulpits a decade later. After being first licensed only to preach, she was fully ordained at the age of thirty-six in Marlborough, Massachusetts, in 1872, the same year that *Woman's Journal* published its first issue in Boston. Though she and her husband later moved to Pennsylvania before eventually returning to Massachusetts, she remained close to the Boston feminists, coming to know especially well those who, like herself, traveled on the lecture circuit on behalf of the Women's Christian Temperance Union. Bowles's lectures touched on many subjects other than temperance, one of her most popular being "Strong-Minded Housekeeping," a plea to women to dispatch their domestic chores in a trice and use the time saved to work on behalf of social causes, especially suffrage. The triumvirate of authors who brought forth the monumental *History of Woman Suffrage*—Stanton, Anthony, and Gage—attested to Bowles's forcefulness and effectiveness by calling her work "striking evidence of the growing self-assertion of the sex."

In speaking before the Fortnightly, Bowles, like other feminists before her, cited examples from the dawn of history to contemporary patents to furnish what she called irrefutable proof that woman was endowed with the inventive faculty. Her lecture was punctuated with stories of several successful inventors, including Harriet Hosmer, who had sculpted Queen Isabella for the Chicago fair. Hosmer's mechanical skills were the kind women needed, said Bowles, and made the case for giving schoolgirls courses in manual training. At the close of that first lecture, Livermore rose to tell the audience that many women *had* invented but didn't get credit and mentioned that a general with whom she worked during the Civil War personally knew many women whom scheming men robbed of their inventions. Henry Blackwell, Lucy Stone's husband and one of the main sources of financial support for *Woman's Journal*, told of a shipbuilder who made a fortune by implementing his wife's suggestion to use copper rather than iron nails in the iron sheathing of his boats. The enthusiastic response of her audience guaranteed that "Women as Inventors" would become a staple in the repertory of speeches Bowles delivered to church auxiliaries, suffrage meetings, and women's clubs for the next decade.

Now seasoned propagandists, the feminists forwarded copies of her speech to the press, and various periodicals, including *Scientific American* and the *New York Tribune*, adapted much of it for their own articles on the subject. In its coverage, the *Tribune* included a graceful admission that, contrary to the common assumption that women submitted the most outrageous schemes to the Patent Office, "[i]n this respect the women inventors do not differ from the men" and repeated Bowles's favorite anecdote of her encounter with an old Vermont farmer who asked her testily: "You women may talk of your rights, but why don't you invent anything?" She shot back: "Your horse's feed bag and the shade over his head were both of them invented by a woman." When the laconic Vermonter countered, "Do tell!" Bowles squared her shoulders and retorted, "Yes, I *do* tell, and I think it is good to tell these things." Wherever Bowles went, she told "these things."

The unnamed *Tribune* writer decried the "great amount of ignorance of the inventive genius of women" but contributed to it himself by alleging that women had only *recently* entered the field, that before 1860 they had taken out "scarcely half a dozen" patents, a figure less than a fourth of what the Patent Office's own lists indicated. (I call the writer male, regardless of what reporter was responsible for it, since the entire article is taken almost word for word from one written by George Ethelbert Walsh and published three months before in *Patent Record*). This kind of statistical error, which the lists of women inventors were intended to eliminate, was bad enough in that it was being perpetuated by apparently well-meaning writers like the *Tribune* journalist. But it was far worse coming from the pens of those who used statistics to undermine women's competence at anything beyond childbearing.

If the nineteenth century was "woman's century," as Livermore and Willard referred to it in *A Woman of the Century*, then why did most of society still question women's ability? Could it be "woman's century" when Iowa University Professor G. T. W. Patrick could still write at its close, in *Popular Science Monthly*, that the small number of women patentees didn't surprise him one bit. Women, said he, were "less adapted to the plodding, analytical work of science, discovery, or invention" and therefore pursued "old rather than new lines." Then came his clincher: "Her tendency is toward reproduction, while man's is toward production."

It was obvious that society's lesser expectation for girls began in the crib, an expectation that hadn't changed much since 1876, when a feminist noted: "When a little girl opens her bright eyes in the sunlight, there is no variety of options." Two decades later, Frances Willard sadly noted little progress: "When we see a boy the question instantly springs up, 'What are you going to do?' but when we see a girl it is 'What are you going to be?' " Those two questions, asked so early, she warned, cast the die for a child's destiny.

Women could be forgiven for concluding that, although they had come a long way, they had certainly not *arrived.*

# 10

## PATENTING
## KNOW-HOW

*B*y the end of the century it was clear that, though women as a class had not yet arrived, women inventors who dared to take the patenting plunge had gained a knowledge of business and a sense of independence that few other women of the period enjoyed. Gradual state-by-state removal of legal barriers not only gave married women patentees the right to sell patent rights without spousal approval but also allowed them to keep their own earnings. Both were strong incentives for them to enter the business world. Energized by their own ambition, initiative, tenacity, and aggressiveness—traits most of society still regarded as pushy or defeminizing—they were supported by their sister inventors, catered to by a variety of women's rights groups plying their own agendas, and encouraged by those whose business depended upon invention—from patent lawyers to publishers of technical magazines.

Among the inventors themselves were a surprising number of editors, writers, journalists, prominent clubwomen, and community leaders who had inventions of their own—Cynthia Westover Alden being a prime example—and who were eloquent in their advocacy of greater opportunities for their gender. The support of the suffragists continued to be unwavering, if not always to the liking of the inventors, since it often took the form of bemoaning the fact that so few were engaged in such work, which they attributed to women's lack of political power, and belittling inventions of a domestic nature, which they viewed as further evidence of women's imprisonment within a narrow sphere. Although women inventors might have preferred more of an emphasis on the positive (and therefore welcomed the efforts of Charlotte Smith and Ida Tarbell to establish that the number of patenting women was actually much higher than generally supposed), still they were glad of the excellent coverage their inventions—particularly those of a non-domestic nature—received in suffragist newspapers and tracts. The suffragist press not only reported the news about women's inventions but encouraged other "right-thinking" women to buy their products and even apprised potential patentees of commodities ripe for invention, including domestic ones. This hint appeared in *Woman's Journal:* "Cannot some of our women devise an overshoe that will keep our feet dry when we are compelled to be out in the rain? I for one should consider such a shoe a great boon." In return, suffragists hoped that the news they purveyed of successful inventors, whose natural abilities society's preconceived expectations had not squelched, would tempt the timid to bolt from their restricted spheres and to aspire to business careers.

Help also came from magazines devoted to mechanics and invention whose publishers appreciated that articles on women inventors would likely attract women as subscribers and, once they patented, as advertisers. These magazines were sources not only of publicity but also of information and advice, which helped inventors to become more sophisticated about what they invented and more knowledgeable about shepherding their products through the patenting process. *Patent Record* advised prospective patentees to conduct thorough searches in the state of the art: "The more intimate a woman becomes with the history of past inventions, the better prepared she will be for making suitable inventions herself." *Scientific American*—for whose Munn & Company offshoot Judge Charles Mason, former commissioner of patents, became legal advisor—continued to publish advertisements of lawyers and agents.

Most of the advertisements in such invention magazines also appealed to inventors of both genders by using get-rich-quick tales. Typically, one of Washington's largest patent agencies, Victor Evans and Company, solicited: "Have You Ever Made . . . An Invention? Of Course You Have! There are so many things in everyday life that could be made to work better by a little study that you must have thought of ways of improving them. If you have done anything of that kind WHY DON'T YOU GET A PATENT?" After disposing of reservations about expense ("[Y]ou may be able to sell it the day after its receipt for fifty thousand"), about simplicity ("[T]he idea of protecting the toes of boys' boots with copper tips was childishly simple, but it paid the inventor half a million dollars"), and about risky investment ("Investing in a patent on a useful invention, no matter how simple, may return you a hundred thousand the first year"), Evans & Company promised to return the fee if it didn't secure the patent and to advertise the product in *Patent Record* if it did. It prodded readers to write for further information—wouldn't cost a dime.

*New Ideas,* first published in August of 1895, made a special appeal to women, noting in its inaugural issue that it hoped its readers would be "active, energetic men and women in all branches of human activity" and introducing in its next issue the column "New Ideas for Ladies," which became a special feature. Though the column described new inventions by and for women, it also carried stories of women working in unusual fields. The various sections of one column, for instance, carried these subheadings: "Court Stenographer," "A Girl Sculptor," "A Woman Invents a Tire," "Lady Inventor," "A Versatile Inventor," and "An Expert Woman Telegrapher." Another editor of the column encouraged women with: "The statement that women are defective in inventive talent is so often given the lie that it should be relegated to obscurity along with the other fallacies of space writers"; and couldn't curb a bit of self-congratulation: *"New Ideas* has stirred up the lady inventors in a remarkable degree, or else the 'new woman' is forging rapidly to the front of the way at the Patent Office." After scanning the most recent list of patents granted and finding thirteen women's names, the "New Ideas for Ladies" columnist added—not so modestly—that so many were for devices suggested in the magazine's own "Patents Wanted" column, that "[w]e feel justified in believing that *New Ideas* had something to do with it." The column then published the names of the thirteen women and their inventions. The column also dispensed advice. Inventors should avoid sour grapes when another made a fortune from an idea one thought was one's own, it

A favorite magazine for inventors.

Columns such as this in *New Ideas* magazine spurred women to invent.

advised. "Remember," cautioned the editor, "the latter knew how to present the new idea to the public, while it never occurred to the former."

In its efforts to seek clients for its best advertisers, *New Ideas* flogged readers' interest with stories like the one about the client who reaped colossal returns because of O'Meara & Company's "liberal, honest, and strongly in the interest of their clients" methods of doing business. O'Meara & Company also made its own direct appeals to women in its Patent Guide, "The Inventor's Head," and since it required no models and only a rough lead pencil sketch and a description ("that anyone can make") from which the company would make "the most elegant Patent Office drawings and specifications [you] have ever seen," it presumably had a special attraction for women with limited capital. In return for giving O'Meara one's patent business, one received a list of prospective capitalists, manufacturers, and dealers who could be helpful when it came time to sell the patent rights. Like Munn, O'Meara's "spacious offices" were, not surprisingly, "directly across from the United States Patent Office." That must have been a busy corner, indeed, for, in addition to Evans, O'Meara, and Munn, C. B. Steele and

Using a sewing machine to sharpen a knife.

Company, "Counsellors-at-Law and Attorneys for Inventors" and publishers of "Inventor's Circular," also crowed about their preferred location "opp. Northwest Corner U. S. Patent Office."

Specifically fishing for women clients, at least one lawyer accommodated them by substituting "Inventress" for the customary "Inventor" on their applications; *Industrial Review* also cast its net their way: "The lady readers of *Industrial Review* will be interested . . ."; *Patent Record* devoted space to advising its "clever women inventors" that "[o]ther women brain workers may at times indulge in dreaming or theorizing, but the woman inventor, however high the flights of her fancy, must always come back to the practical"; *Inventive Age*, whose editor, James Dubois, had been commended by Charlotte Smith for his "courtesies extended to us in giving a list of the women inventors that

Or to beat an egg.

came under his observation," proclaimed that "the door of invention admits her [woman] to a wide field of useful employment where she is in absolute equality with men."

Solicitations for women clients appeared in more than invention magazines, for, according to publisher Edward Bok of *Saturday Evening Post,* an examination of all magazine subscription lists showed that by 1890 seven eighths of the subscribers were women, an astonishing statistic even when one realizes how many magazines dealt with the home. Thomas P. Simpson, a Washington, D.C., agent, for example, placed an advertisement where he knew it would catch a woman's eye—in *Domestic Monthly*: "No pay asked for patent until obtained. Write for Inventor's Guide." Several patent attorneys placed ads in the magazine *Success*, edited by Orison Swett Marden, whose will-to-success philosophy made the magazine a practical guide to the techniques used by prominent men and women to achieve success in fields ranging from business to philanthropy. It had a woman as assistant editor and such feminist contributors as Mary Livermore, Julia Ward Howe, and Frances Willard. No wonder patent attorneys thought to place ads in such a venue.

When a woman needed more than legal advice, she might try to find a sympathetic mentor, and it was in this spirit that Leonie Callmeyer of Madison, New Jersey, sent a sketch of her toy boat, whose rocking motion she hoped to drive by electricity, to inventor Oberlin Smith, the prominent New Jersey mechanical wizard who was president of the Society of Mechanical Engineers, author of numerous articles in technical journals, and, probably most important to Callmeyer, an advocate of women's rights whom Charlotte Smith had cited favorably in *Woman Inventor*. According to James Gandy, a scholar familiar with Smith's technical skill and his advocacy of woman suffrage, Callmeyer undoubtedly felt that Smith's interest in women would guarantee a sympathetic ear and a respectful evaluation of her proposed invention. Smith indeed took time to study her drawing, explained that it would take some time to perfect and manufacture, but judged it "would make a pretty toy and one which probably might sell." He cautioned her to make a thorough search to assure that her idea was indeed new and to allow several weeks to prepare her application and from one to six months for the Patent Office's reaction, "this delay being due to the niggardliness of Congress in providing the Patent Office with sufficient funds to carry on its business properly."

Smith also generously suggested a better location for the power source ("a small battery located and concealed in the base") and a possible manufacturer: "In general, if you wish to invest some capital in starting into the manufacture of a thing of this kind, the best way would be to go to the makers of such apparatus, such as Queen & Co.

of Phila., or the Novelty Electric Co., 30 N. 4th Street, Phila., who would doubtless be able to put it into practical shape for you." While no record exists of Callmeyer's letter of response, she apparently became so excited after experimenting with his suggestion for using an on-off switch to activate a pair of electromagnets that she believed she had discovered perpetual motion, for in a subsequent letter Smith soberly scotched such a conclusion by pointing out that two metals attracted each other only because of stored power. "Perpetual motion," he clarified, was "an absurdity," for "Dame Nature is very shrewd and declines to be cheated every time." When one notes the comment in *Patent Record* a few years later that "[o]ne or two women have even sent in models for machines claiming to solve the mystery of perpetual motion, but as the Patent Office has excluded all patents of this nature from consideration, the applications were rejected," one wonders if perhaps Callmeyer's application was one of those. No record exists of a patent for her toy, but within a few years, showing that ingenuity was not a switch to be turned off, she patented an ingenious means for detecting whether or not someone had opened a sealed envelope.

Most women felt that a patent attorney, though not required, would guide their applications more effectively than an agent, and by the end of the century, they could even retain the first woman patent attorney, Edith Griswold. Griswold learned mechanical drawing at New York Normal College, where she studied civil, mechanical, and electrical engineering and learned mechanical drawing. The firm of patent lawyers where she worked as a draftsman urged her to attend law school, and after graduating from New York University Law School, she opened an office on Lower Broadway and registered to practice in Washington so that she could also represent her clients at the seat of patent power. A writer interviewing Griswold in 1899 for the "About Successful Women" column in *Success* noted that the prosperous attorney whose unswerving drive propelled her to the top of her profession was particularly "tall and well formed," the result, said Griswold, a practicing dress reformer as well as an attorney, of discarding her corsets. Despite patent law's hard work and long hours, Griswold recommended her profession as a far more lucrative business for talented and capable women than hammering typewriter keys. She told others aspiring to enter such an unusual field:

> I think I would not have been in this business to-day, except that I
> always had a natural taste for mathematics and mechanics. When I
> was graduated from Normal School in 1883, I went to a school where
> girls are taught civil engineering. Within three months, I was teach-
> ing a class of boys in trigonometry! I don't know whether boys
> fancied a woman teaching or not, but I enjoyed showing them that
> there are a few things that they can learn from our sex.

In their eagerness to receive patents, women viewed postponement or
outright rejection of their applications as vexatious but surmountable
roadblocks, and when necessary, they reexplained, amended, compromised, wheedled, whimpered, accused, and as a last resort, rolled out
big political guns to guide their applications through the dense under-
growth of bureaucracy. A good many tried to leapfrog over examiners'
heads to reach the commissioner of patents himself, but the latter
routinely forwarded such pleas to the examiners. The few applications
that various commissioners dealt with personally are still in their files,
mute testimony to inventor outrage, resourceful promotion, and artful
maneuvering.

Though most applicants relied upon attorneys familiar with procedures to draw up formal "specifications," some saved the fifty-dollar
standard fee and banked on "How to Patent" books; a few even
expected the Patent Office itself to reframe applications into a form
acceptable to the examiners. If a hitch developed, inventors often
either dumped their local lawyers in favor of Washington counsels,
discharged them for incompetence or chicanery, or reverted to handling their own cases.

Clara Ellsworth of Cincinnati retained a Cincinnati attorney to
forward her application for a "ventilated collar for ladies' neckwear,"
an application on which she had firmly replaced the "himself" with
"herself" in the phrase "verily believes himself to be the original, first,
and sole inventor of the new and useful improvements." When the
examiner ruled against her, she dismissed her Ohio attorney in favor
of one from Washington, who, she thought, could pilot her application
through the treacherous reefs and shoals, but the examiner still insisted
her patent was too similar to other neckwear improvements already
patented. Ellsworth then wielded what political clout she could muster
by persuading her Ohio senator to champion her cause. Senator Joseph
B. Foraker, wary of encroaching upon executive branch affairs but

cognizant of his obligations to his constituent, explained to the commissioner that Ellsworth could market the collar only if she secured the patent and discreetly asked "if there is any likelihood of her application being acted upon in the near future." Three days later the examiners allowed her claims; within a month, the patent was issued.

Dora Rencher attempted a similar approach with Congressman William King of Utah, who asked the commissioner to forward to him copies of patents the examiners had used to support their denial of his constituent's "Dress-cutter" application. The commissioner, obviously accustomed to taking special care of congressional requests, passed the letter to the examiners, who responded that though the application had been "exceedingly informal" (apparently a Patent Office buzzword for a loving-hands-at-home-styled request), the reason for the denial of patent was that it "showed no originality of invention." Sorry, no patent.

Lulu Murphy of Gold Hill, Nevada, disappointed that her state's Senator Newlands had not obtained favorable action, wrote straight to the White House. It was not the President who was her quarry, however, but the First Lady. Describing herself as the outraged member of a family who had fought in every war since the Revolution ("I am poor, through no fault of my own, though connected with the best people in our country"), Murphy went on to describe her invention, which was an emergency ration compound of powdered milk combined with coffee and sugar to which only hot water needed to be added. The White House referred the letter to the secretary of the interior, and he to the commissioner, but despite Murphy's protestations that, as "the mother of sons raised to be brave and noble enough to face death to keep our standing as the First Nation of the globe" she should be granted patent protection, the examiners rejected her application on grounds that she had disclosed neither the "proportions" nor all the steps—key requirements for patenting—and that a British invention preceded her application.

Patent attorneys themselves were not above name-dropping to sway the commissioner of patents. In his query to Commissioner Duell about the rejection of the application of a Mrs. Benjamin (whom he did not further identify) for a spool and needle holder, a property his client could sell if she had the patent, a lawyer name-dropped that his good friend *Speaker Reed* (which he underlined for further emphasis) assured him that the commissioner would "do whatever [he] can properly do for the matter." Patent records of the next five years show that no Mrs. Benjamin received a patent. Miss Letitia Geer of New York, "very much discouraged since receipt of the last office communication," persuaded her attorney cousin to ask the commissioner (addressed as "Friend Duell") to reverse the patent examiners' objection that her "handle to medical syringes" was too similar to a German one. Edward Geer, arguing that the foreign patent worked on a "diametrically opposed principle" from his cousin's, may have laid the groundwork for her receipt of a patent three months later, but though both of the above case letters are among the commissioner's papers rather than in the patent application file where most of them went, there is no evidence of the commissioner's influence in either the denial or acceptance.

Since ineffective attorneys and agents ran the gamut from unethical behavior to negligence to outright larceny, disappointed applicants considered them fair game and took their complaints to the top. In response to one complaint, the Patent Office reprimanded a company that called itself "The National Patent Office" for leading clients to assume it was the official agency. Another seething citizen sent this flyer to the patent commissioner as an example of an agency luring clients by advertising virtually automatic patents:

> Send me your inventions. I will get your patents for you. Thousands of inventors make out their applications, and wonder why they don't get their patents. It is because their attorneys do not tend to their business. . . . I have the advantage of a knowledge of the inside workings of the Patent Office possessed by a very few, which is of course all turned to the benefit of my clients.

Two women who ascribed the rejection of their patents to attorney negligence were hopping mad. Roxsey V. Hicks of Pittsburgh, Pennsylvania, asked the commissioner about her application for a "collapsible luggage carrier" since her attorney "seems never to give any satisfaction as to what the actions on it are and I am very anxious to know for fear I might lose it as I did another one. Please let me know if you have received it and how it is progressing." No patent was forthcoming. Ohioan Katie Miller sought vengeance against an attorney who, though dismissed, still pretended to be a member of a prominent Saint

Louis legal firm. While that firm acknowledged that he used to work for them, "[h]is 'carryings on' have been so disgusting and revolting to us that we are loth to drag our names into it, even to make this complaint." Katie Miller was not "loth," however, and grumbled that the miscreant had fleeced her of the twenty dollars she had sent for her application fee and that she had to come up with another in order to get in under the wire of the Patent Office deadline. Though she obtained the patent, she demanded restitution from the wayward attorney.

Margaret Chase DeForest's husband asked the commissioner on her behalf to track down the "Shaft Supporter for Carriages" application she had entrusted to her lawyer, who, according to his wife's charitable judgment, "must be absent-minded, as his standing was considered very good at the time she employed him." Did the commissioner have any idea where the lawyer was? Since the name of Mrs. DeForest never appeared on the patent rolls, the answer was apparently negative.

In addition to letters from cousins and husbands on behalf of woman applicants, the commissioners' files yield a letter from a wife about her husband's patent. Demanding that the commissioner investigate alleged bribery by attorneys who kept "on the good side of the examiners . . . [by paying] unscrupulous examiners . . . a good annual fee," she added this warning: "Please keep this private as my husband would be much annoyed at the liberty I take in addressing you."

Though some lawyers were indeed unscrupulous, self-representation also carried its own hazard. Josephine Holmes's case is a classic example. With high hopes for her special insulated grip or holder for irons, she forwarded her application and within a month received a rejection that advised that three other patents for similar objects predated hers, blamed her for a too "informal" and "unofficial" oath, enclosed a copy of "Rules of Practice," and advised her to "secure competent assistance" to prosecute her application. Holmes, a recent Norwegian immigrant, had not only mistakenly believed that her gender robbed her of becoming a citizen ("My brothers of age are citizens—because of sex. I enjoy no such honor") but also that without citizenship she could not take the oath that she was the sole inventor of the iron. Learning that she was not proscribed from taking the oath, she promised that if it were returned she would execute it "faultlessly." After still another rejection, Holmes, by then conversant with "Rules of Practice," railed at the examiner's suggestion that she stop representing herself and hire an attorney: "All my money being earned by no easy labor as an ironer, I can ill afford to pay fifty dollars as asked to 'secure competent assistance.' " The beleaguered examiner still couldn't make head or tail of the application: "The language of the applicant's specification and claims is confused and ungrammatical making it difficult to understand. . . . See Rule 45." One can almost hear Holmes ruffling through the manual.

Having amended her claims slightly and treating the examiner as someone whose intelligence was, at best, marginal, Holmes explained that her iron was extremely simple, in no way similar to the two to which he had likened it, and she enclosed an illustration of her holder in actual use. Sniffing that in all her "extensive acquaintance with the laundry business in Sioux City, Chicago, New York, and Philadelphia," she had never met anyone who liked the holders the examiners described, she added, "I put myself hard to work to supply this deficiency, or great want, for my own private use; without having seen or knowing the existence of any of the patented holders to which you have directed my attention."

By the end of the first year's correspondence, the examiner apparently threw in the towel and decided to give the applicant the benefit of the doubt, and he simply dictated the words he would accept in an amended application. That should have been the end of it, but Holmes, unwilling to compromise by accepting his wording, wrote directly to the commissioner: "If you will pardon my humble opinion, *anyone* skilled in this line knows my handle is the best. . . . I can name dozens of friends here who would be very reluctant indeed to part with or work without my holder." She surmised the examiner never got the "full and comprehensive idea" of her invention since it was "at best but a small affair" and her application was "among a large lot of other papers through which he must hurriedly pass."

When the examiner once again urged the obdurate inventor to seek competent help, she reluctantly accepted the wording he had proposed she use—but still complained: "I have to state that inasmuch as I cannot afford to employ an attorney to prosecute my case, I have adopted the only alternative left me." The patent for the sad-iron holder, such as it was, was granted April 23, 1883. Designed for small "polishing irons" as well as the larger "smoothing irons," it boasted two pieces of wood hinged together and covered with a protective soft chamois or sheepskin leather tacked around the wood handle to protect the ironer's hands (since wool does not conduct heat). Holmes, however, had one more letter in her!

Correctly suspecting that her previous letters to the commissioner had been rerouted to her examiner, "where that would be the last of it," she vented her anger to the commissioner's boss, the secretary of the interior. She charged that the examiner was trying to feather his own nest through kickbacks from the Washington lawyer to whom he had referred her, despite the fact that she knew perfectly well how to state her own claims. This deportment was certainly "not in accordance with the strict, just, and honorable rules of the Patent Office." Further, suspecting that someone had destroyed her earlier letters, she intoned ominously, "copies can be furnished." As if to bear out this warning, an almost identical letter, dated four months later, still reposes in the commissioner's files. The commissioner obviously brought her letter to the attention of the examiner, who attached this exculpatory note:

> The case as originally presented was very defective, without letters of reference to design and the different parts of the device. The description meager and without reference to the drawing or descriptive parts shown, the oath was informal and the specific [?] without any claim for the parts deemed 'new.' [These] imperfections were pointed out to the applicant, but obviously with little effect.

The inventors' reliance upon patenting to deliver them from financial despair resonates in their entreaties to the commissioners to intervene on their behalf, and Marie Merganthaler's anguish, certainly unique to her in its voice, is not atypical in its content. She applied for a patent for a "tab" that attached children's waists to another garment, having already contracted with a prominent manufacturer to make them, but he reneged when the patent was denied. According to the examiners, Merganthaler's device was too similar to those patented by two other inventors, who also happen to have been women—Laura Cooney, who had patented an attachment for suspenders, and Agnes Harris, for a garment supporter. At a stalemate with the examiners, Merganthaler poured out her financial woes to the commissioner:

> If you only knew how I am situated financially, not *one dollar* I can call my own, and nothing but debts staring me in the face, and no prospects of any one helping me along. No end of sickness in my household, which you well know takes a hold of the hard earnings of a good husband who was always willing to give up his money for this patent which we lived in hopes of getting. Oh, how I wish, and pray, you would change your mind and *grant* me the allowance. . . . Please have pity for a poor woman. . . . If I wasn't in such *dreadful need*, and a sick woman I would not want to trouble you.

The commissioner's secretary noted on the outside of the letter only: "Ansd. April 21, 1900," giving no indication of the outcome, but from a later Merganthaler communication and her patent application file, one learns that her petition was again denied. Almost a year later, the inventor reminded the commissioner of her previous letter, explained she had had to file a new application for a "new combination never before used by others," bragged of the effectiveness of her device ("If this tab was not good for anything, *everybody* would not be asking for it, as they do"), and declared that the manufacturer must have learned about her process through "collision [*sic*] with a Patent Office employee" who had allowed the manufacturer access to "room 105," where the application was kept. In sum, it was an inside job.

Feeling that her fiscal plight might engender more action than allegations of official betrayal, she concluded her letter with the former:

> I beg of your good kindness, to grant me this *patent*, as I am the *first and sole owner* and inventor of this tab. . . . I am perfectly honest in my appeal to you, and only ask what is really *mine* and belonging to nobody else. . . . I am *very much in need*, and one kind deed from you will help me and my *family*. . . . If you let me have the allowance, will you return this letter to me, as a *keepsake*. I hope I can look at it with *pride* in *future years*, and know just by explaining my case to you, brought me my fortune and happiness with my dear family.

The Patent Office was immune to such imprecations; so the "new combination never before used by others" must have been persuasive on its own. Nine months later, Merganthaler received the patent, with her attorney as co-patentee, obviously as a fee. The letter that she hoped to have returned as a "keepsake" of her plucky fight, alas, resides in the commissioners' records at the Federal Records Center but is incorporated here to memorialize her struggle.

Getting a patent was one thing; successfully marketing the product was another, especially when some of the very women who had the economic means to market were the same ones who cringed over such self-promotion. Though earlier feminists hoped they had put the issue to rest, most of society still considered that a woman's engaging in business signaled her husband's inability to support his wife and would cause both to lose caste. Ellen Demorest, inventor and chatelaine of Demorest's chic New York emporium, tried to spur women on, urging them to disregard such qualms: "A woman thoroughly educated in math, with some natural business qualification and minus the pride as to a woman's being in business, may choose her own position in the world. It is not want of ability to make money with most women who need to maintain themselves, but false pride."

Similarly, Mary Livermore, who had long maintained that marriage was not the *"only* legitimate business of women," argued that women should receive training to endow them with the "firmness and fibre . . . to stand on their own feet, self-supporting, happy in themselves, and helpful to the world." This was easier for Livermore to say than for most women, for she enjoyed the support of an extraordinary husband. When his wife was considering a career as a traveling lecturer at the age of fifty-one, he rendered this unusual spousal vote of confidence: "It is preposterous for you to continue baking and brewing, making and mending, sweeping, dusting, and laundering, when work of a better and higher order seeks you." Admitting that it would take two or three women to do what housework she did alone, he added fondly, "You need not forsake your home, nor your family; only take occasional absences from them, returning fresher and more interesting because of your varied experiences."

Livermore's experience was exceptional. In fact, such deviation from the conventional domestic arrangements was as suspect at the close of the century as it had been two decades before, when, as Sarah Stebbins noted in *Demorest's Monthly* in 1876, men feared that if women engaged in concerns beyond their homes they would lose their femininity. The regressive Stebbins approvingly described such femity as "weakness that looks for protection" and makes women "the charm, the delight, and the lodestones of the hearts and homes of men."

Circumstances hadn't changed much since then. If a woman fretted or grieved in her cage, she was faulted for chafing at her lot and jeopardizing her protected status, and it didn't help that self-proclaimed experts like the author of "The Psychology of Woman" in *Popular Science Monthly* were still, in 1898, deeming woman's childbearing and rearing responsibilities "too sacred to be jostled in the struggle for existence" and her "passivity and calmness" too delicate to be "plunged too suddenly into duties demanding the same strain and nervous expenditure that is safely borne by man." Reflective women wondered if perhaps passivity, calmness, and softness masked dependence, if charm were not a trade-off for competence, if being a lady required exchanging opportunity for genteel poverty.

Toward the end of the century, women who had made names for themselves tried to stiffen the determination of those who hadn't. Candace Wheeler, successful both as a patentee and businesswoman, spoke from experience: "It should be as much a matter of course for a woman to be educated with reference to a profession as for a boy to prepare himself by special study for his future." Harriet Strong, an inventor singularly successful in business, counseled: "I'd train every girl so that instead of prefacing some innovation by saying, 'A man suggested this,' she would rely upon her own judgment." Margaret Knight, already a feminist superstar for inventing a paper bag–making machine in 1870, was demonstrating again how even a woman with no formal education could be as astute in business as she was creative in inventing. Teaching herself everything she needed to know about contract negotiation and licensing, the shrewd capitalist was now making handsome profits from recent patents for shoe-cutting machines she had invented for the industry that ranked second only to textiles in the number of women it employed. She combined four of those patents with those of another Massachusetts inventor in such an intricate series of remunerative settlements with Boston investors that at the end of five years she still owned "eight 24ths of each invention"— which she forthwith sold to another investor who in turn sold it to the Boston Rubber Company.

But these were unusual women for their time. Limited by centuries of protection, groomed to shrink from hardship, narrowed by their limited education and shielded from contact with public affairs, most Victorian women had little opportunity to develop the keen intuition and shrewd managerial skills needed to further their inventions. Inventor Adeline D. T. Whitney would have done well to acquire such skills. But the financial security provided by an inheritance from her father, Enoch Train, a wealthy ship merchant who had founded the packet line between Boston and Liverpool, spared her the need for them, as did the income she received from her career as a prolific and well-published author of poetry. Whitney also wrote moralistic children's stories in *Wide Awake* magazine (which had also published those of Amanda T. Jones) and children's books for Houghton, Mifflin & Company.

Being a writer of children's books, Whitney had a vested interest in having children learn to read early and well. Like many modern reading specialists, she emphasized the importance of tactile as well as visual recognition of each letter's peculiar characteristics, and to this end invented alphabet blocks with raised lettering, which teachers and parents praised elaborately and encouraged her to market. Without the prod of financial need, however, she never sought an agency or channel through which to introduce them to the public, viewing her patent instead as an anchor to windward. She told Ida Tarbell, "[I]t is there, to remain until called for." She never called for it.

Others, however, felt that prod, and feminist leaders tried to inoculate them against fear of entering business. One of the most impatient with their timidity was Frances Willard, who first earned her feminist credentials through membership in New York's Association for the Advancement of Women, which sponsored Sorosis (of which she became vice president). She later founded the largest of all women's organizations, the Woman's Christian Temperance Union, became president of it in 1878, and served as such for the remaining twenty years of her life, while using the organization's journal, *Our Union*, to propound her suffrage as well as temperance views. Like Mary Livermore, her co-author of *A Woman of the Century*, Willard was a lecturer who delivered hundreds of speeches, one of her standard being on the theme of women and business. But unlike some of the other noted feminists of her day, Willard had a way with slogans that attracted conservative women: "Protecting the home" (mainly from the evil effects of alcohol) grew to "For God and Home and Native Land," the nativist pitch designed to attract those who feared that immigrants would subvert American virtues. Having enlisted the conservatives, she tried to interest them in a life beyond the home, a life in which they were capable of earning their own money, promoting other social reforms, and gaining for themselves the ultimate political power, the right to vote. Although Willard herself supported the more radical wing of suffragists headed by Lucy Stone, she managed to skirt the briar patches of debate over their demands and to preserve the fragile bond she had established with the more tradition-minded women, at the same time that she sought to usher them into a new and more practical sphere where business and politics, she promised, need not be "unwomanly."

In her 1897 *Occupations for Women,* Willard exhorted "every true woman" to grasp firmly in her hand "an honorable bread-winning weapon with which she may hold her own in this world of relentless competition." A patent, of course, was such a weapon. Women had a special aptitude for invention, said Willard, citing no less an authority than Thomas Edison, "Mr. Inventor" himself, who admitted that "women have more fine sense about machinery in one minute than most men have in their whole existence." There was, Willard argued, nothing unsuitable about business: "If one finds it necessary to do anything for money, why not stand up squarely and face the fact and do the work that comes to be done. . . . the day is fast passing when the world will put up with poor work because it is done by the 'weaker' sex." Of all the occupations women might enter, none was more fitting than invention, for "[i]f genius is eternal patience . . . then women should be successful as inventors, for nothing requires more patience than invention."

Nor did the preponderance of men's inventions over women's discourage Willard, for women's time would come; inventing opportunities abounded in whatever milieu woman was employed. "There is always room at the top, particularly in invention," uttered the sage, who loved to support her belief that patience and persistence would always win out with the story of patient Jennie Wertheimer of Cincinnati, the "persevering little woman" bank employee whose scheme to make commercial paper for forgery-proof bank checks required long days and nights of development and supplications to thirty national paper manufacturers before she found one who would pay her a royalty for its use. Because Jennie Wertheimer had not shirked hard work, preached Willard, she achieved her goal. Inventors who didn't mind the work but lacked the capital often found it more advantageous to sell their ideas to someone else rather than to go through the patenting procedure. Since there is no record of Wertheimer having received a patent, perhaps she allowed a manufacturer to patent her process.

For those who had already received patents, invention magazines, particularly *Inventive Age* (which was inaugurated in the 1890s to capitalize on industry's need for new products in that era of rapid growth) provided a venue for communicating with prospective buyers. In its "New Patents for Sale" column, Catherine Deiner advertised the rolling pin for which she had received a patent only the month before: "Improved rolling pin is for sale. It consists of a rolling pin with an adjustable sleeve, which when placed on the pin gives the operator four cake cutters, making it possible to rapidly cut up dough into cakes without waste. It can be used in bakeries and families." In its "Novelty Manufacturers Take Notice" column, two weeks after the magazine carried a news article on her flower pot, Kate Tudor advertised: "My improved Flower Pot is worth a careful examination by manufacturers of sheet metal. Best thing out. Correspondence solicited." Two months later, she advertised: "The Whole of Patent 451, 645, issued May 5th, 1891, for Flower Holder. May be used as often as desired. Securely retains the flowers and will keep them fresh for a long time. Just the thing for use in decorating. For full information address Mrs. Kate B. Tudor, cor. Hanson and West Hanson Sts., Lexington, Ky." Luella A. Agney similarly followed up *her* news item with an ad to sell her "Bread Raising Cabinet": "Can be cheaply constructed and will sell rapidly as it is needed in every household." Texan Mrs. Mary D. McDonnell, obviously aware of the de rigueur full-busted look of the period, touted a bodice "which gives to the poorest, most undeveloped form, a tapering symmetrical figure that, in appearance, even nature cannot surpass" and hoped to sell rights or find "a partner with some capital to join me in the manufacture of said Waist."

Some aggressive businesswomen were so sure of favorable action on their patent applications that they signed up clients during the waiting period. The *Patent Assignment Digest* in the National Archives provides evidence of many such creative contracts. Mary Schneider, for example, sold Brinkmeyer Brothers of Saint Louis entire rights to her "Washing Fluid" ("a new and useful Composition of Matter for Laundry Use in Washing Clothes") for a thousand dollars fully nine months before receiving a patent. Sarah Shields sold two designs, one for a "Ladies Costume" and the other for a "Ladies' Wrap," to the Butterick Publishing Company in advance of their patent grants. The agreement to buy Lizzie Howard's "Design for Stitch or Center for Shawls" alerted buyer John Holmes that she had applied for the patent only "this day," and Holmes was fortunate that the patent did ensue, because such was not always the case. When Lucretia Hermann heard that her claims for her "journal bearings" patent had been "allowed," she enthusiastically sold the rights to two New York investors for nineteen hundred dollars. Since no patent is listed in her name, she probably had to return the money—it would depend on the terms of the contract.

Women inventors learned a good deal about sharp financial deals. Long before prolific inventor Harriet Tracy became prosperous and easily disposed of rights to her inventions for goodly sums, she consummated one of the more creative selling arrangements when she gave a mortgage deed of one-half interest in her "Folding Adjustable Stoves for Cooking" in return for payment of rent on her premises at 111 East 31st Street, New York, for the next eight months. Martha Kellogg combined the dressmaking patents of another family member with hers and sold them as a single package for seven thousand dollars. A representative of the Missouri Glass Company in Saint Louis paid Clevelander Elizabeth S. Hunt only five dollars for a patent on a jar for preserving fruits and seventy dollars for an "improved" jar, but Elizabeth Harley, whose patented darning last caused such a stir at the Centennial, sold her invention for a then whopping fifteen hundred dollars. Amelie Hackelberg and her partner sold her packing boxes to a New York company in return for a 20 percent royalty based on the selling price of the boxes, the right to purchase any boxes they wished at 15 percent off, and guarantees that the company would "use all means to promote the introduction of the invention and its applications, to advertise the same and to contract for their manufacture, use and sales and to keep full and accurate books of accounts of all boxes made or sold."

Then there were local rights. Eunice Hood, who invented a garment-cutting apparatus, negotiated a series of regional licensing agreements by selling half her rights to one person, licensing another to use the device in the state of Ohio for five years for seven hundred dollars, allowing two others free reign in two specified counties in Pennsylvania for two hundred dollars, charging another one hundred dollars for similar privileges in two Ohio counties and one in West Virginia, and selling still another the rights to the entire city and county of Philadelphia plus the whole state of New Jersey for five thousand dollars.

Texan Leonia Mabee's records are similarly intricate. For only one hundred dollars, she sold state of Texas rights to a "Bed-Drawer Attachment for Bedsteads," but later, for ten thousand dollars, she sold half her rights in all the remaining states to a Pine Bluff entrepreneur. A year later, she pledged her remaining half interest (nationwide except for Texas) in exchange for stock worth thirty-four thousand dollars to help capitalize the Mabee Extension Bed Company of Chicago. Outside investors put up the remaining sixty-six thousand dollars of the one hundred thousand she needed altogether.

After giving her attorney Wyoming rights, Eliza Harding allowed other agents to sell her "Abdominal Supporter" in specified territories. Lydia Bonney kept Chicago as her personal fiefdom for her "Undergarment for Women and Children" but sold rights for every other part of the country. Chicagoan Emily Gross allowed an agent to take over her "Improvement in Stone Pavements" only if he paid her eighty dollars within sixty days, rented a suitable office in Chicago to carry on the business, printed circulars and descriptions, brought the invention to the public, and promised to pay her 50 percent of any offers he received to purchase territories or rights.

Patentees sometimes made other provisos in assigning rights to their patents. San Franciscan Mary Blauvelt gave her husband California rights for her "Dressmakers Marking and Cutting Gage." New Yorker Susan R. Knox, who had obtained a trademark on a fluting machine that bore her own name and portrait, required several pages to record her complex partnerships with a male inventor of a similar fluting iron, several independent investors, the National Household Goods Manufacturing Company, the American Machine Company, and a marketing agency. She eventually sold her patent and trademark rights to the fluting machine and its improvements to North Brothers Manufacturing Company of Pennsylvania. Bostonian Minnie Kelch, two years after she had received a patent for her "Hand Telephone Support," found financial backing from two investors who joined her as sole shareholders in the Adjustable Telephone Support Company of New Jersey.

As has been shown in previous chapters, inventing women learned to defend themselves from rival claims, but one more example is in order. Saint Paul, Minnesota, residents Pauline Erickson and Annie Davis were pitted against each other for credit (and thus patent rights) for "inventing" a knitted infant garment. Both agreed that Davis had provided yarn to knitting ace Erickson to duplicate in knitting the chest-protecting baby garment Davis had devised in cloth. They differed, however, on the terms. Knitter Erickson argued that Davis had implied that she would share in the patent if she worked out the knitting: "If you can make it," Davis told her, "*we* will get the patent; there is money in it and it will pay you to try." Davis, to whom a prospective buyer had already offered six thousand dollars for patent rights, claimed it was a no-strings business deal: fifty cents for two weeks' knitting and "no reason under the sun" for sharing the patent with the person whose only contribution was "mechanical knitting."

When Davis tried to buy off knitter Erickson with a paltry two dollars, the latter spurned the money and blustered that by knitting, raveling, and reknitting *she* had reduced an otherwise useless invention to practical form and that by illustrating her patent application with drawings of Erickson's knitted improvements, Davis was a "crafty, designing spirit . . . [who used] artifice, false representation and base deceit." The hearings played out against a backdrop of Erickson's Knitting Guild and Ladies Aid Society members testifying like a Greek chorus: "I saw her knitting on it at our Society meeting; she said she was working on a patent"; "I stopped by her house; she was too busy working on her patent to talk to me"; "She said she was knitting this for a patent." When Erickson put into evidence her wee knitted garments, one with tiny steel needles still holding the crucial stitches, the examiners, no doubt sons of knitters, decided on behalf of the valiant stitcher whose labor had made the invention possible and gave her full rights.

By participating in each step of the entire patenting process, from application to marketing, women inventors had gained invaluable business experience. In the course of defending the originality of their concepts, suing to halt encroachment on their patents, and establishing reputations as aggressive patent-rights negotiators, they had emerged as feisty entrepreneurs, personifications of the "new woman" who would surely come into her own in the next century.

# 11

# ''NEW WOMEN''
# IN A NEW CENTURY

*A*s the twentieth century dawned, Ada Bowles was still delivering her "Women as Inventors" lecture, a particular favorite with the now ubiquitous women's organizations networking the country. Women's clubs had become the undisputed pipeline to millions. Since the day in 1899 that fifty clubs linked themselves together as founding members of the General Federation of Women's Clubs on the twenty-fifth anniversary of Sorosis, the number of clubs had climbed astronomically until in 1902 it had reached 3,358; hundreds, if not thousands, more remained unfederated. Every village had a woman's club, and cities swarmed with them. It was not at all unusual for a woman to enjoy membership in multiple clubs and attend meetings as often as her Civil War forebears had frequented their aid societies. Something was afoot, and it's no wonder that in the 1890s *Scribner's Magazine* ran a series on "The Unquiet Sex" and that in the new century's first decade former president Grover Cleveland found support—though not among club members—in imputing to clubs the subversion of women from their household interests. When he wrote in *Ladies' Home Journal,* "I believe that it should be boldly declared that the best and safest club for a woman to patronize is her home," the president of Sorosis merely chortled, "We have tipped the teapot"; but Ada Bowles sharply upbraided him in *Woman's Journal:* "Women are simply learning the lesson that men learned long ago, of the superior efficiency of organized effort over isolated individual endeavors. . . . Mr. Cleveland can no more check the march of progress in this direction than he could persuade women to cease travelling by railroad and go back to the chaises and stage-coaches of our grandmothers' day."

Though leaders of the 1890s had considered their advancement of such epic proportions that they saluted the nineteenth century as "woman's century," the beginning of the twentieth century held forth more promise—and more challenges—than ever before. With the vote still to be won, but opportunities for careers outside the home expanded, Sorosis founder and lifetime honorary president "Jennie June" Croly was entitled to savor the choices a "new woman" could make. But she was not as committed to true egalitarianism as her twentieth-century sisters would have liked her to be. "In olden times," she told an interviewer for *Success* magazine, "a young woman had no alternative but marriage or a life of domestic drudgery," a destiny that Croly, of course, deplored and had thrown her considerable talents and energies into changing. When it was a question of total emancipation, however, she hedged: Men would remain the leaders, she told *Success,* "as is proper." Such a line was exactly compatible with the tone taken by *Success,* which was always keen to publicize the accomplishments of the daring as long as it could assure its readers that such trailblazers had not forfeited their femininity in the process. The now-venerable Croly ("The crown she wears is of frosted silver, but it becomes her") was a heroine in the *Success* mold, and its pages extolled her as a pioneer of her sex who had set countless numbers of her sisters on the path to noble usefulness and had "held aloft for a whole half-century the gentle banner of woman's emancipation from her ancient chains." While not everyone wanted to hold aloft such a "gentle" banner, the general mood among reformers at the turn of the century was conciliatory in the Croly manner.

That mood was reflected in the General Federation of Women's Clubs. The conservative middle-class housewives who were the backbone of its membership devoted so many of their local club programs to cultural affairs that its national leaders almost despaired of redirecting members' energies toward national issues, among them advancing woman's equality. In 1904, the newly elected president of the General Federation made a good try: "Ladies, you have chosen me your leader. Well, I have an important piece of news for you. Dante is dead. He has been dead for centuries, and I think it is time we dropped the study of the Inferno and turned the attention to our own." Despite such pressure, most members considered clubs a social outlet rather than an opportunity to forward the goals of their sex. In taking on "good works" projects, the membership basked in the prevalent theory of women's moral superiority and was lukewarm to woman suffrage, which the General Federation didn't endorse until 1914.

The clubs were unequivocal, however, in their support of women in business. They fanned interest in women inventors by providing a platform for speakers such as Bowles to argue that it was no longer acceptable for a woman with original ideas to plead that patenting was outside her sphere, or that she could ill afford the financial risks, or that she lacked business knowledge. As one new woman proclaimed, "We have just said 'Good morning' to the new century. . . . Let it be your first duty to show the world that you are not made of air bubbles. . . . We may never be able to mould public opinion, but we may be helpful in scraping off some of the mold."

With universal suffrage still two decades away, there was plenty of mold to scrape, including the ancient fungus clinging to the Yale alumnus who planned a "sketch" on invention for the Yale Bi-Centennial Book and, in the following words, asked the patent commissioner to send him any data he might have on the part women had played: "Someone, Shakespeare, I believe, has said that women are ingenious but never invent, and I want to see whether his prognosis is confirmed by the *post mortem*." Though I am not sure, I suspect his knowledge of Shakespeare was as moldy as the commissioner of patents' math skills turned out to be. In his annual report for 1900, the commissioner, while correctly supplying the last official total of 5,535 women inventors as of March 15, 1895, misplaced the decimal when he calculated: "It is fair to estimate that out of every one thousand patents one is granted to a woman." Even as an estimate, it was not "fair." Since the cumulative number of patents issued by that date was 560,000, women's patents accounted for one out of every *hundred*, not one out of every thousand. His error would live on. Almost three decades later, Joseph Rossman (a patent examiner), in an article for the *Journal of the Patent Office Society*, compounded the commissioner's error by repeating it without correction. And variations on it would also find their way into print with some regularity, even in the writings of the supposedly well intentioned.

Perhaps aware of the commissioner's erroneous figures, *Woman's Journal* referred any doubting Thomases to the patent lists themselves: "A time-honored fallacy abroad asserts that although women may imitate, they cannot invent.... Facts indicate otherwise. The printed lists issued by the government prove women's ability along this line." The British journal *Cassier's* had also studied the patent lists and concluded that while most of the "fair sex" had invented articles of dress, cookery, or domestic economy, the "fertile brain of American womanhood" had demonstrated ingenuity of an astonishing breadth and character. When women became free to make their own way in the world and to employ their powers to the best of their ability, predicted *Cassier's*, they would become "mean rival[s] of the lordly sex."

Feminists recognized, however, that such rivalry was still a remote prospect since even the correct ratio, one out of a hundred, fueled the arguments of women's rights antagonists that physiological differences between men's and women's brains made it *impossible* for the latter to invent. It was enough to make Lillian Towslee, a well-known woman doctor, fulminate: "What woman's brain lacks in weight it may make up in finer texture. . . . Women have shown their ability in handling intricate subjects, and have taken the highest honors at the best universities in Europe and America." In addition to the ludicrous arguments of the phrenologists that it was futile to educate women because the effort was wasted on their inferior brains, it was also held that advanced education for women was dangerous, because it turned them into nervous wrecks—a theorem to which even a few women had subscribed in the previous century. There was Mary Elizabeth Wilson Sherwood, for example, a New York social luminary at one time in her life, tireless organizer of the enormous Metropolitan Sanitary Fair in 1864, and, when hard times hit, contributor of verses and stories to magazines and newspapers, as well as counselor on etiquette and manners to the newly elevated Gilded Age rich. Sherwood had recommended educating a girl only if "she were equal to it" since women were happiest in their sphere—marrying early and becoming thoroughly domestic women. "With some women brain work is impossi-

Florence Parpart's Street Cleaner, 1900.

ble," certified Sherwood, for "[i]t produces all sorts of diseases, and makes them at once a nervous wreck." To combat such arguments still making the rounds in the twentieth century, Dr. Towslee countered that education was the *remedy*, not the cause of nervousness: "A strong will, an absolute purpose, exalts the spirits, diminishes dyspepsia, hysteria, melancholia, and all diseases akin to hypochondriasis."

The large gap between education for women and men continued to distress feminists, who certainly could not have been cheered by Emma Hewitt's pronouncement (apparently meant as encouragement) in *Queen of the Home* that no special education was needed for inventing solutions to "difficulties that have baffled all efforts so far." *Patent Record* took a line similar to Emma Hewitt's, stating that while most observers attributed the increased number of women's inventions to better opportunities for girls to participate in manual training classes, the survey of women inventors it conducted showed that "daily toilers in the various lines of industry" with only limited education were more successful in inventing than those who enjoyed all the educational advantages. The magazine was not necessarily a reliable source, for it had made an egregious error in stating in 1899 that as recently as "ten years ago" a woman's name appeared on Patent Office lists no more than three or four times a year. Ten years before 221 patents had been issued to women. More mold on math skills? *Patent Record*'s error, like the commissioner's, had a life of its own: the widely read *Literary Digest* reprinted it; a *New York Post* writer gave the same figure; and *Scientific American Supplement*, in turn, reprinted the *Post* article.

Each, failing to conduct separate research, had recycled the lower figure. Perhaps *Patent Record* tried to atone the next year: "The world now realizes that there are female geniuses in our midst as well as male geniuses." No thanks to *Patent Record.*

By the turn of the century, all married women had gained property rights formerly reserved to their unmarried sisters—rights to own, manage, and dispose of their property without gaining consent of their husbands—legal rights crucial for patenting women. One inventor of the period who exploited those rights quite effectively was Florence Parpart, whom *Patent Record* (proving it wasn't *all* bad) identified as the inventor of a "[r]emarkable piece of machinery . . . now at work on the streets of New York . . . [which] performs the various functions of street-cleaning." While Cynthia Westover Alden had invented a simple dump cart a decade before, Parpart developed a more efficient sweeper, and *Patent Record* swooned over the "young and pretty" inventor who had previously invented a pneumatic corset already on the market and a collapsible boat, several hundred of which she sold to Klondike prospectors. As a newspaperwoman (another similarity to Alden), she had studied how presses printed, folded, bound, and counted newspapers as they rolled off, then applied that technology to street sweeping. A single operator could sprinkle, sweep, load, and compress dirt from two miles of street in the time it normally took twenty-five or thirty men at two dollars a day to sweep by hand. As the horse-drawn wagon moved forward, the driver pressed a foot pedal to spray water and dampen but not saturate the dust; a huge rotating broom attacked the dirt, gathered it, and rolled it up an incline to the wagon, where a powerful screw compressed it. With the entire process carried on inside a protecting apron, said *Patent Record,* no dirt scattered to the sidewalks "to the decided inconvenience of pedestrians."

Parpart, though ingenious, lacked capital to market the machine until she enlisted support from prominent New Yorker Hiram D. Layman, who backed her financially and whose name she allowed to appear ahead of hers on the patent. With his backing, she manufactured and sold the machines and engaged in street contracting businesses in New York; Boston; Chicago; Omaha; Milwaukee; San Francisco; Cambridge, Massachusetts; Camden, New Jersey; Greensburg and Altoona, Pennsylvania; and Portsmouth, Ohio. *Patent Record* expounded on the rarity of the field in which she excelled, concluding that it demonstrated that the inventive profession was "just as much adapted for the woman as man" and that a woman could accomplish great things if she set about her "self-imposed task . . . in a systematic way." She was, they agreed, a "shining example of a bright woman and worthy of emulation of the rest of her sex."

The story might rest there, but official patent lists give it a special ending. Within four years Florence Parpart was enjoying more than business benefits from her erstwhile sponsor. In a patent for an improvement of the machine, Hiram Layman's name still appeared first as co-patentee, but after Florence Parpart's name were the words: "By marriage, now Mrs. F. W. Layman." Ten years later, the Laymans co-patented a refrigerator attachment; *her* name preceded his. Four years later, he alone patented a steam radiator but assigned half rights to his wife. Five years later, in 1919, the patent list recorded that Hiram Layman's patent for a collapsible trash receptacle (half of whose rights he had again assigned to his wife) was "wholly assigned to F[lorence] P[arpart] Layman, executrix." His trash receptacle was thus his last excursion into patenting, and while such an object may not appear to be the consummate bequest, it must have seemed so to a widow who had met her intended over a street cleaner. As to whether the widow's ingenuity was rekindled after her loss, records indicate no further patents.

One would not expect Charlotte Smith, whose ardent interest in women inventors sprang from her desire to elevate the status of working women, to disappear entirely. And she didn't. She was so hopeful of the outcome of her proposal for a permanent building to exhibit women's work, including their inventions, that she was ready to distribute 500,000 pamphlets and 100,000 copies of an illustrated souvenir of Washington with the building's design on it before she learned that the funding would not go through. Discouraged with that project but ready for others, she moved to Boston, where she became as familiar a figure at the State House as she had been on Capitol Hill. Her activities there were as various as ever, ranging from a demand for a tax on bachelors to one for a tax that would enable worthy families to buy their own homes with state funds and repay them as they could.

Still president of the Women's National Industrial League, Smith organized the Woman's Board of Trade in Boston in 1907 to provide any Massachusetts woman "of good character and financial credit" opportunities to exchange and distribute valuable business information, to advance the industrial and commercial interests of its members, and, as in Washington, to exhibit women's work. Boston had a proud tradition of working women, and in lauding those pioneers, Smith did not forget the patentees among them, including Lavinia ("Madame") Foy of corset fame, once listed by *Inventive Age* as the most prolific woman patentee (for gaining ten patents between 1863 and 1878) and well known as a symbol of American women's "genius and intelligence." Smith praised Foy for rising to such business prominence that she could eventually employ two hundred girls to fill the orders for her corsets, which brought her an annual income of twenty-five thousand dollars.

Controversy continued to dog Smith in Boston as it had in Washington, for within the Woman's Board of Trade's first few weeks of existence, a group of members complained to a local newspaper writer that her organization was run for "graft" and was going "to pieces." In response, the apoplectic Smith certified that she alone had financed its start, that a mere three dissidents had been forced to resign, and that the remainder of the two hundred or so members met regularly and amicably. She castigated the papers for the villainous story and appealed to public-spirited men with practical experience as financiers, merchants, and manufacturers to help the new organization, which she characterized as "but an infant in swaddling clothes." Still complaining that there were not "husbands enough to go around" (one of her constant themes), Smith urged women to learn to support themselves, but wanted them to have as much special help as they needed to make it in the commercial world.

Also stepping into the twentieth century was *Saint Nicholas*, still under the editorship of its founder, Mary Elizabeth Mapes Dodge. Still seeking to spur children to invent, *Saint Nicholas* now invoked the glories of America's past to inspire the young to emulate their inventive forebears and stake their own positions along the continuum of "Yankee ingenuity." In "How the Government Promotes Ingenuity," part of the magazine's continued effort to foster problem-solving skills in its columns, *Saint Nicholas* reduced the awesome Patent Office to the status of a "faithful servant" happy to remit a free set of printed rules and instructions, which came complete with a pen drawing of a machine that "many a youngster with a taste for mechanics or mechanical drawing would prize." For ten cents girls and boys could obtain a full-size engraved copy of any patent's drawing and description; for five dollars (surely a cost parents would subsidize), an annual subscription to the *Weekly Patent Gazette;* for another five dollars, engraved copies of *every* new patent in a particular classification, new or old. *Saint Nicholas* announced: "Some of the bright and ambitious boys and girls of the country have already found out the ways and uses of the Patent Office, and the rest are welcome there as fast as they learn to come." Given that her son was by this time a prominent inventor, one can well imagine that editor Dodge entertained high hopes for the future inventing efforts of her magazine's readers.

As boys and girls dreamed of forwarding their ideas to the faithful servant in Washington, "patent-minded" women planned the same attack. Now caught up in the home economics movement, they logically continued to invent in the field feminists growled was already overstocked. But the same household "novelties" and labor-saving contrivances dismissed by feminists were avidly solicited in the ads for patenting agents and attorneys in the magazines. Such innovations afforded the housewife, as *Patent Record and Monthly Review* (a new name for the same magazine) put it, "all the happiness out of life that she deserves." While encouraging women with "There is no monopoly of sex in the field of invention," the same magazine simultaneously limited their field: "Few inventions are more profitable than little matters of feminine utility"; nursing was a "fine field for inventors" since "members of the fair sex are, no doubt, especially qualified by nature for those occupations which call into play the tenderer emotions and sympathies." Similarly, *New Ideas* opined: "A woman should certainly know what utensils are needed in the kitchen."

Hoping that a contest would stimulate more women to invent such household contrivances, the Boston's Women's Educational and Industrial Union offered a prize for the most ingenious labor-saving device for the home, to be judged by a two-person panel consisting of Ellen Richards, the Massachusetts Institute of Technology professor known for her work in sanitary chemistry and for founding the home economics movement, and Dwight Porter, professor of hydraulic engineering at the same institution and the editor of *American Kitchen Magazine.* In response to reader queries, *Woman's Journal* published inventors' names and products, and advised, "Doubtless any of them will be glad to tell where her invention may be had," but, unless I missed finding it mentioned, the *Journal* did not publish the grand-prizewinner's name.

Work-saving though such new gadgets might be, weary housewives could with cause complain that as long as household perfection was still considered their optimum goal, technological progress gave them no new leisure. As Anna Brackett wrote in *The Technique of Rest,* "We keep multiplying our conveniences only to multiply our cares." The situation reminded her, she added, of the old farmer who wailed as he ruefully contemplated his potato patch, "It does somehow seem as if every time a man invented a new machine to save us work, the Lord invented another bug!"

Although most women invented household gadgets, soft-spoken Birmingham, Alabama, belle Mary Anderson invented decidedly beyond the domestic perimeters. On a visit to New York to spend some of the wealth she had recently inherited from an aunt, she disregarded the cold of a frigid New York winter and climbed into a New York streetcar to survey the urban scene. The sight that touched the sympathetic Southerner most, however, was that of the shivering streetcar motorman repeatedly emerging from his car to wipe snow from the car's front glass. The problem was routine in cold weather. Before starting their runs on icy days, motormen often drew a carrot stick, half an onion, or a tobacco plug across the glass to form a film to lessen the formation of ice crystals. Engineers tried to solve the problem by splitting the windshields in the middle to allow the motorman a clearer view and provide a slot through which he could scrape off the frost by hand, but the hand still got cold. As Anderson watched the motorman performing his chilly work, she had an idea for how he could execute the task from within the shelter of the car and quickly set it down in the sketchbook she carried in her bag. Her ingenious plan allowed the motorman to manipulate a lever while remaining inside the car vestibule, which lever would in turn activate a swinging arm outside the vestibule that mechanically swept off the ice and snow. When the weather turned fair, the wiper was easily detached. Though Anderson lacked engineering training and her Alabama friends tittered that she was "oh, so impractical," she nonetheless gained a patent on her wiper, commissioned a local firm to make a model, and tried to sell rights to a prominent Montreal business. When the shortsighted company decided her invention had little commercial value, the miffed inventor, lacking both the spur of financial necessity and experience in pressing issues, pursued the idea no further and allowed the patent to expire. Lovely Southern young women were not expected to be canny businesswomen, and she wasn't.

Though Anderson never made the fortune she might have had she persevered, the story of her invention endured. Fifty years later, in her obituary, *Time* magazine couldn't resist the paradox of the nonmechanical woman who invented "the first patented windshield wiper—hand operated device for streetcars." Anderson herself never made such sweeping claims, saying only that her invention was an "improvement" over previous wipers and not a completely original concept, a fact the more cautious *New York Times* acknowledged in hedging that she was "reputed" to have invented the "original fan-shaped windshield wiper." The game Trivial Pursuit doesn't equivocate. "What woman invented a windshield wiper in 1903?" it asks. Mary Anderson is the answer.

By the next year, managers of the Louisiana Purchase Exposition, better known as the Saint Louis World's Fair, and a Board of Lady Managers consisting of twenty-three prominent matrons from every section of the nation opted to break with the tradition of having a woman's building. Activists felt that women had developed sufficiently extensive networks of their own since the last large fairs in Atlanta and Nashville that they no longer needed such a building as a place to rally women to such causes as suffrage, temperance, and dress reform. As for showing women's work separately from men's, they had come to feel unequivocally that such exhibitions always connoted inequality, the need for women's work to be judged by different—probably lower— standards. That might have been acceptable in the nineteenth century, but not in the twentieth. An *Oakland Tribune* writer explained it to her readers: "All products of feminine genius and industry, for the first time in the history of expositions, are placed on the same footing as those of the sterner sex. The same conditions and tests, the same standards of excellence that apply to man's work apply also to the work of women."

"Mainstreaming" women's inventions at the fair, so that they competed for awards in the same way women's products had to compete with men's in the marketplace, was a change most exhibit judges applauded. One called previous exposition exhibits of "the so-called strictly feminine" works too "showy" and said that Saint Louis offered a woman the opportunity to display "as she really is, the fellow-student, the fellow-citizen, and partner of man in the affairs of life." Initial enthusiasm for joint displays paled, however, the moment it became apparent that men were winning most of the prizes.

Edith Griswold, the country's first woman patent attorney and sole female judge on the awards committee of the Machinery Department, despaired that no women at all exhibited in her department, even though the Patent Office's impressive summary of women's inventions authenticated their inventive skill in machinery. Alas, she sighed, "I almost feel that the least said about women exhibitors in the Machinery Department at the Louisiana Purchase Exposition, the better." Over in Mines and Metallurgy, it was the same story: though several women had indeed patented mining and smelting processes, none volunteered a model for exhibition. A woman judge on that committee quipped that it was a question of gender roles: "In all our fairy stories, dwarfs and elves live below the earth and deal with mines and their dark belongings; the fairies live above." Another juror was irked that in the Equipment for Sewing and Making Wearing Apparel display women appeared only as machine *operators* rather than inventors even though everyone knew that many sewing machine improvements were the suggestions of women. Despite the disappointment, the doggedly optimistic president of the Board of Lady Managers thought women had shown their mettle: "[Women's] strength and powers have been tested . . . their undeniable right to education and training is being acknowledged, their consequent recognition as a factor for increased usefulness is being accorded, and their development is swift, their progress sure."

Before leaving the subject of the World's Fair at Saint Louis, I should note that Aerial, the daughter of 1880s patentees "Madame Carlotta" and Carl Myers, described by a contemporary as the "perfect compound of the studious habits of the father and the somewhat more daring characteristics of the mother," dazzled the crowds in Saint Louis by pedaling her father's inflated, cigar-shaped "Sky Cycle" through the air of a large auditorium without ever brushing against the walls or roof. Today, the legend of Aerial's earlier years lives on. *The Big Balloon Race,* a children's book published in 1981 and somewhat loosely based upon seven-year-old Aerial's trip in her mother's "basket" during a balloon race in 1884, places her on board as a stowaway whose adroit balloon maneuvers snatched victory from the jaws of defeat and thus won her mother's forgiveness for the danger her extra weight caused.

In 1905, *Woman's Journal* excitedly reported another aerial feat involving a woman. George E. Heaton, who had patented two bicycles and a railroad velocipede a few years before when he and his wife lived in Michigan, had just completed a successful test flight of his airship *California Messenger*, powered by a two-cycle, eighteen-horsepower engine that he credited to her. He bragged to the press that his wife, no novice to invention after patenting a color press used to produce color card samples for paint factories, was perfectly capable of making suggestions about a different engine:

> Yes, it was Mrs. Heaton's idea. . . . [T]he more I pondered over it the more I became convinced that she was right. We planned it together, and you see the result. Here is an engine weighing but fifty-five pounds that generates eighteen-horse power and that requires no cooling apparatus. In these essentials it is perfect. I believe that this type of engine, which my wife and I have jointly patented, will eventually be exclusively used for airships. It will also be used in automobiles.

Mrs. Heaton acknowledged that the engine was her idea but added, "Mr. Heaton perfected it so as to make it what it is today." A persistent search of patent records yields evidence of neither her color card sample nor a jointly or singly patented engine, but sometimes, either from overweening optimism or in an attempt to discourage copiers, inventors claimed *having* a patent when one had only been applied for. Patentee or not, Mrs. Heaton (probably Lizzie, since there are marriage records for a sixteen-year-old Lizzie Abraham and twenty-year-old George Heaton on July 30, 1889, in Kalamazoo, where they formerly lived) is credited with such feats of derring-do that she is included in this work to honor her sheer bravado. One of her most dramatic ventures came about by accident, when she was working on a test flight of the *California Messenger* at Oakland's Idora Park. The airship, restrained by tethering cables, rose to treetop level to allow photographers to get good shots before its final ascent. Suddenly the cables snapped and the machine soared into the sky like a rocket, bearing with it the plucky Mrs. Heaton. According to onlookers, it suddenly stopped rising, then descended "like a flash" before evening out to a slow and safe descent. When the occupant emerged from the airship, she limned this scenario of events to a reporter who translated it into an article under the headline BITES GAS BAG AND IS SAVED:

> As soon as I realized that the ropes had parted, I saw my only danger lay in the machine going toward the [San Francisco] bay. At once, I applied the rudder and steered her about. But I was going upward all the time at a terrible rate. I climbed on my seat and bit a hole in the gas bag. This split about a foot and the gas rushed out. The machine turned downward and dropped straight about eight hundred feet, but I had the presence of mind enough to stick to my seat. Then she righted and I simply steered her till I found a good place to land.

On one test flight, Mrs. Heaton watched from below as her husband rose from the very street where they lived (Park Avenue, Oakland, where he listed his occupation in the city directory as "bicycles"). The slightly built inventor climbed onto the platform dangling below the cigar-shaped bag, shouted to his assistants to cut the airship loose, and allowed it to rise about 150 feet before cutting in the engine that drove the propellers. Soaring above the anxious crowds, including his quaking wife, he sailed his airship both before and behind the wind, made complete turns with ease, and after traveling a mile from his starting point, headed home and landed in the identical site from which he had risen. In another ascent, he took his two little girls up for a short distance while his wife snapped pictures of them from below. He was elated with the performance of the airship and confident that his engine would revolutionize the manufacture of gasoline engines. Had his airship been ready for the Saint Louis Fair, he was sure he'd have won the $100,000 prize in the airship competition.

The Heatons continued to test and demonstrate the capabilities of the airship to the astonishment and delight of their rapt audiences. However, at the San Jose Fourth of July celebrations, one of Mr. Heaton's flights had an inglorious, headline-making ending when it sank in San Francisco Bay after ascending to 500 feet. He had once allowed that his ship was not designed to go above 250 feet, enough to clear the tallest buildings, and opined that that was "about as far up in the heavens as I think it is necessary to go." He was right about that—at least as far as his own craft was concerned. When rescue teams picked up Heaton, his first thought was of his wife: "I knew also that Mrs. Heaton who has been my faithful assistant in all my experiments was eagerly awaiting my return. . . . My greatest anxiety to-day was for my wife. As for myself, I felt safe, but I knew that she would be worried." Though Heaton reported that his airship "was in nowise injured by the ducking," Enos Brown, of *Scientific American,* sealed the airship's doom by headlining his article on the sinking THE HEATON AIRSHIP FAILURE. The *Messenger* and its resourcefully inventive team subsequently disappeared from the headlines.

The occasional exception like Mrs. Heaton notwithstanding, there were still very few women who had experience with machinery. But one of the best was the still-active Margaret Knight, who had concentrated on machinery for the shoe industry at the end of the last century. The new century saw her train her mechanical skills on the development of rotary engines and motors for automobiles, optimistically assigning parts of her patent rights to a family company in Saratoga Springs, New York, where several of her nephews and nieces lived. She continued daily visits to her Boston experiment rooms at 100 High Street until her death in 1914, when her hometown Framingham newspaper reported that her silent Knight motor was "heralded all over the world as the latest refinement in automobile motors"—an assessment with which the probate court did not agree when it appraised her half interest in the "Resilient Wheel" patent (the other half had been assigned to a nephew at the time of patenting) as "worthless." With her remaining assets listed as "Cash in Framingham National Bank: $185.68," "Cash in Framingham Trust Co.: $1.37," and "Household furniture: $58," it was obvious that the tall, strongly built, gentle-voiced, white-haired woman who looked younger than her seventy-five years, the fruitful inventor who had once earned a queenly "competence," retained little material wealth at the end. It was a far cry from the electrifying moment when she saw her photograph in that mecca of all patentees, the Patent Office, an experience she loved to relate: "Imagine my surprise when, on going to the Patent Office in Washington, I discovered that my picture was hanging on the wall. It was placed there, I was told, through the efforts of my attorney, as a tribute to the first woman to receive a patent."

The Patent Office has no record of the presence of any such photograph; so it may be that it was an adroit and temporary maneuver by the attorney who represented her so ably in her interference suit in 1870. Of course, she was not the first woman patentee, a fact her attorney must have known. One must assume that the attorney simply gulled the uneducated mill-child-turned-inventor extraordinaire into believing the honor was hers. Naïveté and meager education, however, had never quashed her inventive skills or her entrepreneurship. Both Robert Lovett, the author of biographical material on Knight in *Notable American Women,* and Marilyn Ogilvie, in her *Women in Science: Antiquity Through the Nineteenth Century,* ascribe Knight's uniqueness as an inventor not only to the number of her inventions and their focus on heavy machinery but also to her ability to bridge enormous gaps in her education. That said, Ogilvie amends the compliment to say that Knight understood so little about basic mechanical principles that she never knew *why* her machines worked. It wasn't the kind of question that would have kept Knight up nights! To her it was the how, not the why, that mattered.

Other women also invented in unusual fields, and though their numbers continued to be few, writers interested in women's progress tried to accentuate the positive. Orison Swett Marden, the editor of *Success* magazine and now of *The Consolidated Library* (a sort of encyclopedia), included a section on "Women as Inventors" in the latter, giving the accomplishments of many of the more prominent women inventors and forecasting that more women would become involved in invention as soon as their "faculties are sharpened and quickened by their closer contact with the actualities of life."

Mary Logan knew exactly what "actualities" would be most helpful—and they all came under the rubric of improved education for women. Logan was the widow of a prominent Civil War general whom she had often accompanied to the front. A vivacious and witty speaker, she was an erstwhile editor of *Home* magazine (which carried the usual variety of household articles but also emphasized national affairs), a sometime contributor to *Cosmopolitan* magazine, and a mover and shaker at the Columbian Exposition in Chicago. Willard and Livermore gave Logan this accolade: "There is no woman of to-day with more personal influence on the public." In her 1912 book, *The Part Taken by Women in American History,* written in collaboration with her daughter, Mary Logan Tucker, Logan seemed surprised not by woman's advancement, which was only her due, but by the failure of the world to acknowledge her talents: "That queer turn for original, utilitarian mental progress has probably always been woman's capability as well as man's, but woman's recognition in this field was slow to come."

Recognition would continue to be slow, and even some of the old standbys could no longer be relied upon for help. *New Ideas,* so dependably supportive of women's inventive efforts in the past when it defended women inventors against charges that they occupied themselves exclusively "with curling tongs and clothespins," had changed hands and replaced the "New Ideas for Ladies" column with one called "Beauty Makers for Our Ladies," brimming with tips for alleviating furrows between and bags beneath the eyes. The new editors of *New Ideas* even sniped at feminist activists by aiming a backhanded "compliment" at the inventor of a clip-on perforated stewpan lid: "[S]he was the sort of woman who believes in improving her own sphere—if ever so little—rather than breaking the grocer's window." With "help" like this, taboo (as opposed to window) -breaking women were delighted to discover a new supporter in an unexpected quarter.

Historian and Catholic theologian John Augustine Zahm, writing as "H. J. Mozans" in *Woman in Science,* bolstered his study of women's contributions with new facts. He examined the evidence their patents afforded and quarried statistics not only from the already published lists of women inventors up to March of 1895 but from an additional list of 3,615 women patentees covering the next fifteen years, which brought the cumulative total of patenting women to 8,596 as of 1910. I have not discovered any "official" list covering the years between 1895 and 1910, but it is obvious that *someone* kept a regular count. Writing in 1913, Mozans states that no reports were available after 1910. Of course, anyone who wished to search for what sounded like women's names in the annual lists of the Patent Office could, but Mozans did not say that he had done so himself.

After studying descriptions of women's inventions dating from Mary Kies's 1809 patent through those most recently recorded, Mozans praised women for tackling articles remote from their customary home enterprises, devices that "at first blush would seem to be quite alien to the genius and capacity of woman," such as:

> improvements in locomotive wheels, devices for reducing straw and other fibrous substances for the manufacture of paper pulp, improvements in corn huskers, low-water indicators, steam and other whistles, corn plows, a method of constructing screw propellers, improvements in materials for packing journals and bearing, in fire alarms, thermometers, railroad car heaters, improvements in lubricating railway journals, in conveyors of smoke and cinders for locomotives, in pyrotechnic night signals, burglar alarms, railway car safety apparatus, in apparatus for punching corrugated metals, desulphurizing ores

and so on. Mozans condemned society for its negative opinion of their accomplishments and for erecting barriers against the "depreciated sex" but was optimistic that as institutions of higher learning became more available to them, they would "bid fair to rival men in what they have long regarded as their peculiar specialty." Not surprisingly, suffrage clubs were quick to add *Woman in Science* to their list of required reading.

Though Mozans thought acceptance of professional women was imminent, very few were able to challenge men's monopoly in architecture. Men were still sputtering that "ladies" would not engage in a profession that required them to mount ladders—to which one of the new breed replied that as far as she could gather, there was nothing wrong with climbing, only being *seen* climbing:

> Climbing a ladder is condemned as unwomanly, but so was riding a bicycle or being seen on the top of an omnibus not so very long ago, and yet we are now all seemingly reconciled to these unwomanly practices. Besides, the ladder question could only be raised by persons who are in ignorance of the portion of a lifetime that an architect spends upon a ladder, and as this is so infinitesimal it is unworthy of consideration.

By the end of the new century's first decade, only about fifty women were recognized as "trained architects," though others had acquired training through apprenticeship, tutoring, or correspondence schools rather than by crashing the still-closed gates of the generally male-

Future patentee Anna Keichline at fourteen.

Anna Keichline's "kitchen construction" patent, 1926.

dominated university architecture departments. "Land Grant" universities, which, by offering industrial and mechanical education, qualified for federal lands through the 1862 Morrill Act, had to accept
women without bias, however, and among those early women architects was my mother, Ohio State University's first woman to receive
the degree of Bachelor of Civil Engineering in Architecture. Florence
Hite graduated in 1904; she was not an inventor, but one of her
daughters is.

Anna Keichline, of Bellefonte, Pennsylvania, who graduated in 1911
from Cornell's School of Architecture (Cornell was also one of the Land
Grant colleges), was that state's first registered woman architect.
Keichline was never deterred by stereotypes—or ladders. And apparently she was as charismatic as she was determined. Family members
recall that classmates decided not to participate in their own graduation if the college denied her an architectural degree because of her
gender, but since she was not Cornell's first woman architect, this story
may be apochryphal.

Spotting their daughter's industry, inventiveness, and craftsmanship
early, Keichline's parents gave her a home workshop equipped with the
finest carpentry tools. Public recognition first came at fourteen, when

an admiring *Philadelphia Inquirer* reporter said that her craftsmanship in making the oak card table and walnut chest that took first prize at the Centre County Fair was equal to that of a highly skilled mechanic. He captioned his story MAY DEVOTE LIFE TO INDUSTRIAL ART. The accompanying photograph showed the pert schoolgirl, not bent over her tool bench, where she normally spent every spare moment, but standing demurely in sailor dress with middy blouse, her hair topped by a sporty bow and pulled back into a ribbon-tied braid. At Cornell, where she was the only woman in her drafting class, she became a great favorite for her wide range of interests, puckish humor, penchant for vivid story telling, talent, and, above all, industry. No one could say that advanced education had ennervated this bright graduate student! This is how she later recalled those college years:

> At college we worked, many times, three and four days and nights without stopping; most always in those stretches I took time to make coffee and sandwiches for the fellows, then they carried my board to the dormitory, where I could draw all night. Now after years of practice, I realize that I have never thought of hours, time is divided into jobs, a floor plan, a model, specifications, until the job is done.

As an architect, Keichline not only designed residential and public buildings in several cities other than her native Bellefonte but also gained seven patents, two of which involved time- and motion-saving kitchen designs. Keichline felt women had a special aptitude for domestic architecture, especially kitchens, and the year after she graduated from Cornell she received the first of her patents, for a combined sink-washtub with a drainboard that folded against the wall when not in use. When she patented again, her architectural training and kitchen experience merged to produce a planned kitchen.

Keichline, conjuring up a typical example of extra steps taken by the cook, described her laying down her spoon, opening the cabinet door to remove the box of baking powder, taking off the lid, ladling out a spoonful, replacing the lid on the box, setting the box on the shelf, and then closing the cupboard door: "Imagine a carpenter going through this procedure to get a brad!" she quipped. In her patent for "kitchen construction," she explained that "people seem to have been content to place one box upon another, install a few shelves and drawers and call it a Kitchen Cupboard, or to elaborate somewhat on this and call it a

Kitchen Cabinet and to carry out this same unstudied scheme with all other Kitchen Equipment." She, however, designed everything from range to sink and cupboards in between to "involve the minimum amount of labor on the part of the housekeeper and to reduce the operative cost." One particular innovation was counter space built around a motor shaft to which tools for such tasks as grinding coffee, beating eggs, and peeling potatoes were attached. The countertops sloped to facilitate cleaning; the stove front extended to the floor to lessen floor space to be cleaned; cabinets were low enough to provide access without a ladder, high enough to eliminate stooping, and glass-doored to make their contents visible; the cook measured out loose materials stored in deep doors or cupboards through a small valve that could be operated by one finger.

In coming years, Keichline patented a variety of devices, but though she also served as a special agent with military intelligence during World War I and was later active with President Hoover's Better Housing Conference, the focus of her interest remained the designing of buildings. In fact, her active architectural practice absorbed her so completely that she never consummated sales of her patent rights. Instead, from her home office, where she often developed blueprints in the bathtub and dried them on the back porch, she set forth in her own car (a settlement fee from one of her clients) to oversee construction of her projects, mounting ladders with no compunction.

Despite her relative lack of attention to them, Keichline's patents manifest a breadth of interest and a wellspring of ingenuity. For clients with children, she designed a half-hexagon "portable partition," a divider that could be installed in any corner to provide a playhouse or toy storage that was doored, windowed, and even eaved, the exterior real enough looking to "facilitate the play of children . . . and add to the delight . . . [of] 'playing house.'" Her fireproof building blocks of hollow clay, concrete, or other suitable material, scored with notches and breaking slots to reveal predetermined fracture lines bricklayers could use to obtain desired shapes, were not only cheaper and lighter but could be filled with insulating or sound-deadening material, ordered in a broad assortment of colors, arranged in a wide variety of patterns, and used to reinforce walls in tornado or flood districts. For a small apartment, she patented a bed that folded up into a wall; for an apartment building, an ingenious system for heating it with compressed air piped into radiators. The compressed air also performed such functions as agitating clothes and drying dishes in their respective washers; then, after contracting as it cooled, the air was valved out to create a suction that operated a vacuum-sweeping line.

With increased urbanization in the twentieth century, raising children in cramped urban quarters demanded extra ingenuity, and a number of women tinkered with ideas for multifunctional furniture such as Keichline's folding bed and collapsible playhouse. They were particularly fruitful in the field of children's furnishings and devised portable, folding, or collapsing cribs, cradles, prams, swings, slides, and feeding chairs that could be adapted for other functions.

Adeloe Nadaeu, to name only one of dozens, combined a cradle's properties with those of a rocking chair and converted one to the other by simply rearranging the folding sides, a combination *Patent Record* called a boon to those in tight quarters, for when child outgrew cradle, cradle became chair. Then, as mentioned in the Introduction, there was actress Lillian Russell, who invented a rigid and durably constructed combination dresser-trunk that could both withstand the rigors of a theatrical tour and provide easy access to her costumes and makeup on those occasions when, as her patent said, "the interval between acts is very short." But for every true innovator like Keichline or Russell, there were thousands who trod well-worn tracks to inventions for the household. Ida Tarbell shrugged, saying: "It requires no eye of a lynx to see that the ways of woman the world over are very different from the ways a hundred years ago . . . [but] whatever the stir on the surface, below, the same great occupation, the woman's profession, claims her as it always has."

While the "woman's profession" might have claimed the exclusive attention of most, a good many managed to engage in money-making adventures on the side. In *Occupations for Women*, Willard (who had listed the publisher of the *Beekeepers' Journal* as a prominent "Woman of the Century") commended beekeeping, for example, as an excellent field for women since it appealed to women's nurturing side and had therapeutic effects as well. In the words of a Washington writer quoted by Willard: "The busy little workers, leaving their hives to gather nectar from the beautiful flowers, the dainty white combs that they build, the exhilaration of swarming, all appeal to woman's poetical nature. Not only this, but bees take their owner out into the sunshine

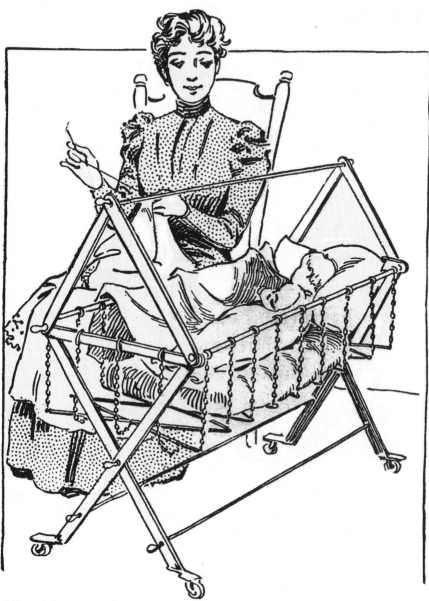

Folding crib for easy storage.

where heaven's own breezes put color in faded cheeks." *New Idea Woman's Magazine* (originally a dress pattern paper but broadened to include other aspects of women's lives and not to be confused with "invention magazine" *New Ideas*) reiterated this line of thinking, stating that a beekeeper could not only gain abundant health but also "considerable sums of the coin of the realm." Such encouragement was

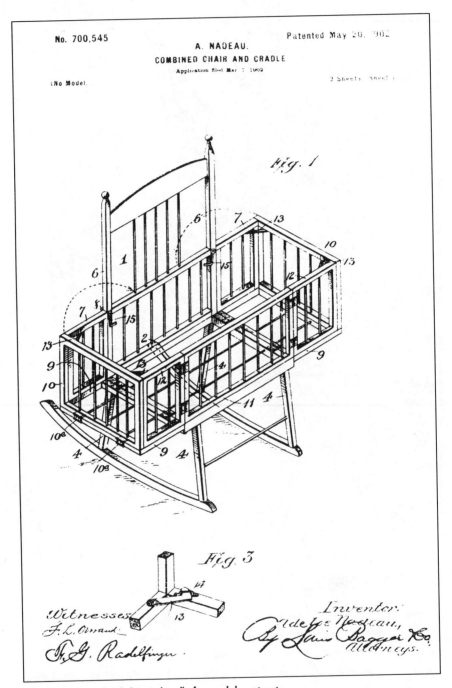

No. 700,545

A. NADEAU.
COMBINED CHAIR AND CRADLE

Application filed Mar 7 1902

(No Model)

Patented May 20, 1902

2 Sheets—Sheet 1

*Fig. 1*

*Fig. 3*

Witnesses
F. L. Orrand
T. G. Radelfinger

Inventor
Adeloe Nadeau,
By Lain Bagger & Co.
Attorneys.

**Adeloe Nadeau's combined chair and cradle for crowded apartments.**

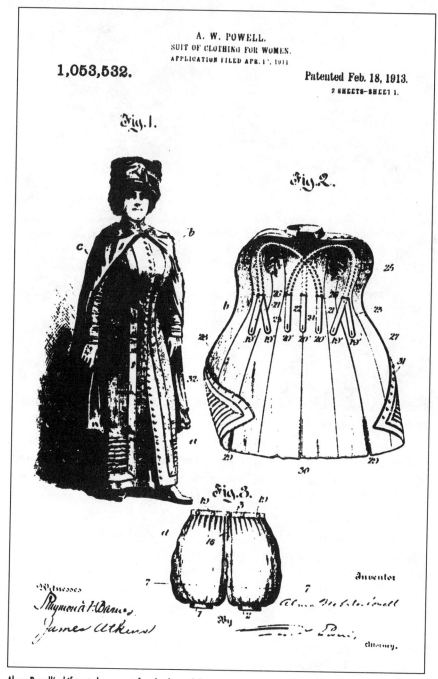

Alma Powell's bifurcated garment for the busy clubwoman.

Girls sew and cook; boys build.

responsible for recruiting even more farm wives to maintain colonies, sell honey for extra income, and invent a large variety of combs, carrying cases, feeding troughs, and protective cloaks. It might be "woman's work," but it paid.

Laundry was also still very much a part of woman's realm, and Proctor and Gamble knew that despite technological advances, it remained an abomination. Still, in a book of laundry hints, it urged on any would-be slackers with the admonition that having clean clothes was "the one great privilege of rich and poor alike." Laundry manual writer Lydia Balderston saw no reason a woman should not use a machine to save time and energy for the "better, broader things in life" but supplied the following awesome list of items she deemed essential for the well-appointed laundry room:

AGATE PAN OR BASIN FOR STARCHING
BOSOM BOARD
CLOTHES BASKET
CLOTHES BOILER (TIN WITH COPPER BOTTOM)
CLOTHES HORSE
CLOTHES LINE
CLOTHES PINS
CLOTHES PIN BAG
CLOTHES PROPS
CLOTHES STICK
CLOTHES WRINGER
CUP FOR MEASURE
DUSTER FOR LINES
DROPPERS
FLANNEL
FUNNEL
HEAVY CLOTH FOR TUBS AND BOILER
HEAVY IRONS
HEAVY PAPER
IRON HOLDERS
IRON REST
IRONING TABLE AND BOARD covered with canton flannel or
    coarse blanket and a fine cotton cloth. A drawer is convenient
    for holders.
PINS
POLISHING IRON
SAUCEPAN FOR STARCH
SCRUBBING BRUSH
SET TUBS, THREE OR FOUR, OR MACHINE
SKIRT BOARD
SMALL PIECES OF MUSLIN AND CHEESE-CLOTH
SMALL POINTED IRONS
STRAINER FOR STARCH
SPRINKLER
TEASPOON
WASH BOARD
WATER PAIL
WAX

Since even in the new century, which began with such promise, most women still refused to test the waters beyond their domestic confine. And the "anti's" roasted the same old chestnuts: that women had less ability than men; that only men climbed to the highest rung of the ladder of genius; that, lacking genius, women could never become responsible citizens. Ergo, no vote. This was too much for Alice Stone Blackwell, the only child of Henry Blackwell and Lucy Stone, who abandoned much of the cautious conservatism of the Boston group after her mother's death in 1893. Not even the most "ultra advocate of a restricted suffrage," she wrote in *Woman's Journal,* would even consider limiting the vote to persons of genius, for if genius were any indication of the potential for civic responsibility, then why did Thomas Edison literally have to be hauled to the polls during a hotly contested school election—hauled there to cast his first vote in fourteen years! This was the same Edison whom Willard had quoted as authority for saying that women had a better sense of machinery than men. There went *that* argument!

As feminists surveyed the first decade of the century, they saw some bright spots. It was hopeful that an increasing number of the most able young women were able to gain professional degrees. It was a sign of progress that women's inventions had been removed from overprotective custody and mainstreamed at the Saint Louis fair. It boded well for inventors that feminists helped to correct the impression that women invented only household devices. But, on the other side of the ledger, by still regarding girls as housekeepers in training and their higher education a frill, society continued to deny women the encouragement to seek wider opportunities. By harping on biological gender differences, society perpetuated the myth that women couldn't invent, or, at the very least, couldn't invent anything beyond their "sphere." These were more than enough negatives to constitute a full agenda for the years ahead.

# 12

# HOPE SPRINGS ETERNAL

*W*hile activists such as Alice Stone Blackwell continued to attack theories about gender differences in inventiveness by emphasizing women's inventions in more "masculine" fields, the majority of women continued to patent prosaic "housewifely" devices so relentlessly that even when the European war loomed on the horizon, only a small number were prompted to invent anything remotely military.

With the home economics movement in full swing, it is no wonder that women seized upon the statistical evidence of time lost on the job through inefficiency, which Lilian and Frank Gilbreth's time and motion studies confirmed, and applied it to the work most of them did—housekeeping. In her *The Psychology of Management,* Gilbreth said it was all a matter of putting one's mind to the task, though she stated it a bit more circuitously—"the effect of the mind that is directing work upon that work which is directed." Applied to what might today be called "interactive" housekeeping, it was the same old appeal for efficiency, *woman's* efficiency, a subject the Beecher sisters had pretty well covered—but not laid to rest—when they chastened the incompetent decades before.

Being a good housekeeper was still so coveted a stamp of approval for women that they welcomed the introduction of an actual stamp to single out those products that would aid them in their pursuit of domestic excellence. When *Good Housekeeping* magazine published its first issue in 1885, it pledged to fulfill a mission of producing and perpetuating household perfection, and in the new century demonstrated its good faith to women readers by establishing the Good Housekeeping Institute Experiment Station as a central headquarters to which consumers could apply for help "toward the higher life of the household." In 1902, it added an "Ironclad Contract" to guarantee the reliability of any product advertised within its pages. Eight years later, the institute established laboratories to test products without charge, allowing those that met the institute's standards of excellence to appear on the institute's "Tested and Approved List" and display the coveted oval seal that stated "Tested and Approved by the Good Housekeeping Institute Conducted by Good Housekeeping Magazine."

In 1915, William Randolph Hearst, the magazine's new publisher, convinced Dr. Harvey W. Wiley, the director of the Food and Drug Administration, to head the institute. The presence of Wiley, a hero to members of the General Federation of Women's Clubs, whose political clout had helped him lobby successfully for passage of the 1905 Pure Food and Drug Act, would certainly confer credibility upon the seal. His devoted clubwomen supporters, however, were distressed to see him leave government service—so much so that one newspaper marked his departure with this headline: WOMEN WEEP AS WATCHDOG OF KITCHEN QUITS AFTER 29 YEARS. At least, the women comforted themselves, he would seek tougher standards for consumer products in his new position.

Laura Hicks was one of the many inventors whose products enjoyed increased sales after winning the *Good Housekeeping* endorsement. Eager to capitalize on the commercial potential of the seal, she gave it prominent placement on the package of her washing mitt, which, when slipped over the hand, provided a corrugated surface for rubbing delicate fabrics. Like sad-iron inventor Mary Potts, she was aware that calling attention to her gender was, in this case, a bonus, and stated explicitly on the package that the mitt was "a woman's invention." She also used a jingle ("Here's a handy little washing mitt. Nothing Takes Its Place. For washing out your Hosiery, your Lingerie and Lace") and some additional ad copy, one woman to another ("All women like to 'fuss over' their finery. It will prove a joy to women in her home, to every traveler and to every schoolgirl"). This was clearly a woman dedicated to marketing!

In those prewar years, stylish matrons embarked on a perpetual search for the perfect corset to relocate, compress, and uplift their flesh into a wasp-waisted, Gibson Girl silhouette, spurred on by the pronouncements of such esteemed fashion arbiters as *Delineator* magazine, which declared that no woman could be well dressed without her corset. "If her flesh is loose and flabby," wrote a *Delineator* authority, "they [corsets] compress it within reasonable limits. If it is hard and firm they push it here and there as skillfully as a masseuse till it is out of harm's way. . . . One should always have at least two pairs of corsets—and wear them on alternate days. The day's rest allows the bones to come back into their normal position after they have been somewhat strained by active use." Of course, one always wore a "corset cover" over the apparatus.

When the rage for plunging necklines on evening dresses hit at the same time fashion mavens began to find the flat-chested look de rigueur, the new imperative was to find a way to secure and even restrain the bust without unsightly straps. Inventors tried such gimmicks as running elasticized ribbed bands around the top edges of their tubular undershirts or flattening the bosom with breast bands, but it was not until Mary Phelps Jacobs, who some years later adopted the more beguiling name "Caresse" Crosby, was so exasperated by her corset cover peeking from her neckline that a backless brassiere was invented. Though she had not yet married Harry Crosby and was still Jacobs at the time she patented, I shall use her later name, Caresse Crosby, because it was under that name that she recalled her inventive experiences in the autobiography she dramatically titled *The Passionate Years.* During her Manhattan debutante year, she wrote, she was dressing for a ball one night, when the "eyelit embroidery of my corset-cover kept peeping through the roses around my bosom." She took action and asked her maid to assemble two pocket handkerchiefs, pink ribbon, needle, thread, and pins. The invention was born:

> There before the glass I pinned the handkerchiefs together on the bias and Marie stitched the pink ribbons to the two points below my breast bone. The ends of the handkerchiefs I knotted round my waist

> and then Marie, grasping the idea and the ribbons, pulled them taut
> and made them fast to the knot behind, the practice being to flatten
> down one's chest as much as possible so the truth that [I] had breasts
> should not be suspected.

Crosby pronounced the brassiere perfect: "The result was delicious. I
could move more freely, a nearly naked feeling, and in the glass I saw
that I was flat and I was proper." When friends flocked to her dressing
room to inspect the invention, they were so impressed that they begged
Marie to sew one for them, but when word leaked beyond her immediate circle and even a perfect stranger asked Marie to make one for her,
Crosby trundled the modest Marie to a patent attorney to whom she
discreetly modeled the sample *over* her maid's uniform. He quickly
grasped the principle, and he and Crosby coined the name "Backless
Brassiere." In the patent claims, Crosby described the garment's novelty ("does not interfere with any design of evening gown that may be
chosen"), its commercial one-size-fits-almost-all practicality ("the size
and shape of a single garment will be suitable for a considerable variety
of different customers"), its comfort ("freedom from bones so that it
may be finished with laces or embroideries for wear beneath a sheer
waist or diaphanous gown"), its versatility ("may be worn even by
persons engaged in violent exercises such as tennis"), and, finally, its
ability to do the job ("does not confine the person anywhere except
where it is needed").

When she received her patent about a year later, Crosby established
a secret "sweat shop" (secret, she explained to readers of her autobiography, "owing to undue prejudice about what young ladies could or
could not do to turn a longed-for penny"), elevated the faithful Marie
to partnership, rented two sewing machines, hired two Italian girls,
and demonstrated her first products to important figures in the mer-
chandising world. They bought a few, but either didn't push them
enough or encountered the resistance of a general public for whom the
concept was too revolutionary. Even the inventor "felt rather like an
anarchist."

Crosby had meanwhile found love with Richard Peabody, the man
who became her first husband, and occupied first with approaching
nuptials and then with her marriage, she shelved her invention. Her
interest in it revived a few years later when she met an old beau who,
he slyly let it be known, worked for Warner Brothers Corset Company,

which made brassieres, known in the trade as "jewel cases." At his urging, she showed his employers her patented invention and accepted their offer of fifteen hundred dollars for the rights to her patent, a figure that seemed to her "not only adequate but munificent." Indeed, she reveled in her "opulence." Like many woman inventors, she was unduly grateful for small favors, for that sum was minuscule compared to the estimated fifteen million dollars Warner Brothers would make on the brassiere; but Crosby, a descendant of Robert Fulton, modestly put her invention in perspective: "I believe my ardour for invention springs from his loins. I can't say that the brassiere will ever take as great a place in history as the steamboat, but I did invent it."

After World War I, Crosby, divorced from her first husband, moved to Paris. It was there that in the 1920s she wrote several volumes of verse and with her second husband, banker and poet Harry Crosby, founded Black Sun Press to encourage such writers as Ezra Pound, Hart Crane, James Joyce, and D. H. Lawrence; in the 1930s, her Crosby Continental Editions published, among others, Ernest Hemingway, William Faulkner, and Dorothy Parker. When she died in 1970, her *New York Times* obituary stated that in her autobiography, written in 1953 when she was sixty-one, she had chalked up several goals reached—America's first Girl Scout, holder of the woman's record for the 220-yard dash, and inventor of the backless brassiere—and also claimed indirect responsibility for founding Alcoholics Anonymous. As for this last, however, she made no such claim in her book, but she did say that her first husband, once a hopeless alcoholic himself, had laid the groundwork for it. Recognizing that true alcoholics were never cured, he founded the Keeley Institute in the early 1920s to treat chronic alcoholics with psychotherapy rather than drugs, helping them to maintain sobriety through lifelong counseling. As for the brassiere invention, it received a measure of publicity in a recent *Life* magazine cover story on the one-hundredth anniversary of the birth of the brassiere. Though Crosby is cited as being one of the many claimants to the title of first-with-the-bra, the laurels went to Parisian corset maker Herminie Cadolle for her 1889 "soutien-gorge." Crosby's was not the first brassiere, per se, but as the first backless one, it was revolutionary.

Sarah Gossard must have hoped for the same commercial success when she reinvented a centuries-old garment—the corset—along ana-

tomical lines. Although there was no dress reform movement comparable to the one of the 1870s, when dress reform committees could make
or break an inventor's "healthful undergarment" by giving or with-
holding approval, or even to the one of the 1890s, when Annie Jenness
Miller lectured on rational dress, twentieth-century on-the-go women
patronized those who catered to their demands for garments that
combined freedom of movement with firm support. Like earlier reformers, Gossard had learned that many of women's ills were directly
attributable to improper corseting, and she aligned the steel boning of
the corset with the wearer's muscles, enabling the body to be compressed into a fashionable form with a minimum of discomfort. Looking at her garments with a twentieth-century eye, one wonders at the
slavishness to fashion that prompted women to accept steel boning in
the first place, but in the next few years advertisements for Gossard
garments so filled fashion magazines that the name "Gossard" became
almost as generic to corsetry as Ellen Demorest's "Imperial" was to
skirt "elevators" over half a century before.

Not all inventors of the period restricted themselves to the "feminine sphere," but when El Dorado Jones moved outside it, she found
the male business world so hostile that she banished the entire gender
from any participation in the company she founded to market her
inventions. Jones, once a schoolteacher in Moline, Illinois, who found
selling insurance far more lucrative than teaching ("She never wrote
a policy under $50,000," reported a friend), had a propensity for
tinkering with iron and soon found inventing even more remunerative
than insurance. Her most successful products were tiny, lightweight
electric irons packaged demurely in cretonne-beribboned containers,
an ingenious travel ironing board with a compartment for the flatiron,
and a collapsible hat rack. All were targeted for women's use, and she
employed only women, all over forty, to manufacture them. The
worldwide success of her El Dorado Inventions, Inc., particularly the
irons, gained her not only fame and fortune but also tenders from
businessmen to purchase her business. But Jones snapped that she
wouldn't sell her business to men because they were "mean" and
"low," not to mention "avaricious and mercenary and everything else
despicable."

Maintaining that she never married because she could ill afford a
husband, she divulged the secret of her commercial success: "The only

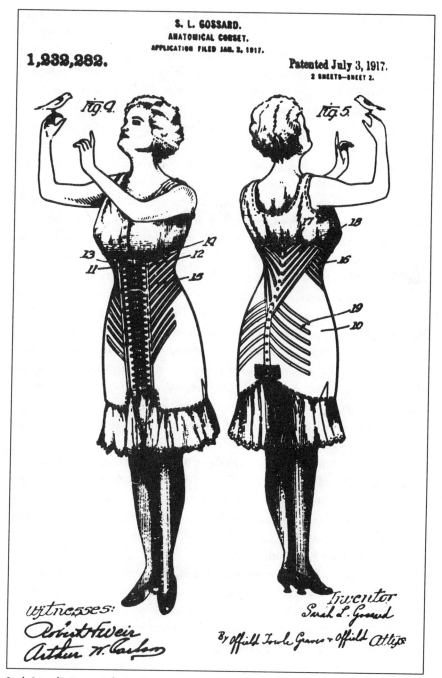

Sarah Gossard's "anatomical corset."

way to get along is to seek the difficult job, always do it well, and see that you get paid for it properly. Oh, yes, and don't forget to exploit men all you can. Because if you don't, they will exploit you." That frequently voiced bias undoubtedly contributed to Jones's eventual financial ruin, for around 1917 she moved to New York to court financial backing from the aviation industry for her recently patented exhaust attachment to a gas engine. The attachment had significantly lessened or "muffled" the racket by conditioning and cooling exhaust gases from automobile engines, and she was so convinced that it could as easily reduce the deafening noise of airplane engines that she broached no disputes about her claims. She antagonized the businessmen with her usual lack of diplomacy and was therefore in no position to capitalize on the *New York Times*'s report of the invention's relatively successful test at Roosevelt Field, Long Island, and its forecast that the Jones attachment could "have a bearing on the future of American aeronautics." But prospective customers had had enough of Jones; there were no takers. When her funds ran out, she moved to increasingly cheaper quarters until, at the end of her rope, she appealed to city welfare agencies for aid. A neighbor who got no answer when she called to take Jones to dinner one evening summoned another neighbor, who climbed through the window to find Jones dead in her bed in the dingy ground-floor tenement apartment.

The once-wealthy inventor, who over a period of several years in Moline had listed herself variously in the city directory as manager, treasurer, president, and vice president of Sun Utilities Company and an officer of the Moline Muffler Manufacturing Company, died at age seventy-one in a twenty-dollar-a-month flat. Friends from the American Woman's Association at 353 West 57th Street, where Jones lived before her funds ran out, claimed her body at the city morgue, held a funeral, cremated her, and shipped her ashes to relatives in Ferguson, Missouri. The Moline newspaper, ranking her prejudice against men of greater interest than her inventions, captioned its obituary notice: WOMAN INVENTOR KNOWN AS MAN HATER; PRODUCTS INCLUDED IRON, MUFFLER. El Dorado Jones was no heroine to the feminists, for their leaders counted many men among their ardent supporters, and they understood only too well that women's advancement depended upon converting the men who controlled the state legislatures, the final hurdle in the battle for ratification of the national suffrage amendment.

Unlike Jones, inventor and businesswoman Harriet Strong did prove a worthy heroine, successful not just in commerce but in the public arena as well, for she had precisely those persuasive skills that Jones lacked. By the middle of the century's second decade, Strong had become southern California's staunchest supporter of the Newlands Bill for appropriating government funds for water conservation, a project so significant that beside it, she said, "the Panama Canal sinks into insignificance." Strong vowed to officials that in the years since she patented her plan for storing water in canyons, no other system had evolved to match it, and urged the government to implement long-range flood-control plans based on her principles. The government stalled. Since women could vote in California (though not yet nationally), Strong mobilized members of women's clubs and suffrage organizations to vote to protect the rich foothill agricultural area from the gravel and debris that rampaging floodwaters dumped on them.

Fully informed about arian and riparian rights, she never missed a flood-control meeting, and when she once found herself the only woman in a meeting to which no representatives of women's organizations had been invited, she lashed out: "I protest against women having no voice here . . . women are citizens; they are not as they were twenty years ago!" The local Whittier, California, newspaper said of the outburst, "She practically hurled a bomb into the meeting," an assessment shared by her daughter some years later:

> Mother threw in the first monkey wrench . . . maybe nearer a bomb. . . . We listened to all these [speeches] and then Mother got busy. And Mother's getting busy was busy indeed. . . . I never saw such wire pulling in my life. She was fighting the Chamber of Commerce and the Board of Supervisors. But one after another fell into line. . . . She might boil with indignation [but] she had the brains to think of a way out and the courage and perseverance to carry her ideas to completion.

In this same period, Edith Griswold, the engineer and patent attorney last noted as a judge at the Saint Louis World's Fair and now president of the Women Lawyers Club, wrote a thirteen-part series on women inventors in *Women Lawyers' Journal.* Griswold began the series by giving the patent number, the inventor's name, and a short descriptive paragraph about each of the thirty-six patents issued to women in the preceding month, intending to do the same in each succeeding column. She changed the format, however, because the number of women's patents increased and the journal's limited size did not. Being unable to go into such detail must have pained her since she had a good many women clients, but in subsequent issues she did manage to make up for the lack with a more personal approach that made use of her own observations. In one column she wrote, "It is interesting to watch the work of women inventors, for we find their inventions almost invariably relate to practical improvement in those devices which are in use by them or those whom they are serving." Writing of inventors so engrossed in their inventions that they bored listeners with details, spent every waking moment tinkering and depleting their savings, she noted, "In my thirty years' work among inventors I have never even heard of a woman belonging to this class, but I have known of many men there." When she described how one woman attached wheels to her suitcase to ease the burden of carrying it and sighed, "May it endure beyond the stage of being laughed down by the simple ones," one would like to tell her that it did! In a more intimate vein, she wrote: "The stout woman will be glad to hear . . . of a swimming suit for women, having a bust supporter concealed by a portion of the combined jacket and skirt"; of two women who sold their patents for menswear to Cluett, Peabody & Co., she put in her oar that "manufacturers may find something new in women's inventions even for men"; of several mechanical patents, she said they epitomized "the diversity of occupations of interests of women in the mechanical world of ideas."

To be found in Griswold's columns are the names of several inventors already known to readers of this book: Mary Phelps Jacob, who "has invented a brassiere made of two bias pieces of material sewed together in front and provided with straps, so that a brassiere is virtually only the front of a waist"; Helen Blanchard, who had a new electrical heating device to attach to a sewing machine which would remove the curl from the two edges to be sewn together; and Florence Parpart, who had a new refrigerator patent. In one column she marked the recent death of Margaret Knight: "an example of a woman whose brain could work as readily on mechanical household lines as on household lines. . . . [T]he true test of Miss Knight being a successful inventor is answered by the fact that most of her patented inventions were taken up by manufacturers."

With the European war now of greater concern to Americans, the only wartime influence Griswold could spot ("The war has set brains working to make something catchy in the way of games—women have not had the courage to stay out of this fight") were two games: Victory War Puzzle and a war-themed card game, its four suits marked "Artillery," "Cavalry," "Infantry," and "Engineering Corps" and individual cards marked "ambulance," "wagon-train," "airship," and the like.

In 1917, just before America entered the war, a notable professor predicted in *Scientific Monthly* that woman, whose role was determined by the "steadfast race-fostering qualities of the female," could never exhibit the "inventive faculties of the restless male." But with America's entrance, a good many observers postulated that war would stimulate women to make major inventive contributions. If they did, said Mary Ogden White, in an article titled "Has the War Made Women Inventors?" in *Woman Citizen* (the inheritor of the pro-suffrage mantle of *Woman's Journal*), it would not be the first time women had answered the call. They had invented since the beginning of time, she thundered, and war would only shed "much needed light" upon their innate creative genius.

Outraged by the "befuddled insistence" of opponents of woman suffrage that superior inventive power inhered only in men and therefore empowered them with the divine right to vote, she validated her claims for women with mention of the items described in Griswold's study: a system of electrical distribution and control; electric engine starters; an automatic lubricator for a journal box; a new form of rivet; a parachute garment to be worn by aeronauts; a portable warming appliance for the beds of patients. She might also have cited several more recent mechanical inventions: May Conner's hay-handling device that lifted and deposited hay in its winter storage area by means of a power-driven fork; Ida Forbes's electrical water heater, which was portable and therefore available for a wide variety of uses; and Emma Barchard's method of trapping condensation from an air compressor. All of these boded well for women's ability to contribute to the war effort.

But none were as startling as Harriet Strong's suggestion. With demand for food production increasing because of the vast quantities of food needed abroad for refugees as well as troops, Strong shocked conservationists with a plan to increase crops by diverting Colorado

River water onto vast tracts of unused (or at least undercultivated) land through a gigantic, coordinated, government irrigation project—which some hopefully called "making the desert bloom." Her fourfold plan to guarantee adequate water for current users, to control floodwaters, to safeguard the resource from "foreign meddling and interference," and to develop new lands for as many as a million people included a blockbuster suggestion—the conversion of the Grand Canyon into a "mammoth irrigation tank" (as headlines in the *Los Angeles Tribune* described it). It was an extension of her patented principle of placing the top of each dam above the lower line of the dam above it to distribute the water's weight and pressure. To her angry critics Strong replied that using the "grandest canyon on earth" for water conservation was a worthy object, "the most important war measure before the American people today."

The enthusiastic Whittier Chamber of Commerce promised that each new dam would generate enough electricity to pay for itself and pointed out that the project was "free from all personal, private or incorporate interests" since Strong's patents had expired and she was contributing her plans and specifications "as a personal offering" to the government. Added the Chamber: "Many competent people occasionally make sporadic efforts in certain directions, but none of them, so far as [we] know have, like her, followed them up for a quarter of a century or more."

By 1918, Strong was in Washington, girding for a fight with private interests who hoped to buy cheap electricity from federally supported municipal dams. Her son-in-law, Congressman Frederick C. Hicks of New York (whose wife, the former Georgiana Pierrepont Strong, had died in Washington a few months before) pushed for an early resolution of Strong's proposal to dam the Colorado River as a wartime expedient and arranged for her to appear before the House of Representatives Committee on Water Power. She began with "I come before you unheralded except where my voice has been heard for 'the greatest good to the greatest number'" and then presented her bona fides: member of the Los Angeles Chamber of Commerce since 1893; chairman of the Whittier Chamber of Commerce Flood Control and Conservation Committee; author of numerous articles on the control of floods for publication ("I told the world for the first time how to handle the waters of the Colorado in this canyon for the great benefit of the Nation"); and patentee of two systems for storage reservoirs in mountain canyons.

She demanded that the United States government itself implement the plans to avoid having private speculators use her discovery for personal gain. When a committee member asked whether her plan might destroy the canyon's scenic grandeur, she replied that the reservoir would be suitable for boating and fishing (precisely the same defense that would later be used to argue for the construction of Hoover—later Boulder—Dam). When Congress turned down her daring Colorado River plan, Strong, proud of her identity as a woman inventor (she once advised women to rely upon their own judgment and never preface an innovation by claiming, "A man suggested this"), attributed the rejection to masculine resistance to the superiority of a woman's plan and, despite the federal government's rejection, continued her battle for long-range water planning for the remainder of her life.

During the war, women were involved in many home-front activities, but there was not the burst of inventing activity one might have expected. Still, there were some notable exceptions. *Club Woman* reported that even Mary Cassatt, the expatriate artist who had lived in Paris for two decades, devoted herself to war work and invented a hammock for a fractured leg, an appliance for a fractured arm, and a splint for a "dropped wrist." Probably the best known inventions were in a conventional field—dress reform—a field in which the General Federation of Women's Clubs had already sown the seed by going on record at its 1914 Biennial Convention in Chicago as favoring simpler, more becoming, and more modest designs in women's clothing, even to the point of "standardized" dress. To those who equated uniformity with loss of individualized style, the federation explained:

> Standardization is a principle and not a uniform; it does not mean adopting a single form of dress for every single occasion, but it does mean that women ought to accept a form of street clothes as unchangeable as the man's suit. Women's clothes will not, even then, look alike for the difference in color, trimming, fabric, and things of that sort, will make the variety, which is evidently so acceptable to women's eye.

Concluding that women should spend their precious time and energy on weightier questions than what to wear, headquarters referred the issue to individual club discussion. When war brought the issue to a head, *General Federation Magazine* provided an ideal forum for protagonists of each side, among them a neophyte to the cause of standardization, May Rhoads. Couturier to New York's fashionable elite, Rhoads was converted when she heard Carrie Chapman Catt and Anna Howard Shaw (president and honorary president, respectively, of the National American Woman Suffrage Association) speak at a suffrage meeting. Here were two women, she thought, who sacrificed their whole lives to the cause of elevating women to noble social interests while her greatest accomplishment had been to decorate her clients so distinctively that Sunday newspapers described "her" clothes rather than their wearers. Convinced that life was "more than meat and the body more than raiment," she shifted her focus to the "earnest woman instead of the other kind."

*Her* kind of earnest women, she said in her patent for a washable, modest, and feminine garment, were: "women working on the farm or in the machine shop, running elevators, driving motor cars, serving as conductors or motormen, or, in short, laboring in any one of the manifold capacities opened to women by modern social and industrial conditions . . . [which] until recently, had been almost exclusively confined to men." The problems were monumental. Women wanted to "look like women" off the job while enjoying the on-the-job security of work clothes that wouldn't tangle in machinery and belting. Since women objected to wearing male clothing for "considerations of natural modesty" and "practical sociologists have seen the danger of permitting them to do so," Rhoads explained that her charter was to fashion a garment that, when worn going to and from the workplace, gave a neat and refined appearance and attracted "no unreasonable attention" but at work made her "readily distinguishable from a man even at a considerable distance."

Employers, with no suitable dressing rooms, were unprepared for the tide of women workers. But clad in a Rhoads dress, an employee arriving at work in conventional attire needed to display no trace of immodesty or even a hint of lingerie. She simply unbuttoned the outer skirted smock, rolled it up, tossed it in her locker, and pitched in for work in a below-the-knee, bloomered garment. At the end of the

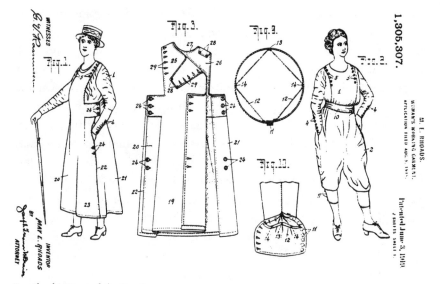

May Rhoads' "Dress of the Hour."

workday, she slipped the skirted smock back on. Delighted clients christened it the "Dress of the Hour," and Rhoads promptly trade-marked the name.

The Rhoads dress truly was of its time, representing a revolt against ostentation, the need to conserve textiles for wartime needs, the major changes that had occurred in women's work, and a reassessment of the very purpose of woman's daytime dress. The General Federation of Women's Clubs, in propagandizing more simple, practical, economical, sober, and sane clothing in its magazine, not only gave official sanction to the dress but furnished Rhoads an ideal pulpit from which to preach her gospel of change. In the federation magazine, Rhoads hailed nine-teenth-century dress reformers as "fearless insurgents" who success-fully liberated the torso from corsets and legs from heavy skirts but failed to realize the perfect combination of freedom and beauty "that is now so happily realized in the dress of the hour." During wartime, said Rhoads, "[w]hen so many of our most cherished theories are undergoing the fierce fire of the crucible," it was even more imperative that women dethrone the "despot Fashion" and release their bodies from constricting and limiting clothing.

New York's C. H. D. Robbins Company, exclusive manufacturer of the "Dress of the Hour," introduced it to the garment trade in *American Cloak and Suit Review* as having won approval "by leading members and officers of the Federation of Women's Clubs who have enthusiastically endorsed and commended it to their members throughout the United States and Canada." The designer's wartime association with the Women's Apparel Unit of the Women's Overseas Hospitals, U.S.A., a nationwide organization of women in the garment trades formed to raise money to sponsor a French refugee center, furnished Rhoads the chance to rub shoulders with industry leaders. These were the women who, according to an article in *Woman Citizen*, "could push and pull strings, and presto, clothes are made," and who could give Rhoads unlimited entrée to women merchandisers and financiers, women's wear trade publication editors such as the chairman of the *Dry Goods Economist*, and women representatives of mail-order houses.

Not only did the prominent fashion magazines laud the dress's combination of style and utility, but Universal Film Company pictured the dress and the story of its creation in an animated monthly shown in ten thousand theaters and *Woman Citizen* showed a woman outfitted for frontline overseas "gas unit" duty in an adaptation of the Rhoads dress. In another issue of *Woman Citizen*, in a segment of its regularly featured "Making the Dress Fit the Task" column, Rhoads, now totally infused with the feminist canon, denounced the past, when "[a] woman's dress expressed the exact measure of her husband's worldly success, his station in life, and his consequent ability to maintain the women of his family in picturesque idleness." Women had now "outgrown the immaturities of thought and feeling that to the doubters seemed so fundamentally and ineradicably feminine," she said, and their dress should express their new stature.

*Woman Citizen* was the perfect vehicle for the Robbins Company's full-page advertisements touting the dress's practicability "now that women have found and are called to so many useful occupations" and urging readers, "If your local dealer or favorite shop does not have 'The Dress of the Hour,' write to us and we will tell you the nearest shop that sells it." Franklin Simon & Company, which sold the dress through its mail-order department, sponsored a special two-day display and advertised: "This Wonderful New Dress embodying beauty, utility, practicability and representing the SPIRIT OF THE TIMES will be shown on a living model [so that] the great number of women of New York and nearby localities who have become interested in this Dress will thus be enabled to see its actual beauty and practicability." The popularity of her dress soared as shops opened special departments devoted exclusively to women in government service or at work on the home front as "farmerettes," chauffeurs, factory workers, and so forth, but Rhoads was not alone in her forward-thinking designs. Best and Company showed "feminine and graceful" outfits designed by former *Vogue* editor Mrs. C.M. Ingersoll, for the specific needs of "The Land Army of America"—presumably those women who heeded the call of the Department of Agriculture to participate in the planting, cultivating, and harvesting of crops. Such farm work required practical clothing. Ingersoll's resembled a riding costume of light cotton twill ("tough stuff khaki"), consisting of trim-fitting breeches topped by a "coat blouse." Puttees could be ordered separately.

A variation on the costume came from Marjorie True Gregg, a young Coloradan who had graduated from Radcliffe College in 1905, stayed to teach history at two private schools for girls in the Boston area, then, as she later put it, "dropped it [teaching] for a business venture." That venture was designing a garment to fit women's needs, from housecleaning to business—what she called in her 1918 patent a "nethergarment." When war broke out, she capitalized upon its potential use by members of the Woman's Land Army by emphasizing in her advertising brochure that her trousered "Putnees," manufactured by the Blakeslee Company in Malden, Massachusetts, were "Practical Garments for Agricultural Workers."

In her patent, Gregg claimed her garment needed only one fixed closure for all sizes, withstood hard usage, remained in position during strenuous exercise, lent itself to easy laundering, and provided "a neat appearance for the wearer's knee." In an interview in *Woman Citizen,* Gregg explained that the war forced her to put her "Radcliffe-trained brains for a whole year into the evolution of trousers for women" and explained to the reporter:

> Even women's riding trousers have been designed to accentuate the bigness of her hips and the smallness of her ankles. They have left no possible reserves for her knock-knees if she has them.

It is all very well to dress woman up like a paper doll, as the man costumier does; but he has made no provision for her stooping over, when the masculine trouser is distinctly unbecoming because the fullness is all in the wrong place, and there is no provision for her lifting her arms without having to come apart at the waistband. Then think how her usefulness is hampered by her lack of pockets.

Gregg considered it a "genuine ethical contribution to the world's progress to give a woman the right kind of clothes in which to carry on her part of the world's work." Franklin Simon, which featured the "Dress of the Hour," also advertised Gregg's contribution, a series of "Practical Garden Clothes for Women Farmers," which included several tops—a generously pocketed blue or khaki tabard, a pocketed shirtwaist of white madras, a blue or khaki smock—as well as a khaki hat and, her special patented invention, blue or khaki "Putnees," which could, at the adjustment of a knee strap, become either breeches or bloomers. Though Gregg felt her patented garment was adaptable to either sex, it appealed only to women. Gregg later served overseas with a YMCA unit in the French Pyrenees and eventually settled in New Hampshire. There, in addition to her church work and organizing and writing for children's Christmas pageants, she designed many of the popular wooden toys manufactured by a local toy mill operated by her sister and brother-in-law and for a while used her ingenuity to create and manufacture tiny dollhouse dolls she called "Real People Dolls."

As the war continued and the countdown began for the woman suffrage amendment still pending in state legislatures, a Detroit businesswoman cited women's wartime contributions as further justification for its ratification, and urged women to seize the whip hand in business activities rather than settle for second place. "There are," she asserted, "just as many women per hundred who are specially capable in all directions as men." And, at war's end, Carrie Chapman Catt saw women becoming so empowered that she fondly hoped: "In another generation the woman who knows how to make bread or an apple pie will be as extinct as a dodo." Time would tell.

# 13

# SAME SONG, SECOND VERSE

*W*hen the war ended, the suffrage amendment was still blocked, and the questions about women's competence were still being asked. *Were* women really as capable as men? That perennial question ("Are Women Inventive?") headed an article in *Woman Citizen*—an auspicious place for an affirmative answer, especially since its author, Florence King, carried impressive professional and feminist credentials. When King responded to the question, she not only responded in the affirmative but told women that if they wanted proper credit in the history books, they should see to it themselves since no one else was interested in setting the record straight.

King was an outspoken suffrage leader in New York's Fifth Assembly District, where she had once attracted attention with her slide lectures on the qualities upon which famous women leaders and innovators had relied to achieve success. She was also a university graduate in mechanical and electrical engineering, a successful patent attorney, and the first woman to win a case in the United States Supreme Court. *Woman Citizen* bragged that this victory, achieved against "the most brilliant lawyers America could produce," put a giant British corporation out of business. In addition, King was attorney for the first "all-woman" patent, Minnie Agnes Phelps's 1906 "Combined

Toaster and Warming Oven," witnessed by Jennie Fiske and Cora Schriver. And if all of the above were not enough, King was founder and first president of the Women's Association of Commerce, a federation of businesswomen's clubs and professional leagues formed in the closing year of World War I to encourage women to greater heights in their professional lives. King told those who attended the association's first annual convention that women must accept new responsibilities and refuse to tread the "beaten path so long followed by men" and reiterated the message that a woman "emerging from the age-old traditions of the past into the sunlight of a new day" must prove to the world by her competency and achievements "that the masculine sex has no monopoly on genius." Though some might have thought her rhetoric too strong, King managed to pursue her professional and her feminist goals while remaining, as the *Chicago Herald* put it, a "refined gentlewoman" and a fitting refutation of arguments against women's entrance into professions.

In answering "Are Women Inventive?" King conceded the overwhelming plurality of men's inventions but rejected any implication that this smaller number connoted lesser genius in women, echoing the refrain of her predecessors: As the world recognized the equal distribution of genius between the genders, as society more willingly invested in women's inventions, as women's educational opportunities and training expanded, women would patent more often. Illustrating the breadth and complexity of women's patents, King showed patent drawings of devices and systems in fields far beyond domestic perimeters, and supplemented them with her own assessment of the magnitude of the achievement they represented.

Included were patent drawings of a corncrib from Lizzie Dickelman of Forest, Ohio, which, said King, were a response to War Food Administrator Herbert Hoover's plea for farmers to conserve precious crops. The oldest of nine children and possessor of only a high school diploma, Lizzie Dickelman went into her father's sheet metal manufacturing company, took over the business upon his death in 1917, and in that year received four patents for various grain-storage devices. By 1920 there were four more patents, including the oblong corncrib King praised, which was perforated from the inside out to deflect rain while still allowing air to flow through naturally. She sold her crib in every state and many foreign countries and earned this encomium from

King: "To invent a device is one thing but successfully to place it upon the market is another. Lizzie H. Dickelman has been able to do both and her product finds its market among the men."

King saluted products that found a market among men, but it goes without saying that money could be made inventing for women. May Rhoads successfully converted the "Dress of the Hour" she had patented for war workers into the epitome of peacetime chic. While the 1918 Rhoads dress was built on basic breeches and blouse in serviceable fabric, she had a surprise for the women of the twenties—black satin breeches topped with a black satin waist. In this, she guaranteed, "[y]ou can do your housework . . . bothered by no troublesome skirts." Over this last word in housework elegance, the woman-on-the-go had but to slip on a tailored overslip—navy blue serge for a tailored look or "Georgette crepe, banded about the skirt with wide black silk braid" for heading out to tea, the matinee, or a restaurant. Rhoads had also added a coat, "strictly and smartly tailored, from its huge collar to the slender belt." Advertising in 1920 in *The Independent Woman,* the magazine of the recently formed National Federation of Business and Professional Women's Clubs, Rhoads noted that she was president of the Better Dress Club for Better Business Women, gave her address— 23 West 30th Street, New York—and urged readers to write for details about membership. The wartime work-dress transformed into wear-everywhere costume for the busy professional woman must have sold well since Rhoads's full-page advertisement continued to appear in subsequent issues.

By August 1920, thirty-five states had finally ratified the Woman's Suffrage Amendment. Thirty-six were needed, and it was a struggle right down to the wire. As Tennessee's state legislature met in special session, wags asked coyly, "Will Tennessee make it a perfect 36?" Brigades of "Suffs" bearing yellow roses, and "Antis" bearing red ones, besieged the capitol, filled the galleries, and spilled onto the floor of the House chamber. Pro-suffragists, noting that brewers and distillers feared that women, if given the vote, would cast it for Prohibition, called the Antis tools of the liquor lobby. Antis, in turn, labeled the suffragists Bolshevik "hatchet women" bent on chopping down the rights and protection of women; snickered that Carrie Chapman Catt's husband was "Tom Catt"; warned of the possibly dire consequences of enfranchising black women; and accused their rivals of bestowing "personal favors" to curry legislative support for suffrage while they themselves delivered only loaves of crusty, home-baked bread. At the end, ratification would have failed had not one delegate changed his vote after his mother wrote: "I have been watching how you stood, but have not noticed anything yet. Don't forget to be a good boy and help Mrs. Catt put the 'rat' in ratification." Harry Burn was a good boy. His vote assured Tennessee's ratification, and the long struggle was over. Now women had the vote, and, since feminists had long argued that women's disenfranchisement had thwarted their creative instincts, they looked forward with interest to see what changes would occur in coming years. In the meantime, they wanted to establish the truth about women's patenting record to date.

King had been persuasive about women's inventive capacity, but how much did the public at large know about women inventors? A member of their own sex, Inez McFee, whose *Stories of American Inventions* was published the following year, began her book auspiciously enough with "The boys, and girls who have an inventive turn of mind and are ambitious to become scientists or inventors, need have no fear as they turn these pages, reading what others have done in the great world of invention." But when one did turn those pages, one found no mention of women among the inventors whose "energy, perseverance, pluck, courage, and application untiring" she extolled. As King said, if women wanted the record set straight, they would have to do it themselves.

Part of that job would fall to Mary Anderson, who, by 1922, was director of the Women's Bureau, an agency that had been inaugurated as a war service and converted in peacetime to furthering working women's welfare. Anderson had begun her own working life as a stitcher in a Chicago shoe factory, serving much of that time as president of the Chicago Boot and Shoe Workers Local. She later became an organizer and eventually an officer of the National Women's Trade Union League, then entered government though her wartime appointment to a subcommittee on women in industry, which was arranged by labor leader Samuel Gompers. When the Department of Labor set up the Women in Industry Service, later called the Women's Bureau, she became its assistant director—the first time, applauded *Woman Citizen*, that a trade union woman had received an appointment to an administrative office in a national executive department. She told that periodical that the "peculiar problems surrounding women in industry have never received enough attention. . . . Woman's Bureau has its work cut out for it."

When Anderson became director of the bureau in 1920, public appreciation of women's wartime work was still fresh, and she felt it was an opportune time to assess their recent contributions in various fields, among them invention. As she wrote in the cover letter she sent to the secretary of labor when submitting study number twenty-eight, *Women's Contributions in the Field of Invention: A Study of the Records of the United States Patent Office,* so many people had asked about women's accomplishments in this field that the bureau had conducted a study of 5,000 patents issued to women in ten randomly selected years between 1905 and 1921. Anderson's 1923 report resonates predictably with Anderson's and her cohorts' feminist rhetoric and arouses a historian's curiosity to see the raw data from which it issued, particularly the letters sent and received that described women's inventive impulses, their successes, and their frustrations. Only the report remains; sadly, the raw data were not preserved.

The purpose of the study, said the compilers, was to resolve whether women had made material contributions to the sum total of creative achievements, whether they had "designed, devised, discovered, and invented to reduce labor, to forestall danger, disease and death, to embellish life with creative comforts, and to enrich humanity with new stores of knowledge." Recognizing that the public was generally aware of the spectacular successes of a few inventive women but ignorant about the creative abilities of women in general, they purposely chose not to focus on those exceptional women but to measure the number and analyze the quality of *all* of women's inventions within a given period, selecting the years 1905, 1906, 1910, 1911, 1913, 1914, 1918, 1919, 1920, and 1921. Like the count done in 1895, this one classified inventions according to the purpose served. Since such an analysis bypassed important psychological factors that did not lend themselves to statistical analysis, the compilers were well aware that records alone did not measure women's creative achievements.

Still, it was better than no effort, and the report loyally stated: "Inventions by women, like inventions by men, are sparks of creative thought that fly from the friction of necessity, from the blows of emergency, or from the smolder of concentrated research." It also took ample notice of the restrictions society imposed on women, consigning them to the domestic sphere and limiting their access to facilities and materials beyond. Supportive faith kindled men's creativity, the report noted; apathy, skepticism, and often open hostility stifled women's. This, the report commented, led women to be timid about even applying for patents for their inventions and fostered their tendency to allow their male relatives, possessed of a "greater self-confidence born of freedom from restricting customs," to perfect their ideas and secure the patents for them. It was almost a voice-over from Matilda Gage: It was remarkable that women invented at all.

Despite excessive discouragement, however, more and more women, 34 percent more in 1921 than in the preceding six years, safeguarded their ideas with patents in their own names. As a proportion of all inventors, however, their numbers were so modest that Anderson resorted to a sea of aquatic metaphor to depict how drowned out they were by the whole: "the torrential volume" of men's inventions; "so submerged are the patents issued to women in the flood of patents"; "thin streams of water trickling here and there into a strong, steady current . . . less than 2 percent of the volume of water," and so on. In fact, women's inventions accounted for only 1.48 percent of the total, though within that number there were quite an extraordinary variety of devices: 221 contrivances for making work easier on the farm, including cultivators, seed planters, tractors, and windmills; over 1,000 articles for personal wear or use, from hooks and eyes to toothbrushes; 71 articles for office supplies; and 81 improvements to railways.

The answers participants in the study (unfortunately not identified by name or patent number) gave to questions about why they invented are refreshingly straightforward, particularly those from farm women. A Florida inventor of a fertilizer-distributing device attributed her invention to: "Yankee laziness, I reckon. I didn't like the idea of bending my back so much, hence the distributor." A Texas woman with a new and useful improvement on a cultivator tongue wrote, "Having been raised on a farm and seeing that there was needed improvement of cultivator tongues, I made up my mind to improve on the old style tongue." A woman with a sugarcane stripper related, "I was farming in 1916 and planted sugar cane to make molasses. When time came to strip cane, I was short of help and I shirked the old tiresome way of stripping cane. I then studied out a new way. . . . After three trials I had what I needed. I had it to work perfect and I could do with it as much as four persons could do in the length of time in the old way and make a better job of the work of stripping, as it saved labor, prevented backaches, sore hands, and the worn-out tired feeling." A Minnesota woman said of the genesis of her portable smokehouse: "As a farmer's wife my duty was to cure meats for summer use and smoked meat is very much favored in my family. I tried to make mine without expense, and after I completed this device, I used it successfully two years before I obtained a patent on it."

In other fields, a woman who invented a window ventilator answered: "[I was] two weeks ill in bed at home and three weeks in bed in a hospital during a hot, rainy June and early July. I had started it [the ventilator] before, but not until I had to lie in those hot stuffy rooms did I realize how badly it was needed." The woman who developed a telephone muffler had visited a New York hotel: "I could hear a man in the next room while using the telephone. I thought it out, worked it out, made a crude one and went to my patent attorney's office with my crude model and had him test it by using it." In the household field, a woman who invented a reinforced wooden bowl that wouldn't split and spill water on the floor when she made butter approached a company with her patent, but the manufacturer rejected it because it was so sturdy that it would last *too* long.

Automobiles prompted new inventions. Asked what circumstance led her to invent a windshield wiper, one inventor replied that she had once noticed that trolley conductors had wipers for their glass windshields and decided to adapt the same principle to her car. (No, this was not a reply from Mary Anderson, since the year of her patent was not considered in the study.) Another woman invented a combined license plate holder and signal device because she was "impressed with the fact that must be obvious to anyone, that at present it is practically impossible to read the number [on the rear] of a moving automobile at night. It is, of course, of the highest importance that it should be made possible for officers and for citizens to be able to make out the number as it is speeding away at night."

The responses themselves revealed a marked diversity in the background and training of the respondents, ranging from some who could scarcely write to obviously educated women committed to "scientific" cooking, preserving, canning, and cleaning. Among the latter was the inventor of a kitchen cabinet, who identified herself as a home economics teacher:

> I was living in one room and taking my meals anywhere I wished. Many times I desired to get my own breakfast and suppers in my room, as many persons do, in order to save time, to reduce living expenses, and to have a chance to eat some of my own cooking. I desired a piece of furniture in my one room which would give the service of an entire kitchen but at the same time be an attractive piece of furniture for a living or bed room. I designed such a cabinet, had it made and furnished as a piece of mahogany furniture and found after using it that it answered my purpose perfectly. Knowing that thousands and thousands of women were similarly situated, I thought I would get my device manufactured and placed on the market.

Their replies shed no new light on their gender's "genius" for inventing, but the overall study disclosed one persistent underlying theme — the difficulty and cost of patenting and marketing the invention. Most were gloomy about women's prospects for exploiting their inventions, and "not a few," said the report, asked if some institute or agency might not introduce inventors to prospective buyers. That section of the report is an almost exact parallel to the discouragement voiced by correspondents to Charlotte Smith's *Woman Inventor* three decades before: the tough, often galling, efforts to raise capital to promote their inventions, and the scant, often grudging, recognition of their accomplishment if they were successful despite those odds. And of course the agency they were suggesting was the very one Charlotte Smith had promised one of her readers but had been unable to get the government to fund.

General press coverage of the study was supportive, quoting profusely Anderson's more trenchant paragraphs and arriving at conclusions similar to those of the study, which in turn were similar to those that had been voiced for a century. In the words of *Equal Rights* magazine: "As opportunities are gradually opened to women along these lines, with the development of recognition given women's work everywhere, the Women's Bureau feels that it will not be long before women as inventors will be recognized as their other work has been, and that the entire country will benefit."

No observers expressed surprise that "Household" led the list of patent classifications, with 27.5 percent of the total, and that "Personal Wear and Use" came in second with 21.7 percent; even the accelerated increase in inventions by women in recent years was to be expected. Nor was it news that women patented in a wider range of activities. In sum, women had come a long way; given opportunity, they would probably go further. It sounded as if the congregation might be repeating the same litany forever.

Three years after the Woman's Bureau study, Patent Office assistant examiner Joseph Rossman published a study of woman inventors in the *Journal of the Patent Office Society*. Even though he repeated the commissioner's miscalculated 1900 statistics, he said that according to psychological tests for invention conducted by George Washington University's Dr. F. A. Moss, women's mental grasp of what actually constituted invention was equal to, and sometimes greater than, men's. But understanding what constituted invention and actually inventing were two different things, and the reason for women's lesser achievement in the field of invention, said Rossman, was that society, under the "erroneous notion that woman's place is in the home," had almost extinguished her spark of creativity. The litany went on! But Rossman saw a ray of hope: Women of the twenties were breaking the ties of societal conventions that bound them and were demanding the same opportunities as those enjoyed by men.

Like the *Scientific American* writer who was staggered by Beulah Louise Henry's sheer "diversity of invention," Rossman allotted so much of his article to this descendant of Patrick Henry that he must have deemed her the very embodiment of the new twenties woman whose creative spark had not been doused by society. Henry, whose admirers called her "Lady Edison," more for the quantity than the impact of her inventions, was the most prolific woman inventor of the twenties and continued to patent in subsequent decades. *Scientific American* credited her with a remarkable (and inaccurate) forty-seven patents by 1924. Henry was the subject of a good many interviews over the decades, and the number of patents grew accordingly until Stacy Jones, ace patent reporter for the *New York Times*, reporting on

Henry's latest invention in 1962 (a combination mailing and return envelope manufactured in continuous strips and therefore easily addressed by machine), noted that though Henry had lost count of the number of her patents, the Patent Office had not; records showed her 1962 invention was her forty-fifth.

Henry's inventive career began when, at fifteen, she patented a vacuum ice-cream freezer. By the end of the 1920s she had already patented such diverse items as a telephone index that attached to the phone and opened like a fan; a "Kiddie Clock" for teaching children the time of day; a machine for placing snap fasteners on clothing; a "Takes the Cake" doll-shaped rubber sponge (a set of which was called "Dolly Dips") with the soap snapped into its center so that youngsters couldn't lose it; and a "Miss Illusion" doll in which interchangeable snap-on wigs transformed blond to brunette, pushing a button changed blue eyes to brown, turning her frock inside out created a new look, and a small mechanism within ("All the time my mind's eye could see the machinery working inside her head") closed her eyes to create the illusion of sleep.

By the thirties, the "tall, blonde and svelte" Henry, who, one smitten reporter wrote, "looks more like Mae West than the movie conception of an inventor," reported she had over sixty patents, including a rubber reducing garment, hair curler, the "Protograph" (a typewriter attachment that gave four original copies without carbon paper), a lockstitch bobbinless sewing machine, and an umbrella with from two to six interchangeable snap-on covers to allow matching the umbrella to that day's garment. When asked the source of her ideas, she chalked them up to some "inner vision" that had impelled her since childhood. "I know," she told one reporter, "less than nothing about the laws of physics, mechanics or chemistry." When another interviewer asked her the same question, she replied that she simply trusted her instincts: "I invent because I cannot help it." To another, she vouchsafed, "I know nothing about mechanical terms and am afraid I do make it rather difficult for the draughtsmen to whom I explain my ideas, but in the factories where I am known they are exceedingly patient with me because they seem to have a lot of faith in my inventiveness. I have my inventions patented in four different countries, and I am President of two newly incorporated companies." To still another, she responded,

"I am an inspirational inventor. I get a complete picture in my mind of what the invention will be like when it is finished and then set to work to get my model-maker to create a model to fit my mind's picture. Inventing is really easy; it's the development work that is heart-breaking."

As for the umbrella, she claimed the idea of snapping the corners of the umbrella to the frame simply came to her at a matinee she attended with her mother:

> That snapper had worried me for a long time. The biggest umbrella men in the country said it could not be done. Of course I did not believe them, because when I start out to do a thing I usually manage to get it done some time. I was putting my gloves on when that snapper in all its details visualized itself against a green drapery. That ended the theater party. Mother wanted to know if I was ill, but I told her it was only the snapper and I asked her to excuse me because I just had to sketch it out on paper before I should forget. Now I have the snappers patented, also the little steel pincers that fasten the seams to the frame.

Learning what kind of snappers to use was one thing. It was quite another to manufacture and market them. Having been turned down by one manufacturer after another in her hometown of Memphis, she finally took the idea to New York umbrella manufacturers, who argued that they couldn't possibly pierce the rib with the kind of snapper she proposed. After a particularly discouraging day, she reported, she went home and "with a stone for a work bench and a hammer and nails for implements, I made a hole in the tip of that steel rib. Then I got a cake of soap and a nail file and modeled the style of snapper that would be strong enough to do duty on a windy day." Armed with proof of its practicality, she had no trouble finding a manufacturer, and received about $50,000 for the idea. Lord and Taylor even displayed her umbrellas in its front window. As she said a good many years later: "If necessity is the mother of invention, then resourcefulness is the father."

If Henry was the most fruitful woman inventor of the twenties (and subsequent decades), one of the most unusual was Marjorie Joyner. Sixty-one years after her 1928 patent, the Forty-fourth National Convention of National Council of Negro Women, in its "Salute to Black Women Who Make It Happen," honored the ninety-three-year-old as one who had done just that, and the *Washington Post* hailed her as the "Grande Dame of Black Beauty Culture." In 1928, however, she was only a thirty-two-year-old who made no money from the machine she had just patented, a permanent waving machine that, she stated in the patent, "will wave the hair of both white and colored people." It consisted of an electrically powered device with cords, metal curling irons, and clamping devices suspended from a dome. Joyner described how the operator first placed flannel around each one-inch square of the patron's hair, wrapped the hair on the iron, placed a special protector against the scalp, and then, when all curling irons were in position, attached the clamps, making sure the cord lengths were adjusted to lift weight away from the patron's head. She then turned on the current. Joyner's patent was for the mechanical device only; successful use depended upon careful training and practice in dividing, wrapping, and heating the curls, then unwrapping and setting the newly "permed" hair when the waving was complete.

Joyner had spent years learning the art. After she arrived in Chicago from Mississippi when she was about twenty, she became affiliated with Sarah Breedlove McWilliams ("Madame") Walker, a self-educated and astute businesswoman who began selling her products door-to-door, then lectured and demonstrated in churches and clubs and successfully established the "Walker Way" for black women to smooth dull, rough hair. The "Walker Way" involved a hot hair-straightening comb, hot-iron curlers, and hair-softening pomades and ointments. Establishing a company to manufacture her products in Indianapolis, she was soon earning a fortune by selling "Walker Way" products through carefully selected "Walker Agents." Also known as "hair culturists," these agents operated in an age before beauty shops proliferated. Dressed neatly in black skirts and white shirtwaist blouses, with Madame C.J. Walker's Hair Grower—along with sixteen other products—tucked neatly into their distinctive black satchels, they carried the tools of their trade with them and dressed clients' hair in their own homes.

As a result of Walker's trip to Paris, Josephine Baker, reigning chanteuse of the twenties, had her hair dressed in the Walker method

Marjorie Joyner, inventor of a permanent wave machine.

and launched such a fad that a French company copied Walker's pomade and christened it the "Baker-Fix." It was the Walker company for whom Joyner worked when she patented, and today she remembers its beginning:

> Well, I was working for Mrs. Walker, and, you know, it was just a necessity to finish our hair after we washed it. We needed to do *something!* We operators might put in a very nice hairdo, but it would never last very long, and in the morning, a customer who looked beautiful when she left my care looked like an accident going some-place to happen. It is important for a woman to show that she takes care of her hair, and that was in my mind when I invented the machine. It would allow a woman to look neat, and that is important. I can't tell you how important!

In the years that followed, during the Depression of the thirties, Joyner stressed the importance of good grooming to those she encountered while working in the New Deal's WPA, CCC, and NYA ("I feel as if I worked for *all* the agencies with letters!"). Trying to find housing and work for young blacks, she made it her mission to instill personal pride in those who pounded the pavements searching for jobs—any jobs. "It was really hard to get work," she recalls, "and if they wanted to get a job, they had to go out looking well, no matter how hard times were. I worked with both men and women. I told them to keep up good grooming, that a good personal appearance helps people get and hold jobs. I even taught them how to walk and sit down. I *still* talk about that. People need to make their own opportunities, and appearance is important."

Joyner became national supervisor of the Mme. C. J. Walker Manufacturing Company's nationwide chain of beauty schools. One of them featured her in a postwar trade magazine advertisement that guaranteed "Easy Terms—Pay While You Learn" and recommended beauty culture to job-seekers:

> Beauty Culture offers post-war security and independent living and an opportunity to serve others. There is tremendous demand for efficient operators. The college is also a supply station for our Chicago Agents and Representatives. All the Mme. C. J. Walker famous preparations may be purchased here. We specialize in teaching Hair Styling, from the nation's most outstanding teachers. Vapoil Cold Curl, Cold Waving and Permanent Waving on pressed hair.

Though Joyner says all beauty operators agree that "hair is hair," white operators have their own trade organization while the group she calls "our people" is the organization she founded in 1945 with Mary McCloud Bethune, the United Beauty School Owners and Teachers Association, a parent group comprising about twenty-five accredited schools in America whose graduates make up the Alpha Phi Pi Omega sorority and fraternity. Joyner takes pride in its selective membership: "We have always been very particular about who joins—they have to have good moral character as well as getting a state license."

While over six decades have passed since she patented her machine, Joyner reprises the steps: giving each strand "three main twists," a technique she still teaches her students and one she vows she will be teaching until the day she dies, and heating the hair to give a lasting curl. Though her machine was successful, no profits passed to the inventor. Mr. Ransom, the Harvard-educated lawyer who, she asserts, helped Walker build the company, told her the patent belonged to the company. She is unfazed:

> I never got a penny from it, but that's O. K. I never paid any attention to how they used it. The Lord has directed me in what I've done. I don't have a whole loaf of bread, but I have a thick slice. I have my health; I have a beautiful house of my own; I've worked seventy-three years in this house, and the walls are covered with pictures of people I have known, and I have wonderful memories of them. Every day I go down to the Chicago *Daily Defender*, our only black paper, because I am president of their charities. I've ridden at the head of their Bud Billiken parade and picnic for sixty years. The second Saturday in August.

Asked what she thought of women in business, Joyner didn't hem and haw: "Why, they just have a whole lot of common sense; they can bridge the gap men don't see. There is nothing a woman can't do. Men might think they do things all by themselves—but a woman is always there guiding them or helping them. You can tell people that!"

Beulah Henry typified independent women inventors struggling to patent and market their inventions; Joyner typified the employee whose brainchild belonged to her employer. The "corporate" woman patentee became more common as the century progressed, since the number of women who gained advanced degrees reached a height in the years immediately preceding and following World War I not to be matched until the 1970s. As more women acquired degrees in science and engineering, they qualified for research positions with access to the finest testing facilities, and companies hired them for the specific purpose of developing new processes and products and acquired patent rights to whatever they developed under the company aegis. While working women had in the past often sold their patent rights to employers if they were lucky, the "corporate" inventor, employed for the purpose of inventing, was a relatively new breed.

One of them was Olive Dennis, and her field was railroading. While a number of women had firsthand experience from living near railroad tracks or junctions and had patented a variety of devices—the *Boston Transcript* had noted their increasing numbers in 1910—there was no female counterpart to Henry Bessemer, whose steel rails the Pennsylvania Railroad first installed in 1863; to Samuel F. B. Morse, whose telegraph enabled dispatchers to pinpoint each train's exact location and assure engineers that the track was (or was *not*) clear ahead; to George Westinghouse, who proposed halting speeding trains with air and put air tanks on each car to deliver the pressure at the engineer's signal; to Eli H. Janney, whose "knuckle coupler" (so called because it resembled a human hand with fingers curled) allowed the brakeman to wield a long lever rather than stand between two cars when attaching them ("shaking hands"). But with all that progress in railroading, filthy cars and woefully inadequate ventilation still plagued passengers. When Dennis emerged from graduate school, she joined the Baltimore and Ohio Railroad and devoted her entire working life to improving such conditions.

As far back as 1852 *Scientific American* said that lack of ventilation made railroad travel the most unpleasant means of transportation. If windows were open, smoke and cinders blew in; if they were shut, passengers felt stifled; screens kept out cinders but offered no protection from drafts. Among the many inventors who had tried to solve the problem was Augusta Rodgers, who capped the smokestack with a device to funnel smoke and cinders into tubes that, in turn, discharged them toward the ground, where they provided additional traction to the wheels. Others devised a variety of screens and wind deflectors—to no avail.

It is no wonder, then, that by the 1920s B & O employee Dennis decided to forget the window and install a ventilator right into the side wall of the car itself. She was no ordinary employee with a tip in the suggestion box but the first woman member of the American Railway Engineering Association, the woman about whom the association's chairman responded after hearing her first report, "I wish to say on behalf of the Association that it was presented ably, clearly and concisely, indicating a thorough knowledge of the subject." She was a science and mathematics graduate of Goucher College, recipient of a masters in mathematics and astronomy from Columbia, and only the second woman to graduate with a degree in civil engineering from Cornell, where she remembered hearing a bystander snipe as she walked by in the commencement procession: "Now what the heck can a woman do in engineering?"

Dennis was confident she could do plenty if someone would only hire her, but after repeated rebuffs in finding work, she was forced to conclude that no one expected a woman to know anything about practical engineering work. She finally landed a draftsman's job in the bridge section of the Baltimore and Ohio Railroad, a railroad she had previously known only as a Baltimore commuter—"the acid test of any railroad." The employment of a woman engineer raised eyebrows until an article in the company's house organ, *Baltimore and Ohio Magazine*, aptly titled "Can a Woman Be a Civil Engineer?" diffused the doubt. In that article Dennis engagingly described how as a small child she lingered on the way to school to watch construction workers operating derricks and cranes; how her interest in dolls was restricted to constructing furniture for them; how she built toys from the day she first learned to drive a nail; how, at ten, she ruined her father's finest tools building a model trolley car, complete with seats that turned over and steps that moved up and down; how her youthful absorption in her civil engineer brother's books prompted her to learn about building bridges; how she withstood the cold during a six-week stint in surveying camp because she had trained the previous December by laying out Ithaca's railroad and liked being out-of-doors, freezing weather or not. Gender, she said, was no impediment: "There is no reason that a woman can't be an engineer simply because no other woman has ever been one; a woman can accomplish anything, if she tries hard enough."

The young "lady engineer," as most newspaper reporters called her, quite captivated one interviewer, who gushed that she had "a delightful personality and is an interesting conversationalist; to meet her is to like her. Besides her knowledge of bridge construction, she is a talented pianist and singer; she understands several languages and dearly loves to knit socks." To learn whether knitting socks was her only "feminine" attribute, a male colleague piped up, "Ask her if she's afraid of mice." "No," responded the intrepid Dennis, "I'm not afraid of mice or snakes—but I'm horribly afraid of bugs! Ugh!" That apparently qualified her to be a "real" woman, despite her engineering degree.

Fourteen months after she joined B & O, the railroad's president, forecasting intensified competition from automobiles and buses and eager to improve his line's service to the women who comprised almost half its users, selected her to study the problems firsthand. As a consumer advocate, she rode over forty-four thousand miles the

Olive Dennis's patented B & O "Blue China."

first year, mainly in day coaches, and if she felt nervous about taking on the new responsibilities, she consoled herself with the thought that any woman with the nerve to tackle courses in an engineering college as the only woman in the class would be able to handle the lesser challenge.

In riding the rails, Dennis observed that women in the dining cars were sensitive to the restful ambience created by tables attractively set with flowers, linen napkins, and smart china; so in honor of the hundredth anniversary of the company's founding, she designed and patented what became B & O's famous "Blue China," eminently appropriate for the newly redecorated "colonial" dining cars. Each piece featured at the center a scenic location along the rail lines, and each was bordered by scenes of motive power the company had employed, from the horse-drawn car to *Tom Thumb* to the double-unit diesel-electric. They became such favorite collectors' items that at the railroad's centennial celebration in 1928, the Fair of the Iron Horse, the company sold 1,900 souvenir dinner plates and took orders on $4,000 worth of orders for other pieces. Today, the china is still popular with visitors to B & O's Railroad Museum in Baltimore. In addition to writing a descriptive book on the Blue China, Dennis researched, for other company booklets, such sites along B & O's right-of-ways as the blockhouses federal troops used to guard the bridges during the Civil War, and pored over thousands of Brady, Poe, and Gardner photographs to gather material for the company's archives.

It was in her capacity as consumer advocate, as she checked on rail passengers' complaints that the removable ventilators and screens limited passengers' vision and made it difficult to raise and lower windows, that she decided to build her new small ventilator right into the sash below the window. This meant that each individual passenger could control the air flow, shutting out summer rain when needed or, as her patent stated, introducing a "comfortable breath of fresh air . . . in even the coldest weather without drafts on the occupants of the seat behind." B & O was delighted with her ingenuity, and a member of its law department to whom Dennis went with her patent affadavit pronounced her a "wonderful girl." He no doubt meant it as a compliment—that despite her advanced degree, her career in railroading, and her inventive skills, she was still all woman—and a young one at that.

A strong advocate of a college education and of Cornell's civil engineering program in particular, Dennis told a writer for her alma mater, "[T]he general training my engineering course gave me is invaluable. It helps in my approach to a problem, my analysis of what is wrong with a car, or a method of operation, and my reasoning to a concrete suggestion for improvement." Her concrete suggestion proved such a boon to improved circulation that when the first mechanically air-conditioned car, the B & O's diner *Martha Washington*, went into regular service in 1930, she was justifiably proud that her long advocacy of proper ventilation had pioneered a new form of climate control.

Dennis was an innovator in other ways as well. Two years after the epic flight of the *Spirit of St. Louis*, B & O, aware that airplanes would compete with railroad service, offered special connections to enable travelers to go one way by rail and return by air, and asked Dennis, ever the observant engineer but nervous about the new form of travel, to take one of the first trips to decide what passengers might need for more comfortable air travel. She reassured herself that the plane had three engines, "any one of which was equivalent to the one which carried Lindbergh across the Atlantic."

In her years as "Engineer of Service" Dennis enhanced both the appearance and the operation of the railroad, from sleeper service ("Sleep like a kitten on the B & O") to light-lunch counters in coaches, from ventilators to new seat upholstery, from clean lavatories to plane and bus connections between strategic points. Dennis encouraged other young women to get engineering degrees and never felt that her gender had stood in the way of her advancement. She modestly called herself only "a giver of suggestions," but one writer, discussing the contributions of women engineers, saw the matter quite differently: "When you ride the B & O, observe the excellent passenger service and equipment, the efficiency of operation, the charm of the cars; interiors and furnishings—[it's] all a credit to Olive W. Dennis, a woman 'railroading' engineer."

Despite Olive Dennis's success in the field, few other women graduated in engineering, and those who did tended toward electrical rather than civil engineering. One *New York Times* writer thought he knew why. In a burst of chauvinistic "humor," he opined that women preferred to become electrical engineers because that specialty sounded cleaner, while civil engineers, "who by the sound of the name ought to have perfect manners," got "quite dusty putting up skyscrapers and building tunnels." This was progress?

# 14

# DEPRESSION, WAR, AND PEACE

*W*ith the Depression of the 1930s bringing mass unemployment, slogans such as "Don't steal a job from a man" and "Get the Men Back to Work" so discriminated against women in the work place that even single women who traditionally worked in offices, factories, stores, schools, and the government had a hard time hanging on to their jobs. It was even worse for married women. Twenty-six states actually prohibited employing them. *Scribner's* carried articles titled "Must Married Women Work?" and "Shall Married Women Be Hired?" The Civil Service ruled that it would employ only one member of a family, and, while it didn't specify that that employee had to be male, the largest number the agency dismissed were, not surprisingly, working wives. It was clear that unless forced by dire necessity to become the family breadwinner when a spouse was laid off or had his wages cut, married women were to be kept out of the labor market. College deans warned their students that these were bad years to be thinking about careers, even in nursing and teaching, fields traditionally made up of women.

Within only a few years, however, World War II came, and the pendulum swung the other way. Women were recruited to fill jobs—with the understanding that it would be only for the duration. Almost five years later, when the war was over, so were their jobs. They were expected to go quietly. In the postwar realignment of occupations, the new slogan was "Give the job to a vet." After making major gains in manufacturing and technical work, women were forced to retreat to such typical "women's jobs" as teaching and office work or, of course, just staying home—leaving them both frustrated and deeply embittered. The times did not spur women to invent.

Nor did those who had done so in the past get any recognition from Esse Virginia Hathaway, whose book, *Partners in Progress,* came out in 1935. In the foreword, she told her readers that the book would include men and women who were "first to lead out in medicine and science, in mechanical inventions, and in a better understanding of their fellow human beings," but the only women's names in the mechanical inventions section were there because they were spouses. The index told the story. Samuel Morse, having married twice, accounted for two women into the index: "Lucretia Walker, marrying Morse" and "Griswold, Sara Elizabeth, Morse's second wife." Since, as Florence King had said, women themselves would have to set the record straight, it's particularly galling when women like Hathaway failed to do so. Fortunately, the Women's Bureau was still around, trying to do just that.

The bureau must have hoped to recommend invention as a money-making option when it assembled a collection of articles on women's inventive activities and compiled a bibliography on the subject. Most of the articles described the experiences of women who displayed their inventions at the National Inventors Congress in Chicago in 1937 and in New York two years later. If the bureau was counting on the press to applaud women's efforts, it would have been encouraged by *Washington Star* writer James Miller's article, "All Inventors Are Not Male" and the *Christian Science Monitor*'s interviews with women who were hopeful about their business prospects. On the other hand, *Literary Digest*'s article telling how Beulah Henry ascribed the success of her patents to her "Inner Vision" would hardly stimulate other would-be inventive women. Nor would articles dispensing the same old bromides, that it was only natural for women to invent, as the *Providence Journal* put it, "mostly devices for the enhancement of beauty or for the simplifying of household duties." If the bureau expected to find that invention was a promising field of employment for women, it was sorely disappointed, for reports showed that, aside from Henry, few inventors were able to find investors to buy patent rights or back them financially.

Despite the dim prospects, a writer in an article in *Independent Woman*, the new magazine for women in business begun by the National Federation of Women's Clubs, encouraged ingenious women to hire a good attorney to storm the gates of the Patent Office, "the last domain to open its doors to women." Author Ruth Arel even had a specific lawyer to recommend: the ardent advocate of women's causes, Washington attorney Marie K. Saunders, who could, guaranteed Arel, read blueprints of complicated machinery "as easily as her morning paper." Saunders was also president of the Woman Patent Lawyers' Association, and it was in this capacity that she masterminded the barrage of letters that forced organizers to scrap their original plans for the Patent Banquet celebration of the hundredth anniversary of the 1836 Patent Act, which, next to the original law of 1790, was the most significant piece of patent legislation passed to that date. Originally to be excluded from the banquet and permitted only to appear after dinner to hear the speeches, women were, instead, well represented after Saunders made the issue public.

While the Depression discouraged many women who would otherwise have elected to pursue advanced degrees, many of those who had previously earned their credentials were able to keep their jobs. Among them was a young woman who at nineteen had already topped her Bryn Mawr Bachelor's degree in physics with a masters in science. Katharine Blodgett emerged at the height of World War I with such a brilliant academic record (and a thesis topic—on the action of gases in gas masks—so appropriate at the time) that General Electric Research Laboratory in Schenectady hired her as its first woman scientist and assigned her to assist the prominent Dr. Irving Langmuir. When Langmuir astonished the scientific world by describing the properties of monomolecular films on water and then learning to transfer those layers to solid substances, he credited most of the experimental work to the twenty-one-year-old Blodgett, a "gifted experimenter [with a] rare combination of theoretical and practical ability."

Langmuir, nominated for a Nobel Prize as early as 1927 and winning it for "surface chemistry" in 1932, had opened numerous doors for Blodgett, most notably to Cambridge University's Cavendish Labora-

Katherine Blodgett in the General Electric laboratory.

tory, where in 1926 she became the first woman to earn a Ph.D. in physics. Returning to Schenectady, she worked with Langmuir first on high-vacuum tubes and then, in the later 1930s, on an expansion of the study he had begun fifteen years before, which established that oily substances spread out on water in a film only a single molecule thick. Since the film reduced the glare from the water, it would undoubtedly also reduce the glare on glass if one could find a way to use the floating film to coat it. Blodgett successively lowered metal and glass plates into the oil-slicked water until she built up a series of thin, gelatinous layers of almost infinitesimal thickness. Finally, by selecting the exact thickness needed to neutralize light rays reflecting from the glass, she found a way to create "invisible glass," not the kind of glass used for showcases, which was ordinary glass arranged at an angle so that its reflected light didn't catch the eye of bystanders, but, instead, glass coated with a film that reduced the reflection (and thus the glare) from its surface.

Of that 1938 discovery, *New York Times* reporters predicted that the new product would make windows "disappear," relieve eyeglass wearers of the reflections from stray beams of light, and make possible new feats of photography. Blodgett herself reminisced of her discovery, "You keep barking up so many wrong trees in research. It seems sometimes as if you're going to spend your whole life barking up wrong trees. And I think there is an element of luck if you happen to bark up the right one. This time I eventually happened to bark up one that held what I was looking for."

The next problem confronting Blodgett was to find a way to measure the thickness of the film layers she built up, since even the most finely calibrated devices of her time could measure nothing thinner than one ten-thousandth of an inch. Her barium stearate film layers, however, were so thin that if one were to pile thirty-five thousand of them, one on top of another, they would still be no thicker than an ordinary piece of paper. Since the films reflected different colors of light depending upon their thickness (one thickness appearing blue while another looks green, for instance), Blodgett recognized that color could provide the answer. Blodgett explained, as she often did in her talks on science to schoolchildren, that as soap bubbles changed in size according to how much they were inflated, their color varied with the thickness of the bubble. She simply decided to use refracted light as a gauge of thickness by recording the color of each successive layer of film to determine its thickness. Her invention made it possible to apply films in the exact thickness required to make glass "invisible."

The public, with its insatiable appetite for intimate details about the woman behind the invention, wondered whether the "famous lady chemist" was a "stick-in-the-lab scientist" or an all-around just-plain-folks woman. The woman author of *American Women of Science* reassured the ambitious young: "Like so many of our successful women of science she has been able to master a laboratory without losing a home, and to develop a passion for the invisible molecule without losing in any sense her appreciation for the visible beauty of a single rose." A female newspaper scribe made her even more adorable: "skimpy five feet tall . . . with a dash of the pixie . . . [and] a tip-tilted nose . . . no slave to the laboratory" but with interests ranging from "the profundities of algebraic equations to the frivolities of wood-chopping for fun." Her dread of snakes was but an endearing flaw: "It is reassuring to the average unscientific human to ferret out that the woman who calmly manipulates molecular films only one-millionth of an inch thick, to eliminate refracted light on glass plates, is thrown into a shrieking panic on meeting face to face with a common garter snake." In 1939, revulsion against icky creatures seemed to be necessary to certify that a woman scientist had not lost her femininity by donning a white lab coat. There it was: for Dennis, bugs; for Blodgett, snakes. No one, however, could cast Blodgett as domestic. She cooked only when she had to; she sewed "once in a blue moon." Her life was the laboratory. And yet, the temptation to cast women in domestic roles remained so strong that the company mail deliverer found it hard to believe that this woman whom he saw each day in her pin-striped cotton dress and white cotton stockings was the recipient of hosts of awards and honors and one of the country's leading scientific lights. According to Ruth Shoemaker of General Electric's Hall of History, Blodgett's striped cotton dress and sensibly low-heeled shoes made her look, at least to him, like some kind of "matron" on the housekeeping detail.

Things were not quite so difficult for women in less unconventional fields, though they certainly weren't treated the way men were. Inventor "Merry Hull" (whose real name was Gladys Whitcomb, later Geissman) was a gifted young industrial designer, one of four to win a thousand-dollar 1939 prize from Lord and Taylor for applying ingenuity and artistry to commercial products—in her case, gloves. After attending a professional glove school, Hull decided to create a pair of handmade gloves for her sister, and these became the prototypes for the award-winning "finger-free" gloves, the first basic pattern change in gloves in over a century. Hull's revolutionary change added a third dimension to gloves: insertions that made the glove conform to the hand's anatomy and provided comfort and flexibility. Hull explained her changes: "No one seems to believe that the hand has thickness as a dimension. The tips of the fingers, however tapered, do not come to a point. They are U-turned. Yet all glove fingers end in V-points. Likewise the wall of the palm continuing the little finger has definite thickness. . . . I have put walls into my gloves which allow the hand and the fingers full freedom. You don't have to ease into my gloves. You just slip them right on."

She patented the new glove; copyrighted the "finger-free" name; sold rights to the Daniel Hays glove firm, which introduced the glove in 1938; and saw it featured in all the major specialty stores in the country. The public attention her ingenuity and commercial success attracted would have been welcome had it not given more weight to her attractive appearance than to her mechanical ingenuity. Even at

"Merry Hull" (Gladys Whitcomb Geissmann) with machinery for cutting her "Finger-Free Gloves."

the Waldorf-Astoria award ceremony, the presenter, overcompensating for any possible doubts the audience might have that the decidedly comely designer before him was also a mechanical prodigy, volunteered that Hull did not "draw merely pretty pictures" but had so carefully drafted the plans for the machinery to cut the glove forms that the gloves required almost no snipping or finishing. Even a member of her own sex, *New York Times* reporter Kathleen McLaughlin, in an article titled "Fragile Bit of Femininity," opined that the inventor of the new glove was "pretty enough to double for a chorus girl in the year's best revue" and pointed out that most people would think it "comic" that this young woman, with "honest smudges on her nose and a heap of man-sized tools at her elbow," earned her living designing machinery and furniture. The new magazine *Invention and Finance* pictured Hull on the cover of its December 1939 issue and gave good coverage to her invention in an accompanying, anonymous article, but the author nonetheless borrowed the same show-biz metaphor: "[Hull] would look swell in the front line of a chorus—yet she has the brain of an inventor." It's no wonder that Hull complained that such attitudes deterred women from entering the fertile and profitable field of industrial design!

"Merry Hull," however, had had enough parental encouragement during her early years that she was relatively immune to what others thought and said about her. She had first learned to work with her hands from her father, a manual training instructor who taught her to tool, sew, and paste leather; to file, solder, and shape metals; and to set stones for costume jewelry. When he built a room for her, she designed the furniture. She was born in Oklahoma and grew up in Ohio, where she attended Ohio Wesleyan College for three years before switching to Ohio State University, where she got her degree. After graduation she went to New York as a free-lance artist specializing in shoe drawings and industrial designs for furniture and automobile accessories until she designed the award-winning gloves. Hull maintained that knowledge of machinery was crucial to anyone in the field of industrial design and, to prove it, went to the machine shop herself to file and shape the new machinery, cutting completely new dies for her gloves since they departed so radically from those previously manufactured.

To those who still thought it "comic" for a woman to work in industrial design, Hull responded, "You've got to have the grit to stand the laughs and live them down." It was a good field for women, she told a reporter, for women knew "instinctively" what would work and what wouldn't in the house. They would understand, for instance, how easily and how quickly furniture could be cleaned, how much storage space could be incorporated into furniture without spoiling its lines, how low a sink or oven could be without breaking the back of the person (almost certainly female) using it. As Hull put it, "Women designers don't have to be told that. Men do." Like Olive Dennis, who once said that her improvements to railroad travel sprang from her "instincts as a homemaker," Hull had found that being a woman had its advantages. Her gender helped her to see opportunities for invention, and it did draw attention to her and her product—albeit not always the kind she would have preferred.

As the decade of the 1940s began and war loomed close, yet another woman joined the chorus of those assailing the notion that only males were capable of invention. Dr. Maude Glasgow, a woman's and public health advocate, concluded that nature had bestowed upon woman such a biological supremacy that she was "sovereign in the field of creative energy." Her book title said it all: *Subjection of Women and Traditions of Men.* Her purposes in writing the book, she explained in the preface, were to depict the adverse environment in which women were confined and to show that, despite such barriers to their progress, the headway they had made in the last half century was generated by their own "initiative, energy and political acumen." The contents of her book reverberated with déjà vu: Like Matilda Gage, she declared that primitive women's rudimentary, prehistoric inventions changed the face of civilization; like Mary Lockwood, flailing at the Smithsonian to display examples of those implements in the 1893 Woman's Building, she pointed to ancient artifacts as proof of women's genius; like Ada Bowles, she argued that genius was not confined to one sex ("It is a human quality and just as likely to appear in one sex, as the other, given the favorable environment"); like *Woman's Journal,* she remarked upon the difficulty if not impossibility of a woman's daring to produce a mechanical invention in the face of men's prejudice and hostility; like Elizabeth Cady Stanton, she saw women squandering their energy on household labors while men sat idly by ("Since historic times man has always enjoyed more spare time than women"); like Frances Willard, she mourned the lack of technical training for women; like Mozans, who copied it from everybody else, she re-credited the cotton gin to Katherine Green. Finally, while celebrating the "decrease in hostility toward the working of the feminine brain outside the strictly proscribed limitations in which she was for so long held prisoner," Glasgow, convinced like Mary Anderson that the country could ill afford the loss of even one woman with inventive genius, ended the book by giving her suggestions about how government could minimize such losses: expand opportunities for research and facilities, give easier access to patent procedure facilities, and offer special help to women in marketing and prompting their patented creations.

The year Glasgow's book was published coincided with the celebration of the 150th anniversary of the original patent act of 1790, and certainly, it was hoped, the events surrounding that celebration would quickly dispel any doubts that women were still being held back. Charles F. Kettering, inventor of the self-starter, director of General Motors Research, and chairman of the Patent Law Sesquicentennial, was toastmaster. Thomas Midgely of the Ethyl Corporation was in charge of the program. In the past century and a half, about twenty thousand patents had been granted to women, and yet when the *Washington Post* ran the headline WINE, WOMEN AND SONG IN PATENT FETE TONIGHT, it wasn't talking about women patentees. In smaller print it clarified: "Food, music and pretty girls will help salute progress." Needless to say, the "pretty girls" were not patentees. The *Evening Star* launched its coverage by proclaiming: "Science combined forces with modern culinary art and feminine beauty last night. . . ." But what were the feminine beauties doing? The paper described how "formalities of the laboratory were forgotten . . . as attractive young women modeled gowns emphasizing latest developments in industrial science." *That's* what women were doing at the celebration of the Patent Act.

New York "cover girl" models moved about to the banquet's theme song, "Beautiful Dreamer," dressed in outfits representing those industries that, presumably, made America great: "Miss Printing" in a newspaper skirt topped by a bodice of maps and a tiara and epaulets of playing cards; "Miss Celluloid" in a black celluloid dress adorned with motion pictures and filmstrips; "Miss Communications" in a necklace of telephone dials, a bodice striped with ticker tape, and a skirt embroidered with telephone wires and poles; "Miss Metals" in a sparkling gold, silver, and bronze outfit that sported airplane-wing epaulets; and "Miss Patents" in a gown of patent facsimiles topped by an American eagle hat. Air route maps covered "Miss Aviation" as best they could; adding machine streamers and cash register keys dramatized statistics on "Miss Accounting Machines" 's black chiffon dress; futuristic flower pots of vegetables and streamers of the latest patented frozen foods hung on "Miss Foods"; hundreds of rubber bands draped the gown of "Miss Rubber" and a rubber tire crowned her head. "Miss Automobile," bedecked with speedometers, gas gauges, and automobile gadgets, supported a steering wheel on *her* head. In the finale, "Miss

Chemistry" brought down the house in her glass test-tube-studded jacket, her gown embroidered with chemical formulas and her hat shaped like a chemist's retort.

The food was a gastronomic flight of fancy concocted by the Mayflower Hotel's chef, whose "Reaper Rolls" (sugar-coated with a picture of the McCormick Reaper) and "Carborundum Canapés" remained his own carefully guarded secret. He did disclose, however, that the evening's special cocktail was copied from a snakebite remedy patented by Joshua Smith of Coffee County, Georgia, in 1888, which he had doctored or laced to make "even tastier," that the "Aluminum Nuts" were peanuts roasted in a colored powder, that the dots and dashes in the "Telegraph Soup" were long and short crackers, that "vacuum tubes" were stuffed potatoes, that those were alligator pears crossed with anchovy paste to look like light bulb filaments in the "Incandescent Salad," and that the phonograph record that accompanied the molded "Airplane Ice Cream" was really cake.

Although President Roosevelt had proclaimed that April 10 be set aside as "Inventors' and Patents Day" and Undersecretary of Commerce Edward Noble remarked upon the diversity of the assemblage of twelve hundred inventors, industrialists, Patent Office officials, and a sprinkling of legislators, the published guest list was not diverse enough to include any women's names, though there may have been some present who were not listed in the newspapers: It's hard to believe Marie Saunders would have let this one get away!

While men celebrated "their" inventive progress, nothing was said of women's contributions. But the press didn't entirely ignore women. A *New York Times* writer concluded that despite psychological tests that revealed women's mental grasp and understanding of invention to be equal to, if not greater than, that of men, the overall figures still reflected no *substantive* gains. But the reporter did note that in fields where women had gained greater opportunities for research and experiment their patents covered a far broader range than in the past, and he cited such products as dyes, airplanes, airplane landing brakes, a robot pilot, internal combustion engines, turbines, mercury vapor lamps, oil burners, puncture-proof auto tires, radios, machine tools, calculating and voting machines, and mining and chemical apparatus. Another *Times* article saluting the increasing number of women inventors singled out Blodgett's invention for improving range finders, telescopes, eyeglasses, camera and projecting lenses and gave it the ultimate accolade for the period—that *Gone With the Wind* had given even greater pleasure to millions of viewers because it was projected on theater screens through lenses made of the nonreflecting glass she had invented. Gladys Whitcomb ("Merry Hull") was also lauded. After improving upon the gloves she had previously patented, she decided that high heels were the primary cause of women's foot discomfort and, applying the same anatomical principles to footwear that she had applied to gloves, redesigned shoes so that they had a flexible arch section, a firm heel support, and a heel cavity filled with a shock-absorbent substance.

In the months after Germany's invasion of Poland caused war to break out in Europe in September 1939, the United States, already recognizing the probability of involvement in what was to become the century's second world war, took many measures aimed at bolstering its economy. Among those actions was the Commerce Department's establishment of the National Inventors Council in 1940. Headed by Kettering of General Motors and staffed with the nation's foremost technologists, its purpose was to help inventors convert ideas into practical applications. The War Department urged inventors to use their wits to "surprise overconfident aggressors" and listed fields in which inventions were needed.

To enlist even children in the invention effort, American Institute, founded over a century before to foster American inventive genius, sponsored more than thirty thousand junior science and engineering clubs, and an *American Magazine* writer alerted parents, "Don't be skeptical if your son or daughter comes home late for dinner some night and offers this explanation: 'I've been working in the school lab on a little invention I thought up.'" The author himself visited clubs with "dozens of boys and girls in smocks and white coats working away at scientific brain teasers," but, though he may have *seen* girls, he interviewed only "short-pants scientists," such as the "bright-eyed lad of fifteen" working on transmitting sound on a beam of light. Noting that businesses encouraged children to be inventive, he concluded promisingly: "No boy or girl who shows genuine promise in a science club is likely to lack a job." It would certainly be no thanks to him if any girl were to so benefit. Nor was the woman author who wrote *Famous Inventors for Boys and Girls* in 1941 any help in stimulating girls to inventive effort. Promising (in her title) inventors for boys *and* girls, she offered girls no role models—just the same old jazz: Edison, Bell, Morse, Bessemer, McCormick, and so forth. Not a woman in the lot.

It must have amazed the National Inventors Council when it received a suggestion for an antijamming communications device from none other than Hollywood screen goddess Hedy Lamar and her partner, George Antheil, a film score composer. The sultry movie star's inventive streak was a well-kept Hollywood secret; one modern reporter puts it, "Hedy was more than Tondelayo, but it didn't quite suit MGM's Publicity Department to let the news out." Lamar was well aware of how she'd been positioned: "Any girl can be glamorous. All you have to do is stand still and look stupid."

The story behind the patent could have been grist for another Hollywood movie. Having met Antheil at a party at Janet Gaynor's, Lamar learned of his expertise in sound synchronization and other mechanical devices and invited him to her Benedict Canyon home to talk business. Business turned out to be the "secret communications system" they patented, a primitive "frequency hopping" radio signaling device so basic in concept that even today it is applied to satellite communication. Lamar, better famed for her nudity in the 1933 Czech film *Ecstasy* than for any prowess as a thespian (much less an inventor), was for three years the petted wife of a wealthy Austrian arms dealer whose company, among other arms deals, supplied munitions for Italy's invasion of Ethiopia. As his wife, she learned about designs for military materials and even suggested a radio-controlled torpedo herself, but discovered that it was too easily jammed.

When the Nazis invaded Austria, the then Hedwig Keisler abandoned her husband ("I couldn't be an object; so I walked out"). She went to London, where Louis B. Mayer signed her for Metro-Goldwyn-Mayer and brought the newly christened "Hedy Lamar" to Hollywood to wow American audiences in such movies as *White Cargo* and *Samson and Delilah.* It was in 1940 that she confided to composer Antheil her scheme for a remote-controlled radio system that would allow signals to be transmitted without danger of detection, deciphering, or jamming, a device they hoped the War Department could use against the Nazis. Antheil grasped the basic concept and realized that he could as easily synchronize microsecond hops between radio frequencies as he

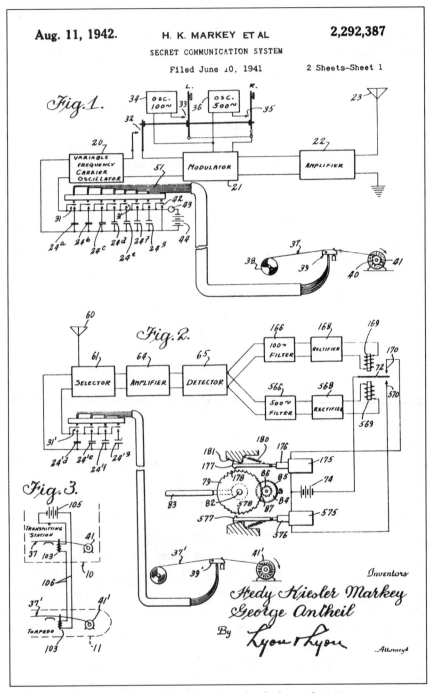

"Secret Communication System" invented by Hedy Kiesler Markey (Hedy Lamar), 1942.

synchronized player pianos. The slotted paper rolls and the eighty-eight frequencies he then proposed (identical to the number of piano keys) reflect his musical experience. Two years after being urged by the Inventors' Council to reduce their concept to a patentable state, Lamar and Antheil did, she in the name of Hedwig Keisler Markey (because she had by this time married Gene Markey).

The War Department, however, never adopted their method, until many years later when, long after their patent had expired, Sylvania independently developed a system based on a similar concept but substituting electronic operation for Antheil's paper rolls. It was, of course, perfectly proper to do so, but Lamar grumbles. Now in her seventies and living in Miami, she recently told a reporter from *Forbes* magazine that though her original intention was to make a wartime contribution, she wouldn't have minded some recognition: "I can't understand why there's no acknowledgment when it's used all over the world. . . . Never a letter, never a thank you, never money. I don't know. I guess they just take and forget about a person."

When the United States actually entered the war in December 1941, many gender stereotypes crumbled. Women took on "male" jobs as bus drivers, police officers, barbers, lifeguards, and gas station operators, and desperate employers, many of whom had banned them from the workplace only ten years before, recruited them for work in shipyards, steel foundries, electrical companies, and aircraft plants. At the Goodyear Aerospace Corporation, women who had gained experience in engineering, designing, drafting, tooling, and other fields from working on Corsair fighter planes and B-29s formed their own "inventors club" to improve production methods; but, for the most part, the search for ideas was conducted gender-blind. This, after all, was wartime. Some already established women inventors were engaged in wartime research. Katharine Blodgett, previously cited for the nonreflecting glass that had enhanced the showing of *Gone With the Wind,* found critical new wartime uses for the thin film with which she had worked for two decades. Coating periscope and aerial camera lenses with it greatly increased their efficiency; putting it on aircraft wings sped de-icing; adding it to smoke screens made them more impenetrable. As she told a radio interviewer, there was no end to discovery: "Each year I learn some new ways . . . and wonder why I never learned them before. They consist mostly in tackling the problems to which I used to say, 'I can't,' and I usually find that they are not so difficult as I thought they would be." B & O inventor Olive Dennis became a wartime engineering consultant on railroad transportation at the Office of Defense Transportation, even participating in a two-way radio broadcast with British railroad women who "manned" rail networks as switch tower operators, train crew members, and crossing watchmen.

It was fifty-year-old businesswoman Lillian Greneker, however, who won wartime inventing laurels by solving one of the defense industry's critical problems: how to make a destructible form for molding the rubber fuel tanks needed for navy planes and submarines. Since these hollow, bulbous tanks (or cells) were made by gluing and vulcanizing sheets of rubber over a form, the mystery was how to remove the form from inside the completed fuel tank without damaging the tank itself. The U.S. Rubber Company of Saugatuck, Connecticut, to whom the navy had awarded a fuel cell contract, had already experimented unsuccessfully with plaster reinforced by wire or burlap and also with plywood strips (curved, carved, and hooked together). It finally decided to try paper. That decision led them to Greneker, whose expertise in manufacturing lifelike and flexible mannequins from cellophane or laminated paper had earned her the soubriquet of "Paper Lady."

Her mechanical instincts had also led her to invent a product she called "Fingertips," which can best be described as elongated thimbles that fit over each finger so that miniature tools or brushes could be attached to them. She boasted that "Fingertips" would enable housewives to peel oranges, pit grapefruit, or scrape pans "with an ease and efficiency never before possible"; would allow artists to have available five brushes, each with different-colored paint; and etchers to work with five different tools—all without laying one implement down to pick up another. And, with her flair for promotion—not surprising since she was a dancer, musician, actress, artist, house builder, designer, and wife of the public relations director for the Shubert Theater—she rented the preview room at Radio City Music Hall to introduce her invention to friends and the press, had a promotional film made, and talked about it to everyone who would listen. Many did. The *New Yorker* described it in its "Talk of the Town," slyly noting, "Mrs. Greneker can, and does, talk for hours about her invention"; Pathe News featured it in a newsreel; newspapers, in this country and abroad, portrayed Greneker with outstretched fingers, each tipped with a different implement. It was ingenious, but despite her efforts, she was unable to market it successfully.

The opposite was true with her mannequins. Her Greneker Corporation, which she had established in Pleasantville, New York, had scarcely been able to keep up with demand—until war came. Knowing of her expertise with paper, U.S. Rubber's experimental engineer, Herbert Polleys, invited her to visit his plant to see if she could come up with a solution to making a destructible form. The timing was serendipitous. Because the war had sharply curtailed her mannequin business and she needed to find other employment for her workers, she was eager for new business. The first meeting between company engineers and inventor, however, got off to a poor start: The engineers wanted advice on how to use paper; Greneker was convinced that, despite their previous lack of success with plaster, she had a solution, one that required plaster. She left in a huff, headed for a building supply store to buy a length of rope, recruited a local Italian plasterer who made birdbaths with an offer of work in a national defense industry, and set him to work in her workshop mixing plaster. As he began to pour the plaster into a large leg mold left over from one of her mannequins, she suspended the rope from a ceiling fixture above and watched it fall naturally into coils as it embedded itself in the wet plaster below. She left one end sticking out. She and the artisan leveled and smoothed the plaster (now webbed with rope) to a uniform half-inch thickness and let it set. It was now possible, she surmised, to seam two identical forms to make a cylindrical mold over which workers could stretch and vulcanize the rubber sheeting. When that was done, one had only to yank the rope, shatter the plaster, and tug the pieces through the hole at the top—leaving the outer rubber fuel tank intact. She called in the engineers.

Having them witness that "rope trick" was a moment she savored, so much so that four decades later, when she was almost ninety, she wrote (in what was probably planned as an autobiography but never finished): "It was too easy! . . . [T]he men hated the rope; [they said] only a woman would think of that. They seemed even to be embarrassed, having to handle it so delicately. '[It's] like sewing,' they said." Engineer Herbert Polleys, however, was not among the scoffers and quickly dispatched to Pleasantville the company's precious wooden form for a mold for the fuel cell needed for the Grumman Hellcat fighter plane so that Greneker and her assistants could take its measurements and make the first production model. When that model was a complete success, Polleys sent under armored guard the model for the huge ("the size of a grand piano") fuel tank for Sikorsky planes and submarines and begged her to work at full speed. Greneker recalled:

> I opened the large doors in the back of my studio and in a well protected truck with armoured guards the precious model was rolled off into the snow. We had to wait for daylight to get it into the studio. It was enormous and held five hundred gallons. What a mold to make! . . . In 24 hours we had a cast perfect in size, and from then on every 24 hours we turned out five; we worked all day and all night. . . . Planes flew over to watch for our safety. Word went around that Mrs. Greneker was going into the defense business. Idle gardeners, workmen, mostly 4-fs came from all over.

The method of making forms for fuel tanks, the invention she called "Pullcord" and for which she obtained three patents in 1944 and 1945, not only kept the Greneker Corporation busy throughout the war but also brought royalties to the inventor for many years, more money than she made from her better known mannequin business. Several years after the war, when Greneker asked engineer Polleys for a business reference for a new venture, he responded with a strong endorsement, crediting her with personal direction of all the technical work, development, and most of the production responsibilities for the fuel cell forms. She was, he vouched, "conscientious and completely able to cope with any engineering changes and did an excellent job; in fact, from our view-point she apparently ran the entire business and ran it well. Her reliability in meeting tight schedules was exceptional and many improvements in form construction and in their making process were due to her imaginative and progressive ability."

Polleys remained a lifelong friend, and in 1977, when they were both in their eighties, Greneker, who by this time had an enviable reputation as a sculptor to add to her other laurels, turned to him again for advice about the patentability of an improvement she had devised to "Fingertips," which she had patented thirty-eight years before. Polleys, mindful of her age, wrote back, "Patents often take years to clear. . . . So what are your future plans? Why not retire and live on your past glories?" But then he closed with "I do feel . . . the idea is *basically good!*" That was encouragement enough for Greneker to consult a second patent attorney after the first dismissed her improvement as too closely related to "Fingertips" and advised her curtly, "I am closing my file on this matter." Though the second pleaded that "the implement you have invented does present us with certain difficulties with respect to patentability" and offered not to charge her if she decided to abandon the application, Greneker instructed him to pursue the patent. After a few amendments insisted upon by the Patent Office, she received her patent. She was eighty-five. When she asked her attorney a few months later whether it was too late for a Canadian patent (it was), he helped her to draw up a licensing agreement with a Canadian associate. If she went ahead with this venture, she apparently made no money from it, and within a few years she moved to California, where she died in 1990—at age ninety-five.

Although few other women made such distinctive wartime contributions as Greneker, they did provide a few other inventions for the military effort, such as the "Torpedo Discharge Means" invented by Henrietta Bradbury, a black woman with no technical experience who had an idea for something that might have proved effective had it ever been adopted. And there was a variety of garments designed for the needs of servicemen and patented by Florence Biggs. But even in wartime there was the usual flurry of nonmilitary inventions, such as Julia Auerbach's "Detatchable self-adjusting corset strap," Anna Barba's "egg-turning device for incubators," and Minnie Blau's "educational device" for teaching arithmetic.

With the close of the war, what little progress women had made during those years was eroded in the return to the status quo. When their country needed them, all discussion about women's innate unfitness for certain work was suspended for the duration, and women acquitted themselves admirably in nontraditional work. When their country didn't need them, it was back to "Woman's place is in the home." It is true that some women voluntarily retreated from the workplace to resume their war-interrupted family lives, but others had no choice but to forfeit their jobs to returning veterans. Some companies simply resurrected Depression policies of denying jobs to married women. By the end of 1946, two million women had been fired from heavy industry—over eight hundred thousand from the aircraft industry alone—and the few who managed to survive the cuts received only a small percentage of the pay men would receive for the same work. Those exiled from the labor force were so indelibly marked by the wartime experience of tasting freedom and independence and discovering their own capabilities that they were often listless in the numbing confines of the suburbs.

There, the reluctantly uprooted Rosie the Riveters, plus those who had always planned to leave work after their men returned from war, swelled the ranks of those already "at home." Companies that had reconverted to peacetime production of domestic appliances lost no time in propagandizing them to *stay* there. Their advertisements (and the magazines that carried them) declared that shiny floors, clean clothing, and home-baked confections were once again fitting criteria of "real women." Writer Sheila Rothman notes with sorrow in her book *Woman's Proper Place* that the war was "not so much a transforming experience as an interruption, after which women returned to pursue an inherited role." War appeared to have restored homemaking to an even more exalted status. Those women who nonetheless insisted on working outside the home had their psyches dissected by leading psychologists who seized upon the slightest indication of maladjustment, neuroticism, or emotional deterioriation to illustrate the price such "unnatural dissenters" had to pay for abdicating their domestic "thrones."

With so many obediently retreating to domestic nests, there were soon thousands who would need Merry Hull's latest invention—an expandable garment for children. Hull's own motherhood had not only altered her domestic arrangements but also refocused her career. Converting her former workroom into her son's bedroom/playroom, she carried on business at home. When she noticed that John Christopher Geissman outgrew his clothing almost as soon as she had bought it, the ingenious inventor began designing clothing with hidden cuffs and tucks that, when let out, allowed his clothing to grow with him. By the time he was four, she described in her patent a scenario familiar to legions of parents:

> The rapid growth of children, particularly boys, has always resulted in ill-fitting clothes. . . . the garment gives the appearance of having

shrunk. The legs of the garment appear to be and are too short, the bib is below the chest of the child and the waistband is nearer the hips than the waist. Unless the garment is purposely too large when originally purchased, about the only thing that can be done at this stage, which usually arrives when the garment is still in good condition, is to discard it or save it for a younger child, and replace it with a new garment.

Hull's newly designed overalls, trousers, and playsuits, which also had the advantage of opening flat for ironing, were called "Merry Mites," a line so successful that she set up a factory in Chambersburg, Pennsylvania, and hired an Ohio industrialist to help her step up production to meet the growing demand. I was one of those eager buyers myself, and from my favorite emporium, Best and Company, I purchased any number of "Merry Mites" for my two youngest children, never suspecting that I would one day be writing about their inventor.

By far the most unusual invention with which a woman was involved in those postwar years was the brainchild of a dedicated aeronautical husband who, with his wife's help, fabricated and then patented jointly the first nonrigid, heavier-than-air device ever to fly, the "flexikite" that became one of the most important discoveries in aeronautics, the paraglider later known as the "Rogallo Wing." Francis Rogallo had long been interested in kites and from childhood had designed and flown his own, always exasperated that the troublesome cross sticks (essential to a rigid kite) poked holes in the covering or broke when the kite crashed.

After graduating from Stanford and progressing to an advanced degree in mechanical engineering (aeronautics), then working on parachutes at Langley Field, he wondered whether he could devise something as limp as a parachute that would fly like a glider. The questions turned to action after the first of his three children reached kite-flying age and he saw his conventionally built kites fall victim to broken sticks. His kite experiments coincided with his professional interests, as it happened. By the late 1940s, Rogallo was chief of the wind tunnel branch of the National Advisory Committee for Aeronautics, stability research section, and hoped for government-sponsored research to develop a cheaper, simpler, and more practical aircraft, which would enable a person with average skills to own and operate his own machine. While a good many persons had private planes, their cost was prohibitive to the average citizen. When the government turned down his request but had no objection to his conducting thermodynamic tests at home on his own time, Rogallo made those tests a family project. To study the basic principles, they built kites.

Francis Rogallo's wife, Gertrude, saw nothing unusual in this. Born and raised in Hampton, Virginia, where the Langley Research Center (now part of NASA) was established in 1917, she had been around "aeronautical people" (as she describes them) all her life. Her uncle was one of the first Coast Guard officers to be given flight training and the only one to serve overseas in World War I. The whole Rogallo family pitched in on the kite project, and the work began. What emerged was a limp piece of cloth with shroud lines like a parachute. Filled with a breeze, however, the batwing-shaped kite took off and remained as stable and maneuverable as its rigid counterpart.

After almost two years of experiments in which the Rogallo family worked on design alternatives to prevent the kites' swooping dives and tested them by sending them aloft along the shores of the Hampton River, they wanted to test them in a wind tunnel. Since Francis Rogallo had access to the country's major tunnel in his "working life"

Gertrude and Francis Rogallo in 1988 with their original kite.

The Rogallo Wing used for hang gliding, Kitty Hawk, N.C. 1975.

but was not free to use it for what was essentially a family affair, the family simply adapted part of their house to the purpose by setting up a large electric fan in the kitchen, opening appropriate doors on the first floor and flying their kites in the doorway between living room and porch. They tried everything from a potato chip bag (moderately successful) to discarded glazed chintz kitchen curtains, which Gertrude Rogallo cut into the prescribed shape and ran up on her sewing machine. When the latter proved effective because the glaze reduced the fabric's porosity and deterred air from leaking through and breaking its "lift," they rigged an eighteen-inch square with nylon shrouds that wouldn't tangle. They had their kite, their "flexible wing."

There was no question in Francis Rogallo's mind then or later that he and his wife were equal partners. In a letter to an official of the National Air and Space Museum twenty-five years after the original experiments, he spoke of his wife as his "collaborator and constant companion in these experiments," public acknowledgment that would have warmed the hearts of those nineteenth-century woman's rightists who groused that men always stole women's ideas. He went on to describe their early work:

> After several years of sporadic thinking about the possibility of human flight with flexible wings, I built in early August of 1948 some small paper wings with a weight suspended below them on threads and was able to get good glides from them in our living room.
>
> The successful flights of these paper gliders encouraged Mrs. Rogallo and me to construct several truly flexible wings of cloth, much larger than the little paper gliders. Following in the footsteps of most of the early pioneers of flight, we decided to test these wings as kites in an open field near our home. On Sunday, August 15, 1948 we accomplished the first really successful flight of one of our flexible wings. It was flown as a kite on Merrimac Shores, Hampton, Virginia, a site of historical interest because of the battle of the Merrimac and Monitor, the world's first iron clad warships.

Gertrude Rogallo recalls that they themselves immediately grasped the aeronautical potential of what they called their "flexible wing," realizing its importance for the government space program, then in its infancy. At the time of filing for the patent, however, they could not interest the government, and their attorney recommended that it would be easier to get a patent if they simply called it a flexible kite.

With the government showing no interest in applying the principle of the invention to space work, the Rogallos decided that a kite business was in order. "In fact," Gertrude Rogallo says now, "I was able to spend more time on it than he was, and when we got into the kite business it was considered to be my business." It became a virtual cottage industry. Neighbors first cut the simple chintz components, then, in an attic workroom under her supervision, they assembled the kites and rigged the nylon shroud lines. A neighborhood woodworker made winders for the "flight lines"; another neighbor made the red silk bags that held the kites and doubled as wind sock tails when the kite was in flight. They sold the kites locally, in toy and gift shops, through a mail-order catalog, and in some New York stores such as Altman's and F.A.O. Schwarz. It sold for five dollars, its package proclaiming: "Swoop it! Loop it! Maneuver it! World's first flexible heavier-than-air craft." Creative Playthings in Princeton, New Jersey, purchased the right to manufacture five thousand of them.

Moving from chintz to quarter-inch cotton mesh laminated between sheets of plastic, the local kitemakers were soon bogged down with orders, and by 1952 the Rogallos licensed a promoter who had done well by "Silly Putty" to take on the Rogallo Flexikites. When a *New York Times* writer spied the Flexikite (by this time made from Dupont Mylar) in a New York toy exhibition, he reported that children loved it because they could maneuver it like an airplane, crash it repeatedly, and still make it take off again undamaged, even in the rain. The prescient reporter saw further value far beyond the playground for the "No sticks, no framework, no tail" kite: Since radar could detect its aluminumized surface and it could carry a radar antenna to broadcast signals, he said, it would be an ideal locator for a downed life raft or plane.

In 1958, seven years after the original patent, the government finally became interested in applying the flexible wing principle to air and spacecraft, and the Rogallos assigned it all rights—without fee. In the next decade the Air and Space Administration continued to work with the "Rogallo Wing" (and improvements to it that Francis Rogallo also patented and also assigned to the government) and learned it could land a space capsule without parachutes by extending flexible wings from the capsule to slow its re-entry. In 1968 NASA awarded both Rogallos a large cash award for their contributions. Despite the later fame of the invention, including the number of technical papers it spawned, Gertrude Rogallo reminds, "The initial work was done by the two of us at home." The kites were, after all, just proof of a principle, a principle with many more applications than the wing's most common one—sport hang-gliding. Advanced models have recovered separated shuttle boosters. They may even be able to recover boosters and engines out of orbit, though, to date, that has not been tried.

William Sleeman, Jr., an aerospace engineer who worked with Francis Rogallo for many years and has known the couple for decades, says that Gertrude Rogallo was far more than a helpmeet in her husband's early experiments:

> Gertrude is an exceptionally bright woman. She comes from a well educated family and was Headmistress of St. Andrews Day School in Newport News—a real educator. She was a co-inventor in every sense of the word. You know that when you get a patent, the idea must be "reduced to practice," and she certainly was part of that

process. Gertrude understood what Rog was trying to do, even though she will tell you she doesn't know much about aeronautics. She grew up in aeronautics! Sure, she stitched the kite on her machine, but that wasn't her only contribution.

Rog wasn't just being gallant in putting her name on that patent, though I must say after many years of working with him, he *is* generous in giving others credit. Gertrude's name is there because it belongs there. Theirs was a complete partnership.

The importance of Gertrude Rogallo's contribution to their joint invention seemed to get lost in the shuffle, however, when on National Aviation Day in 1988, Francis Rogallo received an impressive plaque commemorating the fortieth anniversary of the development of the Rogallos's flex-wing. Gertrude Rogallo was presented with a sewing kit—as if she, like some latter-day Scarlett O'Hara, had done no more than think of another use for old curtains! As an inventive woman was once again typecast as some sort of clever homemaker par excellence, it underscored men's chronic inability to accord women the honor they so easily bestow upon their own sex. This would not have surprised Eleanor Metheney, an exponent of women's rights who informally polled working women about their most common complaints and reported the results in *Independent Woman,* the official publication of the National Federation of Professional Women's Clubs. In a nutshell, she concluded, "It's a man's world, and it's not fair to women. . . . [Men] always think they know more than any woman ever could."

# 15

## THE MODERN
## WOMAN INVENTOR

$\mathcal{I}$t seems reasonable to expect that women who had developed mechanical talents in defense work would patent new industrial machinery when the war was over, but there is no evidence that this occurred. Though a few women scientists, who had gained entry into their fields during wartime personnel shortages and managed to stay on in their jobs afterwards, did account for important patents in later years, in general women's postwar exodus from the labor market paralleled the return to home and hearth that followed both the Civil War and World War I. Even after they gradually began to go back to work again in later years, a superficial examination of the annual lists of patents granted in the sixties and seventies (superficial because lists are not arranged by gender) reveals that though women's names appeared more frequently than in the past, their inventions not only continued to make up a very small percentage of the whole but continued, with some notable exceptions, to be "women's things." To make matters worse, inventors had apparently ceased to be the heroines they once had been to their sisters. In contrast to the period when proponents of women's rights had celebrated women inventors as paradigms of their gender's inventive genius and hailed the commercially successful as model business

strategists, the latter-day observance of women's ingenuity, even during the women's movement of the sixties and seventies, has been
piecemeal at best.

Worse still, the more things might be thought to have changed, the
more they remained the same. In the fifties, Stacy Jones, who covered
patent affairs for the *New York Times*, calculated that the ratio of
women's patents to men's was still the same as it had been in 1900—
one out of every one hundred (at least he didn't recycle the commissioner's error). The result was that the hackneyed "Why don't women
invent?" query was heard once again as if no one had ever asked it
before. Nor did the proffered explanations ever deviate from the accustomed track—that women did invent but no one gave them credit.
Women themselves were not much help. Blanche McKeown, writing
in *American Mercury* in 1955, described how cleverly a woman's
inventive mind worked but exited with the kind of comment that
rested on the assumption that woman's mind turned only to "women's
things": "No one knows for sure who invented the safety pin, but it's
ten to one it was not a man." About a year later, another writer for the
same magazine, this one male, painted the subject in only slightly
more flattering shades: "While it is true that the major inventions have
been fathered by men, it is also true that some inventions have been
mothered by women."

It wasn't a rave notice, but it helped, for it wasn't only feisty
feminists of the nineteenth century who had to stave off doubters of
their inventive capacities. Half a century after a writer in *Popular
Science* proclaimed that women were predisposed to reproduction
rather than production, Clarence Tuska, director of RCA Patent Operations and an admittedly "old-fashioned" man, pointed out in his 1957
book, *Inventors and Inventions*, that though women *could* invent and
some even *did* invent, it was preordained that their number would be
few since the Lord intended them to be mothers rather than inventors.
Let them produce and rear the inventors, spake Tuska, "that should be
sufficient." Aware that he would be censured if he didn't supply names
of *some* women inventors, he unearthed three worthy of mention: Eve,
"credited in the Bible with starting something in the garden of Eden";
Moses' mother, "inventive in an emergency"; and patentee Katharine
Blodgett for her discovery that a thin film spread on glass surfaces
reduced the reflection of light. Tuska attributed Blodgett's expertise to

the fact that she had an advanced academic degree, but instead of concluding from her example that a woman, if given adequate educational opportunities, could be as successful in inventing as a man, he worried lest a career as a patentee might displace the "career chosen by nature." Despite the perpetual discouragement of the ubiquitous Tuskas of the universe, those women who did invent and patent seemed to have mastered the business aspects better than some of their earlier sisters, and Rose Marie Reid of swimsuit fame impressed even Tuska himself because of the lucrative contracts she negotiated for patent rights to her inventions.

Since it is difficult to detect a chronological theme that ties together inventors' experiences in the past four decades, it is more appropriate to examine women's inventions in the context of their field, from "domestic" to highly scientific. With the postwar baby boom still churning as women flung themselves headlong into maternity, diaper pickup and delivery trucks swarmed into suburbia, their Didee Dee, Kiddie Wash, and Baby Bundle logos broadcasting their intent to lighten mother's workload. But their charges were steep, and more than one inventor thought of the obvious, a disposable diaper. Not that it was a new idea. As early as 1887, patentee Maria Allen overlaid a triangular diaper with cotton wadding to which she added a sheet of perforated paper ("to give free circulation"), covered both with a third layer of fine gauze fabric, and then stitched all three together. After applying the prepared diaper to the infant in the usual way, she placed an ordinary cotton diaper on the outside. Voilà, said Allen, "This improved diaper is for the purpose that when it becomes soiled it may be thrown away and replaced by a clean one." It was too expensive for everyday use, but must have been useful when traveling.

When rubberized fabrics "went to war" in the 1940s, mothers, faced with finding alternative means of coping with messy diapers, slavishly knit diaper covers, heavy yarn "soakers" that absorbed the overflow and siphoned away wetness from the body. Soakers remained the staple of every layette until snug, rubberized pants returned to the market. But rubber pants had their drawbacks too: putting them on over cloth diapers encased babies in their own effluvium; pants leaked at the legs, and mothers still had mountains of diapers to wash. Marion Donovan, like other mothers, moaned, "The baby was always wet and cold, and I had too much laundry" and decided to try putting absorbent material

inside plastic. Cutting and folding shower curtains into plastic envelopes into which she slipped absorbent material, Donovan substituted snap closures for diaper pins, patented the resultant "Boater"
diaper in 1951, and, when no manufacturer bought the idea, made
them herself and sold them to department stores. The soaring sales of
the "Boater" signaled the birth of the disposable-diaper industry.
Donovan sold her company for a million dollars, but, like many another ingenious woman, had other inventions up her sleeve: a multiple
skirt hanger and a zipper pull that allowed a woman to close her back
zipper without assistance—both successful.

In the years when it appeared that the majority of American womanhood was re-entrenched—quite properly, said Tuska—in domesticity, one might expect that profit-minded designers like Merry Hull,
who had begun her working life as an industrial designer and bowled
over the media with her successful glove patents, would turn their
inventing talents to domestic problems—especially when they could
invent things that reflected their own changing interests and concerns.
As once she had capitalized on her parental frustrations to design
expandable clothing for toddlers, the no-longer-pencil-slim inventor/
businesswoman now turned her inventive talents to "foundation garments," applying her knowledge of anatomy to relieve the sufferings
of the girdle-bound, which were obviously something she knew firsthand. As she explained in her patent:

> Seldom are they [corsets] able to accommodate such normal positions
> of the body as sitting, bending, kneeling, stooping, and stair-climbing
> without binding or painfully constricting one or more of the critical
> areas of the anatomy.... At times they produce unnatural shapes like
> cylinders or so compress the flesh that an unattractive roll is pushed
> up and out over the waistline. The indiscriminately applied pressures
> generated by these garments can and do reduce the wearer to agony,
> particularly when they multiply as the foundation is driven into a
> sitting position.

Ann Moore's invention of a child-carrying "Snugli," like Hull's
corset, certainly could fit the stereotype of "a typical woman's invention," but the inspiration for it came from her service in the Peace
Corps. While many inventors (male and female) had previously patented various versions of a carrying strap or baby sling, Moore credits

the natives of Togo, West Africa, with giving her the idea for hers. As Peace Corps volunteers in the early 1960s, Ann, a pediatric nurse, and her husband, Mike, a Yale graduate on a teaching team, were struck by the contentment of the African babies who spent long hours snuggled up happily against their mothers' backs in fabric harnesses. While many American mothers feared spoiling their babies with too much handling, this was not true of the Togolese, and volunteers and medical teams ascribed the babies' emotional security to the close bonding they enjoyed with their mothers. Giving birth to a baby daughter two months after her return to the United States, Moore wanted that same closeness to her infant daughter Mandela (named for the African leader), and tried to duplicate the African effect by wrapping a piece of fabric around her child and adding a small pouch to prevent her from slipping through. It was in this printed calico prototype of the "Snugli" that Ann slung seven-month-old Mande on her back as she and Mike, his backpack loaded with diapers, flew to Alabama to join Martin Luther King on his famous march from Selma to Montgomery on March 25, 1965. The newspaper that printed a picture of Mande on her mother's back captioned it "The Littlest Marcher."

Though Moore found the carrier convenient, she described its disadvantages to her mother in Ohio, and the latter, drawing on thirty years of sewing experience, cut and sewed an old sheet into a contrivance consisting of one pouch inside a larger one (with zippers on each), then attached straps to crisscross Moore's shoulders, cut and bound openings through which the baby's legs could swing freely, and added a restraining waistband that Moore could tie in the front as she transported her child on her back, Togolese fashion. By four the next morning, Lucy Aukerman had made the first "Snugli"—so ingeniously that only subtle refinements have been made in all the years since. Eventually, in response to the discovery that many users rested newborn infants against their chests (to tend the infants more easily) and then switched them to their backs as the babies matured, she designed a "Snugli" that could readily be used in either position.

Back in Colorado, the new mother stuck Mande in her pouch for her daily rounds, delighted that she could continue to be active. As the family moved from community to community while Mike Moore worked for a series of federal War on Poverty programs, the parents, without a car, bicycled everywhere with Mande and attracted envious

Ann Moore, inventor of the "Snugli," with mementos of her African experience.

attention from other baby-toters who asked for her mother's Ohio address. Since most of the customers were similarly peripatetic young sixties couples, "Snuglis" customers were much in evidence at peace rallies and civil rights marches. Aukerman filled the two or three orders a month by cutting them at the kitchen table and stitching them on her own machine, but by 1966, when Moore designed a better head support, they found that each sale was generating from five to ten more orders. As the advantages of "Snuglis" spread by word of mouth, a thriving cottage industry developed, with Aukerman depending upon neighbors in the nearby farming community to help when they were not planting or harvesting. It was undoubtedly time to get a patent, and though Moore had conceived the idea, her mother had translated it into a usable product. They reached a consensus that Lucy Aukerman should apply since, as Moore recalls, "It didn't really matter to me whose name was on the patent because we worked on it jointly, but Mother was where she could work with a patent attorney. Anyhow, I am interested in the creative part and know nothing about business angles."

The patent described the "Snugli" as a "pouch-like infant carrier that is comfortable to wear, safe, versatile, inexpensive, easy to use, sanitary, washable, rugged, trouble-free, and decorative," stressed the advantages of having both hands free while carrying the child, and attributed the origin of the pouch to "the more primitive peoples . . . [where] most of the womenfolk had many duties to perform in addition to tending their infant children." Previous rigid-frame inventions for carrying children "piggyback" were already on the market, but since they neither allowed access to the very young child for frequent feedings and diaper changings nor adjusted for an infant's rapid growth, the soft "Snugli" proved a great popular success.

One writer heard about the carrier from a friend and plugged it in an article on the Outward Bound program for the *Whole Earth Catalogue*, a publication dedicated to "alternative energy and life styles, ecology, working with nature and doing more with less." This was "Snugli" 's natural constituency, and when sales climbed from a manageable fifteen to twenty-five a month to three hundred, the cottage industry so mushroomed that the Moores incorporated it in 1972, with Mike as president and Ann as director of consumer relations. Aukerman assigned patent rights to her daughter, and as the whole family toured the country to boost their product, groups promoting a variety of child-rearing techniques that bonded children to their parents, such as natural childbirth and breast-feeding, immediately recognized "Snugli" 's potential. Department store buyers, however, equated the backpacking apparatus with a "hippie" look until *Consumer Reports* bestowed upon "Snugli" its highest rating for soft carriers, especially for babies six months old or younger. When that stamp of approval erased buyers' doubts, Mike recalls, "Why, it was like pigs coming in to somebody making a pig call."

For young families who couldn't afford the $55 handmade "Snuglis" from Lucy Aukerman's Ohio operations, "Snugli" had identical ones made by machine in Lakewood, Colorado, in 1979—offered for sale at $35—and the next year added diaper bags with snap-down changing pads to the line. Carla Cohen of Washington, D.C., remembers that before "Snugli" had become commonplace on the American scene, people who couldn't see her son's head above the rim of his "Snugli" would stare at her as if she were a freak and "just barge right up to

Fig. 2.

Tracing an idea: 1890s—1980s.
(above and opposite, left to right)

Patent drawings (above, left and right).

peer in to make sure the baby was all right." But when the straight-
arrow *Wall Street Journal* featured the "Snugli" in an article titled,
"Baby-Carrier Maker Succeeds Playing It Close to the Vest," "Snugli"
wearers were no longer outré. Sales hit four and a half million dollars
in 1982; two years later, six million dollars. Ann, who had had two
more daughters during the years of development—each lovingly
pouched—looked at "Snugli" 's success in more personal terms: "It
encompasses a whole philosophy of parenting. It's tied into a deeper
human relationship between parent and child. Our kids all seem to
have a lot of inner strength—I'd like to think it was because of our
parenting. . . . I feel we're contributing to the well-being of babies. So
if the future holds a world of more loving adults . . . well, that's
exciting."

While workers at the factory made carriers, the Moores managed
the business from offices in a former dog kennel near their home in
Evergreen, a mountain suburb outside Denver, and when Lucy Aukerman retired from the Ohio operation, her husband ran the branch

The Prototype: inventor Ann Moore and her daughter in Selma, Alabama, 1965.

The modern "Snugli," the author's daughter and grandson, Lorrie and Peter Lorenz.

office in a converted chicken house on the family farm. It remained essentially a family operation until 1985, when, after a good many offers to sell, the Moores, finding the business lucrative but stressful and facing the prospective expiration of their patent, sold their company to Gerico, a Huffy Company. Gerico has honored the "Snugli" philosophy of bonding parent and child in each of its several models, from the original denim double-pouch soft baby carrier to one with breast-feeding cutouts for easy, private nursing and an inner seat to make it possible for the pouch to cradle a child from infancy to two years. There are even deluxe models with extra quilting, padding, and color choices. There is another interesting twist to the "Snugli" story. Foreign marketing of the business was so successful that today Westerners have sold the baby carriers to natives in oil-rich Cameroon, Nigeria, and Gabon, thus returning the garment that had its origin in Africa to its first home.

For inventor Ann Moore, the sale of "Snugli" was not the end of her inventive career, for she has translated that carrier's backpack technology into Airlift, a padded, portable, and adjustable carrier for oxygen (in either liquid or cylinder form). Determined to free the thousands tethered to canisters, Moore designed this new backpack to give greater mobility to patients, and to the parents of children who need a steady supply of oxygen. For further convenience, she designed a shoulder/ hand bag and a carrier to fit on the back of a wheelchair or walker. For those using liquid oxygen, she contrived a ventilated carry pouch. Manufacturers of oxygen products are now recommending "Airlift" to their users, but Moore, rather than handling manufacturing and sales ("I am just no good at business—but give me a new idea and I'm *off!*"), turns that over to her husband and their third partner, Leslie Beauparlant, while she posits more "What ifs?" and continues to churn out solutions.

While there was no feminist cheering section in the sixties and seventies to weed out and publicize the names of women inventors, reporters still hoped that women's inventions would provide material for good feature stories, if only because of their rarity. In 1973, when a *Los Angeles Times* writer titled his piece "More Women Submit Patents," one would think, on the face of it, that he had sighted an optimistic trend. His conclusions, however, could have been written almost a century before: Women's immediate domestic sphere was the source of inspiration for most of their ideas, ideas they simply rerouted "from the kitchen to the Patent Office."

But by the time he wrote, the kitchen where women inventors were working was not necessarily their own, for many of them had found work in food industry laboratories and kitchens. Monitoring the escalating numbers of women in the work force, the food industry recognized those working women—liberated, perhaps, but not from fixing dinner—as potential buyers for the time- and motion-saving "convenience foods" their food-testing laboratories were developing. This new work force had developed when business—particularly the service industries—boomed in the postwar years. Because of the low birth rate during the Depression, economists feared a severe labor shortage unless businesses hired and trained college-educated women. By the 1960s not only the government but even magazines normally dedicated to deifying housewifery enunciated a new dictum: Woman's place might well be the office. With the twin pressures of Betty Friedan's book *The Feminine Mystique* warning suburbanites that they would wither on the household vine unless they took jobs with intrinsic satisfactions, and economists pleading that the nation needed its women for economic growth, it's no wonder so many went to work.

To tap this steadily growing market, General Foods had already stocked its arsenal with instant-mix Postum and Maxwell House, Birds Eye frozen foods, Jell-O, and Minute Rice and was now trying to arrive at a formula for the perfect quick bread stuffing. "In the bird" mixes—which the cook stuffed into the fowl's cavity before roasting—were already available, but General Foods was looking for an outside-the-bird, top-of-the-stove, cook-in-fifteen-minutes, tastes-like-Granny's-on-Thanksgiving bread stuffing that would convert stuffing from holiday fare to an everyday side dish. Developing the ideal mixture was a job for its main technical center at Tarrytown, New York. There, among the 850 researchers—many of whom held doctorates and other advanced degrees as chemists, protein engineers, biologists, and tasters—Ruth Siems, with a bachelor of science in home economics from Purdue University, was to work out the recipe for what became one of the company's top sellers, Stove Top Stuffing. Ellen Richards, who so forcefully paved the way for home economics training for women at the turn of the century, would only have shrugged, "Well, of course!"

With years of company experience in flavor blends, the research team assigned to the project (two were Siems's supervisors and one was a food technologist) easily perfected the chicken broth base and gauged the correct amount of dried onion, parsley, and celery to add, but with no experience in bread, they needed to develop a scientific formula for the specific size and consistency of bread crumbs to combine with the vegetable/chicken broth. Since it was Siems who developed the bread crumb formula without which the "stand recipe" specifying the proper proportion of the basic components could not have been made, it was her name that headed the list of the product's patentees. Since she feels that her contribution was so singular that the whole project would have been quietly disposed of had she not worked out the recipe, she wonders whether she might have been considered the single patentee if she had been a man. "I suppose," she says, "*technically*, I was a co-holder; it was just too difficult for them to call me the *inventor* of Stove Top."

At any rate, her directions for the new product were simple: "Simmer the flavor packet with water and butter for five or six minutes. Add bread, stir, cover, let stand five minutes." General Foods chose the name "Stove Top Stuffing," and with such advertising slogans as "quick and easy to prepare" and "on top of the stove without a bird" and "delicious any time you serve chicken," they made Stove Top the leading brand. Company officials and publications saluted Siems's key role in the development of the "stand" recipe, but both Siems and her product manager felt that her work had not been adequately recognized. Since Siems's prototype recipe was chosen from a large field, including one submitted by a professional chef employed by the company, she was understandably outraged to read a newspaper article in which a company vice president was quoted as giving credit for the recipe to the chef, whose membership in the Escoffier Society seemed to have outweighed the actual facts. Siems, with a what-can-you-expect-from-corporate-politics shrug, chalks the snub up to the fact that, as a woman home economist in research, she had "zero or negative clout."

On the plus side, she did receive a plaque engraved with the first page of the patent, and the satisfaction of knowing that she was the "Stove Top Lady." And her career did advance. Prior to Stove Top, she'd had only one promotion in twenty years; after Stove Top's multimillion-dollar success, she received several promotions and was cited in the house organ as the "key figure in the development of Stove Top Stuffing," and a "co-holder of the Stove Top patent [whose] creative ability has added an extra dimension to the functionality of the Food Products Laboratories." Though her jobs improved, she still felt that her employers kept her at least one grade level below male peers with similar education, experience, and intelligence—a situation she felt was "par for most women at the Tech Center."

In addition, Siems learned that the financial rewards of corporate inventing were minimal at General Foods: twenty-five dollars upon application for the patent; one hundred when the patent was obtained. Though the company normally gave large bonuses to research managers for products that yielded large profits, they offered her none since she was not a manager, only a home economist. When her name was later submitted for such recognition, she was told that in inventing she was "only doing her job." While not wanting to appear greedy for credit for her inventive work, Siems is nonetheless incensed that, being "only a woman"—and a home economist at that—she was denied the monetary and patenting laurels that she would have received had she been a man. She was born "twenty years too soon," she thinks, and admires the women of today for having the courage to expose discriminatory policies instead of quietly accepting them in order to hang on to their jobs. They are helped, of course, by equal employment legislation that forces employers to steer clear, on pain of court action, of gender discrimination. Still, she knows that discrimination is difficult to prove.

Siems's resentment and frustration were fueled not only by her conviction that she was relegated to less prestigious and lower-paying jobs because of her gender, but also by the treatment she received when Philip Morris took over the company in 1985 and decided to retire everyone over fifty. When Siems, banking on the value of her over thirty-three years of service to General Foods and her invention of one of the company's most successful products, angrily refused the retirement package, her boss—ironically, the very Stove Top project manager who had at least seen to it that her name appeared first on the patent—told her that her job had been eliminated. Today, she summarizes her feeling about her work in corporate research with a telling anecdote. When the one-billionth package of Stove Top Stuffing came off the Dover, Delaware, line, the company passed out T-shirts to mark the occasion. Since no one thought to send one to the product's inventor, she ordered one for herself. Across its front was emblazoned: "With Stove Top 1984—1 Billionth Package"; on its back were the words, "Stuff It." To which the unheralded inventor replies, "Touché. My feelings exactly!"

Though quick-fix food and inventions to ease household burdens always found a ready market, their effect upon the morale of harried housewives appeared negligible, a paradox that "Jennie June" Croly had noted a century before when she concluded that women who were relieved of some burdens simply spent more time on the ones that were left. When Ruth Schwartz Cowan examined household technology's influence in her 1983 book, *More Work for Mother*, and a later article whose title—"Less Work for Mother?"—seemed less than encouraging, she found that despite the proliferation of motors and microchips, the average 1980s housewife spent as many hours of unpaid work in the home as had her early-twentieth-century counterpart. This appeared to be a reformulation of the principle Northcote Parkinson had observed about administrative bureaucracy, that work expands to fill the time available.

But in this case it was housewifery that was expanding; as drudgery lessened, expectations escalated. With the introduction of electric vacuum cleaners, housewives, once content to beat their rugs twice a year, cleaned them every week, or even daily. As automatic washers and driers made laundering less burdensome, persnickety housewives washed more often until by the eighties they were processing roughly ten times (in weight) as much as their mothers. With the advent of family cars, mothers carpooled children who once walked to school and shopped for products a deliveryman once sold on his rounds, tasks that did nothing to decrease the accumulating indoor work. Inventions, instead of revolutionizing housework, Cowan concluded, simply equipped a woman to carry the burden of a full-time job outside the home *and* a thirty-five-hour work week in the home—without seriously endangering her health (not her physical health, anyway). Surprisingly, this paradox in no way discouraged inventors from believing that their discoveries would prove exceptions.

One of the overworked and overextended women who fits Cowan's description is Laurene O'Donnell, a mother of three who commutes 105 miles a day to a full-time job. The task she particularly resented was cleaning the aggravating accumulation of glasses her young trio left in the kitchen and bathrooms. O'Donnell considered installing a drinking fountain, but the ones on the market were not only too bulky and unattractive for home use but had to be placed so far back on the sink that the children couldn't reach them. She enlisted the help of Al Litwak, an engineer friend, to design a child-safe, smart-looking, low-profile fountain for the front of a sink. They built several prototypes before resolving leakage and pressure problems, and when the final test proved successful, O'Donnell experienced the rush that comes over every inventor: "one of the most exciting moments of my life—to have gone from an idea to a totally new invention that worked!"

After taking a class in patent procedures, O'Donnell and Litwak decided to hire a lawyer to handle their patent application. When the Patent Office examiners later denied the patent, O'Donnell did what other infuriated inventors (including myself) have done: She headed straight for Washington for a face-to-face confrontation with the ex-

Laurene O'Donnell and "Aqua Spring," her home water fountain.

aminers, ready to do battle for her idea. O'Donnell remembers "sitting in that office with the standard government-issue furniture, looking out the window at the planes taking off from National Airport by the Potomac" and hoping desperately that she could convince the examiners to grant a patent for the idea into which she had poured so much time, money, and energy. As she and her lawyer described the product's intended purpose and how it differed from other water fountains, the examiners pelted them with questions but didn't indicate any change in their position.

There was no change: The decision was still negative. After more amendments and a change of attorney ("The first one just couldn't get it right"), she finally received her patent, a moment she savors: "There were times when things got rough and people would tell me that it wasn't worth doing, that I must be crazy to think that someone else hadn't already done something like this. Friends thought I already had enough to do without taking this on; a few people even asked why a *woman* would want a patent! But getting that patent in my hand was a feeling of elation I cannot explain."

The confident inventor, a quality management advisor for Corporate Support at Bellcore (Bell Communications Research), O'Donnell is currently taking business education courses to hone management skills she first acquired in her high school years when for four summers she and a friend ordered supplies, waited on customers, cleaned, prepared food, hired employees, and managed everything but the writing out of checks for a family-owned ice-cream stand. In the marketing study of her own invention that she wrote for one of her business courses, she points out that because a plumbing industry giant's multiswivel spout is inconvenient for children, it should not be highly competitive with her "Aqua Spring" and even sees extending the original concept of a "baby bubbler" to a water fountain for hotel rooms. For now, however, her target market consists of women like herself, working women whose time is at a premium and to whom any functional and convenient fixture to simplify life would appeal—if only she can make them aware of it and price it affordably. Infused with entrepreneurial spirit, she is currently showing her invention to tract builders, plumbing supply houses, and fixture vendors and remains optimistic.

An invention such as a home fountain must seem a mere stopgap to Frances Gabe, a Newberg, Oregon, resident, who has what she deems the definitive answer to the housewife's dilemma—a house devised to eliminate the drudgeries of housework, a house that cleans itself, a *patented* house that fits no previous Patent Office classification, a house that almost literally takes care of itself with sixty-eight separate devices. Looking at her patent, one is reminded of what *New Ideas* magazine said almost a century ago: "It is due to the inventive faculty of women that we owe the majority of devices which lighten and perfect labor in her own domain. This is not remarkable, for from her practical knowledge of the work she is better qualified than her brother of the sterner sex whose conception of what will aid her is only superficial and gained principally from casual observation."

A decade ago when the press learned that the inventor had built a model at the suggestion of the Inventors Council of Oregon and was in the process of building the entire self-cleaning house for herself, they decided she and it were both big news. The inventor was indeed eminently quotable: "[O]ver the years I've talked to literally thousands of women about cleaning. Only four said they actually enjoyed housework. Cleaning is backbreaking work. It involves stooping, and I say, 'Stoop, stoop, stooping is *stupid*!' " To the editor of *The Technological Woman*, she explained, "Men decided a few centuries ago that any job they found repulsive was women's work. . . . Housework is a thankless, unending job, a nerve-twangling bore. Who wants it? Nobody. With my jaw set hard I was determined that there had to be a better way! Some way, somewhere, I would find it." To a *Los Angeles Times* reporter investigating what she had wrought, she elaborated:

> I'm trying to take a lot of misery out of life. I want to leave the world a better place. What's the fun of cleaning house? It just gripes me every time I dust, scrub floors and clean walls. . . . For God's sake, Why should women waste half their lives cleaning the house? It's damn foolishness! All a woman has to do in the self-cleaning house is push a series of buttons and zowie—the work is done. . . . No carpets in this house. Carpets are dust collectors. I hate them. . . . Why waste time loading a dishwasher, then unloading it and putting them in the cupboard? Why can't dishes be washed in the cupboard and save time?

Gabe had indeed installed her dishwasher in a cupboard. Soiled dishes went directly from table to cupboard for washing and drying, and stayed there until needed—no putting in, no taking out, no stacking. Gabe sloped the floors in all four corners so that when the rotating fixture in the ceiling sprayed water onto the composition furniture and the resin-covered walls, ceiling, and floors, the water ran right off; blowers dried what remained. It was a bit like an automatic car wash. Her porcelain bathtub, shaped like a reclining chair, was always warm since its base was both heat register and body dryer. Sink, tub, showers, and toilets were self-cleaning; a drain in the fireplace carried off ashes.

The inventor and builder, by her own admission a "bossy kid" who couldn't get along with her stepmother, virtually grew up on construction sites because her father, an architect and building contractor, took her to work with him so often. After the war, when her electrical engineer husband could find no work, she started and managed a

Frances Gabe, inventor of the self-cleaning house.

building repairs business for thirty-five years. In business, she made a composite of her other given names and became Frances Gabe because her husband, from whom she later separated, was embarrassed by her construction work and didn't want his name associated with it.

She has suffered through some difficult years, especially the eighteen years it took to recover from blindness that remained undiagnosed and struck her at the time of her first child's birth, and the months she managed the business from her bed because of a broken back, but, Gabe says, "You either struggle and come up or you go down. I didn't have it in me to go down. I didn't know where down was. The struggle has been pure hell. I think women need to know that. The struggle is what gave me . . . the guts to keep on going when half the town was calling me nuts. Any damn fool who tries to do something impossible like a self-cleaning house is crazy!"

Like her father, Gabe often took her own two children to building sites. She's proud that they are both able builders but sighs that they and her grandchildren feel cheated out of having a cookie-baking mother and grandmother. Now seventy-four years old and living in the prototype house she built herself, the inventor has proved the Gabe Self-Cleaning House *works*, that it is a boon not only to burned-out housekeepers but to the elderly or handicapped who want to remain in their own homes but need push-button efficiency. She's ready to "get rid of the whole thing," but for a price: "I'm taking my miniature working model to INPEX, the Inventors New Products Exposition in Pittsburgh, and I sure hope to sell my patent rights. I've worked on it long enough!"

Throughout the history of the Patent Office, a large proportion of women's patents have consistently been issued to clothing improvements or construction, and, while many women moved into many other areas of invention, others found financial success in converting years of personal and professional sewing experience into patenting devices to help others sew clothing with a professional touch. Dorothy Young-Kirby decided to show others how she sewed straight seams and spaced topstitching evenly. Having taught sewing and written *Dot Young's Sewing Book for Girls*, she decided, in retirement, to capitalize on her experience. Finding that stitching guides already on the market were ineffective, she invented the "Dot Young Sewing Guide," which, because it adjusts to accommodate all thicknesses of fabrics and edges, makes it possible, she vouches, for *anyone* to sew professionally. Working within a strict budget for promoting her idea, she found two retired patent attorneys to help her and consulted many business men and women who gave her free advice. She received her patent in 1968, the same year her husband died, and threw herself into establishing a business to prevent herself from becoming just another grieving widow.

That she succeeded is shown by the fact that sixteen years later, sales, boosted by six mail-order houses, hit the quarter million mark. Young-Kirby could look back on a business that had turned out to be far more than an outlet for her grief: "I have no money worries. Besides, inventing keeps me young." In 1986, when her original seam guide no longer fit the newer machines, she patented one with a magnetized rubberlike material that grips the plates of newer machines. She jobs out the components to companies specializing in magnetic products, has them assembled in one place, packaged under her direction, and receives a royalty on each guide sold. Describing this flourishing business venture as "educational, challenging and exciting" despite its ups and downs, Young-Kirby's words of advice to other inventors—"The inventor needs faith in her product, a determination to see her invention on the market, and a willingness to go the extra mile to see it get there"—could have come straight from the pen of

Dot Young-Kirby with her adjustable seam-guide.

Charlotte Smith. Young-Kirby adds, "Something I would like to see organized as a result of your book on women inventors is a National Association of Women Inventors, even if we only met every two years and were a small group. I would like to know other women inventors." One knows that Smith would have printed that in bold type in *The Woman Inventor* and invited Young-Kirby to Washington!

Not all women inventors of the postwar decades worked on such gender-restricted projects, but when they moved into broader fields, they were often limited in their ability to make money from the fruits of their labors. The greatest opportunity for those whose scientific training qualified them to invent in technical areas lay in corporate or government-sponsored research laboratories. Those laboratories, however, required their employees, as a condition of employment, to assign the patent rights to any future discoveries they might make to the company under whose aegis they developed them. Katharine Blodgett, for instance, worked for and assigned rights to General Electric; Olive Dennis assigned hers to B & O. There were others, however, who did not sign away their rights. Two women chemists, Elizabeth Hazen and Rachel Brown, who worked for a state-supported public health laboratory and co-patented one of the most widely acclaimed wonder drugs of the post–World War II years, kept the right to dispose of the profits as they saw fit.

Hazen and Brown's work was stimulated by the wartime need to find a cure for the fungus infections that afflicted many servicemen. Scientists had been feverishly searching for an antibiotic toxic enough to kill fungi but safe enough for human use, since, unfortunately, the newly trademarked "wonder drugs" such as penicillin and streptomycin and later, Chloromycetin and Aureomycin killed the very bacteria in the body that controlled fungi. It was to discover a fungicide without that double effect that Brown, of New York State's Department of Health at Albany, and Hazen, senior microbiologist at the Department of Health Laboratories in New York, began their long-distance collaboration. Based upon Hazen's previous research at Columbia, where she had built an impressive collection of fungus cultures, both were convinced that an antifungal organism already existed in certain soils.

They divided the work. Hazen methodically screened and cultured scores of soil samples, which she then sent to her partner, who prepared extracts, isolated and purified active agents, and shipped them back to New York, where Hazen could study their biological properties. On a 1948 vacation, Hazen fortuitously collected a clump of soil from the edge of W. B. Nourse's cow pasture in Fauquier County, Virginia, that, when tested, revealed the presence of the perfect microorganism. In farm owner Nourse's honor, Hazen named it *Streptomyces noursei*, and, within a year, the two scientists knew that the properties of their substance distinguished it from previously described antibiotics. After further research they eventually reduced their substance to a fine yellow powder, which they first named "fungiciden," then renamed "nystatin" (to honor the New York State laboratory) when they learned the previous name was already in use. Of their major discovery, Brown said lightly that it simply illustrated "how unpredictable consequences can come from rather modest beginnings."

There was nothing unpredictable, however, about the pharmaceutical world's keen interest in the not yet patented drug. According to patent law, an inventor must apply for a patent within a year after publicly disclosing the invention, and, since the two scientists *had* talked about it at a regional meeting of the National Academy of Sciences in Schenectady, there was no time to spare. Brown recalled the issue:

> If we had an antibiotic that was useful, we were responsible in some way to see that it was made available. But we were in no position to carry out the evaluation in humans, in no position to even prepare enough material for the tests in the first place. Obviously, it had to be patented before any company would take it on, but how could we make sure they would carry through?

Brown and Hazen turned for help to Research Corporation, established in 1912 to hold patent rights for individuals who agreed to donate their proceeds to the public interest, in return for which the corporation handled their patent application and arranged for licensing. Brown and Hazen assigned half their royalties to support Research Corporation's grants program in the physical sciences and the other half to establish the Brown-Hazen Fund to help young college and university students pursue the biological sciences, particularly microbiology, immunology, and biochemistry. The patent applied for, Research Corporation licensed E. R. Squibb and Sons to manufacture nystatin for five years, and Squibb used its sophisticated industrial technology to convert what was previously manufactured in a laboratory into a mass-produced drug. Brown and Hazen regularly visited the New Jersey plant to make suggestions about extraction, purification, nutrient broths, cultures, and so on. Hazen told a friend, "It's my baby, and I'm going to look after it."

It took six years, from 1951 to 1957, to get the nystatin patent. The Patent Office first balked because the drug was unpatentable until successful human trials proved its "utility," and then because an article in a professional journal implied that the inventors had in fact disclosed their research more than a year prior to applying for the patent—an action that would have nullified their application. Hazen countered successfully that the paper described only one of many processes attempted by the pair in the course of their experimentation. Still they waited for the patent. Since the American patent system protects the person or company who invents first rather than the one who patents first, Squibb could be certain that no one could steal the process if the drug went on the market while the patent was still pending. It appeared in 1954 as Mycostatin, in a number of forms such as oral and vaginal tablets and ointment. As Mysteteclin, it was combined with tetracycline in capsule form.

Elizabeth Hazen and Rachel Brown, inventors of Nystatin fungicide.

Shortly afterward, the drug made news when doctors for German President Theodore Heuss asked that Mycostatin be ferried by air and thence by courier to their patient, whose lung inflammation forced him to postpone a projected state visit to President Eisenhower. Sending the drug was more a measure of enthusiasm for its "wonder" status, however, than of its appropriateness for the treatment of a site not accessible to the fungicide.

Three years later, when the patent was finally issued, the news reached Rachel Brown as she was reading the *New York Times* and spotted a photograph of Hazen and herself accompanying an article headlined THE FRUITS OF RESEARCH. While the long delay in gaining the patent had been exasperating, Squibb had used the time well, unraveling snags in the drug's manufacture so that the moment protection was assured the company was ready with a much improved nystatin, which generated sizable royalties for the full seventeen years of its patent protection. In its first year, it paid Research Corporation $135,000 in royalties; by 1980, when the patent expired, it had paid the corporation a cumulative total of $13 million.

In order to honor nonchemist Hazen as a co-winner with Brown of its Chemical Pioneer Award, the American Institute of Chemists changed its bylaws. The inventors, having won many similar laurels, encouraged other women to enter the field in which they excelled. Brown recruited promising candidates for the Health Department by delivering her favorite "War Among the Microbes" speech to high schools, colleges, and service clubs, telling how she had planned to major in history until, with a science requirement to fulfill, she took a chemistry course in Mount Holyoke's noted chemistry department— with the surprising result that she "fell in love with it," especially its "ordered pattern and precision." While she herself had enjoyed her career, she was frank to point out: "You must be willing to sacrifice some things. . . . I wouldn't recommend it to everyone, but if they are naturally curious, if they think they might enjoy it, or even if they really enjoy cooking, they should give Chemistry a try." Brown never spelled out what sacrifices she herself had made, but considering that the most common goals for young women of the period were marriage and motherhood, we may hazard a guess: Neither Brown nor Hazen ever married. The long hours required by research would have gotten in the way of the time needed to run a home and rear children, especially in an era that didn't even pay lip service to the idea of men and women sharing in such responsibilities.

When Brown was fifty-six and Hazen seventy, Squibb awarded "the girls" (as their male Albany laboratory mentor affectionately, however inappropriately, called them) its first $5,000 Squibb Award in Chemotherapy, in recognition of their discovery of the first "broadly effective antifungal antibiotic safe enough for human use"—though that described only one of its uses. It also prevented spoilage of bananas and livestock feed and, in a particularly innovative application of its mold-destroying potential, rescued otherwise ruined murals and manuscripts that had been damaged when the Arno River in Florence, Italy, overflowed. It was almost too much to expect that the male reporter interviewing Brown twenty years after her discovery would not feel it incumbent upon him to wrestle with what seemed to him an incongruity—a woman scientist who was a "womanly" woman. To no one's surprise, he found it necessary to report that he felt her "kindly grandmother" appearance contradicted "the stereotype of a successful career woman in the male-dominated field of science." One wonders what he would have thought of her slight, vivacious, not-quite-five-foot southern partner, Elizabeth Hazen, whose meticulously coiffed hair faithfully maintained its original reddish tinge (albeit chemically), who applied her makeup artfully, selected her size six or eight dresses at expensive shops, and vainly refused to wear a much-needed hearing aid.

Unlike Hazen and Brown, who worked for state-owned laboratories and retained control of their patent rights, many other women scientists worked at laboratories of privately held corporations, to which they automatically assigned their rights. One of the best examples is Gertrude Elion, the 1989 Nobel Prize co-winner in medicine, whose major achievements, most in collaboration with George Hitchings, have been in developing drugs crucial to treatment of cancer and viruses: Purinethol and Thioquinnine for treating acute leukemia; Imuram, which made possible widespread kidney transplants by helping the body suppress its immune reactions and thus preventing rejection; Zyloprim, which treated gout and excess uremic acid resulting from chemotherapy and radiation treatment of cancer; and Zovirax, for treating herpes infections. Since Elion was employed by Burroughs-Wellcome, a major pharmaceutical company, she was *expected* to discover and patent. And she did—forty-five times.

Daughter of a dentist father and a mother who was a housewife, Elion grew up in the Bronx, skipping enough elementary school grades to advance to high school at twelve and to college at fifteen, a precocity that led her classmates to consider her "different" but not to ostracize her from their activities. At Hunter College she declared chemistry as her major the first year. "When I was fifteen, I already knew from my high school courses that I loved science," says Elion now, "but that year I was so devastated by my grandfather's death from cancer that majoring in Chemistry seemed the logical first step in committing myself to fighting the disease."

Graduating summa cum laude from Hunter in 1937 in the bottom of the Depression, she made the rounds of the few laboratories that had openings, but, despite impressive credentials, found no work. At the end of one interview that she thought was proceeding particularly well, the interviewer finally told her that he couldn't hire her because her attractive appearance would distract other workers. Well aware at the time that the pseudocompliment was simply a cover for staking out laboratories as male preserves, Elion is *still* indignant at the gambit: "That is *such* a stupid argument. Maybe I was young and 'cute' (after all, I was only twenty then), but I've learned over the years that when you put white lab coats on chemists, they all look alike! Believe me, when I later reached a position where I did the hiring, I never took looks into consideration!" But that opportunity was in the future; at the time she had no recourse but to find any kind of job. She finally landed a three-month job with the New York Hospital School of Nursing after having spent six weeks at a secretarial school. It was not an auspicious start for finding a cure for cancer.

The break came when a man she met at a party allowed her to work in his laboratory—without pay. Seizing the opportunity, she worked for nothing at first, for twelve dollars a week for six months, and finally for twenty dollars a week for the next year and a half, long enough to finance courses for her master's degree from New York University. Degree in hand, she taught high school chemistry for two years but felt she didn't have enough patience for teaching, little realizing then that in the scientific career she planned she would have far more severe

Dr. Gertrude Elion, 1988 Nobel Prize Winner in Medicine.

tests of endurance—waiting for test results, waiting for confirmation, waiting even for the right moment to announce results (not to mention waiting for a job). Since no laboratory job was on the horizon in the 1930s, she had to wait until 1943, when the country was at war, for one to appear.

An employment agency with which she had previously registered called that year to ask if she was still interested in laboratory work. "Interested???" says Elion. "Of *course* I was still interested—it was all I ever wanted to do. It wasn't until men went to war, though, that they finally found they needed me! War changed everything. Whatever reservations there were about employing women in laboratories simply evaporated." Elion learned firsthand what women before her had also discovered when they were pressed into service in wartime—that "genetic disabilities" would be forgotten for the duration.

Elion spent the remaining wartime years in the laboratories of A & P and Johnson and Johnson, but it was drug research she was interested in, and so in 1944 she made a "cold call" on Burroughs-Wellcome to ask for lab work. She was referred to Dr. George Hitchings, who was looking for an assistant; when she saw a woman microbiologist in the laboratory, she knew her gender would be no obstacle. As she heard Hitchings describe the research he was conducting on nucleic acids and realized her job would involve her in it, her mind was made up: "I didn't understand half of what he was saying, but his description of his work so enthralled me that I knew then and there that I'd give my life to finding out about it. And I have done just that—mainly working on purines, the building blocks of nucleic acid. I have to admit, too, that after working for slave wages, I was mightily impressed with the $50 a week pay." Elion started work immediately, relishing her research so much that on the few occasions when she didn't cart it home at night her mother asked if she was sick. When the company moved from New York to Research Triangle Park in North Carolina, she, like most of the other employees, picked up stakes and followed.

After retiring in 1983, she has continued as a consultant for scientific research and maintains a company office from which she sallies forth to worldwide conferences and meetings. Meeting her in her office for the first time, I began and then quickly withdrew the question I was ready to ask—whether her gender had held her back from career advancement or recognition. After all, she *had* won the Nobel Prize! She was eager to think about it anyhow. "Since my work is in no way defined by gender," she answered, "I don't feel that what honors and recognition have come my way have anything to do with my being a woman—I certainly hope that no one thinks I have been singled out just because I am a woman!" She then grinned as she added, "On the other hand, that's not to say that it isn't time women *were* recognized!" Elion is pleased with the message her honors and her position (as head of experimental therapy, which included organic chemistry, enzymology, immunology, virology, and metabolic studies) have telegraphed to prospective female employees—that Burroughs-Wellcome accepts and promotes women on their own merits.

That she has attracted other gifted scientists is obvious. I heard a number of Burroughs-Wellcome scientists say with pride—and awe—"Trudy Elion hired me!" As I threaded my way through the company's labyrinth of laboratories and maneuvered past beakers, bubbling broths, and test tubes to interview several women chemists, virologists, and a medical doctor, I was impressed with the balance between their collegial camaraderie and their solitary laboratory vigils. Currently the best known of Burroughs-Wellcome's patents is AZT, since 1987 the only drug approved by the Food and Drug Administration to combat the AIDS virus directly. Although the compound had been around for years, its usefulness as a specific treatment against the Human Immunodeficiency Virus (HIV) was unknown before group leader of chemistry Janet Rideout decided to include the compound among the twelve she sent to retro-virus specialist Martha St. Clair to test on her laboratory mice. St. Clair remembers the day of discovery: "Before I left work that day, I checked my slide and discovered that one of those antibacterial compounds Janet had refused to give up on actually inhibited the growth of the virus. I told one of my colleagues, and by the next morning, everyone was racing to the laboratory to see what had happened. It was a moment every researcher savors!"

Senior associate virologist St. Clair, like Elion, had identified her chosen field as early as seventh grade, and when she had the chance to do drug research fourteen years ago became "so hooked" that she never returned to finish her Ph.D. program at Duke. "Where else could I have such respect, freedom and responsibility?" asks St. Clair. "I've never been treated differently because I am a woman. I learned the bottom line is to pay attention to your productivity!"

When the new drug was patented, the name of Rideout, who earned both a B.S. and M.S. from Mount Holyoke and a Ph.D. from the University of New York at Buffalo, was listed first among the five inventors, a position reserved for the scientist who initiated the project. While fully cognizant of and grateful for the work of the others,

Rideout feels that being first confers well-deserved official and public acknowledgment of the patience she needed to "hang on to that compound" and the sixth sense she had that it might just be the one the research team was looking for.

Company chemist Lilia Beauchamp had a pharmacist father who bought her a chemistry set when she was a child, thus giving her enough support in her choice of science as a major to make up for the lack of encouragement girls then received in school. After taking a master's in organic chemistry and being hired by Burroughs-Welcome in 1957, she joined the research program on Zovirax, a compound used to treat infections caused by the herpes virus, and then went on to other drug research projects. Beauchamp finds that the search for drugs that will heal patients has a far greater appeal than other jobs she might have taken. Hearing from clinical studies that a drug on which she has been working has helped a child with pneumonia is the kind of impetus she needs to keep up with all the latest technological developments in her field. Indeed, everyone at Burroughs-Wellcome seems driven by passion for what they're doing.

Chemist Susan Daluge, married and the mother of one, calls her job of making and testing compounds over and over grueling work: "For me, it's the thought that I *might* discover something to help sick people that keeps me at it, but I do pay a price. My research has become the second child I might otherwise have had." In saying this, she puts her finger on the dilemma faced by many women in science who have been lucky enough to find absorbing careers yet find that long hours in the laboratory, plus the time they need to put in reading the literature at night, severely limits the time they have for their families. As another woman scientist at the laboratory said, echoing a long-standing feminist complaint: "What we scientists need is a 'wife' at home to take care of all the stuff we have to do after we get there!"

Erna Schneider Hoover's ability to pursue such a career while still enjoying family life with her husband and three children makes her all the more remarkable. Even with a husband who assumed equal responsibility, creative scheduling, and excellent child care, often in shifts, it wasn't easy. Hoover is also unusual in that her career path was quite indirect. She moved from honors work in medieval history and philosophy at Wellesley to a doctorate in philosophy and foundations of mathematics at Yale to a teaching job at Swarthmore and eventually to a scientific job at Bell Laboratories in New Jersey. There she developed and patented the first computer used to switch telephone calls.

When she started work at Bell in 1954, the company was already planning to replace telephone switches controlled either by hard-wired relay equipment or electronic mechanical means with switches operated by electronic computers. In simplifying both the problem and the solution, the draft for which she drew up while still in the hospital after the birth of one of her three daughters, Hoover explains, "We needed a method to keep the computer from being overloaded when a very large number of persons tried to call at once, and my invention just involved measuring how busy the machine was and regulating the number of calls accepted as a result." Her patent, one of the country's first in the software field, and her general technical contributions to the widely used Electronics Switching Project of the Bell Telephone companies resulted in her becoming the first woman supervisor of a technical department at Bell Laboratories.

When Hoover began at Bell in 1954, she was one of the few women there who had any significant responsibility, since many of those hired during the war either left on their own or were demoted at war's end—a general practice, as we have seen. Hoover—no novice to sexist attitudes in the workplace since the day Yale told her that though her outstanding record warranted her staying on to teach, her gender was an obstacle—simply overlooked the prejudice. "You ignore it and do what you have to do," she explained to a reporter who interviewed her for her alumnae magazine after she had received the Wellesley Alumnae Achievement Award. Hoover credited her "supreme self-confidence" to solid academic grounding, professors who served as role models, and students who "showed they had the ability to run things themselves"—a welcome switch from high school, "where girls were supposed to act dumb even if they were not." Such an atmosphere was probably not available in the 1940s anywhere in academia except at a women's college. Some feel that is still true today—witness the passionate (and ultimately successful) protests of Mills College students against their institution's going coed. Though electrical engineering and computer science are still male-dominated, Hoover sees no reason why other similarly competent, confident, highly motivated young women should not find jobs in these fields, as more and more women are doing. Simply check out the company first, she advises them. Make certain that it has a well-established record of hiring, training, and promoting women.

Since it is so unusual to find more than one woman patent holder in a family (though sisters Sarah Ball and Mary Jackson showed a "smoothing iron" at the 1876 Centennial and Emma and Mary Dietz displayed their "Dust Pan and Crumb Receiver" and a snowplow at New Orleans during the 1880s), I am closing this chapter with inventor Nancy Perkins, great-niece of Anna Keichline, the early-twentieth-century architect and patentee of building construction improvements. Perkins inherited Keichline's consuming interest in design and holds three patents of her own.

Like her great-aunt, Perkins developed her professional interest early and earned a degree in industrial design from the University of Illinois, Champaign-Urbana. Though some job interviewers asked her intrusive questions about her personal life to learn whether such an attractive young woman could be serious about a job or would toss it aside for marriage, she found work she liked as a consultant to Sears, Roebuck and Company. At Sears, it was the company's fifteen-year-old, top-of-the-line canister vacuum cleaner that needed fixing. As company engineers addressed performance (proper motor, air flow, and so on), Perkins, in what she calls "human engineering," focused on weight and comfort of operation, both factors to which men—with their greater upper body strength and (alas) infrequent experience in maneuvering canister vacuums—were less sensitive. As she puts it, "When there are thirty male engineers and project managers sitting around a table, somebody has to be there to say, 'Hey, this is too heavy to be comfortable.' " She was there to say it and subsequently redesigned the handle, bumpers, and wheels to satisfy—both technically and visually—the vacuum's principal users—women. While she capitalized on her knowledge of what appealed to women, she objected to being typecast as a designer of "women's products" and made such an issue of having to work on projects her male superiors considered suitable to her gender ("They assume we women are great at baby bottles and that's *it!*") that they finally assigned her to work on a car battery—in the automotive products division, which was well staked

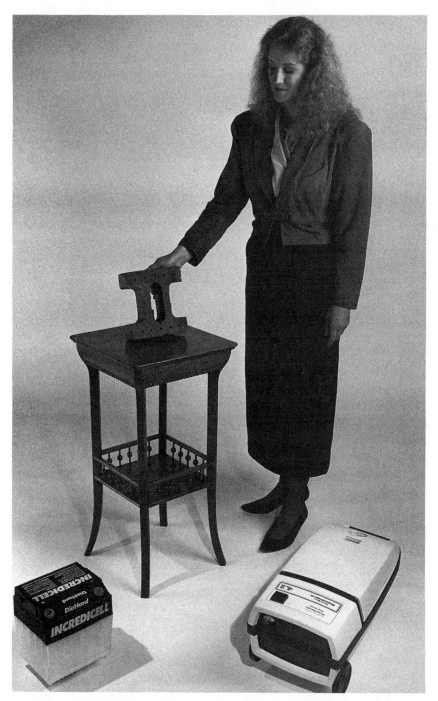

Nancy Perkins with great-aunt Anna Keichline's prize-winning oak table and patented construction brick and Perkins's car battery and vacuum cleaner.

out as a "masculine" enclave. Her subsequent patent for the "Incredicell" automotive battery banished any notion that she was out of place!

Still, men so dominated the whole field of industrial design—with women making up only 7 percent of its professional association's membership—that women were a rarity in top management at design firms. Perkins, an accomplished speaker for industrial designers both here and abroad, solved that problem by starting her own Perkins Design Ltd. in Chicago. She has recently relocated it to her aunt's hometown, Bellefonte, Pennsylvania, and set up shop in a Keichline-designed building. Also, to honor the woman whose career inspired her own, she is now marketing a copy of the 1903 oak card table that brought the fourteen-year-old Keichline her first public praise as an industrial artist.

Perkins has found that since so few women have patents, hers (assigned to Sears) give her respect within her own profession and are a valuable selling point to prospective clients as an indication of her originality and ability to carry an idea through to completion. More important, however, is personal satisfaction and the jubilation common to every inventor whose invention has made "The list," from foremother Mary Kies to the most current patentee whose feminine ingenuity has gained official recognition: "Being on the official U.S. Patent list gives me credibility and authority! The *United States of America* recognizes my creativity! I'm darn proud of it!"

# 16

## PATENTS PENDING?

*E*ver since Mary Kies became the first woman patentee in 1809, it has been evident that commendation—or even passing notice—of a woman's invention could help bring her product to public attention and stimulate business; so when feminists included women's inventions in women's buildings at fairs or praised them in their tracts, bulletins, and newspapers as proof that creativity was not limited to the masculine gender, it was free publicity—manna from heaven to struggling entrepreneurs! Today, women inventors receive notice of a different sort, and it too should stimulate business. Some of the new attention springs from an increasing interest in women's history, which has prompted historians, sociologists, and other researchers interested in gender issues to examine women inventors as a group—though, interestingly, they themselves never acted as a group, despite Charlotte Smith's valiant attempts to forge them into one. The independent and often solitary nature of inventing and protecting their inventions made them so competitive, even so secretive about sharing information, that it undoubtedly dampened any nascent sense of sisterhood. Even though they never acted in concert to press a women's rights agenda, they nonetheless benefitted from whatever gains their sex made. That is still true today; as women's status has improved, women inventors are in a doubly enviable position. Heightened interest in women's affairs focuses welcome attention on them and their products, and now even their government has learned to cherish them as vital assets in the war to reduce foreign competition in technology.

That commercial rivalry began about the turn of the century when a Japanese official who came to the United States to study its patent system concluded that it was the spur of patent protection that gave this nation technological and political supremacy. Japan, too, he vowed, would "have patents." To that end, Japan stimulated its future inventors by offering national prizes to schoolchildren who successfully applied their analytical thinking to invent useful articles. Nine decades later, when roughly half of all American patents issued go to nonresidents, it is the Japanese who receive most of them. To shore up this declining share of patents, which, if unchecked, could make this country a second-rate power, the United States is now trying to groom its students for adult inventorhood in the hope of restoring the nation's competitive edge. Half those students are females, girl students who once sewed and cooked in Home Ec while the boys trooped off to Shop, and they now enjoy equal opportunities to wield tools in Invention Class. Of course, for inspiration, they need female role models. I hope my book will help.

Taking official action in 1988, Commissioner of Patents and Trademarks Donald J. Quigg (since retired) initiated Project XL to prod educators to develop critical and creative thinking programs that would rekindle the spirit of invention. Although some on the sidelines wondered whether creativity was teachable, others, proceeding on the assumption that inventors are made, not born, tried to think of as many ways as possible to put children in problem-solving situations that required inventive solutions. Inventors' organizations encouraged members to visit classrooms to tell their personal stories. *Weekly Reader*, staple of many a grade school classroom, sponsored the *Weekly Reader* National Invention Contest, and its first contest gave birth to a host of new ideas, everything from a suitcase with a zipper on the underside to facilitate retrieval of articles packed on the bottom to elastic shoelaces that don't have to be untied (the latter from a kindergartener). The next year, six-year-old Suzanna Goodin of Hydro, Oklahoma, tired of cleaning the spoon from which she dolloped cat food into her pet's dish, invented an edible spoon-shaped cracker to do the job and, against 200,000 other entries, won one of the two grand prizes, a $500 savings bond and a trip to the National Inventor's Exposition at the Patent Office to exhibit her invention. Quipped the headline of an article in *People Weekly*: NOW THANKS TO SUZANNA GOODIN, PETS CAN CLEAN THE BOWL—AND THEN EAT THE SPOON THAT FEEDS THEM.

The following year, fourteen-year-old Pamela Sica, from Saint Mary Magdalen School in Chadds Ford, Pennsylvania, won the grand prize for her age group for a push-button device that raised the floor of a car trunk to a position high enough that one could retrieve its cargo without bending over and straining one's back. Two intersecting obligations factored Pam's ingenuity: having the family job of carrying in heavy grocery bags from the car and a class report on an invention, required by her English teacher, Susan Ryan, who regularly entered her students in contests. A class poll selected Pam's lifter as one of its entries. After winning first place in her age group, she went to Washington to receive her prize and meet the new inductees into the Patent Hall of Fame as well as the Vice President of the United States. Asked what she would do with her invention, Pam showed that, like her inventing foremothers, she had learned that *conception* was only half the battle:

> Well, my parents and I thought we would see if it could be patented and went to a patent lawyer in Wilmington. From his patent search, I learned I wasn't the only one who had tried to solve this problem! I got piles of pages on other people's patents, and I have to say my idea looked pretty much like some of them. Still, all those others got patents for slight variations, and mine *might* be O.K.
>
> Still, it would be expensive to have someone write up all the mechanical part with all the drawings. Getting a patent isn't cheap. Did you know that?

To help students and teachers involved in such contests, publishers rushed into the breach with books such as Barbara Taylor's *Weekly Reader Presents: Be an Inventor*, whose cover shows both a boy and a girl at a worktable, but whose contents, alas, describe the inventions of many men but only one woman, Becky Schroeder. She was, however, a good choice for children since she had begun her patenting career at fourteen, by slipping a phosphorescent-treated sheet under her writing paper so that she could write in the dark. According to the patent, the uses of phosphorescent writing ranged from hospital charts a doctor

Pamela Sica, *Weekly Reader* Contest Grand Prize Winner, middle school level, and Commissioner of Patents Donald J. Quigg, April, 1989.

could read at night without turning on a light and awakening the patient to situations in outer space travel when the electrical system has to be shut down for recharging. Few youngsters, however, could afford the cost of the legal expertise available to Schroeder; her father is a prominent Toledo patent attorney.

For teachers, Catherine Valentino's *The Invention Convention* outlines steps in preparing for a fair or contest, one of which is to have students write about an inspiring male or female inventor. Since library shelves house literally *yards* of books with titles such as *Heroes of Industry, Men Who Shaped the Future, Men Who Pioneered Invention, Fathers of Industries,* and *Heroes of the Workshop* and almost nothing on heroines and foremothers of invention, a child who decided to write about a woman inventor would be sorely pressed for sources. Undaunted, Jeff Meredith, a fourth grader at Hoover Elementary School in Council Bluffs, Nebraska, who was participating in a contest like those outlined in Valentino's book, decided to write about Margaret Knight since he had read in the "Little Known Inventors of Common Things" chapter of the *Book of Lists 2* that she had invented the machine that made the flat-bottomed paper bag. In checking further, he found that *World Book Encyclopedia* credited the bag to one S. E. Pettee and made no mention of Knight. Jeff decided that as long as he knew Knight had a patent, he would give her as much credit as Pettee. When he read further in *Book of Lists* that Knight had left an estate of only $275.05 when she died in 1914, he concluded that it was no wonder she was obscure. The sad part of Jeff's quest for information about Knight is that while the *Book of Lists* is accurate about her penurious demise, it makes no mention of her remarkable mechanical proficiency, her successful business career in her earlier years, or her eminence as a feminist heroine. At any rate, Jeff, whose paper on Knight was only one aspect of his entry in the contest, emerged a winner of the national contest in his age group—incidentally, in the same year that his brother, Andy, won a similar contest sponsored by *Weekly Reader.*

There *was* a new book on women inventors that Jeff could have used, Ethlie Ann Vare and Greg Ptacek's *Mothers of Invention: From the Bra to the Bomb, Forgotten Women and Their Unforgettable Ideas,* but it had not yet made its way to his local library. Vare, a free-lance journalist specializing in the entertainment industry, and Ptacek, a writer who at various times in his career has been managing editor of *Rock* magazine and senior features editor for *City Sports,* produced a breezy, nonscholarly book of short, lively sketches on women inventors and innovators. Its dust jacket signals the hope it holds out to aspiring girls:

> History is full of women inventors who have been overlooked or cheated out of their due. Ranging from the momentous to the mundane, the discoveries of women have affected all our lives—for better and for worse—in hundreds of ways. How different would the world be without the chocolate-chip cookie? The disposable diaper? Jet-aircraft navigation? The cure for sleeping sickness? This book presents the stories of these women and their inventions, and the one thing they all had in common: They did not let the odds stop them from tinkering with the way things were and coming up with something better.

With a celebration of the 200th anniversary of the passage of the first Patent Act scheduled for 1990, it seemed to the women of the Patent Office, under the chairmanship of Anne Kelly, director of its Office of National and International Application and Review, that this would be an appropriate time to bring their inventing sisters long overdue attention. They kicked off the year's events with a ceremony to open a special exhibit, "Woman's Place Is in the Patent Office." This was a slightly condensed version (because of space limitations) of the exhibition of women's inventions first shown on the Saint Paul campus of the University of Minnesota as "Let Her Works Praise Her" (the words taken from the entrance to the Woman's Building at the Philadelphia Centennial Exposition in 1876). Curated by Professor Fred Amram, a man whose years of teaching creative problem solving at the University of Minnesota had honed his interest in women inventors, and designed by Sandra Brick Pangborn, the exhibit (now on tour) surveys women's technological contributions from kitchen gadgets to high-tech. It uses patent models, products, photographs, and biographi-

"Woman's Place Is in the Patent Office" exhibit.

University of Minnesota Professor Fred Amram with inventions of Heida Thurlow, part of the "Her Works Praise Her" exhibit on women's inventions.

cal material on women inventors, from the earliest to the most recent, to tell the story. Modern inventions included Ruth Handler's Barbie doll and the first breast prosthesis for mastectomy patients, which was also her work; Barbara Askins's photographic process to be used for enhancing photographs taken from spy planes or for sharpening the contrast in old black-and-white photographs; Bette Graham's "Liquid Paper," the messy typist's salvation; and Patsy Sherman's "Scotchguard," the fabric protector she co-invented quite by accident when her team was trying to develop fuel-resistant airplane hoses at 3M Company in Minneapolis and ended up with a coating that proved impervious to stains and dirt.

The featured speaker of the exhibit's opening day was Dr. Stephanie Kwolek, the DuPont Company's much-honored chemist whose 1965 invention of what is technically called "liquid crystal polyamid solution" made possible the development of Kevlar, a high-strength, high-stiffness fiber used for radial tires, airplanes, space vehicles, boat shells, and bulletproof vests. In her audience, as a sign of solidarity, were six other women patent holders from DuPont who had vanned down from Wilmington to lend support and to rise as a proud body when women inventors in the audience were asked to stand.

Though the slant of the program was avowedly feminist, Kwolek eschewed any discussion of gender and hewed to the scientific paper she had prepared. She does, however, have a good deal to say about the subject off the podium. As a young scientist with a degree in chemistry from Carnegie Institute of Technology, she went to work for a DuPont Company laboratory in 1946, intending to work only long enough to finance medical school. The field of low-temperature polymerization process, then in its infancy, was so interesting, however, that she extended her stay—for forty years—even though for the first fifteen years of that time she received not a single promotion. As she puts it now, "My upward progress was definitely limited—there just weren't any women supervisors in research." Promotion came, not surprisingly, at about the same time as the granting of the five patents that led to Kevlar. From that time on, as she continued her inventive career at the company, she had her choice of advancing through either research or management positions and chose the laboratory. She did receive promotions, but the rate of her advancement was not comparable to that of men doing similar work.

She thinks things have changed for the better today—and DuPont's position as one of the top ten companies in the number of women patentees employed there confirms it. Companies cannot possibly attract competent women, says Kwolek, if they don't accept women fully and provide them the training necessary to qualify for promotions on a par with men. No one should have to wait fifteen years! Looking back over the last decades, she believes that World War II was a watershed: "Well, of course, when there weren't enough men to do the work, they needed women—no questions asked! Afterwards, a lot of those women who learned the value of their work during the war, didn't want to return home and stayed in their jobs if they could. Those women paved the way for the rest of us." Kwolek believes that the women's movement of the sixties and seventies, though it often used tactics she disapproved of, had a positive effect in lowering, if not removing, gender barriers. The change that strikes her as most significant, however, is that fathers today expect their daughters to have the same opportunities as their sons. Working within a community of scientists, Kwolek, who has never married, has watched fathers encourage their daughters to take math and science courses so that they are equipped to follow the same career path their fathers have found so rewarding.

Chemist Stephanie Kwolek with sample of fiber used in Kevlar.

"That's where the future is—with those girls," says Kwolek. "But those top students will need to fight the stigma of being called 'grinds,' or whatever they call them today. They should go right ahead and set goals and stick to them. That takes hard work. I admit I never met my goal of being a doctor, but, looking back, I wouldn't exchange it for the happy and productive career I have enjoyed."

Feeling that recognition of women inventors should have come long before, Kwolek was delighted to participate in the Patent Office's efforts to commemorate women's contributions and was gratified that the exhibit included such a broad range of inventions, from domestic to high-tech. Echoing Ida Tarbell's nineteenth-century response to any downplaying of "household" inventions, Kwolek sums up: "Invention is invention. When the Patent Office issues a patent, it says officially 'This is both original and practical.' An industrial invention, though it might be more complicated, doesn't necessarily show any more real ingenuity than a non-industrial one."

At the same ceremony at which Kwolek spoke, the Patent Office's Office of Technology Assessment and Forecast unveiled its in-house answer to the "Does she or doesn't she invent?" question: *Buttons to Biotech: U.S. Patenting by Women, 1977 to 1988*, the first official report on women inventors since 1895. Instead of guessing about the gender of the inventors' first names, as it had done a century before, the Patent Office used a computer to match first names on lists of utility patents (design patents were not counted in the survey) issued to United States residents with the first names most commonly used by women as determined in the 1980 edition of *Name Your Baby*. If one woman's name appeared in a group patent, the patent counted as a woman's.

The new figures tell several important things about modern women inventors. First, according to the 1895 tally almost 70 percent of women patentees had invented within the general "women's" field— from clothing to children's toys—but the newer figures prove that the study is aptly titled *Buttons to Biotech*: Almost 50 percent patented in the field of chemical technologies. In fact, three out of the top six classes of women's inventions relate to biotechnology or pharmaceuticals—the field in which Hazen, Brown, and Elion and her colleagues at Burroughs-Wellcome have been leaders. That women have moved into such high-tech fields further indicates that they have availed themselves of the advanced education that feminists had demanded.

The second important evidence from the study, that over half the women in the study assigned their inventions to either corporations or government agencies, not only shows that more women are being hired by laboratories but also indicates that fewer women are now actually involved in the patenting process itself. Unlike independent inventors, who must raise money to patent, manufacture, and market their products, corporate inventors turn such details over to company professionals so that they can direct their creative energies to solving new problems and, presumably, making new inventions that can be patented. Quite obviously, this bodes well for an increase in the number of women's patents in technological fields.

*Buttons to Biotech* would make more exhilarating reading for feminists if it were not for the third piece of evidence it produced: In the years since 1895, when one out of every one hundred patents granted went to a woman, the figure had risen to an average of only three and a half out of a hundred for the period of 1977 to 1988. Still, within that eleven-year period, the number more than doubled, so that by 1988 5.6 percent were women's patents. Though the percentage had quintupled in a century, the increase still seemed discouragingly small to those who thought that women's educational opportunities had improved far more significantly than such numbers would indicate. The compilers, however, were not discouraged. Charged with peering into the crystal ball and armed with National Science Board indicators that showed more women participating in engineering and science than ever before, they forecast that if women continued to matriculate in such fields, they would undoubtedly contribute to an "upward trend."

Two distinguished institutions will help them to do so. Massachusetts Institute of Technology, which began admitting women before the turn of the century but made no conscious effort to attract them until the 1970s, has recently enrolled a freshman class in which a third are women. Similarly, Pasadena's California Institute of Technology has nearly doubled the number of women admitted to its freshman class, an action hailed by the president of the American Association of University Women as "official recognition of the disadvantages women interested in science have had getting into such colleges." Neither MIT nor Caltech aspire to a percentage much higher than one third, however, until they can draw from a more enriched pool of well-prepared female applicants whose parents—like the fathers Kwolek notices—have encouraged them in science and whose junior high and high school teachers have not shunted them into less demanding courses.

*Buttons to Biotech* came out in January 1990. In April, the National Inventor's Hall of Fame, which had been moved from its cramped quarters in the Patent Office to a new National Invention Center in Akron, Ohio, staged its latest induction as another event in the bicentennial year's celebrations. The three-day event was to culminate in the installation of the newest Hall of Fame honorees (all male), but the kickoff event was planned to give women due respect—if not election into the fraternity of illustrious inventors. Hearing that there were no women's names among the eighty-six Hall of Famers, Susan Buckbee, coordinator of the gifted and talented programs for Summit County Schools, wrote a letter to the editor of the *Akron Beacon Journal* applauding the proposed building and the exhibits planned to mark inventors' "creative and entrepreneurial spirit" but asking, "What message will we give to these girls who comprise our future?" To get the ball rolling for including a woman the *next* year, she asked similarly concerned persons to write to the chairman of the selection committee and helpfully supplied his address.

I had planned to eschew using the first person in writing about the following bicentennial events, but since, as a patentee-cum-historian of women, I have proved to be useful to those wishing to honor women inventors, I shall drop the veil of disinterested third-person.

Some days before the "Women and Invention" luncheon—at which I was fortunate to have been asked to speak—a reporter from the *Akron Beacon Journal* had interviewed me by telephone, and on the morning of the luncheon a front-page story headlined WOMAN INVENTOR SAYS THERE'S LOTS OF UNTAPPED GENIUS IN HER GENDER carried my comments. An auspicious beginning! Over six hundred persons, men and women alike, attended the luncheon, among them high school teachers who brought along girls who were outstanding students in their science and mathematics classes. When I opened my remarks by asking women inventors to stand and not one rose, I asked men inventors to stand. They did, and as I looked out at that sea of dark suits, my point was made: "Well, that's about the way it is!" I spoke of the obstacles inventing women had faced but also wanted to raise my audience's consciousness by focusing on what women inventors had achieved in spite of those societal pressures. After my talk one inspired older woman (older than I, I mean) tapped me on the shoulder and exulted, "It's about time we heard about women. It certainly is fun the way you rattle the timbers!" And it was. Women filled their notepads with names of prominent women inventors, and I daresay the "selection committee" has not heard the last of them.

The next morning's *Beacon Journal* once again devoted front-page coverage to women—and to my remarks. PATENT HOLDER A PROUD PIONEER was the headline of an article that continued on the inside with a column headed "Don't Be Afraid to Pick Up Tools, Woman Patent Holder Declares." The *Youngstown Vindicator* bannered, INVENTOR TRIES TO INSPIRE WOMEN; the *Cleveland Plain Dealer* quoted me to good effect; and local radio and television stations showed me speed-talking to cram as much information on women inventors as I could into what I presumed would be compressed into tiny sound bites. They turned out to be fairly lengthy interviews. Never again will I underestimate the interest in women inventors!

A month later, the Foundation for Creative America, which organized the Patent Office Bicentennial, arranged a symposium on women and invention chaired by Professor Amram with a panel consisting of three women: patent attorney Brereton Sturtevant and two patentees, Nobel winner Gertrude Elion and myself. That night Elion, recently honored by election to the National Academy of Sciences (considered the highest honor accorded to an American scientist or engineer), represented her gender as the only woman among the Third Century Award winners—all of them distinguished innovators in patenting, copyrighting, and trademarking.

In covering the bicentennial year as a whole, the *Washington Post* had included women in an earlier story about local inventors, but its coverage of the celebration itself mentioned women only tangentially—"We've had much talk, many galas, museum shows, youth awards, discussions of women inventors and minority inventors, a laser show and the U.S. Marine Corps Band"—and went on to bemoan the ebbing of the inventiveness the Edisons, Marconis, and Goodyears represented. On the radio, Karen Leggett included another woman patentee and me among the inventors she taped for her week's WMAL radio broadcasts on inventors and inventions. At the Library of Congress, in an exhibit that is now traveling to science museums around the country, women's contributions to America's creative heritage were noted by citing several of their important inventions on wall displays and including women in videotaped interviews with inventors. *Good Housekeeping* gave women inventors timely endorsement, if not the seal of approval, by selecting the best products invented by women since 1900. I can guarantee that such publicity helps because I received a slew of queries about my own invention, which was mentioned. Edmund Andrews apprised *New York Times* readers of some of women's more interesting inventions. Such notice was indeed a welcome change from the centennial celebration one hundred years before, all invitations to which had begun with "Dear Sir . . ."

Despite the overall increase in the number of women inventors and the fact that the majority has graduated from household devices to technology (which would please Gage and Stanton), the extremely low percentage of their patents compared to men's—that miserable 5.6 percent—still rankles! It's easy to understand how years—centuries, actually—of discrimination anesthetized their ambition and thwarted their ingenuity, but there are also enough success stories, if they only knew them, that could show that if women want to be inventors, they can be. But, since society is not yet conditioned to encourage women, they must depend upon themselves. That icon of businesswomen and inventors, Harriet Strong, gave advice that is as trenchant today as it was in 1895. The "scorn of the petticoat," she warned, will never be wiped out until women take responsibility for their own progress and become "not only the mothers but the educators of the men."

As educators, women themselves must set the historical record straight about their past achievements and must raise their gender's expectations for an equal share of future honors. It won't be easy, for, in spite of the many social, political, and economic advances made in women's position, society develops ingenious new ways of trying to limit women to domestic roles. For instance, there's the "mommy track" in business. There's still a backlash from the Equal Rights Amendment campaign—the fear that gender equality would undermine the traditional role of wife and mother, that success in business is incompatible with womanhood. Some women who need to earn an income outside the home soon distinguish between taking a job—which they think is all right—and committing themselves to a career—which they think is not. There is also the resurfacing of old theories about gender spheres under the guise of new "scientific" evidence, which allegedly confirms that each gender's neural synapses and hormonal makeup are so unique that biology, not biography, accounts for differences in intellectual and creative ability. To no one's surprise, those differences do not favor women. Are these "findings" not the same "depreciatory allusions to [woman's] intellectual powers" that Matilda Gage bewailed in 1883—differences that tended to "hamper the expression of inventive genius"? Beryl Benderly seems to think so. In her recent book, *The Myth of Two Minds: What Gender Means and Doesn't Mean*, she weighs the professed "hard" scientific evidence of masculine inventive superiority against the documentation of culture's adverse impact upon women's creativity and concludes that cultural aspects far outweigh genetic factors. She warns biological determinists not to discard half the national pool of talent—women's. "Science knows," she remonstrates, "a certain amount about our genes, bodies, hormones, tissues, and brains, about our history and evolution, but almost nothing about the limits of either male or female minds."

There is good news on the women and invention front. The Patent Office's statistical update in the wake of the cutoff date in *Buttons to Biotech*, indicates that the counterparts of the inventors whom Chicago

Fair organizers in 1893 called "women in unusual occupations" are patenting in increasing numbers—and are therefore accounting for a higher percentage of the total.

There is other good news. In February 1991, the Inventors' Hall of Fame in Akron notified Gertrude Elion of her election to the Inventors' Hall of Fame, the first woman to be so honored. Obviously delighted to be the very first of her gender to be included in the roster of the nation's most illustrious inventors, she spoke of a future in which promising young women will be steered into science and mathematics courses that will equip them to have a career such as hers. "I may be the first woman in the Hall of Fame," she advised, "but I know that I certainly won't be the last." And she won't. At long last, the public recognition accorded Elion gives a decent burial to that age-old query, "Can women invent?"

# PATENTS OF
# WOMEN INVENTORS
# CITED IN TEXT

NOTE. I have been unable to locate patents for all the inventors named in the text, but the following are numbers, titles, and dates of patents issued to most of them. In the case of some multiple patentees, only certain patents have been selected.

Adams, Elizabeth: #1,940, "Method of Manufacturing Corsets to be Worn by Females During Pregnancy or Suffering Umbilical Hernia or Abdominal Weakness," January 21, 1841

Allen, Maria E.: #355,368, "Diaper," January 4, 1887

Allison, Emeline: #467,906, "Doubling and Winding Device for Domestic Use," February 2, 1892

Anderson, Mary: #743,801, "Window-cleaning Device," November 10, 1903

Auerbach, Julia: #1,271,259, "Detatchable Self-adjusting Corset Strap," July 2, 1918

Aukerman, Agnes L.: #3,481,517, "Infant Carrier," December 2, 1969

Averill, Carrie B.: #1,039,009, "Baby Carrier," September 17, 1912

Baldwin, Anna E. Corey: #78,640, "Improved Process of Treating Milk to Obtain Useful Products," June 9, 1868; #93,582, "Improvement in Milk-separators," August 10, 1869; #93,583, "Improvement in Milk-coolers," August 10, 1869; #212,423, "Improvement in Cow-milkers," February 18, 1879

Ball, Sarah E.: #348,373, "Combined Work Table and Basket," August 31, 1886

Barba, Anna E.: #1,277,530, "Egg Turning Device for Incubators," September 3, 1918

Bateson, Frances G. (Frances Gabe): #4,428,085, "Self-cleaning Building Construction," January 31, 1984

Beasley, Maria E.: #202,919, "Improvement in foot warmers," April 30, 1878; #226,264, "Life-raft," April 6, 1880; #245,050, "Barrel-hoop Driving Machine," August 2, 1881; #256,951, "Machine for Driving Hoops upon Casks," April 25, 1882; #258,191, "Life-raft," May 16, 1882

Beauchamp, Lila M.: #4,714,475, "Anti-viral Compounds," December 9, 1987

Bettes, Sephora Louise: #377,663, "Ruling Attachment for Blackboards," February 7, 1888

Biggs, Florence: #1,275,837, "Wrist Mitt," August 13, 1918; #1,275,838, "Helmet Cap," August 13, 1918; #1,282,528, "Sweater," October 22, 1918

Blanchard, Helen Augusta: Sewing Machine improvements: #141,987, August 19, 1873; #152,721, July 7, 1774; #161,471, March 30, 1875; #161,472, March 30, 1875; #162,019, April 13, 1875

Blau, Minnie: #1,279,504, "Educational Device for Teaching Arithmetic,"

Blauvelt, Mary: #141,849, "Dressmakers' Marking and Cutting Gages [sic]," August 19, 1893

Blodgett, Katharine B.: #2,108,641, "Surface Treatment of Materials," April 12, 1935; #2,220,660, "Film Structure and Method of Preparation," March 16, 1938

Bonney, Lydia: #171,467, "Improvement in Undergarments," December 28, 1875

Bradbury, Henrietta: #2,320,027, "Bed Rack," May 25, 1943; #3,390,688, "Torpedo Discharge Means," December 1, 1945

Breadin, Anna M.: #400,738, "School Desk," April 2, 1889

Brigham, Emeline T.: #71,692, "Improved Pessary," December 3, 1867

Britain, Clarissa: #37,851, "Floor Warmer," March 10, 1863; #39,460, "Improvement in Ambulances," August 11, 1863; #40,157, "Improvement in Boilers," October 5, 1863; #41,274, "Improved Lantern Dinner-pail," January 19, 1864; #43,087, "Improvement in Vegetable Boilers," June 14, 1864; #44,080, "Improved Dish-drainer," June 14, 1864; #44,393, "Improvement in Lamp-burners," September 27, 1864

Brooks, Caroline S.: #187,095, "Improvement in Methods of Producing Lubricated Molds in Plaster," February 6, 1877

Brown, Harriet: #392,493, "Dress Waist," November 8, 1888; #392,494, "Method of Making Dress-waists," November 11, 1888

Brown, Rachel F., and Hazen, Elizabeth L.: #2,797,183, "Nystatin and Method of Producing It," June 25, 1957

Burns, Elizabeth A.: #100,497, "Improvement in Desulphurizing Ores," March 8, 1870

Callmeyer, Leonie P.: #482,073, "Means for Detecting the Opening of Sealed Envelopes," September 6, 1892

Campbell, Gertrude: #276,770, "Monthly Protector," May 1, 1883

Carpenter, Mary (see: Hooper, Mary Carpenter)

Chapman, Laura: #151,090, "Improvement in Lap-tables," May 19, 1874

Chilton, Annie H.: #456,613, "Horse Detatcher and Brake," July 28, 1891; #515,651, "Combined Horse Detacher and Brake," February 27, 1894

Clark, Clara P.: #156,278, "Improvement in Corsets," October 27, 1774; #164,905, "Improvement in Skirt Supporters," June 29, 1875; #174,481, "Improvement in Suspender-fastenings," March 7, 1876; #235,403, "Underwaist," December 14, 1880

Clarke, Clara J.: (design patent) #35,978, "Dresser," July 15, 1902

Cochran, Josephine G.: #355,139, "Dish Washing Machine," December 28, 1886; #391,782 (co-patented with Jacob Kritch), "Dish Washing Machine," October 30, 1888; #512,683, "Dish Cleaner," January 16, 1894

Cole, Henrietta: #55,469, "Fluting Machine," June 12, 1866

Collins, Mary: #554,019, "Child Carrying Strap," February 4, 1896

Colvin, Margaret Plunkitt: #120,717, "Improvement in Washing Machines," November 7, 1871; #199,693, "Improvement in Clothes-pounders," January 29, 1878; #202,792, "Improvement in Clothes-pounders," April 23, 1878; #248,712, "Clothes-pounder," October 25, 1881

Connelly, Anna: #368,816, "Fire Escape," August 23, 1887

Conner, May: #1,214,010, "Combined Egg Beater and Potato Masher," January 30, 1917; #1,229,036, "Hay Handling Device," June 5, 1917

Converse, Susan Taylor: #166,190, "Improvement in under-clothing for women," August 3, 1875; #167,436, "Improvement in Under-garments," September 7, 1875; #189,609, "Improvement in under-garments," April 17, 1877

Cooney, Laura S.: #562,582, "Suspenders," June 23, 1896

Cooper, Henrietta: (unnumbered patent), "Straw, Leghorn, Whitening," November 12, 1828

Coston, Martha J., Administrix of the last will and testament of B. Franklin Coston, deceased: #23,536, "Pyrotechnic Night Signals," April 5, 1859; Martha Coston in her own name: #115,935, "Improvement in Pyrotechnic Night Signals," June 13, 1871

Cox, Mary: #577,127, "Useful Improvement in Knife-sharpeners," February 16, 1897

Daluge, Susan: #4,761,475, "Anti-bacterial Compounds," August 2, 1988

Deiner, Catherine: #448,476, "Rolling Pin," March 17, 1891

Delzell, Hattie: #579,295, "Flower-Pot," March 23, 1897

Demorest, Ellen C.: #259,105, "Floor for Elevator Shafts," June 6, 1882; #264,935, "Puff for Headdress," September 26, 1882

Dennis, Olive: (design patent) #72,673, "Plate Design," May 31, 1927; #1,693,108, "Ventilator," November 27, 1928

Dickelman, Lizzie: #1,219,267, "Grain Storehouse Construction," May 15, 1917; #1,226,477, "Metal Building Plate," May 5, 1917; #1,247,511, "Elastic Crib," November 20, 1917; #1,328,132, "Ventilated Storage Warehouse," January 13, 1920; #1,336,945, "Grain Storage Construction," April 13, 1920; #1,339,437, "Grain Storage Bin," May 11, 1920; #1,419,236, "Door and Door Frame for Grain Bins," June 13, 1922

Dockham, Clarissa Ellen: #556,881, "Bicycle Skirt," March 24, 1896; #568,339, "Combination Suit," September 29, 1896

Donovan, Marion: #2,556,800, "Diaper Wrap," June 12, 1951; #2,575,163, "Diaper Cover," November 13, 1951; #2,575,164, "Diaper Housing," November 13, 1951; #2,575,165, "Diaper Cover," November 13, 1951

Edson, Temperance P.: #48,539, "Self-inflator Raising Sunken Vessels," July 4, 1865

Elion, Gertrude B.: (a few are listed) #2,697,709, "6- MERCAPTOPURIN," December 21, 1954; #2,746,961, "6- CHLOROPURIN," May 22, 1956; #2,884,667, "6-THIOGUANINE", May 5, 1959; #3,056,785, "IMURAN," October 2, 1962; #3,666,856, "Purine Derivatives," October 2, 1962

Ellsworth, Clara B.: #668,040, "Ventilated Collar for Ladies' Neckwear," February 12, 1901

Evard, Mary E. A.: #76,314, "Improvement in Broiling Apparatus," April 7, 1868; #76,315, "Improvement in Cooking Stove," April 7, 1868

Everhard, Mary M.: #445,443, "Kneading Bread," January 27, 1891

Everson, Carrie J.: #348,157, "Separating Sulphides in Ore from the Gangue," August 24, 1886; #474,829, "Improvement by adding to buoy-stock," May 17, 1892

Fitch, Nancy M.: #281,625, "Kiln for Firing Pottery, &c.," July 17, 1883; #395,128, "China Kiln," December 25, 1888

Fitz, Ellen E.: #158,581, "Globes," January 1, 1875

Flynt, Olivia P.: #146,175, "Improvement in Undershirts," January 6, 1874; #173,611, "Improvement in bust-supporter," February 15, 1876; #156,018, "Improvement in Dress-protectors," October 20, 1874; #156,019, "Improvement in Skirts," October 20, 1874

Forbes, Ida R.: #1,251,210, "Electric Hot Water Heater," December 25, 1917

Ford, Ellen M.: #215,815, "Improvement in Boxes and Covers for Firing Decorated Porcelain," May 24, 1879; #262,391, "Portable Furnace to Facilitate the Means of Firing Decorated China, glass &c.," August 8, 1882

Foster, Mary F. and Thomas, Anna W.: (design patent) #9,310, "Fan," May 23, 1876

Foy, Lavinia: #35,930, "Improvement in Corset Skirt-supporters," July 22, 1862; further improvements in next decade: #39,908, #39,909, #39,910, #39,911, #41,987, #45,296, #54,323, #79,647, etc.

Frackelton, Susan Stuart: #349,935, "China-firing Apparatus," September 28, 1886; #386,395, "Apparatus for Firing China," July 24, 1888

French, Evelyn F., and Milton Clifford: #234,265, "Sound-Deadening Attachment for Railway-Cars," November 9, 1880

French, Julia Blanche: #152,357, "Bedsteads," June 23, 1874; #164,290, "Bedsteads Containing Drawers, Interior Safe, etc.," June 8, 1875; #317,333, "Combined Wash and Bath Tub," May 5, 1885; #348,321, "Top or Tank for Toilet, Laundry, and Refrigerating Purposes," August 31, 1886

French, Elizabeth J.: #167,162, "Improvement in Electro-therapeutic Appliances," August 31, 1875

Fry, Laura A.: #399,029, "Art of Decorating Pottery Ware," March 5, 1889

Fuller, Georgiana: #438,537, "Catamenial Sack," October 14, 1890

Geer, Letitia: #622,848, "Medical Syringes," April 11, 1899

Geissmann, Gladys Whitcomb: #2,125,673, "Glove Construction," April 2, 1938; #2,194,934, "Glove," March 26, 1940; #2,226,604, "Glove," December 31, 1940; #2,377,141, "Footwear," May 29, 1945; #2,545,272, "Glove," March 13, 1951; #2,654,093, "Child's Garment," October 6, 1953; #2,671,220, "Baby's Garment," March 9, 1954; #2,921,586, "Foundation Garment," January 19, 1960; further foundation garments: #2,958,327, #2,971,515

Ghirardini, Maria L.: #141,217, "Rails for Street Railways," July 29, 1873

Goodman, Agdalena S.: #6,423, "Improvement in Broom-brushes," May 8, 1849

Gossard, Sarah L.: #11,232,282, "Anatomical Corset," July 3, 1917; #1,302,915, "Hospital Mattress," May 6, 1919

Gregg, Marjorie True: #1,272,034, "Nethergarment," July 9, 1918

Greneker, Lillian L.: #2,081,071 (this one only is with E. L. Scovil), "Ornamental Object," May 18, 1937; (design patent) #109,058, "Display Mannikin," March 29, 1938; #2,151,846, "Finger-Fit Implement," March 3, 1939; #2,165,473, "Display Figure," July 11, 1939; #2,165,474, "Ornamental Display Device," July 11, 1939; #2,165,475, "Display Structure," July 11, 1939; #2,165,476, "Display Head," July 11, 1939; #2,181,320, "Display Form," November 28, 1939; #2,215,550, "Display Form," September 24, 1940; #2,309,447, "Display Device," January 26, 1942; #2,343,292, "Destructible Form," March 7, 1944; #2,364,710, "Destructible Form," December 12, 1944; #2,369,892, "Destructible Hollow Form," February 20, 1945; #2,381,663, "Display Head," August 17, 1945; #2,418,551, "Hollow Article and Making of Same," April 8, 1947

Griswold, Catherine A.: #56,210, "Abdominal Skirt-supporting Corset," July 10, 1876; improvements in the next few years: #61,825, #115,825, #116,786, #157,445, #171,012, #181,330, #201,177, etc., through 1889

Gross, Emily: #188,357, "Improvements in Stone Pavements," March 13, 1877

Gugliemi, Winifred Hudnut (professionally known as Natacha Rambova): #1,575,263, "Combined Coverlet and Doll," March 2, 1926

Hackelberg, Amelie: #203,727, "Improvement in Packing-cases or Boxes for Bottles," May 14, 1878

Harding, Eliza: #140,778, "Improvement in Abdominal Supporters," July 15, 1873

Harley, Elizabeth G.: #156,702, "Improvement in Darning-lasts," November 10, 1874; #296,002, "Safety Attachment," April 1, 1884

Harris, Agnes E.: #542,851, "Garment Supporter," July 16, 1895

Hawks, Elizabeth: #64,102, "Auxiliary Air-chamber for Stoves," April 23, 1867; #161,612, "Improvement in Summer-stoves," April 6, 1875

Hazen, Elizabeth L., and Brown, Rachel F.: #2,797,183, "Nystatin and Method of Producing It," June 25, 1957

Henderson, Mary Foote: #481,070, "Armed Unicycle," August 16, 1892; #572,163, "Bicycle Attachment," December 1, 1896

Henry, Beulah: #1,565,145, "Radio Doll," December 8, 1925; #1,492,725, "Parasol," May 6, 1924; #1,723,482, "Sealing Device for Inflatable Bodies," August 6, 1929; #1,551,250, "Doll," August 25, 1925; #1,889,657, "Duplicating Device for Typewriter Machines," August 30, 1932; #2,022,286, "Movable Eye Structure for Figure Toys," November 26, 1935; #2,610,784, "Continuously-attached Envelopes," September 16, 1952; #3,018,033, "Direct and Return Mailing Envelope," January 23, 1962

Hercht, Pauline B.: #567,979, "Cycling Skirt," September 22, 1896

Hibbard, Susan: #177,939, "Improvement in Feather Dusters," May 30, 1876

Hicks, Laura M.: #1,132,475, "Washmitt," March 16, 1915

Higgins, Mary E.: #580,491, "Improved Bloomers," April 13, 1897

Holcombe, Elizabeth J.: #249,937, "Vaginal Irrigator and Urinal," November 22, 1881

Holmes, Josephine M.: #289,536, "Sad-Iron Holder," December 4, 1883

Hood, Eunice: #363,237, "Apparatus for Cutting Garments," May 17, 1887

Hooper, Mary Carpenter: #99,158, "Sewing Machine," January 25, 1870; #112,016, "Improvement in Sewing-machine Feeding Mechanisms," February 21, 1871; #131,739, "Sewing Machine," October 1, 1872; #171,774, "Improvement for Machines for Sewing Straw Braid," January 4, 1876; #455,403, "Mosquito-trap," July 7, 1891

Hoover, Erna S.: #3623,007, "Feedback Control Monitor for Stored Program Data Processing System," November 23, 1971

Hornbrook, Thiphena P.: #32,367, "Beehive," May 21, 1861

Hosmer, Harriet: #214,142, "Improvement in Processes of Making Artificial Marble," March 8, 1879

Howard, Lizzie: (design patent) #11,028, February 18, 1879

Howarth, Sarah S.: #617,693, "Bicycle Attachment," June 27, 1899

"Hull, Merry" (See Geissmann, Gladys Whitcomb)

Hunt, Elizabeth: #170,172, "Improvement in Fruit Jars," November 23, 1865; #182,119, Improvement in Preserving-Packages for Fruits, &c.," September 12, 1876

Irwin, Harriet M.: #94,116, "Improvement in the Construction of Houses," August 24, 1869

Jackson, Mary, and Ball, Sarah: #177,643, "Self-heating Smoothing Iron," May 23, 1876

Jacobs, Mary P.: #1,115,674, "Brassiere," November 3, 1914

Johnson, Nancy M.: #3,254, "Ice Cream Freezer," September 9, 1843

Jones, Amanda Theodosia: #139,547 (assigned to her by Leroy C. Cooley), "Fruit Jars," June 3, 1873; #139,580, "Improvement in Preserving Fruit Vegetables &c." (with Leroy C. Cooley), June 3, 1873; #140,247, "Exhaust Air from Cans" (assigned to her by Cooley), June 24, 1873; #140,508, "Improvement in Fruit Jars," July 1, 1873; #225,839, "Oil-burner," March 23, 1880

Jones, El Dorado: #1,111,686, "Attachment-Plug," June 1, 1915; (with Ray P. Upton) #1,229,471, "Exhaust Attachment for Gas Engines," June 12, 1917; (#1,142,769, "Electrically-Heated Appliance," June 8, 1915, was patented by Albert J. Block and assigned to Jones)

Jones, Mary Scott, and Naly, Sarah L.: #499,244, "Bicycle Seat," June 13, 1893

Joyner, Marjorie S.: #1,693,515, "Permanent Wave Machine," November 27, 1928

Kehlenbeck, Selma: #522,018, "Baby Carrier," June 26, 1894

Keichline, Anna W.: #1,047,072, "Sink," December 10, 1912; (design patent) #46,679, "Toy," November 24, 1914; #1,612,730, "Kitchen Construction," December 28, 1926; #1,647,733, "Portable Partition," November 1, 1927; #1,653,771, "Building Block," December 27, 1927

Kellogg, Martha: #261,359, "Tracing Wheels," July 18, 1882; #435,182, "Tailors Measures," August 26, 1890; #502,436, "Dress Stays," August 1, 1893; she assumed rights to Frank Kellogg's #290,889 for "rules and measures" and #480,589 for "seam presser"

Kies, Mary: (unnumbered patent), "Straw Weaving With Silk or Thread," May 5, 1809

Kirby, Dorothy Young: #3,401,658, "Stitching Guide," September, 17, 1968; #4,449,465, "Universal Stitching Guide," May 22, 1984

Kirwin, Eliza: #514,717, "Catamenial Sack," February 13, 1894

Knight, Margaret: #109,224, "Improvement in Paper-feeding Machines," November 15, 1870; #116,842, "Improvement in Paper-bag Machines," July 11, 1871; #220,925, "Improvement in Paper-bag Machines," October 28, 1879; #306,692, "Clasp," October 14, 1884; #311,662, "Spit," February 3, 1885; #436,358, "Sole Cutting Machine," September 16, 1890; #436,359, "Machine for Cutting Soles," September 16, 1890; #521,413, "Reel," June 12, 1894; #524,278, "Feeding Attachment for Sole-Cutting Machine," August 7, 1894; #716,903, "Compound Rotary Engine," December 30, 1902; #717,869, "Rotary Engine," January 6, 1904; #720,818, "Rotary Engine," February 17, 1904; #743,293 (With J. M. Benjamin, Boston), "Automatic Tool for Boring or Planing Convex or Cylindrical Surfaces," November 3, 1904; #1,105,761, "Resilient Wheel," January 23, 1912

Knox, Susan: #53,633 (co-patented with William C. Corrister), "Improvement in Fluting-machines," April 3, 1866; #59,913, "Improvement in Fluting-machines," November 20, 1866

Kwolek, Stephanie L.: #3,287,323, "Process for Production of a Highly Orientable, Crystallizable, Filament-forming Polyamide," November 22, 1966

Landman, Max (re invention of Eva Landman): #2,024,105, "Umbrella," December 17, 1935

Laumonier, Celine: #168,402, "Improvement in Combined Traveling Bags and Chairs," October 5, 1875

Lawson, Margaret Hobbs: #491,057, "Bicycle-Garment," January 31, 1883

Mabee, Leonia: #460,022, "Bed-Drawer Attachment for Bedsteads," September 22, 1891

Macdonald, Anne L.: #4,548,055, "Method of Hand-Knitting a Patterned Fabric," October 22, 1985

Markey, Hedwig Keisler: #2,292,387, "Secret Communication System," August 11, 1942

Mather, Sarah P.: #3,995, "Submarine Telescope," April 16, 1845; #43,465, "Submarine Telescope," July 5, 1864

McLaughlin, Mary Louise: #526,669, "Method of Decorating Pottery," September 25, 1894

Merganthaler, Marie: #714,317, "Device for Securing One Wearing Artical [sic] to Another," November 25, 1902

Miller, Katie V.: #462,720, "Telegraph Table," November 10, 1891

Montgomery, Mary Jane: #41,167, "Improved War-Vessel," January 5, 1864; #42,958, "Improvement in Locomotive Wheels, May 31, 1864; #47,831, "Improved Table for Hospitals," May 23, 1865; #54,580, "Improved Apparatus for Punching Corrugated Metals," May 8, 1866

Moore, Ann (see also Aukerman for original "Snugli" patent): #3,481,517, "Infant Carrier," December 2, 1969; #4,434,920, "Soft Orthopedic Pouch-

Type Infant Carrier," March 6, 1984; #4,739,913, "Backpack Type Carrier for Portable Oxygen Dispensers," April 26, 1988

Mossman, Sarah: #39,667, "Improvement in Military Caps," August 25, 1863

Mountain, Hannah B.: #136,749, "Improvement in Life-Saving Mattresses," March 1, 1873

Myers, Carlotta [Mary], and Carl E.: #318,575, "Guiding Apparatus for Balloons," May 26, 1885

Nadeau, Adeloe: #700,545, "Combined Chair and Cradle," May 20, 1902

Naly, Sarah L., and Jones, Mary Scott: #499,244, "Bicycle Seat," June 13, 1893

Nash, Alice: #570,676, "Bicycle Suit," November 3, 1896

Neal, Sarah C.: #520,699, "Folding Crib," May 29, 1894

Nolan, Mary: #186,604, "Improvement in Building Blocks," January 23, 1877; #186,660, "Artificial Stone Composition," March 20, 1877

O'Donnell, Laurene H.: #4,552,306, "Drinking Fountain Device and Combination Sink and Drinking Fountain Device," November 12, 1985

Palmer, Anna L.: #213,588, "Combined Aspirator," "Concealed Uterine Cauterizer," and "Vaginal Syringe," March 25, 1879

Parpart, Florence W., and Layman, Hiram: #649,609, "Street Cleaning Machine," May 15, 1900; "Refrigerator," 1914

Perkins, Nancy: [design patent] #284,463, "Battery Container," July 1, 1986; [design patent] #288,014, "Hand Vacuum Nozzle and Housing," January 27, 1987; #289,213 [design patent], "Cannister Vacuum," April 7, 1987

Perry, Elizabeth W.: (design patent) #8,310, "Design for Fans," May 1, 1875

Phelps, Minnie Agnes: #838,053, "Combined Toaster and Warming Oven," December 11, 1906

Philbrook, Emmaline: 175, 154 (not in book) "Equipoise waist 177, 882 spring clasp (not in book) 184, 545 (not in book) undergarment 286; #385,570, "Underwaist," July 3, 1888; #503,436, "Underwaist," August 15, 1893

Potts, Mary F.: #103,501, "Improved sad iron," May 24, 1870; #113,448, "Improvement in Sad Irons," April 4, 1871; #103,501, "Improved Sad Iron," May 24, 1870; #506,252 (with J. H. Austin), Sadiron," October 10, 1893

Powell, Alma Webster: #1,053,532, "Suit of Clothing for Women," February 18, 1913

Reid, Rose Marie: #2,372,855, "Brassiere," April 3, 1945; (design) #144,515, "Bathing Suit," April 23, 1946; #2,418,987, "Garment," April 15, 1947; #2,431,505, "Bathing Suit," November 25, 1948; (design) #151,714, "Bathing Suit," November 9, 1948; #2,535,018, "Garment," December 19, 1950

Rhoads, May E.: #1,305,307, "Woman's Working-Garment," June 3, 1919

Rideout, Janet L. (with four co-patentees): #4,724,232, "Treatment of Human Viral Infections," February 9, 1988

Rodgers, Augusta M.: #113,348, "Car Heater," April 4, 1871; #114,605, "Improvement in Conveyors of Smoke and Cinders for Locomotives," May 9, 1871; #119,790, "Improvement in Conveyors," October 10, 1871

Rogallo, Gertrude, and Rogallo, Francis: #2,546,078, "Flexible Kite," March 20, 1951; #2,751,172, "Flexible Kite," June 19, 1956

[Romney], Caroline Westcott: #164,408, "Improvement in Chemises," June 15, 1875

Rood, Nettie G.: #225,765, "Wardrobe-bed," March 23, 1880; #256,860, "Portable Summer-House," April 25, 1882

Russell, Lillian: #1,014,853, "Dresser-Trunk," January 16, 1912

Ruth, Sarah: #81,412, "Horse Bonnet," August 25, 1868; #134,564, "Sunshade for Horses," January 7, 1873

St. Clair, Martha H. (with four co-patentees): #4,724,232, "Treatment of Human Viral Infections," February 9, 1988

Saul, Sarah E.: #47,134, "Improvement in Churns," April 4, 1865; #54,964, "Boiler for Culinary Purposes," May 22, 1866; #116,502, "Improvement in Seesaws," June 27, 1871; #182,485, "Improvement in Metallic Casings for Lead Pipes," September 19, 1876

Schneider, Mary: #392,885, "Washing Fluid," November 13, 1888

Schrader, Ella M.: #643,543, "Garment Form," February 13, 1900

Schroeder, Becky J.: #3,832,556, "Luminescent Backing Sheet for Writing in the Dark," August 27, 1974; #3,879,611, (continuation of previous patent), April 22, 1975

Sherwood, Rebecca: #40,577, "Reducing Hemp, Flax &c. to Fibrous Substances," November 10, 1863; #45,440, "Improvement in Reducing Straw and Other Fibrous Substances for the Manufacture of Paper-pulp," December 13, 1863

Shields, Sarah: (design patent) #14,572, "Dress," December 25, 1883; (design patent) #14,561, "Wrap," January 22, 1884

Siegel, Sarah: #128,761, "Improvement in Steps for Berth," November 9, 1872

Siems, Ruth, et al.: #3,870,803, "Instant Stuffing Mix," March 11, 1975

Simpson, Louisa B.: #206,628, "Apparatus for Destroying Vegetation on Railroads," July 30, 1878; #213,255, "Apparatus for Destroying Vegetation on Railroads," March 11, 1879

Sittig, Lena: #476,761, "Skirt-protecting Garment," June 7, 1892; #489,103, "Combined Cloak and Skirt Protector," January 3, 1893; #520,225, "Skirt Protecting Garment," May 22, 1894; #532,601, "Skirted Trousers," January 15, 1895

Sterling, Charlotte Higgins: #130,761, "Dish-Washer," August 20, 1872

Stigale, Elizabeth Mary: "Method of Preserving Flowers," April 27, 1869; #97,984, "Rail for Ornamental Fences," December 14, 1869; #112,748, "Improvement in Floral Brackets," March 14, 1871

Stiles, Elizabeth W.: #167,586, "Improvement in Reading and Writing Desks," September 7, 1875

Strong, Harriet W. R.: #306,188, "Device for Raising and Lowering Windows," October 7, 1884; #307,687, "Hook and Eye," November 4, 1884; #352,719 "Window Sash Holder," November 16, 1886; #374,378, "Dam and Reservoir Construction," December 6, 1887; #528,823, "Method of and Means for Impounding Debris and Storing Water," November 6, 1894

Stryker, Elizabeth V.: #460,605, "Fly-Net for Horses," October 8, 1891

Suplee, Hannah G.: #94,924, "Sewing Machine Needle," September 14, 1869; #115,656 (with John H. Mooney), "Improvement in Sewing-machines," June 6, 1871; #250,998, "Pattern and Lining for Garments," December 13, 1881

Tassey, Emily E.: #180,286, "Improvement in Apparatus for Raising Sunken Vessels," July 25, 1876; #183,998, "Improvement in Dredging Machines," December 5, 1876; #184,996, "Improvement in Siphon Propellor-Pumps," December 5, 1876; #194,997, "Improvement in Propulsion of Vessels," December 5, 1876

Thomas, Anna W., and Foster, Mary F.: (design patent) #9,310, "Fan," May 23, 1876

Thomas, Mary E.: #420,840, "Electro-Magnetic Abdominal Support," February 4, 1890; #444,735, "Voltaic Insole," January 13, 1891

Thomas, Norma: #663,942, "Cake Beating Machine," December 18, 1900

Thurlow, Heida L.: (design patent) #273,755, "Covered Frying Pan or Similar Article," May 8, 1984; #4,494,274, "Cookware with Covers Having Metal Handles," January 22, 1985; (design patent) #282,436, "Kettle," February 4, 1986; (design patent) #289,001, March 31, 1987; (design patent) #298,100, "Food Warming Stand," October 18, 1988

Tillinghast, Mary: #268,149, "Needle Woven Tapestry," November 28, 1882

Tracy, Harriet R.: #74,865, "Improvement in Crib Attachment for Bedsteads," February 25, 1868; #266,661, "Folding Adjustable Stoves for Cooking," October 3, 1882; #272,103, "Fire Escape," February 13, 1883; #434,849, "Elevator," August 19, 1890; #469,367, "Sewing Machine," February 23, 1892; #470,960, "Safety Device for Elevators," March 15, 1892; and others involving sewing: #470,796; #471,035; #471,036; #471,037

Tudor, Kate B.: #451,645, "Flower-holder," May 5, 1891

Walton, Mary E.: #221,880, "Locomotive and Other Chimneys," November 18, 1879; #327,422, "Elevated Railway," February 8, 1881

Watrous, Emma: #377,444, "Trellis Support," February 7, 1888; #382,628, "Underwaist," May 8, 1888

Westover, Cynthia M. [Alden]: #468,588, "Improved Dump Cart," January 9, 1892

Wheeler, Candace: #268,332, "Embroidery and Embroidering," November 28, 1882; #271,174, "Fabric for Needle-woven Tapestries," January 23, 1883

Whitner, Mary A. E.: #158,555, "Improvement in Stereoscopes," January 5, 1875

Whitney, Adeline D. T.: #257,630, "Alphabet Blocks," May 9, 1882

Wilcox, Margaret A.: #426,486, "Combined Clothes and Dishwasher," April 29, 1890; #482,772, "Combined Cooking and Hot Water Heating Stove," September 20, 1892; #495,284, "Radiator," April 11, 1893; #496,078, "Bake-Pan," April 25, 1893; #509,415, "car heater," assigned to Wilcox Water Heater, November 28, 1893; #509,987, "Dough Mixer," December 5, 1893

Wood, Eliza: #416,087, "Mop-wringer Pail," November 26, 1889; #466,909, "Mop Pail and Wringer," February 24, 1891

Woodhouse, Sophia: (unnumbered patent), "New and Useful Improvement in the Manufacture of Grass Bonnets and Hats," December 25, 1821

Woodward, Mary Ann: #6,375, "Rocking-Chair Fan Attachment," April 24, 1849.

# NOTES

The notes that follow contain shortened bibliographical references. For full information, please see the bibliography at the end of the book.

Any uncited description of an invention is taken from the the patent itself. Patent numbers, when I know them, are listed under inventors' names in the appendix.

Abbreviations

| | |
|---|---|
| CC— | Centennial Commission |
| CM— | Carl Myers folder at Library of National Air and Space Museum of the Smithsonian Institution |
| DoA— | Digest of Assignment of Property Rights and Patents, 1837–1900, National Archives |
| HH— | Harriet Hosmer Papers, Schlesinger Library |
| HWRS— | Papers of Harriet Strong, Huntington Library |
| LPEC— | *Final Report of the Louisiana Purchase Exposition Commission* |
| LG— | Lillian Greneker Papers, Schlesinger Library |
| MSS qF946— | Laura Fry papers, Cincinnati Historical Society |
| MSS qF946 RMV— | Mary Louise McLaughlin papers, Cincinnati Historical Society |

NEWC— Papers of the New England Women's Club, Schlesinger Library

NO— *Report and Catalogue of the Woman's Department of the World's Exposition, Held at New Orleans, 1884–1885*

PAF— Patent Assignment Files, National Archives

PCP— Papers of the Commissioner of Patents, Federal Records Center

PIC— Patent Interference Case Files, 1835–1905, National Archives, Federal Records Center

ToP— Transfer of Patents Index, National Archives

WCFI— *Women's Contributions in the Field of Invention: A Study of the Records of the United States Patent Office*

# INTRODUCTION

PAGE

xix "My wife suggested the . . .": Testimony taken in *Gilbert M. Richmond* vs. *Susan M. Hibbard, PIC* #5, 184.

xx LANDMAN UMBRELLA: "Windshield Umbrella," *Invention and Finance,* May–June 1936, pp. 6–7.

xx "If it had been . . .": Cited in [Charlotte Smith], "Why I Became Interested in Woman Inventors," *The Woman Inventor,* April 1890 [1891], p. 3.

xxi–xxiii GREENE STORY: "derived from a much . . .": "Sketch of the Life of the Late Eli Whitney, With Some Remarks on the Invention of the Saw-Gin." *Southern Agriculturalist,* August 1832, p. 395; "What! Allow such a . . .": Ibid., p. 397; "At this momment, the . . .": "Anecdote Relative to the Origin of Whitney's Saw-Gin." *Southern Agriculturalist.*" September 1832, p. 468; "mountains of established laws . . .": Matilda Joslyn Gage, *History of Woman Suffrage,* Volume I, p. 112; "fear of ridicule because . . .": [Charlotte Smith], "Women Inventors," *The Woman Inventor,* April 1890 [1891], p. 4; "Had she done so, . . .": Willard, *Occupations for Women,* p. 350. The list of Greene materials is long, but for the purpose of this study, the best material is: M. B. Hammond, "Correspondence of Eli Whitney Relative to the Invention of the Cotton Gin," *American Historical Review,* October 1897, pp. 90–99; Denison Olmsted, *Memoir of Eli Whitney, Esq.,* New York: Arno Press, 1972; Annie Nathan Meyer, *Woman's Work in America,* New York: H. Holt and Co., 1891; Rep. ed.; New York: Arno Press, 1972; and Jeannette Mirsky and Allan Nevins, *The World of Eli Whitney,* New York: Macmillan, 1952.

xxiii "Had she done so . . .": Willard, *Occupations for Women,* p. 350.

xxiii "like a man, seized . . .": Conwell, p. 246. The talks were given from 1877 until his death in 1927.

xxiii "his wife made up . . .": Ibid., p. 255. Case and Case's *We Called It Culture* has good material on Chautauqua and Conwell.

# 1: FOREMOTHERS OF AMERICAN INVENTION

PAGE

3 "for cleaning and curing . . .": Frederick B. Tolles, "Masters, Sybilla" in *Notable American Women, 1607–1950,* p. 508; additional information on Masters, particularly on the development of a mill for grinding the corn: Samuel H. Needles, "The Governor's Mill and the Globe Mills, Pennsylvania," *Pennsylvania Magazine of History and Biography,* October 1884, pp. 285–90.

6 METCALF BONNET: "I could easily earn . . .": Betsey [Metcalf] Baker, West Dedham, Mass., February 11, 1858, letter to her sister-in-law, Mrs. Jesse Metcalf, cited by Roger Bowem, "Betsey Baker Was a Bonnet Maker," *Yankee,* March 1967, p. 71; location: Linda Eppich, Assistant Curator for Collections, John Brown House, Rhode Island Historical Society, to ALM March 18, 1988.

6 KIES: Edward P. Thompson, "Women as Inventors," *Inventive Age,* September 1894, p. 177. Thompson attributes the information of the Madison letter to descendant Marietta Kies; the remainder is credited to her grandson and oldest child, George W. Pike, who in 1894 lived in South Killingly, Connecticut. The secessionist movement reached its peak at the Hartford Convention in 1814.

7–8 WETHERSFIELD BONNET: "superior in color and . . .": Adams and Stiles, vol. 1, p. 651; additional information in *History of American Manufacture,* 1864, p. 271; patent quoted and described in Abbie Dunn, "Our Wethersfield: Bonnet-Maker Sophia," *Wethersfield [Conn.] Post,* [date uncertain, c. 1976], n.p.; "an extraordinary specimen of . . .": Diary notation of March 6, 1821, in Adams and Adams, *Memoirs,* vol. 5, p. 319.

8–10 INVENTIONS: "We deem the telescope . . .": Gage, *Woman as Inventor,* Woman Suffrage Tracts, #1, p. 20; "invented the hand-crank . . .": "Make Mine Peach," *Santa Barbara,* July, August 1988, p. 66; "not so wise as . . .": "Women as Inventors," *Harper's Bazaar,* n.d., n.p., cited in Gibbes, p. 492.

10 "The God who made . . .": Burnap, p. 48.

11 PATENT AGENCIES: Advertisement in *The Inventor,* January 1, 1857, p. 141.

11–12 SCIENTIFIC AMERICAN: "suitable for Sunday reading": *Scientific American,* September 26, 1846, p. 5; "directly opposite the Patent . . .": "Information as to the Patentable Novelty of Inventions," Ibid., August 24, 1861, p. 121;

"Women can also apply . . .": "Information Useful to Patentees," Ibid., December 7, 1861, p. 363. "Any one," however, did not include slaves since the Patent Office's position was that, lacking citizenship, slaves were legally incompetent to receive the patent and to transfer their interest to others. Even free colored men, also lacking citizenship, fell into the same category and could therefore not defend a patent against infringers in the United States courts.

13   "My brother has gone . . .": Advertisement of J. Hollingsworth reproduced in Johnson, *Farm Inventions,* p. 100.

14   WOMEN WORKING THE FARM: "I don't expect you . . .": "Letters from an Illinois Farm, 1864–1865" (letters between Louise Jane Phifer and Corporal George Browne), *Illinois State Historical Society Journal,* Winter 1973, pp. 400–401.

14   PATENT OFFICE FAIR: *Proceedings Attending the Opening of the Patent Office Fair,* Washington, D.C.: n.p, 1864, p. 5; "It would be strange . . .": Ibid., p. 20.

19   COSTON'S EARLY LIFE: Coston, *Signal Success,* p. 11; "the very queen of . . .": Ibid., p. 23; "no good recipes for the . . .": [Coston, Martha], "Letter from Mrs. Coston to the officers authorized to test the Coston Night Signals at sea on a long cruise," Washington, D.C., June 1, 1859, reprinted in *The New Century for Women,* May 13, 1876, p. 13.

19   ATLANTIC CABLE: Sarah Bridges Stebbins, "Women in Business," *Demorest's Monthly Magazine,* September 1876, p. 456.

19–21   BRITAIN: "by her kindness, industry . . .": "Niles Female Seminary," *Niles Republican,* September 9, 1843, p. 2. Additional advertisements gave tuition charges: "Niles Female Seminary," *Niles Republican,* August 10, 1844, and March 7, 1846; re floor warmer: "found to my great . . .": Clarissa Britain to Commisioner of Patents, June 5, 1863, in PAF for patent #37,852; "utterly worthless": July 9, 1863, Ibid.; "rules and directions for your . . .": letter from commissioner, July 25, 1867, Ibid.; "the female half of . . .": letter from Mason, Fenwick and Lawrence, attorneys to Commission of Patents, August 26, 1863, PAF for patent #40,157; "She was a fine . . .": Obituary, [*Saint Joseph, Michigan] Saturday Herald,* November 8, 1895.

21–22   SHERWOOD: "exceedingly vague that . . .": "Argument on Appeal by Gale Salden Alden, PIC #1864B; "a pretty strong soapy solution": testimony of John Sherwood in Ibid.; "[S]he was attending to . . .": Laura Freeman's testimony in Ibid.; "She [Sherwood] said she . . .": additional testimony, name illegible, in Ibid, compounded from several pages of answers; "some in small sheets . . .": Ibid.

22   "perfect passion for engineering": Gage, "The Cotton Gin Invented by a Woman," *The Revolution,* April 30, 1868, p. 259.

23   "Let Every Woman Be Her Own Adviser," Ibid., May 1868, p. 83.

## 2: AFTER THE WAR: INVENTING WITHIN WOMAN'S SPHERE

PAGE

25 "sleepy old Johnstown": Cady diary entry of August 28, 1884, cited in Juster, p. 3.

25 DOMESTIC INVENTIONS: Juster, p. 4.

26 FARM WOMEN: "My weary limbs are . . .": E. B., *The Household*, vols. 11, 12, 1878–79, cited without further information in Juster, p. 146; "I am fifty years . . .": letter from Eliza A. Wood to Charlotte Smith, Easton, N.Y., May 5, 1891, reprinted in *Woman Inventor*, vol. 1, #2, June 1891, p. 3; "There are times when . . .": Jennie E. Hooker, "Farmer's Wives and Daughters," in *Farmer*, p. 177.

27 BALDWIN: Phyllis Schlafly, "National Defense," *Daughters of the American Revolution Magazine*, November 1988, p. 617. Schlafly incorrectly dated the invention as 1886.

29 FARM LIFE: "[M]any are the books . . .": from a reprint of a segment in the Cornell Reading Course for Farmers' Wives that appeared in the *American Kitchen Magazine* in October 1900 and March 1901, cited in Juster, p. 101; "The first thing in . . .": Mrs. H. M. R., "Household Management," *American Agriculturalist*, April 1869, p. 191; "An Overworked Farmer's Wife," Ibid., October 1869, p. 381; "I only wonder that . . .": diary entry, July 29, 1877, in Lensink, Kirkham and Witzke, Karen Pauba, " 'My Only Confidante'- The Life and Diary of Emily Hawley Gillespie," *Annals of Iowa*, Spring 1980, p. 304.

30 BUTTER: "expenditure of considerable physical force": "Butter Making," *People's Journal*, August 1854, p. 289; appetite for butter: Charles F. Benjamin, "How the Government Promotes Ingenuity," *Saint Nicholas*, May 1901, p. 618; "the finest butter neatly . . .": "Ladies at the Fall Fairs," *American Agriculturalist*, September 1868, p. 344; "spend it as she thinks . . .": H. M. Robinson, "A Few Words to the 'Men Folks,' " Ibid., December 1869, pp. 459–60.

31 JOB OPPORTUNITIES FOR WOMEN: Penny, *Think and Act*, p. 158.

31 HOUSEWORK: "at least two domestics . . .": Croly, *Talks on Women's Topics*, p. 35.

32 SOROSIS: "If a sufficient number . . .": Margaret Manton Merrill, "Sorosis," *Cosmopolitan*, June 1893, p. 153; "for its full, appropriate . . .": Wells, *Unity in Diversity*, p. 4; "Sore-eye Sissies": Mott, *A History of American Magazines*, vol. 3, p. 91; "the unfortunate fact of . . .": Merrill, op. cit., p. 157.

33–34 DEMOREST: "Personally, she is the . . .": Elm Odou, "Deserving Women of America," n.d., n.p., from an article in the scrapbook of Ellen Demorest's sister, Anna Mary Curtis Morris; dress patterns: Smith, *Successful Folks,* pp. 428–31; "a mere school girl's . . .": "A Novel Enterprise," undated article in the Morris scrapbook; "evangel to preach a . . .": another untitled and [c. 1872] newspaper article in Ibid; "great business world, where . . .": Elm Odou, "Deserving Women of America," n.d., n.p., in Ibid.; "I do not . . .": Ibid.

34–35 WOMEN AND HOUSEWORK: "It is no degradation . . .": Burnap, p. 137; "however lowly": Cornelius, p. 19; Stanton: "Woman's Work," *The Revolution*, August 27, 1868, p. 120; "a natural instinct of . . .": Croly, *Talks*, p. 118; "good girls": Ibid., p. 85; "I hate living in . . .": Croly, *For Better or Worse*, p. 197; "good women, faithful wives . . .": Ibid., p. 197.

36 MUNN & COMPANY: *United States Patent Law. Instructions How to Obtain Letters Patent for New Inventions*, p. 14; "In our practice as . . .": "Female Inventive Talent." *Scientific American*, September 17, 1870, p. 184.

37 "Inventors, as you read . . .": Snook, pp. 1, 4, 5, 7.

38 BIRTH CONTROL: Clinton, pp. 153–56.

38 EVARD STOVE: Burr, p. 587 and *New Century for Women*, July 15, 1876, p. 75; Credit rating: *Credit Ledgers of R. G. Dun & Co.*, Virginia vol. 24, p. 205.

39–42 HAWKS: "no particular occupation except . . .": *Testimony in Behalf of Elizabeth Hawks* before the Commissioner of Patents. Troy, N.Y.: A. W. Scribner & Co., Printers, 1870, in PIC #174, p. 3; further quotations from Ibid., pp. 4, 5, 14; spiritualism: Braude, passim; "debilitated state of health . . .": letter from Elizabeth Hawks (signed "Per I. P. Hawks"), Troy, N.Y., July 25, 1867, to Commissioner Theaker, in PAF; "baked differently from what" in *Testimony*, p. 35; "every housekeeper in the . . .": from the patent; letter blaming lawyer: Elizabeth Hawks, Troy, N.Y., December 21, 1866, to Commissioner Theaker, in PAF; "at the earliest possible . . .": letter from Elizabeth Hawks, Troy, N.Y., February 25, 1867, to Commissioner Theaker, in Ibid; "It has been approved . . .": letter from Elizabeth Hawks (signed "Per I. P. Hawks"), Troy, N.Y., July 25, 1867, to Commissioner Theaker, in PAF; "the personal matters of . . .": letter from examiner (name illegible), United States Patent Office, January 31, 1867, to Elizabeth Hawks, in PAF; "[P]lease forward as soon . . .": letter from Elizabeth Hawks, Troy, N.Y., April 4, 1867, to Commissioner Theaker, in PAF; "genius of women applied . . .": Gage, *Woman as Inventor*, #1, p. 18; "It requires no deep . . .": decision of the commissioner in favor of John Goodfellow, May 12, 1871, n.p., PIC, #174.

43 WOMEN AND ARCHITECTURE: "climbing ladders [and] mingling . . .": Vaux, pp. 236–37; "To the Ladies of . . .": Tuthill, dedication; "One of the greatest . . .": Stowe, p. 257.

43–45 IRWIN HOUSE: "for the dirt to . . .": Eleanor Cochran McMahon, "Morrison Sisters Make History: Six Daughters Marry Famous Leaders in Old Mecklenburg," *Charlotte Observer,* November 7, 1934; "the most economical, most . . .": Beverly Heisner, "Harriet Morrison Irwin's Hexagonal House: An Invention to Improve Domestic Dwellings," *North Carolina Historical Review,* April 1981, p. 118; "a new era in . . .": *Southern Home Magazine,* February 17, 1870, p. 2., reprinted in Blythe and Brockmann, p. 380; "Who is Harriet Irwin?": Marie Adams, "Harriet Morrison Irwin's House Still Stands," in "The Chatter Box," *The Charlotte News,* December 7, 1962.

46 IRWIN: "Educate the women . . .": in McMahon; general biographical material: Laura Brown, p. 18; "keeping house": 1870 Census, Mecklenburg County, Charlotte Township, Archives of the United States; Patent: the family was well represented at the signing—her sister-in-law, Mary Ann Irwin Osborn; the husband of Eugenia Erixena Morrison, and Isabella Morrison Hill, in Laura Brown, p. 19.

47 "The planning of houses . . .": 1876 editorial cited in Torre, p. 60; "[O]ne invention does not . . .": "American Notes," *Journal of the Society of Architectural Historians,* May 1957, p. 66.

## 3: NEW FIELDS OF INVENTION

PAGE

48 "engrave lines of character . . .": "Female Inventive Talent," *Scientific American,* September 17, 1870, p. 184.

49 Gage on Genius and Minerva: *Woman as Inventor,* #1, pp. 21, 28.

49–50 COSTON: Testimonials: *Coston's Telegraphic Night Signals,* passim; "We hear much . . .": Coston, *Signal Success,* pp. 271–72; "stranded upon the world . . .": Ibid., p. 3.

50–51 COMMENTS ON KNIGHT: "Every shopper who loads . . .": Heyn, p. 46; International acclaim: [Charlotte Smith], "Women Inventors," *The Woman Inventor,* April 1890 [1891], p. 4; "persistency and remarkable competency . . .": Mozans, p. 350; "woman Edison": "Was Notable Woman," *Framingham [Mass.] Evening News,* October 13, 1914; "Margaret E. Knight House," in Sheer and Kazickas, p. 105.

51 "It is only . . .": "A Lady in a Machine-Shop," *Woman's Journal,* December 21, 1872, p. 463, cited by Hanaford, pp. 652–53.

51–52 KNIGHT'S EARLY YEARS: see Knight entry in *Notable American Women,* p. 339; "my health being rather . . .": Testimony of Margaret E. Knight, Boston, May 5, 1870, in PIC #272.

52 KNIGHT'S WORKING EXPERIENCE: "Their dress is objectionable . . .": quoted in

Penny, *The Employments of Women*, p. 376; "a keener eye than . . .": "A Lady in a Machine-Shop," *Woman's Journal*, December 21, 1872, p. 463, cited in Hanford, p. 652.

53–55 KNIGHT CASE: "The idea of a . . .": testimony of Charles Yates, of Columbia Paper Bag Co., Springfield, Boston, May 13, 1870, in PIC #272; Deposition of William C. Abbot: Boston, May 12, 1870, in Ibid.; "I have from my . . .": testimony of Knight in Ibid. (Biographical material in *Notable American Women* states that Knight was born February 14, 1838, which would have made her thirty-two at the time of the suit in the fall of 1870, but in her deposition, she gave her age as thirty-three); Exhibits list and diary notations (February through September, 1867) in Ibid.; "not perfect bags, since . . .": in Ibid.; "She told me she . . .": deposition of Eliza G. McFarland, Boston, May 11, 1870, in Ibid.

55 DECISION OF EXAMINERS: "whenever it suited him . . .": "Before the Examiners-in-Chief on appeal," United States Patent Office, September 3, 1870, no. 377, in PIC #272; "inexperience in business, as . . .": Ibid.; "most notable character": in *Decisions* of the Commissioner of Patents for the Year 1871, p. 37.

55–56 KNIGHT'S BUSINESS VENTURES: "satisfaction of the covenants . . .": agreement reached June 27, 1878, for patent #220,925, in DoA, vol. K-4, p. 104 (full details of the agreement are in TIP, Liber vol. H23, p. 134–37 and X23, p. 224).

56–57 MINING: "A Winter on the . . .": *History of Nevada County, California*, p. 74; "two restaurants, four stores . . .": letter from "Snowball" in *San Francisco Enquirer*, July 25, 1868, cited in Fatout, p. 106; "ready to shuffle off . . .": *Grass Valley Union*, December 23, 1868, cited in Ibid., p. 109; "rebellious ore": *History of Nevada County, California*, p. 196.

57–58 BURNS PROCESS: "became absorbed in other . . .": "The New Process," in "Local Intelligence," *Nevada City Transcript* [Nevada City, Calif.], July 20, 1869; "Meadow Lake will soon . . .": "The New Process," in "Local Intelligence," *Nevada City Transcript*, July 20, 1869; "company of influential and . . .": "Rich Result of the Burns Process," *Nevada City Transcript*, July 20, 1869; Demise of Meadow Lake: "Letter from Meadow Lake," September 27, 1873, *San Francisco Chronicle*, October 2, 1873, Fatout, p. 116.

58–59 WOMEN AND SEWING: "stitched entirely away": Davis, pp. 123–34; "[T]he needle has proved . . .": Hamer [Brown], pp. 27, 30–31.

59–60 INFLUENCE OF SEWING MACHINE: "create a social revolution . . .": "Sewing Machines," *Scientific American*, July 17, 1852, p. 344; "do all that human . . .": International Exhibition *Official Catalogue*, p. 38; "Servant in the House": Lewton, in Smithsonian *Annual Report*, pp. 559–83; "sickly worn-out aspect": *How to Ruin Your Health*, p. 39.

60–61 BLANCHARD: [Charlotte Smith], "Women Inventors," *The Woman Inventor,* April 1890 [1891], p. 4; "Miss Helen Augusta Blanchard," *Portland Express Herald,* January 13, 1922; "a benefactor of her . . .": "Blanchard, Miss Helen Augusta," Willard, *American Women,* vol. 1, p. 97.

61–63 TRACY: "It was a matter of . . .": letter from Harriet Tracy to the Commissioner of Patents, [December 1872], n.p., in PIC #753; "Women cannot always do . . .": letter from Harriet Tracy to the Commissioner of Interferences, in Ibid.; "confidence woman," in Ibid.; ". . . moment of flash of . . .": letter from Harriet Tracy to the Commissioner of Patents, [December 1872], in Ibid.; "My case is so . . .": Letter from Harriet Tracy to the Commissioner of Interferences, New York, October 28, 1872, in Ibid.

63–64 ABOUT CARPENTER: "a great deal of . . .": "The Carpenter Self-Threading and Self-Setting Needle for Sewing Machines," *Scientific American,* October 10, 1870, p. 164; "not an inch of . . .": "A Woman's Genius," *Inventive Age,* December 1895, p. 187.

64–65 PATENT SUIT: "this vile perjurer": in separately printed book of Mary Carpenter Hooper's testimony (p. 191), in PIC #7,506; "That was Mrs. Carpenter's . . .": testimony of Henry McCabe, Ibid., p. 103; "I took that machine . . .": Ibid., p. 190; "eight or nine, I . . .": Ibid., pp. 14–15.

65 BACKGROUND ON JONES: Eleanor Smith, *Psychic People,* p. 49.

66–67 JONES'S INVENTION: "trenchant words": Jones, *Psychic Autobiography,* p. 231; "Now I confess this . . .": Ibid., pp. 297–98; Canning: Bitting, passim, ch. 1; "No spirit told me . . .": Jones, p. 339; "a traffic in the . . .": Jones, p. 380.

67–70 JONES'S BUSINESS: "to manufacture, sell and . . .": incorporation papers listed in official documents section of bibliography (a list of stockholders and their subscriptions accompanies the document); Spiritualism: Braude, passim; "This is a woman's . . .": Jones, p. 414; "At the start each . . .": "These are Real 'New Women,'" *New Ideas,* September 1895, p. 70; "Of course, all this . . .": quoted in May, pp. 310–11; "as much my own . . .": Jones, p. 380.

## 4: CENTENNIAL SISTERHOOD

PAGE

71 PATENT FIGURES: *Women's Contribution in the Field of Invention,* p. 23.

72 LIVERMORE: "potencies and possibilities of . . .": Livermore, *Story of My Life,* pp. 484–85; "new sense of the . . .": Howe on Livermore, *Boston Transcript,* n.d., cited in "Mrs. Howe on Mrs. Livermore," *Woman's Journal,* June 10, 1905, p. 90; "verdant," days: Livermore, Ibid., p. 479; "Here was a . . .": Ibid., p. 436.

74 "[It] is a question . . .": [Stanton], in *The Revolution*, January 14 and November 24, 1869.

74 "a division in the . . .": *The Revolution*, [December 18, 1869?], cited in Griffith, p. 139.

75 LIVERMORE AND WOMAN'S JOURNAL: Stanton, Anthony, and Gage, vol. 3, p. 274; "morning star of the . . .": Blackwell, *Lucy Stone*, preface; "brilliant a coterie of . . .": Livermore, *Story of My Life*, p. 482; "Our sisters, of whatever . . .": Julia Ward Howe, "Salutatory," *Woman's Journal*, January 8, 1870, p. 4.

75 WOMAN'S JOURNAL: "pleasant, prettily fitted up . . .": Howe, "Our Office," *Woman's Journal*, January 8, 1870, p. 4; "noble band of pioneers": Antoinette S. Blackwell, "Forty-seventh Anniversary of Founding of Woman's Journal," *Woman's Journal*, January 6, 1917, p. 3.

76–78 CENTENNIAL PLANNING: "ostracized from our country's . . .": Mrs. Ellen Coll Long, "Extracts from an Appeal to the Women of Florida, *The Herald of the Centennial*, [Providence, R.I.], February 1875, p. 2; "more timid sisters": Gillespie, p. 282; "theologians claim woman . . .": Stanton, *Eighty Years*, p. 314; "Let every woman in . . .": Antoinette Brown Blackwell, speech extracted in "Women and the Centennial," *The Herald of the Centennial*, November 1875, p. 74; "no better than if . . .": William Dean Howells, "A Sennight of the Centennial," quoted in Bishop and Coblentz, p. 312.

78–81 HOSMER: "We had a fright . . .": only the first part of this letter from Hosmer to Gillespie is cited in the report of the Women's Centennial Executive Committee (p. 3), but the last sentence is added in Burr, p. 570; "[K]nowing what barriers must . . .": Hosmer quoted by Reverend R. B. Thurston in his chapter on her in Parton, Greeley, et al., p. 584; "Americans may now boast . . .": Gibson quoted by Thurston, Ibid., p. 586; Early life: Margaret Ferrand Shorp, "The White Marmorean Flock," *New England Quarterly*, June 1959, p. 149; "Every medical college closed . . .": Margaret T. Skiff quoted in "Woman's Education," *Success*, August 1898, p. 16; "I observed a degree . . .": Lydia Maria Child, "Harriet W. Hosmer." *The Ladies' Repository*, January 1861, p. 7; "positive, piquant, and unique,": Thurston in Parton, Greeley, et al., p. 597; "I felt that I . . .": Hosmer quoted in Hanaford, pp. 321–22; "an object of peculiar . . .": Jane O. DeForest, "Women and the Fine Arts, *Arthur's Home Magazine*, August 1876, p. 408.

81–82 PATENTEES: Gillespie, p. 18; Not all inventors were listed in the official catalog but their work was described by attendees. Deborah Jean Warner lists seventy-nine in "Women Inventors at the Centennial," in Truscott, p. 103. Ingram uses the figure seventy-four but gives no actual listing, pp. 103, 105.

82  SUPLEE: (Suplee ran advertisements for several months, beginning in 1877) See *Sewing Machine Journal*, May 1878, p. 8.; "big success": "Philadelphia Notes," *The Sewing Machine Journal*, December 1877, p. 5; "Madame Suplee": "Ladies Corner," Ibid.; "[N]o one who can . . .": Ingram, p. 347; "Yankee training and Chinese . . .": Deborah Jean Warner, "The Women's Pavilion," in Post, p. 167.

82  "the manacles which are . . .": Arsenath Coolidge, "Humor of the Centennial," *Woman's Journal*, May 27, 1876, p. 170.

82  INDEPENDENCE DAY: "injustice and oppression," Stanton, *Eighty Years*, p. 311; General description of the event, Ibid., pp. 312–13; Anthony as Commissioner of Patents: "Progress of Woman's Rights," *Scientific American*, 1873, vol. 28, p. 7.

83  ALLISON: "as smooth and clean . . .": quoted without citation in Dee Brown, *The Year of the Century*, p. 144; Stanton's comments: Stanton, *Eighty Years*, p. 315; "If she does nothing else . . .": Trout, p. 111 (Trout was secretary of the Board of Finance for the Centennial); "She is no low . . .": Bailey, p. 80. Another good source on Allison is Hanaford, p. 646.

83–86  DESCRIPTIONS OF EXHIBITS: Emma Molloy, "Woman versus Whiskey in Philadelphia," *Woman's Journal*, July 1, 1876, p. 209; "Centennial Notes by a Maine Woman," *Woman's Journal*, July 15, 1876, p. 230; Siegel: "happy thought . . . a neat and . . .": "The Centennial: Patents," *Demorest's Monthly*, July 1876, p. 367; Harley Darner: Ingram, pp. 346–47; Colvin: "the successful result of . . .": official catalog, p. 87, and Warner, in Post, p. 167; Pierce: Ingram, pp. 345–46; "rather inventive turn of . . .": "The Women's Pavilion," "Centennial Notes #21," *Friends' Intelligencer*, October 21, 1876, p. 556.

86–87  PRESS: "There are a few . . .": "Woman and the Centennial," *Woman's Journal*, July 29, 1876, p. 243; "how insipid the lives . . .": "How Does It Sound the Other Way?" *Woman's Journal*, March 24, 1876, p. 208; "gauged by higher standards . . .": "The Woman's Pavilion," *The Centennial Eagle*, August 8, 1876, pp. 109–10; "the industry and nerve . . .": "The Women's Pavilion," "Centennial Notes #21, *Friends' Intelligencer*, October 21, 1987, p. 554; *Arthur's Illustrated Home Magazine*: "only the inferior and . . .": "Our First Visit," Ibid., July 1876, p. 398, and a follow-up article, "The Great Centennial Exhibition: The Woman's Department," in the August issue hooted at the "abominations of worsted embroidery" on p. 452; "commenced at a very . . .": *Leslie's Historical Register*, p. 158; "those pests of journalism": Brown, *The Year of the Century*, p. 143.

87  ADVERTISEMENTS: *New Century for Women*: Slade: November 11, 1876, p. 211; French: Ibid, August 19, 1876; Whitener: January 5, 1875.

88 WELLS: "Why does she not . . .": "Inventions and Patents," *The New Century for Women*, June 10, 1876, p. 34. The baby chair was made by the Occidental Manufacturing Company at 50 Gane Street, Henry Wills, Managing Director; "Jane Wells was the . . .": Erma Bombeck, "Men's Inventions = Women's Laments," *Los Angeles Times*, March 18, 1986, part V, p. 2.

88 "originality in construction in . . .": Centennial Commission, *Reports and Awards, Group VII*, p. 36.

89–90 POTTS: Some material on Potts from research done by Edna Glissman cited in Fred Amram, "Collecting Inventions by Women," *The Antique Trader Weekly*, March 30, 1988, pp. 76–77; "[W]e thk [think] if . . .": *Credit and Reporting Ledgers of the Mercantile Agency*, Iowa 51, February of 1870, p. 97, in R. G. Dun & Co. Collection; Trade cards are in the Warshaw Collection at the Smithsonian Institution.

90–92 BROOKS AND "BUTTER LADY" SCULPTURE: "undoubtedly the cream of . . .": Burr, p. 615; Other descriptions in "The Woman's Pavilion," *The Centennial Eagle*, August 8, 1876, p. 109, and from Dale P. Kirkman, "Caroline Shawk Brooks: Sculptress in Butter," *Phillips County Historical Quarterly*, March 1967, p. 9; "Thousands wondered how she . . .": Burr, p. 591; "shapeless golden mass": Ibid., p. 706; Demonstration in Ingram, p. 706; "unconscious artist of the . . .": "The Woman's Pavilion," "Centennial Notes #21," *Friends' Intelligencer*, October 21, 1987, p. 557; "the work itself is . . .": *Leslie's Historical Register*, p. 156; "exquisite head carved in . . .": McCabe, p. 219; "substantial and progressive farmer . . .": *Biographical and Historical Memoirs of Eastern Arkansas*, p. 753.

93 COSTON: Endorsements: *Coston's Telegraphic Night Signals*, n.p.; "[S]he stands today the . . .": Sarah Bridges Stebbins, "Women in Business," *Demorest's Monthly Magazine*, September 1876, p. 456.

94–95 STILES: Good descriptions of the deak can be found in Burr, p. 587, Ingram, p. 334, and "The Great Centennial Exhibition: The Woman's Department," *Arthur's Illustrated Home Magazine*, August 1876, p. 452.

96–98 NOLAN: "Nolanum," *Missouri Republican*, June 4, 1876; "Nolanum is a novel . . .": CC, *Reports and Awards, Group XXI*, p. 43; "Your favor giving text . . .": letter of Mary Nolan, St. Louis, March 7, 1877, to A. J. Goshorn, Director General, Centennial Exposition, and her signed receipt for medal and diploma, July 22, 1977, in CC, Bureau of Awards, Department of Records, City of Philadelphia; "recognized its possibilities . . .": letter, St. Louis, July 17, 1916, William C. Breckenridge to FranklinF.Hoppe, Breckenridge Papers; "little lame Irish woman . . .": Ibid. (an examination of Nolan's listings in the St. Louis City Directory show the variety of her occupations: In 1871, she listed as her address the Catholic Book Store at 822 Washington Avenue; she did not list herself in 1872; in 1873, she added to her bookseller occupation "publisher Central Magazine at 1023 Washington Avenue" but omitted mention of her erstwhile association with *Inland* magazine; she continued listing her work at *Central* until 1878, when she listed "Street paving"; in 1879, it was simply "Building material." By 1881, though *Central* had ceased publication, she called herself "proprietor of Central Magazine"; two years later she was "artiste"; two years later, "artist." In 1884, she was, quite legitimately, "authoress," for her book *Biddy Finnegan's Botheration, or That Romp of a Girl,* in whose introduction she wrote, "A little nonsense now and then is relished by the best of men," was published that year. There are no listings after 1886; Directory listings: *Edwards St. Louis City Directory,* 1886–72; *Gould St. Louis City Directory,* 1873–1901.)

98–99 INLAND AND CENTRAL MAGAZINES: "gentlemen members of the . . .": "Editorial," *Inland Monthly,* May 1872, p. 149; "for what it is . . .": "To the Press," Ibid., August 1872, inside back cover; Marietta Holley ("Joseph Allen's Wife") "My Idees About Free Love," Ibid., September 1872, pp. 401–6; "strictly Christian morality": "Editorial," *Central Magazine,* August 1872, p. 280; "a lady . . . should . . .": "Editorial," *Inland Monthly,* August 1973, p. 135; "unripe essays on crude . . .": "Editorial," Ibid., August 1973, p. 135; "when we have perfected . . .": "Portable Reservoirs," *Central Magazine,* January 1873, p. 66.

99–100 NOLAN'S LATER YEARS: "Miss Mary Nolan who . . .": *Credit Ledgers of R. G. Dun & Co.,* St. Louis, Mo., vol. 5, 1882–1883, no. 41, p. 234; "Miss Mary Nolan who is . . .": Ibid.; St. Louis Fair subscriber list: Francis, p. 373.

100–101 FRENCH: Charges for instruction: advertisement in French, n.p.; "as strong as it . . .": Ibid., p. 101; Baking powder advertisement, Ibid., n.p; "Set up a current . . .": Ibid., p. 109.

101 "mottoes worked in worsted . . .": Mrs. S. J. Cowen, Chairman, "The Exposition," in *The Spirit of "Seventy-Six",* March 1877, pp. 135–36.

101–2 HANAFORD: "The question is sneeringly . . .": Hanaford, p. 641; (Hanaford, who included herself among the century's women leaders, gave this self-evaluation: "Has always been a student, and always will be," Ibid., p. 477.); "Some woman with sufficient . . .": Ibid., p. 648.

102 "synergistic effect": Warner, in Post, p. 173.

# 5: PATENTING DRESS REFORM

PAGE

104–5 WOMEN'S HEALTH: "[I]f, on the whole . . .": Clarke, p. 12; "that part of their . . .": Ibid., p. 44; "The brain is dependent . . .": Ibid., p. 96; "Does it not look . . .": Elizabeth Stuart Phelps, "A Word for the Silent," *The*

*Independent,* January 1, 1874, pp. 1633–34; "Looking over families and . . .": "Sex in Education," *Woman's Journal,* November 8, 1873, p. 352.

105–6 WOMEN'S DRESS: "Women are in bondage. . . .": quoted in Blackwell, *Lucy Stone,* p. 109; "Heigh ho . . .": Park, p. 59; "indicate to their neighbors . . .": *Albany Register,* cited without date in Papachristou, p. 45; "vagabondizing over the country . . .": *New York Herald,* September 7, 1853, cited in *Ibid.,* p. 45; "Well, if Lucy Stone . . .": quoted in Blackwell, *Lucy Stone,* p. 104; "three years of petty . . .": Ibid., p. 106; Hoop skirts: Crawford and Crawford, p. 9; "What incredible freedom I . . .": Stanton, *Eighty Years,* p. 201.

106–7 EARLIER REFORM: "that wholesome discontent which . . .": Lucy Stone, in "The Progress of Fifty Years," in *Eagle,* vol. 2, p. 59; "We could go upstairs . . .": Stone quoted in "The Rational Dress Movement: A Symposium," *Arena,* October 1894, p. 306; "trip them into eternity . . .": Harmon, p. 10.

107–9 HEALTH ISSUE: "injurious to society": Phelps, *What to Wear,* p. 44; "shipwreck[ing] our young daughter . . .": Livermore, "What Shall We Do With Our Daughters?" reprinted in *Story of My Life,* p. 622; "Unloose your corset strings. . . .": Fowler, p. 15; "[c]orsets that embrace the . . .": Clarke, p. 25; "enough to drag the . . .": Kellogg, p. 19; "To thousands of elder . . .": Richards and Elliott, pp. 292–93.

109–10 BOSTON COMMITTEE: "When I want anything . . .": Ibid., p. 294; "in our drawing-rooms . . .": Phelps, p. 9; "You should see us . . .": letter to John Greenleaf Whittier in Essex Institute, Salem, Mass., cited in Bennett, p. 64; Dolls: "Dress Reform Meeting in Boston," *Frank Leslie's Illustrated Newspaper,* June 20, 1874, p. 229; good descriptions in Deborah Jean Warner, "Fashion, Emancipation, Reform, and the Rational Undergarment," *Dress,* vol. 4, 1978, p. 24; "suspend[ing] every single article . . .": Phelps, p. 89.

110–12 FLYNT: "natural circulation, perfect respiration . . .": Flynt, p. 4; "girls go to college . . .": Frances C. Russell, "The Coming Dress," *Woman's Journal,* December 17, 1892, p. 404; "I will [invent], for . . .": Flynt, p. 14; "unattainable to Dress Reformers . . .": Abba Woolson to Olivia Flynt, Concord, N.H., August 21, 1874, copied and enclosed in Woolson to Wolcott, May 18, 1875, in NEWC, folder 57; "The laws that regulate . . .": letter from Mrs. O. P. Flynt to Mrs. A. G. Woolson, received by Mrs. Woolson August 21, 1974, and copied by her in Ibid.; "I am sure that . . .": Abba Woolson to Olivia Flynt, Concord, N.H., August 21, 1874, copied and enclosed in Woolson to Wolcott, May 18, 1875, in Ibid.; "Mrs. Flynt's thunderings seem . . .": Abba Woolson to Miss Peabody, Concord, N.H., March 2, 1875, in Ibid.; "with more forbearance and . . .": Abba Woolson to Mrs. Wolcott, Maine, May 18, 1875, in Ibid.

113 HUTCHINSON COPYRIGHT: Abba Woolson to Miss Peabody, Concord, N.H., February 28, 1875, and April 21, 1875, NEWC, folder 57; copyright also discussed in Sprague, pp. 19–20.

113–15 CONVERSE: "the results of years . . .": Susan Converse to Mrs. Wolcott, Woburn, Mass., May 17, 1875, NEWC, folder 57; "as forcible as a . . .": Converse to Wolcott, Woburn, Mass., May 17, 1875, in Ibid.; "with any kindness of . . .": Converse to Wolcott, Woburn, Mass., May 17, 1875, in Ibid.; "In zeal for . . .": appended to letter of Converse to Wolcott, Woburn, Mass., May 17, 1875, in Ibid.; "I think the sooner . . .": Kendall to Wolcott, Cambridge, Mass., November 29, [1875], in Ibid.

115 "I have worn the . . .": Martha G. Ripley, "Bondage: Woman's Dress," *Woman's Journal*, August 10, 1878, p. 249.

115–16 OTHER INVENTORS: Clark's advertisements appeared regularly in *Chautauquan, Jenness-Miller Magazine, Woman's Journal*, etc.; most additional ads are from the "Corsets" file of the Warshaw Collection; George Frost: "Equipoise Waist," *Household Companion*, January 1893, p. 30.

116 Society is accustomed to . . .": Martha Williams, "Hygienic Dress," *Woman's Journal*, February 1, 1873, p. 35.


## 6: PUBLICIZING, PROSELYTIZING, AND EDUCATING: UPLIFTING THE POSITION OF WOMEN BEGINS

PAGE

118 "If a women was . . .": Ardie Bee, "Women Never Invent Anything," *Woman's Journal*, July 3, 1875, p. 210.

118 *The Chautauquan:* Tarbell, *The Ways of Woman*, p. 83.

118–21 TARBELL: "Invention is an invention . . .": Tarbell, "Women as Inventors," *Chautauquan*, March 1877, p. 355; "an enviable result" Ibid., p. 357; "dishes grew on trees": Mary Lowe Dickinson, "Clerical Pursuits," *Chautauquan*, December 1876, p. 135; "one of our noblest": "Women as Inventors," *Chautauquan*, March 1877, p. 355; "the most delicate, complex . . .": Tarbell, *All in the Day's Work*, p. 75; "I was able to . . .": Ibid., pp. 75–76; "the *first* and *only*": Tarbell, "Women as Inventors," *Chautauquan*, March 1877, p. 355; "An article that will . . .": Ibid., p. 355; "The world sensibly says . . .": Ibid., p. 357; "Girls are so entirely . . .": Quoted without source in Ibid., p. 337; "If she can learn . . .": Ibid., p. 357.

122 "a serious tax on . . .": *Petition to the Honorable Senate, United States*, n.p.; the model requirement remained until 1880, when it was abandoned more for lack of space than out of concern for cost.

122–23 HOSMER: "purely private and confidential . . .": letter from Hosmer to M. Cole, Rome, June 30, 1877, HH; "When Harriet Hosmer took . . .":

"Bowles to Fortnightly," *Woman's Journal*, March 1899, requoted in "Women Inventors," *Scientific American*, August 19, 1899, p. 123; "Anyone can do sculpture . . .": cited without source in Ruth A. Bradford, "The Life and Works of Harriet Hosmer, the American Sculptor," *New England Magazine*, November 1911, p. 269.

124–25 WOMEN'S HIGHER EDUCATION: "existing customs and methods . . .": "The Education of Girls," *Woman's Journal*, January 5, 1870, p. 10; "If Harvard College can . . .": "The Better Education of Women," *Woman's Journal*, January 20, 1872, p. 29; "It is not my . . .": *Last Will and Testament of Sophia Smith*, Northampton, Mass., 1871, pp. 10–11, cited in Flexner, p. 129.

125 WELLESLEY: "established for the beneficial . . .": CC, *Reports and Awards*, *Group XXVIII*, p. 47; Background: Glascock, pp. 14–15.

125 "life's great purpose . . ." Beecher quoted in Sklar, p. 182.

126 Breadin's teaching experience is recounted in a letter to Charlotte Smith, "The Women's Record in the World of Invention," *The Woman Inventor*, June 1891, p. 2.

128–30 FRACKELTON: Awards: "Susan S. Frackelton, Potter, Is Dead at 85," *New York Times*, April 16, 1932; "The first thing to . . .": Frackelton, pp. 16–17; "a notable example of . . .": Carolyn Halsted, "America's First Woman Potter," *Success*, October 1898, p. 15; "to her own temperament . . .": Willard and Livermore, vol. 1, p. 288.

131 MCLAUGHLIN'S WORK: Egg cups: Laura A. Fry, "American Pottery" [Condensed from a paper read before the Art Congress of the Atlanta Exposition, October 8, 1895], *Young Ladies' Magazine*, 1896, pp. 97–100, in MSS qF946 RMV, Exhibits: "Women's Pavilion," CC, *Official Catalogue: Department of Machinery*, pp. 183, 185, 195; "sensation of the hour": "[unknown title]," *Cincinnati Enquirer*, February 20, 1878, courtesy of Cincinnati Historical Society.

131 MCLAUGHLIN'S EARLY BACKGROUND: "Miss McLaughlin Tells Her Own Story," a paper read by McLaughlin at the Meeting of the Porcelain League, April 25, 1914, from Cincinnati Artists File, Cincinnati Art Museum Library, reprinted in *Communications-Ceramic Industry*, p. 218, in MSS qF946 RMV.

131–32 INVENTION: "Success depends on knowing . . .": H. Taine, cited by McLaughlin [or MacLaughlin], *China Painting*, frontispiece; "something I would like . . .": McLaughlin to Ross Purdy, editor of the Bulletin of the American Ceramic Society, Cincinnati, January 24, 1938, in MSS qF946 RMV; "I even knew the secrets . . .": cited anonymously in "War Among the Potters," *Cincinnati Daily Gazette*, October 7, 1880; "not worth the paper . . .": quoted in Ibid.

132–33 FRY: *Young Lady's Magazine*: Kenneth E. Smith, *Laura Anne Fry* (paper presented in Fine Arts Department, Ohio State University], n.d., p. 8, in

MSS qF946 RMV; "most meritorious piece of . . .": Medal citation, H. H. Fry (Laura's sister) to Ross Purdy, Camp Dennison, Ohio, August 30, 1938, in Ibid; "Since I used my . . .": Laura Fry to Kenneth E. Smith, Terrence Park, Ohio, in Ibid.; Sprayer: Smith, *Laura Anne Fry*, p. 6, in Ibid.

133 "Women are inclined sometime . . .": McLaughlin quoted in Weiman, p. 416.

133 "I take this opportunity . . .": Laura A. Fry, "American Pottery," in p. 12 of manuscript in MSS qF946 RMV.

133–35 GAGE: *North American*: The suffrage debate began with an article by Francis Parkman in the October 1878 issue, the women's replies followed in the November number; "in their personal character . . .": *Scientific American*, quoted without specific citation in Gage, "Woman As an Inventor," *North American Review*, May 1883, p. 478; "any sketch of American . . .": Ibid.; "The feminine mind is . . .": Ibid.; "one of the most . . .": Ibid., p. 487; "A very slight investigation": Ibid., p. 483; "trained to seclusion, dependence": Ibid., p. 488.

135 "[a] peculiar neurotic condition . . .": William Hammond, "Dr. Hammond's Estimate of Women," *North American Review*, August 1883, p. 137. Women's angry rejoinders were published in "Dr. Hammond's Estimate of Women," *North American Review*, October 1883, pp. 495–519.

136–38 NEW ORLEANS EXPOSITION: "of an industrial nature . . . requiring . . .": description of Boston exhibit included in NO, p. 46; Maud Howe used the metaphor of tangled threads in "Woman's Work at the Exposition," *Industrial America*, March 14, 1885, p. 63; "a task about equivalent . . .": Indiana Commissioners Mrs. A. M. Noe and Mrs. Mary S. Judah, in NO, pp. 77–78; "one of the most . . .": "Woman's Work at the Exposition," *Industrial America*, March 14, 1885, p. 63; "that shall do credit . . .": Erminnie A. Smith, Lady Commissioner for the State of New Jersey, "To the Women of the State of New Jersey," November 19, 1884, in Ibid., pp. 58–59; Iowa collections: Ibid., pp. 89–90; "a crude, uncultivated civilization": Commissioner Mrs. S. C. Elliott of Nebraska, Ibid., pp. 108–9; New Hampshire: Ibid., pp. 42–43; Virginia: Ibid., p. 186; Illinois Commissioner Mrs. C. C. Hughes, in Ibid., pp. 82–83; Illinois: Ibid., pp. 83–84; California: *Oakland Tribune*, February 14, 1885, and NO, pp. 134–35; Pennsylvania: Ibid., pp. 65, 69; New York: Ibid., p. 53;

138 "interesting range": Howe in Ibid., pp. 13, 14.

138 COMMISSIONER-GENERAL: Colonel Frank Morehead quoted in *New Orleans Picayune*, March 4, 1885.

138 "when majors wrote for . . .": Henry Steele Commager, cited in Meigs, p. 261.

139 "the greatest story teller . . .": Torrence, p. 14.

139 "Boys and Girls of . . .": Advertisements in 1883, 1884, and 1885 issues.

139–40 "ELSIE'S INVENTION": "[M]elt the rocking chair . . .": Charles Ledyard Norton, "Elsie's Invention," *Saint Nicholas,* November 1888, p. 65; "Elsie has made an . . .": Ibid., "in the matter of . . .": Ibid.

141 "With a skip and . . .": Mary P. Jacques, "Washing Dishes," in "Housekeeping Songs," Ibid., October 1888, pp. 948–49; "First your iron smooth . . .": Jacques, "Ironing Song," Ibid., March 1883, p. 364.

141 "How far may girls . . .": Mary A. Livermore, "Co-operative Housekeeping," *Chautauquan,* April 1886, p. 399.

141 LIST OF WOMEN INVENTORS: Cost and time: letter of J. B. Marvin, chief of Draftsman's Division, Patent Office, Department of the Interior, to Charlotte Smith, February 14, 1890, reprinted in *The Woman Inventor,* April 1890 [1891], p. 3; Omissions: Autumn Stanley in "The Patent Office Clerk as Conjurer," in Wright, *Women, Work and Technology,* pp. 119–136. By comparing names on the annual published list with Patent Office records for 1876, Stanley reveals the extent of omissions in that year alone (but hedges over calling the omissions intentional despite the *implication* of the word "conjurer") and surmises that compilers concentrated on searching classifications where they *expected* to see women's names. While her statistics for 1876 are irrefutable, she mistakenly says that alphabetical lists of each year's patents were not available until the 1870s and cites two names as omissions which *should* have been omitted: Martha Coston's 1859 patent #23,536 for "Pyrotechnic Night Signals," which Coston chose to receive it as "Administrix of the last will and testament of B. Franklin Coston, deceased" and several by Mildred Blakey, who, despite the feminine sounding name, was a man.

143 "something which must be . . .": Willard, *Occupations for Women,* p. 139.

143–44 UNIONIZATION: Kenneally, pp. 19, 37; Henry, pp. 36–37; "one of those hopeful . . .": Ibid., p. 52; "There was a time . . .": T. V. Powderly, letter to Elizabeth A. Bryant, secretary of the Women's National Industrial League, Scranton, February 8, 1883, Powderly Papers.

144–45 SMITH: Leaflets and her letter of May 15, 1886, are in PCP, box 123; "how earnest and persistent . . .": letter from former commissioner M. Montgomery to Charlotte Smith, March 30, 1891, reprinted in *The Woman Inventor,* April 1890 [1891], p. 3.

## 7: INVENTING OUTSIDE AND BEYOND WOMAN'S SPHERE

PAGE

146–47 JONES OIL BURNER: Described: Jones, *Psychic Autobiography,* p. 384; navy tests: "stood around agape": Ibid., 389; Jones's partner: Ibid., p. 409;

"invite the ridicule of . . .": Amanda T. Jones, "Oil Burning Utilities and Futilities: Atomization Previous to Ignition: Is It a Necessary Evil?" *Steam Engineering*, August 10, 1903, p. 556; Autobiography: Jones, p. 425.

148 "tough and wiry": Beard, p. 110; "[t]he constant din of . . .": quoted in Gage, "Woman As an Inventor." *North American Review*, May 1883, p. 486.

150 WALTON: "I sawed pieces of . . .": testimony of Mary Walton, October 24, 1879, p. 9, PIC #7,130; "When you stopped your . . .": Ibid., pp. 9–10; "The most noted machinists . . .": "Successful Women Inventors," *Woman's Journal*, August 22, 1891, p. 268.

150–52 EVALUATION OF EVERSON: "it only required the . . .": Hoover, p. 5; "There is probably no . . .": Megraw, p. 5.

152–54 SEARCH FOR EVERSON: "pierce the veil of . . .": "Carrie Jane Billings Everson," *Engineering and Mining Journal*, January 15, 1916, p. 129; "little woman . . .": Ibid., p. 130; "quiet, self-sacrificing woman . . .": H. C. Parmelee, "Carrie Jane Everson and the Flotation Process," *Metallurgical and Chemical Engineering*, January 15, 1916, p. 69; "Mother of New Gold . . .": Arthur Chapman, "Mother of New Gold Treating Process Lost," *Denver Times*, November 12, 1915; "Denver nurse who, while . . .": Ibid.; "Dr. Everson and Not His Wife Found Ore Method," *Denver Times*, November 18, 1915; "She was a woman . . .": in "Carrie Jane Billings Everson," p. 130.

155 "[I]t appears possible that . . .": letter of M. E. Dayton, Chicago, March 1, 1886, to commissioner of patents and subsequent letter, in PAF.

155–56 EVERSON'S LATER YEARS: "So far, the experiments . . .": "Petroleum in Treating Ores," in "Mines and Mining," *Herald-Democrat*, quoted in [*Denver*] *Daily News*, Denver, November 2, 1889; "General Mining News: Oregon," *Engineering and Mining Journal*, November 15, 1890, p. 581; "Mrs. Everson Died As Court Sought Her Aid," *Denver Times*, November 29, 1915.

156–57 LATER COMMENTS ON EVERSON'S PROCESS: "in the position of . . .": Parmelee, p. 69; the flotation expert was T. H. Rickard; see his book, pp. 35–36; "amateur experiments . . . [of an] intelligent . . .": "The Everson Myth," *Mining and Scientific Press*, January 15, 1916, p. 78; "young Colorado school teacher": Ralph Keeler, "Colorado School Teacher Was First to Find Key to Flotation Process," *Rocky Mountain News*, December 17, 1933; "because it was an . . .": "Flotation Pioneer?" *Rocky Mountain News*, June 8, 1952.

157 DESCRIPTIONS OF MYERS: "as if it were . . .": *Berkshire Courier* of Great Barrington, n.d., cited in Mary Myers, *Aerial Adventures*, p. 103; "with no more concern . . .": cited without source, Ibid., p. 108; "Mlle. Carlotta may be . . .": *Daily Saratogan*, August 8, 1882, cited in Ibid., p. 66.

157–58 MYERS: "handsome and highly intellectual": Hardin and Willard, p. 504; "No more cheering place . . .": "NOTE THE CHANGE IN LOCATION" flyer from Frankfort, N.Y., May 20, 1889, CM. Descriptions of other events: David W. H. Pickard, "Carl Myers and His 'Sky Cycle,' " *The Airpost Journal,* November 1976, pp. 45–46; "A Balloon Lawn Party," *Aeronautics,* January 1894, p. 42. (the cover of this issue shows such a lawn party); "of a foot-passenger selecting . . .": Moffett, p. 101.

158 "The small, light balloon . . .": Carlotta Myers, "A Woman's Balloon Trip," *Air Scout,* April 1911, p. 23; "an abundance of health . . .": Myers, p. 5.

158–59 EXPERIMENTS: Myers, Ibid., p. 134; "rapturous sensations of floating . . .": Ibid., Preface, n.p.

159 MYERS, CURRENT ASSESSMENT: Interview with Claudia Oaks: March 27, 1989; Captain Roger Pineau, former director of the Navy Museum, however, omitted any mention of the pair in his important exhibition of ballooning, and says that since the Myerses were admittedly exhibition balloonists, they were entertainers rather than scientists; Interview with Roger Pineau, March 1, 1989.

159–60 EXHIBITIONS: "Queen of the Air": flyer from the Office of Prof. Carl Myers, Frankfort, N.Y., in CM; "prayers ascended with the . . .": "The Ever Glorious Fourth," [Little Falls, N.Y.] *Journal and Courier,* July 6, 1880, in CM; number of ascents: advertising flyers from Balloon Farm; "pretty as a picture . . .": *Berkshire Courier* of Great Barrington, n.d., cited in Myers, p. 103; "simple flannel dress of . . .": *Albany Argus,* n.d., in Myers, p. 79; "Ah me! How aeronautical . . .": Myers, p. 79; "neat-fitting gaiters": *Watertown Daily Times,* n.d., in Myers, pp. 56–57; "Even my nobby sailor . . .": Myers, p. 58.

160–62 STRONG: Background: Joe Da Road, "Harriet: a 'Strong' Woman," *Whittier Daily News,* September 27, 1984; "The pink and white . . .": Harriet Strong, "Thirty Years Ago" [an address at the beginning of her second year as president of Ebell Club in 1895], reprinted in *The Clubwoman,* November 1926, pp. 7, 8.

162–64 STRONG: "plushiest wagon ever to . . .": Marilyn Jensen, "A Legendary Lady: Harriet Strong," *California Highway Patrolman,* May 1987, p. 48; School record: report on Strong from Young Ladies' Seminary, Bernicia, Calif., 1858–60, HWRS, folder 852; All letters to her husband: "My husband is far . . .": Nebraska City, June 28, 1865; "Must I say goodbye . . .": Nebraska City, June 30, 1865; "You say not one . . .": Nebraska City, July 11, 1865, "You have told me . . .": Los Angeles, September 4, 1876, HWRS, folder 843. "I hope you will . . .": Charles to Harriet Strong, Galena, Nev., October 26, 1878, in Ibid., folder 647.

164 DEATH OF HUSBAND: "Please inform Mrs. C. . . .": Western Union telegram from John Painter Coe to Dr. Mitchell, April 11, 1883, HWRS, folder 21; "Everyone thinks Papa's brain . . .": Harriet R. Strong to her mother, Oakland, Calif., February 12, 1883, Ibid., folder 754.

165 INVENTIONS: "We send you by . . .": Sargent & Company, New Haven Manufactory, to Mrs. H. W. R. Strong, Oakland, Calif., September 22, 1884, HWRS, folder 35.

165–66 STRONG AT RANGE: "She did not turn . . .": Bertha H. Smith, "Harriet W. R. Strong: Walnut Grower," *Sunset*, April 1911, p. 413; crops: "The Work of One Woman," *Southern California Business*, November 1926, p. 26.

## 8: CELEBRATING WOMEN'S INGENUITY: EXPOSITIONS, FAIRS, AND PATENT OFFICE LISTS

PAGE

167 "not as [man's] rival . . .": "Inventive Faculty in Women," *Woman's Journal*, May 3, 1890, p. 138.

167–68 THE CENTENNIAL OF THE PATENT OFFICE: "Dear Sir . . . The Executive . . .": *Proceedings and Addresses Celebrating the Beginning of the Second Century*, p. 25; Press accounts: "The Patent Men," *Evening Star* [Washington, D.C.], April 9, 1891; fashion: "Some Notable Costumes," *Evening Star* [Washington, D.C.], April 9, 1891; *Post* coverage: "A Very Brilliant Scene: Reception to a Vast Gathering in the Rotunda of the Post Office Reception to Begin at Nine-thirty," *Washington Post*, April 9, 1891; "Many Men with Brains . . .": Ibid.; "the widow with four . . .": "Flying Machines Are Coming," Ibid., April 10, 1891.

168 "The man who . . .": Mason quoted in *Proceedings and Addresses*, p. 411.

169 "Women as Inventors: They Have Turned Their Bright Ideas into Actual Results," *Washington Post*, April 9, 1891.

171 CHARLOTTE SMITH: "Let us cheer on . . .": [Charlotte Smith], "A Word of Encouragement," *The Woman Inventor*, April 1890 [1891], p. 4; Smith at meeting: "Final Business Session," *Washington Post*, April 11, 1891.

171–72 SUPPORTERS: "staunch defender of woman" and other praise for supporters: *Woman Inventor*, vol. 1, no. 2, June 1891, p. 1; "surpass the scope of . . .": The Hon. John W. Daniel, "The New South As an Outgrowth of Invention and the American Patent Law," in *Proceedings and Addresses*, p. 131; "[T]o-day the women of . . .": *Woman Inventor*, vol. 1, no. 2, June 1891, p. 1; "The editor of *Woman* . . .": Ibid., p. 2.

172 "How many women's inventions . . .": [Charlotte Smith], "Women's Inventions," Ibid., April 1890 [1891], p. 1.

172 EGLIN: "You know I am . . .": Ibid., p. 3; Eglin's plans: "Many Men with

Brains: Inventors Gather to Celebrate the Patent Centennial," *Washington Post*, April 9, 1891.

172–73 PRESS RESPONSE: "We Took the Banquet," *Woman's Tribune*, n.d., cited in *Woman Inventor*, vol. 1, no. 2, June 1891, p. 2.

173–74 BROWN DRESS-CUTTING: "My patents were said . . .": "A Voice from the East," letter from Harriet O. Brown to Charlotte Smith, April 25, 1891, reprinted in Ibid., p. 3; Regarding the delay in getting a patent, letters exchanged between the patent examiner and Brown's attorneys in the Spring of 1888 indicate that the former needed to be assured about the newness of her system: PAF; "I have defeated them . . .": "A Voice from the East," in *Woman Inventor*, vol. 1, no. 2, p. 3.

175 "picked up the tangled . . .": Charlotte Smith captioned "Cheering Words from Our Admirers" to the April 23, 1891, letter she received from Mary E. Thomas, Thomas Battery Company, Cardington, Ohio, and reprinted in Ibid.

176 "I receive so many . . .": letter from Eliza A. Wood to Charlotte Smith, Easton, N.Y., May 5, 1891, reprinted in Ibid.

176 "partner who has money . . .": letter of Mrs. Emma Watrous of Homer, Cortland County, N.Y., to Editor Charlotte Smith, April 27, 1891, reprinted in Ibid.

176–77 "since reading your paper . . .": letter from Maria Littleton to Charlotte Smith, Sandusky, Ohio, April 26, 1891, reprinted in Ibid.

177 "Mrs. Smith personally knew . . .": "Charlotte Smith Dead at 75 Years," *Boston Post*, December 4, 1917.

177–78 CHICAGO FAIR: "In 1492 a woman . . .": *Boston Transcript*, reproduced without date in "World's Fair Notes," *Woman's Journal*, April 8, 1893, p. 209; "feminine ferocity": Griffith, p. 203; Congressional action: Badger, pp. 78–79; "I am truly grateful . . .": "A Woman at the Fair," *New York Daily Tribune*, June 16, 1893.

179 "personal artistic service": Louise Bethune, "Women and Architecture," *The Inland Architect and News Record*, March 1891, p. 20.

180 SMITH: "[l]arge and rather stout . . .": *Pittsburgh Union Leader*, March 18, 1892, cited in Weiman, p. 508; Yale affair: Ibid., pp. 510–11.

180 "Men are fickle and . . .": "Woman and Her Ways," *Chicago Times*, May 8, 1893.

180–81 LOCKWOOD: "the thorny path . . .": "Woman as an Inventor: Shall She Be Given a Representation at the Columbian Exposition?" *Inventive Age*, March 22, 1891, p. 6; Background: "Sketch of Mrs. Mary S. Lockwood," *Daughters of the American Revolution Magazine*, December 1922, pp. 710–11; Call to the DAR: *Washington Post*, July 13, 1890, cited in Ibid., p. 710; Lockwood sketched some of her background in a letter to Palmer cited in Weimann, p. 393; "bonnets, trimmings, dresses . . .":

F. T. Bickford letter, quoted by Mary Logan in letter to Bertha Palmer, August 10, 1891, cited in Weimann, p. 429; "visible sign of diligent . . .": Lockwood, in "Woman As an Inventor," March 22, 1891, p. 6.

181 INVENTIONS ROOM: King, p. 511; Ellen M. Henrotin, "An Outsider's View of the Woman's Exhibit," *Cosmopolitan,* September 1893, p. 562; "unusual and interesting lines . . .": Farmer, p. 492; "existing misconceptions . . .", Ibid, p. 493.

182 PRESS COMMENTS: "that gifted Cincinnati girl": "World's Fair Notes," *Woman's Journal,* July 29, 1893, p. 237; Cochran: "I wish that women . . .": "World's Fair Notes," *Woman's Journal,* September 9, 1893, p. 288; "so perfect in its . . .": "World's Fair Notes," *Woman's Journal,* July 29, 1893, p. 236.

183 TRACY: "A car falling through . . .": J. O. Woods, General Manager, "The Tracy Gravity Safety Elevator with Automatic Platforms," an advertising brochure distributed at the Chicago World's Fair (and probably elsewhere), Box 5, "Sewing," Warshaw Collection, Smithsonian Institution; "it seems presumptuous for . . .": cited without source in Weimann, *The Fair Women,* p. 431; Tracy trade card in Box 5, "Sewing," Warshaw Collection; "But wonders have not . . .": Justus O. Woods, General Manager, Tracy Sewing Machine Co., "The Tracy Lock-Stitch and Chain Stitch Sewing-Machine: A Triumph of Mechanical Genius," an advertising brochure in Ibid; Press coverage: "A Woman's Merited Honor," heading for three articles combined in a hand-out distributed at Chicago World's Fair, 1893 in Ibid.

184 CHILTON: "World's Fair Notes," *Woman's Journal,* September 9, 1893, p. 288.

184 ROMNEY: *Eagle,* vol. 2, p. 579.

184–85 STRONG: Canal project: *Water Power Hearings,* p. 786. Pampas sales: Harriet Russell Strong to Georgina Strong, Chicago, July 22, 1893, HWRS, folder 90.

185 "By crackey! not a . . .": Holley, pp. 251, 279, 286.

185 "the senate and house . . .": "One Woman's Utopian Dream," speech of Mrs. Ruth G. D. Havens of Washington, D.C., at opening of Woman's Building at the Chicago World's Fair, reported in *Chicago Times,* May 2, 1893.

186 "[I]f one possessed of . . .": Laura DeForce Gordon, "Woman's Sphere from a Woman's Standpoint," in *Eagle,* p. 75.

186 "vacant niche in the . . .": Willard and Livermore, vol. 1, Preface; "Queen Bee": Ibid., vol. 2, p. 716.

186 WOMAN AND INVENTION: "Women as Inventors," *New York Tribune,* August 8, 1898; Dr. Ellen A. Wallace, "Woman's Widening Field," *Success,* December 1897, p. 31.

187 MEAD: "a sorry task at . . .": letter of Leon Mead, N.Y., to commissioner of patents John Seymour, March 30, 1893, PCP, box 120; "bright and glorious": Leon Mead, "Women as Inventors," *Chautauquan*, January 1894, pp. 464–65.

187 ATLANTA WOMAN'S BUILDING: "filled with the wonders . . .": remarks of the president of the exposition at the laying of the cornerstone, April 22, 1895, in Cooper, p. 54; "I have no doubt . . .": Clark Howell on behalf of the Masonic Order at the laying of the cornerstone, April 22, 1895, in Cooper, p. 54. Another excellent source is: Kent A. Leslie, *The Woman's Building at the Cotton States and International Exposition (1895): A Cultural Construct*, unpublished manuscript, December 6, 1982, Appendix, table 2; original is in the Atlanta Historical Society.

187–88 ATLANTA WOMEN: "singularly blessed with . . .": Cooper, p. 50; "I'm tired of being . . .": "What Women Are Doing for the Exposition," *Atlanta Constitution*, March 31, 1895; Grant: *The Atlanta Exposition and South Illustrated*, p. 177; Senate Pass to the Reserved Gallery, John Marshall Slayton Papers; "a charming picture with . . .": "Big Day for Dames," *Atlanta Constitution*, October 21, 1895.

188–89 CENTENNIAL EXHIBITORS: Ella Haller's fruit jar, Mary Carpenter's feeding mechanism for a sewing machine and a sewing machine, Hannah Suplee's sewing machine, sisters Mary Jackson's and Sarah Ball's self-heating smoothing iron, Mary Potts's sad-iron, Henrietta Cole's fluting machine, Mary Blauvelt's dressmaker's marking and cutting gauge, and Ellen Fitz's globe. The model for Mary Whitner's stereoscope, advertised but not displayed in Philadelphia, was also in Atlanta. Source: State of Georgia Archives.

189 "gladly and proudly welcome . . .": letter from Mrs. William A. Grant, chairman, Committee, Patents and Inventions, to "Dear Madam": Atlanta, July 11, 1895, John Marshall Slayton Papers; Miller's address label, dated September 10, 1895, in Ibid.

189 THEME SETTINGS: "Some of the Inventions of Women," *Atlanta Constitution*, August 31, 1895.

190 "semi-contemptuous reference": "A Delayed Recognition," in "New Ideas for Women," *New Ideas*, March 1897, p. 310.

190 "woman's attention is devoted . . .": "Women as Inventors," *Portland Oregonian*, n.d., cited in *New York Daily Tribune*, September 8, 1895, p. 25.

190 Material on women's committee: Correspondence from Mrs. S. G. Ratterman to Major J. W. Thomas, President, Tennessee Centennial Exposition, Nashville, February 26, 1897, in TCEP, box 5 f 4, "invaded and mastered this . . .": *Catalogue of the Tennessee Centennial Exposition*, n.p., from material supplied the author from the Nashville Room of

Nashville Public Library; "an integral part of . . .": "In Woman's Building," *Nashville American*, May 4, 1897. Though the *Nashville American* proudly pointed out that the 137 models from the Patent Office were not shown at Chicago, most had probably been exhibited in Atlanta and were shipped on to Nashville: "Women Had the Floor," *Nashville American*, May 4, 1897.

190 "the freemasonry among women": source was the speech dedicating the Woman's Building, but I don't have a full quotation.

## 9: STILL A LONG WAY TO GO

PAGE

191 "domestic shrine": Mrs. Effie Pitblado, "Not Things But Women," in *Eagle*, p. 794.

191 "this vicious dogma . . .": quoted from Ward's *Dynamic Sociology*, in "Lester F. Ward," *Woman Voter and Newsletter*, June 1913, p. 19.

192 WOMEN AND HOUSEHOLD INVENTION: "A woman knows intuitively . . .": "Women as Inventors," *New York Tribune*, August 8, 1898; "[W]ho knows better than . . .": George Ethelbert Walsh, "Women Inventors," *Patent Record*, March 1899, p. 9; "[f]rom [a woman's] practical . . .": "Glass Oven Doors," *New Ideas*, November 1896, p. 246; "Why should [women] not . . .": A Woman Cleans Chicago Streets," *Success*, January 1898, p. 64.

192 WOMEN'S HIGHER EDUCATION: "as something in the nature . . .": Mrs. Joseph Cook, "The Improvement in Girls," *Success*, November 1900, p. 469; "scarcely compatible with the . . .": Penny, *How Women Can Make Money*, p. 17; "the tramp of progress . . .: "Woman's Education," *Success*, August 1898, p. 16.

193 NORTHFIELD SEMINARY: Emily Huntington, "Domestic Training for Girls," *Harper's Bazaar*, February 15, 1890, p. 125; "But what of women? . . .": Ibid., p. 124.

193 INVENTION SCHOOLS: Hon. W. H. Ruffner, in *Va. Ed. Journal*, cited in "Schools of Invention," *Industrial News*, March 1881, p. 52, and referred to in "Women to the Front," *Success*, May 27, 1899, p. 442.

193 HOUSEKEEPING IN COLLEGES: Ainsley Crawley, "The Social Side of Women's Colleges," *Jenness-Miller Monthly*, October 1895, p. 10; "from the thraldom of . . .": "College Notes," *Godey's Magazine*, September 1896, p. 334.

193–94 "The education of females . . .": Emma Willard, "A Plan for Improving Female Education, an address to the public, particularly to the members of the Legislature of New York," quoted in Brackett, *Technique of Rest*, p. 15.

196 CLEANSING AGENTS: Balderston, p. 8. Although this list appeared in 1900, many references to these same reagents appeared in earlier books.

196 "clear headed and sensible": obituary notices supplied by the Willard Library of Battle Creek, Mich. Margaret Colvin died on August 1, 1894.

196 POTTS'S IRONS: "labor-saving machine": Johnson, Introduction; "a convenient article for . . .": Ibid., advertisement, n.p.; "the most popular and . . .": "Two Old Time Ottumwa Inventors," [Ottumwa] Saturday Herald, May 27, 1899.

197 "cramped by untoward circumstances": Wheeler, Yesterdays, p. 210.

197–98 WHEELER VS. TILLINGHAST: Tillinghast testimony, PIC #8,252, n.p.; "acquired her special . . .": preliminary statement of Wheeler in Ibid.; "The inventions sought to . . .": in "Dissolution of Interference," May 13, 1882, in Ibid.

198 "natural field": "Interior Decoration as a Profession for Women," Outlook, 1895, cited by Stern, 301; "We added interior decoration . . .": Wheeler quoted in Ibid., p. 293.

198 TILLINGHAST AND STAINED GLASS: Gibbes, pp. 470–71.

200 DRESS: Elizabeth Stuart Phelps, "The Decollete in Modern Life," Forum, August 1890, p. 677; Annie Jenness Miller: "[n]o man of equal . . .": advertisement for lecture for 1890 in the Advertising Department of Jenness-Miller Magazine, February 1890, p. 1; "right to the ballot-box . . .": Annie Myers, Home Dressmaking, p. 180.

200–202 DRESS REFORM AT CHICAGO: "No one is asked . . .": "The Rational Dress Movement: A Symposium," Arena, October 1894, p. 307; other comments cited by Miss Iris B. Martin, "The Bondage of Custom," in Ibid., p. 306; "just like people who . . .": "Dress Her Theme," Chicago Times, May 17, 1893; "The Queen of Spain . . .": Mrs. Celia B. Whitehead in "Eight Months of Experiences in the Syrian Costume," in Arena, October 1894, pp. 325–26.

202 GROWTH OF BICYCLE INDUSTRY: United States Patent Office, Annual Report of the Commissioner, 1897, p. xix; "due to the enormous . . .": Ibid., p. xiii; "gives them a kind . . .": "The Bicycle as Life-Giver," Success, June 1898, p. 33.

203 SITTIG: "She cannot get them . . .": letter from Sittig attorney, September 26, 1894, in PAF; Sittig rainwear: "Mrs. Sittig's Novelty," The Brooklyn Eagle, July 3, 1892; "miraculous waterproof" appears in "Some of the Inventions of Women," Atlanta Constitution, August 31, 1895, p. 7; Sittig suit: "A New Bicycle Skirt," Brooklyn Times, February 22, 1895; "as gracefully and modestly . . .": "The Cycle Club's Reception," Brooklyn Eagle, February 24, 1895.

203–7 WOMEN'S BICYCLE INVENTIONS: "Combination Cycling and Walking Skirt," New Ideas, November 1896, p. 246; "eminently proper": "Lady Patentees," *New Ideas,* May 1897, p. 342; Henderson also invented "A Woman's Tricycle," *New Ideas,* September 1895, p. 70; "The curs require one . . .": "Women's Patents," *New Ideas,* August 1899, p. 783.

207–8 WESTOVER: "first wheelbarrow to collect . . .": "Mrs. Alden Dead; A Social Worker," *New York Times,* January 9, 1931; "on speaking terms with . . .": Willard and Livermore, vol. 2, p. 761; Electric railways: *Annual Report of the Commissioner of Patents for 1897,* p. xviii; Public interest in invention: letter from Westover's lawyer to commissioner of patents, [1891], in PAF; "cart to dump as . . .": *Womanlist,* Weiser and Arbeiter, pp. 104–5.

208 WESTOVER PUBLICATIONS: Nickname: "Cowboys and Indians Liked Her," *Success,* July 8, 1899, p. 541; "habit of self-dependence, the . . .": Alden, *Bushy: A Romance Founded on Fact,* Introduction, n.p.; Press notices: Alden, *Manhattan: Historic and Artistic,* n.p.; In an earlier issue of the book, co-authored with Carolyn Faville Ober in 1892 and published by Lovell, Coryell & Co. of New York, her father's company advertised: "Westover & Son. Collectors of Mineral and Geological specimens and dealers in shells, corals, and Mosses from the Pacific coast—orders promptly filled. Santa Monica, Los Angeles County"; Press notices appear on inside covers of various of her Bushy books.

208–10 WESTOVER LATER CAREER: "essentially womanly . . . very handsome . . .": in "Cowboys and Indians Liked Her," *Success,* July 8, 1899, p. 541; Wedding: "Newspaper Workers Married," *New York Times,* August 17, 1896; Other material in Cameron, *Biographical Cyclopaedia of American Women,* vol. 1, p. 378; "Early Days in New York," *New York Times,* May 2, 1896; "progressive womankind": "New Field for Women," *New York Tribune,* March 26, 1900; "It is my firm . . .": Alden, *Women's Ways of Earning Money,* p. 166; "Though I often had . . .": Ibid., preface, p. 23; "breezy, confident, and reassuring": Margaret E. Sangster, editor's introduction to Ibid., p. 9; "cooking for sixteen farm . . .": Ibid., p. 17.

210 WESTOVER BROOKLYN YEARS: "Mrs. Alden Dead; A Social Worker," *New York Times,* January 9, 1931; Blind babies: "willfully altered": "Littleton Defends Sunshine Society," Ibid., July 31, 1914; "Books Found Wrong in Sunshine Society," Ibid., November 8, 1913; "I do not care . . .": "Littleton Defends Sunshine Society," Ibid., July 31, 1914.

211 "when careers for women . . .": "Mrs. John Alden, Friend of Blind Babies, Dies at 70," *Brooklyn Daily Eagle,* January 8, 1931.

211 CHARLOTTE SMITH: "extravagantly grotesque": "Charlotte Smith's Ideas," *New York Times,* July 26, 1897; Exhibition: letter from Charlotte Smith, Arlington, Va., to Commissioner of Patents Charles H. Duell, October 18, 1898, PCP, box 124; Other materials from Smith in this box are: *Memorial of the Woman's Industrial League of America,* [October 1898] and

*An Appeal to the Roman Catholic Church, and to the Bishops of the Protestant Episcopal Church of the United States in Convention Assembled,* October 1898.

211–13 BOWLES: "striking evidence of the . . .": Stanton, Anthony and Joslyn, vol. 3, p. 194; Description of Bowles's first lecture to Fortnightly: "Women as Inventors," *Woman's Journal,* March 18, 1899, p. 88; "You women may talk . . .": Ibid., and repeated in "Women Inventors," *Scientific American,* August 19, 1899, p. 123, and *New York Tribune,* June 19, 1899, p. 5; "great amount of ignorance . . .": "Women as Inventors," *New York Tribune,* June 18, 1899, part II, p. 6; George Ethelbert Walsh, "Women Inventors," *The Patent Record,* March 1899, p. 9.

213 "less adapted to the . . .": G. T. W. Patrick, "The Psychology of Woman," *Popular Science Monthly,* October 1898, pp. 215–16.

214 CHILDREN: "When a little girl . . .": Jean Arnold, "Science for Women," *Woman's Journal,* June 10, 1876, p. 186; "When we see a . . .": Willard, *Occupations,* p. 5.


## 10: PATENTING KNOW-HOW

PAGE

216 "Cannot some of our . . .": "An Invention Wanted," *Woman's Journal,* January 18, 1890, p. 18.

216 "The more intimate a . . .": George Ethelbert Walsh, "Women Inventors," *Patent Record,* March 1899, p. 9.

216–17 VICTOR EVANS AND COMPANY: "Have You Ever Made . . . An Invention?": *Patent Record,* May 1899, p. 3; Guaranteeing a patent: see advertisement in Ibid., December 1899, p. 26.

217–19 "NEW IDEAS FOR LADIES" COLUMN: *New Ideas,* February 1896, p. 100; "The statement that women . . .": "Attachment for Chairs," Ibid., February 1896, p. 100; "[w]e feel justified in . . .": Ibid.; "the latter knew how . . .": Ibid., September 1896, p. 216.

219–20 PATENT AGENTS: "liberal, honest, and strongly . . .": "$2,500,000 Made by One of O'Meara & Co.'s Clients," *New Ideas,* May 1897, p. 339; "Counselors-at-Law and Attorneys for . . .": *Inventor's Circular.* C. B. Steele & Co: Washington, D.C., 1871.

220–21 APPEAL TO WOMEN CLIENTS: "Inventress": James Layman provided this identification for both fire escape patents of Barbara Fox from Napoleon, Ind., and for Cincinnatian Louise Fein's "self-acting" brakes to slow the descent of her fire-escape platform; he may have done so for others. "The lady readers of . . .": "Comments on Foreign Topics," *Industrial Review,* April 1883, p. 105; "[o]ther women brain workers . . .": "Clever Women Inventors," *Patent Record,* December 1899, p. 26; "courtesies extended to us . . .": *Woman Inventor,* March 1890 [1], p. 3; "the door of invention . . .": J. A. Minturn, "Women as Inventors," *Inventive Age,* December 1893, p. 5.

221–22 MAGAZINE STATISTICS: Bok cited in "Woman's Column," February 4, 1890, p. 4.

222 *"Patents:* Thomas P. Simpson . . .": *Domestic Monthly,* February 1893, p. 28. No address was given; perhaps one could write the editor.

222–23 CALLMEYER: Background on Smith: James W. Gandy, Bridgeton, N.J., to Anne Macdonald, January 21, 1990; "would make a pretty . . .": letter from Oberlin Smith, Bridgeton, N.J., to Leonie P. Callmeyer, Madison, N.J., May 10, [1893], Oberlin Smith Letter Copies, 1892–1904; "In general, if you . . .": letter from Oberlin Smith, Bridgeton, N.J., to Leonie P. Callmeyer, Madison, N.J., May 10, [1891], Ibid.; "Dame Nature is very. . . .": Ibid.

223 "[o]ne or two women . . .": George Ethelbert Walsh, "Women Inventors," *Patent Record,* March 1899, p. 9.

223–24 GRISWOLD: "tall and well formed": "A Woman Patent Solicitor," *Success,* March 4, 1899, p. 245; all further quotations from Ibid.; Background material: "Miss Griswold, the Only Woman Patent Lawyer," *The Patent Record,* November 1899, p. 8; Willard, *Occupations,* p. 453; Margaret Ingels, "Petticoats and Slide Rules," *Midwest Engineer,* no. 5, 1952, p. 2.

224–25 ELLSWORTH: "verily believes herself to . . .": altered oath is in Ellsworth file in PAF; Letter from Examiner Purvis, United States Patent Office, July 10, 1900, to Clara B. Ellsworth in Ibid.; "if there is any . . .": letter from Senator J. B. Foraker to Commissioner of Patents Duell, January 14, 1901, PCP, box 119.

225 RENCHER: "exceedingly informal": "Examiner's Report in the Matter of the Application of DORA RENCHER, for patent for Dress Cutter," n.d., PCP, box 120.

225 MURPHY: "I am poor, through . . .": letter from Lulu N. Murphy, Gold Hill, Nev., to Mrs. Theodore Roosevelt, May 5, 1904, Ibid., box 126; Cover notations of May 24, 1904, on outside of Murphy's letter, Ibid., box 127.

226 "do whatever [he] can . . .": George Gunton, N.Y., to Patent Commissioner Duell, September [9?], 1898, Ibid., box 119.

226 "very much discouraged since . . .": letter from Edward Winslow Geer, N.Y., to Commissioner of Patents Charles H. Duell, January 23, 1899, Ibid.

226 "Send me your . . .": letter of Robert Gow of Washington, D.C., February 5, 1897, Ibid.

226 "seems never to give . . .": letter of Mrs. Roxsey V. Hicks, 4644 Gangwish

Street, Pittsburgh, Penn., to Patent Commissioner Duell, June 30, 1899, Ibid., box 120.

227 "[h]is 'carryings on' have . . .": letter of Katie V. Miller of Lewisburg, Ohio, to John E. Higdon of Higdon and Higdon, April 18, 1892, Ibid., box 121.

227 "must be absent-minded, as . . .": letter of Cleus T. DeForest, N.Y., to Patent Commissioner Mitchell, August 9, 1890, Ibid., box 119.

227 "on the good side . . .": letter from Mrs. A. Young, Erie, Penn., to Patent Commissioner M. V. Montgomery, September 11, 1885, Ibid., box 125.

227–28 HOLMES: "secure competent assistance": letter of Examiner [Williams?], United States Patent Office, December 2, 1881, to Josephine Holmes, in PAF; "My brothers of age . . .": letter from Holmes, Philadelphia, December 12, 1881, to Commissioner of Patents in Ibid.; "All my money being . . .": letter from Holmes, Philadelphia, March 29, 1882, to "Sir" [probably Commissioner of Patents] in Ibid.; "The language of the . . .": Examiner [Williams?], United States Patent Office, April 6, 1882, to Holmes in Ibid.; "extensive acquaintance with the . . .": letter of Holmes, Philadelphia, September 30, 1882, to Commissioner of Patents, Ibid.; "If you will pardon . . .": letter from Holmes, Philadelphia, April 6, 1883, to Commissioner of Patents, Ibid.; Advice to get legal help: Whittaker and Barbur, United States Patent Office, April 16, 1883, to Holmes, Ibid.; "I have to state . . .": letter of Holmes, Philadelphia, April 23, 1883, to Commissioner of Patents, Ibid.

229 HOLMES AND THE COMMISSIONER: "where that would be . . .": letter of Holmes, Philadelphia, July 5, 1883, to Commissioner of Patents Marble, PCP, box 121; "The case as originally . . .": letter from Chief Examiner, U.S. Patent Office to E. M. Marble, Commissioner of Patents, August [n.d.], 1883, Ibid.

229–30 MERGENTHALER: Letter of Marie Merganthaler, Albany, N.Y., to Commissioner of Patents Duell, April 17, 1900, Ibid., box 120; "If you only knew . . .": letter of Marie Merganthaler, Albany, N.Y., to Commissioner of Patents Duell, April 17, 1900, Ibid.; "new combination never before . . .": letter of Marie Merganthaler, Albany, N.Y., to Commissioner of Patents Duell, February 16, 1901, Ibid.; "I beg of your . . .": letter of Marie Merganthaler, Albany, N.Y., to Commissioner of Patents Duell, February 16, 1901, Ibid.

231 "A woman thoroughly educated . . .": from an untitled and undated newspaper article [c. 1872] in the scrapbook of Ellen Demorest's sister, Anna Mary Curtis Morris, 1861–1889, Schlesinger Library, ALM 875.

231–32 WOMEN IN BUSINESS: "only legitimate business of . . .": "Superfluous Women," lecture quoted in Livermore, The Story of My Life, p. 493; "It is preposterous for . . .": Ibid., p. 486; "weakness that looks for . . .": Sarah

Bridges Stebbins, "Women in Business," *Demorest's Monthly Magazine,* September 1876, p. 455; "too sacred to be . . .": G. T. W. Patrick, "The Psychology of Woman," *Popular Science Monthly,* October 1898, pp. 224–25; "It should be as . . .": Wheeler, *Yesterdays,* p. 421; "I'd train every girl . . .": Strong quoted by Lavinia Griffin Graham, "Advocates Schools for Women Farmers," *Los Angeles Examiner,* [c.1920s?] (original undated in HWRS, folder 854).

232 KNIGHT: Shoe industry: Abbott, p. 148; Knight's patent transactions can be traced in DoA, vol. K8, pp. 80, 208, 243, 257; vol. K9, pp. 28, 29.

233 WHITNEY: Background in Willard and Livermore, vol. 2, p. 768; "[I]t is there, to . . .": Whitney quoted in Ida M. Tarbell, "Women as Inventors," *Chautauquan,* March 1877, p. 357.

234 WILLARD: "an honorable bread-winning weapon . . .": Willard, *Occupations,* p. 11; "women have more fine . . .": Ibid., p. 353; "If one finds it . . .": Ibid., p. 80; "if genius is eternal . . .": Ibid., p. 353; "There is always room . . .": Ibid.; "persevering little woman": Ibid., p. 163.

235 ADVERTISEMENTS: "Improved rolling pin is . . .": "New Patents for Sale," *Inventive Age,* April 21, 1891, p. 6; "my improved Flower Pot," "Novelty Manufactures Take Notice," Ibid.; "Securely retains the flowers . . .": "Novelty Manufactures Take Notice," Ibid., June 30, 1891, p. 5; "Can be cheaply constructed . . .": "New Patents for Sale," Ibid.; "which gives to the . . .": Ibid., April 21, 1891, p. 6. I have been unable to find a patent for such a waist. It may possibly have been previously patented under her maiden name.

236–38 SELLING PATENT RIGHTS: Mary Schneider: DoA, vol. S-20, p. 232; Sarah Shields: Ibid., p. 219; Lizzie Howard: Ibid., vol. H-10, p. 162; Lucretia Hermann, Ibid., vol. H-14, p. 188; Tracy: Ibid., vol. T-5, p. 75 (other examples of Tracy contracts are in Ibid., vol. T-5, pp. 75, 231, 253; and vol. T-9, pp. 45, 46, 49); Martha Kellogg: Ibid., vol. K-10, p. 138; Hunt: Ibid., vol. H-9, p. 216; Harley: ToP, liber vol. Y-21, p. 66; "use all means to . . .": Hackelberg, ToP, liber vol. R-23, pp. 341–42; Elizabeth Hood: DoA, vol. H-16, pp. 26, 229; vol. H-17, pp. 146, 188, 238, 288; Mabee: Ibid., vol. M-18, pp. 220, 256, 289; Eliza Harding: Ibid., vol. H-9, pp, 212, 231; Lydia Bonney: DoA, vol. B-9, p. 32; Emily Gross: ToP, liber vol. F-23, p. 279; Blauvelt: PAD, vol. B-9, p. 138; Knox: DoA, vol. K-2: pp. 229, 237; vol. K-3: pp. 159, 170, 250, 251; vol. K-5: p. 13; vol. K-8, p. 56; Minnie Kelch: Ibid., vol. K-5, p. 90.

238 ERICKSON-DAVIS CASE (All material in PIC #19,138): "If you can make . . .": testimony of Pauline Erickson, August 27, 1897, p. 9; "no reason under the . . ." and other testimony: in *Brief of Annie Davis* p. 8; "crafty, designing spirit . . .": *Brief of Pauline Erickson,* p. 2; "I saw her knitting . . .": Erickson record, pp. 31–40.

## 11: "NEW WOMEN" IN A NEW CENTURY

PAGE

240–41 WOMEN'S CLUBS: Statistics: Mott, vol. 4, p. 356; *Scribner's Magazine*, the series in 1897–98; "I believe that it . . .": Grover Cleveland, "Woman's Mission and Woman's Clubs," *The Ladies' Home Journal*, May 1905, pp. 3–4; "We have tipped the . . .": cited in Ross, p. 51; "Women are simply learning . . .": Ada S. Bowles, "Cleveland on Women's Clubs," *Woman's Journal*, May 13, 1905, p. 74.

241 "held aloft for a . . .": "Fifty Years a Journalist," *Success*, April 1900, p. 136.

242 "Ladies, you have chosen . . .": Rhetta Childe Dorr, *A Woman of Fifty*, New York: Funk and Wagnalls, 1924, p. 119, cited in Hymowitz and Weissman, p. 220.

242 REASONS FOR NOT PATENTING: Katharine Dooris Sharp, "The Woman and the Inventor," *Woman's Journal*, November 25, 1905, p. 189.

242 "We have just said . . .": Lena Keith Marsh on "Culture and Art," in Turner, p. 12; "We may never be . . .": Ibid., p. 17.

242 "Someone, Shakespeare, I believe . . .": letter from Judge Charles [?] Townsend, New Haven, to H. H. Seamans, Clerk to the Patent Commissioner, January 7, 1900, PCP, box 124.

242 NUMERICAL ERROR: "It is fair to . . .": *Annual Report of the Commissioner of Patents, 1900*, p. xi; Joseph Rossman, "Women Inventors," *Journal of the Patent Office Society*, September 1927, p. 21.

243 "A time-honored fallacy . . .": "Women Inventors," *Woman's Journal*, November 28, 1903, p. 382.

243–44 WOMEN'S BRAINS: "fertile brain of American . . .": James Johnson, "Women Inventors and Discoverers," *Cassier's*, October 1909, p. 548; "What woman's brain lacks . . .": Lillian G. Towslee, M.D., "Why Women Should Practice Medicine," in Lena Keith Marsh on "Culture and Art," in Turner, pp. 146–47; "she were equal to . . .": Sherwood, p. 41; "With some women brain . . .": Ibid., p. 75; Barbara A. Welter, in her essay on Mary Elizabeth Wilson Sherwood in *Notable American Women*, notes that the biographer of her grandson, playwright Robert E. Sherwood, judged that his grandmother "had a strong mind weakly used": vol. 3, p. 285; "A strong will, an . . .": Towslee, in Turner, p. 147.

244 "difficulties that have baffled . . .": Hewitt, p. 443.

244–45 FIGURES ON WOMEN INVENTORS: "daily toilers in the . . .": quoted from a December 1899 *Patent Record* article, in "Women as Inventors," *Literary Digest*, January 6, 1900, p. 7; Olive F. Gunby, "Women Inventors," in *New Pork Post*, reprinted in *Scientific American Supplement*, no. 1325, May 25, 1901, p. 21242; "The world now realizes . . .": "Women as Inventors," *Patent Record*, May 1900, p. 8.

245 LEGAL RIGHTS: "The Legal Status of Women," published by the Suffrage Association [unnamed], 1897, cited by Katharine Crawford "Legislation and Woman," *New Idea Woman's Magazine*, March 1903, p. 39.

245–46 PARPART: "[r]emarkable piece of machinery . . . now . . .": "A Woman's Remarkable Invention," *Patent Record*, September 1900, p. 8; Other material on Parpart appears in a separate article on the same page: "A Woman's Great Work."

246–47 SMITH: "The Woman's Exposition," *Patent Record and Monthly Review*, February 1902, p. 29; Activities in Boston: "Dogs at $100, Babies at $2.00," *New York Times*, April 11, 1911; "of good character and . . .": *Woman's Board of Trade Report*, 1908, p. 3; "genius and intelligence": Ibid., p. 11; Lavinia Foy: Edward P. Thompson, "Women as Inventors," *Inventive Age*, September 1894, p. 177; "but an infant in . . .": *Woman's Board of Trade Report*, p. 5.

247–48 SAINT NICHOLAS: " 'Yankee invention' is a . . .": Jennie Day Haines, "The Wonderful Century," *Saint Nicholas*, February 1901, p. 339; "faithful servent . . .": Charles F. Benjamin, "How the Government Promotes Ingenuity," Ibid., May 1901, p. 616; "Some of the bright . . .": Ibid., p. 618.

248 ENCOURAGEMENT TO PATENT DOMESTIC ITEMS: "all the happiness out . . .": "A Fine Field for Women Inventors," *Patent Record and Monthly Review*, February 1900, p. 11; "Few inventions are more . . .": "Inventions Wanted," Ibid., March 1902, p. 11; "fine field for inventors": Ibid., February 1900, p. 11; "There is no monopoly . . .": "Lost Chances," Ibid., May 1900, p. 8; "A woman should certainly . . .": "A Woman's Invention," *New Ideas*, June 1900, p. 19.

248–49 BOSTON COMPETITION: "Prize Offered to Women Inventors," *Woman's Journal*, September 20, 1902, p. 300; "Doubtless any of them . . .": "Women Inventors," Ibid., January 17, 1903, p. 400; "Another Woman's Invention," February 21, 1903, p. 58.

249 "We keep multiplying our . . .": Brackett, *The Technique of Rest*, pp. 43–44.

249–50 ANDERSON: "oh, so impractical": Blanche McKeown, "She Invented the Windshield Wiper," *The* [Birmingham] *Record*, January 1956, p. 11; Lack of interest in invention: letter from Dinning & Eckenstein, Montreal, to Mary Anderson, June 20, 1905, courtesy of Birmingham Public Library; General background on Anderson: Clarke Stallworth, "Southern Belle Invented Wiper for Windshield," *Birmingham News*, February 20, 1977, and Lynn Reeves, "Concern Gave Boon to Drivers," n.d., n.p., clippings courtesy of Birmingham Public Library; "the first patented windshield . . .": "Died: Mary Anderson," *Time*, July 6, 1953, p. 72; "original fan-shaped windshield wiper": "Miss Mary Anderson," *New York Times*, June 30, 1953.

250 "All products of feminine . . .": "Interesting Notes for Women," *Oakland Tribune*, December 4, 1904.

250–51 SAINT LOUIS FAIR: "the so-called strictly . . .": Mrs. Richard P. Bland in LPEC, p. 450; "I almost feel that . . .": Edith J. Griswold in Ibid., pp. 497–98; "In all our fairy . . .": Mrs. M. G. Scrutchin in Ibid., p. 501; Sewing machines: Mrs. F. K. Bowes in Ibid., p. 465; "[Women's] strength and powers . . .": Ibid., p. 522.

251–52 AERIAL MYERS: "perfect compound of the . . .": Hardin and Willard, p. 506; Croll, passim.

252–53 HEATON: "Yes, it was Mrs. . . .": *Berkeley* [California] *Gazette*, [n.d.], reprinted in *Woman's Journal*, December 31, 1904; "like a flash": "Bites Gas Bag and Is Saved," *Los Angeles Times*, February 19, 1904; "Heaton's Airship Soars Over Oakland: Successful Flight Is Made by 'California Messenger,' " *San Francisco Examiner*, December 5, 1904; "Airship Proves a Success," *Oakland Tribune*, December 6, 1904.

253–54 FLIGHTS IN THE *MESSENGER*: "about as far up . . .": "Heaton's Airship Soars Over Oakland: Successful Flight Is Made by 'California Messenger,' " *San Francisco Examiner*, December 5, 1904; *San Jose Mercury* articles: "California Messenger, Heaton at Agricultural Park," July 2, 1905, p. 4, col. 3; "Baseball and Airship Today," July 2, 1905, p. 12, cols. 3–4; "Inaugural Celebration," July 3, 1905, p. 2., cols. 3–4; "I knew also that . . .": "Airship 'Messenger' Drops into Bay: Heaton Ascends to Height of 500 Feet," *San Francisco Examiner*, February 13, 1905; Enos Brown, "The Heaton Airship Failure," *Scientific American*, February 25, 1905, p. 159.

254–55 KNIGHT: "heralded all over the . . .": "She Was Notable Woman," *Framingham* [Mass.] *Evening News*, October 13, 1914; Evaluation of estate and effects of Margaret E. Knight, Probate Court for Middlesex County, Commonwealth of Massachusetts, April 20, 1915, provided by Paul J. Cavanaugh, Register of Probate Court, East Cambridge, Mass.; "Imagine my surprise . . .": "She Was Notable Woman," *Framingham* [Mass.] *Evening News*, October 13, 1914; Evaluations of Knight: Robert W. Lovett, "Knight, Margaret E.," in *Notable American Women: 1607–1950*, vol. 1, p. 340; Ogilvie, p. 111.

255 "faculties are sharpened and . . .": Marden, vol. 7, p. 377.

256 "There is no woman . . .": Willard and Livermore, vol. 2, p. 471; "That queer turn for . . .": Logan, p. 883.

256 NEW IDEAS: "with curling tongs and . . .": "Female Mind Keen Upon 'Notions,' " *New Ideas*, August 1899, p. 778; "[S]he was the sort . . .": "Lid for Stewpans," *New Ideas*, June 1912, p. 8.

256–57 ZAHM/[MOZANS] ON WOMEN'S PATENTS: Zahm [Mozans], p. 346; "at first blush would . . .": Ibid., p. 351; "improvement in locomotive wheels . . .": Ibid., pp. 345–56; "Depreciated sex": Ibid., p. 348; "bid fair to rival . . .": Ibid., p. 346.

257 "Climbing a ladder is . . .": Ethel M. Charles, "A Plea for Women Practising Architecture," *American Architect and Building News,* April 19, 1902, p. 21.

259–60 KEICHLINE: Background: Martha E. Rich, secretary of the class of 1911 in the *Cornell Alumni News,* [1943]; Keichline's grand-niece, Nancy Perkins, has supplied the following materials: "May Devote Life to Industrial Art," *Philadelphia Inquirer,* October [19], 1903; "At college we worked . . .": Keichline quoted in Eleanor Morton, "More About the Advantages of Having a Woman as Architect for the Home," n.d., "Imagine a carpenter . . .": "Anna Keichline Dies at Home," *Central Valley Times,* February 5, 1943.

260–61 KEICHLINE INVENTIONS: Brick: Anna W. Keichline, "A Tile Designed to Effect a Scientifically Built Wall," *Bulletin of the American Ceramic Society,* September 1931, passim, pp. 287–292; Other material is from the patents.

262 NADEAU: "Combination Chair and Cradle," *The Patent Record and Monthly Review,* September 1902, p. 17.

262 "It requires no eye . . .": Tarbell, *The Ways of Woman,* p. 5.

262–63 "The busy little workers . . .": W. L. Hutchinson, in *Home Magazine,* cited without date or page in Willard, *Occupations,* p. 108.

263 "considerable sums of the . . .": Sarah E. Slater, "Profitable Industries for Women: The Apiary." *New Idea Woman's Magazine,* October 1903, p. 34.

266 LAUNDRY: "the one great privilege . . .": Vail, p. 7; "better, broader things of . . .": Balderston, p. 140; Equipment list: Ibid., p. 133.

268 "ultra advocate of a . . .": Alice Stone Blackwell, "Genius and Suffrage," *Woman's Journal,* August 16, 1913, p. 260 (in another article on the same page, Blackwell rebutted the arguments of a Professor Starr of Chicago [not further identified] that "no woman has ever invented anything of value" by citing Bowles's talk before Boston's Fortnightly club: "Women as Inventors," Ibid.); Edison quoted in Willard, *Occupations,* p. 353.

## 12: HOPE SPRINGS ETERNAL

PAGE

269 "the effect of the mind . . .": Gilbreth, *The Psychology of Management,* p. 1.

269–70 GOOD HOUSEKEEPING: Paul Holzman, "Celebrating 80 Years of the Good Housekeeping Seal," *Good Housekeeping,* February 1990, pp. 76–77; "Harvey W. Wiley, Pioneer Consumer Activist," Ibid., pp. 145–46; "toward the higher life . . .": Paul Holzman, "Ninety Years of the Good Housekeeping Institute," Ibid., p. 72. The institute, now with a staff of seventy, continues to evaluate products.

270–71 HICKS: Her package was in the "Let Her Works Praise Her" exhibition of women's inventions at the Goldstein Gallery in Saint Paul in 1989.

271 "If her flesh is . . .": Helen Berkeley-Loyd, "You and Your Corset-Maker," *Delineator*, October 1910, p. 293.

271–73 CARESSE CROSBY: "eyelit embroidery of my . . .": Crosby, p. 62; "The result was delicious . . .": Ibid., p. 63; "owing to undue prejudice . . .": Ibid., pp. 62–63; "felt rather like an . . .": Ibid., p. 64; "not only adequate but . . .": Ibid., p. 64.

273 SALE: Kenneth Lasson incorrectly puts the figure at $15,000 in *Mouse-traps and Muffling Cups*, p. 95; "I believe my ardour . . .": Crosby quoted without citation by Lasson, p. 95.

273 OBITUARY: "Caresse Crosby, Publisher, Dies," *New York Times*, January 25, 1970; Alcoholics Anonymous and Richard Peabody: Crosby says her husband was "a forerunner of the famous AA," Crosby, p. 92. Other material on Peabody is "Prohibition Booms Mr. Peabody's Business of Curing Hard Drinkers, Yet He's an Advocate of Repeal," n.p., n.d. [1922?], courtesy of Anne Conover, author of *Caresse Crosby*; Claudia Glenn Dowling, "Ooh-La-La! The Bra," *Life*, June 1989, p. 91.

274–76 JONES: "She never wrote a . . .": "El Dorado Jones, 71, Former Moline Manufacturer, Dies in New York," *Moline Daily Dispatch*, November 28, 1932, p. 4; Potential sales: "Woman Inventor Dies in Poverty," *New York Times*, November 27, 1932; "avaricious and mercenary and . . .": "El Dorado Jones, 71"; "The only way to . . .": Ibid.; "have a bearing on . . .": " 'Fog Eye' for Plane Pierces Mist Test," *New York Times*, October 15, 1930; Registry: R. L. Polk & Co.'s Moline City Directory, R. L. Polk & Co., 1913–1917; Death: "Woman Inventor Dies in Poverty," *New York Times*, November 27, 1932, and "Claim Miss Jones's Body," Ibid., November 30, 1932; "Woman Inventor Known as . . .": "El Dorado Jones, 71."

277 STRONG ON WATER CONSERVATION AND FLOOD CONTROL: "the Panama Canal sinks . . .": Harriet W. R. Strong, "Source Conservation of Storm Water," *The Whittier News*, Twenty-fifth Anniversary Edition, January 1913; "Whittier Woman for Control of Floods," [Whittier] *News*, August 11, 1915; Harriet Strong, "Source Conservation," *The Woman Citizen*, July 1914, p. 21.

277 WOMAN ACTIVIST: "I protest against women . . .": "Woman Makes Herself Felt," [Los Angeles] *News*, May 10, 1916; "She practically hurled a . . .": "Flood Control Board Confer on Bill," [Whittier] *News*, January

1, 1913; "Mother threw in the . . .": Harriet R. Strong, [c. 1925?], HWRS, folder 760.

277–79 GRISWOLD SERIES: The issues appeared between November 1913 and April 1915; Griswold didn't sign the first article but did the others (first was "Women Inventors," *Women Lawyers' Journal*, November 19, 1913, pp. 15–16). All other material appeared under her name: Ibid., December 1913, pp. 21–22; "It is interesting to . . .": Ibid., December 1914, p. 19; "In my thirty years' . . .": Ibid.; "May it endure beyond . . .": Ibid., February 1914, p. 35; "The stout woman will . . .": Ibid., January 1914, p. 27; "manufacturers may find something . . .": Ibid., November 1914, p. 83; "the diversity of occupations . . .": February 1915, p. 35; "has invented a brassiere . . .": Ibid., January 1915, p. 27; "novel garment for women": Ibid., November 1914, p. 83; Blanchard: Ibid., May 1914, p. 59; Knight death: "an example of a . . .": Ibid., December 1914, p. 19; Knight patent: Ibid., May 1915, p. 51; War games: Ibid., January 1915, p. 27.

279 "steadfast race-fostering qualities of . . .": excerpt from Professor Spencer Foster's article in *Scientific Monthly*, reprinted in "Mental Ability and Sex," *New York Tribune*, March 3, 1917.

279 "much needed light": Mary Ogden White, "Has the War Made Women Inventors?" *Woman Citizen*, June 9, 1917, p. 35.

279–80 STRONG: "foreign meddling and interference": "Use Grand Canyon as Mammoth Irrigation Tank, Urges Woman," [Los Angeles] *Tribune*, September 1, 1917; "grandest canyon on earth": H. W. R. Strong, "Should Grand Canyon Be Dammed: A Flood Suggestion," *The Times Illustrated Magazine*, [1917], p. 852; "free from all personal . . .": Resolution of the Whittier Chamber of Commerce signed by Paul J. Denninger, Vice President, in HWRS; "Many competent people occasionally . . .": James W. Reagan to M. J. Haig, Secretary, Whittier Chamber of Commerce, October 18, 1917, Ibid., folder 850.

280–81 STRONG AT HEARINGS: "I come before you . . .": *Water Power Hearings*, p. 773; "I told the world . . .": Ibid., p. 774. The patents themselves are reproduced in the hearings report on pp. 787–794.

281 "A man suggested this": Strong cited in Lavinia Griffin Graham, "Advocates Schools for Women Farmers," *Los Angeles Examiner*, [c.1920s?], original undated in HWRS, folder 854; rejection of plan: Harriet Strong, "To the Taxpayers and Bond Owners" [pamphlet], Los Angeles, January 15, 1919, Ibid., folder 850. In 1926, Strong, 82, died in an automobile accident on her way from Los Angeles to her Whittier ranch.

281 CASSATT: "Women in War Work," *Club Woman* [published by Detroit Federation of Women's Clubs], April 1918, p. 292.

281–82 STANDARDIZATION IN DRESS: "Standardization is a principle . . .": "Standardization—What It Means," *General Federation Magazine*, March 1918, pp. 21–22; "more than meat and . . .": "War, Women and Clothes," Ibid., October 1918, p. 18; "earnest woman instead of . . .": Rhoads quoted in "Making the Dress Fit the Task," *Woman Citizen*, August 17, 1918, p. 232; other quotations are from the patent; additional information: Florence King, "Are Women Inventive?" *Woman Citizen*, July 3, 1920, p. 133; "fearless insurgents": May E. Rhoads, "The New Dress," *General Federation Magazine*, October 1918, p. 25.

283–84 ADVERTISING RHOADS DRESS: "by leading members and . . .": advertisement: "C. H. D. Robbins Company, New York, Announces the Introduction of 'The Dress of the Hour,' " *American Cloak and Suit Review*, September 1918, p. 61; "could push and pull . . .": "The Women's Apparel Unit of the Women's Oversea Hospitals, U.S.A.," *Woman Citizen*, August 24, 1918, p. 251; "Gas unit": "Fashions for Women Citizens," *Woman Citizen*, August 24, 1918, p. 255; "A woman's dress expressed . . .": May Rhoads, "As the Designer Sees It," in "Fitting the Clothes to the Task" (usually this column was titled "Making the Dress Fit the Task"), *Woman Citizen*, November 23, 1918, p. 533; "now that women have . . .": "Introducing 'The Dress of the Hour,' Fashion's Most Recent Creation," *Woman Citizen*, September 21, 1918, p. 335 (the advertisement, with a few variations in content and size, appeared throughout 1918); Franklin Simon display: "This Wonderful New Dress . . .": *Woman Citizen*, October 19, 1918, p. 417.

285 INGERSOLL GARMENT: "On and Off the Market," *Woman Citizen*, February 9, 1918, p. 216; "A Costume Especially Designed for the 'Land Army of America,' " Advertisement of Best and Company, *Woman Citizen*, March 23, 1918, p. 322.

285–86 GREGG: "dropped it [teaching] for . . .": in 25th Reunion Report, Radcliffe College, class of 1905, courtesy of Radcliffe College Archives; "Practical Garments for Agricultural . . .": advertising brochure for "Putnee": "Trousers for Women: Practical Garments for Agricultural Workers," Ibid.; "Radcliffe-trained brains for a . . .": "Putting Pockets on the Eternal Feminine," in "The Clothes and the Work," *Woman Citizen*, April 6, 1918, p. 374; "genuine ethical contribution to . . .": Ibid.; Franklin Simon: "Practical Garden Clothes for Women Farmers," Advertisement for Franklin Simon and Company, Ibid., May 14, 1918, p. 462; Obituaries of Marjorie True Gregg, Carroll County *Independent* and Carroll County *Pioneer*, April 25, 1968, courtesy of Radcliffe College Archives.

286 "just as many women . . .": "Detroit Business Women Meet," *Woman Citizen*, July 27, 1918, p. 176.

286 "In another generation the . . .": Carrie Chapman Catt, "An Eight-Hour

Day for the Housewife—Why Not?" *Pictorial Review,* November 1918, p. 28.

## 13: SAME SONG, SECOND VERSE

PAGE

287–89 KING: "Suffragist Reaches Out," *New York Times,* February 18, 1911; "Want Woman Made Judge," *New York Times,* November 26, 1922; "most brilliant lawyers America . . .": "Women and Big Business," *Woman Citizen,* July 27, 1918, p. 171; "beaten path so long . . .": Ibid., p. 170; "refined gentlewoman": *Chicago Herald,* quoted in Ibid.; Comments on inventions: Florence King, "Are Women Inventive?" *Woman Citizen,* July 3, 1920, passim, pp. 133–34; "To invent a device . . .": Ibid., p. 134.

289 "You can do your . . .": "The Dress of the Hour," Advertisement, *The Independent Woman,* September 1920, p. 19.

290 "I have been watching . . .": quoted in Flexner, p. 323.

290 "The boys, and girls . . .": McFee, Preface, p. iii.

291 "peculiar problems surrounding women . . .": "Industrial Women's New Milestone," *Woman Citizen,* August 3, 1918, p. 195.

291 WOMAN'S BUREAU STUDY: Mary Anderson, letter of transmittal to The Hon. James J. Davis, Secretary of Labor, Mary Anderson, ed., WCFI, inside cover; Purpose of study: p. 3; "designed, devised, discovered, and . . .": WCFI, p. 1.

291–92 "Inventions by women, like . . .": part of WCFI reprinted in Joseph Rossman, "Women Inventors," *Journal of the Patent Office Society,* vol. 10, 1927, p. 26; limiting circumstances: WCFI, p. 9; "greater self-confidence born . . .": Ibid., p. 5.

292 AQUATIC METAPHORS: WCFI, p. 2.

292–94 LETTERS: "Yankee Laziness, I reckon . . .": Ibid., p. 17; "Having been raised on . . .": Ibid.; "I was farming in . . .": Ibid.; "As a farmer's wife . . .": Ibid.; "[I was] two weeks . . .": Ibid., p. 24; "I could hear a . . .": Ibid., p. 33; Windshield wiper: Ibid., p. 27; "impressed with the fact . . .": Ibid., p. 28; "I was living in . . .": Ibid., p. 35.

294–95 "As opportunities are gradually . . .": "Women's Inventive Genius," *Equal Rights,* August 25, 1928, p. 230.

295 TESTS: F. A. Moss, "Psychological Test for Invention," *Journal of the Patent Office Society,* April 1927, pp. 348–56, cited in Rossman, "Women Inventors," pp. 28–30; "erroneous notion that woman's . . .": Ibid., p. 18.

295–97 HENRY: "diversity of invention": "A Study in Feminine Invention," *Scientific American,* October 1924, p. 160; number of patents: Stacy V. Jones, "Inventive Woman Patents 2-Way Envelope," *New York Times,* January 27, 1962; "[A]ll the time my . . .": "Beulah Henry Has Patented Thirty-three Novelties," *American Magazine*, April 1925, p. 75; "I know nothing about . . .": "Lady Edison," *Literary Digest*, May 8, 1937, p. 21; "I invent because I . . .": Aubrey D. McFayden, "Beulah Louise Henry," *Journal of the Patent Office Society*, August 1937, p. 606; "I know less than . . .": "A Study in Feminine Invention," p. 260; "I am an inspirational . . .": Ruth Arel, "Paging Lady Edison," *Independent Woman*, July 1937, p. 198; "That snapper had . . .": "A Study in Feminine Invention," p. 260; "with a stone for . . .": "Beulah Henry Has . . .", p. 75; "If necessity is the . . .": Elizabeth M. Fowler, "Beulah Louise Henry Has Been Called 'Lady Edison,' " *New York Times*, January 27, 1962.

298  "Grande Dame of Black . . .": Barbara Feinman, "Oprah, Winningly," *Washington Post*, December 4, 1989.

298–99  BACKGROUND ON WALKER: Ives, pp. 52–55, and *Notable American Women*, vol. 1, pp. 533–35.

299  "Well, I was working" and all subsequent Joyner quotations are from an interview with the author, April 25, 1990.

300  "Beauty Culture offers . . .": Advertisement, circa 1945, in a trade publication, courtesy of Fred Amram.

301  GRADUATE EDUCATION: Background: Smith-Rosenberg, p. 34.

301  RAILROADS: "Inventions by Women," a reprint from *Boston Transcript*, n.d., n.p., *International Inventor*, August 1910, p. 11; "Ventilation of Railroad Cars," *Scientific American*, July 17, 1852, p. 345.

301–3  DENNIS: "Olive Dennis First Woman to Present Report at American Railway Engineering Association Meeting," *Baltimore and Ohio Magazine*, June 1929, p. 19; "Now what the heck . . .": Olive W. Dennis, "Modernization of Railroad Passenger Facilities," *Cornell Engineer*, November 1949, reprinted in *Baltimore and Ohio Magazine*, January 1949, p. 22; Job hunting: Olive W. Dennis, "From a Woman's Viewpoint," *American Railway Engineering Association Bulletin*, no. 425, June–July 1941, p. 9; "the acid test of . . .": "Can a Woman Be a Civil Engineer?" *Baltimore and Ohio Magazine*, January 1921, p. 35.

303  DENNIS BIOGRAPHICAL MATERIAL: Adelaide Handy, "Woman Designer of Bridges Has Enhanced Rail Travel," *New York Times*, December 22, 1940, sect. 3, p. 4; Anabel E. Hartman, "Olive Wetzel Dennis" [in memoriam], *Goucher Alumnae Quarterly*, Winter 1958, pp. 34–35.

303  DENNIS AS ENGINEER: "There is no reason . . .": "Can a Woman Be a Civil Engineer?" *Baltimore and Ohio Magazine*, January 1921, p. 35; "a delightful personality and . . .": Ibid.; Singing: Dennis reported regularly in the *Baltimore and Ohio Magazine* on the Women's Music Club's performances, first formed in 1927 with company help and support of friends who bought tickets for benefit concerts.

304–5 DENNIS AS CONSUMER ADVOCATE: Olive W. Dennis, "From a Woman's Viewpoint," *American Railway Engineering Association Bulletin,* #425, June–July 1941, p. 10; China: Dennis, "Modernization of Railroad Passenger Facilities," p. 22; China designs: "Decorations of New Dining Car China Tell the Story of the Baltimore and Ohio," *Baltimore and Ohio Magazine,* August 1927, passim, pp. 28–31; Sales: Olive W. Dennis, "What the 'Iron Horse' Carried Away in Souvenirs," *Baltimore and Ohio Magazine,* January 1928, p. 30; The descriptive booklet "Concerning the Blue China," with no attribution to Dennis, is available from the B & O Railway Museum in Baltimore; Archival material: Dennis, "From a Woman's Viewpoint," p. 15.

305 PATENT AND ENGINEERING: "wonderful girl": George W. Haulenbeck, "Among Ourselves," *Baltimore and Ohio Magazine,* January 1928, p. 67; "[T]he general training my . . ." Dennis, "Modernization of Railroad Passenger Facilities," p. 22; Air-conditioning: Dennis, "From a Woman's Viewpoint," p. 12.

305 "any one of which . . .": "Olive W. Dennis, Sweeps the Cobwebs Off the Sky," *Baltimore and Ohio Magazine,* January 1929, p. 37.

306 EVALUATION: Modesty: "a giver of suggestions": Dennis, "From a Woman's Viewpoint," p. 16; "When you ride the . . .": Margaret Ingels, "Petticoats and Slide Rules," *Midwest Engineer,* August 1952, pp. 12–13.

306 "who by the sound . . .": "Women Engineers," in "Topics of the Times," *New York Times,* December 6, 1940.

## 14: DEPRESSION, WAR, AND PEACE

PAGE

307–8 DEPRESSION: Hymowitz and Weissman, p. 307.

308 "first to lead out . . .": Hathaway, Foreword, p. 1, and Index.

308 WOMEN'S BUREAU COLLECTION: Women's Bureau, U.S. Department of Labor, *Women as Inventors,* n.p. [late 1930s] (the book is in the library of the United States Patent Office); Press: James Nevin Miller, "All Inventors Are Not Male," *Washington Star,* July 17, 1938; "Women as Inventors," *Christian Science Monitor,* June 25, 1935; " 'Lady Edison': Woman Inventor with Fifty-two Patents Ascribes Success to Inner Vision," *Literary Digest,* May 8, 1937, p. 21; "devices for the enhancement . . .": "Women Inventors," *Providence Journal,* June 16, 1937.

309 SAUNDERS: "the last domain to . . .": Ruth Arel, "Paging 'Lady Edison,' " *Independent Woman,* July 1937, p. 198; "Patent Banquet": Ibid., p. 199.

309 BLODGETT: Background: Vincent J. Schaeffer and George L. Gaines, Jr., "Obituary, Katharine Burr Blodgett," *Journal of Colloid and Interface Science,* July 1980, p. 271; also in Goff; "gifted experimenter [with a] . . .":

cited in "Public Information" (release), General Electric Company, Corporate Research and Development, p. 3. Courtesy General Electric Company.

310 INVISIBLE GLASS: "Glass 'Invisible' by Use of Film," *New York Times,* December 27, 1938; Clock dial: "Research" in "Footnotes on Headlines," *New York Times,* September 4, 1939; Robert D. Potter, "Practical Uses of Invisible Glass," *Science Digest,* July 1940, p. 63; "You keep barking up . . .": Blodgett quoted in Yost, p. 207.

311 COLOR GAUGE: Waldemar Kaempffert, "Oil Film Gauged by Color," in "Current Developments in Science: Notes from the Laboratories," *New York Times,* June 12, 1938 (this was written about research being conducted before Blodgett's patent); Blodgett's explanations: Dr. Katharine B. Blodgett, "A Gauge That Measures Millionths of an Inch," in Reynolds and Manning, pp. 258–262.

311–12 BLODGETT: "Like so many of . . .": Yost p. 213; "skimpy five feet tall . . .": Kathleen McLaughlin, "Creator of 'Invisible Glass' Woman of Many Interests," *New York Times,* September 24, 1939; "matron": interview with Ruth Shoemaker, General Electric Hall of History, March 12, 1989.

311–15 HULL: "No one seems to . . .": "Introducing . . . The Merry Hull 'Finger Free' Glove," *Invention and Finance,* December 1939, pp. 3, 10; "draw merely pretty pictures . . .": "Four Designers Win Service Awards," *New York Times,* April 22, 1939; "pretty enough to double . . .": Kathleen McLaughlin, " 'Fragile Bit of Femininity' Wins Fame as Industrial Designer," *New York Times,* April 30, 1939; "She would look swell . . .": "Introducing . . . The Merry Hull 'Finger Free' Glove," p. 3; "You've got to have . . .": Hull quoted by McLaughlin; "instincts as a homemaker": Olive W. Dennis, "Modernization of Railroad Passenger Facilities," *Cornell Engineer,* November 1949, reprinted in *Baltimore and Ohio Magazine,* January 1949, p. 22.

315 GLASGOW ON HEALTH: "The Owen Bill," *Women Lawyers' Journal,* November 1913, pp. 13–14; "sovereign in the field . . .": Glasgow, *Life and Law,* Preface, p. v.

315 GLASGOW: "initiative, energy and political . . .": Glasgow, *The Subjection of Women,* Preface, p. ii; "It is a human . . .": Ibid., p. 273; "Since historic times man . . .": Ibid., p. 275; "decrease in hostility toward . . .": Ibid., p. 281.

316–17 PATENT ACT'S 150TH ANNIVERSARY: 1940 patent figures: "Women Gaining in Patent Rolls," *New York Times,* August 11, 1940; "Food, music and pretty . . .": "Wine, Women and Song in Patent Fete Tonight," *Washington Post,* April 10, 1940; "Science combined forces with . . .": "Patent Law Banquet's 1,200 Guests Dine on Special Dishes," [Washington,

D.C.] *Evening Star,* April 11, 1940; Models and menus: "Laud Genius of U.S. Inventors," *Washington Post,* April 11, 1940; "Patent Law Banquet's 1,200 Guests Dine on Special Dishes," [Washington, D.C.] *Evening Star,* April 11, 1940.

317–18 INCREASE IN PATENTING: "Women Gaining in Patent Rolls," *New York Times,* August 11, 1940.

318 "surprise overconfident aggressors": Stuart Chase, "Uncle Sam: Calling All Inventors," *The Rotarian,* January 14, 1941, p. 28.

318 CHILDREN: "Don't be skeptical if . . .": "Our Teen-Age Edisons," *American Magazine,* July 1941, p. 216; Eberle, Contents page.

319 "Hedy was more than . . .": Alice Brannigan, "Radio's Golden Era: Broadcasting and Wireless in the Pages of History," *Popular Communication,* March 1989, p. 14.

319–21 LAMAR: "I couldn't be an . . .": Lamar cited by Fleming Meeks, "Hedy Lamar, Inventor," in "Science and Technology," *Forbes,* May 14, 1990, p. 138; "Any girl can be . . .": Lamar cited by Brannigan, p. 13; "I can't understand why . . .": Lamar cited by Meeks, p. 137; "Never a letter, never . . .": Ibid., p. 138.

321–22 BLODGETT: "Each year I learn . . .": "Katharine B. Blodgett," in uncited source from General Electric History Foundation, p. 53.

322–24 GRENEKER: "with an ease and . . .": "Chores Made Easy by Fingertip Tools," *New York Times,* March 9, 1937; "It was too easy": personal notes, from LG, p. 116; "[T]he men hated the . . .": Ibid., p. 120; "the size of a . . .": from a manuscript dated December 1984 and titled "Some of the Background Leading to My Invention 'Fing-R-Tips,' " LG, p. 6; "I opened the large . . .": personal notes, LG, pp. 116–17; "Pullcord" and royalty information from "Some of the Background Leading to My Invention 'Fing-R-Tips,' " p. 6.

324–25 GRENEKER *(postwar):* The following material is courtesy of the Mannequin Museum: "conscientious and completely able . . .": H. R. Polleys, Developing Engineer, Engineering Department (United States Rubber Co.), to Mr. John F. Bowman, Jr., June 5, 1951; "Patents often take years . . .": letter from Herbert R. Polleys to Lillian Greneker, February 13, 1977; "I am closing my . . .": John L. Welch of Morgan, Finnegan, Pine, Foley & Lee, N.Y., to Lillian Greneker, February 22, 1978; "the implement you have . . .": Daniel M. Rosen of Yuter, Rosen & Dainow, N.Y., to Lillian Greneker, February 7, 1979.

325–26 EFFECTS OF WAR: Theresa Wolfson, "Aprons and Overalls in War," *The Annals of the American Academy of Political and Social Science,* September 1943, cited without page in Hymowitz and Weissman, p. 314; "not so much a . . .": Rothman, p. 224.

327–28 ROGALLO BACKGROUND: Material is from Rogallo Biographical File, National Air and Space Museum Archive, Smithsonian Institution, and from the author's interview and telephone conversation with Gertrude Rogallo, October 18, 1988.

327–32 GERTRUDE ROGALLO: "collaborator and constant companion . . .": Francis M. Rogallo to Frank H. Winter, Kitty Hawk, N.C., June 6, 1973, Rogallo Biographical File; "After several years of . . .": Rogallo to Winter, May 15, 1973, Ibid.; "I was able to . . .": Gertrude Rogallo to ALM, letter, October 18, 1988; Kite business: Charles McDowell, Jr., "It's Limp But It Flies," *Richmond Times-Dispatch Magazine*, December 18, 1949; Mary E. Ames, "The Man Who Invented the Flexible Wing, the Hang Glider & Succeeded in Mating a Jet with a Parachute," *American Kite*, p. 37; "No sticks, no framework . . .": "Flexible Kite for Signalling," in "Notes on Science," *New York Times*, March 14, 1954; "Wide Variety of Ideas Covered by Patents Issued During the Week," *New York Times*, August 17, 1968; "The initial work was . . .": Rogallo to ALM; "She is a particularly . . .": William Sleeman, Jr., telephone interview with ALM, April 14, 1989; Ceremony: "KDH Ceremony Pays Honor to Several Flight Aspects," *The Coastland Times*, May 10, 23, 1988, p. 3A.

332 "It's a man's world . . .": Eleanor Metheney, "Inventory of Frustrations," *Independent Woman*, January 1949, p. 14.

## 15: THE MODERN WOMAN INVENTOR

PAGE

334 1950S PATENTS: Stacy V. Jones, "Inventive Woman Patents 2-Way Envelope," *New York Times*, January 27, 1962.

334 "No one knows for . . .": Blanche McKeown, "It Was a Woman's Idea," *American Mercury*, August 1955, p. 84.

334 "While it is true . . .": Joe Giovanni, "Women Are Inventors Too," *American Mercury*, May 1956, p. 59.

334 TUSKA: "that should be sufficient": Clarence D. Tuska, *Inventors and Inventions*, New York: McGraw-Hill, 1957, p. 48; "career chosen by nature": Ibid., p. 49; Rose Marie Reid: Tuska, *Independent Inventors and the Patent System*, p. 4.

335 "The baby was always . . .": Micki Siegel, "Mothers of Invention," *Good Housekeeping*, September 1984, p. 72.

337 "The Littlest Marcher," caption to photograph accompanying Page H. Wilson, "They Came, They Marched . . . For the Right of All to Vote," *A.D.A. World*, April 1965, p. 3. Courtesy of the inventor.

338 "It didn't really matter . . .": Moore, in interview with ALM, April 13, 1989.

339–40 "SNUGLI" PUBLICITY: "Soft Carriers," *Consumer Reports*, November 1975, pp. 669–71; "Why, it was like . . .": Eric Morgenthaler, "Baby Carrier Maker Succeeds Playing It Close to the Vest," *Wall Street Journal*, April 23, 1982.

339–40 "just barge right up . . .": Carla Cohen, interview with ALM, April 9, 1989.

340 "It encompasses a whole . . .": Morgenthaler, "Baby Carrier Succeeds"; "I feel we're contributing . . .": Siegel, p. 76.

341 HUFFY COMPANY: 1989 catalog, *Soft Baby Products for Today's Parents*, Gerry Baby Products Company, a Huffy Company. Courtesy of the company.

342 "I am just no . . .": Moore, interview with ALM, April 13, 1889

342 "from the kitchen to . . .": "More Women Submit Patents," *Los Angeles Times*, December 11, 1973.

343 "I suppose *technically* . . .": letter from Siems to ALM, February 16, 1989; Additional direct quotations are from this same letter or a follow-up telephone conversation with ALM.

344 ADVERTISING: "General Foods," *Madison Avenue Magazine*, [March 1974], p. 18. Courtesy of the inventor.

344–45 RECOGNITION: The inventor supplied the author with these communications: General Foods bulletins dated February 1973, September 7, 1976; letter from J. D. Thompson, Director of Research-Europe, General Foods Europe, February 13, 1973, letters from J. Brendan Ryan, Product manager, General Foods Corporation of March 10, 1972, and February 16, 1973; Company chef: cited in David F. White, "The Flavor of General Foods," *New York Times*, June 5, 1977, n.p., reprint, courtesy of the inventor.

345–46 HOUSEWORK: Ruth Schwartz Cowan, "Less Work for Mother?" *American Heritage of Invention and Technology*, Spring 1987, passim, pp. 57–61.

347–48 O'DONNELL: "sitting in that office . . .": Laurene O'Donnell, interview with the author, January 21, 1990; all subsequent direct quotations are from this interview or a subsequent telephone discussion a week later; Marketing study: Laurene H. O'Donnell, "Aqua Spring Marketing Study," December 2, 1989, courtesy of the inventor.

348 "It is due to . . .": "Glass Oven Doors," *New Ideas*, November 1896, p. 246.

349–51 GABE: "[O]ver the years I've . . .": Gabe quoted in Abrams and Bernstein, p. 290; "Men decided a few . . .": Frances Gabe, "The Gabe Self-Cleaning House," in Zimmerman, p. 75; "I'm trying to take . . .": Charles Hellinger, "Push Button Scrubbing: Inventor Building 'Self Cleaning' House," *Los Angeles Times*, November 1, 1981, part I, p. B3; Other material on Gabe: Micki Siegel, "The Best Inventions by Women Since 1900," *Good Housekeeping*, February 1990, pp. 140–43, Gerri Hirshey, ed., "A Self-cleaning House?" in "Woman's World," *Family Circle Magazine,* July 1979, pp. 4, 22; Kristin McMurran, "Frances Gabe's Self-Cleaning House Could Mean New Rights of Spring for Housewives," *People,* March 1982, pp. 38–39; "Frances Gabe and Her Self-Cleaning House," *The Lightbulb,* vol. 9, issue 2, 1979, cover and pp. 11–12; "You either struggle and . . .": Tepper and Tepper, p. 192; "I'm taking my miniature . . ." and other background material throughout: Interview with ALM, April 21, 1990.

351 YOUNG-KIRBY: Background: Micki Siegel, "Mothers of Invention," *Good Housekeeping,* September 1984, p. 72; "The inventor needs faith . . .": letter from Young-Kirby to ALM, July 20, 1989.

353–54 BACKGROUND ON NYSTATIN: *"Streptomyces noursei":* press release from the Public Information Department, E. R. Squibb & Sons Division, Olin Mathieson Chemical Corporation, October 28, 1955. Other material in "A Brief History of Nystatin": Mount Holyoke College Library/Archives; "Rachel Fuller Brown: Distinguished Woman Scientist, Co-Discoverer of First Antifungal Antibiotic," press release, Research Corporation, N.Y., January 18, 1980, courtesy of Mount Holyoke College Library/Archives.

354 BROWN AND HAZEN: "how unpredictable consequences can . . .": David Salisbury, "A Chemist's Discovery Saved Priceless Murals," *Christian Science Monitor,* October 1, 1975, p. 20; "If we had an . . .": Brown quoted by Baldwin, p. 80; "It's my baby, and . . .": Hazen quoted in Baldwin, p. 99.

356 DRUG IN GERMANY: "U.S. Drug Flown to Heuss in Bonn," *New York Times,* February 24, 1955.

356 "The Fruits of Research": Stacy V. Jones, "Antibiotic Said to Be Effective Against Some Fungus Diseases," *New York Times,* June 29, 1957.

356 RESEARCH CORPORATION PROFITS: 1957 figure: Yost, p. 77; 1980 figure: "Rachel Fuller Brown," *Medical Mycological Society of the Americas,* Bulletin #35, February 1980, n.p., Courtesy of Mount Holyoke College Library/Archives.

356 BROWN: "fell in love with . . .": Salisbury, p. 20; "ordered pattern and precision": Brown quoted in Yost, p. 68; "You must be willing . . .": Brown quoted in Salisbury.

357 "the girls": cited in Baldwin, p. 77.

357 "broadly effective antifungal antibiotic . . .": release from the Public Information Department, E. R. Squibb & Sons Division, Olin Mathieson Chemical Corporation, October 28, 1955, n.p.

357 PERCEPTIONS OF BROWN AND HAZEN: "the stereotype of a . . .": David Salisbury, Hazen described in Baldwin, p. 110.

357–61 ELION: Quotations are from interview with ALM, July 6, 1989.

361  OTHER BURROUGHS-WELLCOME SCIENTISTS: All quotations and material from interviews with ALM, July 6, 1989.

362–63  HOOVER: "We needed a method . . .": Erna Hoover, correspondence and interview with ALM, November 16, 1989, and December 12, 1989; "You ignore it and . . .": Hoover quoted by Jean Pinanski Dietz, "The Medievalist Who Helps Make Telephones Work," *Wellesley*, Spring 1990, pp. 7, 34; Advice: interview with ALM.

364–66  PERKINS: Background: Lisa Krohn, "Against All Odds," *Magazine of International Design*, September/October 1986, p. 38; Visual impact of design: Nancy Perkins, presentation to the Fourth Symposium on Human Factors and Industrial Design in Consumer Products, Saint Paul, Minn., May 20–22, 1985, p. 89; "human engineering aspect": Perkins, letter to ALM, July 19, 1989; "When there are thirty . . .": Perkins quoted in Krohn, p. 41; Other quotations from interview with the inventor and subsequent correspondence and discussions.

## 16: PATENTS PENDING?

PAGE

368  JAPAN: "have patents": quoted in *The Story of the United States Patent and Trademark Office*, p. 3.

368  PROJECT XL: "Project XL" and "Can You Teach Invention to Children? If So? How?" *Inventor Assistance Programs Newsletter*, November 1987, pp. 1, 3; Commissioner Quigg quoted in "Share of U.S. Patents Issued to Foreigners Grew Again in 1988," *Wall Street Journal*, March 26, 1989.

368–69  *WEEKLY READER* CONTEST: David Stipp, "Who Says the Idea of Child Inventors Is Patently Absurd?" *Wall Street Journal*, January 9, 1986; "Now Thanks to Suzanna . . .": reprinted in "Inventions," *Weekly Reader*, n.d., n.p., p. 5.

369  SICA: "Well, my parents and . . .": Pamela Sica, interview with ALM, August 5, 1989.

369–70  SCHROEDER: April Koral, "A Young Inventor Sheds Light on a Tricky Problem," *Seventeen*, April 1977, p. 104. Ms. Schroeder had also spoken of her experiences at various conferences on encouraging the young to experiment.

370–71  JEFF MEREDITH ON KNIGHT: Jeff Meredith, "A Tribute to an Inventor." Courtesy of Jeff Meredith.

371  OTHER BICENTENNIAL INVENTION CONTESTS: National Elementary Chess Championship, Invent America!, Silver Burdett & Ginn Invention Convention, *Weekly Reader* National Invention Contest, Mathcounts Foundation, Westinghouse Science Talent Search, TEAMS (sponsored by the Junior

Engineering Technical Study, Inc.), Future Problem Solving Team, National Talent Network's Cognetics Team, and Odyssey of the Mind.

371 "History is full of . . .": Vare and Ptacek, dust jacket.

372 "WOMEN'S PLACE IS IN THE PATENT OFFICE": There was also an exhibit of inventions by minority inventors, curated by Patricia Slurby.

374–75 KWOLEK: "My upward progress was . . .": this and all subsequent quotations of Stephanie Kwolek are from an interview with ALM, October 5, 1990.

376–77 BUTTONS TO BIOTECH: Background material: Jane S. Myers, Director, Office of Documentation Information, interview with ALM, March 18, 1989; 1895 figures: *Buttons to Biotech*, p. 5; Statistics: Ibid., passim. The overall number of women's patents in the eleven-year study was 18,248 or 3.6 percent of the 501,491 U.S.-origin patents, Ibid., p. 2; Increase of women in engineering and science: *Science and Engineering Indicators—1987*, National Science Board, Washington, D.C.: Government Printing Office, 1987, pp. 62–63, cited in *Buttons to Biotech*, p. 16; "upward trend": Ibid, p. 16.

377 "official recognition of the . . .": Sharon Schuster, quoted in Jay Matthews, "Worried About Science's Future, Caltech Enrolling More Women," *Washington Post*, March 11, 1990.

377–78 INDUCTION 1990, AKRON: "creative and entrepreneurial spirit": Susan Buckbee, "Opportunity to Nurture Spirit of Invention," Letter to "Voice of the People," *Akron Beacon Journal*, March 28, 1990; Newspaper coverage: Marilyn Miller Roane, "Woman Inventor Says There's Lots of Untapped Genius in Her Gender," *Akron Beacon Journal*, April 4, 1990; Roane, "Patent Holder a Proud Pioneer," *Akron Beacon Journal*, April 7, 1990; "Inventor Tries to Inspire Women," [Youngston, Ohio] *Vindicator*, April 4, 1990; "It's about time we . . .": unidentified guest to ALM; Prior to the event, another local paper covered the story: Karen Koch, "Luncheon Honoring Women Inventors Kicks Off Induction Festivities," [Akron, Ohio] *West Side Leader*, March 6, 1990; Brian E. Albrecht, "Crowning Ceremony: 10 Inventors to Be Inducted in Akron to Hall of Fame," *Cleveland Plain Dealer*, April 7, 1990.

378–79 PATENT OFFICE BICENTENNIAL: Symposium: *Official Program*, Bicentennial Celebration, pp. 14–15; Elion: "60 New Members Elected to Academy of Sciences," *New York Times* [national], May 13, 1990; *Program*, Third Century Awards Ceremony, Washington, D.C.: Foundation for a Creative America, May 10, 1990; Coverage: "we've had much talk . . .": Henry Allen, "The Patent Truth of a Bygone Era," May 11, 1990; Micki Siegel, "The Best Inventions by Women Since 1900," *Good Housekeeping*, February 1990, pp. 140–43; Edmund L. Andrews, "An Exhibit of Inventions by Women," *New York Times*, January 20, 1990.

380 "scorn of the petticoat": Harriet Strong, "Thirty Years Ago" [an address at the beginning of her second year as president of Ebell Club in 1895], reprinted in *The Clubwoman*, November 1926, pp. 7, 8.

380 "depreciatory allusions to [woman's] . . .": Gage, "Woman as an Inventor," *North American Review*, May 1883, p. 489.

380 "Science knows a certain . . .": Benderly, Epilogue, p. 285; Benderly also used the phrase "biology rather than biography," which I paraphrased, Ibid., p. 234.

# BIBLIOGRAPHY

## PERIODICALS

\* = author is a patentee.

Adams, Marie. "Harriet Morrison Irwin's House Still Stands." In "The Chatter Box," *The Charlotte News*, December 7, 1962.

"The Afro-American and What He Is Doing: An Inventor." *The Afro-American*, September 7, 1895.

"Air-Inflated Skirts." *The Inventor*, May 5, 1857, pp. 259–60.

"Airship in the Clouds." *Oakland* [California] *Tribune*, February 18, 1905.

"Airship Proves a Success." *Oakland Tribune*, December 6, 1904.

"Airship 'Messenger' Drops into Bay: Heaton Ascends to Height of 500 Feet." *San Francisco Examiner*, February 13, 1905.

Albrecht, Brian E. "Crowning Ceremony: 10 Inventors to Be Inducted in Akron to Hall of Fame." *Cleveland Plain Dealer*, April 7, 1990.

Aldrich, Michele L. "Women in Science." *Signs: Journal of Women in Culture and Society* 4, no. 1, Autumn 1978, pp. 126–35.

Allen, Barbara. "Spring Cleaning." *American Kitchen Magazine*, March 1902, pp. 220–21.

Allen, Donna. "Women Who Made the World Work." *American Ingenuity at Work*, Tampa, Fla.: Tampa Bay Inventor's Council, March 1988, n.p.

Allen, Henry. "The Patent Truth of a Bygone Era." *Washington Post*, May 11, 1990.

"American Notes." *Journal of the Society of Architectural Historians,* May 1957, p. 66.

"American Railway Engineering Association Nominates Officers." *Railway Age,* January 11, 1941, pp. 151–52.

Ames, Mary E. "The Man Who Invented the Flexible Wing, the Hang Glider & Succeeded in Mating a Jet with a Parachute." *American Kite,* Fall 1988, pp. 34–37, 39–40, 44.

Amram, Fred M., and Morgan, Jane A. " 'Inventor' Is a Masculine Word." *Journal of Creative Behavior* 14, no. 3, pp. 161–173; also in *U.S. Woman Engineer,* December 1980, pp. 1–5, 34.

———. "Women's Contribution to the History of Technology." Unpublished manuscript, General College, University or Minnesota, 1984.

———. "Woman's Work Includes Invention." *The Woman Engineer,* Spring 1981, pp. 29–33, 78–83; reproduced almost identically in *Proceedings of the International Conference on the Role of Women in the History of Science* 2, August 15–19, 1983, pp. 1–5.

———. "Collecting Inventions by Women." *The Antique Trader Weekly,* March 30, 1988, pp. 75–78.

———. "The Innovative Woman." *New Scientist,* May 1984, pp. 10–12.

"Anecdote Relative to the Origin of Whitney's Saw-Gin." *Southern Agriculturalist.*" September, 1832, pp. 467–689.

"An Honor for Super Slurper." *Agricultural Research,* January 1976, pp. 12–13.

"Anna Keichline Dies at Home." *Central Valley Times,* February 5, 1943.

Andrews, Edmund L. "An Exhibit of Inventions by Women." *New York Times,* January 20, 1990.

Andrews, William D., and Andrews, Deborah C. "Technology and the Housewife in Nineteenth-Century America." *Women's Studies* 2, no. 3, 1974, pp. 309–28.

"Another Woman's Invention." *Woman's Journal,* February 21, 1903, p. 58.

Arel, Ruth. "Paging Lady Edison." *Independent Woman,* July 1937, pp. 198–99.

Arnold, Jean. "Science for Women." *Woman's Journal,* June 10, 1876, p. 186.

"Ashes Removed Without Dust." *The Patent Record,* October 1900, p. 14.

"At St. Louis in 1904." In "Interesting Notes for Women," *Oakland Tribune,* December 4, 1904.

"Attachment for Chairs." In "New Ideas for Women," *New Ideas,* February 1896, p. 100.

"Baby's Crib Goes in Trunk." *New Ideas,* August 1899, p. 744.

Ballinger, Willis J. "Spinster Factories: Why I Would Not Send a Daughter to College." *Forum,* 1932, pp. 301–5.

"A Balloon Lawn Party." *Aeronautics,* January 1894, p. 42.

"B & O Women on the Air and in the News." *Baltimore and Ohio Magazine,* May 1943, p. 22.

Banks, Elizabeth. "The Educated American Drudge." *North American Review,* September 1900, pp. 433–38.

"Baseball and Airship Today." *San Jose Mercury and Herald,* July 2, 1905.

Bassett, Preston R. "Carlotta, the Lady Aeronaut of the Mohawk Valley." Reprinted from *New York History,* April 1963, pp. 365–90.

Baxter, H. "No Centennial for Women." *Woman's Journal,* July 19, 1873, p. 232.

Bee, Ardie. "Women Never Invent Anything." *Woman's Journal,* July 3, 1875, p. 210.

Benjamin, Charles F. "How the Government Promotes Ingenuity." *Saint Nicholas,* May 1901, pp. 613–18.

Berkeley-Loyd, Helen. "You and Your Corset-Maker." *Delineator,* October 1910, p. 293.

Berkman, Sue. "Models of Inventive America." *Historic Preservation,* October–December 1977, pp. 21–23.

Bethune, Louise. "Women and Architecture." *Inland Architect and News Record,* March 1891, pp. 20–21.

"Beulah Henry Has Patented Thirty-three Novelties." *American Magazine,* April 1925, pp. 75–76.

"The Bicycle as Life-Giver." *Success,* June 1898, p. 33.

"Big Day for Dames." *Atlanta Constitution,* October 21, 1895.

"Bites Gas Bag and Is Saved." *Los Angeles Times* [date illegible, c. 1904]

Blackwell, Alice Stone. "Cleveland on Women's Clubs." *Woman's Journal,* May 13, 1905, p. 74.

———. "Forty-seventh Anniversary of Founding of Woman's Journal." *Woman's Journal,* January 6, 1917, p. 3.

———. "Genius and Suffrage." *Woman's Journal,* August 16, 1913, p. 260.

———. "Women as Inventors." *Woman's Journal,* August 16, 1913, p. 260.

Blackwell, Antoinette Brown. Speech extracted in "Women and the Centennial." *The Herald of the Centennial,* November 1875, p. 74.

Bombeck, Erma. "Men's Inventions = Women's Laments." *Los Angeles Times,* March 18, 1986, part 5, p. 2.

"Books Found Wrong in Sunshine Society." *New York Times,* November 8, 1913.

Boone, Andrew W. "Talent Scouts for War Ideas." *Nation's Business,* February 1943, pp. 22–23, 78.

Bowen, Roger. "Betsey Baker Was a Bonnet Maker." *Yankee,* March 1967, pp. 71–73, 108–9.

Boyd, Mary Sumner. "Women Workers After the War." *Woman Citizen,* December 2, 1918, p. 612.

Bradford, Ruth A. "The Life and Works of Harriet Hosmer, the American Sculptor." *New England Magazine,* November 1911, pp. 265–269.

Brannigan, Alice. "Radio's Golden Era: Broadcasting and Wireless in the Pages of History." *Popular Communication,* March 1989, pp. 14–15.

"Bread Raising Cabinet." *Inventive Age*, May 5, 1891, p. 9.

Breeze, Winna. "Skirts." *Woman's Journal*, June 7, 1873, p. 178.

"A Brilliant Banquet." *Washington Post*, April 11, 1891.

"A Very Brilliant Scene: Reception to a Vast Gathering in the Rotunda of the Post Office to Begin at Nine-thirty." *Washington Post*, April 9, 1891.

Brown, Enos. "The Heaton Airship Failure." *Scientific American*, February 25, 1905, p. 159.

Bruce, H. Addington. "Books About the Soul." *New York Times Saturday Review of Books*. November 26, 1910, pp. 661, 666.

Buckbee, Susan. "Opportunity to Nurture Spirit of Invention." Letter to "Voice of the People." *Akron Beacon Journal*, March 28, 1990.

"Burning of the Old and Opening of the New Scientific American Offices, New York." *Scientific American*, February 11, 1882, pp. 81–82.

"Butter Making." *The People's Journal*, August 1854, p. 289.

"Button Fastener." *New Ideas*, November 1896, p. 246.

"Buttonhole Guide." *New Ideas*, May 1897, p. 342.

"Cake-Beating Machine." *New Ideas*, February 1901, p. 14.

"California Messenger, Heaton at Agricultural Park." *San Jose Mercury*, July 2, 1905, p. 4, col. 3.

Cameron, Laura B. "Educate to Marry." *New Ideas*, December 1896, p. 264.

"Can A Woman Be a Civil Engineer?" *Baltimore and Ohio Magazine*, January 1921, p. 35.

"Cannot Tamper with this Paper." *New Ideas*, October 1897, p. 428.

"Caresse Crosby, Publisher, Dies." *New York Times*, January 25, 1970.

"The Carpenter Self-Threading and Self-Setting Needle for Sewing Machines." *Scientific American*, October 10, 1870, p. 164.

"Carrie J. Everson and Flotation." *Mining and Scientific Press*, January 15, 1916, p. 82.

"Carrie Jane Billings Everson." *The Engineering and Mining Journal*, January 15, 1916, pp. 129–32.

"The Centennial." *Demorest's Monthly*, July 1876, p. 367.

"The Centennial Exposition." *The United States Centennial Welcome*, June 15, 1876, pp. 2–3.

"The Centennial Lap Table." *Industrial News*, May 1883, p. 84.

"Centennial Notes." *Arthur's Illustrated Home Magazine*, February 1876, p. 121; April 1876, p. 233.

"Centennial Notes by a Maine Woman." *Woman's Journal*, July 15, 1876, p. 230.

"Centennial of Invention." *Washington Post*, April 8, 1891.

"Centennial Traveling Suits." *Harper's Bazaar*, May 27, 1876, p. 339.

Chapman, Arthur. "Mother of New Gold Treating Process Lost." *Denver Times*, November 12, 1915, p. 1.

Charles, Ethel M. "A Plea for Women Practising Architecture." *American Architect and Building News,* April 19, 1902, pp. 20–22.

"Charlotte Smith Dead at 75 Years." *Boston Post,* December 4, 1917.

"Charlotte Smith's Ideas." *New York Times,* July 25, 1897.

Chase, Stuart. "Uncle Sam: Calling All Inventors." *The Rotarian,* January 14, 1941, pp. 26–28.

"C. H. D. Robbins Company, New York, Announces the Introduction of 'The Dress of the Hour.' " *American Cloak and Suit Review,* September 1918, p. 61.

"Cheering Words from Our Admirers." *Woman Inventor* 1, no. 2, June 1891, p. 3.

"Chemists See Film on Langmuir Work." *New York Times,* June 4, 1939.

Child, Lydia Maria. "Harriet W. Hosmer." *The Ladies' Repository,* January 1861, pp. 1–7.

"Chores Made Easy by Fingertip Tools." *New York Times,* March 9, 1937.

"City Briefs." *The Columbus* [Ohio] *Dispatch,* [1945?]. Courtesy of Alumni Office, Ohio Wesleyan University.

"Claim Miss Jones's Body." *New York Times,* November 30, 1932.

"Clarissa Britain." Obituary. [Saint Joseph, Michigan] *Saturday Herald,* November 8, 1895.

Clark, Clifford E., Jr. "Domestic Architecture as an Index to Social History: The Romantic Revival and the Cult of Domesticity in America." *Journal of Interdisciplinary History* 7, Summer 1976, pp. 35–56.

Claudy, C. H. "What Inventors Are Doing." *Scientific American,* April 13, 1912, pp. 338–39.

"Clever Carlotta." *The Daily Saratogan,* August 6, 1890.

"Clever Women Inventors." *The Patent Record,* December 1899, p. 26.

"Clever Wives." *Home Comfort,* June 1898, p. 9.

"Clothes Dryer and Bread Raiser." *New Ideas,* July 1900, p. 960.

"Club Founder Auto Victim." *Los Angeles Times,* September 17, 1926.

Cohen, John Sanford. "Cotton States and International Exposition." *Godey's Magazine,* October 1895, pp. 340–57.

"Combination Cane and Whip." *The Patent Record and Monthly Review,* September 1902, p. 6.

"Combination Chair and Cradle." *The Patent Record and Monthly Review,* September 1902, p. 17.

"Combination Cooking Utensil." *New Ideas,* August 1902, p. 9.

"Combination Cycling and Walking Skirt." *New Ideas,* November 1896, p. 246.

"A Comfortable Rocking Chair." *New Ideas,* March 1900, p. 13.

"The Coming Centennial." *Woman's Journal,* August 27, 1867, p. 276.

"Comments on Foreign Topics." *Industrial Review,* April 1883, p. 105.

"Congress of Invention." *Atlanta Journal*, October 23, 1895.

Cook, Mrs. Joseph. "The Improvement in Girls." *Success*, November 1900, pp. 469–70.

Coolidge, Asenarth, "Humor of the Centennial." *Woman's Journal*, May 27, 1876, p. 170.

"A Costume Especially Designed for the 'Land Army of America.' " Advertisement of Best and Company, *Woman Citizen*, March 23, 1918, p. 322.

Cowan, Ruth Schwartz. "Less Work for Mother?" *American Heritage of Invention and Technology*, Spring 1987, pp. 57–63.

"Cowboys and Indians Liked Her." In "About Successful Women." *Success*, July 8, 1899, p. 541.

Cowen, Mrs. S. J. "The Exposition." *The Spirit of "Seventy-Six,"* March 1877, pp. 135–36.

Crawford, Katharine. "Legislation and Women." *New Idea Woman's Magazine*, March 1903, pp. 38–40.

"Cutlery Etc." *Harper's Bazaar*, May 9, 1868.

"Cycle Club Reception." *Brooklyn Eagle*, February 24, 1895.

"A Dangerous Trip." *The Daily Saratogan*, August 6, 1890.

"Decorations of New Dining Car China Tell the Story of the Baltimore and Ohio." *Baltimore and Ohio Magazine*, August 1927, pp. 28–31.

DeForest, Jane O. "Women and the Fine Arts." *Arthur's Illustrated Home Magazine*, August 1876, pp. 407–410.

DeKoven, Mrs. Reginald. "Bicycling for Women." *Cosmopolitan*, August 1895, pp. 386–94.

"A Delayed Recognition." In "New Ideas for Women." *New Ideas*, March 1897, p. 310.

Dennis, Olive W. "First Public Concert, Baltimore & Ohio Women's Music Club." *Baltimore and Ohio Magazine*, May 1927, pp. 19, 27.

———. "From a Woman's Viewpoint." *American Railway Engineering Association Bulletin*, no. 425, June–July 1941, pp. 9–16.

———. "Modernization of Railroad Passenger Facilities." *Cornell Engineer*, November 1949, pp. 7–9, 34, 36. Reprinted in *Baltimore and Ohio Magazine*, January 1949, pp. 22–23.

———. "What the 'Iron Horse' Carried Away in Souvenirs." *Baltimore and Ohio Magazine*, January 1928, p. 30.

"Detachable Handle." *Inventive Age*, May 1893, p. 6.

"Detroit Business Women Meet." *Woman Citizen*, July 27, 1918, p. 176.

Dickinson, Mary Lowe. "Clerical Pursuits." *Chautauquan*, December 1886, pp. 135–38.

"Died: Mary Anderson." *Time*, July 6, 1953, p. 72.

Dietz, Jean Pinanski. "The Medievalist Who Helps Make Telephones Work." *Wellesley*, Spring 1990, pp. 7, 34.

"Dr. Hammond's Estimate of Women." *North American Review,* October 1883, pp. 495–519.

"Dogs at $100, Babies at $2.00." *New York Times,* April 11, 1911.

"Doll Walker." *New Ideas,* December 1896, p. 262.

"Don't Paint Your Face!" *Success,* November 11, 1899, p. 832.

"Door Adjuster." *New Ideas,* March 1897, p. 310.

"Door Check." *The Patent Record and Monthly Review,* June–July 1901, p. 10.

"Dough Kneader." *The Patent Record and Monthly Review,* March 1902, p. 22.

"Dough Kneader." *Industrial News,* November 1883, p. 212.

Dowling, Claudia Glenn. "Ooh-La-La! The Bra." *Life,* June 1989, pp. 87–92, 94, 97, 98.

"Dr. Blodgett Wins AAUW Award." [Washington, D.C.] *Evening Star,* March 29, 1945.

"Dr. Blodgett Wins Achievement Prize." *New York Times,* March 29, 1945.

"Dr. Everson and Not His Wife Found Ore Method." *Denver Times,* November 18, 1915, p. 1.

"The Dress of the Hour." Advertisement. *The Independent Woman,* September 1920, p. 19.

"Dress Her Theme." *Chicago Times,* May 17, 1893.

"Dress Reform Meeting in Boston." *Frank Leslie's Illustrated Newspaper,* June 20, 1874, p. 229.

"Dress Reform—A Suggestion." *Woman's Journal,* August 31, 1878, p. 275.

"Dress-Skirt Lifter." *New Ideas,* October 1897, p. 422.

"Dresser." *The Patent Record and Monthly Review,* September 1902, p. 18.

[Duffey, Mrs. E. B.]. "Exhibits of Woman's Work." In "The Great Centennial Exhibition." *Arthur's Illustrated Home Magazine,* December 1876, pp. 684–85.

———. "Women's Work in the World." *Arthur's Illustrated Home Magazine,* November 1876, pp. 613–15.

Dunn, Abbie. "Our Wethersfield: Bonnet-Maker Sophia." *Wethersfield* [Conn.] *Post,* [date uncertain, c. 1976]. Courtesy of Wethersfield Historical Society.

"Early Days in New York." *New York Times,* May 2, 1896.

"East Favors Suffrage." [Los Angeles] *Express,* January 14, 1911.

"Editorial." *Central Magazine,* August 1872, p. 280.

"Editorial Notes." *Woman's Journal,* January 8, 1870, p. 4.

"The Education of Girls." *Woman's Journal,* January 5, 1870, p. 10.

"El Dorado Jones, 71, Former Moline Manufacturer, Dies in New York." *Moline Daily Dispatch,* November 28, 1932, p. 4.

"Ellen Louise Demorest Dead." *New York Times,* August 11, 1898.

Ellis, Linda. "A Mother of Invention Makes a Splash." *Insight,* Spring 1990, pp. 19–20.

"The End of Volume Second." *People's Journal,* October 1854, p. 353.

"Engineering and Signalling." *Railway Age*, January 12, 1946.

"The Eternal Feminine." *New Idea Woman's Magazine*, October 1901, p. 15.

"The Ever Glorious Fourth: Immense Celebration in Little Falls." [Little Falls, N.Y.] *Journal & Courier*, July 6, 1880.

"The Everson Myth." *Mining and Scientific Press*, January 15, 1916, p. 78.

"The Exposition News." *New York Weekly Recorder*, August 25, 1895.

"An Exposition of Brains." *The Patent Record*, May 1898, p. 9.

Falk, James W. "Celebrating America." *Insight*, Spring 1990, pp. 3–4.

"Farmhouse Fashions in Dress." *Domestic Monthly*, March 1893, p. 28.

"Fashionable Women." *St. Louis Sunday Herald*, April 15, 1856.

"Fashions for Women Citizens." *Woman Citizen*, August 24, 1918, p. 255.

"Fastening Device." *The Patent Record and Monthly Review*, March 1902, p. 14.

"Female Mind Keen Upon 'Notions.' " *New Ideas*, August 1899, p. 778.

"Female Inventive Talent." *Scientific American*, September 17, 1870, p. 184.

"Feminine Gossip." *New Ideas*, July 1901, p. 954.

"Few Late Patents to Women." *New Ideas*, September 1895, p. 70.

"Fifteen Thousand Patents Secured Through Our Agency." *Scientific American*, December 14, 1861, p. 377.

"Fifty Years a Journalist." *Success*, April 1900, p. 136.

"Final Business Session." *Washington Post*, April 11, 1891.

"Finding Capital for Inventors." *The Patent Record*, May 1898, p. 9.

"A Fine Field for Women Inventors." *Patent Record*, February 1900, p. 11.

"Flexible Kite for Signalling." In "Notes on Science." *New York Times*, March 14, 1954.

"Flood Control Board Confer on Bill." *Whittier News*, January 13, 1915.

"Flood Control Meeting Is Called." *Whittier News*, April 19, 1916.

"Flotation Mother's, Son Says." *Rocky Mountain News*, November 19, 1915, p. 1.

"Flotation Pioneer?" *Rocky Mountain News*, June 8, 1952.

"Flying Machines Are Coming." *Washington Post*, April 10, 1891.

" 'Fog Eye' for Plane Pierces Mist Test." *New York Times*, October 15, 1930.

"For Drying the Hair." *New Ideas*, July 1901, p. 954.

"Four Designers Win Service Awards." *New York Times*, April 22, 1939.

Fowler, Elizabeth M. "Beulah Louise Henry Has Been Called 'Lady Edison.' " *New York Times*, January 27, 1962.

Francis, Mary C. "Over One Hundred Thousand Women Stenographers." *Success*, January 28, 1899, p. 149.

"A Free Trip to the Paris Exposition." *The Patent Record*, January 1900, p. 19.

Fritschner, Linda Marie. "Women's Work and Women's Education: The Case of Home Economics." *Sociology of Work and Occupations* 4, May 1977, pp. 209–34.

"From a High Source." *Atlanta Journal*, October 12, 1895.

"From Little Inventions." *The Patent Record,* October 15, 1898, p. 11.

"Fruit Juice Extractor." *The Patent Record and Monthly Review,* September 1902, p. 8.

*Fry, Laura A. "American Pottery" (condensed from a paper read before the Art Congress of the Atlanta Exposition, October 8, 1895). *Young Ladies' Magazine,* 1896, pp. 97–100.

Gage, Matilda Joslyn. "The Cotton Gin Invented by a Woman." *The Revolution,* April 30, 1868, pp. 259–60.

———. "Woman an Inventor." *The Revolution,* September 7, 1868, pp. 165–60.

———. "Woman as an Inventor." *North American Review,* May 1883, pp. 478–89.

Garrigues, H. J. "Woman and the Bicycle." *Forum,* January 1896, pp. 578–87.

"General Foods." *Madison Avenue Magazine,* n.d., pp. 17–18. Courtesy of inventor Ruth Siems.

"Getting Under Way: The Atlanta Exposition Is Interesting If Still Incomplete." *New York Tribune,* September 29, 1895.

Gilroy, Roger. "Letting the Housework Slide." *Washington Post Magazine.* January 7, 1988, pp. 7–8.

Glasgow, Maude. "The Owen Bill." *Women Lawyers' Journal,* November 1913, pp. 13–14.

"Glass 'Invisible' by Use of Film." *New York Times,* December 27, 1938.

"Glass Oven Doors." *New Ideas,* November 1896, p. 246.

"Gossip of People and Events." In "Woman's World." *Atlanta Journal,* September 7, 1895.

Gougar, Helen M. "A Successful Invention." *Woman's Journal,* August 24, 1889, p. 267.

Griswold, Edith J. "Women Inventors." *Women Lawyers' Journal,* November 19, 1913, pp. 15–16; December 1913, pp. 21–22; January 1914, p. 27; February 1914, p. 35; March 1914, p. 43; April 1914, p. 51; May 1914, p. 59; June 1914, p. 67; November 1914, p. 83; December 1914, p. 19; January 1915, p. 27; February 1915, p. 35; April 4, 1915, p. 51.

Gunby, Olive F. "Women Inventors." *New York Post.* Reprinted in *Scientific American Supplement,* May 25, 1901, pp. 21241–42.

Haines, Jennie Day. "The Wonderful Century." *Saint Nicholas,* February 1901, p. 339.

Halsted, Carolyn. "America's First Woman Potter." *Success,* October 1898, p. 15.

Hammond, William A. "Dr. Hammond's Estimate of Women." *North American Review,* August 1883, pp. 495–517.

Hartman, Anabel E. "Olive Wetzel Dennis" [in memoriam]. *Goucher Alumnae Quarterly,* Winter 1958, pp. 34–35.

"Harvey W. Wiley, Pioneer Consumer Activist." *Good Housekeeping,* February 1990, pp. 145–46.

Haulenbeck, George W. "Among Ourselves." *Baltimore and Ohio Magazine*, January 1928, p. 67.

"Have You Ever Made . . . An Invention? Of Course You Have!" *Patent Record*, May 1899, p. 3.

[Hayes, Joanne M.]. "A Woman's Place *Is* in the Patent Office." *Inventors' Digest*, September/October 1990, pp. 6–7, 16.

"Heaton's Airship Soars over Oakland: Successful Flight Is Made by 'California Messenger.' " *San Francisco Examiner*, December 5, 1904.

Heisner, Beverly. "Harriet Morrison Irwin's Hexagonal House: An Invention to Improve Domestic Dwellings." *North Carolina Historical Review*, April 1981, pp. 105–23.

Hellinger, Charles. "Push Button Scrubbing: Inventor Building 'Self-Cleaning' House." *Los Angeles Times*, November 1, 1981, part 1, p. B3.

Henrotin, Ellen M. "An Outsider's View of the Women's Exhibit." *Cosmopolitan*, September 1893, pp. 560–66.

"Hints to Inventors." *The Patent Record and Monthly Review*, December 1902, p. 102.

Hirshey, Gerri, ed. "A Self-cleaning House?" In "Woman's World." *Family Circle Magazine*, July 1979, pp. 4, 22.

"Hitchings, Elion: Nobel Brings Fame, but Saving Lives Is Greatest Reward." *Wellcome News*, Special Nobel Prize Issue, [1988]. Courtesy of Burroughs-Wellcome.

[Holly, Marietta]. "My Idees [sic.] about Free Love" *Inland Monthly*, September 1872, pp. 401–16.

Holzman, Paul. "Celebrating 80 Years of the Good Housekeeping Seal." *Good Housekeeping*, February 1990, pp. 76–77.

———. "Ninety Years of the Good Housekeeping Institute." *Good Housekeeping*, February 1990, pp. 72–74, 134, 137–8.

"Hon. George W. Murray, the Lone Star of the Race in Congress." *The Afro-American*, April 29, 1893.

"How Does It Sound the Other Way?" *Woman's Journal*, March 24, 1876, p. 208.

"How to Make Good Wives." *The Cook: A Weekly Handbook of Domestic Culinary Art for All Housekeepers*, April 6, 1885, p. 1.

Howe, Julia Ward. "Salutatory." *Woman's Journal*, January 8, 1870, p. 4.

———. "Our Office." *Woman's Journal*, January 8, 1870, p. 4.

Huntington, Emily. "Domestic Training for Girls." *Harper's Bazaar*, February 15, 1890, pp. 124–25.

"Ideas That Make Money." *Christian Science Monitor Magazine*, January 10, 1942, p. 15.

"Improved Puff-Box." *New Ideas*, December 1897, p. 460.

"Improved Traveling Bag." *New Ideas*, September 1896, p. 214.

"Improvement in Lime-Kilns." In "New Inventions." *The Patent Right Gazette*, November 1872, pp. 4–5.

"Improvement in Car-Couplings." In "New Inventions." *The Patent Right Gazette*, June 1872, p. 7.

"In Aid of Her Sex." *Chicago Times*, May 16, 1893.

"Inaugural of Celebration." *San Jose Daily Mercury*, July 3, 1905.

"In a Woman's Realm." *New York Weekly Recorder*, September 18, 1892.

"Industrial Women's New Milestone." *Woman Citizen*, August 3, 1918, p. 195.

"Information as to the Patentable Novelty of Inventions." *Scientific American*, August 24, 1861, p. 121.

"Information Useful to Patentees." *Scientific American*, December 7, 1861, p. 363.

Ingels, Margaret. "Petticoats and Slide Rules." *Midwest Engineer* 5, 1952, pp. 2–4, 10–16.

"The Inland Monthly in Court." *Missouri Republican*, March 29, 1874.

"Instrument to Draw an Ellipse." *New Ideas*, November 1900, p. 15.

"In the Woman's Building." *Atlanta Journal*, March 7 and 23, 1895.

"In the Woman's Building." *Nashville American*, May 4, 1897.

"Introducing . . . The Merry Hull 'Finger Free' Glove." *Invention and Finance*, December 1939, pp. 3, 10.

"Invalid Bed Lift." *Industrial News*, September 1883, p. 171.

"Invalids Easily Removed." *New Ideas*, November 1900, p. 15.

"An Invention Wanted." *Woman's Journal*, January 18, 1890, p. 18.

"Inventions and Patents." *The New Century for Women*, June 10, 1876, p. 34.

"Inventions and Patents for Sale." *The Patent Record and Monthly Review*, June 1904, p. 30; December 1904, p. 38.

"Inventions by a Woman." *Woman's Journal*, August 6, 1904, p. 251.

"Inventions by Women." *International Inventor*, August 1910, p. 1.

"Inventions by Women." *New Ideas*, May 1898, p. 533.

"Inventions Wanted." *Patent Record and Monthly Review*, November 1899, p. 8; March 1902, pp. 10–11.

"Inventive Faculty in Women." *Woman's Journal*, May 3, 1890, p. 138.

"Inventor Tries to Inspire Women." [Youngston, Ohio] *Vindicator*, April 4, 1990.

"Inventors, Attention!" *Science Digest*, March 1942, p. 94.

"Inventors and Inventions." *New York Times*, December 14, 1890.

"Inventors' Trials: Struggles of Those Who Have Accomplished Great Things." [Washington, D.C.], *Evening Star*, April 4, 1891.

"Irrigating or Watering Cart." *New Ideas*, March 1897, p. 319.

Ives, Patricia Carter. "Patent and Trademark Innovations of Black Americans and Women." *Journal of the Patent Office Society*, February 1980, pp. 108–26.

Jackson, Katherine Gauss. "Must Married Women Work?" *Scribner's*, 1935, pp. 240–42.

Jacques, Mary P. "Drying and Ironing." in "Housekeeping Songs." *Saint Nicholas,* October 1888, pp. 548–49.

———. "Clear Starching." in "Housekeeping Songs." *Saint Nicholas,* September 1888, pp. 864–65.

———. "Washing Dishes." in "Housekeeping Songs." *Saint Nicholas,* October 1888, pp. 948–49.

Jensen, Marilyn. "A Legendary Lady: Harriet Strong." *California Highway Patrolman,* May 1987, pp. 48–50.

Johnson, James. "Women Inventors and Discoverers." *Cassier's,* October 1909, pp. 548–52.

Jones, Amanda Theodosia. "Oil Burning Utilities and Futilities: Atomization Previous to Ignition: It Is a Necessary Evil?" *Steam Engineering,* August 10, 1903, pp. 554–57.

Jones, Stacy V. "Antibiotic Said to Be Effective Against Some Fungus Diseases." *New York Times,* January 29, 1957.

———. "Inventive Woman Patents 2-Way Envelope." *New York Times,* January 27, 1962.

Kaempffert, Waldemar. "Oil Film Gauged by Color." In "Current Developments in Science: Notes from the Laboratories." *New York Times,* June 12, 1938.

"Katharine Blodgett Honored at Elmira." *New York Times,* June 13, 1939.

Kaye, Frances W. "The Ladies' Department of the *Ohio Cultivator:* A Feminist Forum." *Agricultural History* 50, July 1976, pp. 414–23.

"KDH Ceremony Pays Honor to Several Flight Aspects." *The Coastland Times,* August 23, 1988, p. 3A.

Keeler, Ralph. "Colorado School Teacher Was First to Find Key to Flotation Process." *Rocky Mountain News,* December 17, 1933.

Keichline, Anna W. "A Tile Designed to Effect a Scientifically Built Wall." *Bulletin of the American Ceramic Society,* September 1931, pp. 287–92.

Kennard, June A. "The History of Physical Education." *Signs: Journal of Women in Culture and Society* 2, no. 4, Summer 1977, pp. 835–42.

King, Florence. "Are Women Inventive?" *Woman Citizen,* July 3, 1920, pp. 130–33.

Kirkman, Dale P. "Caroline Shawk Brooks: Sculptress in Butter." *Phillips County Historical Quarterly,* March 1967, pp. 8–9.

"Knife Cleaner." *New Ideas,* October 1897, p. 422.

"Knife Sharpener." *New Ideas,* February 1897, p. 342.

Koch, Karen. "Luncheon Honoring Women Inventors Kicks Off Induction Festivities." [Akron, Ohio] *West Side Leader,* March 6, 1990.

Koral, April. "A Young Inventor Sheds Light on a Tricky Problem." *Seventeen,* April 1977, p. 104.

Kosterman, Carol. "For the Love of Science," *Leader,* April 14, 1988, p. 28.

Krohn, Lisa Krohn. "Against All Odds." *Magazine of International Design,* September/October 1986, pp. 38–43.

"Ladies at the Fall Fairs." *American Agriculturalist,* September 1868, p. 28.

" 'Lady Edison:' Woman Inventor with Fifty-Two Patents Ascribes Success to 'Inner Vision.' " *Literary Digest,* May 8, 1937, pp. 20, 22.

"A Lady in a Machine Shop." *Woman Inventor,* December 21, 1872, p. 463.

"Latest Inventions by Ladies." *New Ideas,* September 1896, p. 216.

"Laud Genius of U.S. Inventors." [Washington, D.C.] *Evening Star,* April 11, 1940.

"Laundry-Work." *Arthur's Illustrated Home Magazine,* October 1876, p. 563.

Leach, Joseph. "Harriet Hosmer: Feminist in Bronze and Marble." *Feminist Art Journal,* Summer 1976, pp. 9–14.

Lensink, Judy Nolte: Kirkham, Christine M.; and Witzke, Karen Pauba. " 'My Only Confidente'—The Life and Diary of Emily Hawley Gillespie." *Annals of Iowa,* no. 45, pp. 288–313.

"Let Us Dress as We Choose." *Woman's Journal,* May 11, 1878, p. 152.

"Letter from Mrs. Coston." *The New Century for Women,* May 13, 1876, p. 13.

"Lid for Stewpans." *New Ideas,* June 1912, p. 8.

"Literary Intelligence." *New York Times,* January 4, 1867.

"Littleton Defends Sunshine Society." *New York Times,* July 31, 1914.

Livermore, Mary A. "Woman as an Inventor." *Woman's Journal,* January 6, 1900, p. 4.

"Local Brevities." *Missouri Republican,* November 2, 1875.

Lockwood, Mary S. "Woman as an Inventor: Shall She Be Given a Representation at the Columbian Exposition?" *Inventive Age,* March 22, 1891, p. 6.

Long, Ellen Coll. "Extracts from an Appeal to the Women of Florida." *The Herald of the Centennial,* [Providence, R.I.], February 1875.

"Lost Chances." *The Patent Record,* May 1900, p. 8.

"Madame Jones' Patent Bustle." *The Patent Record,* November 1872, p. 10.

"Make Mine Peach." *Santa Barbara,* July–August 1988, p. 66.

"Making the Dress Fit the Task." *Woman Citizen,* August 17, 1918, p. 232.

"Many Men with Brains: The Inventors Gather to Celebrate the Patent Centennial." *Washington Post,* April 8, 1891.

"Mary Louise McLaughlin." *Bulletin of the American Ceramic Society* 17, no. 5, May 1938, pp. 217–25.

Mason, Otis Tufton. "Woman as an Inventor and Manufacturer." *Anthropological Series* 1, New York: D. Appleton & Co., 1894. Reprinted in *Popular Science Monthly,* May 1895, pp. 92–103.

Matthews, C. T. "Influence of Women in Architecture." *American Architect and Building News,* January 1, 1898, pp. 3–4.

Matthews, Jay. "Worried about Science's Future, Caltech Enrolling More Women." *Washington Post,* March 11, 1990.

"May Devote Life to Industrial Art." *Philadelphia Inquirer* October [19], 1903.

McDaniel, Susan A.; Cummins, Helene; and Beauchamp, Rachelle. "Mothers of Invention? Meshing the Roles of Inventor, Mother and Worker." *Women's Studies International Forum* 2, no. 1, pp. 1–12. Elmsford, N.Y. Pergamon Press, 1988.

McDougall, Sarah. "Beulah Henry Has Patented Thirty-three Novelties." *American Magazine,* April 1925, pp. 75–76.

McDowell, Charles, Jr. "It's Limp But It Flies," *Richmond Times-Dispatch,* December 18, 1949.

McFayden, Aubrey D. "Beulah Louise Henry." *Journal of the Patent Office Society,* August 1937, pp. 606–608.

McGaw, Judith A. "Women and the History of American Technology." *Signs: Journal of Women in Culture and Society,* Summer 1982, pp. 799–828.

McGovern, Chauncey M. "Impossible Inventions." *The Patent Record,* October 1899, p. 2.

McKay, Martha N. "Women as Architects." *The Western,* January 1880, pp. 22–39.

McKeown, Blanche. "She Invented the Windshield Wiper." *The Record,* January 1956, pp. 11–12.

McLaughlin, Kathleen. "Creator of 'Invisible Glass' Woman of Many Interests." *New York Times,* September 24, 1939.

———. " 'Fragile Bit of Femininity' Wins Fame as Industrial Designer." *New York Times,* April 30, 1939.

McMahon, Emma Cochran. "Morrison Sisters Make History: Six Daughters Marry Famous Leaders in Old Mecklenburg." *Charlotte Observer* (Junior League ed.), November 7, 1934.

McMurran, Kristin. "Frances Gabe's Self-Cleaning House Could Mean New Rights of Spring for Housewives." *People,* March 1982, pp. 38–39.

Mead, Leon. "Women as Inventors." *Chautauquan,* January 1894, pp. 464–67.

"Mechanical Inventions and Designs." *Inventive Age,* July 1896, p. 102.

"Mechanical Powder Puff." *New Ideas,* October 15, 1902, p. 9.

Meeks, Fleming. "Hedy Lamar, Inventor." In "Science and Technology." *Forbes,* May 14, 1990, pp. 136–38.

Meler, Meg. "Mothers of Invention." [Minneapolis] *Star Tribune,* June 5, 1988.

"Memorial and Petition to the Members of the Centennial Celebration." *The Woman Inventor,* April 1890 [1891], p. 2.

"Mental Ability and Sex." *New York Tribune,* March 3, 1917.

Merrill, Margaret Manton. "Sorosis." *Cosmopolitan,* June 1893, pp. 153–58.

Merrington, Marguerite. "Woman and the Bicycle." *Scribner's,* May 1895, pp. 702–704.

Metheney, Eleanor. "Inventory of Frustrations." *Independent Woman,* January 1949, pp. 12–15.

Miller, James Nevin. "All Inventors Are Not Male." *Washington Star,* July 17, 1938.

"Minnesota's Day in the Woman's Congress." *Atlanta Journal,* March 25, 1895.

Minturn, J. A. "Women as Inventors." *Inventive Age,* December 1893, p. 5.

"Miss Dennis Honored." *Baltimore and Ohio Magazine,* November 1930, p. 67.

"Miss Griswold, the Only Woman Patent Lawyer." *The Patent Record,* November 1899, p. 8.

"Miss Helen Augusta Blanchard." *Portland Express Herald,* January 13, 1922.

"Miss Mary Anderson." *New York Times,* June 30, 1953.

"Miss Gertrude Haynes, Vaudeville Star." *The Patent Record,* May 1899, p. 3.

"Modern Inventions." *New Ideas,* March 1897, p. 319.

Molloy, Emma. "Woman Versus Whiskey in Philadelphia." *Woman's Journal,* July 1, 1876, p. 209.

"More Women Submit Patents." *Los Angeles Times,* December 11, 1973.

Morgenthaler, Eric. "Baby Carrier Maker Succeeds Playing It Close to the Vest." *Wall Street Journal,* April 23, 1982.

"Mrs. Alden Dead: A Social Worker." *New York Times,* January 9, 1930.

"Mrs. Everson Died as Court Sought Her Aid." *Denver Times,* November 29, 1915, p. 1.

"Mrs. Howe on Mrs. Livermore." *Woman's Journal,* June 10, 1905, p. 90.

"Mrs. John Alden, Friend of Blind Babies, Dies at 70." *Brooklyn Daily Eagle,* January 8, 1930.

"Mrs. Julia Ward Howe." From the *Boston Traveller.* Reprinted in the *New York Times,* October 18, 1885.

"Mrs. Lena Sittig." *New York Times,* August 28, 1913.

"Mrs. Sittig's Novelty." *The Brooklyn Eagle,* July 3, 1892.

Myers, Mary. "A Woman's Balloon Trip." *Air Scout,* April 1911, p. 23.

Needles, Samuel H. "The Governor's Mill and the Globe Mills, Pennsylvania." *Pennsylvania Magazine of History and Biography,* October 1884, pp. 279–99.

"The Negro as an Inventor." *A.M.E. Church Review* 2, no. 14, April 1886, pp. 397–411.

"New Baseball and Airship Today." *San Jose Mercury and Herald,* July 2, 1905.

"A New Bicycle Skirt." *New York Times,* February 22, 1895.

"New Can Opener." *New Ideas,* January 1912, p. 6.

"New Culinary Aids Devised by Women." *New York Times,* March 16, 1941.

"New Fields for Women." In "Only Woman's Page." *New York Tribune,* March 26, 1900.

"New Ideas." *New Ideas,* September 1896, p. 214.

"New Inventions Patented by Women." *New Ideas,* December 1896, p. 216.

"Newspaper Workers Married." *New York Times,* August 17, 1896.

Nolan, Mary. "Portable Reservoirs." *Central Magazine,* January 1873, p. 66.

"Nolanum." *Missouri Republican*, June 4, 1876.

Norton, Charles Ledyard. "Elsie's Invention." *Saint Nicholas*, November 1888, pp. 65–67.

"Notable Triumphs." *Success*, December 1897, p. 31.

"Notes and Comments." *Domestic Monthly*, February 1893, p. 8.

"Notes of Inventions." *The Patent Record*, September 1899, p. 31.

"Now It's the Women." *Washington Post*, April 11, 1891.

"Of Interest to Women." *Brooklyn Eagle*, July 16, 1892.

Ohl, J. K. "The Southern Exposition at Atlanta." *Chautauquan*, June 1895, pp. 555–61.

"Olive Sweeps the Cobwebs Off the Sky." *Baltimore and Ohio Magazine*, January 1929, pp. 36–37, 42, 43.

"Olive Dennis First Woman to Present Report at American Railway Engineering Association Meeting." *Baltimore and Ohio Magazine*, June 1929, p. 19.

Oman, Anne. "Mothers of Invention." *The Washington Woman*, May 1984, pp. 18–22.

"On and Off the Market." *Woman Citizen*, February 9, 1918, p. 216.

"One Hundred Years." [Washington, D.C.], *Evening Star*, April 8, 1891.

"One Woman's Utopian Dream." In "Woman and Her Ways." *Chicago Times*, May 2, 1893."

"Opinions of the Press." *Central Magazine*, September 1872.

"An Opportunity to Sell Patents." *Patent Record*, January 1900, p. 19.

"Our Centennial Exhibit." *Arthur's Illustrated Home Magazine*, June 1876, pp. 291–94.

"Our Country and the Scientific American." *Scientific American*, December 14, 1861, p. 377.

"Our First Visit." *Arthur's Illustrated Home Magazine*, July 1876, pp. 397–99.

"Our Teen-Age Edisons." *American Magazine*, July 1941, pp. 56, 116.

"Outlines Plans for Control of Floods: Mrs. H. W. R. Strong Prepares Paper on System for Check Dams and Storage Reservoirs." *Whitter* [Calif.] *News*, April 18, 1916.

"An Overworked Farmer's Wife." *American Agriculturalist*, October 1869, p. 381.

Owens, Martha J. "How Many Women Are Going into Business?" *Chautauquan*, June 1895, pp. 337–40.

Paine, Judith. "The Women's Pavilion of 1876." *Feminist Art Journal*, Winter 1975–76, pp. 5–12.

Parmelee, H. C. "Carrier Jane Everson and the Flotation Process." *Metallurgical and Chemical Engineering*, January 15, 1916, pp. 67–69.

"The Passing of Uncle Sam's Old Curiosity Shop." *Mentor*, September 1925, pp. 3–12.

"Patent Law Banquet's 1,200 Guests Dine on Special Dishes." [Washington, D.C.] *Evening Star*, April 11, 1940.

"The Patent Men." [Washington, D.C.] *Evening Star,* April 9, 1891.

"Patents Recently Secured." *The Patent Record and Monthly Review,* December 1900, p. 7; August 1902, p. 11.

"Patents Granted to Women." *New Ideas,* November 1896, p. 246.

Patrick, G. T. W. "The Psychology of Woman." *Popular Science Monthly,* October 1898, pp. 209–25.

"Prohibition Booms Mr. Peabody's Business of Curing Hard Drinkers, Yet He's an Advocate of Repeal," n.d. [1922]. Courtesy of Anne Conover, author of *Caresse Crosby.*

"Peace Reigns Again." *Chicago Times,* May 4, 1893.

"Penwiper." *New Ideas,* August 1896, p. 198.

Phelps, Elizabeth Stuart. "A Word for the Silent." *The Independent,* January 1, 1874, pp. 1633–34.

Phifer, Louisa Jane. "Letters from an Illinois Farm, 1864–1865." *Journal of Illinois State History,* no. 66, Winter 1973, pp. 387–403.

"Philadelphia Notes." *The Sewing Machine Journal,* December 1877, p. 5.

"Phoebe on the Warpath." *Chicago Times,* May 3, 1893.

"The Physical Life of Woman." *Demorest's Monthly,* November 1872, pp. 338–39.

"Pineapple Knife." *New Ideas,* September 1896, p. 216.

"Plea for a Homely Branch of Industry." *Harper's Bazaar,* June 10, 1876, p. 379.

" 'A Pneumatic Figure for the Dressmaker's Use." *New Ideas,* May 1900, p. 922.

" 'Positive Stand' on War is Urged." *New York Times,* November 19, 1939.

Potter, Robert D. "Practical Uses of Invisible Glass." *Science Digest,* July 1940, pp. 61–64.

"Practical Garden Clothes for Women Farmers." Advertisement for Franklin Simon and Company. *Woman Citizen,* May 14, 1918, p. 462.

"Presidents, Actors, Millionaires Try Their Hands at Invention." *Literary Digest,* March 24, 1928, pp. 53–61.

"Prize Offered to Women Inventors." *Woman's Journal,* September 20, 1902.

"Project XL" and "Can You Teach Invention to Children? If So? How?" *Inventor Assistance Programs Newsletter,* November 1987, pp. 1, 3.

"The Progress of Invention." *The Patent Record and Monthly Review,* September 1904, p. 10.

Pursell, Carroll. "Women Inventors in America." *Technology and Culture,* July 1981, pp. 545–49.

"Putting Pockets on the Eternal Feminine." In "The Clothes and the Work." *Woman Citizen,* April 6, 1918, p. 374.

"Rail Joint." *The Patent Record and Monthly Review,* August 1802, p. 11.

"The Rational Dress Movement: A Symposium." *Arena,* October 1894, pp. 305–326.

"Recent Deaths." *Boston Evening Transcript.* October 14, 1914.

"A Recent Invention." Reprinted from the *New Orleans Daily Picayune*, n.d. *Woman's Journal*, September 7, 1895, p. 285.

"Recent Inventions of Women." *New Ideas*, February 1896, p. 100.

"Recent Patents Described." *The Patent Record*, February 1900, p. 5.

"Recently Patented Inventions." *Scientific American*, June 1, 1895, p. 348.

"Recently Secured Patents." *The Patent Record and Monthly Review*, December 1902, p. 11.

Reeves, Lynn. "Concern Gave Boon to Drivers." Undated and unassigned newspaper article. Courtesy of Birmingham Public Library.

"Research." In "Footnotes on Headlines." *New York Times*, September 4, 1939.

"Revolutionized Farming, Diapers: Super Slurper Becoming Thirstier." [Houghton, Michigan] *Mining Gazette*, February 9, 1977, n.p. Article courtesy Donald Kelly, United States Patent and Trademark Office.

Rhoads, May E. "As the Designer Sees It." In "Fitting the Clothes to the Task." *Woman Citizen*, November 23, 1918, p. 533.

———. "The New Dress." *General Federation Magazine*, October 1918, pp. 25, 31.

Richards, Ellen. "The Place of Science in Woman's Education." *The American Kitchen*, 7, no. 6, September 1897, pp. 224, ff.

———. "Value of Science to Women." *Woman's Journal*, July 7, 1900, pp. 212 ff.

Riegel, Robert. "Women's Clothes and Women's Rights." *American Quarterly*, Fall 1963, pp. 390–99.

Ripley, Martha G. "Bondage: Woman's Dress." *Woman's Journal*, August 10, 1878, p. 249.

Roane, Marilyn Miller. "Patent Holder a Proud Pioneer." *Akron Beacon Journal*, April 7, 1990.

———. "Woman Inventor Says There's Lots of Untapped Genius in Her Gender." *Akron Beacon Journal*, April 4, 1990.

Roberts, Helene E. "The Exquisite Slave: The Role of Clothes in the Making of the Victorian Woman." *Signs: Journal of Women in Culture and Society* 2, no. 4, Spring 1977, pp. 554–69.

Robinson, H. M. "A Few Words to the 'Men Folks.' " *American Agriculturalist*, December 1869, pp. 459–60.

Roche, Mary. "Decorating Ingenuity." *New York Times Magazine*, February 11, 1945, p. 34.

Rold, Joe Da. "Harriet: a 'Strong' Woman." *Whittier Daily News*, September 27, 1984.

Rossiter, Margaret W. "Women's Work in Science." *Isis*, September 1980, pp. 381–90.

Rossman, Joseph. "Women Inventors." *Journal of the Patent Office Society* 10, 1927, pp. 18–30.

"Rotary Oven Plate." *The Patent Record,* December 1899, p. 12.

Russell, Frances E. "The Coming Dress." *Woman's Journal,* December 17, 1892, p. 404.

―――. "Dress and Health." *Woman's Journal,* December 29, 1894, p. 409.

―――. "Summer Dress Reform Notes." *Woman's Journal,* June 30, 1894, p. 202; July 7, 1894, p. 211.

Ryder, Emma Brainerd. "A Woman's Invention." *Woman's Journal,* August 21, 1875, p. 268.

Sabin, Florence R. "Women in Science." *Science* 83, no. 2141, 1936, pp. 24–26.

"Safety in Stepladders." *New Ideas,* March 1900, p. 892.

"Safety Window Cleaning Chair." *Industrial News,* October 1881, p. 190; November 1881, p. 213.

St. Clair, Annie. "Canning." *Demorest's Monthly Magazine,* June 1877, p. 333.

Salisbury, David. "A Chemist's Discovery Saved Priceless Murals." *Christian Science Monitor,* October 1, 1975, p. 20.

Sanford, Mary Williams. "The Tyranny of Fashion." *Woman's Journal,* June 8, 1872, p. 178.

[Scarborough, William]. "Sketch of the Life of the Late Eli Whitney, With Some Remarks on the Invention of the Saw-Gin." *Southern Agriculturalist,* August, 1832, pp. 392–403.

Schell, George P. "Analysis of Current Electrochemical Patents." *Electrochemical Industry,* July 1903, p. 395.

Schaeffer, Vincent J., and Gainers, George L., Jr. "Obituary, Katharine Burr Blodgett." *Journal of Colloid and Interface Science,* July 1980, pp. 269–71.

Schlafly, Phyllis. "National Defense." *Daughters of the American Revolution Magazine,* November 1988, pp. 616–24, 628, 630.

Schlesinger, Elizabeth B. "The Nineteenth Century Woman's Dilemma and Jennie June." *New York History,* October 1961, pp. 365–79.

Sears, Anna W. "The Modern Woman Out of Doors." *Cosmopolitan,* October 1896, p. 630.

"A Select Bibliography of Inventions and Inventors." *Libraries,* May 1928, pp. 247–50.

"A Self-cleaning House?" In "Woman's World." *Family Circle Magazine,* July 1979, pp. 4, 22.

"Sewing Machines." *Scientific American,* July 17, 1852, p. 344.

"Sex in Education." *Woman's Journal,* November 8, 1873, p. 352.

"Shaping Many Drugs from a Basic Concept." *Medical World News,* 1967, pp. 41–46, 86–95.

"Share of U.S. Patents Issued to Foreigners Grew Again in 1988." *Wall Street Journal,* March 26, 1989.

Sharp, Katharine Dooris. "The Woman and the Inventor." *Woman's Journal,* November 25, 1905, p. 189.

"She Invented Pepsin Chewing Gum." *New Ideas,* June 1900, p. 938.

"She Was Notable Woman." *Framingham* [Mass.] *Evening News,* October 13, 1914.

Shorp, Margaret Ferrand. "The White Marmorean Flock." *New England Quarterly,* June 1959, pp. 147–67.

Siegel, Micki. "Mothers of Invention." *Good Housekeeping,* September 1984, pp. 72, 74, 78, 80.

———. "The Best Inventions by Women Since 1900." *Good Housekeeping,* February 1990, pp. 140–43.

"60 New Members Elected to Academy of Sciences." *New York Times* [national section], May 13, 1990.

"Sketch of Mrs. Mary S. Lockwood." *Daughters of American Revolution Magazine,* December 1922, pp. 710–11.

"The Skirt, Male or Female?" *The Woman Citizen,* September 27, 1919, p. 418.

"Skirt Maker." *New Ideas,* March 1912, p. 6.

Slater, Sarah E. "Profitable Industries for Women: The Apiary." *New Idea Woman's Magazine,* October 1903, pp. 34–37.

Smith, Bertha H. "Harriet W. R. Strong: Walnut Grower." *Sunset,* April 1911, pp. 412–15.

[Smith, Charlotte]. "Memorial and Petition to the Members of the Centennial Celebration." *The Woman Inventor,* April 1890 [1891], p. 2.

Smith, Charlotte. "Western Magazine and Western Literature." *The* [St. Louis] *Daily Times,* January 25, 1875.

———. "Woman's Work." *Inland Monthly,* July 1876, pp. 962–64.

[———]. "Women's Inventions." *The Woman Inventor,* April 1890 [1891], p. 1.

[———]. "The Women's Record in the World of Invention." *The Woman Inventor,* June 1891, p. 2.

[———]. "A Word of Encouragement." *The Woman Inventor,* April 1890 [1891], p. 4.

Smith, Helen Evertson, "Woman's Own Art." *Domestic Monthly,* September 1892, pp. 1–2.

"Society's Gala Day." *Atlanta Constitution,* October 23, 1895.

"Soft Carriers." *Consumer Reports,* November 1975, pp. 669–71.

"Some Afro-American Inventors." *The Afro-American,* November 2, 1895.

"Some of the Inventions of Women." *Atlanta Constitution,* August 31, 1895.

"Some Late Patents By Women." *New Ideas,* August 1896, p. 198.

"Some Notable Costumes." [Washington, D.C.] *Evening Star,* April 9, 1891.

"Some of the Inventions of Women." *Atlanta Constitution,* August 31, 1895.

"Sorosis." *Cosmopolitan,* June 1893, pp. 153–58.

Stallworth, Clarke. "Southern Belle Invented Wiper for Windshield." *Birmingham News,* February 20, 1977.

"Standardization—What It Means." *General Federation Magazine*, March 1918, pp. 21–22.

Stansell, Christine. "Women on the Great Plains." *Women's Studies*, no. 4, 1976, pp. 87–98.

Stebbins, Sarah Bridges. "Women in Business," *Demorest's Monthly Magazine*, September 1876, pp. 454–57.

"The Sterling Dishwashing and Drying Machine." *The* [Gambier, Ohio] *Weekly Argus*, December 14, 1876.

Stevens, Leo B. "Mothers of Invention." *Washington Times*, July 30, 1984.

Stipp, David. "Who Says the Idea of Child Inventors Is Patently Absurd?" *Wall Street Journal*, January 9, 1986.

"Straw Bonnets." *Harper's Monthly*, October 1864, pp. 576–84.

Strong, H[arriet]. W[illiams]. R[ussell]. "Source Conservation." *The Woman Citizen*, July 1914, p. 21.

———. "Can the U.S. Feed the World?" *New American Woman*, December 1917, pp. 3–4.

———. "Should Grand Canyon Be Dammed: A Flood Suggestion" *The Times Illustrated Magazine*, [1917?], p. 852.

———. "Source Conservation of Storm Water." *The Whittier News*, Twenty-fifth Anniversary ed., January 1913.

———. "Thirty Years Ago." An address at the beginning of her second year as president of Ebell Club in 1895. Reprinted in *The Clubwoman*, November 1926, pp. 7–8.

"A Study in Feminine Invention." *Scientific American*, October 1924, p. 260.

"A Study of Women as Inventors." *Current Opinion*, July 1918, p. 38.

"Successful Women Inventors." Reprinted from *India Rubber News. Woman's Journal*, August 22, 1891, p. 268.

"Suffragist Reaches Out." *New York Times*, February 18, 1911.

"Susan S. Frackelton, Potter, Is Dead at 85," *New York Times*, April 16, 1932.

"Swell Bicycle Receptions." *Nashville American*, May 3, 1897.

Switzer, Lucy. "Dress Reform Notes." *Woman's Journal*, May 6, 1893, p. 139.

"The Talking Side of the Chicago Exposition." *Chautauquan*, November 1893, pp. 226–27.

Tarbell, Ida M. "Women as Inventors," *Chautauquan*, March 1877, pp. 355–57.

"Teakettle." *New Ideas*, March 1897, p. 310.

Tharp, Louise Hall. "Bonnet Girls." *New England Galaxy*, Winter 1960, pp. 3–10.

"These are Real 'New Women.' " *New Ideas*, September 1895, p. 70.

"They Demand a Vote." [Chicago?] *Journal*, n.d., 1893. Original in the Strong papers, folder 854.

Thompson, Edward P. "Women as Inventors." *Inventive Age,* September 1894, p. 177.

"Those Who Wish to Buy Inventions." *The Patent Record,* January 1900, p. 18.

"Three Dimensional Glove." *The Ohio State University Monthly,* October 1938, p. 9.

"Tinkerers End 'Picnic Slide.' " *Christian Science Monitor,* April 11, 1938.

"To Inventors!" *Patent Record,* June 1899, p. 29.

"To the Editor." *Woman's Journal,* June 30, 1888, p. 204.

"Toilet Appliance." *New Ideas,* May 1897, p. 342.

"Toilet Vaporizing Apparatus." *The Patent Record,* February 1900, p. 21.

"Transactions of the United States Patent Office." *The Inventor,* April 1, 1857, p. 245.

Tricker, Janice. "Sex, Science, and Education." *American Quarterly,* no. 26, 1964, pp. 353–66.

"A Trip to Mount Vernon." *Washington Post,* April 11, 1891.

"28 Women Form Inventors Club." *New York Times,* July 10, 1941.

"$2,500,000 Made by One of O'Meara & Co.'s Clients." *New Ideas,* May 1897, p. 339.

"Two Old Time Ottumwa Inventors." [Ottumwa] *Saturday Herald,* May 27, 1899.

"A Union of Inventors: Brainy Men Trying to Organize a National Association." *Washington Post,* April 10, 1891.

"U.S. Drug Flown to Heuss in Bonn." *New York Times,* February 24, 1955.

"Use Grand Canyon as Mammoth Irrigation Tank, Urges Woman." [Los Angeles] *Tribune,* September 1, 1917.

"The Value of Small Inventions." *The Patent Record,* January 1899, p. tk.

Van Rensselaer, Susan. "Harriet Hosmer." *Antiques,* October 1963, pp. 424–28.

Veblen, Thorstein. "The Economic Theory of Woman's Dress." *Popular Science Monthly,* December 1894, pp. 198–205.

"Ventilation of Passenger Cars." *Inventive Age,* June 28, 1892, p. 1.

"Ventilation of Railroad Cars." *Scientific American,* July 17, 1852, p. 345.

"A Very Brilliant Scene." *Washington Post,* April 9, 1891.

"A Voice from the East." *Woman Inventor* 1, no. 2, June 1891, p. 3.

Wallace, Ellen A. "Woman's Widening Field." *Success,* December 1897, p. 31.

Walsh, George Ethelbert. "The Inventors' World of Marvels." *Gunton's Magazine,* March 1902. pp. 232, 242.

———. "Women Inventors." *The Patent Record,* March 1899, p. 9.

"Want Woman Made Judge." *New York Times,* November 26, 1922.

"Wants and Supplies." *Inventor and Manufacturer,* March 1872, p. 13.

"War Among the Potters." *Cincinnati Daily Gazette,* October 7, 1880.

"War, Women and Clothes." *General Federation Magazine,* October 1918, pp. 18–19.

Ward, Lester. "Genius and Woman's Intuition." *Forum,* June 1890, pp. 401–408.

Ward, Susan Hayes. "In-Door Employments for Women." *Chautauquan,* February 1887, p. 262.

Warner, Deborah Jean. "Fashion, Emancipation, Reform, and the Rational Undergarment." *Dress* 4, 1978, pp. 24–29.

———. "Science Education for Women in Antebellum America." *Isis,* no. 69, 1978, pp. 58–67.

"Washing Machine." *The Patent Record and Monthly Review,* June–July 1902, p. 10.

Welter, Barbara. "Anti-Intellectualism and the American Woman, 1800–1860." *Mid-America,* no. 48, 1961, pp. 258–70.

"What Is a Patent?" *The Patent Record and Monthly Review,* September 1904, pp. 16–17.

"What Mrs. Alden Writes Us." *Sunshine Bulletin,* March 1902, inside cover.

"What the Press Says of the 'Woman Inventor.' *Woman Inventor* 1, no. 2, June 1891, p. 2.

"What the Inventors Are Doing." *The Patent Record and Monthly Review,* June–July 1902, p. 28.

"What Women Are Doing for the Exposition." *Atlanta Constitution,* March 31, 1895.

Wheeler, Emily F. "A Business Education for Girls." *Chautauquan,* October 1886, pp. 3–5.

"Whips." *The Patent Record and Monthly Review,* June–July 1902, p. 10.

White, David F. "The Flavor of General Foods." *New York Times,* June 5, 1977. Reprint courtesy of inventor Ruth Siems.

White, Mary Catherwell. "The Week's Work." *New Ideas Woman's Magazine,* February 1903, pp. 85–88.

White, Mary Ogden. "Has the War Made Women Inventors?" *Woman Citizen,* June 9, 1917, p. 35.

Whitney, Lillian. "Blessed by Drudgery." *The Household Companion,* April 1893, p. 102.

"Whittier Woman for Control of Floods." *Whittier News,* August 11, 1915.

"Why I Became Interested in Woman Inventors." *The Woman Inventor,* April 1890 [1891], p. 3.

"Wide Variety of Ideas Covered by Patents Issued During the Week." *New York Times,* August 17, 1968.

Williams, Martha, M.D. "Hygienic Dress." *Woman's Journal,* February 1, 1873, p. 35.

Wilson, Page H. "They Came, They Marched . . . For the Right of All to Vote." *A.D.A. World,* April 1965, p. 3.

"Windshield Umbrella." *Invention and Finance,* May-June 1936, pp. 6–7.

"Wine, Women and Song in Patent Fete Tonight." *Washington Post,* April 10, 1940.

Wolfinger, Florence. "The Versatile Mrs. Greneker: Her Rope Trick Was a World War II Secret." *Patent Leader,* December 14, 1965.

"Woman and the Centennial." *Woman's Journal,* July 29, 1876, p. 243.

"Woman and Her Ways." *Chicago Times,* May 16, 1893.

"A Woman as Inventor." *Woman's Journal,* June 30, 1888, p. 204.

"Woman at the Fair." *The Illustrated World's Fair,* August 1893, p. 614.

"A Woman at the Fair." *New York Daily Tribune,* June 16, 1893; July 2, 1893.

"Woman-Built Coffee Pot." *New Ideas,* March 1914, p. 8.

"A Woman Cleans Chicago Streets." *Success,* January 1898, p. 64.

"A Woman Inventor." *Woman's Journal,* January 26, 1907, p. 13.

"Woman Inventor Dies in Poverty." *New York Times,* November 27, 1932.

"Woman Makes Herself Felt." [Los Angeles] *News,* May 10, 1916.

"Woman out of Her Element." *New York Times,* May 1, 1895.

"A Woman Patent Solicitor." *Success,* March 4, 1899, p. 245.

"Woman Wronged." *The Revolution,* April 9, 1868.

"Woman's Canning and Preserving Company." *Domestic Monthly,* February 1893, p. 29.

"Woman's Congress Resumed Today." *Atlanta Journal,* September 30, 1895.

"Woman's Contribution in the Field of Invention." *Mentor,* September 1925, p. 13.

"Woman's Education." *Success,* August 1898, p. 16.

"The Woman's Exposition." *The Patent Record and Monthly Review,* February 1902, p. 29.

"A Woman's Genius." *Inventive Age,* December 1895, p. 187.

"Woman's Genius." *New York Times,* November 16, 1913, sect. 6, p. 624.

"A Woman's Great Work." *The Patent Record,* September 1900, p. 8.

"Woman's Industrial League." *New York Times,* September 15, 1882.

"A Woman's Invention." *The Centennial Welcome,* September 15, 1876, p. 6.

"A Woman's Invention." *New Ideas,* June 1900, p. 11; March 1902, p. 9.

"A Woman's Invention." *The Patent Record,* July 1900, pp. 21–22.

"A Woman's Invention." *Woman's Journal,* June 30, 1888, p. 204; October 28, 1893, p. 342; April 20, 1907, p. 64; December 31, 1904, cover.

"A Woman's Inventions." *New Ideas,* January 1, 1900, p. 855.

"Woman's Inventive Genius." *Equal Rights,* August 25, 1928, pp. 230–301.

"A Woman's Labor-Saving Device." *New Ideas,* November 1901, p. 954.

"Woman's Pavilion." *Arthur's Illustrated Home Magazine,* April 1876, p. 193.

"The Woman's Pavilion." In "Centennial Notes." *Friends' Intelligencer,* October 21, 1876, pp. 554–57.

"Woman's Pavilion." *The Centennial Eagle,* August 8, 1876, pp. 108–10.

"The Woman's Pavilion at the Centennial Exhibition." *The United States Centennial Welcome,* October 15, 1876, pp. 1, 2.

"Woman's Real Needs." *Inland Monthly,* April 1873, pp. 211–12.

"A Woman's Remarkable Invention." *The Patent Record,* September 1900, p. 8.

"Woman's Skirt Invented by Mrs. Sittig: Exhibited at Brooklyn Cycle Club." *New York Times,* February 24, 1895.

"A Woman's Tricycle." *New Ideas,* September 1895, p. 70.

"Woman's Work." *The Revolution,* August 27, 1868, p. 120.

"Woman's Work at the Exposition." *Industrial America,* March 14, 1885, p. 63.

"Woman's Work at Wisconsin Fair." *Woman's Journal,* September 15, 1888, p. 294.

"Woman's World." *The Atlanta Journal,* October 21, 1895.

"Woman Wronged." *The Revolution.* April 9, 1868.

"Women and Big Business," *Woman Citizen,* July 27, 1918, pp. 170–71.

"Women and Their Work." *Harper's Bazaar,* April 18, 1868, p. 394.

"Women as Inventors." *Portland Oregonian,* n.d. Reprinted in *New York Daily Tribune,* September 8, 1898.

"Women as Inventors." *Christian Science Monitor,* June 25, 1935.

"Women as Inventors." *The Patent Record,* May 1900, p. 8.

"Women as Inventors." *Literary Digest,* June 30, 1923, p. 7.

"Women as Inventors." *New York Tribune,* June 19, 1899.

"Women as Inventors." *Woman's Journal,* February 15, 1873, p. 56; August 18, 1888, p. 88; March 18, 1899, p. 88; February 24, 1900, p. 58.

"Women as Inventors: They Have Turned Their Bright Ideas into Actual Results." *Washington Post,* April 9, 1891.

"Women as Sanitary Inspectors." *New Ideas,* February 1896, p. 100.

"Women Had the Floor." *Nashville American,* May 4, 1897.

"Women in War Work." *Club Woman,* April 1918, pp. 287–92.

"Women Inventors." *Woman's Journal,* November 28, 1903, p. 382.

"Women Inventors." *Providence Journal,* June 16, 1937.

"Women Inventors." *Scientific American,* August 19, 1899, p. 123.

"Women Inventors." *New Ideas,* March 1900, p. 892.

"Women Inventors," *The Patent Record,* March 1899, p. 9; August 1899, p. 7.

"Women Inventors." *Domestic Monthly,* August 1895, p. 24.

"Women Inventors' Mutual Aid and Protective Association of the United States of America." *Woman Inventor* 1, no. 2, June 1891, p. 2.

"Women Not Inventors." *The Patent Record and Monthly Review,* June–July 1902, p. 30.

"Women of 1939." *Independent Woman,* January 1940, pp. 4, 29–30.

"Women Pledged to Save Food." *Los Angeles Sunday Times,* July 1, 1917.

"Women to the Front." *Success,* May 27, 1899, p. 442.

"Women Gaining in Patent Rolls." *New York Times,* August 11, 1940, Sec. 2, 5:4.

"Women Engineers." In "Topics of the Times." *New York Times,* December 6, 1940.

"Women Employees in the Patent Office." *The Woman Inventor*, April 1890 [1891], p. 3.

"The Women's Apparel Unit of the Women's Oversea Hospitals, U.S.A." *Woman Citizen*, August 24, 1918, pp. 250–51.

"Women's Inventions." *Woman's Journal*, January 17, 1903, cover.

"Women's Printing." *Missouri Republican*, November 27, 1874.

"Women's Special Work as Exhibited at Nashville." *New Ideas*, May 1897, p. 342.

"Wonderful Growth of the Electric Railway in the United States." *Scientific American*, May 18, 1895, p. 315.

"Work Holder for Sewing Machine." *The Patent Record*, May 1899, p. 13.

"The Work of One Woman." *Southern California Business*, November 1926, pp. 26, 32.

"World's Fair Notes." *Woman's Journal*, April 8, 1893, p. 209; July 29, 1893, p. 237; September 9, 1893, p. 288.

"You Men." *Woman's Journal*, June 15, 1872, p. 186.

Zimmerman, Barbara Baker, and Carstonsen, Vernon. "Pioneer Women in Southwestern Washington Territory: The Recollections of Susanna Marie Slover McFarland Price Ede." *Pacific Northwestern Quarterly*, October 1976, pp. 137–50.

## SECONDARY SOURCES

* = author is a patentee.

Abell, Mrs. L. G. *Woman in her Various Relations*. New York: R. T. Young, 1853.

Abbott, Edith. *Women in Industry: A Study in American Economic History*. New York: D. Appleton and Company, 1910. Reprint ed., New York: Arno Press, 1969.

Abrams, Malcolm, and Bernstein, Harriet. *Future Stuff*. New York: Penguin, 1989, p. 290.

Adams, John Quincy. Edited by Charles Francis Adams. *Memoirs of John Quincy Adams, Comprising Portions of His Diary from 1795 to 1848*. 12 vols. Philadelphia: J. B. Lippincott and Company, 1875.

Adams, Sherman W., and Stiles, Henry R. *The History of Ancient Wethersfield*. 2 vols. [Somersworth, Conn.]: New Hampshire Publishing Company in collaboration with Wethersfield Historical Society, 1974; facsimile of 1904 ed.

*Alden, Cynthia Westover. *Bushy: A Romance Founded on Fact*. New York: Morse, 1896.

———. *Manhattan: Historic and Artistic*. New York: Morse and Company, 1897.

———. *Women's Ways of Earning Money*. New York: A. S. Barnes and Company, 1904.

——— and Ober, Carolyn Faville. *Manhattan: History and Artistic New York*. New York: Lovell, Coryell and Company, 1892.

Andrews, John B. and Bliss, W. D. P. *History of Women in Trade-Unions.* New York: Arno Press, 1974.

Babcock, Emma Whitcomb. *Household Hints.* In *Appletons' Home Books.* 6 vols. New York: D. Appleton and Company, 1881.

Bachman, Donna G., and Piland, Sherry. *Women Artists: An Historical, Contemporary and Feminist Bibliography.* Metuchen, N.J.: The Scarecrow Press, Inc., 1978.

Badger, Reid. *The Great American Fair.* Chicago: Nelson Hall, 1979.

Bailey, David. *Estward Ho.* Highland, Ohio: David Bailey, 1877.

Baker, Elizabeth. *The Happy Housewife.* Wheaton, Ill.: Victor Books, 1975.

Baker, Elizabeth Faulkner. *Technology and Woman's Work.* New York: Columbia University Press, 1964.

Baldwin, Richard S. *The Fungus Fighters.* Ithaca, N.Y.: Cornell University Press, 1981.

[Bates, Lizzie]. *Woman: Her Dignity and Sphere.* New York: American Tract Society, [c. 1870].

Baxandall, Rosalyn; Gordon, Linda; and Reverby, Susan, eds. *America's Working Women.* New York: Random House, 1976.

Beard, George M. *American Nervousness: Its Causes and Consequences.* New York: C. P. Putnam's Sons, 1881. Reprint ed. New York: Arno Press and the New York Times, 1972.

Beecher, Catharine E. *The Duty of American Women to their Country.* New York: Harper and Brothers, 1845.

———— and Stowe, Harriet Beecher. *The American Woman's Home, or Principles of Domestic Science.* Boston: J. B. Ford and Company, 1869.

Benderly, Beryl Lieff. *The Myth of Two Minds: What Gender Means and Doesn't Mean.* New York: Doubleday, 1987.

Bennett, Mary Angela. *Elizabeth Stuart Phelps.* Philadelphia: University of Pennsylvania Press, 1939.

Bentley, Susan. *Farm Women in the United States.* University Park, Penn.: Pennsylvania State University, 1984.

Berney, Esther S. *A Collector's Guide to Pressing Irons and Trivets.* New York: Crown, 1977.

*Biographical and Historical Memoirs of Eastern Arkansas.* Chicago: The Goodspeed Publishing Company, 1890.

*Biographical Cyclopaedia of American Women.* Mabel Ward Cameron, ed., 2 vols. New York: The Halvord Publishing Company, Inc., 1924.

*Biography Almanac.* Susan I. Stetler, ed. 3 vols. Detroit: Gale Research Company, 1987.

Bird, Caroline. *Enterprising Women.* New York: W. W. Norton and Company, Inc., 1976.

Bishop, Robert, and Coblentz, Patricia. *The World of Antiques, Art, and Architecture in Victorian America.* New York: E. P. Dutton, 1979.

Bitting, Arvill W. *Appertizing: The Art of Canning.* San Francisco: The Trade Pressroom, 1937.

Blackwell, Alice Stone. *Lucy Stone: Pioneer of Woman's Rights.* Boston: Little, Brown and Company, 1903.

Blanc, Marie Therese. *The Condition of Women in the United States.* n.p., 1895. Reprint ed., Freeport, N.Y.: Books for Libraries Press, 1972.

Blythe, LeGette, and Brockmann, Charles Raven. *Hornet's Nest: The Story of Charlotte and Mecklenburg County.* Charlotte, N.C.: McNally of Charlotte, 1961.

Bourne, Frederick Gilbert. *American Sewing Machines.* New York: n.p., 1895.

Brackett, Anna Callendar. *The Technique of Rest.* New York: Harper and Brothers Publisher, 1905.

————. *Women and the Higher Education.* New York: Harper and Brothers, 1893.

Braude, Ann. *Radical Spirits: Spiritualism and Women's Rights in Nineteenth Century America.* Boston: Beacon Press, 1989.

Browne, Charles Albert, and Weeks, Mary Elvira. A History of the American Chemical Society. Washington, D.C.: American Chemical Society, 1952.

Brown, Dee. *The Year of the Century.* New York: Scribners, 1966.

Brown, Kenneth A. *Inventors at Work: Interviews with Sixteen Notable American Inventors.* Redmond, Wash.: Tempus Books of Microsoft Press, 1988.

Brown, Laura Morrison. *Historical Sketch of the Morrison Family.* Charlotte: Presbyterian Standard Publishing Company, 1919.

Brownlee, W. Elliot, and Brownlee, Mary M. *Women in the American Economy: A Documentary History, 1675–1929.* New Haven: Yale University Press, 1976.

Burnap, George. *Lectures on the Sphere and Duties of Woman and Other Subjects.* Baltimore: John Murphy, Printer and Publisher, 1841.

Byrn, Edward Wright. *The Progress of Invention in the Nineteenth Century.* New York: Munn & Company, 1900. Reprint ed., New York: Russell and Russell, 1970.

Burr, Samuel J. *Memorial of the International Exhibition.* Hartford: L. Stebbins, 1877.

Burt, McKinley. *Black Inventors of America.* n.p.: National Book Company of Educational Research Associates, 1969.

Cahoon, Haryot Hold. Cynthia M. Westover Alden, ed. *What One Woman Thinks.* New York: Tait, Sons and Company, 1893.

Callen, Anthea. *Women Artists of the Arts and Crafts Movement.* New York: Pantheon Books, 1979.

Carden, Maren Lockwood. *The New Feminist Movement.* New York: The Russell Sage Foundation, 1974.

Case, Victoria, and Case, Robert O. *We Called It Culture.* Garden City, N.Y.: Doubleday and Company, 1948.

*Chicago and the World's Columbian Exposition.* New York: A. Wittemann, 1893.

Clarke, Edward Hammond, Dr. *Sex in Education; or, a fair chance for the girls.* Boston: J. R. Osgood and Company, 1873.

Clinton, Catherine. *The Other Civil War.* New York: Hill and Wang, 1984.

Cohart, Mary, ed. *Unsung Champions of Women.* Albuquerque: University of New Mexico Press, 1976.

Cole, Doris. *From Tipi to Skyscraper.* Boston: i. press inc., 1973.

Collins, Archie Frederick. *Inventing for Boys.* New York: Frederick A. Stokes Company, 1916.

Conover, Anne. *Caresse Crosby.* Santa Barbara, Calif.: Capra Press, 1989.

Connett, Henry, and Fraser, Arthur C. *Patents on Inventions.* New York: Burke, Fraser and Connett, 1884.

Conwell, Russel H. *Acres of Diamonds.* Kansas City, Mo.: n.p., 1968.

Coolidge, Orville W. *A Twentieth Century History of Berrien County, Michigan.* Chicago: Lewis Publishing Company, 1906.

Cooper, Grace Rodgers. *The Invention of the Sewing Machine.* Washington, D.C.: Smithsonian Institution Press, 1968.

Cooper, Walter G. *The Cotton States and International Exposition and South, Illustrated.* Atlanta: The Illustrator Company, 1896.

Cornelius [Mrs.] *The Young Housekeeper's Friend.* Boston: Charles Tappan, 1841.

*Coston, Martha J. *Signal Success.* Philadelphia: J.B. Lippincott Company, 1886.

**Coston's Telegraphic Night Signals Patented in the United States and Europe.* New York: S. W. Green, Printer, 1880.

Cowan, Ruth Schwartz. *More Work for Mother: The Ironies of Household Technology from the Open Hearth to the Microwave.* New York: Basic Books, 1983.

Croll, Carolyn. *The Big Balloon Race.* New York: Harper and Row, 1981.

Croly, Jane C. *For Better or Worse: A Book for Some Men and All Women.* Boston: Lee and Shepard, Publishers, 1875.

———. *Sorosis: Its Origin and History.* New York: Press of J. J. Little and Co., 1868.

———. *Talks on Women's Topics.* Boston: Lee and Shepard, 1869.

———. *Thrown on Her Own Resources or What Girls Can Do.* New York: Thomas Y. Crowell and Company, 1891.

Crosby, Caresse. *The Passionate Years.* New York: Dial Press, 1958.

Crow, Duncan. *The Victorian Women.* New York: Stein and Day, 1972.

Davies, Margery W. *Woman's Place Is at the Typewriter.* Philadelphia: Temple University Press, 1982.

Davis, Mary Elizabeth [Maragne]. *The Neglected Thread: A Journal from the Calhoun Community, 1836–1840.* Columbia [S.C.]: University of South Carolina Press, 1951.

DeBono, E. B. *Eureka.* London: Thomas and Hudson, 1974.

Degler, Carl. *At Odds: Women and the Family in America from the Revolution to the Present.* New York: Oxford University Press, 1980.

Delaney, Janice; Lupton, Mary Jane; and Toth, Emily. *The Curse: A Cultural History of Menstruation.* New York: New American Library, 1976.

Dennis, Olive W. *Railroad 'Rithmetic: Supplementary Railroad Transportation Problems for Elementary Schools.* Baltimore: B & O Railroad, 1949.

Depew, Chauncy M., ed. *1795–1895: One Hundred Years of American Commerce.* New York: D. O. Haynes and Company, 1895.

Dexter, Elisabeth. *Colonial Women of Affairs: A Study of Women in Business and the Professions in America Before 1776.* Boston: Houghton-Mifflin, 1984.

Diaz, Abby Morton. *A Domestic Problem: Work and Culture in the Household.* Boston: J. R. Osgood, 1875; Reprint ed., *Women in America.* New York: Arno Press, 1974.

Dorland, William A. Newman. *The Sum of Feminine Achievement.* Boston: The Stratford Company, 1917.

Dorr, Rhetta Childe. *A Woman of Fifty.* New York: Funk and Wagnalls, 1924.

Douglas, Ann. *The Feminization of American Culture.* New York: Knopf, 1977.

Eagle, Mary Kavanaugh Oldham, ed. *The Congress of Women Held in the Woman's Building, World's Columbian Exposition, Chicago, U.S.A.* 2 vols. Chicago: W. B. Conkey Company, 1894.

Earl, Fannie Kennish. *"The World's Fair": An Evening Entertainment for Young People's Church and Temperance Societies.* Lake Wales, Wis.: n.p., 1891

Eberle, Irmegarde. *Famous Inventors for Boys and Girls.* New York: A. S. Barnes and Company, 1941.

Ehrenriech, Barbara, and English, Deidre. *For Her Own Good: 150 Years of Experts' Advice to Women.* Garden City, N.Y.: Anchor Press, 1978.

Elliott, Maud Howe, ed. *Art and Handicraft in the Woman's Building of the World's Columbian Exposition.* Chicago: Rand, McNally and Company, 1894.

Ellis, John, M.D. *The Great Evil of the Age: A Medical Warning.* n.p. [c. 1870].

Farmer, Lydia Hoyt. *The National Exposition Souvenir: What America Owes to Women.* Buffalo: Charles Wells Moulton, 1893.

Fatout, Paul. *Meadow Lake: Gold Town.* Lincoln: University of Nebraska Press, 1969.

Ferguson, Eugene S., and Baer, Christopher. *Little Machines: Patent Models in the Nineteenth Century.* Greenville, Del.: Hagley Museum, 1979.

Fink, Deborah. *Open Country, Iowa: Rural Women, Tradition and Change.* Albany: State University of New York Press, 1986.

Flexner, Eleanor. *Century of Struggle.* Cambridge, Mass.: Belknap Press of Harvard University Press, 1975.

Flinn, John J. *The Best Things to Be Seen at the World's Fair.* Chicago: Columbian Guide Company, 1893.

*Flynt, Olivia. *Manual of Hygienic Modes of Under-Dressing for Women and Children.* [Boston: self-published], 1873.

Foner, Philip S. *Women and the American Labor Movement.* New York: The Free Press, 1982.

Fowler, Orson Squire. *A Home for All or the Gravel Wall and Octagon Mode of Building,* New York: [Fowler and Wells], 1853.

————. *Tight Lacing, or the Evils of Compressing the Organs of Animal Life.* New York: Fowler and Wells, 1852.

*Frackelton, Susan Stuart. *Tried by Fire: A Work on China-Painting.* New York: D. Appleton and Company, 1885.

Francis, David R. *The Universal Exposition of 1904.* St. Louis: Louisiana Purchase Exposition Company, 1904.

Frankfort, Roberta. *Collegiate Women: Domesticity and Career at the Turn of the Century.* New York: New York University Press, 1977.

Franklin Institute. *Proceeds Relative to the Establishment of a School of Design for Women.* [Philadelphia, 1850].

*French, Elizabeth J. *A New Path in Electrical Therapeutics.* Philadelphia: Published by the author, 1973.

Fuller, Edmund. *Tinkers and Genius: The History of the Yankee Inventors.* New York: Hastings House, 1955.

Gage, Matilda Joslyn. *Woman as Inventor.* Woman Suffrage Tracts, #1. Fayetteville, N.Y.: F. A. Darling, 1870.

Gerdts, William H., Jr. *American Neoclassic Sculpture: The Marble Resurrection.* New York: Viking Press, 1973.

Gibbes, Emily Olivia ["By a Woman"]. *Gleanings, a Gift to the Women of the World.* Privately printed, 1892.

Giedion, Siegfried. *Mechanism Takes Command: A Contribution to Anonymous History.* New York: Oxford University Press, 1948.

Gilbreth, Lilian M. *The Psychology of Management.* New York: Sturgis and Walton, 1914.

Gillespie, Elizabeth Duane. *A Book of Remembrance.* Philadelphia: J. B. Lippincott, 1901.

Gilman, Charlotte Perkins. *The Home: Its Work and Influence.* New York: McClure, Phillip and Company, 1903.

Glascock, Jean, ed., *Wellesley College 1875–1975: A Century of Women.* Wellesley, Mass.: Wellesley College, 1975.

Glasgow, Maude. *Life and Law.* New York: G. P. Putnam's Sons, 1914.

————. *The Subjection of Women and the Traditions of Men.* New York: M. J. Glasgow, Publisher, 1940.

Glazer, Penina M., and Slater, Miriam. *Unequal Colleagues: The Entrance of Women into the Professions.* New Brunswick, N.J.: Rutgers University Press, 1986.

Goff, Alice G. *Women Can Be Engineers.* Youngstown, Ohio: n.p., 1946.

Goldman, Eric. *The Crucial Decade and After: America, 1845–1970.* New York: Alfred A. Knopf, 1966.

*The Good Housekeeping Woman's Almanac.* New York: Newspaper Enterprise Association, Inc., 1977.

Gordon, J. E. *Structures: Or Why Things Don't Fall Down.* New York: Plenum, 1978

Gowans, Alan. *Images of American Living: Four Centuries of Architecture and Furniture as Cultural Expression.* New York: Harper and Row, 1976.

Hanaford, Phebe A. *Daughters of America; or, Women of the Century.* Augusta, Me.: True and Company, 1876.

Hanson, John Wesley. *Wonders of the Nineteenth Century.* Chicago: W. B. Conkey, 1900 [1899].

Harmon, Ellen Beard. *Dress Reform: The Physiological and Moral Bearings.* New York: Davis and Kent, Printers, 1862.

Harper, Ida Husted. *The Life and Work of Susan B. Anthony.* 3 vols. Indianapolis: n.p. 1908.

*\*Harriet Hosmer: Letters and Memoirs.* Cornelia Carr, ed. New York: Moffat Yard and Company, 1912.

Hathaway, Esse Virginia. *Partners in Progress.* New York: McGraw-Hill Book Company, Inc., 1935.

Hayden, Dolores. *The Grand Domestic Revolution: A History of Feminist Designs for American Homes, Neighborhoods, and Cities.* Cambridge, Mass.: Massachusetts Institute of Technology Press, 1981.

*\*Hazen, Elizabeth Lee. *Laboratory Identification of Pathogenic Fungi Simplified.* Springfield, Ill.: Thomas, 1970.

Heilbrun, Carolyn. G. *Reinventing Womanhood.* New York: Norton, 1979.

Henry, Alice. *The Trade Union Woman.* New York: Burt Franklin, 1915. Reprint ed., New York: Lenox Hill Publishing and Distributing Company, 1973.

————. *Women and the Labor Movement.* New York: George H. Doran Company, 1923. Reprint ed., New York: Arno Press, 1971.

Hess, John L. *The Taste of America.* New York: Penguin Books, 1977.

Hewitt, Emma C. *Queen of the Home: Her Reign from Infancy to Age from Attic to Cellar.* Philadelphia: Miller-Magee Company, 1889.

Heyn, Ernest V. *Fire of Genius.* Garden City, N.Y.: Anchor Press/Doubleday, 1976.

Hiley, Michael. *Victorian Working Women.* Boston: D. R. Godine, 1980.

*History of Berrien and Van Buren Counties, Michigan.* Philadelphia: D. W. Ensign and Company, 1880.

*History of Herkimer County, New York.* George E. Hardin and Frank H. Willard, eds. Syracuse, N.Y.: D. Mason and Company, 1893.

*History of Nevada County, California.* n.p.: Thompson and West's, 1880. Reprint ed., Berkeley, Calif.: Howell North Books, 1970.

Holley, Marietta. *Samantha at the World's Fair.* New York: Funk and Wagnalls Company, 1893.

*Home Decorative Work.* Minneapolis: Buckeye Publishing Company, 1891.

Hoover, Theodore J. *Concentrating Ores by Flotation.* San Francisco: Mining and Scientific Press, 1912.

Horowitz, Helen. *Alma Mater.* New York: Knopf, 1984.

Horner, Charles F. *Life of James Redpath.* New York: Baise and Hopkins, 1926.

*How to Ruin Your Health with the Sewing Machine* [By a Physician]. Baltimore: Turnbull Brothers, 1874.

Howe, Julia Ward. *Sex and Education: A Reply to Dr. E. H. Clarke's "Sex in Education".* Boston: Roberts Brothers, 1874. Reprint ed., New York: Arno Press, 1972.

Hughes, Marija Matich. *The Sexual Barrier.* Washington, D.C.: Hughes Press, 1977.

Humphrey, Grace. *Children of Necessity.* Indianapolis: Bobbs-Merrill Company, [c. 1925].

Huntington, Emily. *The Little Housekeeper.* New York: Anson Randolph and Company, 1897.

*The Hygiene of the Sewing Machine: A Brief Inquiry into the Causes and Disorders Arising from the Use of Machines, with Some Suggestions as How They May Be Avoided* [By a Physician]. Baltimore: Turnbull Brothers, 1874.

Hymowitz, Carol, and Weissman, Michaele. *A History of Women in America.* New York: Bantam Books, 1978.

Ingram, J. S. *The Centennial Exposition, Described and Illustrated.* Philadelphia: Hubbard Brothers, 1876.

*Irwin, Harriet [Mrs. James P. Irwin]. *The Hermit of Petraea.* Charlotte, N.C.: Hill and Irwin, 1871.

Johnson, Helen Louise. *The Enterprising Housekeeper.* Philadelphia: The Enterprise Manufacturing Company, 1896.

Johnson, Patricia A., and Kalven, Janet. *With Both Eyes Open: Seeing Beyond Gender,* New York: Pilgrim Press, 1988.

Johnson, Paul C. *Farm Inventions in the Making of America.* Des Moines: Wallace-Homestead Book Company, 1976.

*Jones, Amanda Theodosia. *A Praire Idyl.* [Chicago]: James McClung, and Company, 1882.

———. *A Psychic Autobiography.* New York: Greaves Publishing Company, 1910.

———. *Rubaiyat of Solomon and Other Poems.* New York: Alden Brothers, 1905.

Kellogg, John Harvey, M.D. *The Evils of Fashionable Dress and How to Dress Fashionably.* Battle Creek, Mich.: The Office of the *Health Reformer,* 1876.

Kelley, Mary. *Private Woman: Public Stage.* New York: Oxford University Press, 1984.

Kenneally, James J. *Women and American Trade Unions.* St. Albans, Vt.: Eden Press Women's Publications, Inc., 1978.

Kennedy, Susan Estabrook. *If All We Did Was to Weep at Home: A History of White Working Class Women in America.* Bloomington, Ind.: Indiana University Press, 1979.

Kidwell, Claudia. *Cutting a Fashionable Fit: Dressmaker's Drafting Systems in the United States.* Washington, D.C.: Smithsonian Institution Press, 1979.

———. *Women's Bathing and Swimming Costume in the United States.* Washington, D.C.: Smithsonian Institution Press, 1968.

——— and Christman, Margaret. *Suiting Everyone: The Democratization of Clothing in America.* Washington, D.C.: Smithsonian Institution Press, 1974.

Kilgore, Carrie B. *Sewing Machine.* Philadelphia: J. B. Lippincott Company, 1892.

King, William C. *Woman: Her Position, Influence and Achievement Throughout the Civilized World.* Springfield, Mass.: King Richardson Company, 1902.

Lasson, Kenneth. *Mousetraps and Muffling Cups.* New York: Arbor House, 1986.

Lears, T. J. Jackson. *No Place of Grace.* New York: Pantheon Books, 1981.

Leavitt, Judith W., ed. *Women and Health in America.* Madison, Wis.: University of Wisconsin Press, 1986.

Lewis, Dio. *Curious Fashions.* New York: Clarke Brothers, 1883.

———. Mrs. A. B. Doutz, comp. *Our Girls.* Indianapolis, Ind.: J. G. Doughty, Printer, 1869.

Jeffrey, Julie R. *Frontier Women: The Trans-Mississippi West, 1840–1880.* New York: Hill and Wang, 1979.

Jensen, Joan M. *With These Hands: Working the Land.* New York: The Feminist Press, 1981.

Juster, Norton. *So Sweet to Labor: Rural Women in America 1865–1895.* New York: Viking Press, 1979.

Livermore, Mary A. *My Story of the War: A Woman's Narrative of Four Years Personal Experience.* Hartford: A. D. Worthington and Company, 1889.

———. *The Story of My Life.* Hartford: A. D. Worthington and Company, 1899.

———. *What Shall We Do With Our Daughters?* Boston: n.p., 1883.

Logan, Mary. *The Part Taken by Women in American History.* Wilmington, Del.: Perry-Nalle Company, 1912.

Lynes, Russell. *The Domesticated Americans.* New York: Harper and Row, 1957.

Maas, John. *The Glorious Enterprise.* Watkins Glen, N.Y.: American Life Foundation, 1973.

Marlow, Jean. *The Great Women.* New York: A & W Publishers Inc., 1979.

Marden, Orison Swett, ed. *The Consolidated Library.* 12 vols. Washington, D.C.: Bureau of National Literature and Art, 1906.

Matthews, Glenna. *"Just a Housewife": The Rise and Fall of Domesticity in America.* New York: Oxford University Press, 1987.

May, Earl Chapin. *The Canning Clan: A Pageant of Engineering Americans.* New York: The Macmillan Company, 1937.

May, Rollo. *The Courage to Create.* New York: W. W. Norton and Company, 1975.

McCabe, James D. *Illustrated History of the Centennial Exhibition.* Philadelphia: National Publishing Company, 1876.

McFee, Inez N. *Stories of American Inventions.* New York: Thomas Y. Crowell Company, 1921.

McGroarty, John Steven. *History of Los Angeles County.* 3 vols. New York: The American Historical Society, Inc., 1923.

*McLaughlin, M. Louise. *The China Painter's Handbook.* Cincinnati: self-published, 1911.

————. *China Painting: A Practical Manual for the Use of Amateurs in the Decoration of Hard Porcelain.* Cincinnati: Robert Clarke Company, 1877, 1889.

————. *Pottery Decoration Under the Glaze.* Cincinnati: R. Clarke and Company, 1880.

Megraw, Herbert A. *The Flotation Process.* New York: McGraw-Hill Book Company, 1918.

Meigs, Cornelia, ed., *A Critical History of Children's Literature,* London: Macmillan, 1969.

Meyer, Annie Nathan. *Woman's Work in America.* New York: Henry Holt and Company, 1891. Reprint ed., New York: Arno Press, 1972.

Mintz, Steven. *A Prison of Expectations: the Family in Victorian Culture.* New York: New York University Press, 1983.

Moffett, Cleveland. *Careers of Danger and Daring.* New York: The Century Company, 1924.

*Montgomery Ward and Company Catalogue and Buyer's Guide,* no. 56. Northfield, Ill.: Gun Digest Company, 1894–95.

Moore, Katharine. *Victorian Wives.* New York: St. Martin's Press, 1974.

Morison, Elting E. *From Know-How to Nowhere: The Development of American Technology.* New York: Basic Books, 1974.

Mosher, Clelia D. *The Mosher Survey: Sexual Studies of Forty-five Victorian Women.* New York: Arno Press, 1980.

Mott, Frank Luther. *A History of American Magazines: 1885–1905.* 5 vols. Cambridge, Mass.: The Belknapp Press, 1957.

Moussa, Farag. *Les Femmes Inventeurs Existent.* Geneva: Farag Moussa, 1986.

Myers, Annie E. *Home Dressmaking.* Chicago: Charles H. Sergel, 1892.

*Myers, Mary [By the Lady Aeronaut, Carlotta]. *Aerial Adventures of Carlotta or Sky-Larking in Cloudland, Being Hap-Hazard Accounts of the Perils and Pleasures of Aerial Navigation.* Mohawk, N.Y.: C. E. Myers, 1883.

Napheys, George H. *Modern Surgical Therapeutics.* Philadelphia: D. B. Brinton, 1878.

*Nolan, Mary. *Biddy Finnegan's Botheration, or That Romp of a Girl.* St. Louis: Ev. E. Carreras, 1884.

*Notable American Women: 1607–1950.* Edward T. James, ed. 3 vols. Cambridge, Mass.: Belknap Press of Harvard University, 1971.

*Notable American Women: The Modern Period.* Barbara Scherman and Carol Hurd Green, eds. Cambridge, Mass.: Belknap Press of Harvard University, 1980.

Oakley, Ann. *Woman's Work: The Housewife Past and Present.* New York: Pantheon Books, 1975.

*Official History of the Centennial.* Herman Justi, ed. Nashville: Brandon Printing Company, 1897.

Ogden, Robert C. *Philadelphia and the Centennial.* New York: Hurd and Houghton, 1876.

Ogilvie, Marilyn B. *Women in Science: Antiquity Through the Nineteenth Century.* Cambridge, Mass.: Massachusetts Institute of Technology Press, 1986.

O'Neil, Lois Decker, ed. *The Women's Book of World Records and Achievements.* Garden City, N.Y.: Anchor Press, Doubleday, 1979.

Ormsbee, Agnes Bailey. *The House Comfortable.* New York: Harper and Brothers, 1892.

Ossoli, Margaret Fuller. *Woman in the Nineteenth Century.* n.p., 1855. Reprint ed., Freeport, N.Y.: Books for Libraries Press, 1972.

*Our Famous Women.* Hartford: A. D. Worthington and Company, 1883.

Papachristou, Judith. *Women Together: A History in Documents of the Women's Movement.* New York: Alfred A. Knopf, 1976.

Park, Maud Wood. *Lucy Stone: A Chronicle Play.* Boston: Walter H. Baker Company, 1938.

Parloa, Maria. *Miss Parloa's New Cook Book and Marketing Guide.* Boston: Dana Estes and Company, 1888. Rev. ed., Boston: Bates and Lauriat, 1908.

———. *Miss Parloa's Young Housekeeper.* Boston: Estes and Lauriat, 1894.

Parnow, Elaine. *The Quotable Woman: From 1800–1975.* Los Angeles: Corwin Books, 1977.

Parton, James; Greeley, Horace; et al., eds. *Eminent Women of the Age.* Hartford, Conn.: S. M. Betts and Company, 1869. Reprint ed., New York: Arno Press, 1974.

Penny, Virginia. *The Employments of Women: A Cyclopedia of Woman's Work.* Boston: Walker, Wise, and Company, 1863.

————. *How Women Can Make Money.* Springfield, Miss.: D. E. Fisk and Company, 1870. Reprint ed., New York: Arno and the New York Times, 1971.

————. *Think and Act: A Series of Articles Pertaining to Men and Women, Work and Wages.* Philadelphia: Claxton, Remson, and Haffelfinger, 1869. Reprint ed., New York: Arno and the New York Times, 1971.

Petersen, Karen, and Wilson, J. J. *Women Artists: Recognition and Reappraisal.* New York: Harper and Row, 1976.

Peterson, Harold L. *Americans at Home.* New York: Charles Scribner's Sons, 1971.

Pizer, Vernon. *Shortchanged by History: America's Neglected Innovators.* New York: Putnam, 1979.

Phelps, Elizabeth Stuart. *What to Wear.* Boston: James R. Osgood and Company, 1873.

Post, Robert C., ed. *1876 A Centennial Exhibition.* Washington, D.C.: Smithsonian Institution, 1976.

Potter, William Warren. *How Should Girls Be Educated? A Public Health Problem for Mothers, Educators, and Physicians.* New York: New York Medical Journal, 1891.

Power, Mrs. S. D. *Anna Maria's House-Keeping.* Boston: D. Lothrop and Company, 1884.

Quigley, Dorothy. *What Dress Makes of Us.* New York: E. P. Dutton and Company, [c. 1897].

Ralph, Julian. "Woman's Triumph at the Fair." In *Chicago and the World's Fair.* New York: Harper's, 1893.

Randall, William Pierce. *Centennial: American Life in 1876.* Philadelphia: Chilton, 1969.

Ray, William. *The Art of Invention: Patent Models and Their Makers.* Princeton, N.J.: Pyne Press, 1974.

Rayne, Martha Louise. *What Can a Woman Do.* Petersburgh, N.Y.: Eagle Publishing Company, [c. 1893].

Reynolds, Neil B., and Manning, Ellis L., eds. *Excursions in Science.* New York: Whittlesey House, 1972.

Richards, Laura E., and Elliott, Maude Howe. *Julia Ward Howe.* 2 vols. Dunwoody, Ga.: Norman S. Berg, Publisher, 1915.

Rickard, T. A., comp. and ed. *The Flotation Process.* San Francisco: Mining and Scientific Press, 1916.

Robertson, Patrick, ed. *The Shell Book of Firsts.* London: Ebury Press, 1974.

Rosenberg, Rosalind. *Beyond Separate Spheres: Intellectual Roots of Modern Feminism.* New Haven: Yale University Press, 1982.

Ross, Ishbel. *Crusades and Crinolines: The Life and Times of Ellen Demorest and William Jennings Demorest.* New York: Harper and Row, 1933.

Rossiter, Margaret W. *Women Scientists in America: Struggle and Strategies to 1940.* Baltimore: Johns Hopkins University Press, 1982.

Rothman, Sheila M. *Woman's Proper Place.* New York: Basic Books, Inc., 1978.

Rothschild, Joan, ed. *Machina Ex Dea.* New York: Pergamon Press, 1983.

———. *Women, Technology, and Innovation.* Elmsford, N.Y.: Pergamon Press, 1982.

Roysdon, Christine. *Women in Engineering.* Monticello, Ill.: Council of Planning Libraries, 1975.

Rybczynski, Witold. *Home.* New York: Viking, 1986.

Sachs, Carolyn E. *The Invisible Farmers.* Totowa, N.J.: Rowman and Allenheld, 1983.

Sandhurst, Philip T. *The Great Centennial Exhibition.* Philadelphia: P. W. Ziegler and Company, 1876.

Scharf, John Thomas. *History of St. Louis City and County.* Philadelphia: L. H. Everts and Company, 1883.

Schemmel, August. *How to Make Money Out of Inventions: An American Adviser for Patentees.* Nashville, Tenn.: Le Roi, Printer, 1890.

Schiebinger, Londa. *The Mind Has No Sex?: Women in the Origins of Modern Science.* Cambridge, Mass.: Harvard University Press, 1989.

Sherr, Lynn, and Kazickas, Jurate. *American Woman's Gazeteer.* New York: Bantam, 1976.

Sigourney, Lydia H. *Letters to Young Ladies.* Hartford: William Watson, 1835.

Sklaar, Kathryn Kish. *Catharine Beecher.* New Haven: Yale University Press, 1973.

Smith, Elizabeth Oakes. *Woman and Her Needs.* New York: Fowler and Wells. Reprint ed., *Women in America.* New York: Arno Press, 1974.

Smith, Eleanor Tuohey. *Psychic People.* New York: William Morrow and Company, Inc., 1968.

Smith, Mary Stuart, ed. *Tribute in Song from Virginia Women to Georgia.* Richmond: B. F. Johnson Publication Company, 1895.

Smith, Matthew Hale. *Successful Folks.* Hartford, Conn.: American Publishing Company, 1878.

Smith, Page. *Daughters of the Promised Land.* Boston: Little, Brown and Company, 1970.

Smith-Rosenberg, Carroll. *Disorderly Conduct: Visions of Gender in Victorian America.* New York: Alfred A. Knopf, 1985.

Smuts, Robert W. *Women and Work in America.* New York: Schocken Books, 1971.

Snook, L. D. *Snook's Inventors' Helper.* Dundee, Yates County, N.Y.: n.p., 1879.

*The Spirit of "Seventy-Six."* [Hartford, Conn.]: n.p., 1876.

Spofford, Harriet Prescott. *House and Hearth.* New York: Dodd, Mead and Company, 1891.

Sprague, Julia A., comp. *History of the New England Woman's Club from 1868–1893.* Boston: Lee and Shepard Publisher, 1894.

Stanton, Elizabeth Cady. *Eighty Years and More.* New York: European Publishing Company, 1898.

Stanton, Elizabeth Cady; Anthony, Susan B.; and Gage, Matilda Joslyn, eds. *History of Woman Suffrage.* New York: Fowler and Wells, 1881–1922. 6 vols. Reprint ed., New York: Arno Press, 1959.

Stern, Madeleine B. *We the Women: Career Firsts of Nineteenth-Century Women.* New York: Schulte Publishing Company, 1963.

Stowe, Harriet Beecher. *Household Papers and Stories.* Boston: Houghton, Mifflin and Company, 1864. Reprint ed., 1896.

Strasser, Susan, *Never Done: A History of American Housework.* New York: Pantheon Books, 1982.

*The Successful Housekeeper.* Mrs. M. W. Ellsworth, ed. Detroit: M. W. Ellsworth and Company, 1882.

Tarbell, Ida M. *All in the Day's Work.* New York: Macmillan Company, 1939.

———. *The Business of Being a Woman.* New York: Macmillan Company, 1912.

———. *The Story of My Life.* Hartford, Conn.: A. D. Worthington and Company, 1899.

———. *The Ways of Woman.* New York: The Macmillan Company, 1915.

Taylor, Barbara. *Weekly Reader Presents Be an Inventor.* New York: Harcourt, Brace, Jovanovich, 1987.

*Tennessee Centennial and International Exposition.* Nashville: Brandon Printing Company, 1897.

*The Tennessee Centennial: New York Day, Brooklyn Day.* n.p.: New York State and Brooklyn Commissioners, 1898.

Tepper, Terri P., and Tepper, Nona Dawe. *The New Entrepreneurs: Women Working from Home.* New York: Universe Books, 1980.

Thurston, Robert H. *Evolution of Technical Education in Economics, Politics, Statecraft and Morals; The Work of the Franklin Institute During Seventy-Five Years.* Reprinted from the *Journal of the Franklin Institute,* February 1900.

Tomkins, Mary E. *Ida M. Tarbell.* New York: Twayne Publishers, Inc., 1974.

Torre, Susana, ed. *Women in American Architecture: A Historic and Contemporary Perspective.* New York: Whitney Library of Design, 1977.

Torrence, George P. *James Mapes Dodge*. New York: Newcomen Society in North America, 1950.

Trescott, Martha Moore Trescott, ed. *Dynamos and Virgins Revisited: Women and Technological Change in History*. Metuchen, N.J.: The Scarecrow Press, Inc., 1979.

————. *The Rise of the American Electrochemical Industry, 1880–1910*. Westport, Conn.: Greenwood Press, 1981.

Trout, S. Edgar. *The Story of the Centennial of 1876*. n.p.: S. Edgar Trout, 1929.

Truman, Benjamin C. *History of the World's Fair*. Chicago: Mammoth Publishing Company, 1893.

Turner, Loretta E. *How Women Earn a Competence*. Oberlin, Ohio: News Printing Company, 1902.

Tuska, Clarence D. *Inventors and Inventions*. New York: McGraw-Hill, 1957.

Tuthill, Mrs. Louisa C. *The Yong Lady's Home*. Boston: William J. Reynolds and Company, 1847.

*United States Patent Law. Instructions How to Obtain Letters Patent for New Inventions*. New York: Munn and Company at the Offices of *Scientific American*, 1870.

Vail, Mary Beals. *Approved Methods of Home Laundering*. Cincinnati: Proctor and Gamble, 1906.

Valentino, Catherine. *The Invention Convention*. Morristown, N.J.: Silver Burdett, 1984.

Vare, Ethlie Ann, and Ptacek, Greg. *Mothers of Invention from the Bra to the Bomb: Forgotten Women & Their Unforgettable Ideas*. New York: William Morrow and Company, Inc., 1988.

Vaux, Calvert. *Villas and Cottages*. Franklin Square, N.Y.: Harper and Brothers, 1857.

Van Etten, Frank M. *Van Etten's New Illustrated Sewing Machine Agents' Directory and Manual*. Chicago: F. H. Van Etten, 1880.

Warrior, Betsy, and Leghorn, Lisa, eds. *Houseworker's Handbook*. Cambridge, Mass.: Women's Center, 1975.

Waters, Clara Erskine Clement. *Women in the Fine Arts*. Boston: Houghton, Mifflin, n.d. Reprint ed., Boston: Longwood Press, 1978.

Weimann, Jeanne Madeline. *The Fair Women*. Chicago: Academy Chicago, 1981.

Wells, Mildred White. *Unity in Diversity: The History of the General Federation of Women's Clubs*. New York: General Federation of Women's Clubs, 1953.

Wertheimer, Barbara M. *We Were There*. New York: Pantheon Books, 1977.

Wheeler, Candace W. *Yesterdays in a Busy Life*. New York: Haper and Brothers, 1918.

————. *The Development of Embroidery in America*. New York: Harper and Brothers, 1921.

Wheeler, Gervase. *Homes for the People*. New York: Charles Scribner, 1855.

Whiting, Lilian. *Women Who Have Ennobled Life.* Philadelphia: Union Press, 1915.

*Whitney, Adeline, D. T. *Selections from the Writings of Mrs. A.D.T. Whitney Arranged Under the Days of the Year, and Accompanied by Memorials of Anniversaries of Noted Events and of the Birth and Death of Famous Men and Women.* Boston: Houghton, Mifflin, 1888.

Wilkins, Kay S. *Women's Education in the United States.* Detroit: Gale Research Company, 1982.

Willard, Frances E. *American Women.* New York: Mast, Crowell and Kirkpatrick, 1877. 2 vols. Reprinted in 1893 by Willard, Frances E. and Livermore, Mary A. as *American Women.* New York: Charles Wells Moulton; Reprint ed., Detroit: Gale Research Company, 1973. Also published as *A Woman of the Century.* New York: Nast, Crowell and Kirkpatrick, 1897. 2 vols. Also published as *Portraits and Biographies of Prominent American Women.* 2 vols. Springfield, Ohio: Crowell and Kirkpatrick Company, 1901.

————. *Occupations for Women.* Cooper Union, N.Y.: The Success Company, 1897.

Witherspoon, Margaret Johanson. *Remembering the St. Louis World's Fair.* St. Louis: The Folkestone Press, 1973.

*Womanlist.* Marjorie K. Weiser and Jean S. Arbeiter, eds. New York: Atheneum, 1981.

Marden, Orison Swett, ed. *The Consolidated Library.* 14 vols. New York: Bureau of National Literature and Art, 1906.

*Women in American Agriculture: A Select Bibliography.* Washington, D.C.: U.S. Department of Agriculture, 1977.

*Women of 1923 International.* Ida Clyde Miller, ed. Philadelphia: John C. Winston Company, 1923.

*Women of 1924 International.* Ida Clyde Miller, ed. Philadelphia: John C. Winston Company, 1924.

Woolson, Abba Gould, ed. *Dress Reform: A Series of Lectures Delivered in Boston, on Dress as it Affects the Health of Women.* Boston: Roberts Brothers, 1874. Reprint ed., New York: Arno Press, 1974.

*The World's Fair, Being a Pictorial History.* n.p.: 1893.

*World's Fair Recipe Book.* Philadelphia: Jacob F. Landis, 1893.

Wright, Barbara Drygulski, ed. *Women, Work and Technology: Transformations.* Ann Arbor: University of Michigan Press, 1987.

Wright, Julia McNaer. *The Complete Home: An Encyclopaedia of Domestic Life and Affairs.* Philadelphia: Bradley Garretson and Company, 1879.

Young, John H. *Our Deportment, or the Manners, Conduct, and Dress of the Most Refined American Society.* New York: F. B. Dickerson and Company, 1879.

Yost, Edna. *American Women of Science.* Philadelphia: Frederick A. Stokes and Company, 1943.

————. *Women of Modern Science*. New York: Dodd, Mead and Company, 1959.

Zahm, John Augustine [H. J. Mozans]. *Woman in Science*. New York: D. Appleton and Company, 1913.

Zimmerman, Jan, ed. *The Technological Woman*. New York: Praeger, 1983.


## PAMPHLETS, CATALOGS, AND DIRECTORIES

*The Atlanta Exposition and South Illustrated*. Chicago: Adler Art Publishing Company, 1896.

Baltimore and Ohio Railroad Company Dining Car Department. *Concerning the Blue China*. n.p.: n.d. [c.1927].

*Boyd's Directory of the District of Columbia*. Washington, D.C.: William Ballantyne and Sons, 1886–99.

*Burroughs-Wellcome Co. Establishes $250,000 Endowment at Hunter College*. Press Release, Burroughs-Wellcome, June 1, 1989.

*Catalogue of the First Annual Exhibition of the New England Manufacturer's and Mechanics' Institute*. Boston: n.p., 1881.

*Catalogue of the Tennessee Centennial Exposition*. Nashville: Burch, Hinton and Company, Publishers, 1897.

*Catalogue Woman's Department: Tennessee Centennial and International Exposition*. Nashville: Burch, Hinton and Company, 1897.

Centennial Exposition of the Ohio Valley and Central States. *Official Guide*. Cincinnati: Centennial Guide and Program Publishing Company, 1888.

*Edwards St. Louis City Directory*, n.p., 1886–72.

*Gould St. Louis City Directory*, n.p., 1873–1901.

*Industrial Progress*. San Francisco: Inventor's Institute of America [December 1883].

*Inventor's Advocate*. [Inventors' League of the United States, Inc.]. June 15, 1913.

*Inventor's Circular*. Washington, D.C.: C. B. Steele and Company, [1871].

Inventors' Protective National Union of the United States. *Constitution and By-Laws*. New York: Gray and Company, 1853.

*The Inventor's Manual*. Cincinnati: American Patent Agency, 1879.

*National Inventors Hall of Fame Induction 1990* [program]. Akron, Ohio: National Invention Center. 1990.

*The Official Catalogue of the Cotton States and International Exposition*. Atlanta: Claflin and Mellichamp, Publishers, 1895.

*Official Program*. Bicentennial Celebration, Washington, D.C.: Foundation for a Creative America, 1990.

*Papers Read at the Fourth Congress of Women, Held at St. George's Hall, Philadelphia, October 4, 5, 6, 1876*. Washington, D.C.: Todd Brothers, 1877.

Philadelphia, International Exhibition, 1876. *Catalogue of the Woman's Department*.

Porter, Florence Collen Porter. *Resolution of Sympathy at the Death of Harriet Williams Russell Strong.* Ninth Congressional District, South Pasadena, Calif., September 18, 1926.

*Report and Catalogue of the Woman's Department of the World's Exposition, Held at New Orleans, 1884–1885.* Boston: Rand, Avery, and Company, 1885.

*R. L. Polk and Co.'s Moline City Directory.* R. L. Polk and Company, 1913–17.

Smith, Charlotte. *An Appeal to the Roman Catholic Church, and to the Bishops of the Protestant Episcopal Church of the United States in Convention Assembled.* n.p., October 1898.

[————]. *Memorial of the Woman's Industrial League of America.* [October 1898].

Strong, H[arriet]. W[illiams]. R[ussell]. "To the Taxpayers and Bond Owners" [pamphlet]. Los Angeles, January 15, 1919.

*Third Century Awards Ceremony* [program]. Washington, D.C.: Foundation for a Creative America, May 10, 1990.

"Trousers for Women: Practical Garments for Agricultural Workers." Advertising brochure for "Putnee." Courtesy of Radcliffe College Archives.

Twenty-fifth Reunion Report, Radcliffe College, Class of 1905. Courtesy of Radcliffe College Archives.

U.S. Department of Agriculture, Agricultureal Research Service, North Central Region. *News.* May 23, 1976, and January 25, 1977. Courtesy of Anne Whitehead, United States Department of Agriculture, Agricultural Research Service, Beltsville, Md.

————. *Nomination of Mary Ollidene Weaver, Edward B. Bagler, George F. Fanta, William M. Doane for the Inventor of the Year Award.* Northern Regional Research Center, Peoria, Illinois, Courtesy of Ann Whitehead, United States Department of Agriculture, Agricultural Research Service, Beltsville, Md.

United States Department of Labor, Women's Bureau. *Women as Inventors.* [late 1930s], n.p. Clipping file/scrapbook in Patent Office library.

*A Woman's Place Is in the Patent Office.* [Washington, D.C.]: U.S. Department of Commerce, Patent and Trademark Office, [1990].

*Woman's Board of Trade Report.* Boston: n.p., 1908.

Women's Centennial Committee. *The New Century for Women.* Philadelphia: Woman's Building, International Exhibition, 1876.

## OFFICIAL DOCUMENTS, REPORTS, AND PUBLICATIONS

Andrews, John B. and Bliss, W. D. P. *Report on Condition of Woman and Child Wage-Earners in the United States.* Volume 10: *History of Women in Trade Unions.* District of Columbia: Government Printing Office, 1911.

*Annual Report for 1929.* Board of Regents of the Smithsonian Institution, Washington, D.C.: Government Printing Office, 1930.

Board of Lady Managers of the Louisiana Purchase Exposition. *Report of the Louisiana Purchase Commission.* St. Louis: Board of Lady Managers, 1905.

City of Philadelphia, Bureau of Records. *Centennial Exposition Citations.*

Fairfield, George A. *Report on Sewing Machines.* Washington, D.C.: Government Printing Office, 1875.

*Final Report of the California World's Fair Commission.* Sacramento, Calif.: State Office, A. J. Johnston, Supt. State Printing, 1894.

*Final Report of the Louisiana Purchase Exposition Commission.* Senate, 59th Congress, 1st Session, Document #202. Washington, D.C.: Government Printing Office, 1906.

General Services Administration: National Archives and Record Service. Files of the Office of the Commissioner of Patents, from Approximately 1850 to 1946, Consisting of Correspondence, Orders, Notices, Personnel Records, Attorney Records, etc. Boxes 118 through 126.

*Incorporation of Woman's Canning and Preserving Company.* December 4, 1890, Cook County, Illinois, Office of the Secretary of State, Springfield, Illinois.

International Exhibition [London]. *United States Official Catalogue.* London: n.p., 1862.

Mason, Otis Tufton. *The Birth of Invention* [Smithsonian Institution Report for 1892]. Washington, D.C.: Government Printing Office, 1892.

*New York Tribune Guide to the Exhibition Extra,* no. 35, 1876. *Official Views of the United States Government Exhibits at the Cotton States and International Exposition in Atlanta, Georgia, 1895.* 2 vols. Washington, D.C.: United States Government Board, 1895.

*The People of the State of Illinois Versus Woman's Canning and Preserving Company.* #14286, April 14, 1921, Office of the Secretary of State, Springfield, Illinois.

*Proceedings and Addresses Celebrating the Beginning of the Second Century of the American Patent System at Washington City, D.C..* Washington, D.C.: Press of Gedney and Roberts Company, 1892.

*Proceedings Attending the Opening of the Patent Office Fair.* Washington, D.C.: n.p, 1864.

*Report of the Board of Management of U.S. Government Exhibit in Atlanta, Georgia, Cotton States and International Exposition.* [Washington, D.C.: Government Printing Office], 1897.

*Report of the Board of Trustees of the Schools of the District of Columbia to the Commissioners of the District of Columbia, 1893–1894.* Washington, D.C.: Government Printing Office, 1894.

*Report of C. H. Barney, Commissioner for New Jersey to the World's Centennial and Cotton Exposition.* Trenton: John L. Murray, State Printer, 1885.

*Report of the Board of Commissioners of the Cincinnati Industrial Exposition.* Cincinnati: By Order of the Board, 1870, 1873, 1879.

*Report of the Board of Commissioners, 5th Annual Cincinnati Industrial Exposition, 1874.* Cincinnati: Times Steam Book and Job Printing Establishment, 1875.

*The Story of the United States Patent and Trademark Office,* Washington, D.C.: U.S. Government Printing Office, July 1981.

Tuska, Clarence D. *Independent Inventors and the Patent System,* Study of the Subcommittee on Patents, Trademarks, and Copyrights of the Committee on the Judiciary, United States Senate, Eighty-sixth Congress, Second Session. Study No. 28. Washington, D.C.: Government Printing Office, 1961.

United States Census Bureau. Mecklenburg County, Charlotte Township, North Carolina, 1870 Census. National Archives.

United States Centennial Commission. International Exhibition, 1876. *Official Catalogue: Department of Machinery.* Philadelphia: John R. Nagle and Company, 1876.

————. *Reports and Awards, Group VII.* Francis A. Walker, ed. Philadephia: J. B. Lippincott and Company, 1877.

————. *Reports and Awards, Groups XXI, XXVIII.* Francis A. Walker, ed. Philadelphia: J. B. Lippincott and Company, 1878.

United States Congress. House Committee on Water Power. *Water Power Hearings Before the Committee on Water Power of the House of Representatives, Sixty-fifth Congress, Second Session, March 18 to May 15, 1918.* Washington, D.C.: Government Printing Office, 1919.

United States Department of Commerce. Patent and Trademark Office. *Buttons to Biotech: U.S. Patenting by Women, 1977 to 1988.* Office of Documentation Information, Technology Assessment and Forecast Program, January 1990.

United States Department of Labor. *Women's Contributions in the Field of Invention: A Study of the Records of the United States Patent Office,* Women's Bureau Bulletin 28. Mary Anderson, ed. Washington, D.C.: Government Printing Office, 1923.

United States Patent Office. *Annual Report of the Commissioner of Patents.* Washington, D.C.: Government Printing Office, 1876–1924.

————. *Decisions of the Commissioner of Patents for the Year 1871,* Washington, D.C.: Government Printing Office, 1872.

————. Patent Application Files, 1837–1918, Entry 9, Record Group 241, National Archives, Suitland, Md.

————. Digest of Assignment of Property Rights and Patents, 1837–1900, Entry 28, Record Group 241, National Archives, Suitland, Md.

————. Patent Interference Case Files, 1835–1905, Entry 24, Record Group 241, National Archives, Suitland, Md.

————. *Transfer of Patents* (liber vols.). Federal Records Center, Suitland, Md., Access #55-A-256.

————. *Women Inventors to Whom Patents Have Been Granted by the United States Government, 1790 to July 1, 1888.* Compiled under the direction of the Commissioner of Patents. Washington, D.C.: Government Printing Office, 1888.

————. *Women Inventors to Whom Patents Have Been Granted by the United States Government, July 1, 1888, to October 1, 1892.* Appendix No. 1. Compiled under the direction of the Commissioner of Patents. Washington, D.C.: Government Printing Office, 1892.

————. *Women Inventors to Whom Patents Have Been Granted by the United States Government. October 1, 1892, to March 1, 1895.* Arranged chronologically and by classes. Appendix No. 2. Compiled under the direction of the Commissioner of Patents. Washington, D.C.: Government Printing Office, 1895.

Women's Centennial Executive Committee. *First Annual Report* [February 2, 1874]. Philadelphia. J. B. Lippincott and Company, 1874.

World's Columbian Exposition. *Report of the Committee on Awards of the World's Columbian Exposition.* 2 vols. Washington, D.C.: Government Printing Office, 1901.

## MANUSCRIPT SOURCES

Breckinridge, William C. Papers. Missouri Historical Society Archives.

*Credit Ledgers of R. G. Dun & Co.* Baker Library, Harvard University Graduate School of Business Administration, Boston, Mass.

Dress Reform Committee of the New England Women's Club. Schlesinger Library, Radcliffe College.

Files of the Office of the Commissioner of Patents, from Approximately 1850 to 1946, Consisting of Correspondence, Orders, Notices, Personnel Records, Attorney Records, etc. General Services Administration: National Archives and Record Service. Boxes 118 through 126.

Fry, Laura. Papers. Cincinnati Historical Society Collections, MSS qF946 RMV.

Greneker, Lillian. Papers. Schlesinger Library, Radcliffe College.

————. Papers. Mannequin Museum, Santa Monica, California.

Hosmer, Harriet. Papers. Schlesinger Library, Radcliffe College.

Leslie, Kent A. *The Woman's Building at the Cotton States and International Exposition (1895): A Cultural Construct.* Unpublished manuscript, December 6, 1982. Original in Atlanta Historical Society.

Letter from Dinning & Eckenstein, Montreal, to Mary Anderson, June 20, 1905. Courtesy of Birmingham Public Library.

McCabe, Lida Rose. "The Ceramic Movement: A Work in Which Ten Thousand American Women are Engaged." [c. 1880] Manuscript from the collections of the Cincinnati Historical Society, MSS gM161p RMV.

McLaughlin, M. Louise. Papers. Cincinnati Historical Society Collections, MSS qM161P RMV.

Morris, Anna Mary Curtis. Papers, 1861–1889. Schlesinger Library, Radcliffe College.

Myers, Carl and Mary. Biographical File, National Air and Space Museum Archive, Smithsonian Institution;

*Oberlin Smith Letter Copies, 1892–1904.* Oberlin Smith Society, Bridgeton, N.J. Courtesy of James W. Gandy.

O'Brien, James Frederick. "A Profile of Users of the United States Patent System: 1968 and 1973." A Master's Thesis submitted as a partial fulfillment of Requirements for Master of Science at the Massachusetts Institute of Technology, August 1975. Courtesy of Donald Kelly, United States Patent and Trademark Office.

Palkinghorn, Frank A. *A Biographical Sketch of Amanda Minnie Douglas.* Original typescript in the possession of the New Jersey Historical Society.

Powderly, Terence. Papers. The Catholic University of America, Washington, D.C.

Press Release. The Public Information Department, E. R. Squibb and Sons Division, Olin Mathieson Chemical Corporation, October 28, 1955.

Rogallo, Francis. Rogallo Biographical File, National Air and Space Museum Archive, Smithsonian Institution.

Slayton, John Marshall. Papers. Georgia Department of Archives and History. [Ac 00-070 Box 41/2093-15].

Smith, Kenneth E. "Laura Anne Fry" [Paper Presented in Fine Arts Department, Ohio State University], n.d. Original is in the possession of the Cincinnati Historical Society.

Strong, Harriet. Papers. Huntington Library, San Marino, Calif.

Tennessee Centennial Exposition Correspondence, box 5 f4, State Library and Archives, Nashville, Tenn.

# INDEX

# ILLUSTRATION SOURCES
# AND CREDITS

*xvi.* photo: Dennis Brock/Black Star; *5. Harper's Magazine*, October, 1964, p. 580; *7.* courtesy of Wethersfield Historical Society; *9.* patent drawing; *13.* reproduced from Paul C. Johnson, *Farm Inventions in the Making of America*, Des Moines: Wallace-Homestead Book Co., 1976, p. 100; *16.* patent drawing; *17.* patent drawing; *26.* Library of Congress; *28.* patent drawing; *29. People's Journal*, August, 1854, p. 289; *35. Scientific American*, February 11, 1882, p. 81; *40.* patent drawing; *44.* patent drawing; *45.* Public Library of Charlotte and Mecklenburg County; *53.* Smithsonian Institution; *61.* Francis Willard, *Portraits and Biographies of Prominent American Women*, vol. 1, Springfield, Ohio: Crowell & Kirkpatrick Co., 1901, p. 97; *62.* Smithsonian Institution; *63.* Hagley Museum and Library; *67. Prominent American Women*, vol. 1. p. 762; *68. Domestic Monthly*, January 1893, p. 29; *70. The Historical Register of the Centennial Exhibition*, New York: Frank Leslie's Publication House, 1876, p. 38; *79.* Library of Congress; *84.* patent drawing; *85.* patent drawing; *89.* patent drawing; *91.* J.S. Ingram, *The Centennial Exposition, Described and Illustrated*, Philadelphia: Hubbard Bros., 1876, p. 322; *93.* Library of Congress; *94. Centennial Exhibition*, p. 331; *95. Centennial Exhibition*, p. 332; *97.* Library of Congress; *108. Frank Leslie's Illustrated Newspaper*, June 24, 1874, p. 227; *111.* Olivia P. Flynt, *Manual of Hygienic Modes of Under-Dressing*, Boston [c.] 1877; *114.* Schlesinger Library, Radcliffe College; *122.* Schlesinger Library, Radcliffe College; *127.* patent drawing; *129.* Susan Smart Frackelton, *Tried by Fire*, New York: D. Appleton and Co., 1895, frontispiece; *130.* courtesy of the Cincinnati Historical Society; *142.* United States Patent Office; *143.* courtesy of the Jim Davie Collection, U.S. Patent and

Trademark Office; *148.* patent drawing; *149.* patent drawing; *150.* Library of Congress; *153.* courtesy of *Engineering and Mining Journal; 158.* Smithsonian Institution, National Air and Space Museum; *160.* Mary Meyers ["By the Lady Aeronaut, Carlotta"], *Aerial Adventures of Carlotta or Sky-Larking in Cloudland, Being Hap-Hazard Accounts of the Perils and Pleasures of Aerial Navigation,* Mohawk, N.Y.: C.E. Meyers, 1883; *161.* Collection of George S. Bolster; *162.* from the Archives of the Whittier Museum; *163.* patent drawing; *164.* Smithsonian Institution; *170.* Smithsonian Institution; *171. Prominent American Women,* vol. 1, p. 99; *182.* reprinted from Jeanne Madeline Weimann, *The Fair Women,* Chicago: Academy Chicago, 1981, p. 430; *184.* patent drawing; *188.* patent drawing; *189.* John Marshall Slayton Papers, Georgia Department of Archives and History; *194.* advertisement in *The Chautauquan,* March, 1892, p. 771; *195.* advertisement in Helen Louis Johnson, *The Enterprising Housekeeper,* Philadelphia: The Enterprise Manufacturing Co., 1896; *199.* Candice Wheeler, *Yesterdays in a Busy Life,* New York: Harper & Bros., 1918, frontispiece; *200. New Ideas,* May, 1900, p. 922; *204.* patent drawing; *205.* patent drawing; *209. Prominent American Women,* vol. 2, p. 762; *218. New Ideas,* April, 1898; *219. New Ideas,* May 1900, p. 922; *220. New Ideas,* May, 1897, p. 342; *221. New Ideas,* February, 1901, p. 14; *249. Patent Record,* September 9, 1900, p. 7; *258.* courtesy of Nancy Perkins; *259.* courtesy of Nancy Perkins; *263. New Ideas,* August 1899, p. 744; *264.* patent drawing; *265.* patent drawing; *266.* "A Modern Manuel [sic] Training School," Baker and Cornwall, 1905. Library of Congress; *275.* patent drawing; *283.* patent drawing; *299.* courtesy of Marjorie Joyner; *304.* from the Archives of the B & O Railroad Museum; *310.* GE Research and Development Center; *313. New York Times* Pictures; *320.* patent drawing; *328.* Mary Ames Photo; *329.* National Aeronautics and Space Administration; *338.* courtesy of Ann Moore; *340* patent drawings; *341.* (left) courtesy of Ann Moore, (right) Anne M. Lorenze, Snugli courtesy of Huffy Corp.; *347.* courtesy of Laurene O'Donnell; *350.* courtesy of Francis Gabe; *352.* courtesy of Dot Young-Kirby; *355.* Photography Unit, Wadworth Laboratory; *359.* Världsbilden, Lars Åström; *364.* courtesy of Nancy Perkins, photography, John Holmstrom; *370.* courtesy of United States Patent Office; *372.* courtesy of the Jim Davie Collection, U.S. Patent and Trademark Office; *373.* courtesy of Fred Amram; *374.* courtesy of the Jim Davie Collection, U.S. Patent and Trademark Office.

# ABOUT THE AUTHOR

*

ANNE L. MACDONALD, who has successfully marketed her own patented invention, is the former chair of the history department of the
National Cathedral School in Washington, D.C. She is also the author
of *No Idle Hands: The Social History of American Knitting*. She lives
with her husband in Bethesda, Maryland.